# *Film*

## FORM & FEELING

### DENNIS DENITTO
CITY COLLEGE OF NEW YORK

1817

**HARPER & ROW, PUBLISHERS**
**NEW YORK**

CAMBRIDGE
PHILADELPHIA
SAN FRANCISCO
LONDON
MEXICO CITY
SÃO PAULO
SINGAPORE
SYDNEY

Sponsoring Editor: Phillip Leininger
Project Editor: Jo-Ann Goldfarb
Text Design: Gayle Jaeger
Cover Design: Hudson River Studio
Text Art: J & R Services, Inc.
Production: Delia Tedoff
Compositor: ComCom Division of Haddon
  Craftsmen, Inc.
Printer and Binder: The Murray Printing Company

Film: Form & Feeling

Library of Congress Cataloging in Publication Data

DeNitto, Dennis.
  Film, form & feeling.

  Bibliography: p.
  Includes indexes.
  1. Moving-pictures.  I. Title.  II. Title: Film,
form and feeling.
PN1994.D42  1985      791.43      84–19282
ISBN 0–06–041629–7

84  85  86  87  9  8  7  6  5  4  3  2  1

This book is dedicated
to the memory of
two remarkable women—
Myra Antonelli
and
Josefine Brenner

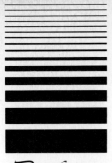

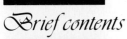

# Brief contents

# Detailed contents

# Preface

*Film: Form & Feeling* was conceived to encompass in one volume introductory material on practically every aspect of cinema studies, apart from the actual technical processes involved in preparing a motion picture. I include the components of film, the function of each member of the filmmaking team, critical approaches, history, characteristics of four genres, and analyses of 18 motion pictures.

In writing this volume, I gave highest priority to three objectives. The first was clarity of expression without oversimplification of concepts. The chapters in Part One were developed on the premise that the reader at first knows little about film beyond exposure to the medium. This premise required defining every new term as it was used and a careful explanation of each principle. Moreover, the overall scheme developed in Chapters 1 and 3 and some of the vocabulary are of my own devising.

Equally important to me as clarity of expression was organizing my material to integrate generalizations and specific examples. To this end, the generalizations in Part One are illustrated mainly by references to the films explored in Parts Two and Three. The analyses of films are based on the criteria and perspectives set forth in Chapter 3 ("Critical Approaches to Film"). For each film examined in Chapters 4 through 9, there is information on both the film itself and the individuals chiefly responsible for its creation. The latter particularizes the principles stated in Chapter 2 on the function of each member of the filmmaking team.

The third of my primary objectives was to supply background material so that a reader will consider a film as more than an isolated entity. For this reason, almost half of *Film: Form & Feeling* consists of historical surveys. I doubt that I am alone in finding that there is a paucity of succinct, clear historical material outside of expensive encyclopedias. Volumes devoted solely to film history are too lengthy and detailed for my purposes. What I have provided are surveys that highlight significant films, filmmakers, and movements, and contain lists of names of filmmakers and titles of motion pictures that can serve as bases for further research. Chapter 4 consists of a survey that emphasizes movements but is also a concise history of what could be called "drama films" (an explanation of why the term is avoided as the designation of a genre appears in the introductory note to Chapter 4). In Chapters 6 through 9 are similar, if briefer, historical surveys of four genres: comedy, documentary, Western, and musical. I regret not having the space to include others, especially animation and the science fiction film.

The introductory notes to parts and chapters go beyond this preface in indicating the book's scope and features and my rationales for inclusions and exclusions. It is necessary, however, that I include here three additional statements on format and content.

The stills in this volume are chiefly frame enlargements taken from my own collection; most of them have never before appeared in print. The exceptions (courtesy of The Museum of Modern Art/Film Stills Archive) are the following: 1.27, 4.26, 4.30, 4.-31, 4.32, 4.34, 4.38, 4.39, 4.43, 4.44, 4.45, 4.46, 4.51, 4.54, 4.55, 4.56, 6.3, 6.5, 6.7, 7.5, 7.9, 8.2, 9.2, 9.4, 9.5. I have preferred to include in Parts Two and Three a series of smaller photographs illustrating the action of a scene analyzed in the text rather than larger but fewer individual stills. Each of the 30 over-size photographs was selected on the basis of a particularly striking composition. In the captions for stills I frequently refer to a shot. Of course, a shot cannot appear on a printed page, and I have used the term to avoid repetition of the cumbersome phrase "enlargement of a frame from a shot."

Instead of a separate glossary that would repeat the definitions in the pages devoted to "camera-editing dynamics," I have compiled an index of technical terms.

There is one last point of which the reader should be aware. I have tried to avoid making assumptions or generalizations about the gender of readers and unnamed members of the filmmaking team. But occasionally, a third-person singular pronoun was indispensable for clarity and accuracy, and I have followed the tradition of using *he* as a universal generic. This is by no means to be interpreted as a slight to female readers or film professionals.

## ACKNOWLEDGMENTS

Acknowledgments are an author's token payments on debts of gratitude, and I owe a great deal to many people for their help in the creating of this volume. Everything that I write on cinema has been influenced by my students at the City College of New York. By asking acute, demanding questions, they have prevented me from ever becoming complacent or esoteric in discussing films. My colleagues in the Film and Video Program—especially Christopher Lukas, Kathleen Collins, and Neil Zusman—have been the source of stimulating conversations on all aspects of cinema, but especially on how esthetic values are grounded in the techniques of filmmaking. Jan Zuckerman, Lelia Lowe, Roman Kisiak, and John Console constitute the staff of the Audio-Visual Division of City College's Cohen Library; graciously and generously they spent time in obtaining and screening films for me.

Gordon Hitchens has assisted so many authors with their work that I am simply the latest in a long line in expressing my appreciation for his enthusiasm and advice. Donald E. Staples (North Texas State University) went over an early version of this book and gave valuable criticism. Others who read the manuscript at various stages and helped to mold the final version (while in some cases reinforcing my natural modesty) include the following: Frank E. Beaver (University of Michigan), David A. Cook (Emory University), Frank R. Cunningham (University of South Dakota), Bruce M. Firestone, Barry K. Grant (Brock University, Canada), John F. Harrington (California Polystate University), Charles R. Hill (Emporia State University), Lloyd Michaels (Allegheny College), Calvin Pryluck (University of North Carolina), Steven C. Runyon (University of San Francisco), Jerome Tanner (Pennsylvania State University), and Orville Wanzer (New Mexico State University).

I have indeed been fortunate in the people with whom I have worked at Harper & Row. For longer than I am sure either of us would like to recall, Senior Editor Phillip Leininger was a paragon of patience and never lost the composure of a genuine gentleman. Jo-Ann Goldfarb, my project editor, combined professional expertise with a charm that persuaded me, even when I was bleary-eyed and harassed by other responsibilities, to meet her deadlines. B. F. Emmer was more than simply a copy editor. He became the superego of my writing style, and I depended greatly on his awesome knowledge of languages to catch errors in the titles of foreign films. I appreciate the efforts of Gayle Jaeger, senior designer, to make this volume as physically attractive as possible.

Finally, there are individuals whose moral support sustained me during periods of frustration and doubt. James J. Greene (City College of New York) has been a close friend for so many years that he now accepts the role of encourager and optimist during each of my writing projects. The same holds true of my brother Ron DeNitto. I will always be grateful to William Herman (City College of New York) for what I learned from him during our collaboration on *Film and the Critical Eye*. My son Daryl has an intuitive understanding of the form and feeling of film and an uncompromising honesty that I depend on to compensate for my own dogmatism. He also deserves credit, praise, and my gratitude for preparing the index of this book. My wife, Elisabeth Brenner, never—well, hardly ever—complained when I retreated to my study for hours at a time. Her contribution to the making of this book was the most intangible yet the most substantial.

Dennis DeNitto

# Note to teachers

*Film: Form & Feeling* is intended primarily as a text-book for college film courses, although it may fulfill other functions. A few suggestions on how this volume could be used in the classroom might be of help to teachers.

The variety of material in this book makes it suitable for introductory film courses, history courses (as a primary text for a one-semester class or a secondary text for a two-semester class), and for genre courses. When a film program consists of a sequence of courses, this one book could be the text for more than a single course.

The major problem that I have encountered in more than two decades of teaching film courses is allotting the time required to analyze properly individual motion pictures and to discuss specific aspects relevant to those works. Reading assignments in various books were necessary since I could not find a single text to serve most of my needs. I have designed *Film: Form & Feeling* to reduce the dimensions of this problem for myself and other teachers.

A similar purpose is served by the detailed analyses of individual films. They offer examples of how different types of motion pictures can be critically explored. If a student has read an essay on a motion picture, investigation of that film can be condensed. On the other hand, I do not recommend that screening in a course be limited to selections from the 18 films analyzed in this volume. There is unquestionable value in a teacher's guiding a class in exploring a work for which students have not been prepared by a reading assignment. For this reason, I confined the films that I analyzed to those released before 1970. I assumed that instructors would prefer to apply their own approaches to more recent works and spend more time on them.

My essays on individual motion pictures can also be of use when a film by a director other than the one I considered is screened or when only one example of a genre is presented. I am not referring only to the material on a filmmaker in the "Background" section of each essay. A student who has studied my pages on Eisenstein's *October* should find it easier to understand dynamic montage in *The Battleship Potemkin*. The same holds true for a genre film. A student will be better able to evaluate the intentions of Richard Leacock in one of his direct cinema documentaries after reading about the approach of Robert Flaherty in *Man of Aran*.

Finally, the characteristics of four genres in Chapters 5 through 9 offer criteria that will assist an instructor in examining comedies, documentaries, Westerns, and musicals.

No textbook can meet every need of an instructor of a single type of film course, much less more than one type of course. Even writing one's own text results only in a partial realization of an impossible dream. What I hope I have accomplished is to produce a volume broad enough in scope and detailed enough in certain areas to be useful and stimulating to both students and teachers.

D. D.

PART ONE

*Foundations*

In the chapters that make up the first part of this book, I examine three important foundations of cinema studies. Anyone who wishes to view motion pictures with active understanding and perception rather than with passivity and casualness should become familiar with these foundations. Chapter 1 is devoted to the components of what appears on the screen and how each contributes to the experience of viewing a film. Chapter 2 surveys the functions of the major members of the filmmaking team. The principles and methods of critically analyzing films is the subject of Chapter 3.

    Although an introductory note to each chapter explains its approach, there are common denominators in this part of the book. Whenever feasible, I illustrate generalizations or definitions by citing specific motion pictures. A majority of these illustrations are drawn from the 18 films examined in Parts Two and Three. I have attempted to make each reference complete in itself. However, when this could not be accomplished succinctly, an asterisk refers to pages elsewhere in the book where there is a more detailed description. Numbered footnotes are reserved for bibliographic and occasional supplementary material. Since in most instances they are irrelevant in Part One, I do not include the date of release of motion pictures that are cited or the original titles of foreign films. This information is supplied in Parts Two and Three and in the index.

# The components of film

## 1

A film, whether solely an entertainment or also a work of art, should possess an organic unity. For example, when experiencing a sound narrative film, we are exposed to various types of stimuli, often simultaneously, even within a few moments of footage. There can be visual images (perhaps in color), words that are spoken and occasionally written (as in signs or a letter shown in a close-up), background music, actors in costumes, settings and props, and other means by which the medium of cinema conveys emotions and ideas to an audience. While these elements of a film may not always be fully integrated, they are organically related in that each component depends on the others to fulfill its functions.

During an initial viewing of a film, the highest priority is usually given to the experience itself in toto. Although we may make judgments, our attention is preoccupied with the feelings aroused by the motion picture, our immediate impressions. After seeing the film and during subsequent viewings, we analyze it, focus on individual elements, and evaluate how effectively each element contributed to the whole. This is a form of dissection, even though the probing instruments include intuition as well as intellect. This violation of the organic unity of a film is necessary, however, if we wish to go beyond unexamined experiences to being able to justify our subjective reactions, to understand why we approve or disapprove of a portion of a film or an entire motion picture, to appreciate the means available to filmmakers in attempting to fulfill their intentions, and to establish valid criteria for judging cinematic works.

Learning to respect the integrity of a film while separating and examining individual elements is a formidable emotional and intellectual practice that requires experience and discipline. Prerequisites for such an approach are an analytic scheme and an understanding of the functions, potentials, and limitations of the components of film. The purpose of this chapter is to supply as clearly, as concretely, and as coherently as possible the knowledge necessary to evaluate and elucidate perceptively individual motion pictures.

The scheme that I devised, with my own headings for major divisions, is inevitably an artificial construct, but it has been effective in helping beginning and advanced students to categorize diverse aspects of a motion picture. Each division of this tripartite system is defined and justified in the opening paragraphs of the pages devoted to it. However, a brief summary of each is appropriate here. "The Narrative Dimension" refers to all elements that unify a sequence of events included in a film. "Camera-Editing Dynamics" defines all techniques and approaches that depend on the processes of shooting and editing for their functioning. "Elements of Presentation" consists of those components appearing on the screen that are physically separate from the camera. This is the objective material on which the shooting and editing processes impose their own dynamics.

## THE NARRATIVE DIMENSION

A narrative in any medium is fundamentally a story. Some narratives are so simple and straightforward that they do not go beyond a sequence of events. Most, however, involve complexities that can be termed *narrative elements*. These consist chiefly of themes, plot, place and time settings, characterizations, and relationships in conflict or harmony.

The content of a narrative originates as a concept in the mind of a creator or creators, even when it is inspired by events that actually occurred, and becomes concrete and dramatic only through the modes of expression of a specific medium. These modes of expression can range from solely the words used by a novelist to the combination in opera of music, words, the human voice, facial expressions and gestures of singers, and such elements of presentation as sets, costumes, and lighting. The medium used to communicate a developed sequence of events profoundly affects the nature of the emotions and ideas conveyed to an audience by the narrative. We have different experiences when we encounter the same story in different media, for example, the legend of Perceval in the poem by Chrétien de Troyes, the opera by Richard Wagner, and the film by Eric Rohmer.

The narrative elements in a film are designated by the same terminology (for instance, *theme, setting, conflict*) as those for a novel, play, or opera. As is also true of these other media, each element is dependent on and interrelated to the others. What makes cinema unique are the other components of a film, the means by which narrative concepts are transformed into a dramatic reality on the screen. Our apprehension of a character, for example, depends on how camera-editing dynamics and elements of presentation are used. For this reason, the use of the term *dimension* helps to emphasize that a narrative is only one facet of a motion picture and cannot be experienced as a self-contained entity. Not all motion pictures have a narrative dimension (obviously, an abstract film does not), but the majority do.

If we consider separately each element of a cinematic narrative, we can mitigate the effects of violating the organic unity of a film by constantly keeping in mind the interconnections among the components of a motion picture and those among individual elements of the narrative dimension.

## THEME

The theme of a film when expressed verbally is an abstraction. It is the dominant or central idea of a motion picture that is dramatized in the film itself. This may be a clear idea in the minds of filmmakers before they begin production, or it may only emerge in the editing process. It may be unequivocal and obvious or ambiguous and subtle.

In this context *Idea* has a broad range of referents. It could be a moral principle, an emotional situation, or an intellectual concept. A theme is not a summary of a story. A summary encapsulates a sequence of events dealing with specific people in specific situations. A theme is a generalization, a universalizing of the specific. For example, the plot of *Smiles of a Summer Night* centers on emotional and sexual relationships among eight individuals. A formulation of its theme might be that illusion is a major component of romantic love, but the older a person gets, the more realism and even cynicism undermine that illusion.

Whenever a person generalizes from concrete action, a degree of subjectivity is inevitable. Three different viewers of a film may arrive at three different interpretations of its theme. The more straightforward and uncomplicated a film is, the more individuals tend to agree on its theme. Few viewers would deny that *Broken Blossoms* demonstrates how innocent feelings can be sullied by people who are cruel and insensitive. On the other hand, there are almost as many interpretations of the theme of Alain Resnais's *Last Year at Marienbad* as critics who have written on this complex film.

Only the most simplistic feature film will contain just one idea. A distinction, therefore, is often made between the major theme and secondary themes, though they are usually interrelated. Distinguishing a major theme from secondary ones can be a matter of personal judgment. For instance, in the analysis of *The Wild Bunch* in Chapter 8, three themes are discussed; critics differ as to which is the major one.

No formulation of a theme, major or secondary, should be considered irrevocable. A fourth viewing of a film may yield a different perception of its ideas than the first viewing. A student of cinema should be open to various views if the individuals offering them justify their interpretations with references to the film that are consistent and logically lead to specific conclusions.

Some critics believe that the potential scope and depth of a theme is irrelevant in evaluating a film and that only the degree to which a theme is realized or the ways in which it is implemented are worthy of consideration. Most critics would argue, however, about the assumption that all themes are equally stimulating and meaningful. Just as there are cliché cinematic modes of expression, there are trite ideas. *The Ten Commandments* is mediocre not simply because Cecil B. De Mille substituted spectacle for imaginative film techniques, but also because his ideas on religious faith are shallow when compared to, say, Robert Bresson's *The Diary of a Country Priest.*

Attempting to formulate the themes of a film is most useful if it is done in two stages: first, soon after viewing a motion picture, when one's impressions are freshest, and second, after a thoughtful analysis of the components of the film, perhaps utilizing pertinent critical perspectives. The latter process can lead to insights and new interpretations that necessitate a revising of one's immediate but unexamined conclusions.

The themes of a film constitute the universal aspect of that work. A motion picture, however, is not a philosophical treatise. To appreciate how intellectual concepts are transformed into dramatic, organic experiences through the medium of cinema requires that we explore the other elements of the narrative dimension.

---

PLOT

*Story* and *plot* are often regarded as synonymous terms. Although each consists of a sequence of events unfolding in time, a distinction between the two should be made. A story confines itself to answering the question, What happened next? All other considerations, such as characterizations and relationships, are secondary. The earliest films were stories that simply presented action, such as a thief being caught while attempting to break into a house or a man rescuing his child from an eagle's nest.

A plot goes beyond action to indicate also why events happen. This more sophisticated type of story depends on the other elements of the narrative dimension to fulfill its function. Of these, the most significant influence is the theme. A plot is the most immediate concrete manifestation of a film's dominant idea or ideas.

A problem of terminology arises with respect to plot when one discusses documentaries. Most contain a narrative dimension, but the emphasis is more on revealing actuality than in developing a coherent plot. It may consist solely of a series of images unified by a commentary, as in *Night and Fog.* It is more accurate, therefore, to refer in a documentary to a *sequence of events* or *sequence of images* rather than to a plot, which usually is reserved for fiction films.

The initial fashioning of a film plot is typically, though not always, the responsibility of a screenwriter. Even when adapting the work of a writer into another medium, the screenwriter must recast the original into a new form that meets the unique requirements of a motion picture. The result can be subject to extensive revision in the production and postproduction stages, especially during editing. What motivates filmmakers as they revise a screenplay is difficult to discover unless, which is rare, there is sufficient documentation on how the film was created. It is possible, however, to reverse the process and to deduce the characteristics of plots in general from the elements of the narrative dimension in completed films. By keeping in mind the omnipresent factor of the demands made by the other components of a film, we can examine the choosing, structuring, and developing of the events that make up the plot of a film.

Even in the simplest plot, the number of events that could be included is multitudinous. As Aristotle pointed out in his *Poetics,* a narrative is an imitation, not a reproduction of reality. If this were not so, 24 hours in the life of a fictional character would require 24 hours of cinematic time. Instead, a film condenses and expands physical time and offers only selected events. The primary criterion for the choice of events is the requirements of the theme; however, the final arbitrator is the creative intuition of a filmmaker. Referring again to Aristotle, the goal is to achieve "unity of action"; that is, if any one action is "displaced or removed, the whole work will be disjointed and disturbed."[1] (Chapter VIII) For example, in *Variety,* the occupation of the main character is pertinent to why he kills his partner, and scenes of him as a trapeze artist are necessary. On the other hand, what Antonio in *The Bicycle Thief* did during World War II is irrelevant to his unemployment after the war and is never mentioned.

Another determinant of what incidents are included is derived from the condition that a fiction film creates a sequence of events that has no existence in time and space beyond what appears on the screen between the first and last shots of a motion picture. *Antecedent action* often precedes the opening of a film. This action consists of events that occurred before the initial scene that are important to an understanding of what follows.

Numerous methods are available to a filmmaker whereby antecedent action can be incorporated into a plot. The simplest device is a title card appearing before the first shot that states relevant information. A voice-over commentary may also serve this function. Another direct method is the use of dialogue. In the opening scene of *Smiles of a Summer Night,* we learn essential facts about Fredrik's present marriage and previous love affair from a spiteful conversation between two of his employees. Flashbacks exist chiefly for this purpose. What has happened to the Chinaman in *Broken Blossoms* during the years between the opening sequence and the second one that is relevant to the plot is revealed in a flashback.

Screenwriters and directors are sometimes ingenious in devising unusual ways of presenting antecedent action to an audience. The newsreel projected on the screen in Welles's *Citizen Kane* reviews the public career of Charles Foster Kane. In the first sequence of *Singin' in the Rain,* Don Lockwood summarizes his rise to stardom in a speech for his fans. A combination of several devices, such as dialogue and flashbacks, may be used to convey antecedent action in a single film. Unity of action should prevail as much in the choice of which past events to include as in the choice of the present ones. In *The 400 Blows,* we need no more information about Antoine's childhood than what he tells a psychologist during a consultation; we can surmise the rest.

*Plot structuring* refers to the ordering of events and the ways in which that ordering contributes to emphasizing certain incidents. The most common approach is a chronological or *linear* sequence of actions. Often this type commences with the development of a crisis or unusual occurrence and ends when the crisis has been resolved or there is a return to normalcy for the characters involved. For example,

*Shane* opens with the appearance of the title character in a valley community and closes when he leaves. Flashbacks may supply antecedent action, as in *Broken Blossoms,* but such excursions into the past occupy a small percentage of the film's cinematic time.

There can be variations of a straightforward linear plot. One of the most frequently used is a *framework* that encloses a central sequence of events: a device that introduces and justifies the main action, usually in the past in relation to the framework itself. An example is the structure of *Variety.* The framework is a prisoner explaining to his warden why he committed murder and ends with his release. The film proper is a dramatization of his experiences. If the framework contains pivotal action in relation to what follows, it is called a *framework story.* In Wiene's *The Cabinet of Dr. Caligari,* the framework story begins with a young man relating a tale; at the conclusion of the film, we return to the young man and discover that he is insane. The last sequence puts everything that happened in the central portion of the film in a special perspective. Occasionally a person who appears in the opening section of a framework comments throughout the remainder of the motion picture. This is what occurs in Bergman's *Wild Strawberries.* In the first scene, Isak Borg is at a desk, writing about the events of a significant day in his life. During the dramatization of that day, in which he appears, his voice is periodically heard off-camera commenting on the action. *Wild Strawberries* is unusual in that there is not a second stage to the framework: We do not return to him at his desk at the end of the film. The criterion for determining if a motion picture with a framework contains a linear plot is whether or not events unfold in chronological order in the major portion of the work, as is true of each of the three examples just cited.

A *nonlinear plot* is one in which the structure is determined by factors other than a chronological sequence. A major category of nonlinear plots consists of surrealistic films in which the ordering of events depends primarily on the associations or unconscious connections supplied by the filmmaker either from outside the action (as in Buñuel's *Un Chien Andalou*) or through a main character (as in *Meshes of the Afternoon,* directed by Maya Deren).

A second category of nonlinear plots comprises

films in which past and present are continually juxtaposed beyond the point of occasional flashbacks to supply antecedent action. Kurosawa's *Rashomon* opens with a framework story in which two men, a priest and a woodcutter, describe an occurrence (the attack by a bandit on a samurai and his wife) to a third person. This occurrence is dramatized five times, from five points of view. At the end of the film, we return to the framework story. This pattern of points of view emphasizes the subjectivity with which people recall experiences.

The subjectivity of our apprehensions of reality is a major theme of many nonlinear plots of this type. French New Wave filmmakers in particular have insisted on the unsubstantiality of memory and sensory perceptions, but perhaps no one has more assiduously mined this theme than Alain Resnais.* To complicate matters, this director often, as in *Last Year at Marienbad,* does not clearly distinguish between genuine memories, faulty though they might be, and fantasies.

Another function of the structuring of a plot is to arrange for the emergence of the climactic moments in a film. A *climax* is a point of heightened intensity that attracts a viewer's fullest attention. Most films have a major climax—the scene toward which everything before it leads and from which everything that follows is a consequence—and also minor climaxes, moments of relatively high intensity in a sequence or even a scene.

Although most motion pictures have only one major climax, some may have two or more. When the narrative spine of a film is primarily action, there is usually a single major climax. In a murder mystery, the climax probably occurs in the scene in which the murderer is identified. When characterization and relationships are as important as the physical action, there can be two separate major climaxes. For instance, the climax of the action of *Smiles of a Summer Night* is the elopement of Henrik and Anne; the climax of character revelation in this comedy is the dinner sequence in which all the guests realize that Anne is in love with her stepson. Naturally, one major climax may serve both functions, as in *Variety* when Huller kills his rival and rejects his wife.

*pp. 375–376

Minor climaxes appear within a sequence or, less frequently, within a scene. In *The Gold Rush,* there is a sequence in which first Charlie and then Big Jim takes refuge from a snowstorm in the cabin of the villainous Black Larsen, who is forced to accept them as guests. The scene in which the starving men draw cards to determine who is to go for help and Larsen leaves is the climax of the sequence, but it is a minor climax of the entire comedy. If unity of action is to be preserved, minor climaxes must be consistent with—and contribute to—preparation for the major climax. Each of the minor climaxes in *The Wild Bunch* prepares the viewer for the fateful decision by Pike Bishop to challenge the bandit leader Mapache, which results in the climactic massacre.

The third aspect of plot that a filmmaker must take into consideration is the degree to which each event is developed. Some events are, of course, more important than others. Generally, the more significant an incident, the greater the detail and cinematic time devoted to it. A climactic scene, for example, is usually carefully developed. On the other hand, a director may choose to understate an important moment in a film or dwell on one that is only peripherally relevant to the major and minor themes of a work. A very brief scene, for example, may give the viewer a vital insight into the motivation of a character. In *Stagecoach,* a dialogue of less than a minute between Doc Boone and the Ringo Kid explains the young man's incredible naiveté about women. A lengthy scene may function solely to create atmosphere and to establish a place setting. In short, a discerning viewer not only pays attention to and questions why an event is carefully developed, but also recognizes that the duration and detailed presentation of the event are not infallible indications of its significance in relation to the whole film.

The plot of a motion picture can be considered a skeleton that establishes the structure of a film, just as the themes determine its function.

## SCENES AND SEQUENCES

It is conventional to divide a film into three dramatic units in order of increasing complexity—shot, scene, and sequence. A *shot* is determined by a mechanical process (an uninterrupted running of the camera). A *scene* or *sequence,* on the other hand, is defined by its dramatic content in relation to the entirety of a film. Duration and number are useful but not infallible criteria for distinguishing among the three. Although a scene is longer than a shot and a sequence is longer than a scene, the enfolding of a scene in an individual film may require more cinematic time than a sequence in the same motion picture. Even though a series of shots usually makes up a scene and a series of scenes makes up a sequence, it is possible for a scene to consist of a single shot and a sequence of a single scene.

In the earliest days of cinema, a scene was defined as a series of shots with the same setting. When a new setting was introduced, a new scene began. With the development of crosscutting, which allowed for the presentation of events taking place at approximately the same time in different settings, this standard became inapplicable. A scene need no longer have a unity of place, but it typically preserves a unity of time and definitely possesses a unity of action. The problem is identifying the smallest dramatic unit beyond the shot combining the unities of time and action. This is not difficult when the action is primarily physical, as with the Indian attack in *Stagecoach.* But when complex human relationships in a limited sphere of time predominate, the boundaries of the scenes blur (for example, the evening of the dinner party at the castle, which constitutes almost half the running time of *Smiles of a Summer Night*). A screenwriter usually indicates scenes while preparing a screenplay. A critic who does not have a screenplay containing these designations has to depend on personal judgment in referring to a scene. The same subjectivity prevails in determining the sequences in a film.

The following is a possible breakdown of the plot of D. W. Griffith's *Broken Blossoms* into its component sequences (indicated by Roman numerals). For Sequence I, there is a listing of scenes (indicated by Arabic numerals). A clearer understanding of what constitutes a sequence can be gained, especially after a viewing of the film, by comparing this breakdown with the plot summary of *Broken Blossoms.* *

*pp. 200–201

I. In China: 1. Street scenes. 2. A Chinaman prays in a temple of Buddha. 3. He attempts unsuccessfully to stop a fight between two British sailors. 4. He departs for England to propagate the "message of peace to the barbarous Anglo-Saxons." II. Three People in Limehouse. III. Encounter Between Lucy and the Chinaman. IV. Battling Beats His Daughter, but She Finds a Haven. V. Discovery and a Vow of Revenge. VI. Two Struggles—One Physical and the Other Emotional. VII. Battling's Revenge. VIII. Battling Kills Lucy and Is Killed in Turn. IX. The Chinaman Finds Peace Through Suicide.

## PLACE AND TIME SETTINGS

Every scene in a motion picture with a narrative has a place setting that is a physical entity, whether or not it is identifiable by an audience. A time setting may be less specific, but unless a film takes place at some vague time in the future, such as Godard's *Alphaville,* it is usually identifiable within an age if it is in the distant past or in a decade within our century. Although in a given motion picture either place or time can be more relevant to the plot, the two form a continuum that orients an audience as to where and when a sequence of events occurs.

If a film has definite and consistent time and place settings, there are many ways in which they can be conveyed to the viewer. The most direct way is through a title card in a silent film or dialogue in a sound film. If there is a commentator or narrator, a statement from that person will suffice (as in the opening sequence of Truffaut's *Jules and Jim*). Place may be indicated obliquely by a landmark, such as the Eiffel Tower in the background of the opening shots of *The 400 Blows.* A time setting is more difficult to suggest indirectly. One method is through the costumes. A historical film may use an important event that the audience will recognize or the appearance of famous personages. Props can also be useful in this respect.

A definite time and locale may be irrelevant to a plot. Fritz Lang's *M* could take place in any city at any time. The passage of time can also be ambiguous. In *The Gold Rush,* there is no indication of whether months or years elapse between Charlie and Big Jim's discovery of gold and their return home.

In later sections of this chapter, the types and functions of physical settings and the ways in which time can be manipulated are surveyed.* There is, however, one facet of a place-time setting that should be considered here.

*Exposition* in cinema is the process of supplying facts necessary to the understanding of a motion picture. Indicating antecedent action by means of a flashback is a form of exposition. Generally, the less exposition required, the more dramatic a work will be. The need for exposition is reduced if an audience is likely to be familiar with a place and a certain time.

Genre films in particular take advantage of the audience's familiarity with background material. A war film usually takes for granted that a viewer is informed about the causes and course of a conflict. Yet certain types of audiences are more knowledgeable about a sequence of events than others. Contemporary Russian viewers are thoroughly acquainted with the circumstances of the 1917 revolt in Leningrad, but even with translated title cards, American audiences are often confused by what is happening in *October*. Problems of exposition are not confined to motion pictures that include foreign locales and relatively distant events. The films of Woody Allen have a universal appeal, but only a New Yorker can appreciate fully the nuances in a number of scenes in *Annie Hall*.

Place and time settings are integral parts of the narrative dimension of any film. A filmmaker who deals with them perfunctorily runs the risk of disorienting the audience and misses the opportunity to enrich the concreteness and expressiveness of a motion picture.

CHARACTERIZATION

Characterization is the means by which an imaginary person in a film is developed and made credible to viewers. Although the term *character* usually refers to a human being, it can include a cartoon figure, an animal (for example, the dog in De Sica's *Umberto D*), or even a physical entity, such as HAL, the computer in Kubrick's *2001*. The following discussion of characterization, however, will be confined to human beings.

Not every person in a film is a character. At

least two criteria must be met. First, the person should be sufficiently prominent and individual to be noticeable and should not simply be a part of the background. Second, the person could not be eliminated from the film without substantially changing the plot or affecting the major and minor themes.

A distinction between two basic types of characters as defined by E. M. Forster in chapter 4 of *Aspects of the Novel* (1927) applies to cinema as well as to literary fiction. A *flat,* or *two-dimensional,* character is one who conforms to a type and is limited to a few characteristics or qualities. For example, in *Stagecoach,* the lieutenant who escorts the coach to its first way station, and Yakima, the wife of the Mexican stationmaster, are flat characters. A two-dimensional character who is sufficiently exaggerated becomes a caricature, as with Roger De Bris, the director, and L.S.D. in *The Producers. Rounded* characters are developed to the point where they have distinct personalities in which the viewer can discern the motivations that prompt their actions and the possibility of inner conflicts. The nine travelers in *Stagecoach* belong in this category.

The most immediate means by which a character is projected on the screen, aside from camera-editing dynamics and such other elements of presentation as lighting, is the physical presence and interpretation of an actor. Typecasting is based on the premise that an audience will assume a correspondence between physical appearance and character. This may be a valid assumption (as with Big Jim in *The Gold Rush*), or it may be misleading (the burly Huller in *Variety* is actually a gentle and sensitive person). Also contributing to a viewer's impression of a character are costume and makeup. Chaplin's Charlie the tramp, for instance, proclaims some of the qualities and contradictions of his nature by his costume. Lon Chaney was a master at using makeup as an adjunct to his creation of a role.

An actor's interpretation includes walk, gestures, and facial expressions. In *Broken Blossoms,* Lillian Gish adopts a hunched posture, a shuffling walk, and a tendency to clutch herself with her arms to indicate Lucy's insecurity. In silent films, actors were confined to physical characteristics, costumes, and makeup in creating characterizations. With the intro-

---

*pp. 55–58, pp. 41–42

duction of sound, actors vastly extended their range through tone of voice and delivery of lines. We need only to hear a single sentence spoken by Lina Lamont in *Singin' in the Rain* to realize that, though physically attractive, she is a crude person of limited intelligence. It is the expressiveness with which fine actors deliver lines and the quality of their voices that so often make dubbing by other actors a device that weakens the effectiveness of a film.

How an actor interprets a speech is as important as what he or she says. The screenplay supplies the basis for this element of characterization. The ways in which spoken words communicate the character of the speaker to an audience are too obvious to require illustration. Only a bit less self-evident is the ability of words to disguise as well as to reveal. This is done either purposely by a character for ulterior motives or because of self-deception. An example of self-deception is the frequent statements by Henrik in the first half of *Smiles of a Summer Night* that his theological studies have armed him against the temptations of the flesh.

The response to a situation of a fictional person is one of the most conclusive means of characterization. Any situation that requires a character to make a choice and to act on it is a test of the emotional makeup of that individual. It may even function as a sort of litmus paper of personality, demonstrating the presence of a trait that has previously remained hidden. The strength of character and courage of the drunken Doc Boone in *Stagecoach* are revealed only when a baby must be delivered at a way station and during an Indian attack. One can examine practically every film with a carefully constructed narrative dimension and discover situations that confirm a viewer's impression of the nature of a character or reveal new facets.

There is a distinction in critical analysis, however, between how a character acts and why. *Motivation* impels or incites the responses of an individual. In real life, we often encounter human actions that appear to be without motivation because of our limited knowledge about the persons involved. Art, in contrast, traditionally has tried to impose a degree of order on human existence. We usually require a plot to have some clues as to why characters act as they

do. The majority of narrative motion pictures, especially before the 1950s, carefully delineate the motivations of major characters. One of the functions of a critic who is elucidating on a conventional film is to point out character motivation that may not be obvious.

The easiest type of motivation to represent is the pressure of external circumstances inciting the actions of a character, as when an honest man steals a bicycle because without it and the job it guarantees, his family may starve. More difficult in cinema is revealing deep rooted, psychological motivations. The presentation of antecedent action, perhaps a flashback or other devices described earlier in this section, is one method. A character's response in one situation may help to explain a response in a different one. For example, in *The 400 Blows*, by observing Antoine's restiveness under the unloving and arbitrary authority of his parents and teachers, we anticipate that he will try to escape from the reformatory. Symbols may suggest a cause for otherwise mysterious effects. Again referring to *The 400 Blows*, only by recognizing the symbolic meaning of the sea can a viewer understand why Antoine feels a compulsion to run to a beach at the end of the film.

Definite indications of character motivation do not have the highest priority in all types of films. A surrealistic work is based on the premise that the intellect cannot apprehend the fundamental motives of human emotions, and this approach can perplex a viewer who insists on logical connections between causes and effects. Another movement also encouraged a nonrational view of motivation. In the fifties, the philosophical doctrine of existentialism attracted the attention of a number of filmmakers, notably French directors like Godard and Resnais. One of the tenets of existentialism is that in an absurd universe, people have the freedom to act by standards of their own making rather than by those of society. As one might expect, films based on existential fiction and drama (and there have been many—for example, Luchino Visconti's *The Stranger,* a version of Albert Camus's novella) have obscure motivations for major characters. This approach, however, has also influenced a wide range of films, including many with original screenplays, from Godard's *Breathless* and

Arthur Penn's *Mickey One* to, more recently, Anton-ioni's *The Passenger*. Most of these unconventional works contain a nonlinear plot.

One of the reasons many viewers are puzzled by a fictional individual who acts impulsively—in ways that are not in accordance with traits revealed earlier in a film—is that they have come to expect consistency in characterization and justifications for radical changes. From this perspective, there are two types of characters. A *static character* is stable throughout a film. The circumstances of his existence may vary during the events of the plot and his re-sponses to these events may reveal his character. His basic nature, however, remains constant or influenced only in small ways. The three major figures in *Broken Blossoms* and Shane in *Shane* are examples of static characters. On the other hand, a *dynamic character* is one who is profoundly affected by a sequence of events. At the end of a film such an individual is very different from what he was at the beginning.

In a fantasy, characters can be metamorphosed by the wave of the wand of a Prospero-like magician. This type of incredible transformation may also occur in certain melodramas and romances. However, in motion pictures we generally require that we not only can observe but also are given insights into a radical change of character. In *Variety,* the amiable, gener-ous Huller becomes a murderer because his love is betrayed. Leo is a "gray person in a gray life" in *The Producers* until he becomes an adventurous swindler under the tutelage of Max.

The point at which a character changes is usu-ally a climactic scene (though not necessarily the major climax of a film) in which he makes a decisive choice. Leo proclaims his emancipation at the Lincoln Center fountain in New York, a scene that Mel Brooks satirizes with melodramatic underscoring. In contrast, the inner conflict of Antonio before he attempts to steal a bicycle in *The Bicycle Thief* is unaccompanied by any dramatizing devices; shots of the desperate man and ones of an unguarded bicycle leaning against a wall on an empty street simply are juxtaposed re-peatedly.

Physical presence and the interpretation of an actor, dialogue, responses to a situation, motivation, dynamic changes—these are the major means by which a fictional person in a film is characterized. Relationships are also significant, but they will be dis-cussed separately. Our concern in this section has been with the narrative dimension, the category into which these techniques usually belong. As with the other elements of the narrative dimension, it cannot be reiterated too often that camera-editing dynamics and elements of presentation can play crucial roles in characterization. In the pages devoted to these two components of film, there are frequently references to how specific devices and approaches convey to an audience—sometimes in vivid, subtle ways that are impossible through the narrative dimension—the character of a person on the screen.

RELATIONSHIPS: CONFLICT OR HARMONY

Until now we have focused on the single individual in a film. We are, however, as interested in how a char-acter deals with the problems of his existence, which usually derive from relationships of various kinds, as in the traits of that character. The two, of course, correspond. The ways in which a fictional person reacts in a relationship usually reveal character; we cannot fully understand a relationship without some insights into the nature of the individual and the forces involved. Conflict and harmony are coupled with rela-tionships because any interplay between the human psyche and external or internal forces results in de-grees of either conflict or harmony.

The broadest perspective from which this as-pect of the narrative dimension can be examined con-sists of three categories: the individual and binding forces that are larger than the self, the individual and other human beings, and the individual and the self. In the first division, a human being interacts in signifi-cant ways with nature, religion, war, a nation, a city, a bureaucracy, or social mores—any binding force that transcends the individual. These are primarily ab-stractions. To be effective dramatically in a motion picture, however, an intangible force must be con-cretely manifested. In *The Gold Rush,* a title refers to "The North, A Law to Itself." What we relate to is what we see: not an abstract "North" but an ava-lanche destroying the villainous Black Larsen.

If a manifestation of an intangible force is a human being, he or she must function simultaneously as a vivid person and a personification or symbol. This is accomplished in a film like Cacoyannis's *Zorba the Greek,* in which a prim young intellectual learns to feel honestly and to act spontaneously through his relationship with the Greek. Zorba is both a credible human being and a personification of the élan vital in nature. Difficulties arise, especially if a conflict is involved, when a character representing an abstraction is flat and limited. This sometimes happens in political and war films. For instance, in the otherwise impressive *Open City* (directed by Roberto Rossellini), the Nazism against which the members of the Italian underground are pitted is exemplified by two Germans, Bergmann and Ingrid. Their cruelty and perversity are so exaggerated that they become caricatures rather than characters.

The relationships of an individual with other human beings (there is a special subdivision for animals) can take a multitude of forms. Harmony or conflict between a man and a woman, between men or women, and between parents and children are the most common. The more complex the relationship, the more we wish to know about the characters. When a conflict arises, the more equally balanced the antagonists, the more exciting the drama. Another variation is when one character remains static and another is dynamic; this can result in harmony, as between Max and Leo in *The Producers,* or conflict, as between Fredrik and his son in *Smiles of a Summer Night.* The only underlying principles that apply to all relationships between human beings in films are that the characters be believable and the conflicts or harmony between them be concrete and dramatic.

An individual's relationship with the self can be one of harmony, as in the case of Jerry Travers in *Top Hat,* but a person with interior conflicts usually attracts our interest. Practically all dynamic characters change as a result of an inner conflict. Most conflicts with external binding forces and other human beings derive from an inability to reconcile opposing emotions. Although interior tensions are crucial to our understanding of a character, no aspect of the narrative dimension is more difficult to project on the screen. Unlike literary fiction, we cannot enter the mind of a character. The interior monologue is usually artificial, as is the use of a commentator. Of the various means

of developing a character in the narrative dimension, dialogue and responses individual to a situation are the most expressive for this purpose. More exceptional are dreams and hallucinations. Camera-editing dynamics—especially subjective shots and elements of presentation, particularly the interpretation of an actor—can give us insights into the interior conflicts of a character that are not stated explicitly. Other devices have also been developed. One of these is the diary, as in Bresson's *The Diary of a Country Priest.* In his later films, Bergman brilliantly uses the spoken monologue (as in *Persona,* when Alma describes a sexual encounter while on a vacation) or a letter (as in *Winter Light*).

An individual's inner conflicts may or may not be resolved by the conclusion of a film. A resolution is either forced upon a person by circumstances (as in *Top Hat,* when Dale's doubts about Jerry are dispersed when she learns his true identity) or if a conscious choice is made (as when Shane decides to leave the valley after ridding it of the scourge of Ryker and his men). At the end of a film, a character can still be debating within himself, as Andreas is doing in the final scene of Bergman's *The Passion of Anna.* Occasionally, a director concludes a motion picture with a symbolic rather than an actual resolution. Fellini is particularly fond of this device; he uses it in the last sequences of, among other works, *Nights of Cabiria, La Dolce Vita,* and *8 ½.*

These categories are not intended to be exclusive of one another. It is not uncommon for one character to encounter all three types of relationships in one film. In *The Wild Bunch,* Pike endures a trek across a desert, debates internally whether or not he should attempt to save a member of his gang, and fights with Mapache and his men. One form of relationship can lead to another. In *Smiles of a Summer Night,* Fredrik's duel with Malcolm results in his accepting the loss of his young wife and in his returning to his former mistress. This film also illustrates how a network of relationships, with varying degrees of conflict and harmony, can exist among rounded characters; in the case of Bergman's film, there are eight such characters.

This survey of the narrative dimension of film has been confined to major elements. Others that are less prominent but also important—such as the point beyond which chance as a principle of determining events in a sequence strains our credulity and the role symbols play in revealing character and relationships —have only been alluded to. There is, however, one general aspect that must be at least briefly considered.

Each rounded character in a film is unique, existing in a special place-time continuum that is the setting for incidents that are distinctive, although not necessarily original. Yet a fictional character may also represent or symbolize a type as well as be a unique individual. The same holds true for a situation. In *The 400 Blows,* Antoine is both himself and a prototype of all youngsters who are neglected and misunderstood by parents and other adults. Although the many relationships in *Smiles of a Summer Night* evolve in Sweden during the spring of 1901, the contrasting attitudes toward love in youth, middle age, and old age transcend a specific time and place.

An analogy inspired by Plato might provide some clarification. The imagination of a filmmaker is like a spotlight directed at fictional characters that causes shadows to appear on a wall behind them. The stronger the light, the more clearly we see the characters and the larger the shadows become. These shadows present no details and are larger than the specific character acting in specific ways. They correspond to the universality of individual characters in a distinctive sequence of events. If the imagination of the filmmaker is weak, the characters are difficult to discern clearly, and their universality is faint or nonexistent.

The degree to which the characters and events in a motion picture possess universality may generally be acknowledged or debatable. Few would deny that *Smiles of a Summer Night* magnificently transcends the particular. Few would maintain that the same is true of *The Producers* or *Top Hat.* Since its release, critics have argued whether the members of the Wild Bunch in Peckinpah's film are exceptional in their pleasure in violence or whether they represent a repressed trait of human nature. An attempt by a filmmaker to invest characters and events with symbolic overtones is no guarantee of universality. One of the functions of film criticism is to help us distinguish between works that are simply pretentious and those that contain genuine intimations of universal emotions and situations.

## CAMERA-EDITING DYNAMICS

Cinema developed the potential of being an art form when filmmakers were able to go beyond simply recording reality to re-creating it through camera movement and editing. These two processes infuse a narrative dimension with the characteristics that are unique to the medium. Because photographing with a motion picture camera and cutting, reassembling, and splicing together developed footage are accomplished in separate stages, shooting and editing are usually treated as distinct entities in cinematic studies.

I feel, however, that from the viewer's perspective the two processes are inextricably bound together. There are decisions confined to one stage, such as types of transitions between shots during editing, but generally the viewer of a final print has no way of ascertaining whether a choice made during shooting or editing determined what appears on the screen. In an introduction to cinema, it is the film itself that is of primary interest. For this reason, I have hyphenated *camera* and *editing.* To emphasize that the essential element of this multifaceted aspect of filmmaking is movement, I have added the word *dynamics.*

### THE SHOT

Practically all motion pictures consist of individual shots joined together by transitions* into scenes and sequences.

**SHOT** A single, uninterrupted (actual or apparent) running of the camera.

The qualifier "actual or apparent" is necessary because occasionally a cut between two shots is so brief that the shots appear as one on the screen.

*Frame*
A shot is, in turn, made up of frames; however, during

───────

*pp. 29–34

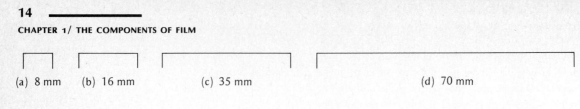

(a) 8 mm    (b) 16 mm    (c) 35 mm    (d) 70 mm

**FIGURE 1.1**

Comparison of four standard gauges (actual width).

the normal running of a projector, a single frame never appears on the screen. To complicate matters, the term *frame* has two referents.

**FRAME** 1. A single image on a strip of film. 2. The perimeter of the screen at any moment the motion picture is being shown.

*Definition of FRAME—1* / What is attached to a projector is a lengthy strip of developed film wound on a reel. The width of the film is measured in millimeters (1mm = 0.03937 inch), and there are standardized widths called *gauges*.

A *reel* is both the spool attached to the projector on which a film is wound and a specific length of film. A full reel (approximately 1200 feet) of 16mm film provides about 30 minutes of screening time.

A projector operates at a consistent speed that determines how many frames per second are projected on the screen. The two conventional speeds are silent (16 to 18 frames per second) and sound (24 frames per second). Variations of speed within a film are discussed under the subheadings "Slow Motion" and "Accelerated Motion."*

Although a shot may consist of any number of frames, a strip of film is made up of a specific number of frames per length. For instance, a foot of 16mm film contains 40 frames. Each frame is basically a still photograph (such as one might take with an ordinary still camera) that is projected on the screen for approximately $\frac{1}{24}$ to $\frac{1}{16}$ second before being replaced by the next image. There are minute variations from one frame to the next that cumulatively create the illusion of motion. This is possible because of a characteristic of human eyesight called *persistence of vision*. The retina of the eye retains an image for a fraction of a second after it disappears. If one image replaces an-

other within $\frac{1}{24}$ second, the human eye does not record any discontinuity between the two images. Motion pictures exist because we have persistence of vision.

An exception to this principle appears to be a *freeze frame,* such as the last shot of *The 400 Blows.* * That single image seems to remain fixed, or "frozen," for a few seconds. Actually, a freeze frame is the same frame repeated (at the rate of 24 frames per second in the case of a sound film) for as many seconds as the image remains.

Although we cannot see a single frame during the screening of a film, we are often exposed to single frames in printed material on cinema. With the proper equipment attached to a still camera, it is possible to photograph a single frame, then enlarge and print it. A *frame enlargement* is one of two types of *stills* (a still is a photograph of a single image in a film). The other type consists of those taken by a still photographer, usually for purposes of publicity, during the production of a motion picture. Stills appear in books, magazines, and newspapers and in advertisements outside movie theaters. Usually there is no indication as to whether a still is a frame enlargement or a production photograph. Unless otherwise noted, however, all stills in this book are frame enlargements.

*Definition of FRAME—2* / In analyzing a film it is useful to have a consistent framework within which the directions of actions can be indicated. No matter how many changes occur during a screening of a motion picture, the perimeter of the screen remains fixed (except as noted below) and is referred to as the *frame,* as in the sentence, "The actor enters frame left." It has become standard practice to designate direction within a frame (in this context) from the viewer's (camera's) left or right, top or bottom.

Sometimes a writer will add the adjective *camera* to *left* or *right* to differentiate from the actor's left or right (which changes depending on whether or not the actor is facing the camera).

**FIGURE 1.2**

Designation of directions for a frame enlargement. (From *Beauty and the Beast,* directed by Jean Cocteau, 1946.)

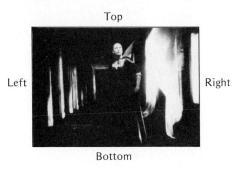

Top

Left        Right

Bottom

The proportions of the perimeter of a screen, or *format,* are designated the *aspect ratio.*

**ASPECT RATIO** The relative proportions of the width and height of the frame (both definitions 1 and 2).

The conventional format is a ratio of 4 (width) to 3 (height) or, more exactly, 1.33 to 1 (called the *academic frame*). For wide-screen systems, the ratio can increase to 1.85 to 1 or even to 2.2 to 1 (Panavision) and 2.55 to 1 (Cinemascope). Television's aspect ratio of 4 to 3 is the standard one. This explains why telecasting a motion picture that was originally photographed for a wide-screen system causes problems.

A wide screen can affect the dynamics of a scene, particularly when groups of actors are involved. This is evident in the fight and dance sequences in *West Side Story,* a Panavision film.

Although it rarely occurs, it is possible to change the format of the shots for a whole sequence, as Abel Gance did in the last sequence of *Napoléon.* * During the silent era, the shapes of individual screen images were altered by means of *masking.*

**MASKING** The use of a shield over a lens to change the shape, usually the width or height, of a shot.

**FIGURE 1.4**

Masking of a shot. (From *Broken Blossoms.*)

One of the advantages of this device is to give an area of a shot prominence without moving the camera closer to the subject.

The major characteristics of a shot are (1) content, (2) distance, (3) angle, (4) duration, and (5) camera movement. A single shot may be described by one of these characteristics or, infrequently, by all five in any appropriate order (for example, a high-angle shot; a lengthy, medium, eye-level, panning shot).

**FIGURE 1.3**

Diagrams of three aspect ratios.

*p. 112

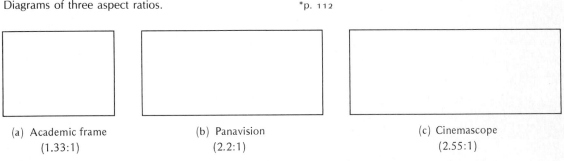

(a) Academic frame      (b) Panavision               (c) Cinemascope
    (1.33:1)              (2.2:1)                     (2.55:1)

### Content

Content includes that portion of reality photographed for the duration of a single shot. The way in which a shot is photographed (that is, its form) is the means used by the filmmaker to influence what a viewer thinks or feels about its content. Although there are rare exceptions, such as microphotography, there is no single, invariable way in which a portion of reality must be re-created. On the other hand, certain types of shots or characteristics of a shot are defined solely on the basis of content, regardless of the form chosen by the filmmaker. The prevalent labels in this category are the *establishing shot,* the *subjective shot,* the *reaction shot,* and a specification of how many individuals appear in a shot.

**ESTABLISHING (OR MASTER) SHOT** An early shot that establishes the setting of a scene or sequence in the viewer's mind. Without this type of primary shot, the viewer would become disoriented as the camera revealed only portions of the setting.

**SUBJECTIVE SHOT** Shot from the point of view of a character in the film rather than that of an observer outside of the action.

This type of shot is discussed more extensively later in this chapter under the subheading "Point of View."*

**FIGURE 1.5**

Establishing shots. (a) From the opening sequence of *Shane.* (b) From the second sequence of *Variety.*

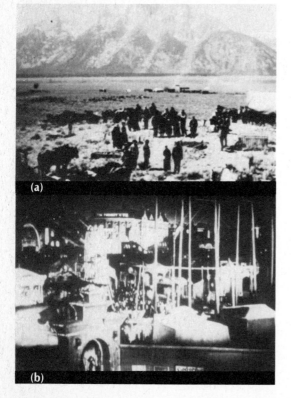

**FIGURE 1.6**

Subjective shot. (a) First shot indicates from whose point of view is the subjective shot. (b) Subjective shot follows. (From *Variety.*)

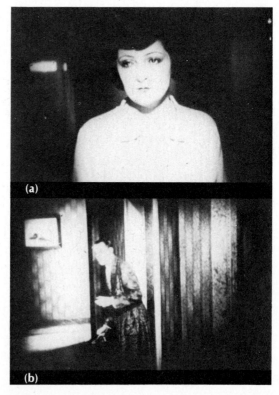

* pp. 42–43

**REACTION SHOT** Reveals the reaction of a person or persons to something presented in the preceding shot.

**FIGURE 1.7**

Reaction shot. (a) A boy jumps out to frighten a young woman. (b) Reaction shot of a young woman. (From *The Mischief Makers,* directed by François Truffaut, 1957.)

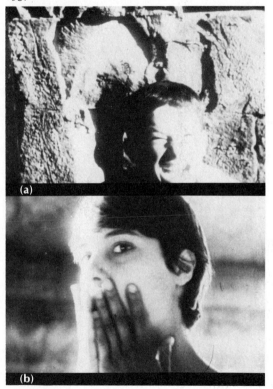

(a)

(b)

**NUMBER OF INDIVIDUALS IN A SHOT** A *one-shot* contains one person (two examples appear in Figure 1.6); a *two-shot,* two persons; and so on. More than four persons in a shot is usually referred to as a *group-shot.*

### Distance

The distance between camera and subject is not indicated by well-defined designations. Instead, there are three general categories, long, medium, and close (and/or close-up). When the scale is the human figure, at least some specificity is possible.

**LONG** Showing the full figure and usually a portion of the setting.

**MEDIUM** Showing the body from approximately the waistline to the top of the head.

**CLOSE** Extending from the shoulders to just above the head. Some writers reject the term *close shot* and use *close-up,* indicating closer distances by *extreme close-up* or, borrowing a term from television production, *tight close-up.*

**FIGURE 1.8**

Human subject. (a) Long shot. (From *Smiles of a Summer Night.*) (b) Medium shot. (From *Shane.*) (c) Close shot. (From *October.*) (d) Close-up. (From *Broken Blossoms.*)

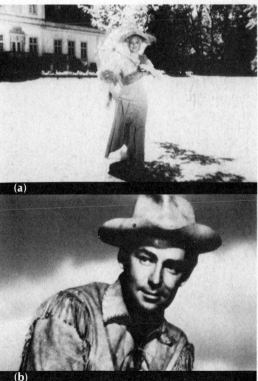

(a)

(b)

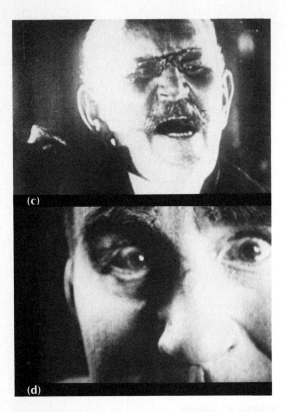

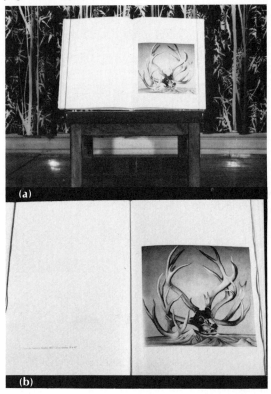

**FIGURE 1.9**

Objects. (a) Long shot of a table and open book on a stand. (b) Medium shot of the book. (c) Close shot of a page of the book. (d) Close-up of a detail on the page. (Photographs by the author.)

**CLOSE-UP** Showing an area of the head (for example, the eyes) or, less often, another small portion of the human anatomy (for example, a hand).

When there is the absence of the scale of a human being in a shot, designations of distances can become extremely subjective. A single shot, however, can function, in a sense, as a benchmark if it is followed by a series of images during which the distance noticeably increases or decreases.

On the other hand, in Figure 1.9, the long shot (a) might be of the wall of a room, including the table and book, the medium shot (b) of the table and book, the close shot (c) of the book, and the close-up (d) of a page in the book.

Another aspect of distance involves the illusion of depth on a two-dimensional screen. Especially for long shots, it is helpful to differentiate between what appears to be closer or more distant from the camera (viewer).

**FOREGROUND** The area closest to the camera.

**BACKGROUND** The area farthest from the camera.

The terms *foreground* and *background* are not only useful in describing a shot, but they are also necessary in understanding the limitations of motion picture photography before the late 1930s.

Filmmakers of the silent era had to take into account the *depth of field* of individual camera units when shooting.

**DEPTH OF FIELD** The range within which a subject is in focus at any given moment. Lenses for cameras are classified according to focal length and diameter of the lens opening. A combination of both these factors

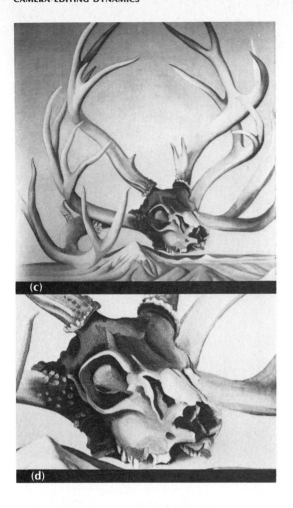

**FIGURE 1.10**

Shift in focus during a single shot. (From *Beauty and the Beast,* directed by Jean Cocteau, 1946.)

determines a shot's depth of field. Any subject or setting outside of the depth of field appears blurred to some degree.

A filmmaker may make the limitation of depth of field an advantage. It is possible to have two subjects within a shot and focus on each in turn. Without the camera or subjects moving, an audience's attention is shifted from one subject to the other.

The restrictions imposed by depth of field were minimized by the development of *deep focus.*

**DEEP FOCUS** Equally sharp definition of objects both close to and distant from the camera, achieved through the use of a special lens and appropriate aperture openings.

This type of motion picture photography allows relationships—emotional as well as physical—within a shot to be observed without the director's calling attention to them by moving the camera or adjusting the lens. The potentials of this device are so impressive that it has been elevated by some critics to the status of a stylistic technique and is occasionally designated as *deep-focus cinematography.* As the Xanadu interiors in *Citizen Kane* demonstrate, deep focus makes clear to an audience with particular vividness how physical settings reflect and influence characterizations. More recent examples include scenes in Kubrick's *2001* (1968), Coppola's *The Godfather* (1972), and Spielberg's *Jaws* (1975).

---

**FIGURE 1.11**

Two interior shots in deep focus. (From *Citizen Kane,* directed by Orson Welles, 1941.)

---

**FIGURE 1.12**

Camera movement between two shots: long (a) to medium (b). (From *Broken Blossoms.*)

As with each characteristic of a shot aside from content, changes in distance create visual dynamics. Movement toward the camera increases the authority of a subject; movement away from the camera diminishes it. This principle applies whether there is camera or subject movement within a shot (discussed later) or between two shots.

Although changes in distance are accomplished usually by camera movement within or between shots, there are three devices whereby it is possible to present a segment of a shot without moving the camera.

A *zoom shot* allows a director to move toward and away from a subject with a static camera by adjusting a varifocal lens (not developed until the mid-

fifties), which enlarges or reduces the image during a shot. A viewer perceives the resultant effect as camera movement, so it could be considered a type of ersatz tracking shot.* Because the camera itself does not move, however, the device is included here. Sam Peckinpah repeatedly uses zoom shots in *The Wild Bunch.* † Masking and a *fixed iris-out* rarely appear on the screen today, but they were common in silent films when it was difficult to move large, heavy cameras and lighting had to be adjusted for each new distance. Masking was described earlier.‡

---

*pp. 26–29
†p. 434
‡p. 15

An *iris-out* is a transition device and will be noted under that heading.* Directors of silent films, however, could begin an iris-out (black diffusing from the edges of the frame in an increasingly constricting circle of light), then fix it at a certain point. What was still illuminated in the circle was intended to be significant. After viewers had time to focus their attention on this portion of the shot, the iris-out continued until the screen was black or there was a cut from a fixed iris-out to the next shot.

### FIGURE 1.13

Fixed iris-out. (From *The Gold Rush.*) This is the end of the shot; it is followed by a cut to the next shot.

### Angle (or camera angle)

The angle at which the camera is pointed at the subject. The main angles are low, eye level, and high.

**LOW ANGLE** The camera is below the subject; the viewer "looks up" at what is being photographed.

A low-angle shot tends to aggrandize what appears on the screen. The expression "looking up to a person" is made visually concrete from this perspective.

On the other hand, a low-angle shot may instill fear in a viewer, or, if it is subjective, it may suggest that a character is gripped by this emotion because the subject is made more imposing.

*pp. 33–34

### FIGURE 1.14

Low-angle shot. (From *Triumph of the Will.*) In this documentary, Hitler is repeatedly photographed from a low angle to encourage admiration of him.

### FIGURE 1.15

Low-angle shot. (From *The Producers.*) Leo is on the floor, with Max standing over him. A subjective, low-angle shot from Leo's point of view reveals the bulky producer as a frightening figure towering over him.

**EYE LEVEL** The camera is neither noticeably above nor below the subject.

This angle establishes a neutral relationship between camera (viewer) and subject; it conveys no inherent emotional connotation. Of course, drama may be instilled into an eye-level shot by other characteristics of the shot, such as a content in which the subject fires a gun directly at viewers.

**FIGURE 1.16**

Eye-level shot. (From *The Great Train Robbery,* directed by Edwin S. Porter, 1903.)

**HIGH ANGLE** The camera is above the subject; the viewer "looks down" at what is being photographed.

This angle has the opposite effect of a low-angle shot: The authority and significance of the subject is diminished. In an emotional sense, the viewer is "looking down upon" the subject.

**FIGURE 1.17**

High-angle shot. (From *The Producers.*) This shot follows the one illustrated in Figure 1.15. Max is looking down (both literally and emotionally) at Leo lying on the floor.

A *reverse-angle* shot depends, for its effectiveness, on the angle at which the camera is pointed at the subject. However, unlike the three angles just defined, this designation cannot be applied to a single shot.

**REVERSE ANGLE** A reversal between two shots of the direction in which the camera is photographing a subject, usually consisting of two people.

This device is most often used when two characters are speaking to each other. First one character is featured, then the other.

**FIGURE 1.18**

Reverse-angle shot. (From *North by Northwest,* directed by Alfred Hitchcock, 1958.) The scene from which these two shots are taken consists almost entirely of a series of reverse-angle shots.

(a)

(b)

Most filmmakers comply with a principle involving the reversal of angles in this type of shot.

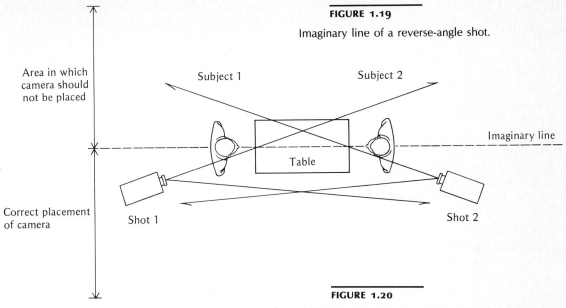

**FIGURE 1.19**

Imaginary line of a reverse-angle shot.

Area in which camera should not be placed

Subject 1

Subject 2

Imaginary line

Table

Correct placement of camera

Shot 1

Shot 2

**FIGURE 1.20**

False reverse-angle shot. (From *The Mischief Makers*, directed by François Truffaut, 1957.)

When photographing two characters who face each other, the director and cinematographer should take the *imaginary line* into account. This line cannot be crossed between two shots without the risk of disorienting the viewer.

Figure 1.20 demonstrates what happens when the filmmaker crosses the imaginary line in positioning the camera or cameras between two shots. The viewer may be confused by the reversal of figures: the young man is on the left in the first shot and suddenly on the right in the second.

Although the short *The Mischief Makers* was Truffaut's first professional film, we assume that the false reverse-angle shot was intentional. A plausible explanation is that Truffaut used this device to suggest that reality is disoriented for two lovers when they embrace.

Usually, two cameras are operating during a series of reverse-angle shots, with alternating shots edited together. When only one camera is available, the scene is photographed from one side and repeated with the camera on the other side; the shots are later edited in proper sequence.

The emotional connotation of most reverse-angle shots is two people who are separated yet at the same time connected in some way. This is midway

(a)

(b)

between the isolation of alternate one-shots and the connectivity of two-shots in which the individuals are together within the frame.

### Duration

Duration is the length of time a shot lasts from beginning to end. An individual shot can last from approximately ½ second (a viewer has difficulty perceiving anything briefer as an individual entity) to hours in avant-garde films such as Andy Warhol's *Empire* (which appears to be, but is not, one shot that is 8 hours long). Although there is no typical duration for a shot, an average of 20 seconds is an educated guess. The more adventurous commercial directors have experimented with unusually lengthy shots. Prominent examples include Bergman (especially in his films of the sixties in which a character delivers a monologue enclosed in one shot that varies from 2 to 5 minutes), Godard (for example, the brilliant moving shot of 10-minutes' duration near the beginning of *Weekend*), and Antonioni (for instance, the famous 7-minute penultimate shot of *The Passenger*).

The vital roles that the durations of shots can play in the rhythm of scenes, crosscutting, and cinematic time are considered under these topics later in this chapter. To prevent confusion with distance, it is preferable to use the adjectives *brief* and *lengthy,* rather than *long* and *short,* when referring in general terms to the duration of a shot.

### Camera movement

Camera movement is one of three categories of movement within a shot. The other two are action within the frame and in-the-camera special effects. All three may operate simultaneously, as when the camera pans (camera movement) along a line of soldiers running toward the camera (action within the frame) in slow motion ("in-the-camera" special effect). We will consider, however, each separately.

When the camera is static and running at normal speed, the movement of subjects within a shot is toward and away from the edges of the frame, toward and away from the camera, or combinations and variations of these two fundamental directions. At a fixed distance from the camera, the center of the frame is the area of greatest stability. Very generally,

motion of a subject away from the center (left or right, up or down) leads to a weakening of authority and of the interest of the viewer. The reverse is also true, similar to the way an actor who wishes the full attention of an audience walks to center stage. Movement toward or away from the camera initiates comparable dynamics. The former action increases the authority of a subject; the latter diminishes it.

*In-the-camera* special effects are those that can be photographed by the camera rather than solely through laboratory processes. Special effects are described later under "Elements of Presentation."* Three in-the-camera effects are relevant here, however, because they depend on forms of motion within the shot.

**SLOW MOTION** Images on the screen appear to move at a slower rate than in reality.

As noted earlier, cameras operate at standard speeds. Projectors should run at the speed corresponding to the standard that was used during shooting. However, if a camera is run at a faster speed than its standard for a portion of the *footage* (amount of film), yet the developed film is projected at the standard rate, movement on the footage will appear to be slower than usual on the screen.

Slow motion can expose details of an action that we would otherwise not be able to observe at normal projection speed. Leni Riefenstahl uses this technique in photographing athletes in *Olympia*. In this case, slow motion reveals the grace of the movements of runners, divers, and others. Another function of slow motion is to call attention to an action by extending it in time, as in the death of Bonnie and Clyde in Arthur Penn's film. Finally, slow motion can dramatize visually the psychological pressure on an individual who is attempting to accomplish something in a limited period of time. In *The Wild Bunch,* Angel, one of the outlaws, is trying to escape from a bandit general and his men. Angel's desperate ride to reach a gate and freedom is photographed in slow motion.

**ACCELERATED MOTION (OR FAST MOTION)** Images appear to move at a faster rate than in reality.

---

*pp. 59–60

This type of special-effect motion has appeared most often in comedies. It can also accentuate mysterious, frightening forces, as in F. W. Murnau's silent film *Nosferatu.* Godard and Truffaut have also utilized this technique for noncomic purposes.

**REVERSE MOTION** A person or object appears to move in a reverse sequence from that seen in conventional motion picture photography.

As with accelerated motion, this device is a staple of film comedy, but it can also be effective for serious purposes. At the conclusion of *Beauty and the Beast,* the Prince and Beauty seem to rise into the sky. As Jean Cocteau points out in his *Diary of a Film* (1946), the two actors jumped from a raised, hidden platform; then the footage was reversed in the final print to create the effect of the characters levitating.

Camera movement chiefly includes *panning, tilting,* and *tracking.* For the first two movements, the camera is attached to a fixed base (tripod); in tracking, the camera itself is in motion.

**PAN** A pan results when a camera on a fixed base has pivoted on a horizontal plane. *Panning* describes this movement; a *pan shot* contains panning as a major characteristic of a single shot. The extent of a pan may be noted in degrees, with the camera in the center of a circle, the beginning of a pan at 0 degrees, and the end indicating the number of degrees the camera has turned on its axis in an uninterrupted motion. For example, in a 180-degree pan the camera pivots half a circle. A swish pan is so rapid that the image is blurred.

On the simplest level, panning reveals more of an exterior or interior than is evident within the confines of the frame of a static shot, so establishing shots frequently include this type of movement. Panning may also establish relationships or supply information. Near the end of *Stagecoach* there is a pan from a solitary coach on a plain to Indians on a hill above, preparing the audience for the attack that follows.

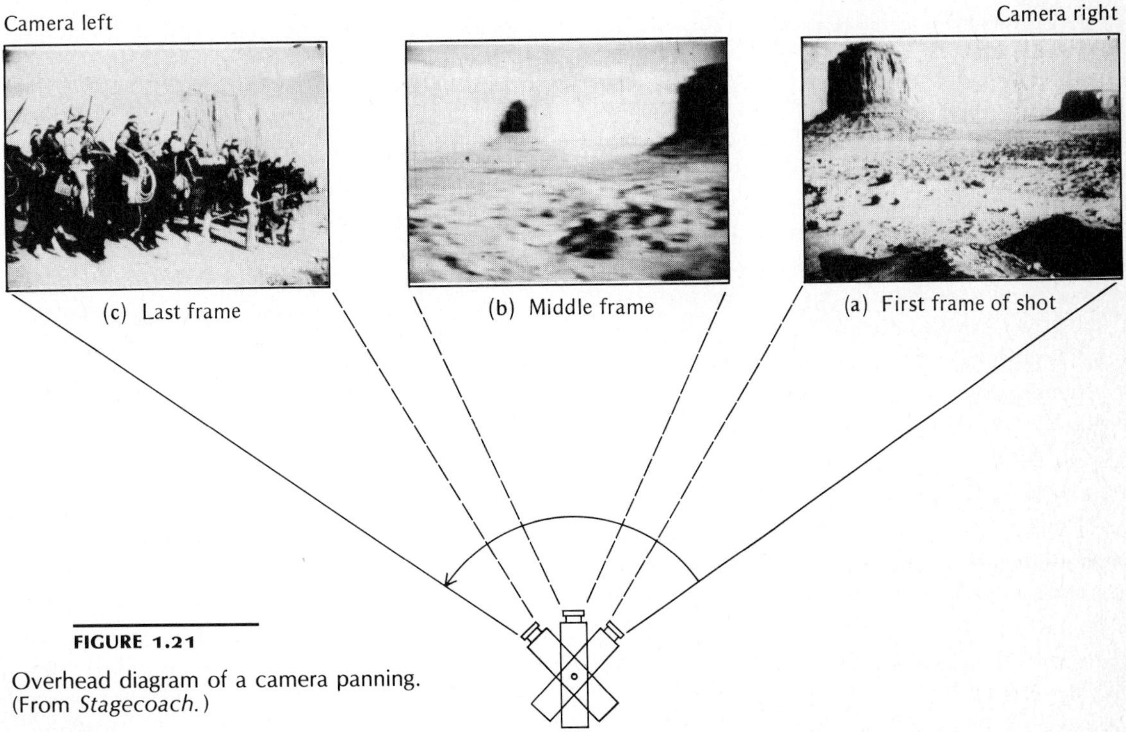

Camera left

Camera right

(c) Last frame    (b) Middle frame    (a) First frame of shot

**FIGURE 1.21**

Overhead diagram of a camera panning. (From *Stagecoach.*)

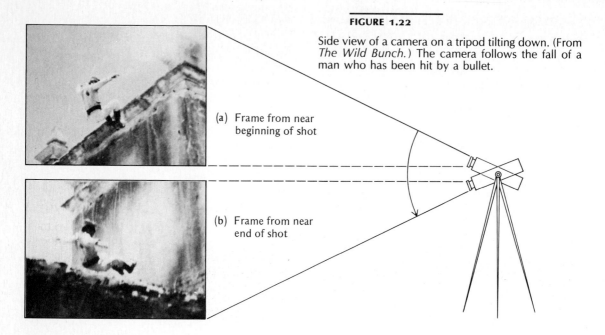

**FIGURE 1.22**

Side view of a camera on a tripod tilting down. (From *The Wild Bunch.*) The camera follows the fall of a man who has been hit by a bullet.

(a) Frame from near beginning of shot

(b) Frame from near end of shot

**TILT** A type of camera movement in which the camera on a fixed base pivots on a vertical plane; *tilting* describes this movement. *Down* or *up* indicates the direction, in relation to the beginning of the shot, in which the camera pivots.

Tilting can add the emphasis of movement to the ability of a static low-angle shot to aggrandize a subject or a high-angle one to diminish it. In *Triumph of the Will,* the director emphasizes the power of the Nazi party by tilting up from an eye-level shot of marching soldiers to a low-angle perspective of a banner containing a swastika. A device so often used that it has become a visual cliché is in a fight scene to tilt down from the victor to the vanquished lying on the ground. Moreover, a tilt has an advantage over a static angle shot in that it follows an action rather than solely indicating a state of being.

**TRACKING (DOLLYING, TRUCKING)** A type of camera movement in space (as distinct from camera movement on a stationary base, as in panning and tilting). The camera travels backward or forward in relation to a fixed subject or keeps a moving subject within the frame as both camera and subject travel at the same or different speeds.

*Dollying* and *trucking* are synonyms for *tracking* from the viewer's perspective because the viewer is usually unaware of the vehicle on which the camera is mounted. To the filmmaker, however, there are distinctions: In tracking, the camera is placed on a platform that moves along tracks, like a train; in dollying, the camera is attached to a dolly (a four-wheeled wagon); in trucking, the camera is mounted on a truck or car. Less frequently used is the term *crane shot,* in which the camera is attached to a crane that moves upward or downward and/or from side to side.

Synonyms for *tracking* that are general and do not refer to the vehicle on which the camera is mounted are *moving shot* and *traveling shot.* However, throughout this book, *tracking* is with very few exceptions the only term used.

Other terminology that distinguishes between types of tracking shots are *tracking in,* which occurs when the camera moves toward a subject, and *tracking back,* which is the reverse movement. When the subject moves away from the camera and the latter keeps pace, the camera is *following the subject.* When the subject moves toward the camera and the latter keeps pace traveling back, the camera is *leading the subject.*

**FIGURE 1.23**

Tracking-in shot. (From *Stagecoach.*) (a) First frame of the shot. (b) Middle frame of the shot. (c) Last frame of the shot. During editing, other shots were intercut.

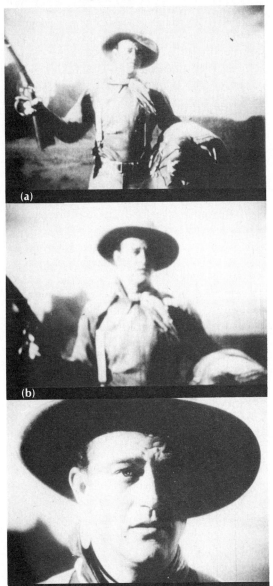

(a)

(b)

(c)

**FIGURE 1.24**

Tracking shot with the camera leading the subject. (From *The Wild Bunch.*) (a) First frame of the shot. (b) Middle frame of the shot. (c) Last frame of the shot.

(a)

(b)

(c)

Tracking has the potential of being the most complicated camera movement. Its fundamental action, tracking in or tracking back from a still subject, causes the same dynamic effect as a subject moving

---

**FIGURE 1.25**

Camera traveling parallel to the setting. (From *Shane.*) (a) Early frame. (b) Later frame. (c) Still later frame (shot continues).

toward or away from a static camera—that is, it increases or diminishes the authority of the subject. (As was pointed out earlier, this type of dynamism can also be achieved with a static camera through the use of a zoom lens.) An emphatic form of this movement occurs when the subject moves toward the camera while the camera simultaneously tracks in on the subject, or the subject moves away while the camera tracks back. In Hitchcock's 1958 film, he induced vertigo in audiences through combinations of forward-zoom and tracking-back shots.

A variation of tracking consists of the camera traveling parallel to the subject. When the subject is stationary and the camera is moving, the function of this motion usually is to reveal detailed aspects of the setting or the subject that could not be encompassed within a static shot.

When both subject and camera are moving and are parallel to each other, the impression is primarily one of kinetic purposefulness. If the shot is of sufficient duration, it induces a strong identification of a viewer with a subject.

Only four prototypical tracking shots have been described here. There are many other possibilities, including a camera circling a subject. Once a camera is removed from a fixed tripod and set in motion, there are many ways within a shot by which a filmmaker can relate the camera to both stationary and moving subjects.

Whether static or including motion, every shot has composition, tone, and rhythms. *Composition* (the putting together of parts to form a whole) in a shot is an integration of a multitude of elements, including shapes, vertical and horizontal thrusts, lines of perspective in space, light and dark areas (or color), and the textures of surfaces. Generally, the composition of a shot determines the esthetic values of an image. A matter of dispute among film theorists is whether or not in a narrative the content of a shot and its relation to previous shots influence our reactions to an individual composition. A comprehensive introduction to this intriguing question can be found in the first chapter of Vladimir Nilsen's *The Cinema as a Graphic Art.* [2] Tone and rhythm are discussed as separate topics later in this section.

**FIGURE 1.26**

Camera tracking parallel to a moving subject. (From *The 400 Blows*.) (a) Early frame. (b) Later frame. (c) Still later frame (shot continues).

Aside from a few avant-garde works, however, films are made up of individual shots joined together by transitions. As with other elements of camera-editing dynamics, the type of transition influences, even if imperceptibly, the reactions of an audience to what appears on the screen. The most common transitions are the cut, the dissolve, and the fade. The superimposition and the wipe are less frequently used. The iris-in and iris-out, once staples of silent films, rarely appear on the screen today. There are also such exotic forms as the swish pan.

*Cut*

**CUT** Instantaneous transition from one shot to another. The last frame of one shot is immediately followed by the first frame of the next shot.

**FIGURE 1.27**

Match-image cut. (From *2001*, directed by Stanley Kubrick, 1964.)

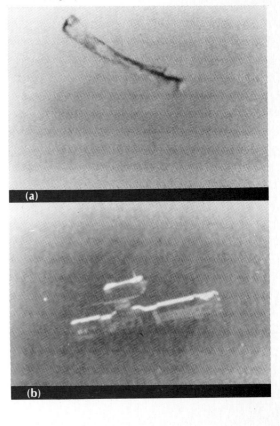

TRANSITIONS

It is possible for a single shot to constitute a motion picture. For example, Michael Snow's *Wavelength* (1967) is composed of one 45-minute zoom shot.

Beyond functioning simply as a connective, the effects of the cut are derived from the relationships between shots. When the subject and/or the movements of two shots match, there can be a smooth transition and an emphasis on continuity. This transition is called a *match-image cut.* Sometimes only the juxtaposition of the two shots indicates their relationship, as in *2001,* where an image of a whirling bone followed immediately by one of a whirling space satellite establishes a correspondence between the two shots.

In a *jump cut,* there is discontinuity between two shots joined by a cut. It is intentional in a professionally edited film, as in a dream sequence.

**FIGURE 1.28**

Jump cut. (From *Wild Strawberries,* directed by Ingmar Bergman, 1957.) These two successive shots are from the first dream sequence in the film.

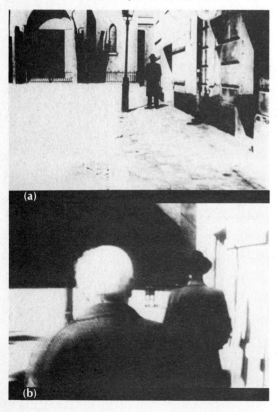

A jump cut, however, is also one of the most frequent errors in pictorial continuity—a smooth flow from one image to the next—made by beginning filmmakers. (This flaw can be remedied by the proper use of a *cutaway,* a shot of an object or subsidiary action occurring at the same time as the main action that serves to cover a break in the continuity of a scene.)

A *reverse-angle shot* * is typically joined to the previous shot by a cut. The subject matter remains the same, but the perspective of the camera changes within a range of 180 degrees.

*Dissolve*

**DISSOLVE** The last image of one shot merges into the first image of the next shot until the former disappears. Dissolves are usually created by optical overlapping in a laboratory.

A dissolve frequently signals that there will be a shift in the time and place settings, but with close associational connections in time and place between the two shots. It is less emphatic than a cut, but without the conclusiveness of a fade. A *match-image dissolve* (as with a match-image cut) joins two images with similar form or content. In *Wild Strawberries*, Bergman uses this type of transition to indicate a shift in the mind of a character (from present reality to the past) as he contemplates a summer house.

It is customary, though not inevitable, that a flashback be introduced by a dissolve. This type of transition can also function to introduce the dreams and fantasies of a character (as in *Variety,* when Huller imagines himself murdering his rival while they are performing their trapeze act), to join together a series of shots that are not in chronological sequence (for example, the five opening shots of *The 400 Blows* †), or to transform the physical appearance of a person (for instance, near the end of *Beauty and the Beast* when Avenant metamorphoses into the Beast).

*pp. 22–24
†pp. 249–250

**FIGURE 1.29**

Dissolve between two shots. (From *Singin' in the Rain.*) This very slow dissolve required 30 frames. (a) Frame 1 of the dissolve. (b) Frame 15 of the dissolve. (c) Frame 30 of the dissolve.

**FIGURE 1.30**

Match-image dissolve. (From *Wild Strawberries*, directed by Ingmar Bergman, 1957.)

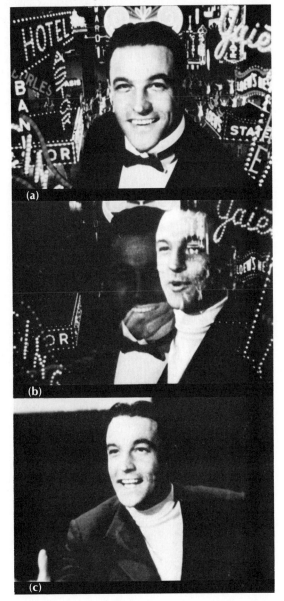

**FIGURE 1.31**

Dissolve between two shots. (From *Beauty and the Beast,* directed by Jean Cocteau, 1946.) (a) Beginning of the dissolve. (b) Middle of the dissolve. (c) End of the dissolve.

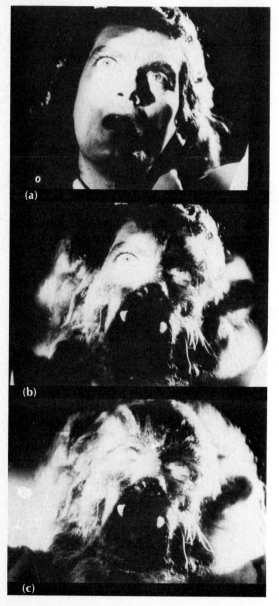

(a)

(b)

(c)

*Superimposition*

**SUPERIMPOSITION** The placing of one image over another. This is usually done in a laboratory, but it can be achieved by running a portion of film stock (undeveloped film placed in a camera) through a camera twice.

This is the most obvious and emphatic method of compelling an audience to see a connection or contrast between two shots. It is not always easy to differentiate between a superimposition and a very slow dissolve. The criterion is whether or not the dual image remains on the screen for sufficient time to be a noticeable entity in itself, as in Figure 1.32.

Of course, if a superimposition is present from the beginning of a shot to its end or if one shot is imposed on a series of shots (this is rare, except when credits are superimposed on action at the beginning of a motion picture), then the device is not a transition but a characteristic of a shot or scene.

*Fade-out and fade-in*

**FADE-OUT (OR FADE TO BLACK)** The last image of a shot gradually dissolves until the screen is blank.

**FADE-IN** The reverse process: The first image of a shot gradually appears on a blank screen.

Fades are the most conclusive transitions. A coupling of both types of fades can occur anywhere within a motion picture, but this is most often reserved for connecting sequences or lengthy scenes. When, as generally happens, a fade-out ends a film, the device is not functioning as a transition.

*Wipe*

**WIPE** A transition between two shots in which a line or edge moves across the screen. As one shot is "wiped off," it is replaced by the next shot.

Because wipes come in such a variety of forms (more than 100 different types), it is a very versatile type of transition. The shape of a wipe can reinforce the content of shots, such as a spiral to join images of a whirlpool. Its disadvantage, unless the effect is desired, is to call attention to itself, thus weakening a fluent movement from one shot to another.

**FIGURE 1.32**

Superimposition. (From *The Seventh Seal,* directed by Ingmar Bergman, 1951.) (a) Near the end of the shot. (b) Superimposition. (c) Beginning of the next shot.

**FIGURE 1.33**

Wipe. (From *Ordet,* directed by Carl Dreyer, 1955.) Between the two shots (a, c), a vertical edge moves from the left to the right of the frame (b); it is completed in 55 frames.

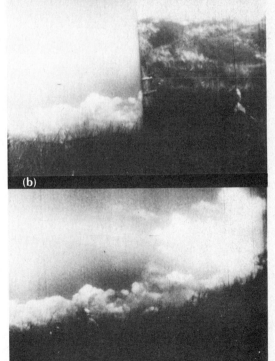

*Iris-in and iris-out*

**IRIS-IN AND IRIS-OUT** An iris effect is achieved by means of a diaphragm in front of a lens that opens and closes. When the diaphragm opens (iris-in), a small circle of light appears on a blank screen, and as it expands to the edges of the frame, it reveals an image. The reverse process constitutes an iris-out.

Although widely used in silent films, especially as transitions between scenes, iris effects rarely appear in sound films, except to give an aura of premodern times (as used by Truffaut in *The Wild Child,* 1970, which has an eighteenth-century setting). An iris-out is also still used at the end of cartoons. Iris effects are sometimes categorized as a type of wipe. The *fixed iris* as a device for focusing on a part of a shot without moving the camera was described earlier.*

**SWISH PAN (ALSO FLASH PAN OR BLUR PAN)** A pan so rapid that the images in a shot or shots are blurred. It is infrequently used as a transition between two shots, but it can be, as in *The 400 Blows* and *West Side Story.* †

### BEYOND SHOTS: TECHNIQUES FOR CONTINUITY BETWEEN SCENES AND SEQUENCES

Although shots are the basic physical units of a film and transitions are the means of connecting shots, a motion picture is more complex than this simple formula suggests. There should also be *continuity* between shots, that is, a logical and emotional development of the film narrative or series of related images. Continuity is achieved through an organic unity between components of the narrative dimension, elements of presentation, and camera-editing dynamics. Certain techniques (in the broadest sense, so that devices, approaches, and qualities are included) of camera-editing dynamics that are made up of shots and transitions have been devised. What they have in common is that their primary functions are deter-

**FIGURE 1.34**

Iris-in. (From *The Cabinet of Dr. Caligari,* directed by Robert Weine, 1919.) (a) Near the beginning of the iris-in. (b) Middle of the iris-in. (c) Near the end of the iris-in.

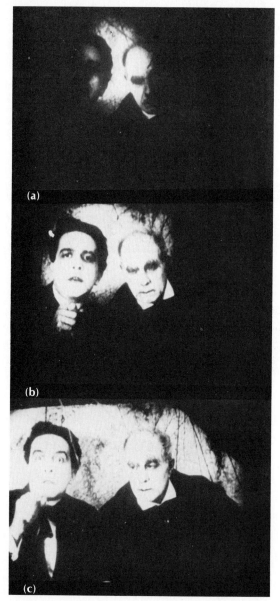

mined by the interrelationships between a series of shots. The remainder of this section is devoted to surveying the nine most important techniques for continuity.

Crosscutting and flashbacks, by definition, require two or more shots. This is perhaps not entirely clear in the case of the flashback, for the device can in itself consist of one shot. Even a single image from the past, however, must be preceded by a shot from the present time of the film that introduces the flashback and another (although there are exceptions) that brings the viewer back to the present. Montage, *mise-en-scène,* cinematic time, and point of view are approaches or characteristics of sequences or of an entire film. Tone and rhythm are qualities of individual shots, but are most identifiable and significant in larger units of a motion picture. A symbol may appear only once in any individual shot; on the other hand, its meaning is derived from the context developed in the film.

Although these nine techniques depend to some degree on the narrative dimension and elements of presentation, they are realized fully only through the dynamics that result from the ways in which the camera is utilized and the process of editing.

### Crosscutting

**CROSSCUTTING (ALSO INTERCUTTING OR PARALLEL EDITING)** A method of editing by means of which the viewer is aware of moving back and forth between related events that are occurring at about the same time, or even simultaneously, in two or more different settings.

At the beginning of the century, when cinema was in its infancy, tentative efforts at crosscutting were attempted (for example, by Edwin S. Porter in *The Great Train Robbery,* 1903). However, it was D. W. Griffith, in the second decade of the century, who developed crosscutting into an integral, expressive technique for creating sophisticated narratives. Film was then released from the straitjacket of a strictly chronological presentation of events. Simultaneous action could be shown on the screen by alternating segments of separate but related strands of nar-

rative in different settings. Thus cinema could share with literature the advantage of disjointing time by means of a visual equivalent of the verbal transition "meanwhile."

The most obvious function of crosscutting is to build suspense. We are familiar with the situation of the camera cutting back and forth between an individual racing to prevent a murder and the murderer threatening a victim. Through crosscutting, a filmmaker can also demonstrate immediately and dramatically points of contrast and similarity between the actions and attitudes of characters in different settings. In *West Side Story,* a "rumble" is arranged for late one night. Various characters, directly or indirectly involved, react differently to the imminent fight between two gangs. This is emphasized by repeated crosscutting among six individuals or groups.*

A synonym for *crosscutting* is *parallel editing.* This term points up that while the function of crosscutting in a sense is determined by the narrative dimension, its form is created during the process of editing. One sequence of events is shot in chronological order; another sequence, intended to be taking place simultaneously or close in time, is shot separately. The footage of both sequences are intercut in the editing room. During this process, the editor, usually collaborating with the director, can take advantage of certain unifying or clarifying devices to make the parallel editing more effective.

Both the separateness and the relatedness of what will develop as two distinct strands of narrative should be established before crosscutting commences. An audience must be prepared to understand what is happening in each setting and the relationship between the settings. In *Variety,* for example, Huller is manipulated into encouraging his wife and partner to go together to a ball that he cannot attend. Without the use of dialogue, a viewer comprehends the situation because of the crosscutting between Berthe-Marie and Artinelli becoming intimate at the party and shots of Huller waking up periodically to look at a clock and to stare at his wife's empty bed.

Two scenes can be so carefully edited that there

*pp. 485–486

are even discernible correspondences between specific actions in different settings. In *Broken Blossoms,* when Battling Burrows is in the ring and the Chinaman and Lucy are together, there is a series of shots of the fighter being knocked down, then rising and flooring his opponent. The intercut shots of the Chinaman also show him winning a victory after an initial defeat, though in the arena of morality rather than fisticuffs, by resisting the temptation to seduce the girl.* Another unifying device is to open and close crosscutting footage with the main characters in the same shots, yet in separate settings for the intervening shots.

The durations of individual shots during crosscutting are usually of great concern to editors and directors, for by controlling the relative duration of the shots, a distinct rhythm can be created. This is especially important in building suspense. An illustration is the typical situation in a Western of the cavalry rushing to the rescue of a beleaguered wagon train. As the excitement intensifies with the ring of Indians tightening around the settlers, whose ammunition is running out, and the cavalry galloping across an empty plain, the shots of each setting become briefer and briefer until the climax of the rescue.

These devices are only a few that increase the effectiveness of crosscutting. Parallel-edited footage is the same as any other footage in one respect: its capability of being molded by diverse cinematic techniques.

### Flashback and flashforward

A flashback presents events prior to the present time of a motion picture. The past includes action antecedent to the film itself, incidents already shown but from different points of view (as in Kurosawa's *Rashomon*), events that occurred within the time span of a motion picture but not appearing earlier on the screen (for example, the dream of the previous night that Anna relates to Andreas in Bergman's *The Passion of Anna*), or a repetition of an event previously viewed (for instance, the ringing of the temple bells in *Broken Blossoms*).

Although dramatized on the screen and perhaps described in words by the off-camera voice of a character existing in the present, a flashback is a subjective experience recaptured in the mind of an individual. It is necessary, therefore, for a director to indicate to which character a flashback belongs. Audiences take for granted that images of the past are being revived by the person whose face last appeared on the screen before a transition to the flashback itself. The dialogue often reinforces this assumption.

An interesting variation is the situation in which a character is describing an incident in the past and a flashback occurs, but the last face seen is that of a listener. This usually signifies that the incident is being envisioned in the listener's mind. An example of this is in the short film *The Secret Sharer,* based on Joseph Conrad's novella. Antecedent events involving a murder are described by the former mate of a ship, Leggatt, who has sought sanctuary with the captain of another boat. The flashback is broken up into a series of images, with a return periodically to the present. What makes the flashback unusual is that just before each of the three shots of the past, which are enclosed by dissolves, the camera is on the captain's face. A viewer's conjecture that this was purposely done is supported by the screenplay, which specifically states: "The ensuing shot . . . is *not* a cut back but [the Captain's] automatic envisioning of Leggatt's words."[3] This is a visual indication of how closely the captain identifies with the "murderer," symbolically an aspect of himself.

The dissolve is the typical form of transition to and from flashbacks. This allows the viewer to become oriented to changes in time and/or place. There is no reason why cuts cannot lead to and from a scene in the past, but they are most suitable when the flashback is brief.

A flashback is created by the same techniques and is governed by the same principles as any other footage. Sometimes, however, a flashback contains distortion to remind an audience that it is subjective, seen from the point of view of the person recalling the past. Hitchcock takes advantage of this approach at the end of *Marnie* when the young woman finally confronts a traumatic experience of her childhood.*

Because flashbacks are from the point of view

---

*pp. 206–207

*p. 127

of the person who is reminiscing, we can never be sure of the accuracy of a remembrance of things past. In Kurosawa's *Rashomon,* this subjectivity is the major theme of the film. We usually trust the essential veracity of flashbacks, as in Welles's *Citizen Kane,* unless there is some suggestion in the dialogue or in the interpretations of the actors that arouses doubts in our minds. This ambiguity is sometimes intentional in experimental films. A third of the way into *Last Year at Marienbad* a perceptive viewer will realize that Alain Resnais does not clearly distinguish between flashbacks and fantasies or a combination of both. Another fascinating expansion of the scope of the flashback is to have characters from the distant past and from the present appear in the same scene or even the same shot. This is done with impressive skill by Alf Sjöberg in *Miss Julie,* a film version of Strindberg's one-act play.*

A flashforward is a leap forward rather than back in time, and it rarely appears in conventional motion pictures. When used, it can function not only to anticipate an event that is presented later in its proper chronological place, but also to communicate speculation about the future on the part of a character. An example of a flashforward that communicates speculation is an incident in the first sequence of *La Guerre est finie* (directed by Alain Resnais) in which the main character, Diego, is in a car speeding to meet a train. He imagines the alternatives that will be open to him when he reaches the train station, and each alternative is projected dramatically on the screen.

#### Montage and mise-en-scène

André Bazin popularized the distinction in cinema between montage and *mise-en-scène* (the latter is often not hyphenated and sometimes is not italicized). He was attempting to develop a terminology that described the two most fundamental stylistic approaches to filmmaking: one to emphasize what is happening within the shot and the other to emphasize the relationship between shots. (This is an oversimplification of the great French critic's intention, but it will serve our purposes.) The word *montage,* from the French verb *monter* ("to assemble"), was readily at hand. As

has been pointed out frequently in this chapter, as soon as the filmmaker shifts an angle or distance or moves the camera between or during shots, the actuality has to be re-created or reassembled. The Russian directors of the silent era made montage the foundation of film esthetics in which even apparently unrelated material that was properly juxtaposed could create in the mind of the audience new relationships that were not inherent in the shots per se. The most important characteristic of montage for Bazin was that through this method directors (assuming they were intimately involved in the process of editing) had considerable power in controlling what audiences saw, thought, and felt.

There was another tradition that dated back to the static camera of the Lumière brothers. In that tradition, the emphasis was on allowing the camera to observe, to present representationally, the actuality photographed. Naturally, the camera eventually moved, and shots had to be joined together. The goal of the director influenced by this tradition, however, was to imitate reality as closely as possible through cinematic form. To a greater degree than in montage, the audience must assume responsibility for perceiving relationships and significances within the shot or scene. To describe this approach, Bazin borrowed a term from the theater, *mise-en-scène* (literally, "placing in a scene"). In cinema, this includes especially what is categorized in the present chapter as *elements of presentation.*

Bazin's binary perspective on film esthetics is useful in focusing on two essential emphases in the creation of motion pictures. Unfortunately, many students of cinema have dealt with montage and *mise-en-scène* as though they were irreconcilable opposites, each having a list of characteristics that constitute the basis of value judgments whereby one type of film is praised and another is criticized. To do justice to Bazin's concept, we must reject unjustifiable interpretations of this duality (some of them fostered by the critic himself) and focus on valid ones.

One unsupportable premise is that *mise-en-scène* reveals more of the content of a scene than does montage. The two approaches differ not in *what* they communicate but *how* they communicate. There is, however, one qualification: One cinematic tech-

---

*p. 167

nique will highlight an aspect of subject matter to a greater degree than another technique. For instance, Eisenstein's type of dynamic montage emphasized conflict in a scene more than, say, if Renoir were using *mise-en-scène* in a similar situation.

Bazin was correct in associating *mise-en-scène* with realism; however, only if one is using this amorphous term as referring not to "real" or "truth," but to the movement of Realism. One of the tenets of Realism is that environment exerts a crucial influence on the formation of the character of an individual or group. In cinema, the relationship of the individual or group to place setting is pointed up with greater clarity by *mise-en-scène* than by montage. It is not surprising, therefore, that a director inspired by the principles of Realism, as were the Italian Neorealists, tends to favor the approach of *mise-en-scène.*

It could be maintained that the Russian directors were as much realists (in the broadest sense of the term) as De Sica and early Rossellini. The former group was not as interested, however, in revealing the relationship of human beings and their environments as in demonstrating the possibilities of change. Their essential ideological intention was to devise cinematic briefs in defense of a social and political philosophy, and this could be done best through montage. Realists, on the other hand, believed that an apparently objective presentation of conditions at a specific time and place was a nondoctrinal argument for ameliorative change. Here, then, are two different "truths" that required different techniques to transform the abstract into the concrete.

Finally, montage and *mise-en-scène* are not exclusive approaches, as is often asserted. Rather, they are complementary ones. This stress on unity rather than diversity has been defended fervently, in theory and in practice, by Jean-Luc Godard. In the essay "Montage My Fine Care," he states:

. . . montage is above all an integral part of *mise en scène.* Only at peril can one be separated from the other. One might just as well try to separate the rhythm from a melody. . . . The montage, consequently, both denies and prepares the way for the *mise en scène:* the two are interdependent.[4]

The French director admits distinctions between the two, but insists that like two sides of a coin, one is only the obverse surface of the other. Perhaps Godard goes to extremes in his analogy to rhythm and melody. Still, his defense of the essential unity of montage and *mise-en-scène* is a welcome corrective to the arguments of those who divide filmmaking into opposing camps.

Having examined the connectives between the two approaches, we can consider differences with greater discrimination. Generally, there is a preoccupation with space in *mise-en-scène,* whereas the essential dimension of montage is time. Less emphatically, it can be suggested that there is a larger degree of concentration on tone and rhythm within the shot in *mise-en-scène;* in montage, these two elements of camera-editing dynamics are manifested chiefly through the relationships of shots. With all the qualifications necessary to point out similarities between the arts, *mise-en-scène* in cinema is a step in the direction of painting and montage is a step in the direction of music.

Applying *montage* and *mise-en-scène* as adjectives descriptive of approaches to filmmaking emphasizes that each serves as "a way or means of reaching something." The director chooses the approach that is most effective in communicating the essence and overtones of the subject matter, and within a film there may be a shift from one to the other. For instance, the newsreel sequence at the beginning of *Citizen Kane* is an example of montage; most of the important scenes in Welles's masterpiece, however, use a *mise-en-scène* approach, which is made particularly effective by use of deep focus. A brilliant example of montage is illustrated later in *The Bicycle Thief,** a Neorealistic work in which *mise-en-scène* predominates.

The sets of stills in Figures 1.35 and 1.36 demonstrate the contrasting effects of these two approaches.

---

**FIGURE 1.35**

Montage approach. (From *North by Northwest,* directed by Alfred Hitchcock, 1959.) One frame from each shot in a portion of a lengthy sequence in which Thorndike (Cary Grant) is pursued by an airplane whose pilot is intent on killing him.

---

*pp. 243–245

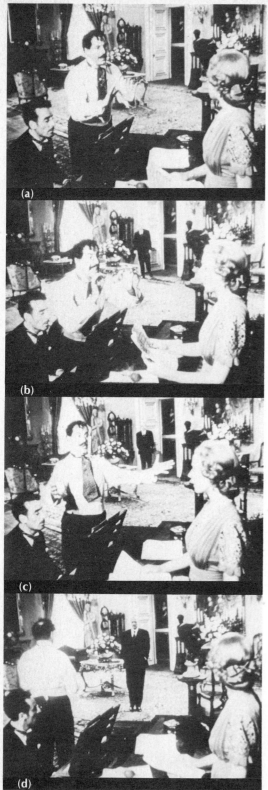

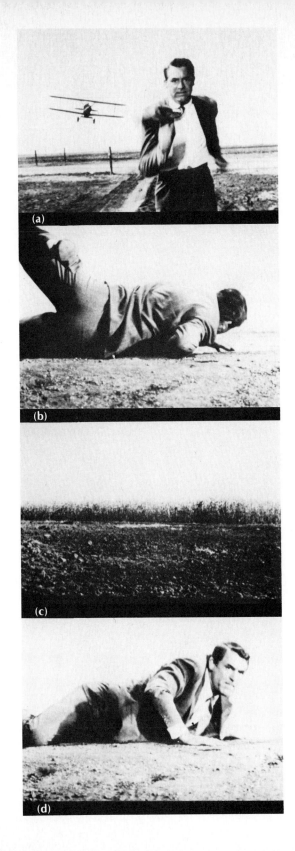

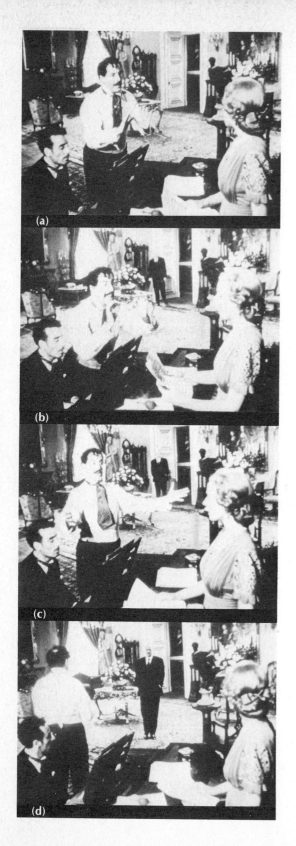

(a)

(b)

(c)

(d)

(e)

(f)

(g)

(h)

## FIGURE 1.36

*Mise-en-scène* approach. (From *Citizen Kane,* directed by Orson Welles, 1941.) The scene consists of one shot taken by a completely static camera (after a slight tracking-in at the very beginning). Note how without moving the camera, director Orson Welles has Kane visually dominate the music teacher who is critical of Susan's singing abilities.

### Cinematic time

In practically all narrative motion pictures, time is manipulated. This is possible because a film is embedded simultaneously in two different types of time. *Physical time* can be defined as the duration of an action or series of actions in actuality as recorded by a clock. *Cinematic time* is the duration of an action or series of actions on the screen. Both modes of time correspond within a shot (exceptions are noted later). However, as soon as there is a transition between shots, there is the potential to condense or expand time, to create the effect of the simultaneity of events, and to move the flow of time forward or backward.

The first problem a filmmaker faces relevant to the contraction of time is whether or not the events included in the film can be presented without manipulation within the 1 ½ hours that constitute the average motion picture. This has been done in such films as Hitchcock's *Rope,* Zinnemann's *High Noon,* and Varda's *Cleo From 5 to 7,* in which there is generally a correspondence between physical and cinematic time. In most films, however, this is impossible, so physical time must be condensed. The only way this can occur within a shot is through special effects, such as the accelerated motion in the *The Gold Rush;* within one shot Charlie shovels snow in 30 seconds, a task that would have taken 30 minutes in reality.

A significant lapse of time during a transition may be taken for granted, indicated verbally, or suggested by visual means. A line of dialogue can reveal a jump forward in time. If it is evening when a flight commander announces to his pilots, "We leave at dawn," and the next shot is of planes taking off, we assume a night has elapsed between the two shots. A narrator may also telescope time (as in Truffaut's *Jules and Jim*). A title card in *The Gold Rush* begins, "The next morning . . ."

Nonverbal means of signaling a condensation of time include contrasting the contents of shots. In *The 400 Blows,* we see the two boys leaving a movie house, there is a swish pan, and they enter another theater. Certain devices have appeared so often that they have become clichés. For example, it is very obvious that a year has passed when there are dissolves between four shots of a tree: with leaves, without leaves, with snow on the branches, and finally, with birds in the branches. The content of a single shot may also function in this way: The pages of a calendar are blown away by the "wind of time," or the hands of a clock jump from 12:00 to 5:00.

Imaginative filmmakers have discovered less trite ways of making an audience aware of leaps forward in time. In Welles's *Citizen Kane,* the sequence at the boarding house in which Charles is a boy ends with a shot of snow falling on a sled; dissolve to the elegantly dressed youngster opening a present of a sled from Thatcher, who says, "Merry Christmas"; cut to Thatcher in his office dictating ". . . and a Happy New Year" for a letter to the 21-year-old Charles Foster Kane. In *West Side Story,* Maria is seen in her new dress; it is presumably late afternoon. Her image becomes a kaleidoscope of colors; semiabstract shapes appear. These shapes resolve into dancers at the high school gym that evening.

No type of transition is in itself an indication that time has been contracted. Cuts, dissolves, wipes, and other transitions may join shots that are separated by seconds or years of physical time. The shots before and after the transition must reveal a notable jump in temporal sequence. We do tend, however, to associate fade-outs and fade-ins with the ending of one time setting and the beginning of a new one.

The expansion of time within a linear plot is less likely to occur, but it can appear. Slow motion confined to a shot or series of shots is one method. Another method is the use of repeated changes in such elements of camera-editing dynamics as angle and distance in a carefully orchestrated montage. In a climactic moment in *The Battleship Potemkin,* a sailor smashes a plate. The act in reality would occupy only 3 or 4 seconds, yet Eisenstein uses 10 different shots to photograph it, thus distending cinematic time.

Recording an action from different points of view also results in a difference between the two modes of time. A speeding car hitting a man happens in a few seconds. If the event were recorded objectively from a high angle and in separate shots from the points of view of the driver, the victim, and an observer, it would take four times as long to elapse on the screen.

A presentation of events occurring at the same time in different settings can be achieved in many ways. Actually, if there is a clear indication, such as the face of a clock in each setting, any two shots in succession can reveal concurrent events without confusing the viewer. Another method is the use of the split screen. Crosscutting is the most elaborate form of creating simultaneous cinematic time.

Moving backward in time in relation to the unfolding present of a film is the function of flashbacks. Most flashbacks involve an expansion of physical time. It usually takes much less time to recall or verbally describe past action in reality than to re-create it on the screen.

Fundamental variations in cinematic time available to filmmakers have been described on these pages. The molding of time in a motion picture can be quite complicated if a number of variations are combined. The films of Alain Resnais, for instance, are often intricate arabesques of time manipulation.

*Point of view*

In cinema there are two perspectives from which point of view may be considered. One is the attitude of audiences and filmmakers toward the characters and events that appear on the screen; the other, the consciousness through which the action of a film is filtered. The point of view of the audience is examined at the end of Chapter 3 under "Audience Reactions and Popular Culture."

By the very fact that filmmakers (from screenwriter to editor) make choices at every stage in the creation of a motion picture, they mold the characters and events in a cinematic work. An *auteur* director imposes his personal views on the material more emphatically than a competent but ordinary director. For example, in *The 400 Blows,* Truffaut utilizes every resource at hand to encourage the viewer's sympathy for the plight of Antoine Doinel.

This first definition of point of view includes the effects of camera-editing dynamics, but it goes well beyond that component of film to involve basic questions of how the special reality of a motion picture is created by filmmakers and reinterpreted by audiences. The second definition is more restricted, depending primarily on camera-editing dynamics, and it is our main concern here.

An omniscient observer who can, within reason, travel anywhere in time and space is most often the consciousness through which the events and characters of a film are presented. The audience thereby assumes an "eye of God" or a "camera eye" perspective, but with one restriction: The audience cannot see into a human being. The mind and emotions of a character must be deduced from dialogue, interpretations of actors, characters' reactions to incidents, and other means described earlier under the heading "The Narrative Dimension—Characterization." This point of view is not entirely objective because the filmmaker determines what will appear in a frame. The omniscient "eye of God," therefore, is selective, objective only to the degree determined by the filmmaker.

Cinema would have remained a limited dramatic art if ways of entering the psyches of characters had not been developed. The narrator or title card for this purpose is a device derived from literary fiction; however, unless it is used discreetly and intelligently, it suggests a failure of imagination on the part of a filmmaker. Another literary device is a variation of the soliloquy. In Woody Allen's *Annie Hall,* the actor looks directly at the camera and verbalizes his feelings.

The subjective shot is the most intrinsically cinematic technique whereby the audience shares a character's point of view. In a subjective shot we see through the eyes of a fictional person; we do not observe the character and the environment from the outside. The difficulty is that consistent subjective shots are disconcerting, as demonstrated in Robert Montgomery's *Lady in the Lake,* a tour de force consisting entirely of subjective shots from the point of view of the character Philip Marlowe. When we move our heads swiftly to see in more than one direction, our brains adjust. When the camera imitates this motion, however, the repeated flashes of images on a large screen are bewildering and dizzying. Most filmmakers settle for occasional subjective shots for emphasis or to indicate the emotional reactions of characters to situations. The latter is particularly striking when the images seen through the eyes of a character are distorted.

Halfway between the omniscient and subjective points of view are clearly indicated subjective experiences of characters, which are projected on the screen, with or without distortion, as objective dramatic scenes. These experiences are often presented as flashbacks, dreams, or personal fantasies. In each case, the audience is usually aware that what appears on the screen is being filtered through the consciousness of a character, who in addition may narrate in a voice-over or appear in scenes.

A provocative variation is the technique labeled the *subjective camera.* It can be said to correspond in literary fiction to the *limited third-person narrator;* that is, the story is told in the third person, but information generally is restricted to what a single character apprehends (for instance, the novels of Thomas Wolfe). The film credited with first taking full advantage of the subjective camera is F. W. Murnau's *The Last Laugh* (1924). Although there are some subjective shots and a dream from the point of view of the doorman, most of the film consists of scenes of him as he encounters significant experiences during two days of his life. Among the films examined in Part Two of this book, this approach is to be found (with some departures in each one) in *The Gold Rush, The 400 Blows,* and *Shane. Shane* is especially interesting in this respect because being aware that a subjective camera is used can radically affect one's interpretation of the work.*

Experimentation with point of view is a characteristic of the bolder post–World War II dramas. Kurosawa's *Rashomon* is one example; many of the works of French New Wave directors have explored its potentials. In Bergman's *The Passion of Anna,* actors appear as themselves before the camera to discuss the roles they are portraying. This is a startling challenge to the conventional premise that the fictional frame of reference, which includes only the

omniscient and characters' points of view, must be preserved.

### Tone

*Tone* is a very difficult term to define when it is applied to a scene, a sequence, or an entire film. *Mood, atmosphere,* and *manner* are often used as synonyms, but they lack the weighty significance of tone. The German word *Stimmung* is closer in meaning, carrying the connotation of the essential spirit of a cinematic experience. Usually the best one can do to convey a sense of the tone of part or all of a film is to search for a series of appropriate adjectives and adverbs.

Every component of cinema contributes to the creation of tone. It is for this reason that the director, the member of the filmmaking team most aware of the role each aspect of a motion picture plays in making up an organic impression, is chiefly responsible for the tone of a work. The director must be aware of how tone is achieved primarily through other camera-editing dynamics but is dependent on the structure supplied by the narrative dimension and the physical tangibility derived from the elements of presentation. An experienced director knows that he feels most comfortable with certain means in attaining the tonal effects he desires. If they are distinct enough to form a recognizable pattern, these means form one of the foundations of a director's style. Success in an individual film will depend on how appropriate and creative the director's choices were and how completely each element was integrated so that a consistent tone is communicated to an audience.

Tone in cinema is basically an emanation of form in that it epitomizes the attitude of the director toward his subject matter. Moreover, like a visual gestalt, it is more than the sum of its parts. Changing one element in a scene, such as the lighting, changes the tone of that scene to one degree or another. The question a critic asks is whether or not or to what degree (in his opinion) the tone is appropriate to the action. For example, in Ken Russell's version of D. H. Lawrence's *Women in Love,* two men are wrestling. The director's use of pyrotechnic camera-editing dynamics results in a fervent, almost hysterical tone that has been considered exaggerated, even vulgar. On the

---

*pp. 419–420

other hand, there are viewers who find a climactic scene in *The Diary of a Country Priest* between the title character and a wealthy woman so subdued in tone as to be ineffective. In a great scene or film, there is a fusion of cinematic elements and action. Beyond the completely effective and completely ineffective cinematic experience, the appropriateness of the tone of a scene or a whole film is often a matter of subjective judgment.

An examination of a few examples is the most expedient method of indicating how tone arises from the unification of form and content. First, we will consider the tone of an entire film. *Singin' in the Rain* is a brash, energetic musical, in keeping with its subject matter, Hollywood in the late twenties. The approach is primarily *mise-en-scène*, especially for production numbers; the rhythm is fast-paced; there is little crosscutting and few abrupt shifts in time; the point of view is generally omniscient; the music is loud and melodic, the lighting high-keyed, the color luminous and bold; and the studio settings are flamboyant. Even the romantic scenes are forceful and bright. In contrast, *The Bicycle Thief* is an intensely realistic story of the plight of an Italian family just after World War II. The camera-editing dynamics are fluid but conventional. Form is entirely subordinated to content, so very few striking images appear on the screen. Because the main theme involves the relationships of individuals to one another and their environment, the *mise-en-scène* approach predominates. Natural sounds are more important than background music. The entire film was shot on location, with most of the action occurring on the streets of Rome. The lighting for this black-and-white film appears natural. *Natural* also is the most suitable adjective to describe the acting by nonprofessionals dressed in ordinary street clothes. The linear plot contains no flashbacks and little crosscutting.

A motion picture may not necessarily preserve a single tone throughout (*Smiles of a Summer Night* is an example), so characterizing the tone of an entire film is a matter of determining its predominant one.

The *Stimmung* of an individual scene or sequence can be defined more easily and its appropriateness evaluated. In *The 400 Blows,* Antoine has run away from home and spends a night wandering through the streets of Paris. Without a word of dialogue (except at the beginning in the search for a lost dog), every cinematic element of the scene—from the background music to the dissolves between shots—contributes to creating an atmosphere of loneliness and sadness. On the other hand, the tone in a single sequence of one setting may be in contrast to that of another; this can be emphasized by crosscutting. In *The Gold Rush,* shots of a forlorn, disillusioned Charlie in his cabin or walking through the dark town are juxtaposed with those of the brightly lit activities in the dance hall on New Year's Eve.

Tone is the fifth dimension of a film: It is an intangible value that affects audiences' reactions to what appears on the screen, often without viewers' being aware of it. Amorphous though it may be, even a small degree of ineffectiveness or inappropriateness in the tone of a scene will make its dissonant presence felt, no matter how brilliant is the concept or execution. For a viewer, it can be like listening to an experienced musician playing an impressive piece on an instrument that is slightly out of tune.

*Visual rhythms*

All human experiences, from the most physiological to the most spiritual, are governed by the ebb and flow of rhythms of various types. Cinema is not an exception; quite the contrary, for it is an art, like music and dance, that unfolds in time. Therefore, unless a film is chaotic, an important structural device is fourth-dimensional patterns. This is easy to recognize in sound, especially background music, but it is less obvious in visuals.

A visual rhythm is repetition in space or time or in any visual element that creates a pattern that subtly or obviously imposes itself on the consciousness of a viewer. This type of rhythm can be confined to one shot or can appear in a scene or a sequence. In a single static shot, it manifests itself, as in a painting or still photograph, in patterns created by the spatial constituents of a composition. In a single shot containing movement, it may appear as the action of a subject (most obviously in a filmed dance) or a form of camera-editing dynamics, such as the camera repeatedly tracking back and forth in depth or an elaborate pan (for example, in *Weekend,* Godard includes a shot that utilizes a 360-degree pan repeated three times).

There are many forms of rhythm created by the juxtaposition, through editing, of individual shots (as Eisenstein recognized when he established *rhythmic montage* as a major method of montage\*). One form depends on content. An image may be repeated with some variations in each shot for a number of times in a scene or sequence. In *Broken Blossoms,* a shot of the street in front of the Chinaman's shop appears six times in a scene that lasts less than 3 minutes. In *October,* Eisenstein repeats one basic action from different perspectives, as in the pulling down of the statue of Alexander III and Kerensky mounting the stairs in the palace of the czars. The duration of shots is another mode. In *The Wild Bunch,* the opening sequence of a bank robbery is effectively structured by an intricate combination of lengthy long shots and brief close shots. Directional cutting with a pattern of contrasting movements is still another possibility. The directors of the "city symphony" documentaries of the twenties (for example, Walter Ruttmann in his *Berlin*) were fond of repeated shots of crowds or traffic moving first in one direction and then the opposite. These are only three examples of individual characteristics of a shot that can create rhythmic patterns when they are repeated in or related to other shots during a scene or sequence.

Transitions also can be a factor. In silent films, the iris-in and iris-out form emphatic patterns between shots, as in Wiene's *The Cabinet of Dr. Caligari.* The dissolve, when used repeatedly, is one form of transition that has an integrity and significance of its own. A series of nonlinear images is structured by the repetition of this transition, as when Antoine wanders through the streets of Paris in *The 400 Blows.*

The more intricate a scene or sequence, the more complex will be various types of rhythms supporting other components of film. The Odessa Steps sequence in Eisenstein's *The Battleship Potemkin* and the biplane attack on Thornhill on an Indiana prairie in Hitchcock's *North by Northwest*† are frequently analyzed because every aspect of each sequence, including various forms of rhythm, reinforces the total effect of memorable cinema.

*Symbols*

Symbolic transformation is a process by which an actual or imaginary object or action can be invested with a significance that goes beyond the functional to intimations of the universal and transcendental. The first criterion of a *symbol* is that it refers to—or is—something that concretely exists, yet suggests associations beyond its immediate function. This definition, however, includes both signs and symbols. A *sign* represents or points to a specific referent; for example, a bell indicating the end of a class period may have pleasurable associations for many students in the class. A symbol, however, embodies a significance that cannot be determined completely by ratiocination (that is, logical and methodical reasoning). A residue of overtones that reason cannot grasp is always clinging to a symbol.

Our interest in these pages is confined to symbolization in cinema. Sounds (including words), objects, and actions can be symbolic in a film. Let us consider each in turn. One of the most famous symbolic words in a motion picture is *rosebud* in *Citizen Kane.* Immediately, we encounter the first major problem that is unavoidable in any examination of symbols: Is the meaning embodied in a symbol inherent, is it created by context, or is it a combination of both? Examples of symbols in each category can be cited. Psychologists refer to objects and patterns of action (for example, the cave and visions of descents into hell) that arise from the unalterable psychic forces of the unconscious. On the other hand, in *Moby Dick,* Herman Melville endowed a whale with significance of his own devising. The inherent and invested meanings of a symbol usually reinforce each other, as is true of *rosebud* in Welles's film.

The word *rosebud* itself arouses emotional associations, such as beauty, vulnerability, and the feminine, with its referent, the bud of a rose. These associations reverberate in our minds even when we learn that *rosebud* refers to a sled. We are dealing, however, with a narrative, and we want to know what *rosebud* means to Charles Forster Kane. The context of the film supplies clues, suggesting that Kane associates the sled with the security of his childhood and the unquestioning, undemanding love of his mother. Thus the intrinsic overtones of the word *rosebud* reinforce

\*p. 225
†pp. 38–39

the meaning invested by context. This premise of the combination of intrinsic and contextual symbolic meaning can be tested in the case of *rosebud* by imagining the sled being named *the thorn.*

Leitmotifs in background music as well as words can stimulate evocative associations in an audience. In *Stagecoach,* for instance, the main theme from "Oh! Susannah" reminds us of the traditions of the South that motivate the attitudes and actions of Lucy Mallory and Hatfield. Natural sounds can also assume symbolic meanings, as with the continual pounding of waves in the island sequences in Antonioni's *L'Avventura* as passions ebb and flow and metamorphose.

Visual symbols are of particular interest in film because, unlike any other medium, they can be molded and made more effective by camera-editing dynamics. An example is the Eiffel Tower in the opening shots of *The 400 Blows.* Once again, there is a mutual reinforcement of intrinsic and contextual meaning. The structure embodies our associations with the city of Paris, and its shape suggests aggressive masculinity. The relationship of these symbolic overtones and their development in the film, as well as the symbolic significance of the sea, are discussed in the analysis of *The 400 Blows* in Part Two.* Other symbolic objects that will be encountered later in this book include the doll in *Broken Blossoms,* the special wine in *Smiles of a Summer Night,* and the gun in *Shane.*

Not only individual objects but settings too can be given symbolic meaning. In *Broken Blossoms,* the Chinaman's room represents a haven of peace and tenderness, whereas the fight ring is invested with the qualities of violence and enmity. Griffith uses cinematic devices such as crosscutting and contrasting lighting to develop the connotative significances of the two settings. Color is another element of presentation that can perform this function. In Antonioni's *The Red Desert,* the changing colors on the walls of the room Guiliana has rented reflect the disintegration of her psyche.

Symbolic action in a film may extend throughout a film or be limited to a scene or even a few minutes. In Bergman's *Wild Strawberries,* the physical trip of Isak Borg from Stockholm to Uppsala is also a journey into his past and his unconscious. In *The 400 Blows,* the significance of the amusement park ride, the "Rotor," once its overtones are recognized, makes the predicament in which Antoine finds himself concrete and vivid for an audience.* In Renoir's *The Rules of the Game,* an elephantine music box is proudly presented by Robert de la Chesnaye at a party in his country house. It symbolizes the artificiality and pretentiousness of the French aristocracy. Significantly, it is "wounded" by a bullet from a gun fired by a gamekeeper who invades the party.

**FIGURE 1.37**

Symbolism. (From *The Rules of the Game,* directed by Jean Renoir, 1939.)

Other examples of various types of symbols that function in different ways are pointed out in the analyses of films in Part Two. In deciding whether or not to agree with the designations and interpretations offered in these analyses, the reader should consider three generalizations.

It is often difficult to know when the identification of a symbol is farfetched and unnecessary. Every word is capable of being symbolic, and every sound and image can be perceived in this way. Yet as Freud remarked to those who were so enthralled by his theories that every object they encountered was either a masculine or a feminine symbol with sexual overtones, "Sometimes a cigar is just a cigar."

---

*pp. 249–250

*pp. 255–256

The first rule that can be applied is that no element of a film should be designated as symbolic unless such an identification helps a viewer to understand the major and minor themes—or any other aspects of the work. This does not involve doubts about the intentions of the filmmaker, for symbolic meanings can arise regardless of the creator's conscious intentions, whether or not a work is primarily entertainment. Finding symbolic overtones in the recurrent presence of the sea in the James Bond film *You Only Live Twice* might be an exercise in ingenuity, but it is hardly profitable. This is not the case for *King Kong* in both versions of the story; the creature is more than simply a monster on the order of Godzilla.

The second precept is to be able to demonstrate by specific references that an interpretation of a symbol or a symbolic pattern is consistent with other elements in the film. Because the overtones of symbols are so amorphous and descriptive phrases can evoke only possible associations, no interpretation can be proved to be incontrovertible; it can only be feasible and consistent.

Finally, one should make a a distinction between symbols that reveal the emotions of characters and symbols that are imposed by the filmmaker as a personal commentary. The latter can be done solely through a cinematic technique. An example is the use of the moving camera by Resnais in *Night and Fog.* For the shots in color (also symbolic) of the concentration camp during the present time of the documentary, the camera constantly moves from left to right, penetrating deeper and deeper into the maze of horror. Finally, the heart of this darkness is reached—the crematories. A different approach is evident in *The Silence.* In an early shot, Ester is masturbating; her head is shown upside down and she breathes in gasps. Near the end of the film, she is in a similar position and is choking when she has an attack that brings her close to death. In the context of the film, Bergman is imposing a symbolic association between narcissistic sex and death.

Camera-editing dynamics are the bloodstream of filmmaking, the approaches, processes, and techniques that sustain and give life to the medium. Any student in any category of cinema studies who does not do justice to this component of film is confining

**FIGURE 1.38**

Symbolism. (From *The Silence,* directed by Ingmar Bergman, 1963.)

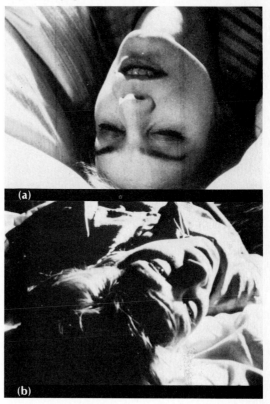

(a)

(b)

himself—to shift analogies—to the shadows on a wall rather than the beings and actions that create the shadows.

## ELEMENTS OF PRESENTATION

*Elements of presentation* is a term used in the theater. In that context it refers to all physical elements that are required to transform the text of a play into a dramatic presentation before an audience. The major elements of presentation in a narrative motion picture are basically the same as in a theater production: actors, sound, sets and props, lighting and color, costumes, and special effects. These elements appear physically on the screen or, in the case of sound, are heard in a movie theater. In principle they exist independently, but in practice, as we have seen, the camera and the editing processes interpose themselves between a performance and what appears on the screen and impose their own dynamics.

These generalizations about cinematic elements of presentation are subject to qualifications that will become apparent when we consider each element individually. For example, in a motion picture, special stock and developing are necessary for color, and inevitably it has a degree of artificiality of tone on the screen that is not encountered on the stage. There are also special effects that can be achieved solely with the camera or through laboratory processes. For the ones discussed in these pages, however, the final effects are chiefly photographed by the camera.

The purpose of this section is to examine each element of presentation in a motion picture. There is one exception. Actors are unique in functioning as an element of presentation as well as being members of the filmmaking team. To emphasize their active rather than passive contribution to a film, I have postponed dealing with actors until Chapter 2.

### SOUND

Since the advent of sound in cinema in the late twenties, controversy has centered on the significance of this element of presentation. The eminent film scholar Siegfried Kracauer wrote in 1960 that "attempts at an equilibrium between word and image . . . are doomed to failure" and that the visuals in a motion picture should always have first priority.[5] On the other hand, Rudolf Arnheim, an equally distinguished theoretician of cinema, represents those (the majority today) who believe that sound entirely transformed the medium into a new form and that "sound film . . . is . . . a homogeneous creation of word and picture which cannot be split into parts that have any meaning separately."[6] Whichever position one takes, it cannot be denied that sound has had a tremendous influence on filmmaking, and an understanding of its characteristics and functions is essential to anyone whose interest in cinema is more than perfunctory.

Before considering aspects of sound, it should be noted that an effective device in a sound film can be the use of silence. Ingmar Bergman has been particularly original in making silence reverberate with meaning. In the memory sequence at the beginning of *The Naked Night,* Frost cries out his anguish, but the sound track is silent. In *The Silence,* the absence of many natural sounds and of background music is symbolic of spiritual sterility. Silence, then, can be as significant and striking as sound if it is used judiciously.

Sound in cinema can be examined by means of two perspectives: principles governing sound in general and the categories of sound. The general principles include the relation of sounds to images, the nonnaturalistic presentation of sounds, and the symbolic use of sounds. This element of presentation is conventionally divided into three categories: the spoken word, natural sounds, and music.

There is no more basic principle for the use of sound in film than its relationship to the visuals. In *Theory of Film,* Siegfried Kracauer postulates four types of sound-image coordinations.[7] *Parallel synchronization* occurs if sound and image carry parallel meanings (what we associate with standard synchronization). *Counterpoint synchronization* occurs when sound and image carry different but related meanings (for example, the face on the screen of a rejected suitor, with grief-stricken eyes and compressed lips, who says that his beloved has not hurt him). In *parallel asynchronization,* the sound is synchronized with images other than those of its source; however, the intrinsic relationship is easily recognized. All commentaries, as in *Night and Fog,* for example, fit into this subdivision. *Counterpoint asynchronization* is the most subtle form of relationship between sound and image. The differences between the two are obvious, but to discern the connections requires imagination and intuition. In Fritz Lang's *M,* a distraught mother repeatedly calls out her missing daughter's name. On the screen appear shots of an empty stairwell, an empty basement, an unoccupied chair in the kitchen, and finally, a ball and balloon that belonged to the murdered girl.

The value of Kracauer's system is not simply to supply us with labels that we can apply to shots and scenes; more important, it focuses our attention on various types of relationships between sounds and images. Thus we can appreciate how a director and his collaborators achieve effects in a specific film.

Another general principle is the nonnaturalistic presentation of sounds. The question relevant to sound in this type of situation is not whether the experience is "real" but whether the sounds are presented naturally. In Ingmar Bergman's *The Seventh Seal,* when Death speaks to the Knight, the scenes are fantasy or hallucinations. Death's voice, however, is that of a human being. The form of the dialogue in these scenes would be nonnaturalistic in presentation if Death's voice had been recorded in an echo chamber or seemed to come from a great distance even though the two figures were physically a few feet apart.

Any sound can be given symbolic overtones. For example, the opening scene of Bergman's *The Passion of Anna* contains the image of a dual sun, a portent of tragedy. On the sound track, sheep bells tinkle. Later, this sound is associated with violence on the island and the slaughter of animals, including sheep.

We can now apply the general principles of sound to its three categories. The spoken word may be in the form of commentary, dialogue, or interior monologue. A commentator supplies information (if confined to this function, the commentator is a *narrator*) and comments on the action. Since we hear but do not see the commentator, sound and image are asynchronized. The rare exception is when a commentator appears before the camera and speaks directly to the audience; an instance is the Narrator in Max Ophuls's *La Ronde.* A commentator may structure diverse material (especially in documentaries), establish a specific point of view (as in Bergman's *Wild Strawberries*), develop suspense (as in Robert Montgomery's *Lady in the Lake*), or move the plot forward (for instance, the voice of Groot in Howard Hawks's *Red River*).

Most dialogue is realistic and in the form of parallel synchronization. However, many variations are possible. The camera may hold for a lengthy shot on an individual while another person is speaking off-camera. This occurs in *The 400 Blows.* We watch the reactions of Antoine as his mother belatedly attempts to establish a warm relationship so that the boy will not reveal her extramarital affair.

The term *interior monologue* should be confined to a specific sequence in which we share the thoughts of a person, hearing the individual's voice accompanied by asynchronized images. A memorable example is the soliloquies delivered by Laurence Olivier in *Hamlet.* This form of spoken word should not be confused with a character's flashback (the character is usually addressing another person and does not comment directly during the dramatic presentation) or with devices such as those used by Woody Allen in *Annie Hall.* In this film, subtitles reveal the actual thoughts of individuals during a dialogue and characters are physically present during the projection on the screen of a memory.

Natural sound encompasses all sounds that are not spoken words or music. (In this context, the concept of music must exclude the singing of birds— surely a type of music, but considered a natural sound —and any rhythmic beat of nonhuman origin, such as ocean waves or wind rustling through trees.) Although most natural sounds simply enhance the illusion of reality, they can assume symbolic proportions. For example, the mournful wail of a foghorn at night may represent lonely human beings seeking solace, as in the last sequence of Bergman's *Scenes From a Marriage.*

Most film music is asynchronized in that we do not see the source of the music on the screen. But this is not always so. We may observe musicians playing instruments or a person singing as we hear the music on the sound track. A radio or phonograph might be visible. Usually, however, music without a visual source accompanies the images. We have become so accustomed to this dimension of sound films that we tend to forget that background music is completely a convention. Only bemused lovers think they hear a string orchestra playing as they embrace in an open field.

The ways in which a composer prepares a motion picture score will be outlined when we consider the activities of this member of the filmmaking team in Chapter 2. Our concern here is the functions of background music in a nonmusical.

The most practical function of background music is to help make transitions between sequences. A fade-out and a fade-in to a new setting are often not enough of a signal to an audience that the perspective has changed in space and/or time. Music can serve, therefore, as an emotional bridge for viewers (in fact, composers refer to *bridge music*).

Background music can also evoke an atmosphere throughout a film. The use of folk songs suggesting a time and place is one method (two examples are the melodies of Irish songs in *Man of Aran* and the folk songs in *Stagecoach*). Lush, sentimental music for a romance and stirring, martial music for an adventure film are conventional examples of this approach. Less obvious is a score in a mood that is in contrast to the content of a film, building up a tension that the director feels is appropriate. In *Night and Fog,* the horrors of the visuals are set against Hanns Eisler's terse, controlled chamber music score.

In addition to creating a special ambiance for an entire film, background music can also heighten the drama of a specific scene or sequence. During a scene in *The 400 Blows,* Antoine wanders alone at night in Paris. The boy's loneliness and sadness are conveyed not only by his actions and expressions but also by a wistful flute solo. Background music can even prepare us for a stirring event before it happens. We are familiar with this device in Alfred Hitchcock's films, as in *Psycho* when the detective Milton Arbogast is climbing the stairs in an apparently deserted house; the background music is a clue that at any moment something unexpected is going to happen. There are also a number of musical anticipations in *Man of Aran.* *

One of the most intriguing roles that background music can play is to comment on the action and characters. This may be done for obvious comic effect; for example, when we view a wedding in a church and hear a funeral march on the sound track. A comic commentary, however, can be subtle. Charles Chaplin in his sound films and Jacques Tati in all his works were masters in utilizing this type of sly musical irony. Naturally, musical commentary is not confined to the comic. In *Beauty and the Beast* there are two separate worlds: the house where the mer-

chant and his bourgeois family live and the fantastic castle of the Beast. With a couple of brief exceptions, there is no background music when the house is the setting for sequences and scenes, but there is almost continual music at the castle. Jean Cocteau is thus able to reinforce the visual impression that the merchant's house is a place of mundane practicality and the castle a setting for imagination and genuine emotions.

Georges Auric, who composed the score for *Beauty and the Beast,* makes use of a technique derived from opera and symphonic tone poems that is a mode of musical commentary. This technique enables the creators of a motion picture to indicate nonverbally a character's feelings and to crystallize in auditory terms the probable reactions of an audience. A leitmotif in music is a theme that is associated with a character or a situation; variations on the theme may reflect changes in either or both. For example, in Fellini's *La Strada,* the melancholy tune that Gelsomina plays on a trumpet becomes associated with her. During the last sequence of the film, the taciturn Zampanò need not say a word to convey his despair after losing her; all that is necessary is for the score to build on her melody.

Innumerable motion pictures illustrate how background music can go beyond being merely an auditory binding between scenes to being a means of intensifying and commenting on the visuals. To cite just a few examples, without the collaboration between S. M. Eisenstein and Sergei Prokofiev, Jean Vigo and Maurice Jaubert, Jean Cocteau and Georges Auric, Orson Welles and Bernard Herrmann, and Ingmar Bergman and Erik Nordgren, *Alexander Nevsky, Zero for Conduct, Beauty and the Beast, Citizen Kane,* and *Wild Strawberries* would be less the masterworks of cinematic art that they are.

### LIGHTING AND COLOR

Light is indispensable in the making of motion pictures, for without it images would not register on film stock. There are basically two types of illumination: natural (usually sunlight) and artificial (electrical)—although the former is often modified by the use of reflectors, silk screens, and floodlights. Generally, outdoor or exterior settings are photographed in natural light, and indoor or interior ones are lighted artificially.

*pp. 358–359

There have been many exceptions. During the heyday of the big studios, for example, it was not an uncommon practice to shoot an entire motion picture, regardless of setting, in a film studio rather than on location or outdoors on studio lot sets.

The second function of lighting in a two-dimensional medium is to increase the illusion of depth in a setting by means of multiple planes of light. This illusion is naturally molded by sunlight when an outdoor scene is photographed. It is far more difficult to produce the same effect for an interior scene. The process of lighting a film set in this respect is fundamentally the same as for a theater set. There is, however, a major difference. The perspective of a theater audience remains fixed, whereas a camera changes a viewer's perspective with each shift of position. Therefore, to preserve an illusion of depth, the lighting must be readjusted for each major change in the placement of the camera. In fact, in Europe during the silent era, it was the practice to reset the lighting for every new shot.

Lighting graduated from a technical necessity to a significant means by which a director can re-create reality when it was recognized that this element of presentation could also function expressionistically. The major ways in which lighting can go beyond simply illumination and perspective include underscoring the tone of a whole film or a specific scene, emphasizing an actor or an object, suggesting aspects of characterization, and creating symbolic overtones.

Considering the necessity or potentials of these functions of lighting, it is understandable why much of the time in shooting a film is devoted to arranging the lighting. This procedure requires a great deal of attention from the cinematographer and the art director, who together bear the responsibility of using the available equipment to implement the director's vision, because they must take the many qualities of light into account. To simplify a description of these qualities, the additional complications involved in color photography will be considered later in this section.

The primary concern in lighting a setting is the intensity and direction of the illumination. The main source of illumination in a shot is the *key light,* with molding and softening effects supplied by *fill light.* When a shot or scene should be bright, cheery, and unshadowed, *high-key* lighting is sought (Figure 1.39). The opposite, *low-key* lighting, results in a veiled, mysterious, shadowed shot or scene (Figure 1.40).

**FIGURE 1.39**

High-key lighting. (From the production number "You Were Meant for Me" in *Singin' in the Rain.*)

**FIGURE 1.40**

Low-key lighting. (From *M,* directed by Fritz Lang, 1931.) The scene takes place at night. The Murderer is talking to a child, whom he intends to make his next victim.

When a key light is turned on an object, such as a face or a gun, the object stands out and attracts our attention. Intensity can also be influenced by the camera shutter speed, the size of the lens opening, the light sensitivity of film stock (ASA), and the laboratory processing.

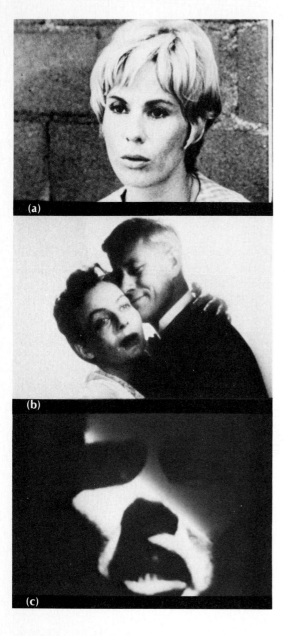

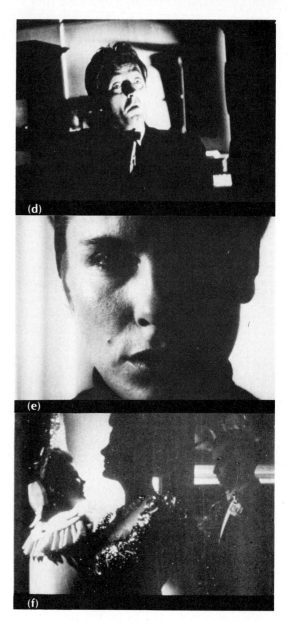

**FIGURE 1.41**

Direction of lighting on the human face. (a) Above and in front, equally diffused. (From *Passion of Anna,* directed by Ingmar Bergman, 1969.) (b) Top. (From *Ordet,* directed by Carl Dreyer, 1955.) (c) Front. (From *The Hour of the Wolf,* directed by Ingmar Bergman, 1966.) (d) Below. (From *The Night of the Hunter,* directed by Charles Laughton, 1955.) (e) Side. (From *Persona,* directed by Ingmar Bergman, 1966.) (f) Back (silhouette). (From *The Magnificent Ambersons,* directed by Orsen Welles, 1942.)

The direction from which light falls on a subject is also crucial, as is evident in Figure 1.41. Lighting from above and in front is most commonly used when photographing a face, for it softens features and casts shadows downward where they are less noticeable (a). From directly above, a shimmer, suggesting spirituality, appears on the top of the head (b). Lighting from directly in front flattens the planes of the face (c). From below, deep, sinister shadows develop on features, and shadows are also cast behind the subject (d). Side lighting leaves half of the face in shadows and the other half brightly illuminated, giving the effect of conflict or moodiness (e). If intense enough, back lighting results in a silhouette (f) or, when carefully controlled, a romantic aura, particularly effective for a woman's hair. The human face has been used as an example, but, of course, the same principles of lighting direction apply to objects or to any combination of human beings and objects.

In describing the effects of lighting from the qualities of intensity and direction, adjectives with emotional connotations are unavoidable. The ability of lighting to stimulate our feelings is derived on the most elementary level from our contrasting associations with light and dark. Light suggests truth, clarity, cheerfulness, and life; dark arouses feelings of doubt, mystery, fear, and death. These associations can be ambiguous. Dazzlingly bright snow is often a symbol of death, and a dark cave can offer the comfort of escape.

It is possible to generalize about the lighting of a whole film on the basis of our responses to light and dark. Comedies and musicals are typically shot in predominantly high-key lighting. Tragedies and melodramas emphasize low-key lighting. On the other hand, most films, especially dramas, include more than one tone or mood, so lighting is usually planned in terms of smaller units—sequence, scene, and shot.

The specific effects that a filmmaker can achieve primarily through lighting can be made concrete by examples. A range of possibilities is indicated in the following illustrations drawn from films analyzed in Parts Two and Three of this book. *The 400 Blows* is predominantly in low-key lighting appropriate to a drama of frustration and conflict. On the

other hand, *Top Hat,* a bright and blithe musical, is photographed in high-key lighting. *Titicut Follies,* a documentary on inmates in an institution for the criminally insane, makes no use of artificial lighting (except for a stage performance), and it is uniformly gray, with little contrast between light and dark tones. To a lesser degree, the same is true of the Neorealistic *The Bicycle Thief.*

In *October,* when Eisenstein wishes to ridicule religious objects, including masks and fetishes, he photographs many of them with lighting from below, making them look grotesque. Bergman used side lighting in *Smiles of a Summer Night* to indicate the conflict within Fredrik, so half of his face and body is in shadows when he first discovers that the two people he cherishes most in the world, his young wife and son, are in love with each other. In a sequence in *Broken Blossoms,* Griffith goes beyond mood and makes his lighting symbolic, crosscutting between the Chinaman's room, a dimly lit abode of romance pervaded by soft shadow, and a fight ring, with very high-key, harsh lighting. Shadows can be an effective means of conveying a sense of symbolic import and mystery. It was for this reason that the device was cultivated by Expressionistic directors (who were concerned with projecting powerful and subjective feelings on the screen). In *Variety,* E. A. Dupont makes use of deep shadows, particularly in the first sequence, which takes place in a prison.

Directors may surprise audiences by reversing stock associations with certain lighting effects, as in the films of Hitchcock, a master manipulator of audience responses. A murder may occur in brilliant daylight, as in the North African marketplace in *The Man Who Knew Too Much* (1956 version), or a sequence in very low-key lighting may convey the expectation but not the realization of danger, as in the Chicago setting of *North by Northwest.*

Color motion pictures depend on basically the same lighting techniques as black-and-white films. There are problems, however, unique to color photography that can only be dealt with separately.

Color was a potential element of presentation in motion pictures from the beginning of the century. By the end of the first decade, two techniques were available. Hand coloring involved the tedious process of painting each frame of a black-and-white print by hand. Tinting made use of stencils and staining to achieve the same effects. Other experiments, such as directing a colored beam of light on images on a screen, were also attempted.

Photographic reproduction of colors similarly began early. The basic problem was the projection of red, green, and blue, the primary colors of light, which can be combined to make all other colors. The process invented first was the additive: Black-and-white stock was run through a camera at double speed so that alternate frames were photographed through alternate red and green rotating filters. When the projector was supplied with rotating filters and the film was projected at the same speed, the eyes of viewers, through persistence of vision, blended the colors. The first viable additive system was Kinemacolor, patented in 1906 by Charles Urban and G. Albert Smith.

Practically all color motion pictures since the thirties have been made by a subtractive color process. It is based on the principle that what our eyes see as ''white'' light is actually a mixture of the colors of the spectrum. So if a yellow filter is placed between a beam of light and a screen, all colors but yellow will be subtracted, and this color appears on the screen. The process itself is very complex, and there are many variations at different stages, but in the simplest terms, subtractive-color film stock contains three layers of emulsions (a *tripack*), each one sensitive to a primary light color. When exposed, the dyes are activated. During processing, the red, green, and blue content are printed as, respectively, cyan (blue-green), magenta, and yellow—the primary colors of the process. Combinations of these colors create others (for example, red is formed by the presence of yellow and magenta and the absence of cyan). These dyes act as filters that subtract color from the white light of the projection bulb. The blending of subtractive primary colors results in the range of tones we see on the screen.

Two-color prints made by the subtractive process were available in the mid-twenties. The first entire feature in three colors with live action was *Becky Sharp* (1935), directed by Rouben Mamoulian, in Technicolor. In the late forties the superior Eastman Color and Agfacolor (from Germany) were distributed. Since the late sixties most commercial films have been photographed in color.

Anyone looking at a color motion picture with a critical eye is aware that color photography is more varied in tone but essentially almost as artificial as black and white. No process yet devised is able to reproduce the ability of the human eye to distinguish subtle hues and the multiple effects of surfaces and textures on color. Moreover, color photography is affected in individual ways by the intensity and direction of lighting, as well as the use of filters, laboratory dyes, and brand of stock. So this type of film photography is an artifice that should be molded and manipulated with the goal not only of attaining more realistic images of the real world than black and white but also of taking advantage of the intrinsic characteristics of color photography.

A director and a cinematographer especially must take a number of these characteristics into account in arranging the lighting of a film. Color photography tends to prettify what it reproduces, and it may even add a garish tone. This works to the advantage of a musical, such as *Singin' in the Rain,* or a comedy, such as *The Producers;* however, it offers problems when uncompromised realism is the intention of a director. It is hard to imagine *The Bicycle Thief* in color. Robert Altman overcame the color difficulties involved in depicting the brutal life of a frontier town in *McCabe and Mrs. Miller* by restricting the hues as much as possible to grays and browns. Another solution is to combine color and black-and-white photography, as in *The Wizard of Oz* or more recently as Bergman does in *The Passion of Anna* by presenting Anna's dream sequence in black and white in contrast to the rest of the film.

Bright hues tend not only to dominate the lighter hues but also to flatten images, so objects in vivid colors stand out even if they are dramatically unimportant. This can be dealt with by choosing the most significant objects in a scene and making their colors preeminent. Ingenuity is often required in moving harmoniously from one scene to another or if the tone changes from one shot to another.

Individual colors, as well as black and white, are laden with psychological connotations. For example, red is associated with passion and violence, blue with serenity, and orange with aggressiveness. It is on the bases of these associations that a filmmaker can use color expressionistically to reinforce a mood or to suggest symbolic meanings. The tiredness and desperation of the outlaws in *The Wild Bunch* is emphasized by the dominance of black and beige except in sequences of extreme violence, when red blood bursts across the screen. Red develops symbolic proportions in *West Side Story.* In the scene where Tony and Maria meet for the first time at the high school dance, swirls of red and green surround them, anticipating the passion and security that they will cherish in their private world of romance. On the other hand, a splash of red filling the screen introduces the sequence of the rumble that includes the deaths of Riff and Bernardo; here passion results not in love but in violence.

Some of the best–World War II directors, particularly Michelangelo Antonioni, Ingmar Bergman, Stanley Kubrick, and Federico Fellini, have taken advantage of expressionistic uses of color. Generally, however, this aspect of color has been approached with extreme caution by the majority of directors and cinematographers. This is an area of cinema that is largely unexplored, and filmmakers of the future with verve and imagination can still make exciting and significant contributions to it.

### PLACE SETTINGS

The *setting* is the physical environment in which a motion picture takes place. This term refers either to the general locale of an entire film (for example, the setting of *Shane* is the American West) or to a more specific location within that locale (for instance, the two main settings of *Shane* are the Starrett ranch and the town). *Decor* is sometimes used as a synonym for *setting,* but it should be reserved for the furnishings and decorations appearing in a setting. There are other confusions of terminology related to this element of presentation. *Set* is a contraction of *setting;* however, it usually refers to an artificially constructed setting in a studio or on its grounds. *Props* (short for *properties*) are objects that are part of the decor. They can be differentiated as set props, action props, and hand props. Unless specified otherwise, a setting includes its decor.

As noted in the section on lighting, there are two types of settings: those created in a studio or on a studio lot and those outside the studio, when the shooting is done on location. Settings in a studio or a studio lot give filmmakers greater control, especially in lighting, while settings on location usually have greater authenticity on the screen.

The art director is in charge of settings even when the shooting is on location, but an art director's major contribution is in designing and supervising the construction of sets and arranging for their decor. The theater has been the strongest influence on cinema set designs, and numerous art directors developed their talents while working on stage productions. There are, however, important differences. A theater production usually has fewer individual sets than a motion picture. A film setting must be more detailed and realistic because a camera can move in very close to walls and objects, whereas a theater audience remains at a fixed distance from the stage throughout the performance. On the other hand, only what appears on the screen need be constructed for a motion picture. Because lighting for a film set must be readjusted for each scene or even each shot, it can be more refined and subtle than for a stage set, although color in the latter is more natural.

Film settings serve a number of functions. Most obviously, they indicate time and place. A setting can also suggest the circumstances and the tastes of characters in a film. In *The 400 Blows,* the crowded, untidy apartment in which the Doinels live reflects the financial straits and carelessness of the parents. A Western, on the other hand, usually requires that we see vistas of an imposing, potentially threatening nature if we are to appreciate the special difficulties of frontier life. Of course, a director might wish to emphasize the crudity and uncomfortableness of that milieu through suitable interiors, as Robert Altman does in *McCabe and Mrs. Miller.*

Although the place settings in most motion pictures only attempt to convey as authentically as possible the physical world and circumstances of the participants in a drama, they can play a role in expressing the inner feelings of characters. To understand how settings can function expressionistically, it is necessary first to recognize that any set that appears on the two-dimensional screen is inevitably a construct. Its perspective, lighting, and decor are adjusted to the requirements of a camera lens. Whenever necessary, an art director makes use of devices described later in this chapter under "Special Effects," such as matte and mirror shots. The control of physical effects may extend to location shooting.

*Authenticity,* then, is a relative term. We believe on faith in the reality of the place settings for *The Bicycle Thief* or for documentaries, even though we are aware that the eye is easily fooled. Yet we will just as willingly accept distortion and obviously artificial effects in settings if they intensify the emotional impact of a scene. The crucial criterion of acceptance is whether or not we can be convinced that an expressionistic approach is intentional and justified. When confronted with a crude backdrop in an inexpensive Roger Corman horror film, we may be indulgent but remain unconvinced. We recognize, however, that the opening shots in *Variety* contain distorted sets in order to convey the oppressive atmosphere of a prison. The papier-mâché boulders in *The Gold Rush* remind us that this tale of a tramp-turned-prospector is intended as a fantasy.

There are many individual ways in which an art director can have settings function expressionistically, but there are only three general approaches. The first approach is to use a primarily realistic set and to adjust scale, lighting, and props to exaggerate certain characteristics of it so that the ambiance of a situation is intensified. This is what Van Nest Polglase did for the interiors of Xanadu in Welles's *Citizen Kane* to suggest the grandiosity and emptiness of the lives of Kane and his wife in the castle. Examples of this approach also appear in *The Night of the Hunter* (Figure 1.42).

**FIGURE 1.42**

Nonrealistic setting without distortion of the set. (From *Night of the Hunter,* directed by Charles Laughton, 1955.) The scene takes place in the bedroom of two children. The expressionistic tone is achieved entirely through lighting and the nonrealistic proportions of the room.

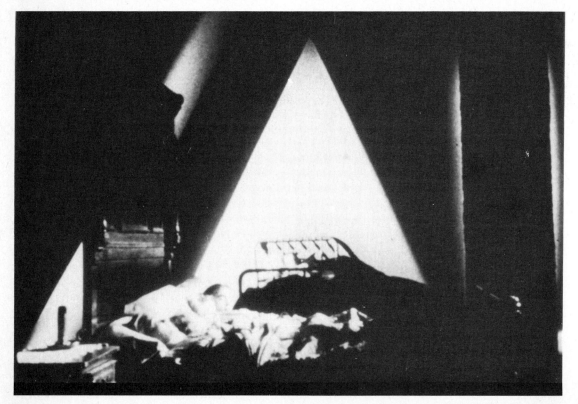

Justification within the plot for a nonrealistic setting is the second possibility. A warrant for such sets in musicals may be that production numbers are appearing on a stage, as in the title number in *Top Hat.* Dreams, hallucinations, and insanity offer other justifications. A fantasy by definition contains fantastic settings; the mysterious castle in Cocteau's *Beauty and the Beast* is a case in point (Figure 1.43).

Finally there can be unusual, even bizarre, sets from the beginning to the end, or at least for most of the duration, of a horror film (for example, the 1924 version of *Dante's Inferno*), when a film takes place in the distant past or future *(The Lost World, 2001),* or when it is predominantly Expressionistic* or Surrealistic† *(The Cabinet of Dr. Caligari* [Figure 1.44], *The Seashell and the Clergyman).*

**FIGURE 1.43**

Nonrealistic setting—fantasy. (From *Beauty and the Beast,* directed by Jean Cocteau, 1946.) Beauty's bedroom in the Beast's castle.

Any setting, portion of a set, or prop, even if intrinsically realistic, can be made symbolic if the director creates the proper context and emotional resonance. Some examples are the Chinaman's upstairs room in *Broken Blossoms,* the Eiffel Tower and the sea in *The 400 Blows,* the staircases in so many Hitchcock films, and the mirrors in practically every major work of Bergman.

No film can exist without place settings, whether real or created in a studio. With imagination, however, a filmmaker can transform a specific setting from a nondescript physical background into a vital, indispensable component of a film.

---

*pp. 102–104
†pp. 113–114

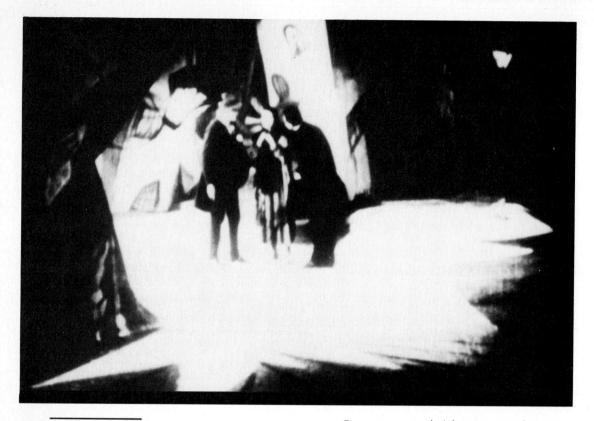

**FIGURE 1.44**

Nonrealistic setting with distortion of the set. (From *The Cabinet of Dr. Caligari,* directed by Robert Wiene, 1919, a classic of Expressionistic filmmaking.)

## COSTUMES

All apparel worn by actors and actresses, including hats, jewelry, and even armor, are costumes and the responsibility of the costume designer. One of the most difficult tasks a designer faces is authenticity when a film does not have a contemporary time setting. Costume designers go to a good deal of trouble to be sure that characters are dressed in styles appropriate to the period designated by a motion picture's plot or to indicate the passage of time. An ingenious example of the latter is a scene in Orson Welles's *The Magnificent Ambersons* in which Joseph Cotton as the young Eugene observes himself in a mirror, each shot in a different style of men's apparel (Figure 1.45).

Costumes may also function in other ways. They can disclose the social class to which a character belongs. Our first view of Fredrik in *Smiles of a Summer Night,* dressed in a stiff collar and a conservative but well-tailored suit, proclaims that he is a successful businessman or member of a profession. The personality of a character within a social class may be reflected by his or her taste in clothes. In Stroheim's *Greed,* the plaid suits and ostentatious jewelry favored by Marcus reveal his essential vulgarity. A change in a character's personality can be conveyed by new tastes in clothes. Lubitsch's *Ninotchka* has as its heroine (played by Greta Garbo) a dedicated Russian Communist who falls in love while in Paris. The first indication that her proletarian attitudes are changing is when she secretly buys an elegant hat, and her surrender to love is self-evident when she goes to dinner in a lovely evening gown instead of her severely functional jacket and skirt.

Within certain contexts, a costume may assume symbolic significance. In a Western, as in *Shane,*

FIGURE 1.45

Passing time is suggested by changes in the apparel of a single male character. (From *The Magnificent Ambersons,* directed by Orsen Welles, 1942.)

white clothes identify a hero and dark clothes a villain. This is not inevitably the case; for example, Hopalong Cassidy always wore black. The doorman in Murnau's *The Last Laugh* is admired by his tenement neighbors while he displays his imposing uniform but is ridiculed when he loses his job (Figure 1.46).

When creating costumes, a designer must take all these potential functions into consideration and also determine how the texture of the materials and the colors will photograph.

FIGURE 1.46

The Doorman's splendid uniform is admired by his neighbors. (From *The Last Laugh,* directed by F. M. Murnau, 1924.)

## SPECIAL EFFECTS

In a comprehensive and highly technical entry in the invaluable *Focal Encyclopedia of Film and Television Techniques* (1969), *special effects* are defined as "certain kinds of scenes which are too costly, too difficult, too time-consuming, too dangerous, or simply impossible to achieve with conventional photographic techniques."[8] The author of this article, Anthony Heightman, classifies these effects into three categories: (1) in-the-camera techniques (the final effects are photographed by the camera), (2) laboratory processes (requiring duplication of the original negative), and (3) combination techniques (primarily rear and front projections).

Laboratory processes are too complicated to discuss here, involving equipment that is difficult to describe without extensive diagrams; the interested reader is referred to the *Focal Encyclopedia* and to material listed in the bibliography at the end of this book. In-the-camera techniques include, first of all, the basic devices of slow motion, accelerated motion, reverse motion, and superimposition. All four were described under "The Shot" in the preceding section. Two other techniques that belong in the category of camera-editing dynamics but were not noted earlier are *pixilation* (a type of animation with live people in which the actors in actual place setting are photographed by the camera operating at a frame at a time; one result can be to make people on the screen "disappear" by removing certain frames from shots) and *day-for-night* effects (shooting in sunlight in such a way that the illusion of evening is created in the developed footage). Although an argument could be made for characterizing the other special effects that will now be considered as forms of camera-editing dynamics, they depend to such an extent on manipulating material in front of the camera that they are more appropriately included here as constituting an element of presentation.

Only the most unsophisticated moviegoer is unaware that miniatures or small-scale models are used in many motion pictures, especially in such genres as war, catastrophe, fantasy, and science fiction films. Kubrick's *2001,* for example, could never have been created without miniatures. A recent development is in the opposite direction, that is, constructing full-scale creatures controlled by computers, as in *Jaws* and the seventies version of *King Kong.*

The most widely used special effect is image replacement—replacing a portion of a setting with specially prepared details or background to save the expense of putting together a complete set. For instance, in a long establishing shot we see two people talking in the doorway of an immense mansion. By means of image replacement, only the doorway need be constructed in a studio. The three methods possible are a split-screen shot, a glass shot, and a mirror shot.

In principle, a split-screen (matte) shot requires two exposures of a negative. The first, using the example of a mansion and its doorway, is of an actual mansion or an enlarged photograph of the mansion with an opaque fiber or metal plate called a *matte* placed in front of the lens or the photograph in such a way that the doorway is blocked out. During the second exposure, a matte covers the remainder of the mansion, leaving only the doorway with the actors standing in it. When the film is processed, the two images will appear as one. It is usually more practical to achieve this effect in a laboratory than to double-expose the negative. The term *split-screen* also refers to one shot in which there are two (or more) distinct images in obviously different locations, as when we see two people talking to each other on a telephone.

In a glass shot, a sheet of transparent glass is painted or a photograph is attached, but a portion of the glass is clear. The subject might be the mansion, with a transparent space where the doorway would be. The prepared sheet of glass is placed in front of the camera in such a way that the transparent space is exactly filled by the studio-constructed doorway and the two actors. On the screen, one fused image appears. In a mirror shot (a variation of which is called the Schufftan process), a mirror reflecting a full-scale live action is combined with a miniature (or vice versa). It would be impractical to photograph the mansion and its doorway by this complicated process, but it could be done. A clear glass at an angle to the camera would present a blow-up of a photograph of the mansion. Where the doorway would be is a mirror reflecting the studio-constructed doorway and the actors. If the angle of the glass and mirror is correct, there would be little distortion, and a composite image appears and is recorded by the camera.

In a combination technique, the third category of special effects, a background scene previously photographed is projected on a screen before which the actors appear. The background can be projected from the rear or from the front of the screen. This method is the one usually used when we see a landscape passing by as actors are sitting in a car (in the studio, the car is stationary).

These are only a few of the techniques and processes used in special effects. In recent years, with films such as *Close Encounters of the Third Kind,* the *Star Wars* series, *Altered States,* and *Tron,* this element of presentation has become increasingly complex and significant, to the extent that for certain types of motion pictures it makes the difference between the film's success or failure.

# The filmmaking team

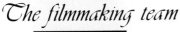

**2**

Surely few media require the cooperation of so many people to produce a single work as the cinema. It is not unusual for the shooting crews and peripheral helpers working on a multimillion-dollar motion picture to involve over 200 people. This does not include others who devote themselves to preproduction and postproduction activities, actors, and *extras* (performers who play minor parts, as in a crowd scene, and are usually hired by the day). It is possible for a single person, such as an animator, to put together a very short work or for a small documentary crew to operate independently. Our concern in this chapter, however, is the production of commercial fiction films.

The term *team* seems to be the most appropriate one to describe all those who contribute to the creating of a motion picture from its conception to its release. *Crew* should be reserved for those who collaborate in the actual shooting and can be limited to an aspect of production, such as a *sound crew*.

A filmmaking team consists of those in charge of an activity and their assistants and technicians. The producer, screenwriter, director, actors, director of photography, art director, composer, and editor are usually the major members of the team. Somewhat less prominent are the costume designer and sound supervisor. A third echelon is comprised of a chief makeup man, supervisor of special effects, script supervisor, casting director, and many others. Also espe-

cially significant, depending on the type of film, may be the choreographer, technical adviser, and second-unit director. With the exception of the screenwriter and some other personnel, each individual in charge of an aspect of filmmaking will have one or more assistants and, in many cases, a crew; for example, there can be eight or more technicians working on lighting and six on sound.

It is convenient to divide the process of making a motion picture into three stages. *Preproduction* encompasses all preparation before shooting; *production* is the actual photographing of a film; *postproduction* includes all procedures involved in transforming developed footage into a print that is projected on the screen of a theater or a TV set. A major member of the filmmaking team—especially the producer and the director—may collaborate on all three stages, but the following breakdown indicates the chief contributing members in each stage: preproduction (producer, screenwriter, art director), production (director, director of photography, actors), postproduction (editor, composer).

Although each contributor is responsible for a specific aspect of filmmaking, the process requires such overlapping of authority that it is often difficult to assign credit for an activity to a single person. For example, without seeing the original screenplay, it is hard to determine how much of the screenwriter's material was retained during production and postproduction.

A new filmmaking team is usually assembled for each motion picture. There have been, however, certain individuals who repeatedly work together. Examples are noted throughout this chapter.

## PRODUCER

The primary function of a producer is easily defined. The producer is responsible for all financial aspects of the making of a film. The qualifying adjective *primary,* however, is important. Types of producers range from those who are solely business people to those who participate in, or even dominate, every stage in the creation of a motion picture from script and casting to editing. The majority of producers tend to be business people and are overshadowed by their directors.

The making and distribution of films in America and Europe since the beginning of the twentieth century is detailed in Chapter 4, but a brief summary will help to elucidate the changes that have occurred in the activities and authority of the producer. What has happened in the United States is fairly typical of developments in most other democracies.

Basically there were three stages. In the earliest years of commercial filmmaking, a company arranged the financing, and a director was usually also the executive producer. With the innovations instituted by Thomas Ince in the second decade of this century,* the producer emerged as a separate and powerful member of the filmmaking team. This approach reached its culmination in the studio system. By the 1920s, the big studios, which were located in Hollywood, had consolidated control of all aspects of the productions under their aegis. The heyday of this dictatorial system was the thirties and forties, when such men as Irving Thalberg, Louis B. Mayer, Harry Cohen, William Fox, Darryl F. Zanuck, and Jesse Lasky—as president or vice-president in charge of production— were autocratic rulers of individual studios. There were also a few prominent companies independent of the studios, most notably those of Samuel Goldwyn, David O. Selznick, and Walt Disney.

In the late forties and early fifties, the reign of the major studios went into decline.† This led to the rise of independent production companies. They were established by directors, actors, and producers who had previously been salaried (such as Sam Spiegel, Hal Wallis, Jerry Wald, and Don Hartman). Today there are generally three types of companies that produce commercial motion pictures, with interconnections and separate interlocking deals that supply a livelihood for hundreds of lawyers and accountants.

First, there are studios owned by conglomerates (for example, Warner Bros., a subsidiary of Warner Communications, Inc., and Paramount Pictures, a subsidiary of Gulf + Western Industries, Inc.). These studios make only approximately 30 percent of the feature films released in the United States; however, they are the major source of financing for small independent companies. Second, there are companies that have connections to bank consortiums and private money sources. They may not have the monetary resources of the studios, but they can become involved in multi–motion picture deals. Among such organizations are Mirisch Corp., First Artists, Roger Corman's New World, and, until recently, Francis Ford Coppola's Zoetrope Studios. Finally, there are the genuine independent producers who often work on one project at a time or at least on a very limited number of projects at various stages of development. Although they are usually incorporated, these producers may work out of a single office with a very small staff. Among the better-known individual producers in recent years (some of whom at one time or another have been associated with a studio) are Ray Stark, Robert Stigwood, Elliot Kastner, Martin Ransohoff, Edward Pressman, and Irwin Allen.

We have been considering the methods of production in the United States. The situation in foreign countries, especially in nondemocratic nations, can be different in many respects. In most communist countries, for instance, all film production is completely controlled by the government, and producers are salaried employees who must conform to the directives and procedures of a state board of cinema. A similar condition existed in Germany, Italy, and Spain when they were governed by dictators.

Aside from countries that have exclusive state control, there have been two main divergences between the development of the motion picture industries in the United States and in European countries. First, the monopoly of the Hollywood studio system was unique. The only European studio that was comparable to Paramount or MGM in the twenties was Germany's UFA,* under the supervision of Erich Pommer, one of the greatest producers in the history of cinema. In England in the thirties and forties, Alexander Korda attempted to imitate a Hollywood studio first through London Film Productions and then through British Lion, but he only partially succeeded. In Italy, Carlo Ponti and Dino De Laurentiis, both in

---

*p. 100
†p. 148

*p. 102

their own country and abroad, individually and together, have built up financial resources that rival those of any company in the United States.

Most European producers have gained international reputations through relatively small companies that are associated with a specific director or type of film. Some examples: in England, Gabriel Pascal (film versions of the plays of George Bernard Shaw) and John and Roy Boulting (British comedies); in France, André Paulvé (films of Jean Cocteau) and Pierre Braunberger (New Wave filmmakers); and in Sweden, Allan Ekelund (films of Ingmar Bergman).

The second distinction is that government subsidies are available in most Western European countries. These subsidies are usually derived from some type of entertainment tax. The United States has never had direct government support of commercial films.

The financing of motion pictures has become more difficult because of continually mounting costs, as illustrated by the following figures for some American films: *From Here to Eternity* (1953), $1.9 million; *Planet of the Apes* (1967), $5.8 million; *King Kong* (1976), $25 million; and *1941* (1979), $40 million. Naturally, these are approximate costs, and the examples are selective. A more general indication of rising expenses is the estimate that a film made in 1943 would have cost about twice as much in 1963; today, only a very modest feature can be made for less than several million dollars. Because of this inflation, an independent producer has difficulty in obtaining financial backing unless there is some guarantee of success through adaptations of popular novels and plays or through the use of actors with established box office appeal.

Obviously the independent producer's life is not an easy one. Why, then, would anyone except a masochist want to enter this field? There is an element of glamour in dealing with "movie people," and there is the possibility, unlikely as it may be, of huge profits. One can also take at face value the statements by certain producers that their greatest satisfaction is being responsible for worthwhile films that would not have been created without their efforts. Also influential is the lack of any special requirements for being a producer; in fact, anyone, with any background, can become a producer. For this reason, no other area of filmmaking contains more crass opportunists and inexperienced individuals who substitute self-aggrandizement for expertise.

Financing a film is a very complicated process, replete with percentages, fixed or changing costs, and trade-offs. There are general approaches, however, with which anyone interested in motion pictures should become familiar. To simplify matters, let us follow a fictitious example through various financial stages in the United States, keeping in mind that the figures quoted could be, depending on circumstances, considerably more or less. An overall budget of $1 million is indeed a modest sum these days ($10.5 million was the average in 1982), but it is a handy number for calculating percentages.

Mr. P, an independent producer, reads *Tarnished Trophies* by John Johnson. He believes the novel, although not a best-seller, could be made into a small but commercially successful film. The first problem for Mr. P is obtaining *front money* (financing for the initial stage of producing). He needs $80,000. Mr. P already has $30,000 and persuades a business associate to invest $50,000, for which the producer gives up 30 percent of his profits. Mr. P can now start operating.

Mr. P contacts John Johnson's agent and negotiates film rights for the novel at $85,000. He does not pay this sum but takes an *option* (a right to buy within a fixed time) on the novel for 6 months. For this privilege he must pay 5 to 10 percent of the purchase price —in this case, $8,000. Mr. P then hires a writer to prepare a screenplay from the novel. This costs $25,-000 (a bargain, for the sum is close to the minimum set by the Writers Guild of America). Mr. P could now move to the next stage, but to increase the interest of a studio, he decides to arrange a *package deal* (commitments from a director and a star in addition to rights and a script). He convinces Mr. D, a well-known director, that *Tarnished Trophies* will be commercially profitable and could enhance D's reputation. They agree that the director will receive a salary of $125,000 if the film is made; however, Mr. P is to pay $20,000 immediately for Mr. D's participation in revising the screenplay. Fortunately, the producer is a close friend of Robert Redacres, and the famous actor commits himself to the film without an advance.

Mr. P has paid out $53,000, plus traveling, overhead, and entertainment costs. His final expense is to hire an assistant with a business background. Together they prepare a general budget for *Tarnished Trophies*. With this document, the screenplay and treatment, and all signed commitments, Mr. P is ready for the most crucial stage in producing the film.

He presents all his material to Mr. V, vice-president in charge of production at United Filmmakers. Mr. V likes what he sees and persuades the executive board of his company to invest $1 million in the film. Mr. V, Mr. P, and their assistants then prepare a detailed production budget; in the case of *Tarnished Trophies*, it runs to 93 pages. The first page is called a *topsheet* and is a summary of the budget. It consists of two sections. The first is a list of the expenses *above the line*, including such items as costs for the story and screenplay and the fees of the producer, director, major actors, and supervising personnel. Mr. P receives a sum of money for himself and his staff as well as a percentage of the profits (we will return later to this item). Mr. D has agreed to a salary of $125,000. Robert Redacres, however, insists on a *participation clause* (once called a *deferment*), which is a salary plus a percentage of the profits. Redacres could demand $200,000 as his acting fee (this is a modest sum; for an expensive production he usually receives $1 million). Because he has faith in the film and wishes to help Mr. P by not subtracting his full salary from the $1 million committed to the film, Redacres will accept a fee of $90,000 plus 10 percent of the *distributor's gross* (defined later). Should the motion picture prove to be commercially profitable, he might receive substantially more than $200,000; if not, he will have gambled away $110,000.

*Below the line* encompasses all other expenses: salaries for the remainder of the cast, technicians, and other personnel; sound; transportation; and other costs. These items are sometimes called *direct costs* and are rarely subject to the type of negotiations typical of above-the-line expenses.

There is a breakdown of all financial arrangements in the contract, even though details cannot be worked out until the film is in production. First, it is anticipated that approximately 50 percent of every dollar taken in at the box office (the *theater gross*) will be kept by the exhibitor. What remains is called the *distributor's gross*. Robert Redacres receives 10 percent of the latter through his participation deal.

From the distributor's gross, United Filmmakers take 30 percent to operate their business (principally for salaries and overhead). They take another 20 percent for distribution costs (for example, prints, advertising, and taxes). The rest is the *net producer's share*. From this sum is subtracted the *negative cost,* which is how much it costs to make the film. In the case of *Tarnished Trophies,* that would be at least $1 million borrowed from the banks.

These figures indicate that the film must take in a minimum of $4 million at the box office just to break even (that is, $2 million to exhibitors, $1 million to United Filmmakers, and $1 million for negative costs). Actually, it comes to more, since we have not included the bank interest on the loan and other expenses. It is usually calculated that, after the exhibitor has taken his share, a film must generate a 2.4 percent ratio to the negative cost. Included in income is not only the U. S. box office receipts but also those from the foreign market and TV rentals. So from all sources, *Tarnished Trophies* will have to take in $4.4 million before there are any profits. These profits are typically divided between the financing-distributing company and the producer—United Filmmakers and Mr. P in our example.

It should be clear now why investment in a film is not a casual affair and why advertising and audience acceptance are so important. If *Tarnished Trophies* depended only on U. S. box office receipts, with an average ticket price of $3 per person, then nearly 1.5 million viewers must pay to see the film for the financing to break-even.

The motion picture industry has often been castigated as being too commercial, and producers have been considered the chief villains in a conspiracy to prevent the medium from realizing its full potential as an art form. An appreciation of the costs involved in making a commercial motion picture, however, can lead one to wonder not that so many films are without redeeming artistic and social values but that so many works of art and worthwhile films have been created by an industry that above all else must produce profits to survive.

## SCREENWRITER

Practically all narrative motion pictures are based on screenplays. Exceptions, such as the films of Andy Warhol, usually can be cited as evidence of how a screenplay is necessary if a film is not to be diffuse and haphazard in development.

In most cases a screenplay is prepared by a screenwriter who is an independent member of the filmmaking team. From the earliest years of cinema, however, there have been directors who wrote their own screenplays. Prominent among those who performed this dual function in the silent era were D. W. Griffith, Erich von Stroheim, Carl Dreyer, and Charles Chaplin. Particularly since World War II there have been increasing numbers of director-screenwriters (Ingmar Bergman is a nonpareil example). Another interesting phenomenon is the director who works repeatedly with a specific writer, such as F. W. Murnau and Carl Mayer, Marcel Carné and Jacques Prévert, Frank Capra and Robert Riskin, John Ford and Dudley Nichols, and Vittorio De Sica and Cesare Zavattini.

Because a screenplay supplies the essentials of the narrative dimension in a motion picture, one might imagine that the screenwriter is a highly respected member of the filmmaking team. The situation is quite the reverse. In the introduction to a volume of interviews with screenwriters, William Froug states that they are "beaten, battered and belittled" and "kept, securely, in the back of the hall."[1]

There are reasons, though they do not constitute justification, for this neglect. Typically, the activities of a screenwriter are confined to the preproduction stage of the making of a film. Moreover, once a screenplay has been completed, it becomes the property of the production company. Unless there is an unusual clause in the writer's contract, changes can be made in a script without the approval of its author. Perhaps most detrimental to the screenwriter's public image is the widely held view that the director is essentially the "author" of a film.

The screenwriter's status and rewards have improved considerably, however, since the 1940s. In the United States, primarily through the efforts of the Writers Guild of America, there are contractual rules governing who is credited for a screenplay and the minimum fees that are paid. Today an outstanding original screenplay can command an impressive purchase price (for example, William Goldman received $400,000 for his screenplay on which *Butch Cassidy and the Sundance Kid* was based). Since the early 1970s, for the first time, critical studies devoted to screenplays and their authors have been published.

What does not exist to date, however, is a comprehensive history of screenwriting. Such a volume surely would include commentaries on the following eminent screenwriters: in Germany, (silent era) Carl Mayer (who set a standard of accomplishment and influence by which all screenwriters have had to measure themselves), Thea von Harbou, and Hanns Krähly; in the United States, (silent era) Anita Loos, Frank Woods, Roy McCardell, and June Mathis, (thirties and forties) Ben Hecht, John Howard Lawson, Norman Krasna, Billy Wilder, Charles Brackett, Dalton Trumbo, Nunnally Johnson, Herman J. Mankiewicz, Joseph L. Mankiewicz, Robert Riskin, and Dudley Nichols, (post–World War II) Ring Lardner, Jr., Abraham Polansky, Frank Tashlin, Frank S. Nugent, I. A. L. Diamond, Walter Brown Newman, William Bowers, Buck Henry, Terry Southern, and Joan Tewkesbury; in France, (chiefly thirties and forties) Jacques Prévert and Charles Spaak, (post–World War II) Alain Robbe-Grillet and Marguerite Duras; in Italy, Cesare Zavattini and Tonino Guerra; and in England, (thirties and forties) Eric Ambler, Emlyn Williams, R. C. Sherriff, Sidney Gilliat, and Lajos Biro, (post–World War II) Harold Pinter, Graham Greene, Robert Bolt, and Terence Rattigan. This is, of course, a highly selective list and does not include (with a few exceptions, such as Wilder, Robbe-Grillet, and Duras) directors who write or collaborate on the screenplays for their own films.

Creating a screenplay is the most private activity in the making of a film, for a writer usually works alone. There are, however, a number of exceptions. Writers can collaborate repeatedly together (examples are Garson Kanin and Ruth Gordon, Betty Comden and Adolph Green, and David Newman and Robert Benton). A producer may insist on evaluating a screenplay at each major stage in its evolution. If any other filmmaker assists the screenwriter, it is likely to be the director.

There are two types of screenplays. The first is an *adaptation:* a screenplay based on a story that has already appeared in another form—for example, a novel, short story, or play. It may adhere very closely to its source, as did Robert Bresson's screenplay for *Diary of a Country Priest,* or it may retain no more than the main theme and a few characters, which was the approach used by Antonioni and Tonino Guerra in the script derived from "Blow-Up," the short story by Julio Cortazar. The merits of a film adaptation should not be judged by its fidelity to the original work. At its best, it is not a facsimile of a source on film, but a re-creation that facilitates every potential for cinematic values inherent in the narrative.

An *original screenplay* is one written solely to serve as the basis of a film. While it is usually more difficult to do because a writer must conceive rather than re-create a narrative, it has the advantage of encouraging the screenwriter from the beginning to imagine sequences and scenes in terms of what the medium of cinema can do most effectively. There is no better advertisement for the benefits to be gained from this type of script than the fact that Welles's *Citizen Kane,* practically all the films of Bergman and Fellini, and most of those of Antonioni were created from original screenplays.

Whether an adaptation or an original, a screenplay (*scenario* and *script* are synonyms) goes through various stages. The earliest stage is the *story outline* (also *step outline* or *synopsis*). The story outline contains a condensed description of the basic elements of the narrative dimension of a potential film. It can range from two to six pages. The second stage is a *treatment.* In essence a rough draft of a screenplay, a treatment indicates place and time settings, fundamental action, characterizations, and relationships. Many professional screenwriters consider a treatment to be superfluous and proceed from a story outline to a screenplay proper.

The screenplay can be in a variety of forms. At its simplest, it contains, in addition to what is in a treatment, dialogue and a breakdown into scenes. At its most detailed, the screen play also includes a listing of shots and may supply suggestions on the characteristics of shots. A *shooting script* is prepared by the screenwriter and director, the director and other colleagues, or the director alone. It is comprised of all the information, such as angles and distances of shots and perhaps transitions, necessary for production. It is sometimes described as a verbal blueprint for shooting. Many directors have a *storyboard* prepared: sketches of projected shots (somewhat like a comic strip) or at least of the main action. The final form of a screenplay is a *cutting continuity.* This is based on the final print and should detail every aspect of a film from the angle, distance, and duration of each shot and the forms of transitions to dialogue and sound effects.

Professional screenwriters disagree as to whether or not a screenplay should go beyond the narrative dimension to notations on the other two components of film. Most screenwriters restrict themselves to the simpler form of screenplay unless encouraged to do otherwise by a producer or director.

Readers should be aware of a problem related to printed screenplays. Within the last few years a number of publishers—most notably Simon and Schuster in their Classic Film Scripts and Modern Film Scripts series and the Grove Press in its Film Book Series—prepare the texts from a cutting continuity or directly from a released print of a film. However, all too often, texts—especially those that were printed before the seventies—are based on shooting scripts. Since changes, even radical ones, occur during shooting and editing, there can be discrepancies between a printed script and a final film print.

One question that can occupy *cinéastes* (French for "film buffs") until the wee hours of the morning is whether or not a great motion picture can be made from a mediocre screenplay. Few would deny, however, that an outstanding screenplay is a giant step toward creating an outstanding film.

## DIRECTOR

The chief responsibility of a director is to coordinate and control the activities of actors, subordinate directors, and technicians in the production period. A director may or may not be directly involved in the preproduction and postproduction stages. Yet of all the members of a filmmaking team, the director has the opportunity to mold to a personal interpretation what finally appears on the screen. The only challenge to this preeminence comes from the producer. Historically, a rise in the power of producers has usually resulted in a lessening of the authority exercised by directors.

Whatever his degree of influence on the makeup of the final print, the director should be completely in command during the actual shooting of a film. Although he may delegate authority to others, he is responsible for the footage "in the can" at the end of a day's work. To fulfill this responsibility, the director must have certain abilities.

Most important of all, the director should know what he wishes to achieve in a specific shot and how it could relate to what comes before and after in the final print. It helps if he is aware of the technical problems involved or at least what is feasible technically with the available equipment and crew. This does not mean that he has to know the wattage of a bulb required in a certain type of spotlight or even the appropriate camera lens. He should be capable, however, of envisioning the effects he requires and communicating that vision to his subordinates. The more the director knows about the technical aspects of filmmaking, the easier is this task.

Careful preparation before the actual shooting is one way a director can avoid wasting expensive time and film stock. This type of preparation can include extensive rehearsals of actors, consultations with key members of a production crew, and the use of a storyboard. Some directors—Fellini and Godard, for instance—purposely limit their preproduction preparations. This approach may be desirable and even necessary in making a documentary. For a fiction film, however, the potential advantages of increased spontaneity on the part of actors and a salutary openness to inspiration on the part of the director have to be weighed against the disadvantages. These include increased production costs and the possibility of footage with varying tones and rhythms that even the most imaginative editing cannot coalesce. Only a very experienced and confident director—or a very inexperienced and foolhardy one—will depend on luck and inspiration as major supports during shooting.

Once shooting begins, a director works under severe limitations and continual pressure. He is supposed to stay within the budget determined during the preproduction stage. The details are the responsibility of the producer, but the director courts disaster if he repeatedly insists on expensive changes and spends twice as much time on shooting as was planned, for each extra day can add thousands of dollars to costs.

Moreover, a director rarely has more than one chance to make use of a single location. Usually all scenes in a specific setting (on location or on a studio stage) are shot together regardless of each one's chronological place in a shooting script. Once the production crews have moved from a location or the order is given to *strike* (dismantle) a set, it is exorbitantly expensive to return to or reassemble a setting, even if the actors are still available. A director, therefore, must be sure that he has all the material for each scene that will be required for properly editing the film.

There are a number of ways in which a director reassures himself that he has taken full advantage of each day of production. First, he insists on as many *takes* (number of times a single shot is filmed) as he feels are necessary to achieve the best results possible under the circumstances. It is not unheard of for a demanding director to require 20 or more takes of a given shot. Second, a director may prepare for unanticipated editing problems by photographing a shot from various camera positions and including a supply of *cutaways* (shots of simultaneous events or backgrounds that are tangential to the main action) that can be inserted between two shots to avoid discontinuity. This is sometimes called *covering footage.* Third, a director and his colleagues will study *rushes* of the previous day's shooting. Rushes (or *dailies*) consist of exposed negative footage printed in a photographic laboratory within 24 hours. The director can judge from the unedited rushes what shots must be redone while crews, actors, and setting are at hand. Recently the importance of rushes has been reduced by the use of video cameras shooting simultaneously with film cameras.

With multiple takes and covering footage, inevitably more film stock is exposed than is used in the final print. This disparity is called a director's *shooting ratio:* the proportional relation of exposed footage to the amount that is included in the final print. Generally, directors differ widely in their shooting ratios and even from one film to another, but an average might be 7 to 1. A filmmaker who does a great deal of preparation during preproduction, such as Alfred Hitchcock, or one with years of experience, such as John Ford, may have an average shooting ratio of 2 to 1. An article on documentary filmmakers suggests that Frederic Wiseman's shooting ratio can be as high as 70 to 1.[2]

Although a director must know what he wants to accomplish during production and how it might be done, almost as important if he is to be successful in his profession is the ability to draw the best from individual members of the filmmaking team. No director can make a feature film entirely by himself. There are various ways in which he obtains the cooperation of his colleagues. A few directors—from all accounts, Erich von Stroheim was of this type—tyrannize the production crews and actors. Most, however, use persuasive means, an approach encouraged by the power of contemporary motion picture unions in most countries of the Western world. On the other hand, it is unusual for a director willingly to share his authority with others, yet still be able to impose his interpretation on a production. Alain Resnais apparently is such an exception.

No subject connected with the activities of individual directors is more difficult to discuss intelligently and concretely than *style.* Although this term cannot be defined with any exactitude, it can be asserted that in any medium an artist who goes beyond the stage of journeyman develops patterns of choices in both content and form. In other words, an artist imposes a vision of reality on the created work that is distinctly personal. The patterns of choices that constitute the style of a director encompass the narrative dimension (for example, Bergman's preoccupation with the inner conflicts of characters that result in journeys into the unconscious), camera-editing dynamics (Welles's use of deep focus or the slow dissolve favored by George Stevens), and elements of presentation (the chiaroscuro lighting in F. W. Murnau's films or the emphasis on place settings in the works of Max Ophuls). The one common denominator of all directors whose styles are unique is imagination, whether retrained,

subtle, and "classic," as in the approaches of Carl Dreyer and Robert Bresson, or flamboyant, overtly dramatic, and "romantic," as is characteristic of Fellini and Sam Peckinpah.

In the "Background" sections of the film analyses included in Part Two and Part Three of this book, the styles of 18 directors are examined individually. The names of numerous other directors are listed and the achievements of major directors are summarized in the historical surveys in Chapters 4 to 9.

## ACTORS

Actors (a designation that refers to both males and females) are unique in that they are simultaneously objects that appear on the screen (and therefore must to some degree be manipulated like any other element of presentation) and also feeling, thinking members of the filmmaking team. This dual function is reflected in the extreme attitudes that directors can take toward them. Erich von Stroheim and Alfred Hitchcock are examples of directors who openly proclaimed that actors should have no will of their own and should be completely submissive to their director. On the other hand, others such as Robert Altman and John Cassavetes depend on their actors to be active collaborators in the creating of a film. Most directors favor a relationship midway between these two extremes: guiding and encouraging, not dictating to actors, yet denying them free rein.

Professional actors should have technique and intelligence, yet their primary stock in trade is their ability to mold their emotions and to project them to an audience. How they do this—in spite of all the teachings of different schools of acting and printed volumes on the subject—is, as with most creative acts, essentially a mystery. Only the vaguest adjectives are applicable (such as *convincing, intense, subtle,* and *imaginative*) when we attempt to explain why a great performance moves us and what the actor did to arouse our admiration. Although we cannot penetrate to the essence of the actor's art, we can examine actors' functions and the conditions of film production with which they must contend or use to their own advantage.

An actor is usually defined as a person who performs in a play or motion picture. The operative word is *perform*. In film an actor assumes an identity not his own (even if there is a close correspondence between his own nature and that of the character), is required to follow a preconceived sequence of action (although rarely photographed in chronological order), and in most sound films delivers lines prepared for him. By this definition, documentaries, with a few exceptions, do not make use of actors, only of people who appear in them. A nonprofessional actor in fiction films is one who has not had previous training in acting and has not performed before on screen or stage, but the difference between a professional and a nonprofessional actor is not clear-cut. One invalid criterion is quality of performance. It is difficult to imagine professional actors being more convincing than Lamberto Maggiorani and Enzio Staiola as, respectively, Antonio and Bruno in The Bicycle Thief.

A far more significant distinction is that between stage and screen acting. This has been a symbiotic relationship, and the development of screen acting cannot be discussed perceptively, especially when considering the silent era of cinema, without references to what was happening contemporaneously in the theater in respect to acting.

In the mid-nineteenth century the rhetorical style of acting was predominant. It required broad gestures, exaggerated facial expressions, artificial phrasing and enunciation, and forceful projection of the voice. With the appearance of realistic drama, a new style emerged that was restrained and abjured theatrical artifice.

These two styles were challenging each other when narrative cinema was born. Most stage actors viewed movies as a vulgar entertainment and considered it beneath their dignity to appear in ''flicks'' unless driven by dire circumstances. The only exceptions at the beginning of the century were filmed excerpts from stage plays (for example, those released by Le Film D'Art Company in France and Famous Players in America).

A disdain for their audience and the need to improvise whole scenes may have encouraged actors to exaggerate their expressions and gestures, but the major factor was the loss of their voices. The rhetorical style seemed more suitable than a realistic one when communication with an invisible audience had to be almost entirely through facial expressions and body movements and when the plots of most motion pictures were melodramatic and sentimental. By the end of World War I, film acting had become more sophisticated, the actors had adjusted better to the requirements of the medium, and the value of the restraints imposed by directors like Griffith and Victor Sjöström had been recognized. Silent-film acting, however, was to remain an amalgam of rhetorical and realistic styles or even abrupt changes from one approach to the other in a single motion picture.

With the advent of sound in cinema, film acting inevitably became more subdued. Given words to speak, actors could now use the more natural style that had become pervasive in the theater since the establishment of the modern drama of Ibsen, Strindberg, Pirandello, Chekhov, Gorky, Shaw, and O'Neill and the propagation of the ideas of Stanislavski and his followers. Moreover, by the 1930s cinema had become more respectable, and stage actors only occasionally felt they debased themselves by appearing on the screen.

The next distinctive method of film acting occurred in the late forties and fifties and again was often influenced by what was happening in the theater. An introspective, unmannered, self-consciously natural, sometimes terse, other times explosive approach became popular in different countries at different times after World War II. This style appeared first most prominently in Italian Neorealistic films (for example, in performances by Anna Magnani, Aldo Fabrizi, and Guilietta Masina). In the United States, it was dubbed *method acting* (based on the Stanislavski ''method''), and both its strengths and its weaknesses were exemplified by Marlon Brando and James Dean. A more extroverted form of method acting developed in Great Britain (for instance, in the performances of Mary Ure, Tom Courtenay, Richard Harris, Albert Finney, and Rita Tushingham).

During the sixties and seventies, no startling new acting style developed on stage or screen. Realism in all its variations was the predominant mode. When appropriate, however, the larger-than-life grand manner in film could still be drawn from older actors such as Laurence Olivier, Orson Welles, To-shiro Mifune, and Simone Signoret. The finest acting transcends contemporary fashions and is as ideal a balance as possible between what the screenplay requires and what the actor brings to the screen from his or her own personality and technique.

Today actors rarely confine themselves exclusively to the theater, the screen, or the third world of television. Only a few, however, have been equally successful in each medium, for there are significant differences between acting on the stage and before a camera. The most daunting of these is lack of continuity. In a play, the actor develops a role along the dramatic lines established by the author. This is usually not true in making a film. Setting up equipment in a locale (on location or in a studio) is so expensive that all scenes taking place in that setting are shot together, regardless of when the scenes occur in the plot. An actor, therefore, may have to appear, to take an extreme instance, in a climactic scene on the first day of shooting and in the opening scene on the last day of production. Sometimes a director is able to shoot the scenes of a motion picture in chronological order. Even in this situation, however, the actors must fragment their roles. Each new major scene usually requires changes in lighting, camera position, and movement of other equipment. An actor may appear before the camera for 10 minutes, then wait an hour before being on again. Not every actor is able to learn the technique of performing in bits and pieces and of recapturing on call a mood developed a week earlier.

Another aspect of screen acting that can disturb an actor trained in the theater is the absence of an audience. An intangible but vital connection is created between members of a theater cast and an audience. The most concrete manifestation of this relationship is applause after a song or production number in a musical or laughter in a comedy. Even for a drama, actors depend on emotional antennae that register the restlessness or attentiveness of the people sitting in the theater. Experienced actors learn to adjust their performances in ways that manipulate to their advantage the responses of a specific audience on a specific evening or afternoon. There is, however, no responding audience when an actor is before the camera, only a director who will offer criticism after a take. Without

hints from an audience, a screen actor must be very sure of what he is doing and have confidence in the other actors with whom he is working.

The screen actor must also learn to deal with the potential intimacy of the cinema. On the physical level, the slightest blemish on the face or perspiration on the forehead, which would go unnoticed on the stage, calls attention to itself on the screen. Actors in a theater are always separated from an audience by the area of the stage itself. In film production, a love scene may be performed with a dozen or more people within a few feet of the actors. Under these circumstances, the performance of an actor trained to project his emotions across the footlights becomes grotesque. A film actor is not performing for a living, responsive audience but for the omnipresent, unblinking, cold eye of the camera. Every movement, the pacing of a scene, and the relationships of the actor to other actors and to a setting must conform to the camera's dictatorial demands. It mercilessly magnifies any emotional and physical defect. An actor's ego must be very strong to endure such scrutiny.

Along with confidence and a certain amount of exhibitionism, the screen actor must develop patience. A shot is repeated until the director is satisfied with the results. Most actors are tolerant, within reason, of frequent takes, because once the director says, "Print it" or "Save it" (indicating that the shot is satisfactory), they know it is unlikely that they will have another opportunity to improve the performance in that moment of the film. In the theater, a weak performance one night can be corrected and developed the next night. On the other hand, when the run of a theatrical production ends, an individual performance exists only in the memory of people who have seen it, whereas a performance in a film survives as long as prints of the motion picture.

A final significant difference between theater and screen acting is the control a performer has over an interpretation of a role. A performance in both media is influenced by forces external to the actor, particularly the director and interaction between actors. In the theater, the actor is present when these molding pressures are applied and he can, if he chooses, object to changes forced on him in his interpretation. In a film production, however, there is a stage at which a performance may be radically modified, and the actor rarely has any say in the matter. During the editing of a film, by cutting out footage, an actor's performance can be improved, transformed in small or radical ways, or, in the case of a minor role, even eliminated. Seeing oneself on the screen in the final print (an opportunity unavailable to a stage actor) can be a satisfying, frustrating, or very disappointing experience for an actor.

Because screen acting is such an introspective, subjective art, it is not always easy, even for professionals in the field, to distinguish between a weak or a fine performance. There are, however, a few criteria of judgment that depend on recognizing, to the extent that this can be done intellectually, the basic components of a performance.

The first of these elements is a combination of physical appearance and intrinsic personality. This is a limitation that an actor accepts and exploits or attempts to transcend. Most actors are reconciled to being typecast (that is, limited to roles that fit a certain screen persona). A few fortunate and gifted ones can extend their range: For example, Jean-Paul Belmondo, most natural in portrayals of extroverted adventurers, could nevertheless convincingly play a shy intellectual in De Sica's *Two Women.*

Whatever the physical appearance and natural personality of an actor, an audience demands above all a convincing performance. John Wayne, for example, was not a versatile actor, yet he was eminently convincing in the Westerns of John Ford. On the other hand, Gunnar Björnstrand can play different and demanding roles with equal credibility and subtlety. There can be no question that Björstrand is a greater actor than Wayne, yet the American is as persuasive as the simpleminded man of action Ringo in *Stagecoach* as the Swede is in playing complex Bergman characters.

Related to plausibility is the actor's responsibility to convey the inner feelings of a character. Some of this burden is carried by cinematic techniques and dialogue supplied by the screenwriter. An actor, however, has a great deal of leeway in body movement, gestures, facial expressions, and delivery of lines. Effective use of these means of communicating emotions to an audience depends on an actor's training

and emotional and intellectual choices. Sometimes an actor will respond in a situation before the camera instinctively, drawing on memories of similar experiences in the past and perhaps making use of acting techniques that help to project emotions naturally and convincingly. Other times an actor will make intellectual choices, coolly and objectively. The cumulative result that appears on the screen is the actor's *interpretation* of a role.

In developing an interpretation of a role, an actor can be helped inestimably by a director. The director not only supplies an objective eye but also has an overview of the whole film and the interrelations of all its elements, including an actor's interpretation. Moreover, the director has the authority during shooting to insist on unforeseen but necessary changes in the screenplay. Usually, a director is in charge of rehearsals before scenes are photographed and also helps actors when difficulties arise during shooting. Few successful directors have not developed techniques for the care and handling of actors.

Interaction with other actors also influences an actor's performance. Most acting consists of responses between two people in a scene. The more one actor gives emotionally, the easier it is for the other to respond. When two actors are attuned to each other, a marvelous interlocking of timing and tone can result. An example is any motion picture in which Katharine Hepburn and Spencer Tracy appeared together. Every movie buff has a mental scrapbook of treasured memories of films in which the screen glowed with the excitement created by two or more actors able to give and take without fear, yet preserve each one's individuality.

The ultimate judge of the effectiveness of an actor's performance is the film theater audience. If that audience is sufficiently enthusiastic, a "mere" actor becomes a star. Determining the qualities necessary to reach this pinnacle of fame and fortune in the movie industry has baffled everyone who has attempted to reach definite conclusions.

Stars have existed in every country in which a film industry developed since 1910, when Florence Lawrence's name first appeared on the credits for a motion picture. It was the studios in Hollywood, however, that created a *star system* so important to the industry that it often took precedence over any other aspect of filmmaking. Especially during the twenties and thirties, each studio cultivated and catered to their stars, but each still treated its stars as commodities, to be used in any way that would be most profitable and, if necessary, bought and sold. Though glamour and fame were the rewards of stardom, the pressures were immense. From Florence Lawrence to Marilyn Monroe, there were stars who could not contend with the artificiality and demands of the "Hollywood Babylon" and committed suicide. Others, like Judy Garland, were driven to repeated nervous breakdowns. Almost as unfortunate for many stars was to lose popularity and to be relegated to those of whom it was asked, "Whatever happened to . . . ?" On the other hand, actors such as Katharine Hepburn, Cary Grant, Bette Davis, John Wayne, Gary Cooper, Joan Crawford, and Henry Fonda had the ability or the true grit to survive and prosper for decades.

One of the more insidious characteristics of the Hollywood star system was the creating and sustaining of a specific persona for each star. Audiences came to demand that the stars on whom they had bestowed the highest approval live up, at least publicly, to images that fulfilled the needs of the audiences rather than the actors. Failures and weaknesses freely confessed with contrition—the stock in trade of Louella Parsons, Hedda Hopper, and their ilk—were permissible. Forbidden was outright defiance of the sort perpetrated by Charles Chaplin and Ingrid Bergman.

The studios encouraged an individual persona for each star by typecasting. The advantage of this system was that a producer could be assured in advance that audiences would accept the physical traits and personality of an actor in a single type of role. It even lessened the need for characterization. However satisfying typecasting was to studios and audiences, some actors rebelled against being confined to one type of role in film after film at the rate of two or three films a year. Bette Davis in the mid-thirties and Olivia De Havilland in the mid-forties fought bitterly with their studios for opportunities to extend their range of roles. More than any other factor, it was the decline of the studios in the fifties that allowed stars to decide for themselves the motion pictures in which they

would act. Today the majority of American stars have incorporated themselves and sign contracts for independent productions.

A fair and sensible writer surveying screen acting will praise the many accomplished and dedicated actors who never quite achieved the status of stars, yet are the backbone of their profession. But genuine movie stars possess an added dimension of personality, skill, and drive that is inevitably fascinating. Despite the false glitter, pretentiousness, and arrogance that can be characteristic of movie stars, without them the history of cinema would lack a certain excitement and glamour.

## DIRECTOR OF PHOTOGRAPHY

In the early years of motion pictures, a director's chief collaborator on the production crew was the cameraman, whose primary task was to operate the camera during shooting. Today a cameraman prefers being called a cinematographer, although the official title is director of photography in the United States and lighting cameraman in Great Britain; in a commercial production, he may only occasionally look through the eyepiece of a camera during shooting. The chief reason for this change is the complexity of modern equipment, which can no longer be handled physically by one person.

The director of photography's chief function is to translate the director's ideas on how shots should be photographed into the practicalities of appropriate types of film stock and lenses, composition, angles and distances, and lighting. Lighting, especially if color is being used, is the chief preoccupation of this member of the filmmaking team, who has been called a painter in light and movement. After consultation with the director and art director, he plans the illumination for each shot or scene. He then informs his electricians of his needs. During shooting, the director of photography supervises the lighting crew and deals with any problems that may arise.

The director and the cinematographer usually have a close relationship. For this reason, a director who finds an outstanding cinematographer will try to use him in film after film. The director must, however, take into consideration the fact that some directors of photography are most effective with a certain type of photography or film (for example, dramatic black-and-white photography, a thriller, or a musical).

In turn, a director of photography must depend on his crews. His electricians have fewer opportunities for individual initiative than the crew members who operate a camera. The camera operator physically manipulates the camera according to the instructions of the director of photography. At times the operator collaborates with the director of photography in working out shot compositions, angles, and distances. The focus puller keeps the camera in focus as it moves or when a zoom lens is used. Another member of this crew loads the camera and places the *clapboard* (also *clapper* or *clapstick*) in front of the camera before (and sometimes after) each take. A hinged portion of the clapboard is snapped sharply on a slate to give the editor a reference mark in synchronizing sound and visuals. On the slate is written in chalk the take number, director, time, place, and other information an editor requires.

Only lately have directors of photography begun to receive the attention they deserve. The best known are usually associated with an individual director and obscured by the shadows the director casts when in the limelight. Yet even the most famous directors, in relatively rare moments of fairness and modesty, admit that without the directors of photography, their achievements might have been less or more difficult to accomplish. The Cinematographers Hall of Fame would have to include Billy Bitzer (for his close collaboration with D. W. Griffith), Edvard Tissé (chief cameraman on practically all of Sergei Eisenstein's films), Karl Freund and Fritz Arno Wagner (the two leading directors of photography in Germany during the twenties), Gregg Toland (for innovative work on *Citizen Kane* and a dozen other major Hollywood films), James Wong Howe (for almost half a century the most consistently ingenious director of photography in Hollywood), Raoul Coutard (the favorite cameraman of the French New Wave filmmakers, particularly Godard and Truffaut), Sven Nykvist and Gunnar Fischer (collaborators of Ingmar Bergman, Nykvist on 19 films and Fischer on 9). Other outstanding cinema-

tographers: in the United States, Lee Garmes, William Daniels, Hal Mohr, Stanley Cortez, Haskell Wexler, Laszlo Kovacs, Vilmos Zsigmond, and Nestor Almendros; in France, Léonce-Henri Burel, Georges Périnal, Jean Backelot, and Henri Decae; in Italy, G. R. Aldo, Gianni Di Venanzo, and Giuseppe Rotunno; in Russia, Andrei Moskvin, Mikhail Kaufman, and Sergei Urusevsky; in England, Jack Cardiff and Frederick Young; and in Mexico, Gabriel Figueroa.

To be an outstanding director of photography requires a unique combination of technical knowledge and artistic sensibility; a capacity for working long, intense hours; and a modesty that permits, in most instances, the major credit for one's efforts to go to the director. It is understandable, then, why there are so few truly prominent directors of photography.

## ART DIRECTOR

The art director's function is to supervise all aspects of place settings. His specific activities include submitting a budget for his needs to the producer, preparing preliminary designs for each set or approving selections for location shooting, supervising the construction of first scale models and then the actual sets, checking that necessary props have been obtained, approving the work of the costume designer (if the art director does not design them himself), and consulting, if necessary, with the special effects director.

When everything is prepared, the director, art director, and others discuss when and how shooting will be done. The director of photography in particular consults with the art director as he plans *set-ups* (camera, lighting, and setting arrangements for each shot). Most of the activities of the art director are completed during preproduction; however, he should be available during production should any difficulties arise.

How the art director's chief responsibilities (settings and props) contribute to the form and feeling of a film were discussed in Chapter 2. Art directors have generally not received the attention from the public given to set designers in the theater, but many have left their mark on the history of cinema. The earliest motion pictures did not have sets, but rather shooting areas with painted backdrops. In the second decade of this century the situation changed. Experts were brought in to design sets and supervise lighting. Among the earliest such art directors were Robert Jules Garnier in France and Wilfred Buckland in Hollywood. Perhaps the most striking sets and props to appear on the screen during the silent era were those in German Expressionistic films, especially ones designed by Walter Röhrig, Hermann Warm, Walter Reimann, and Robert Herlth. At the end of the twenties and in the early thirties, the work of Andrei Andreiev in Germany was also impressive. In France, the spectacular, exotic approach of the Albatros Company under the direction of Alexander Kamenka dominated the decor of French films of the twenties.

In the United States, many young men began their careers in the 1920s and were for decades to contribute to the reputation of Hollywood as the most technically proficient motion picture industry in the world. Among the most prominent were Richard Day, Hans Dreier, Cedric Gibbons, and Van Nest Polglase. The most respected and influential of Hollywood art directors during the thirties and forties was William Cameron Menzies (1896–1957). His ability to create expressive, original designs that personified the tone of an individual film was revealed as early as 1924 in *The Thief of Bagdad* and was sustained in *Alice in Wonderland* (1934), *Things to Come* (1936, which he also directed), *For Whom the Bell Tolls* (1943), *Arch of Triumph* (1948), and many others. His masterpiece of design is generally acknowledged to be *Gone With the Wind*.

France also developed a genius in this field in Lazare Meerson (1900–1938). He was most inspired when contributing to the films of Jacques Feyder and René Clair (including for the latter the classics *An Italian Straw Hat* and *A nous la liberté*). Other outstanding French art directors of the thirties and forties were Alexandre Trauner, Léon Barsacq, and Christian Bérard. Great Britain's most noteworthy art directors of this period were Vincent Korda, Alfred Junge, and Hein Heckroth.

Since the 1950s there have been so many fine art directors that in a very brief survey only a few names can be listed, and for the best known of them, a couple of examples of their work. In the United States, Dean Tavoularis *(The Godfather, The Godfa-*

*ther—Part II)*, Polly Platt *(The Last Picture Show, Nashville)*, Harry Horner *(The Hustler; They Shoot Horses, Don't They?)*, Robert Boyle, George Jenkins, Boris Levin, and Lyle R. Wheeler; in Great Britain, Ray Simm *(Seance on a Wet Afternoon, A Hard Day's Night, Darling)*, John Box *(Lawrence of Arabia, A Man for All Seasons)*, Asheton Gorton *(The Knack, Blow-Up)*, Carmen Dillon *(The Go-Between)*, Richard MacDonald, Ted Marshall, and Jocelyn Herbert; in France, Bernard Evein *(Viva Maria!* and other Louis Malle films, *The 400 Blows, Umbrellas of Cherbourg, Cleo From 5 to 7)*, Jacques Saulmier *(Last Year at Marienbad* and other Alain Resnais films), and Jean Mandaroux *(The Wild Child* and other François Truffaut films); in Italy, Piero Gherardi *(La Dolce Vita, Juliet of the Spirits)*, Piero Poletto *(L'Avventura, The Red Desert)*, Danilo Donati *(Fellini-Satyricon)*, Eliseo Boschi *(Oedipus Rex* and other Pier Paolo Pasolini films), Mario Chiari, and Ottavio Scotti; and in Sweden, P. A. Lundgren *(Smiles of a Summer Night* and a dozen other Ingmar Bergman films).

## COMPOSER

A composer is responsible for creating all the music, both original and adapted, that is heard during a film. His contribution is most prominent when the motion picture is a musical (see Chapter 9), but our principal concern here is with the composer of background music. The chief functions of this mode of sound were discussed in Chapter 1. They include facilitating transitions between sequences, evoking an atmosphere, heightening the drama of a specific scene or sequence, and commenting on the action and characters.

Producing background music for motion pictures requires special skills that many composers of music for the concert hall and opera house are incapable of developing. Although some famous artists have written scores for films, very few, with such exceptions as Erich Wolfgang Korngold and Hanns Eisler, have gained equal renown in both areas of musical composition. An important difference is the sheer amount of music, disregarding evaluations of quality, that a film composer must produce. The length of an average score for a 2-hour motion picture is approximately that of two symphonies. The facility of someone like Miklos Rozsa, who between 1937 and 1973 was responsible for 87 film scores, is astonishing. It is no wonder that film composers do not hesitate to "borrow" themes from anywhere they can find them in music of the past. Furthermore, a film composer must be able, if necessary, to fashion a musical effect within a very limited period of time. It is not unusual for him to have the duration of a shot, perhaps 30 seconds, in which to embellish, say, a violent action. Finally, a film composer cannot be overly protective of his score, any more than a writer can be of his dialogue. Pages of a composition may be dropped or new music added at any time between the completion of a score and the acceptance of the final print.

Like a writer, a composer usually works alone; unlike a writer, his contribution is required after rather than before the production stage. Different composers proceed in different ways. Some prefer to view only a rough cut of a film and then create major themes, which are later molded to the needs of the motion picture. Others depend on a Moviola, producing music precisely to fit a specific scene or shot. At some point, however, a composer must deal with a *timing sheet.* This is prepared by the editor and contains a breakdown to within a second of all dialogue and action. The composer is ultimately required to fashion the music to meet this exacting format.

Most film composers, though by no means all of them, leave orchestration of their themes to an assistant. Many do not direct an orchestra during the recording sessions. It is an arduous task for a conductor simultaneously to direct an orchestra, observe the film projected on a screen behind the musicians, listen to the dialogue on earphones, and watch a second-counter, the readings of which must correspond to the timings marked on the score. On the other hand, a composer usually will insist on being consulted during the process of mixing (combining separate sound tracks into one), especially to check volume settings of background music vis-à-vis dialogue and natural sounds.

It is the responsibility of the director to decide what role background music is to play in relation to the other components of a film. A weak filmmaker depends on music to camouflage visually ineffective footage. A creative director uses background music to complement or reinforce other elements of a film. When this type of music is superfluous, it should be left out. One of the most striking sound tracks in recent years is part of Robert Altman's *Nashville.* Music is performed by actors on the screen, music issues from radios, and natural sounds are skillfully included, but there is no background music. Nor is there background music in Ingmar Bergman's *The Silence* or Alfred Hitchcock's *The Birds.*

A director may decide that the effects he desires can be obtained from extant music rather than an original score, so only an arranger is needed. The score for Kubrick's *2001* consists of music by Richard Strauss, Aram Khachaturian, Johann Strauss, and György Ligeti. Bergman restricts background music to a J. S. Bach cello suite in *Through a Glass Darkly.*

Original scores prepared for an individual film, however, are usually most exciting and effective. A film composer need not be a musical genius to create an exceptional score, but some of the most memorable film music has been the result of a collaboration between an acclaimed composer and an outstanding director. Such collaborations antedate the advent of sound. In the silent era, the premiere of an important motion picture often featured an orchestra that played selections to accompany the film. These were usually excerpts from standard works. More interesting was original background music prepared by well-known composers for silent films, beginning with Camille Saint-Saëns's score for an art film, *L'Assassinat du Duc de Guise* (1908) and including works by Arthur Honegger, Darius Milhaud, Jacques Ibert, and Edmund Meisel.

The development of synchronized sound encouraged some famous composers to write for the screen. A few scores have become concert works, such as Sergei Prokofiev's for *Alexander Nevsky* and *Ivan the Terrible,* Virgil Thomson's for *Louisiana Story,* and Ralph Vaughan Williams's for *Scott of the Antarctic* (1948). Other composers in this category (with only one or two examples given for each) include Dimitri Shostakovich (*Counterplan,* 1932), Arthur Honegger (*Mayerling,* 1936), Darius Milhaud (*L'Hippocampe,* 1934), Georges Auric (*Beauty and* the Beast, 1953; *Moulin Rouge,* 1953; and many others), Hanns Eisler *(New Earth, Night and Fog),* Benjamin Britten *(Night Mail),* Arthur Bliss (*Things to Come,* 1936), William Walton (*Hamlet,* 1948, and Laurence Olivier's other Shakespeare films), Aaron Copland (*Of Mice and Men,* 1939; *Our Town,* 1940), Marc Blitzstein *(Spanish Earth),* and Leonard Bernstein (*On the Waterfront,* 1954).

Professional film composers have, however, made background music an essential component of sound films. Their scores may be issued on phonograph records but are rarely performed in concert halls. Some, however, have gained reputations that extended beyond the motion picture industry of their native country.

The most celebrated film composer to emerge from France was Maurice Jaubert (1900–1940). Before his untimely death early in World War II, he composed delicate, sensitive scores that often featured solo instruments for the films of Jean Vigo, René Clair, Marcel Carné, Julien Duvivier, and Jean Painlevé. Among his best-known scores are those for *Zero for Conduct, Le Dernier Milliardaire, Le Jour se lève,* and *Un Carnet de bal.* Another notable French film composer was Joseph Kosma. Hanss Eisler* collaborated with many French, as well as German and American, directors.

Among Italian composers are Renzo Rossellini, Nino Rota, and Ennio Morricone. More impressive and innovative, however, is the work of Giovanni Fusco (practically all of the features of Antonioni, as well as Resnais's *Hiroshima mon amour* and *La Guerre est finie*). Probably the most eminent of British film composers is Malcolm Arnold, followed by Richard Rodney Bennett, William Alwyn, Peter Maxwell Davies, and John Barry. Mention should be made of a man who was not himself a creative artist or producer, yet who profoundly influenced the development of background music in the British film industry during the thirties and forties. Working as music director under the aegis of Alexander Korda and then J. Arthur Rank, Muir Mathieson persuaded many leading British composers to write for films, including Ralph Vaughan Williams, Arthur Bliss, William Wal-

ton, and Arnold Bax. Mathieson also personally conducted hundreds of film scores at recording sessions.

Hollywood, with its full production schedules and impressive salaries, especially during the heyday of the studios, attracted many film composers. Even a list of only major composers is a lengthy one. At the top of such a list should be the name of Max Steiner (1888–1971), who composed 310 scores between 1929 and 1965. He received three Academy Awards (including one for *The Informer*) and 17 nominations. Among his most successful scores are those for *Gone With the Wind, King Kong, Casablanca, The Big Sleep,* and *The Treasure of Sierra Madre.*

Erich Wolfgang Korngold was a distinguished conductor and composer in Germany and Austria during the second and third decades of this century. In 1936 he came to Hollywood and composed film scores until his death in 1957. He won Oscars for *Anthony Adverse* (1936) and *The Adventures of Robin Hood* (1938). Other scores include those for *A Midsummer Night's Dream, Juarez, The Sea Wolf, King's Row,* and *Of Human Bondage.*

Dmitri Tiomkin writes scores in the melodramatic style of Korngold. His best known are for *High Noon,* which won him the first of three Academy Awards, *Lost Horizon, Red River,* and *The Old Man and the Sea.* Bernard Herrmann made his film debut—an auspicious one—with a score for *Citizen Kane,* then went on to *The Magnificent Ambersons.* Although he has contributed to numerous films, his most exciting compositions have been for those directed by Hitchcock (for instance, *North by Northwest* and *Psycho*) and Truffaut (*Fahrenheit 451* and *The Bride Wore Black*).

Other outstanding film composers who have worked primarily in Hollywood include Elmer Bernstein, John Green, Jerry Goldsmith, Frederick Hollander, Alfred Newman, Alex North, André Prévin, David Raksin, Miklos Rozsa, Victor Young, and Franz Waxman. To this list should be added the name of John Williams for his contributions to *Jaws, Family Plot,* and *Close Encounters of the Third Kind,* among others.

A notable phenomenon since the 1950s, especially in the United States, is the use of jazz and rock themes as the basis for background music. The earliest

*p. 377

jazz scores include Alex North's for *A Streetcar Named Desire,* Elmer Bernstein's for *The Man With the Golden Arm,* and Duke Ellington's for *Anatomy of a Murder.* A rock influence was apparent in the sixties, as evidenced in *Easy Rider* and *Midnight Cowboy,* and has continued to the present. In a special category belongs one of the most popular series of songs in recent years to appear as background music: Simon and Garfunkel's music and vocals for *The Graduate.*

## EDITOR

Although every aspect of filmmaking contributes to the creation of a motion picture, three activities are the most fundamental: screenwriting, shooting, and editing. During the editing process, choices are made among various takes of a shot, the types of transitions between shots are established, the sequence of shots and scenes is decided, and superfluous footage is eliminated. In short, the final content and form of a motion picture are determined. Most filmmakers would agree that the most skillful editing cannot save poorly conceived and photographed material but that a botched job of editing can ruin even brilliant work done in the preproduction and production stages.

Editing is so important that the question of who has the greatest authority during this postproduction stage is significant. There should be a balanced collaboration among editor, director, and producer. The ideal, however, is rarely realized in practice. An editor may have final authority when no one is really concerned about the value of a motion picture (as was the case with B movies made under the Hollywood studio system) or when a director has difficulty in being objective about his footage. Under the studio system, executive producers often made crucial decisions, as David O. Selznick did for *Gone With the Wind.* Most worthwhile motion pictures result, however, from a close collaboration between editor and director, in which the latter has final authority.

Although an editor may be subordinate to others in making major decisions, he still plays a vital role in the overall process. This becomes clear if we follow the stages of editing in a typical commercial feature

motion picture. The editor begins work during production. At the end of a day's shooting, a print is processed from the exposed footage within 24 hours. These rushes are viewed by the director and his associates, and the best takes are chosen. Meanwhile, the editor—or more likely the first assistant—works with a duplicate print, using information on the clapboard shots to number and store every take of every shot. When the instructions from the director arrive, the editor runs the rushes through a synchronizer that matches the visuals with the corresponding sound track, which has been recorded separately (the two are not physically joined until later). The next equipment usually used is a *Moviola.* This is a viewing machine operated by foot pedals that allows the editor to view and hear the synchronized footage and to stop, slow down, or reverse it at will. Defective and superfluous material (such as shots of the clapboard) are eliminated, and *stock shots* (background footage obtained from film libraries, such as the establishing shot of a city skyline or a battle scene) are added.

The next stage cannot commence until production is completed. Following the shooting script and *continuity sheets* (descriptions prepared by the script supervisor of what has been shot and the relation of one shot to another), the editor assembles the component shots of the film. This is accomplished by *splicing* (attaching with transparent tape) lengths of footage. The editor now has a *rough cut* of the film. It is at this point that the director and other consultants enter the cutting room. They work with the rough cut, alternate takes that the editor has put aside, and even rejected footage that has been stored away as potentially usable.

Now the essential process of editing begins. Decisions must be made by those who have final authority as to what footage is kept, added, or eliminated, how long each shot will be (often to within three frames), and what forms of transitions beyond the cut (called *opticals* by editors because they are done in the laboratory) will join shots. It is an arduous process of increasing refinement.

Sound is added by the mixer (see next section).* Individual tracks of natural sounds, dialogue, and

---

*pp. 79–80

background music are combined into a single master sound track, which the editor and his assistants synchronize with the visuals. The last stage of the editing process has been reached. Everyone involved has been using work prints; now the negative film can be cut. From the negative, an *answer print* (the first approved print) is produced. Changes may still be made, however, before final or commercial prints are released for distribution to theaters.

It is difficult to define the principles that govern editing. When questioned about the guidelines of their profession, editors often refer to an intuitive feeling that one choice is "right" and another is "wrong." Rhythm is of prime importance in deciding the length of individual shots. Objectives in creating tone in scenes and sequences frequently determine what footage is included or eliminated. The effects of individual techniques, discussed in Chapter 1 under "Camera-Editing Dynamics," consciously or unconsciously influence the people who are editing a film. An analogy may help to make clear the goals of the editing process. The making of a film can be compared to creating a work of sculpture in clay before it is cast in metal. The screenplay is like the armature or wire framework of the sculpture. Shooting is comparable to placing clay on the armature. Editing is the process of shearing away excessive clay, smoothing out defects, and adding essential refinements.

Although editing is a vital component of filmmaking, few editors are known outside of their profession, with the exception of Alain Resnais, David Lean, Robert Wise, and others who went on to directing. As noted earlier, during the postproduction stage of making a film, the director not only usually has final say in all important decisions but also often receives credit for the editing. Some editors even maintain that they do not have a style of their own.[3]

Perhaps half a dozen editors have been known internationally as major figures in their profession. Only one, Helen von Dongen, has worked exclusively in the genre of the documentary. The others have devoted themselves primarily to commercial fiction films.

William W. Hornbeck (1901–) is an almost legendary figure to film editors. Between 1921 and 1959, he edited more than 60 motion pictures, including

*Rembrandt, The Heiress, A Place in the Sun,* and *Suddenly, Last Summer.* David Lean began his directing career in 1942, but in the thirties he was Great Britain's leading editor, responsible for *Escape Me Never, Pygmalion, Major Barbara,* and *One of Our Aircraft Is Missing,* among others. Other outstanding British editors include Reginald Beck (especially known for his contributions to the films of Joseph Losey), Jim Clark, Anthony Gibbs, Bernard Gribble, Jack Harris, Ralph Kemplen, and Peter J. B. Taylor.

Although Henri Colpi began his editing career in France in 1945, he is usually associated with the New Wave filmmakers of the sixties, particularly Alain Resnais (including *Night and Fog, Hiroshima mon amour,* and *Last Year at Marienbad*). Among other exceptional French editors are Raymond Lamy (editor for practically all of Robert Bresson's films) and Henri Lanoë.

Robert Wise was a highly respected music editor and general editor before becoming a director. He collaborated with Mark Robson (who also moved into the field of directing) on *Citizen Kane* and was sole editor on *The Magnificent Ambersons.* A highly selective list of eminent American editors would have to include George J. Amy (a veteran of almost four decades of editing from the early twenties to the mid-fifties), Folnar Blangsted (another veteran who collaborated with Hawks, Sternberg, Curtiz, De Mille, and Walsh, among others), Gerald Greenberg, Doane Harrison (one of Billy Wilder's favorite editors), Warren Low, Daniel Mandell and William H. Reynolds (two of the most highly respected editors in Hollywood), Ralph Rosenblum (who has worked extensively with Woody Allen and Sidney Lumet), Merrill C. White, Ralph Winters, and Robert L. Wolfe.

With the exception of acting and, to a lesser degree, screenwriting, no other major area of filmmaking has offered more opportunities to women than editing. Women entered this field in the United States when editing first became a profession. Viola Lawrence worked as a film editor from 1916 to 1960. Anne Bauchens was Cecil B. De Mille's favorite editor from 1918 to 1956. Margaret Booth edited major motion pictures from 1924 to 1960, Dorothy Spencer from 1926 to 1974, and Barbara P. McLean from 1927 to 1955. Musicals were the specialty of

Adrienne Fazan, who included among her credits *An American in Paris* and *Singin' in the Rain*.

Since World War II, one of the most highly respected editors in the United States has been Dede Allen, who edited, *The Hustler, Bonnie and Clyde, Alice's Restaurant, Little Big Man, Slaughterhouse Five*, and *Dog Day Afternoon*, among other works. Verna Fields includes among her many credits *Medium Cool; What's Up, Doc?; American Graffiti; Paper Moon; The Sugarland Express;* and *Jaws*. Anne V. Coates has been an outstanding editor in Great Britain since 1947 and received an Oscar for her contribution to *Lawrence of Arabia*.

In France, female film editors have truly come into their own. Cécile Décugis and Agnes Guillemot are ranked by filmmakers in their country with Henri Colpi as the best in their profession. Décugis worked on films directed by Rohmer, Godard, and Truffaut. Guillemot edited 28 features and numerous shorts and TV series between 1953 and 1975, among them Godard's *A Woman Is a Woman, Contempt, Alphaville,* and *La Chinoise*. Other highly respected French film editors are Anne-Marie Cotret (especially for the films of Jacques Demy), Claudine Bouché, Denise De Casabianca, and Martine Kalfon.

## OTHER MEMBERS OF THE FILMMAKING TEAM

In addition to the major contributors to the making of a film already discussed, there are dozens of other people who perform necessary functions. Many of these individuals are members of crews, such as electricians or carpenters who create sets. Others have more specialized responsibilities or are employed only for certain types of films.

*Casting director/* The casting director is responsible for the selection of the actors who will perform in a motion picture. This person is either employed by a studio or hired by a producer for a specific production.

*Choreographer/* A choreographer creates dances for a film and usually rehearses the dancers before shooting. Most musicals contain choreographed dances, and a choreographer is of course required for a dance film. Prominent choreographers are listed in Chapter 9.

*Costume designer/* Although usually supervised by the art director, a costume designer of sufficient reputation can operate quite independently and collaborate directly with the director and producer. The functions that costumes can serve in a film were considered in Chapter 1.*

Each country has had its own leading costume designers, such as Georges Annenkov and Marcel Escaffier in France, Ali Hubert and Anne Willkomm in Germany, Piero Gherardi and Danilo Donati in Italy, and Julie Harris and Cecil Beaton in Great Britain. In Hollywood, the doyenne of costume designers was Edith Head. Almost as well known are Irene Sharaff, who specializes in musicals, and Orry-Kelly, like Head, a veteran Hollywood costume designer.

*Gaffer/* Industry term for the chief electrician. The gaffer is in charge of the director of photography's crew of electricians.

*Gofer (or gopher)/* A person who is sent on errands; in other words, someone employed to "go for" things.

*Makeup artist (or cosmetician)/* The individual who applies makeup to the face of an actor. Most challenging to this member of the filmmaking team is aging a character and making masks for use in horror and science fiction films. Among the best known Hollywood artists in this field are Maurice Seiderman (for example, *Citizen Kane*), Jack Pierce, the Westmores (George and his six sons), and, of the younger generation, Dick Smith and Rick Baker.

*Mixer/* The chief technician of the sound crew. The mixer is sometimes called a *recording director,* though this title is usually reserved for the person employed by a sound studio who is in charge of the sound for all films made on the premises. The mixer begins confronted by as many as 50, sometimes even more, individual tracks of dialogue, natural sounds, and background music. During what can be weeks of effort, the mixer and colleagues (perhaps the director) work at a sound console that allows them to arrange any combination of material on the tracks. Ultimately, they must produce a single optical or, preferable be-

*pp. 58–59

cause its frequency range is so much greater, a magnetic sound track. This is sent to the editor, who synchronizes sound and image.

*Script supervisor/* The person who fills in continuity sheets—information on each shot that might be helpful to the editor—and is responsible for ascertaining that the details of the shots within a scene are consistent. (An older designation is *script girl* or *continuity girl.*)

*Second-unit director/* As assistant to the director, the second-unit director supervises the shooting of scenes that do not require the presence of the chief actors, those involving crowds of extras, stunt work, and rear projection footage.

*Special effects director/* The special effects director is in charge of the crew that creates all required special effects (techniques were described in Chapter 1.*)

*Stunt man (or stunt woman)/* A person who substitutes for an actor when the screenplay calls for dangerous physical action. One of the most famous Hollywood stunt men was Yakima Canutt. His activities in *Stagecoach* are described in the essay on this Western in Chapter 8.† In a motion picture requiring the services of many stunt experts, such as a James Bond film, a *stunt coordinator* is used.

*Technical adviser/* A technical adviser is a specialist whose advice may be needed—for instance, on a historical or catastrophe film.

---

*pp. 59–60
†p. 408

# Critical approaches to film

## 3

Cinema studies is a relatively new field. Its subject has existed for less than a century, and with some exceptions (particularly publications by the Russian directors of the 1920s), serious studies—as opposed to reviews, interviews, and autobiographies—were not written until after World War II. With accelerating momentum, anthologies, introductions, histories, theories, analyses, biographies, screenplays, and other material have been published since the 1950s. While this plethora of printed matter is gratifying to most students of film, it has also led to confusion in terminology and standards of judgment in every respect.

This field is usually divided into four categories: criticism, history, methodology, and theory. Naturally, these categories are interrelated and interdependent. The purpose of this chapter is to examine only criticism and to establish at least a few definitions and guidelines.

## THE FUNCTIONS OF FILM CRITICISM

A useful starting point is the root derivation of the term *critic*. The English word, by way of Latin, has its source in the Greek *kritikos,* "able to discern," in turn derived from *krinein,* "to separate" or "to choose."

We usually do associate with *critic* and *criticism* the function of separating and choosing—in other words, judging. We are most familiar with film criticism on its most mundane level, the newspaper and TV review. We expect from any reviewer at least a description and evaluation of a specific motion picture to help us determine whether or not we wish to see it. Even a lengthier, more sophisticated review or essay in a film magazine offers a judgment of a work. The inevitable question is, What standards does a critic apply in evaluating a film?

It has been said that when a motion picture appears on the screen in a theater, as many versions of the film are viewed as there are members of the audience. This is certainly an exaggeration, but the statement emphasizes the subjectivity of criticism. When typical moviegoers leave a theater and discuss with one another what they have seen, they are acting as critics, using as standards the most immediate level of criticism: what they liked or disliked in a film. A professional critic supposedly differs from a lay person in having more experience in watching films, greater knowledge of most aspects of the medium, and a special facility in expressing personal views. There are other differences, which we will turn to later. Yet when evaluating a motion picture in a review, essay, or book, a critic is basically justifying subjective opinions. Beyond a few fundamentals, such as a minimum of technical facility on the part of the filmmakers and at least an attempt to avoid clichés of any sort, there are few universally accepted, objective criteria for judging the worth of a motion picture.

Subjective standards of evaluation are to be found to some degree in any medium, but they present special difficulties in cinema. Of prime importance is the fact that from the second decade of this century to the present day there have been arguments about whether there should be or can be a distinction between film entertainment and film art. How one defines these terms is crucial. It is not sufficient simply to state that an entertainment holds our attention and gives us pleasure, for a cinematic work of art can have these characteristics, as do the major features of Charles Chaplin. A more defensible thesis is that worthwhile motion pictures give us pleasure (or, returning again to the principle of subjectivity, a film that gives viewers pleasure is worthwhile in their opinion). There are, however, differences between types of pleasure and their significance.

A good entertainment, such as a James Bond film, passes a couple of hours pleasantly and during that time may supply us with material for fanciful identification and vicarious thrills or romance. Sociologists maintain that even this type of film influences our values when certain themes and attitudes are repeated in one motion picture after another. Basically, however, we leave a theater with a glow of contentment and promptly forget what we have seen except for some vivid moments or a particularly interesting character. A film that is a work of art, on the other hand, challenges our attitudes toward ourselves and the world around us. We are forced to confront our feelings and ideas rather than escape from them. Our pleasure is derived from exciting esthetic, emotional, or intellectual experiences, although on the highest level of cinematic art, all three modes of pleasure impinge on our psyches simultaneously. Imperceptibly or impressively, each of us, if responsive, is a different person after leaving the theater. In the same way, an individual does not feel quite the same about human relationships after reading a novel by Dostoevski or see the physical world with the same visual perceptions after concentrating on a painting by Cézanne. There are, of course, degrees of sensitivity in viewers, just as there are degrees of effectiveness in cinematic works of art. Moreover, since a motion picture unfolds in time, even the finest artistic film may have dull moments and an entertainment may contain a scene that electrifies us with its beauty, insights into human nature, or stimulating concepts. When we label an entire film as either an entertainment or art, we are referring to its cumulative effect on us.

Whether a motion picture is predominantly an entertainment or a work of art, two principles can be useful to the critic and help the lay person to judge the judge. First, each film should be evaluated within its own context; that is, every motion picture has individual potentials within its limitations. The critic's essential function as a judge is initially to estimate from what appears on the screen the extent of these potentials, then to determine to what degree the creators have realized the possibilities available to them. This is not simply a question of recognizing the restrictions of a genre (a topic we will return to later) and so avoiding the fallacy of denigrating a fine, unpretentious comedy for lacking the profundities of Bergman's *Persona*. Nor does this mean that a critic has the right to create in his own mind a film radically different from what appears on the screen and compare the two, to the detriment of the latter. Rather, it is the ability of the critic to recognize where filmmakers missed opportunities within their grasp or what choices were made that did not fulfill the potentials of a film. Examples include undeveloped characters, a tone inconsistent with the action of the film, or an actor allowed to be self-indulgent. Any strengths or flaws that work to the advantage or disadvantage of a film within what have been surmised as the filmmaker's intentions is the legitimate concern of the critic, however subjective the bases of such judgments.

The second principle can help to lessen the unsubstantiality of subjective interpretations and is necessary for effective criticism in any medium. Whenever possible, a critic should justify generalizations by specific references to a film. This type of documentation is more difficult to achieve in cinema than in most other media because of two factors: the general unavailability of a print of the motion picture to which the critic can refer a reader and the vagueness of much film terminology.

Thus far this discussion has been confined to the function of a critic in evaluating the worth of cinematic works, "to separate, to choose." Let us move to the closer Greek derivation of the word *critic, kritikos,* "able to discern" or to see, a facility particularly necessary in studying a work of art. The merits of a motion picture entertainment are usually, so to speak, on the surface, although we may not always appreciate the craft—and even possibly the artistry in certain scenes —that contributes to the success of an entertainment. A cinematic work of art, on the other hand, often contains subtleties, innovations, and unique devices that are not noticed by a lay person. A critic, with trained mind and sensibility, not only can see things that a less experienced viewer might miss, but also can elucidate the themes and techniques of a film with greater authority.

The basis of a critic's interpretation of a motion

picture can be divided into three interrelated categories. The first is determined by what a critic discovers about a film through analysis solely of what appears on the screen. Another method is to concentrate on only the factors external to the individual film that are ignored in the first type of analysis. Finally, a motion picture can be elucidated by means of a critical perspective, sometimes based on a comparison of works. Such perspectives are either essentially cinematic (methods of analysis derived from the medium itself, such as genre study) or noncinematic (methodologies and ideologies borrowed from other disciplines, such as philosophy, psychoanalysis, and sociology).

The advantages and disadvantages of each of these approaches and how they can complement one another in a comprehensive interpretation of a film are surveyed in the remainder of this chapter.

In establishing the functions of film criticism, it is expedient to confine references to individual films. One should be aware, however, that all these points also apply to a critic evaluating and/or elucidating a number of films for the purpose of drawing conclusions about common elements, such as themes, techniques, and the style of a director.

### PRIMARY SOURCE: THE FILM ITSELF

An approach in which the critic's evaluation or interpretation of a motion picture is limited to the film itself is usually designated a *formal analysis.* It can reveal valuable insights into the structure of a cinematic work and the functions of the film's components. A major weakness of dealing with a motion picture as a closed system, however, is the resultant disregard of influences of time, place, and individuals that may have been decisive in the film's creation.

A critic engaged in formal analysis must contend with many problems beyond mastering and applying the principles of his approach and the lack of a concise terminology to communicate his conclusions. The following is a list of some of these problems. A good deal of criticism is founded on the writer's memory of the single viewing of a film, for prints are difficult to obtain for intensive study and require special equipment, such as a Moviola. (Video tapes are beginning to ameliorate this situation, and videodisks hold great promise for the future.) Prints can be lost, may be incomplete, and can exist in more than one version. Only recently have published screenplays become accurate and detailed. Information on how individual films were made is scarce. It is often virtually impossible to ascertain who should be credited or blamed for what appears on the screen. The subtitles for foreign motion pictures are usually inadequate.

The critic, then, must make do with what is at hand, for he cannot dispense with justifying his interpretations by specific, accurate references to a film or films. Ultimately, the film itself must be the final test of the validity of a critic's judgments or interpretations.

### SECONDARY SOURCES: MATRIXES AND THEIR DOCUMENTATION

No film is created in a self-contained world consisting only of the filmmaking team and their equipment. Most critics, therefore, do not confine their attention solely to the film itself. A motion picture is molded by individuals living in and affected by their contemporaneous conditions of time and place. In short, it arises from a definite matrix.

*Matrix* is defined as "that which gives origin or form to a thing." It includes for a film every force—small and large, external and internal—that acts on the members of the filmmaking team in conceiving a motion picture and influences the degree to which they realize their intentions. To identify all these forces is, of course, impossible. Critics must settle for the sources that are available and principles of analysis that can help them to reach pragmatic and often only tentative conclusions.

To make this concept of secondary sources manageable, it is necessary to refer to a group of interrelated and interdependent matrixes. One is the biographical; that is, what effects on a specific film or films resulted from the background and experiences of a filmmaker. Other matrixes include the economic, political, religious, and social—in fact, every major component of what anthropologists define as making up a culture: institutional and aggregate forces that differentiate one society from another. It is possible to go further in the direction of refinement by determining the characteristics of each matrix during a period of time and in a nation. Two matrixes not yet specified are especially important in the medium of cinema. The first is the arts. Film is probably the most eclectic medium in drawing inspiration from and incorporating into itself manifestations of contemporary arts. The other matrix is film's own heritage, technology, and methods of production. Cinema learns from its past; technological advances expand the resources available to a filmmaker; and industry practices, especially financial ones, can reinforce or vitiate the possibility of a filmmaker's achieving his intentions.

The value of dividing an inclusive matrix from which a film arises into separate, subordinate ones is to allow the critic to concentrate on those that were most relevant in the creating of an individual film. The political situation in the Soviet Union in 1927 is important in understanding why and how Eisenstein created *October.* It would be fruitless to examine the same type of matrix for Sweden in 1955, when Bergman directed *Smiles of a Summer Night.* The first task of a critic, therefore, who wishes to go beyond a film itself to secondary sources of information is to distinguish between matrixes that are relevant for his purposes and those that are not.

A critic should learn to distinguish between intrinsic manifestations of a matrix, which are evident in the film per se and therefore can be proved to exist, and extrinsic ones, which must be documented by sources external to the film. One of the functions of a critic, in fact, is to point out references within a film to aspects of a matrix that might not be clear to the majority of viewers. This is especially necessary for non-Western films. The works of Japanese director Yasujiro Ozu, for instance, are not appreciated as they should be in the West because the mores of the Japanese families with which they usually deal are unfamiliar to most Occidental audiences. A critic can help by explaining the subtleties in an Ozu film. Another type of film that can often profit from this type of elucidation is the political, as in the struggles between leftists and rightists in the war films of the Polish director Andrzej Wajda.

Other influences of matrixes may not appear concretely in the work itself. Here we enter slippery ground. Any material relevant to the making of a motion picture could be useful; however, analyzing what does not manifest itself in the content and form of a film presents a twofold danger.

First, a critic must guard against allowing secondary sources of information that are unverifiable in the film itself to cloud his judgments and perceptions. This can happen in many ways. Knowing that a director did not have editing rights and that the job was botched by a hack may explain why a film is a failure, but these things should not influence how a critic evaluates a film. The same caution must be exercised when it is known, perhaps through a published screenplay, what a director has eliminated in the editing process; it is a critical fallacy to justify what is shown on the screen by what is not. A final example: A filmmaker may declare his intentions in an interview while making a motion picture. A critic should look for those intentions in the film but, again, can only make judgments on what is realized within the work.

A special situation involving secondary sources of information is adaptations of works of literature. It may be enlightening when a critic examines similarities and differences between the two, provided that the motion picture is nevertheless evaluated and elucidated solely as a work of cinema, as demonstrated by André Bazin's fine essay on Robert Bresson's *The Diary of a Country Priest,* an adaptation of Georges Bernanos's novel.[1]

The second problem in dealing with data gathered from outside the context of the film is documentation. Documentation is especially difficult when attempting to determine the contribution of a particular member of the filmmaking team to a work. A prominent controversy of the early seventies, instigated by Pauline Kael, is the question of to what degree Orson Welles (listed as coauthor) helped to mold Herman J. Mankiewicz's original screenplay for *Citizen Kane* and whether the director alone conceived the brilliant innovations in this masterpiece. Kael's documentation in her essay is inconclusive, and she depends more on hearsay, intuition, and prejudice than on demonstrable facts.[2]

Serious cinema scholarship has developed only

recently, and depositories of secondary material have been established only since the 1950s; consequently, many areas of study have not been explored, and a great deal of significant material has not been printed, much less annotated. Under these circumstances, a critic who assumes the role of historian can take advantage only of what is available and must fulfill his responsibility to his readers by indicating his sources and giving some estimate of their reliability.

## TYPES OF FILM CRITICISM

A critic who attempts to evaluate a film may find it necessary to elucidate it. There is no sharp line of demarcation between the two functions. However, a distinction can be made on the basis of emphasis. The purpose of a review is chiefly to evaluate a motion picture. Critical writing devoted primarily to elucidation can be divided into two additional categories: a comprehensive approach to a film or films and an approach, with many subdivisions, that takes a specific critical perspective.

### THE REVIEW

Most people with even a casual interest in motion pictures come in contact with film criticism most often in the form of the review. As pointed out earlier, every viewer reacts to some degree differently to a film, just as no two people are likely to agree on exactly why Anna Karenina commits suicide or why Frank Sinatra is so skillful at singing popular songs. Any film review, therefore, is a communication in words (and, in television reviews, facial expressions and gestures) of an individual's reactions to a motion picture. Fortunately, there are common grounds, conventions, and standards that can help the reviewer to convey his impressions effectively and help the reader (or television viewer) to evaluate the review. First, let us consider the point of view of the reviewer.

The film reviewer has an advantage over his colleagues in theater and music in that he is dealing with a performance fixed in celluloid. For this reason, he usually can see a film at a special screening arranged by the distributor prior to its premiere, so he has time to think about his impressions and even view it more than once, if he wishes.

A reviewer should record honestly his subjective evaluation of a motion picture. As much as possible, he should ignore extraneous conditions and prejudices—for example, that he suffered from heartburn during the screening or that the producer is an amiable person who has invested his life's savings in the picture. Far more difficult than this is for a reviewer to be able to appreciate the highest excellence of which cinema is capable, yet evaluate an individual film in terms of its own self-imposed scale and scope and determine the degree to which the work's potentials were fulfilled within these limitations. A masterpiece transcends its genre and requires that the reviewer apply standards that are only rarely required. Extraordinary films are rare, and a review is usually concerned with how successful a comedy is as a comedy, a Western as a Western. The reviewer should therefore be familiar with the history and principles of the major modes and forms of cinema if his opinion is to have any validity.

When the reviewer comes to deciding the content and form of his commentary, he must consider factors that should not influence his final judgment of a film but do affect the way in which he communicates that judgment. The most important of these is his audience. A reviewer of integrity never tailors his opinion to fit what he believes are the prejudices and preferences of his readers. He is doing them a disservice, however, if he does not emphasize the information and the aspects of his reactions in which they are most interested and in a form that is most comprehensible to them.

In general, film reviews appear in two different types of periodicals. The first category consists of newspapers and magazines that do not confine themselves to a specialized audience. Readers of these periodicals are likely to be seeking an answer to a pragmatic question: Is the film worth my time and money? The reviewer's chief goals are clarity of expression and concrete justifications of his recommendations. The second category consists of specialized periodicals that are intended for readers who are well informed in a certain field—educational or psychoanalytic journals, for example. Specialized motion picture reviews are most commonly encountered, however, in film magazines, well over 100 of which are currently published in English.

The reviewer for a film periodical is not required, as would be the case in a general review, to define technical terms, explain allusions to artists and films, or justify a critical approach. A reader of this type of review is less interested in whether a film is worth seeing (often, the reader has already seen or decided to see the film before reading the review) than in what the reviewer can reveal that the reader might miss or might fail to appreciate.

No matter what kind of audience a reviewer is addressing, he should always attempt to adhere to the principles of effective writing: careful organization, coherence, correctness, and clarity. A vivid, personable style also helps. Although there are no inflexible rules for organizing a review of a film, reviewers often use certain devices that can be helpful to novices in this area of journalism. The opening sentence should be striking, capturing the attention of the reader. At least a hint of the writer's evaluation of the film should appear in the first paragraph. Plot summaries should be brief, and no surprises in the story should be divulged. Whenever possible, generalizations should be justified by specific, self-explanatory references to the film. Indications of the strengths and flaws in a motion picture are the spine of a review. A personal prejudice or antipathy on the part of the reviewer toward any aspect of a film should be labeled as such. The concluding paragraph should summarize the reviewer's evaluation.

A listing of this sort may seem arid and mechanical. What brings life to writing is the vitality, sensitivity, and knowledge of the writer. But excesses must be avoided. Some reviewers get so carried away with trying to captivate or impress their readers that their opinions get lost in the verbiage. At the other extreme are film writers who seem to believe that the more obscure and esoteric the content and style of their reviews, the more respectful readers will be. The wisest course is to write as honest an evaluation of a film as possible with clarity and liveliness.

Readers also have a responsibility to be neither awed nor arrogantly critical of a reviewer. In most communities, readers have a choice among film reviewers—and always have the option of simply not reading a review. Once a reader has decided that a reviewer's opinions are worthy of consideration, he can very quickly recognize the reviewer's special areas of competence and perceptiveness as well as intellectual and emotional blind spots.

## COMPREHENSIVE APPROACH

In writing an article, a chapter of a book, or an entire volume on a film or the works of a filmmaker, a critic has a choice of two approaches: either to be comprehensive or to confine himself to one or a limited number of perspectives.

In interpreting his subject matter, the critic usually offers judgments on the significance of a film or a filmmaker; however, whereas a reviewer's primary intention is to evaluate, a critic's is to elucidate. This overriding concern should predominate, even though he may make use of information and methods from film history, methodology, and theory.

A comprehensive approach, the first of the two possibilities in this type of film criticism, is characterized by eclecticism. The critic makes use of any suitable perspective and form of cinema studies that can assist in exploring a film or the oeuvre of a filmmaker. In a utopia of critical studies, without restrictions of time and space, the critic could indulge in completely comprehensive analyses. A subject might be an individual film. The critic would deal with each element of each component of the film (based on some schema, such as the narrative dimension, camera-editing dynamics, and elements of presentation); examine the matrixes that influenced the creators of the motion picture; attempt to determine the intentions, extent of realization of those intentions, and contributions of each member of the filmmaking team; and subject the film to repeated scrutiny from every relevant critical perspective. The result might well be a weighty tome of, perhaps, 300 to 400 pages.

Although the idea of shelves of lengthy studies of individual films is intriguing as well as daunting, practical considerations in the publishing industry today make this possibility extremely unlikely. The pragmatic critic must therefore make choices, especially when writing an essay rather than a book, judging what inclusions will yield the most pertinent insights. He must be particularly discriminating when including references to other films and emphasizing critical perspectives that might be useful in elucidating a motion picture. The analyses of films in this book are examples of this type of selectivity determined by limitations of space.

A comprehensive critical approach usually functions best in a study of the work of a director or other member of the filmmaking team. A biographical matrix naturally assumes particular importance. The "Background" sections of the essays on films in Parts Two and Three are often, in miniature, instances of this form of interpretive criticism. More extensive studies are the books listed in the bibliography, such as Birgitta Steene's *Ingmar Bergman* and C. G. Crisp's *François Truffaut.*

### PERSPECTIVES

A critical perspective is a system or doctrine that exists independent of an individual film. It supplies principles and methods of analysis that can lead to insights into an aspect of a single film or group of films to which the principles and methods are applicable. A matrix that influenced a filmmaker in molding the content and form of a motion picture and a critical perspective may correspond, but the function of each is different. For example, a critic may reveal how the tenets of Marxism affected Bertolucci in directing *1900,* a specific film created under unique circumstances. It is a different matter, however, for a writer to apply the principles of Marxist criticism to *1900.* This perspective is a means of interpreting the film, not the forces that influenced the filmmaker. The same principles of analysis can be applied to any film, if their relevance can be demonstrated, even though the filmmaker may not have been aware—at least not consciously—of Marxist ideology.

A student of cinema must be wary of certain pitfalls in making use of a perspective (a couple of these have been mentioned earlier in relation to film criticism but are worth repeating). First, the tenets of a perspective should be thoroughly understood if embarrassing faux pas are to be avoided. Second, the writer should make every effort to avoid the use of specialized terminology unless it is defined and explained; the extent of such clarification should depend

on the probable knowledge of readers in a specific area. Third, a perspective must be demonstrably applicable to a motion picture. An analysis of *Top Hat* based on the tenets of existentialism is hardly likely to increase anyone's understanding or evaluation of the musical. Fourth, a perspective should not operate as an intellectual Procrustean bed in which the aspects of a film that support an interpretation are included and those that contradict it are ignored. The insights gained from the use of an analytical point of view can still be valid even though that approach is not applicable to every facet of a film. No element in that work, however, can be incompatible with an overall interpretation. Fifth, the conclusions drawn from the exercise of a critical perspective, as with any analysis, should be justified as much as possible by specific references to the film. Finally, no absolute interpretation of a film derived from a perspective can supersede all others. A Jungian perspective in examining *Smiles of a Summer Night,* for example, may be as valid as a Freudian one. The number of perspectives that can be applied to a film are limited only by the relevance of each perspective and the richness of the work itself.

These recommendations apply not only to the application of perspectives to one film but also to comparisons of films or of the characteristics of a filmmaker. Furthermore, a lengthy study, without being comprehensive, may make use of more than a single perspective, although one usually predominates. Will Wright's *Six Guns and Society,*[3] for instance, includes the perspectives of genre and the *auteur* theory but for criteria of analysis depends chiefly on concepts borrowed from structuralism.

There are numerous perspectives that are efficacious in film analysis. They can be divided into three main categories. The first two focus on the significance of what appears on the screen; the third focuses on audience reactions.

### *Cinematic perspectives*

The following film perspectives fall under this heading: movements, genres, theories, and national characteristics. Each encompasses principles, methods, and terminology based primarily on the characteristics of cinema as a medium that would be inapplicable to another medium without extensive revisions. Each offers a means by which we can better understand the content and form of a film or the works of a filmmaker.

*Movements/ Movements* are periods in the history of cinema when a certain concept of film production, involving interdependent stylistic techniques and themes, influenced a group of filmmakers. A specific movement is usually associated with an individual country, though this is not true in every case. There have been many cinematic movements, some short-lived, but the most prominent are Realism, Expressionism, Surrealism, Dynamic Montage, French Poetic Realism, Neorealism, *Film Noir,* and the French New Wave. The tenets of each are discussed in Chapter 4. Our interest here, however, is in comprehensive generalizations about this type of critical perspective.

Most cinematic movements are related to and even derive from movements in the other arts. This relationship is obvious in some instances. For example, Expressionism was a movement in the literature and visual arts of Germany more than a decade before tentative manifestations of it appeared in cinema, and a complete realization was not achieved until almost two decades later (in *The Cabinet of Dr. Caligari,* 1919). Sometimes the relationship is more tenuous, as with the influence of the French New Novel *(Nouveau Roman)* and New Theater *(Nouveau Théâtre)* of the early fifties on the film productions of the New Wave *(Nouvelle Vague)* that began appearing in 1959.

Whatever approaches and themes a cinematic movement shared with its counterparts in other arts, it developed its own uniquely filmic form and content. A critic may share with film historians an interest in the origins of a movement and the matrixes that affected its development. He also may find provocative a film theoretician's conjectures on what a movement illustrates about the potentials and limitations of the medium. The critic's chief concern, however, is how knowledge of the principles and practices of a movement helps him to understand the means by which the intentions of a filmmaker were influenced by a movement and the degree of realization of those intentions in individual works. The essay on *Variety* in Chapter 5, for example, uses, among other perspectives, references to the techniques of Expressionism to underscore the counterpoint in the film between objective and subjective realities.

A significant movement flourishes during a limited time span and usually in an individual country, but its effects may spread beyond that time and that place. A device that can be used to distinguish between a movement per se and manifestations of its tenets (usually greatly modified and appearing as elements in a work rather than an encompassing concept of filmmaking) is to capitalize the designation of the movement to indicate the former and to lowercase it to indicate the latter. Cinematic Surrealism, for instance, developed in France during the twenties, most notably in the works of Luis Buñuel and Germaine Dulac. Buñuel has continued to be a Surrealist. Charles Laughton's *The Night of the Hunter* (1955), however, contains elements of surrealism and expressionism.

*Genre/ Genre* is probably the leading candidate as the vaguest word in film terminology. Writers who do meet the challenge of the term define it in one of two ways. The inclusive definition is illustrated by Geduld and Gottesman in their glossary of film terms: "A category, kind, or form of film distinguished by subject matter, theme, or technique."[4] The authors then list 78 "leading genres," including adaptation, biography, epic, gangster, screwball comedy, and whodunit. In another glossary appears a more restricted definition: "A film type, such as a Western or science-fiction film, which usually has conventional plot structure and characters; loosely, a 'formula' film."[5]

Although the referents for *genre* are disputable and amorphous, the term can be useful in supplying critics with perspectives for discerning similarities that certain films share other than country of origin and a member of the filmmaking team (such as a director). A major problem is devising categories that will make manageable the many bases available for comparing motion pictures in order to evaluate and elucidate them. The best-known classification is the one contrived by the Beograd Film Institute, which consists of two principal divisions: structure and technique, and aim and theme.[6] Another possibility is the three categories of form, mode, and subject matter.

*Form* is based on one of three criteria. The first is the distinction between fiction and nonfiction cinema. The second comprises processes of making films other than the conventional use of a camera running at a certain number of frames per second and the projection of the print on a large screen. An alternate form is animation: photographing, one frame at a time, people or objects (pixilation), drawings (cartoons), puppets, or silhouettes; there is also camera-less animation (drawing or painting directly on film frames). In incipient stages of development are computer and holographic films. It is true that television requires a special method of projection, but it has developed into a separate medium from cinema. Videotape also is on its way to becoming a separate medium; however, if it is considered as a subdivision of cinema, it would belong in the category of genre form.

The third criterion is the predominance or reduction of one of the components (or elements of a component) of a film. In a conventional motion picture, the narrative dimension, camera-editing dynamics, and the elements of presentation are more or less in balance. An abstract film, however, eliminates the narrative dimension. Music, an element of presentation, is of such significance in a musical that the actors respond to it by singing and/or dancing (which is not the case with standard background music). The same holds true of opera, operetta, and dance films.

A cinematic *mode* identifies the filmmaker's attitude toward and treatment of his material, regardless of the form or subject matter chosen. The major modes are tragedy, comedy, epic, and fantasy; others are melodrama, spectacle, satire, and parody (although satire and parody are usually considered subdivisions of comedy).

A *subject matter* genre is self-explanatory: a grouping of films that deal with the same or similar subject matter. (An aesthetician would probably prefer the more academic term *iconography:* the pictorial representation of a given subject.) The number of possible headings in this category is vast; the major ones include Western, war, gangster, detective, horror, monster, historical, biographical, religious, thriller, science fiction, and spy pictures. A glance through the subject index in *The American Film Institute Catalogs: Feature Films*[7] suggests that even confining one's scope only to the United States, there are few conceivable themes on which three or more motion pictures have not been released.

The categories of form, mode, and subject matter are obviously not exclusive, and more than one designation within a category can apply to a film. Ralph Bakshi's *The Lord of the Rings* is an animated epic. *Destry Rides Again* is a comedy Western. *The Seventh Seal* is a historical, religious tragedy. Any valid designation of the significant form, mode, or subject matter of a film is justification for comparing this aspect to other films in the genre.

It should be clear from these generalizations on film genre criticism that this approach requires numerous differentiations and qualifications if it is to be of help to a critic and to readers. The response of some scholars is understandable: to jettison the whole elaborate system and restrict the term *genre* to "formula" films (the second definition given earlier). While it is true that the Western, for example, has always adhered to certain conventions, *formula* is too restrictive a word, and it has acquired derogatory connotations that are often unjustified. A tradition undergoes changes, and it is frequently these departures from conventions that are the most revealing to a critic who is attempting to interpret the genre aspect of a film. Moreover, such genres as the documentary and comedy are too diverse in style and content to be reduced to a set of formulae. This restrictive definition of *genre* should therefore be limited to subdivisions of a specific genre, for example, the "screwball comedy" and the "classic Western."

The function of genre criticism is demonstrated in Part Three of this book. Each chapter, with one exception, opens with a survey of the characteristics and history of an individual genre. Documentary (Chapter 7) and musical (Chapter 9) are form genres, comedy (Chapter 6) is a mode genre, and the Western (Chapter 8) is a subject matter genre. The perspective provided by a survey, in addition to other critical approaches, is applied to the films analyzed in each chapter.

*Film theories/* In addition to movements and genres, *film theories,* if their tenets are reducible to criteria for criticism, also can form the bases of cinematic perspectives. J. Dudley Andrew, in his fine study, *The Major Film Theories: An Introduction,* discusses, among others, "the formative tradition," realist film theory, and cinema semiology. Each one has significantly influenced film criticism. Andrew is only cursory in his examination of the *auteur* theory, for he considers it as "properly speaking . . . not a theory at all but a critical method."[8] While this method may be peripheral to a book on theory, it is important to the purposes of this chapter. Each of these four cinematic theories supplies perspectives that can be of value to a critic.

*Formalism* historically is an aesthetic theory that developed as a movement in Russia at about the time of World War I. Its advocates advanced the view that the essence of art lies in the form of each medium rather than subject matter and manifestations of ideologies. Among others, Eisenstein (in both theory and practice), Rudolf Arnheim (from his background in philosophy and psychology), and Béla Balázs (from his experiences in various arts) built their ideas on film on the foundations of Formalism.

A cinematic formalist (one who subscribes to the basic approach but not necessarily all the tenets of the Russian aesthetic movement) is preoccupied with what was described earlier in this chapter as "the film itself"—that is, how camera-editing dynamics and manipulation of the elements of presentation mold the reactions of a viewer to a motion picture. On the other hand, a critic cannot function completely as a formalist except when considering abstract films. This theory can be useful, however, in evaluating and elucidating a motion picture by supplying a vocabulary and critical methods for focusing a critic's attention on *how* a filmmaker expresses his intentions in the medium rather than solely on *what.*

*Realism* as a film theory had its most fervent defenders in Siegfried Kracauer and André Bazin. A clue to the main premise of this aesthetic is the subtitle of Kracauer's *Theory of Film: The Redemption of Physical Reality.* To *redeem* something is to recover or restore it. The author recognizes that no art medium can duplicate reality, only, as Aristotle pointed out, imitate it. For Kracauer, cinema is truest to its inherent nature when it captures on the screen a physical reality that would otherwise have been lost to a viewer.

To achieve this goal, the reality photographed should be as unstaged as possible, should include what is random and fortuitous, and should convey the sense that a film re-creates a fragment of human existence, not a self-contained aesthetic entity. In other words, the less a filmmaker interferes with the redemption of reality, the more "cinematic" will be his work. So Bazin praises De Sica's *The Bicycle Thief* as "one of the finest examples of pure cinema."[9]

Whereas the perspective derived from formalism encourages the critic to analyze the techniques of a film and the ways in which a filmmaker re-creates reality to convey his vision of it, the perspective of realism requires that the critic examine the correspondence between the reality photographed and its representation on the screen.

The *auteur theory* had its origin in the concepts of a group of young French critics who wrote in the fifties for the magazine *Cahiers du Cinéma.* They shared three major dissatisfactions with the state of filmmaking and film studies in their day: the conventionality and artificiality of French films released after World War II, the condescending attitude of the older generation of film critics toward the commercial genre productions of Hollywood, and the view of intellectuals and the general public that cinema was primarily a medium of entertainment created by committees of technicians rather than an art. The most prominent members of the group—François Truffaut, Jean-Luc Godard, Eric Rohmer, and Claude Chabrol—also shared affection and respect for André Bazin (one of the three founders of *Cahiers du Cinéma*) and a determination, realized since the late fifties, to make their own films. What they attempted to do was to reconcile the formalists' emphasis on treatment rather than subject matter (adding an appreciation of craft as well as form) with the realists' focus on the representational, especially the influence of the matrixes from which a film emerges. To a certain degree, they succeeded.

The keystone of the *auteur* theory (more specifically the *politique des auteurs,* literally "policy of authors") was the assertion that the director should be regarded as the author of a film. It is the *auteur* director who imposes his personal interpretation on a reality photographed for a motion picture, even if he must do so craftily and slyly within the restrictions imposed by a studio system. The *Cahiers* critics thus asserted that it was the director who could realize an artistic vision in the medium of film.

Not every director is capable of being an *auteur*. One of the functions of a critic, according to Truffaut and his colleagues, is to identify and to celebrate those who qualify for this cinematic roll of honor. The *auteur* critic studies the oeuvre of a director in search of techniques and themes that are characteristic of the artist's total output. It is on the basis of these distinctive characteristics and their development, rather than the reception of individual films by critics and the public, that a determination is made as to whether or not a director is a genuine *auteur*.

The chief contribution of the *auteur* theory to film criticism, aside from upgrading the role of the director, has been to demonstrate that the style (in the broadest sense of treatment of themes as well as techniques) of a director can be defined. Far less effective has been the attempt of *auteur* critics to rank directors on the basis of their styles. Andrew Sarris, the leading advocate of this theory in the United States, in 1962 postulated in an essay[10] three criteria for judging whether or not a director is an *auteur:* (1) Does he have sufficient technical competence to realize his intentions in the medium? (2) Does he have a distinctive vision of the human condition (Sarris resorts to the more ambiguous term *distinct personality*) that guides him as he re-creates reality? (3) Is there a meaning or a significance that arises from the tension between his vision and the resistance of his material? These are vague standards, open to subjective interpretations. For this reason, *auteur* critics often differ among themselves as to who deserves their approbation.

By downgrading the contributions to a film of other members of the filmmaking team, especially the screenwriter, *auteur* critics often ignore the limitations imposed on a director by his material. There is just so much even the most brilliant director can do with a cliché-ridden plot. Furthermore, a distinctive style is no guarantee of significant results; if it were, Ken Russell and Sam Peckinpah would be considered two of the world's greatest directors. Too often also when *auteur* status has been conferred on a director, even his banal films are automatically praised for the one or two striking cinematic flourishes they might contain.

*Cine-structuralism* and *cine-semiology* constitute the most innovative and exciting theoretical approach to film in recent years. As with practically all important theories, they were based on the work of earlier thinkers. In the case of film structuralism and semiology, concepts developed in noncinematic disciplines were particularly significant. The main impetus came from the writings of Ferdinand de Saussure, who in the beginning of the twentieth century, after studying general linguistics, founded the science of *semiology,* the study of signs. Semiotics is often considered a synonym for semiology, though some linguists insist on a distinction between the two terms. In our time, the most prominent linguistic semiologist has been Noam Chomsky. Other influences were anthropologist Claude Lévi-Strauss's studies of the structure of myths, concepts of perception proposed by various schools of psychology, in psychoanalysis Freud's observations on the dynamics of the unconscious and Jung's ideas on archetypal images and patterns, and various philosophical theories, such as Charles Sanders Peirce's taxonomy of different classes of signs. Also playing a role in the development of cine-structuralism and cine-semiology were prevous film theories, particularly formalism (with its emphasis on how techniques of the medium influence the "meaning" of a motion picture) and the *auteur* theory (the principle that an individual filmmaker can demonstrate a uniqueness and consistency of style from one work to another).

The most dedicated and provocative writer on film structuralism and semiology is Frenchman Christian Metz. His book *Film Language: A Semiotics of the Cinema* is a prime text in the field. Another leading theorist was Metz's countryman Roland Barthes, a literary critic with a special interest in film. An Italian school of cine-semiology has been established, including among its prominent contributors Umberto Eco, Gianfranco Bettetini, and the late director Pier Paolo Pasolini. A similar group preoccupied with cine-structuralism has formed in Great Britain. No book written in English by a member of this group has aroused more interest than Peter Wollen's *Signs and Meaning in the Cinema.* Colleagues of Wollen are

Geoffrey Nowell-Smith, Jim Kitses, Alan Lovell, and Noel Burch. The British publication *Screen* confines itself to articles from a semiotic perspective. In the United States, no one writer has emerged as an authoritative spokesperson for this approach, but among those who have committed themselves to supporting structuralistic and semiotic analysis of motion pictures are Bill Nichols, Brian Henderson, and Will Wright.

Basic to Saussure's formulation of semiology is the relationship between the *signified* (a concept, say, of a house) and the *signifier* (the means by which the signified is communicated, as the word *house*). In a specific instance the two constitute a *sign* (in our linguistic example, the combination of the word *house* and its referent, the concept of a house). In language, the connection between a word and what it signifies is, on the basic level, arbitrary. In Italian, for example, *casa* is the signifier for the concept of a house. In film, however, the situation is different: The signifier and the signified are almost identical. The image of a house on the screen is a two-dimensional ''concept'' of a house and is simultaneously recognizable to an audience as a specific house, a concept made concrete.

Words have both denotative and connotative meanings. For example, this is the denotative definition of a rose: ''Any of numerous shrubs or vines of the genus *Rosa,* usually having prickly stems, compound leaves, and variously colored, often fragrant flowers.'' A single rose given by a man to his wife on their first anniversary, however, evokes associations (that is, connotations) that go beyond the definition of a flower of the genus *Rosa.* If a word in a given context has overtones so complex and subtle that they cannot be contained within rational thought, the word assumes the proportions of a symbol.

Film images also have denotative and connotative meanings. In Lang's *M,* there are three shots of the Murderer looking in a mirror. Each image is a sign in the film which literally signifies an object whose function is to present a reflection of the person who looks into it. (Every object that appears on the screen has such a denotative meaning, which is to say that it is what we recognize it to be.) As *M* unfolds, however, we realize that the mirror image is associated symbolically with the true nature of Hans Beckert, a psychopath, in contrast to the rather amiable appearance he

normally presents to the world. The mirror has thus been invested by the filmmaker with connotative significance. The word *trope* describes a relationship between signified and signifier that allows a sign to possess connotative as well as denotative meaning. Just how a sign with predominantly denotative significance is turned by an artist into a trope is a complex area that semiologists have been exploring since the time of Saussure.

Signs in cinema are the means whereby meaning is communicated from the screen to an audience. A few moments of footage may contain dozens of signs. After all, every identifiable entity that appears on the screen is a visual sign, just as every word on a page is a linguistic sign. Fortunately, it is possible to classify signs into *codes.* A code consists of a group of related signs. In cinema, there are three types of codes. The first is societal: derived from a cultural environment (for example, the way characters in a motion picture dress). Another type of code includes the signs that cinema shares with other media, such as natural sounds in a play, a film, and an opera. Finally, there are codes unique to cinema; visual montage is an example. No matter what the type, codes are not formulae that a filmmaker follows in creating a motion picture. They are critical constructs that enable the student of cinema to explore how what appears on the screen is perceived intellectually and emotionally by viewers.

Most codes can be reduced to subcodes and ever finer distinctions. A subcode of the way people eat is their actions when a family sits down to dinner. A cinematic code is the relation of the camera to the subject during a shot. A subcode would be the angle of the camera in relation to the subject. A further subdivision would be low angles. In fact, the pages of this book devoted to camera-editing dynamics can be viewed as a survey of various cinematic codes and subcategories. Similarly, the section on elements of presentation is constituted primarily of codes shared by cinema and other media, and the matrixes discussed in this chapter correspond generally to cultural codes.

Of all theoreticians in the field of cine-semiology, Christian Metz has gone furthest in systematizing codes. Having established to his satisfaction that film has unique characteristics that differentiate it as a medium from linguistic structures (especially because of an identity between signifier and signified), he turned to problems of how the narrative dimension of a motion picture can be examined from a semiological perspective. In a specific narrative *text* (any organic entity in a medium, such as an individual film in cinema) there are, he proposed, two axes of meaning. The first is the *syntagmatic axis:* significance derived from what follows what—that is, choices of ordering on the horizontal level of time. The climactic sequence in *Smiles of a Summer Night,* for example, begins with a visual presentation of bottles of wine.* Henrik drinks the wine; he smashes his glass and delivers a tirade against the others; he runs out of the room; Anne moves after him, revealing her love for him. The meaning of each event depends on what came before it; there could not be a change in this ordering without creating a different text. The code of eating and the subcode of the wine, the insights into Henrik's character and his relationship with Anne—all are interdependent and developed along the syntagmatic axis.

The *paradigmatic axis* is vertical. It allows a revelation of the potential significance of what appears on the screen based on the organization of associations, not sequence. In Bergman's film, the potency of the wine is associated with the mysterious powers of Mrs. Armfeldt by means of camera-editing dynamics, words and gestures of the actress, and background music. A critic who conceives of Mrs. Armfeldt as a good witch or anima figure is operating on the paradigmatic axis in interpreting the meaning of this scene in this particular text.

The interrelation of the syntagmatic and paradigmatic is emphasized by J. Dudley Andrew: "The full meaning of the text is the complex interweaving of the two axes of selection and organization."[11] And Christian Metz even refers to *"paradigms of syntagmas."*[12] A critic should keep this interrelation of axes of meaning in mind, whether he is exploring the numerous codes in a single text or analyzing a single code (perhaps montage, or marital infidelity) in a number of related texts (for example, the oeuvre of a director).

---

*pp. 310–311

Now that the basic terminology has been introduced, we can examine the function of the approach constituted by cine-structuralism and cine-semiology and the distinctions between the two terms. As a critical perspective, the goal of this approach is to create methods whereby a student of film can investigate how meaning created by the unique medium of cinema is conveyed from the screen to viewers. In essence, Metz and his colleagues are attempting to develop an epistemology of film.

Film structuralism and semiology are often coupled and, indeed, share fundamental premises. The distinction lies in what Metz calls a different "principle of pertinency." He maintains that structural analysis "can trace a single code through several texts. . . . [It] is the study of codes (a code always appears in several texts). . . . [Semiotics] can grasp a single text through all its codes. . . . [It] is the study of texts (a text always involves several codes)."[13] In other words, the cine-structuralists are preoccupied with demonstrating how basic *structures* reveal meanings to be found in many films and the influence on those meanings of codes inherent in a specific culture. Film structuralism, therefore, is akin particularly to the interests of anthropology and psychoanalysis. Cine-semiologists concentrate on how the medium of cinema conveys meanings to an audience as exemplified by an individual film. These interests coincide especially with those of linguistics and the psychology of perception.

In these few pages, we have barely scratched the surface of the theories of film structuralism and semiology. Their goals are ambitious, methods are still being developed, and vital questions still remain unanswered. Unfortunately, for both theories a terminology so dense and inflexible has accumulated that it has become a sort of linguistic coral reef that can sink all but the most knowledgeable readers. The few terms defined here are only the most fundamental ones, and a serious student of this area of cinema theory must be prepared to do extensive background reading before being able fully to understand an essay devoted to how film meaning is communicated.

Another problem of the cine-structuralist and cine-semiological perspective is that identifying and interpreting signs and codes in a film or films helps us to appreciate how meaning is conveyed through the medium of cinema but does not evaluate that meaning. There is a tendency among critics who take advantage of this perspective to associate complexity and multiplicity of signs and codes with richness of significance. This is not always the case. A simple, straightforward shot can often be more effective, more meaningful in itself than one replete with subtle, interrelated tropes. At their present stage of development, cine-structuralism and cine-semiology assist us more in describing and elucidating than in judging works of cinematic art.

Whatever its weaknesses, however, this approach has revitalized film criticism and theory since the 1960s. No one with more than a casual interest in cinema studies can afford to ignore it.

*Other cinematic perspectives/* In addition to the cinematic perspectives just summarized, four others are especially noteworthy. *Marxism,* both as a separate perspective and as a one concomitant with others, has developed its own criteria and methods of analysis in dealing with films. Most interesting is how this approach gives us insights into latent premises underlying motion pictures that do not contain overt sociopolitical meanings. *Myth criticism* in the hands of such a perceptive practitioner as Parker Tyler has gone beyond simply identifying character types and recurrent plot structures to exploring archetypal images and patterns and the ways unique to the medium of cinema by which filmmakers incorporate them, consciously or unconsciously, in specific works. *Phrenomenology* is a school of philosophy founded by Edmund Husserl early in this century. He asserted that the significance of an object is discovered through intuition rather than by analytic methods. A group of French film theorists attempted in the 1960s to apply Husserl's concepts to cinema. They claimed André Bazin as a forerunner, but the main advocates of this approach have been Amédée Ayfre (who died in 1963) and Henri Agel.

*National characteristics* is based on the premise that filmmakers of the same nationality create motion pictures in ways that differ from those of other nationalities. This perspective can be helpful in understanding a national movie industry's influence on what films are made and how they are made. It can offer insights into movements that originate in specific countries, as Siegfried Kracauer demonstrates in his analysis of Expressionism in *From Caligari to Hitler: A Psychological History of the German Film.*[14] It may be possible to go beyond the matrix from which a film emerges to generalizations about the relationship between a filmmaker's oeuvre and his nationality, as Vernon Young suggests in *Cinema Borealis: Ingmar Bergman and the Swedish Ethos.* On the whole, however, a critic using this perspective should proceed with particular caution and be open to many qualifications and exceptions to any comprehensive conclusions.

*Noncinematic perspectives*
Numerous sciences, philosophies, and ideologies supply principles and methods whereby a film or films can be examined from a particular perspective. These perspectives differ from cinematic ones in that they have not developed individual criteria for evaluation and elucidation that apply only to cinema. An example would be existentialism. An understanding of this school of philosophy could assist a critic in analyzing a film adaptation of an existential work of fiction or drama (such as Visconti's *The Stranger,* from Albert Camus's novel) or a film with an original screenplay that contains existential concepts (such as Bergman's *The Seventh Seal*). This perspective, however, will not contribute to the critic's exploration of a film as film. The same principles of existentialism would in the same way apply whether the work being considered is a motion picture, a novel, or a drama.

One of the recommendations discussed in relation to perspectives in general is relevant particularly to a noncinematic one: The tenets of a perspective should be thoroughly understood before applying them to a film or films. This type of background knowledge, however, does not relieve a critic of responsibility for examining the form as well as the content of the subject of his analysis. Examination of the techniques of a film must be based on criteria and methods borrowed from cinematic perspectives to explain how meanings in that work revealed by use of a noncinematic perspective are made vivid and concrete to an audience.

In the analysis of *Shane* in Chapter 8, for example, it is suggested that a Freudian perspective might offer insights into the relationships among the youngster Joey, his parents, and Shane.* The psychoanalyst's theories, however, are of no help in recognizing how the director and his colleagues established that relationship through dialogue, point of view, conventions of the Western, and low-angle shots of Shane.

The chief value of a distinction between cinematic and noncinematic perspectives is to help a critic recognize the limitations and potentials of an individual perspective in elucidating the interdependence between the content and the form of a film. It should be kept in mind, however, that many noncinematic perspectives can be transformed into cinematic ones if an approach based on that perspective can be developed that results in the means for judging and interpreting the components of a film beyond the narrative dimension. This is what occurred in the case of semiology, basically a linguistic science but converted by Christian Metz, Roland Barthes, and others into cine-semiology.

### Audience responses and popular culture

This category of perspectives is designated separately because its objectives are essentially different from those of the other two major types. The justification for applying any cinematic or noncinematic perspective to a film is to assist a critic in revealing forms and feelings within a motion picture. The film is treated as a self-contained entity as it is projected on a screen. The reactions of an audience during a viewing should not affect a critic's evaluation or elucidation of a film.

It is possible, however, for a critic to explore a motion picture primarily in terms of audience responses. This is a difficult area of cinema studies, for the information on which conjectures can be based is not easily obtainable, and conclusions are sometimes impossible to document. The first basic problem is determining the size and makeup of audiences that have viewed a film during a specific time period and in a specific geographic area. The second is focusing on what elements in a film or group of films reflect the characteristics of a culture to which viewers respond or that influence them, as well as how these processes

*pp. 421–422

operate. Such problems are appropriate to the science of sociology, but in dealing with motion pictures, this perspective has developed its own methodology. It would in fact be considered a cinematic perspective if its approach and objectives were not so different.

Aside from the figures of box office receipts on the number of viewers who see an individual film and in what part of a country, not many statistics are available. A critic would want to know, for example, whether or not there is a relationship between a genre and a segment of a national population. Some assumptions seem reasonable, such as that adolescents patronized the "beach party movies" popular in the United States during the sixties. Others are probable but undocumented—for instance, that Westerns appeal chiefly to males and romances to women. Further assumptions depend on so many variables that they can be no more than guesses. A critic studying audience reactions therefore begins with the handicap of having to speculate on the makeup of the audience being analyzed.

Since the late nineteenth century, the terms *popular arts* and *popular culture* have been used to differentiate art, which was subsidized by a discriminating minority, from entertainment that attracted a less sophisticated majority. Though the distinction in film is vague and should be followed by a dozen qualifying statements, a critic who is examining film as a popular art tends to deal more with cinematic entertainments than with works of art. The critic's interest is likely to be in how the largest number of viewers react to what appears on the screen rather than the more subtle, profound, and individual effects.

Scholars of popular culture have demonstrated that a mass medium both reflects and influences the attitudes and beliefs of a large segment of a national population. It is frequently difficult, however, to distinguish between reflection and influence; one can reinforce the other. A few examples drawn from American motion pictures: Negative racial stereotypes—such as the "Yellow Peril" (threats to American society from Oriental immigrants), blacks, and other minority groups—have often mirrored the fears of groups in American society. Many films of the thirties and forties, exemplified by the works of Frank Capra, supported a view of the small American town as a bastion of the virtues and values of democracy. On the other hand, myths of the West and the Western hero were initiated by fiction but developed principally by cinema.

Manifestations in motion pictures of ideas and stereotypes current in a culture may be overt, as in the portrayals in war films of the enemy as ruthless and brutish. Latent meanings, naturally, are more difficult to ascertain. Does *The Graduate,* for instance, support the radical rebellion of youth in the sixties against the life-style of the previous generation, or is the film, under the disguise of opposition to the superficialities of the establishment, a covert defense of basically bourgeois values? When there is evidence of ambiguity, a critic's knowledge of cinematic techniques can be important, for it is possible that a motion picture's camera-editing dynamics and elements of presentation may slyly contradict its narrative themes, as has happened in films made under totalitarian governments.

A critic who is attempting to fathom to what degree audiences have accepted or rejected themes, stereotypes, and beliefs inherent in certain films can encounter perplexing questions. Just what percentage of American moviegoers took seriously the ''Red scare'' films of the fifties? Did the films of proletarian life made by the British Angry Young Men in the sixties reflect a genuine shift in the social structure of England? To avoid farfetched generalizations, the critic exploring this aspect of popular culture should be familiar with the history of the period, be acquainted with the principles of sociology and psychology, and possess a discriminating imagination that recognizes relationships between events of reality and fiction that on the surface appear disparate.

In reaching conclusions on the interactions between motion pictures and their audiences, a critic depends chiefly on either intuition and fairly self-evident influences or on methodological research. The former method suffices when dealing with such obvious imitations of screen styles as dress and home decor. More subtle and profound effects can also be uncovered in this way. Robert Warshow refers to only a few films to substantiate intriguing insights in his essays on the Western and gangster film genres in *The Immediate Experience.* Generalizations with little documentation predominate in Stanley Cavell's *The World Viewed: Reflections on the Ontology of Film.* On the other hand, a more scholarly methodology is to be found in Siegfried Kracauer's *From Caligari to Hitler* and Molly Haskell's *From Reverence to Rape: The Treatment of Women in the Movies.*

It is often difficult for a critic schooled to judge and to interpret films by traditional criteria to adjust to viewing movies solely as artifacts of a culture and to limit the relevance of those works to the degree they reflect and influence the attitudes and beliefs of masses of people. Moreover, conclusions about the role of an individual medium in the popular culture of a certain time and place are so difficult to substantiate that critics who wish to bring greater preciseness, coherence, and standards of judgment to their discipline are often impatient with the use of this perspective.

Yet it is salutary for students of cinema to be reminded that their medium is primarily a popular one. Criticism since World War II has emphasized the art of cinema. This is unquestionably the glory of the medium, but only a snob would scorn another major function of motion pictures: to offer audiences through entertainment a means of escaping from the harassments and problems of everyday life. Nor should a critic underrate the value of a perspective that explores how film entertainment has influenced, often in subtle ways, masses of people's views of themselves, others, and the world in which they live.

The chief goal of this chapter has been to demonstrate that the house of film criticism consists of many interconnecting rooms and that renovation is constantly going on. No one room is an inner sanctum of revealed truth, although a critic may feel more comfortable in one area than another. Dwellers in this mansion, or in any of the other edifices in the complex of film studies, do not usually receive the respect and renown of filmmakers. Nonetheless, it is through their efforts that the significance of the medium as both art and entertainment has been impressed on the consciousness of our time.

PART TWO

# film movements

The definitions, techniques, and perspectives described in Part One are applied in Parts Two and Three to specific films, and the dimension of historical background added.

In Chapter 4, major film movements are examined in a succinct history of narrative cinema. The analyses of films in Chapter 5 illustrate the movements of Realism, Expressionism, Dynamic Montage, Neorealism, and the French New Wave. The format followed for the discussion of individual motion pictures is described in the introductory note to this chapter.

# Film history and movements

A knowledge of film history is essential if a student of cinema is to understand the context in which individual motion pictures are created and the means available to filmmakers at a specific time and place to express their interpretations of reality. Film movements in particular offer insights into how ideas and techniques derived from cinema and other arts and forms of entertainment influenced a group of filmmakers.

The type of films surveyed in this chapter could be called "dramas" if the term had not accumulated so many referents as to be debased completely in value. What is included, then, are fiction narratives, with references to later chapters when a film or filmmaker is associated primarily with a specific genre discussed elsewhere in this book.

A historical survey of 100 pages or so is of necessity restricted, but no major director or movement has been omitted.

## THE SILENT ERA

The earliest motion pictures were predominantly either visual recordings of the everyday activities of people and of important events or travelogues. There were also attempts at dramatization and fiction. Historical events were reconstructed (for instance, *The Execution of Mary, Queen of Scots,* 1895). Georges Méliès used special effects as well as other techniques to tell fictional stories, as in *A Trip to the Moon (Le Voyage dans la lune,* 1902). The Frenchman Ferdinand Zecca was directing episodes from the novels of Victor Hugo and Emile Zola in 1901 and 1902. What this category of motion pictures lacked, however, was a coherent, developed narrative dimension, even within the restrictions of one or two reels, that took advantage of the unique characteristics of cinema. These were the very qualities that Edwin S. Porter began to explore in *The Great Train Robbery* (1903),* and for this reason the 10-minute film is usually considered the first genuine drama in cinema.

## U.S.A.

During the first decade and a half of this century, the advances in the United States of motion picture distribution from nickelodeons (frequently converted stores) to genuine movie theaters was typical of that in other countries. Film companies such as Biograph, Edison, and Vitagraph sprang up and then expanded from production to distribution and finally to ownership of theaters. In fact, in 1909, the Motion Picture Patents Company, a trust, was established by the leading companies to protect their interests from outsiders, though it did not prevent internal battles. Films were made in every genre that entertained audiences. Meanwhile, a young actor and playwright from the theater who was serving his apprenticeship as a film director at Biograph was to revolutionize the medium.

The contributions of D. W. Griffith are delineated later, in Chapter 8.† By the time he completed *The Birth of a Nation* (1915) and *Intolerance* (1916), he had molded a crude form of entertainment into an art. Griffith was committed to preserving the reality he created in front of the camera, but he realized that through camera-editing dynamics he could add narrative depth to his plot, help audiences to "see" emotionally as well as physically. This emphasis on projecting a filmmaker's intensified vision of reality on the screen has come to be called *cinematic Realism.*

Realism in the arts is based on the concept of *mimesis*—an imitation of nature. From this perspective, all motion pictures (with the exception of abstract

---

*p. 385
†pp. 198–200, 204–210

films) are to some degree realistic, for they either consist of or represent (as in animation) an objective reality (even if simulated) that is recorded by the camera. Cinematic techniques, however, allow a manipulation of that reality for dramatic effects. The crucial question is the purpose of those effects. When they go beyond attempting to achieve verisimilitude ("appearing to be true or real"), a component of most films, to a distinct interpretation of reality that a number of directors share and implement in their works, we can refer to the movement of Realism.

A Realistic film focuses on the familiar and the likely; it avoids the improbable, the unknown, and the illusional. Adherents of the movement do not deny the existence of farfetched situations and distorted sense perception; they simply restrict the former and minimize the latter. Discernible causes of manifested effects are emphasized, particularly as they influence an individual's feelings and actions, so environment is a major force and is often presented in detail. The camera is predominantly objective, with a minimum of subjective shots. *Mise-en-scène* is preferred to montage.

The ways in which reality is projected on the screen during a specific period are conditioned by what is envisioned as constituting that reality in contemporary art and entertainment. For this reason, Realism in the United States of the teens and twenties, compared to that of the thirties and forties, was more sentimental and contrived. Realism is relative, and scenes in Griffith's dramas that are amusing today were often considered daring or expressive in his day. We should also keep in mind that, unlike Expressionism in Germany or Neorealism in Italy, Realism in the United States in the silent era was not a self-conscious, conceptual movement. Although influenced by Realism in fiction and stage drama, directors like Griffith and Stroheim believed that they were only taking advantage of what motion pictures did most effectively. Later certain theorists, such as Siegfried Kracauer and André Bazin, maintained that since cinema is most true to its intrinsic nature when realistic, critics should not refer to a "movement" of Realism. There may be some validity in this view, but the label is still useful in differentiating one overall approach to filmmaking from others.

During the second and third decades of this century, radical changes occurred in the motion picture industries on both sides of the Atlantic. In the United States, Griffith, encouraged by lengthy films made in Italy and France, demonstrated through *The Birth of a Nation* that, contrary to the view of motion picture company executives, audiences were prepared to sit through more than one or two reels per movie. The star system was initiated in 1908 by the designation of Florence Lawrence (who was under contract to the Independent Motion Picture Company) as the "imp girl." Thomas Ince in the middle of the teens began insisting on shooting scripts and production budgets and schedules, thus originating the concept of a producer's sharing responsibility for a film with a director. It was not a long step from the rise of influential producers and the economic advantages they offered to the development of studios in the twenties that dominated what appeared in the movie theaters of America.

Griffith is now considered the master director in the United States during the silent era. Only Erich von Stroheim (1885–1957), in retrospective critical opinion, challenges Griffith's preeminence. The Austrian came to this country in 1906 and was an actor and assistant director before making three films at Universal Pictures (*Blind Husbands,* 1918; *The Devil's Passkey,* 1919; and *Foolish Wives,* 1921) and a portion of a fourth one (*Merry-Go-Round,* 1921).

The climax of Stroheim's career as a director was the creation of *Greed* (1923, using his own screen play derived from Frank Norris's novel *McTeague*). While the film was being made at MGM, Irving Thalberg, who had been Stroheim's nemesis when they both worked at Universal, became production supervisor. He was unsympathetic to a 10-hour (at silent speed) film, and at his insistence, over Stroheim's violent objections, the film was "edited" to a fourth of its original length. Although the main plot— a dentist (Figure 4.1) becomes a drunkard and eventually kills his miserly wife then dies in Death Valley— was preserved in a fragmented state, essential subplots, characters, and sequences were eliminated. Even in the mutilated version, however, a viewer is conscious of being exposed to the skeleton of a great work of cinematic art.

**FIGURE 4.1**

*Greed,* 1923, directed by Erich von Stroheim. McTeague (Gibson Gowland), an unlicensed dentist, admires the sign he has purchased to advertise his office. Throughout the film, the sets, props, and costumes are meticulously realistic.

Stroheim went on to direct four other films: *The Merry Widow* (1925), *The Wedding March* (1926–1928, released in two parts), *Queen Kelly* (1928, edited and mutilated by others), and *Walking Down Broadway* (1933, extensively revised and given a new ending). In the decades until his death, he wrote and acted (often with great distinction, as in Renoir's *Grand Illusion*).

In fairness to such production chiefs as Thalberg, with whom the director repeatedly had confrontations, it should be pointed out that Stroheim was arrogant, dictatorial in dealing with actors and crews, cavalier about budgets, and uncompromising in fulfilling his vision of a film. Yet the subtlety and depth of his insights into the psychology of his characters, especially in sexual situations, was unequaled by any contemporary American director, including Griffith. Through his obsession with authenticity, carrying realism as far as possible in his day, he fashioned decors that reflected and reinforced the charged atmosphere of brilliantly realized scenes. Hollywood has ignored or destroyed the talents of many artists, but few cases are more regrettable than its dissipation of the genius of Stroheim.

Three contemporaries of Griffith and Stroheim gained particular prominence as directors during the silent era. King Vidor made *The Big Parade* (1925), a powerful drama of World War I and its horrors despite its sentimental ending. *The Crowd* (1928) is one of the first American films to deal honestly with the subject of unemployment, and it anticipated Vidor's later films of social consciousness. Josef von Sternberg showed in his early films a remarkable gift for striking visual effects, especially in the area of lighting. His *Underworld* (1927) and *The Docks of New York* (1928) are usually remembered as forerunners of the gangster films of the thirties, but each one in itself is a laudable achievement. Although Sternberg went on to make many successful sound films (discussed later in this survey), in the view of many critics he never fulfilled, with the exception of *The Blue Angel* (1930), the promise of these two works and *The Last Command* (1928). Cecil B. De Mille was from the beginning the complete professional, capable of making any type of film, but he had a flair for spectacle, as demonstrated in *The Ten Commandments* (1923) and *The King of Kings* (1927), both biblical epics.

Other notable directors of this period were Maurice Tourneur, who specialized in adapting literary classics (for example, *Trilby,* 1915; *Treasure Island,* 1920; and *The Last of the Mohicans,* 1920, with Clarence Brown as codirector); Rex Ingram, best known for the first version of *The Four Horsemen of the Apocalypse* (1921); William Wellman (for example, *Wings,* 1927); Henry King (*Tol'able David,* 1921, and *Stella Dallas,* 1925, among others); Clarence Brown, who directed Valentino in *The Eagle* (1925) and Garbo in *The Flesh and the Devil* (1927); Frank Borzage (for instance, *Seventh Heaven,* 1927); W. S. Van Dyke; and Fred Niblo. European directors, often to their regret, were lured to Hollywood. The experiences of F. W. Murnau, Mauritz Stiller, and Victor Sjöström are described in the commentaries in this section on drama in Germany and Scandinavia.

## GERMANY

During the twenties only Germany established a motion picture industry comparable to that in the United States. Before and during World War I, production was confined, with a few exceptions, to the conventional staples of commercial cinema. Just before the end of the war, however, a very significant event occurred. In 1917 most of the major film companies were integrated into a combine called UFA *(Universum Film Aktiengesellshaft),* with one-third of its capital derived from government funds. By the early 1920s, its studios had the most advanced and extensive facilities in the world.

Under the leadership of the phenomenal Erich Pommer* (executive producer from 1921 to 1931), UFA developed certain characteristics that, in addition to its facilities, made it a unique organization. Although concerned with making profits, it also supported such noncommercial genres as documentaries, avant-garde works, and animated films. Pommer encouraged a camaraderie among his employees that allowed exceptional talents in every area of filmmaking to express themselves.

UFA and the other film companies were very active, releasing a total of 200 to 300 features a year. There were costume dramas (in which Ernst Lubitsch specialized until he left for Hollywood in 1922), melodramas, comedies, the mountain films of Arnold Fanck, historical pageants (such as Fritz Lang's *Die Niebelungen*), thrillers, and even semipornography (for example, Richard Oswald's *Prostitution,* 1919). Although many of these genre films may have had individual artistic and entertainment values for the age in which they were made, most important from a historical perspective is the industry's promotion of an innovative subject matter for dramas *(Kammerspielfilme)* and one of the most influential movements in the history of cinema (Expressionism).

The term *Kammerspiel* can be translated as "chamber play," and it was the designation originated by Max Reinhardt, the famous stage director, for an intimate drama to be presented in a small theater. In cinema, this intimacy was achieved through the use of cramped, shadowy backgrounds in a lower- or middle-class milieu, emphasis on the psychological conflicts of individuals caught in a net of oppressive social and economic pressures, and plots confined to a limited time and restricted place. Two devices advocated by the screenwriter Carl Mayer, though not always accepted by his colleagues, was nameless characters (designated only by roles) and, more startling, the elimination of titles in these silent films. The latter may

have encouraged visual continuity, but it also led to narrow, oversimplified characterizations.

Typical *Kammerspielfilme* include Leopold Jessner's *Backstairs (Hintertreppe,* 1921, codirected by Paul Leni), Lupu Pick's *Shattered Fragments (Scherben,* 1921), Paul Czinner's *Nju* (1924), and F. W. Murnau's *The Last Laugh.* With the exception of *Nju,* the screenplays for each of these films was written by Carl Mayer. The basic plot of *Shattered Fragments* indicates the story line favored by the screenwriter for this type of drama: A railroadman's daughter is seduced by an arrogant inspector; the young woman's mother dies of exposure while praying for her daughter at a roadside cross; the father, prompted by his daughter, kills the lover and gives himself up. The sole title card appears when the railroadman announces that he is a murderer.

A special category consists of "street films," *Kammerspielfilme*, in which city streets, with their temptations and community spirit, were the main place settings. Two examples are Karl Grüne's *The Street (Die Straße,* 1923) and G. W. Pabst's *Joyless Street.*

Many *Kammerspielfilme* took advantage of some of the techniques initiated by the contemporary movement of Expressionism (as noted later), but its approach was closer to Realism. Whereas Realism focuses on the objective world, Expressionism emphasizes subjective experiences. Although the impulse toward this form of expression manifested itself in the art of previous ages, it was the romantic artists of the nineteenth century who laid the foundation for the movement that emerged in Germany about 1900. More immediate forerunners of Expressionism were, among others, Wedekind and Strindberg in drama; Dostoevski in fiction; Rimbaud and the other French Symbolists in poetry; Vincent van Gogh and Edvard Munch in painting; Nietzsche, Schopenhauer, and Bergson in philosophy; Freud in psychology (*The Interpretation of Dreams* was published in Germany in 1900); and Max Reinhardt through his theater productions. Also influential was Marx's criticism of capitalism. From these diverse sources developed in Germany a more or less coherent interpretation of reality expressed by means of, depending on the medium, certain specific styles and devices.

---

*pp. 211–212

In German cinema, the Expressionistic techniques that became characteristic included dramatic lighting (or *film chiaroscuro*), distortion through special effects (for example, superimposition, slow motion, and stop-action), stylized sets and costumes, an exaggerated acting style, unnatural makeup, unusual camera angles, and abrupt transitions between shots and scenes. These devices and others projected on the screen a character's or director's subjective point of view and created an eerie or threatening *Stimmung* (mood or atmosphere).

The themes favored by film Expressionists were derived principally from those that emerged in works influenced by this movement in the other arts, such as the drama of Georg Kaiser and Ernst Toller; the poetry of Georg Trakl and Ernst Stadler; the fiction of Franz Werfel and Alfred Döblin; the paintings of Franz Marc, Wassily Kandinsky, Oskar Kokoschka, and many others; and the sculpture of Ernst Barlach. Chief among these themes was the need for emancipation from the restrictions of bourgeois values, condemnation of the pressures of mass society that vitiate the freedom of the individual, confidence that the artist can play a role in revitalizing society, and a belief in the validity of insights into human nature that can come from abnormal states of mind, particularly insanity.

A tentative effort to bring Expressionism to the German screen was released in 1913. *The Student of Prague* (*Der Student von Prag,* directed by Stellan Rye) is the story of a young man who sells his mirror image to a mysterious stranger. A year later, Paul Wegener and Henrik Galeen, inspired by *The Student of Prague,* made *The Golem* (*Der Golem*). Unfortunately, this drama of a monster created in a Prague Jewish ghetto has disappeared (Wegener made a second version in 1920).

Other efforts in the direction of cinematic Expressionism were only preludes to the first film indisputably in this style, *The Cabinet of Dr. Caligari* (*Das Cabinett des Dr. Caligari,* 1919, directed by Robert Wiene). In the framing story, a young man relates to an acquaintance a tale concerning Dr. Caligari (Werner Krauss), the master of Cesare (Conrad Veidt), a somnambulist who murders at his bidding. After Cesare dies in an attempt to kidnap Jane (Lil Dagover),

the hero's beloved, Caligari is revealed as the director of an insane asylum. At the end of the film, however, we return to the framing story and learn that it is the young man who is insane and that "Caligari" is actually a benevolent psychiatrist attempting to cure him. The tale is projected on the screen with grotesque sets, chiaroscuro lighting, and stylized acting (see Figures 1.34 and 1.44). When released, the drama caused a sensation in Europe and the United States.

The original screenplay by Carl Mayer and Hans Janowitz did not include a framing story. The screenwriters maintained that the Expressionistic techniques needed no rational justification (a tale told by a madman) and that this plot addition vitiated the film's allegorical meaning: Germany (Cesare) was suspended in a nightmare world when the kaiser and the military (Caligari) dominated the country. The two authors could not persuade Erich Pommer, the producer, and Fritz Lang, who was to have been the director, of the validity of their argument. In a fascinating commentary on the film, Siegfried Kracauer offers his explanation of why the Mayer-Janowitz condemnation of authoritarianism was resisted.[1]

Cinematic Expressionism as presented in Wiene's film led to a problem: Most viewers grew impatient when required to sit through over 2 hours at silent speed[2] of bizarreness. It became evident to filmmakers who wanted to appeal to mass audiences that the approach of Expressionism would have to be integrated with more conventional modes of expression. Very few commercial films after 1919 were as uncompromising in style as *The Cabinet of Dr. Caligari.* In the twenties, manifestations of Expressionism in the silent films of Germany, therefore, appeared in two types of films.

*Caligarism* is the term coined by French critics to describe works in which the techniques of Expressionism are appropriate to the preoccupation of members of the movement with the fantastic, the abnormal, and the grotesque. Realistic scenes are included, but the Expressionistic ones are most prominent. Into this category fit the early films of Lang, especially *Destiny;* most of the early works of Murnau, particularly *Nosferatu;* Wiene's post-*Caligari* dramas, such as *Genuine* (1920), *I.N.R.I.* (1923), and *The Hands of Orlac* (*Orlacs Hände,* 1924); Paul Leni's fantasy *Wax-*

works (*Das Wachsfigurenkabinett,* 1924); Arthur von Gerlach's *Vanina* (1922) and *Chronicles of the Gray House* (*Die Chronik von Grieshuus,* 1925); Arthur Robinson's *Warning Shadows* (*Schatten,* 1923); and G. W. Pabst's *Secrets of a Soul* (1926).

In a second type of German silent drama, Expressionism is subordinated to Realism. Many directors of *Kammerspielfilme* took advantage of some Expressionistic techniques to intensify the psychological implications of their intimate dramas. This combination of styles is discussed at length in the essay on *Variety* in Chapter 5. Other examples include most of the later films of Murnau (such as *The Last Laugh* and *Sunrise*), the silent works of Pabst and E. W. Dupont, Leopold Jessner's *Backstairs* (1921), and Lupu Pick's *Shattered Fragments* and *Sylvester* (1923). Lang preferred after 1921 a fusion of Expressionistic techniques with fantasy and myth, as in *Metropolis,* the Dr. Mabuse films, and *Die Nibelungen.*

What future filmmakers throughout the world learned from Expressionism (which ended as a movement by the mid-twenties) was that subjective states of mind could be projected physically on the screen and that the manipulation of set designs, lighting, camera angles, and other components of cinema could contribute to a tone of danger and charged feelings in a drama. It is in this sense that we refer to the influence of this movement on Bergman, Welles, Hitchcock, Fellini, and others.

The names of most of the prominent directors of Germany's Golden Age were listed in referring to *Kammerspielfilme* and Expressionistic films. Three of these—Fritz Lang, F. W. Murnau, and G. W. Pabst—towered above their contemporaries.

Fritz Lang (1890–1976) had not only a distinguished career but also a long and active one. From 1919 to 1960 he directed 41 feature films in Germany and the United States (and one in France). Although never less than a complete professional in any of his works, his enduring fame rests predominantly on the films he created in Germany between 1921 and 1931.

Lang was born and brought up in Vienna. After studying architecture and then painting in his youth and being decorated for bravery during World War I while serving in the Austrian army, he entered the German film industry. Erich Pommer's Decla-Bioscop

Company employed him as a screenwriter, story editor, and film editor; in 1919 he directed his first film. Two years later he completed a work that established him as one of Germany's most promising directors.

*Destiny* (*Der Möde Tod,* 1921) depicts the efforts of a young woman to persuade Death to return her fiancé (Figure 4.2) and the incarnations of her beloved and herself in three different time and place settings in the past. There is a combination of detailed realism and telling Expressionistic scenes. No one who has seen the film can easily forget the shots of a portion of the wall surrounding Death's residence dissolving and the young woman entering the hall of candles, each one the soul of a human being.

The two-part *Dr. Mabuse, the Gambler* (*Dr. Mabuse, der Spieler,* 1922) ostensibly deals with the nefarious acts of a master criminal, but the actual subject is the decadence and corruption of post–World War I Germany. Lang returned to Dr. Mabuse in two later films. Two years of preparation and 7 months of studio shooting were devoted to the two-part *Die Nibelungen* (1924), a cinematic version of the medieval epic. Setting and design predominate, especially in part one, to the point where the actors appear to be puppets rather than characters.

A more humanized spectacle, enlivened with Expressionistic techniques, is *Metropolis* (1926). The time setting is the future. Workers live in a subterranean portion of the city and produce for the benefit of a small group of aristocratic masters. A revolt of the masses almost destroys the city, but a final reconciliation of "the hand and the mind" is achieved through the mediation of "the heart" (the love interest in the film). The plot at times seems awkwardly constructed —especially in the English version, from which a third of the footage is omitted—and some of the dialogue (title cards) and actions are ridiculous by today's standards. The shots of the city, the underground industries, the mass meetings, and the flood, however, are truly remarkable.

*Spies* (*Spione,* 1928), another master-criminal thriller, and *The Woman on the Moon* (*Die Frau im Mond,* 1929), a science fiction tale with little of the vitality of *Metropolis,* preceded *M* (1931), Lang's first sound film and his most completely realized work of art. The screenplay, by Thea von Harbou, is based on

**FIGURE 4.2**

*Destiny,* 1921, directed by Fritz Lang. The Girl (Lil Dagover) faces Death (Bernhard Goetzke) at the entrance to his mansion and begs that her fiancé be returned to life.

the actual case of Peter Kürten, who in the mid-twenties in Düsseldorf killed 10 children. As the film opens, a German city is in terror of a murderer who, because he follows instinct instead of logic in committing his crimes, has undermined the citizenry's confidence in moral order and authority. Disturbed by police harassment, the various unions of criminals initiate their own search for the outsider, the Murderer. It is the criminals who first capture him, and at a kangaroo court they condemn him to death. Meanwhile, however, the police, through their own methods, have identified the Murderer and have learned of his capture. They arrive just as he is going to be executed.

Lang develops his plot with remarkable fluency and ingenuity. The means by which he crosscuts be-

tween the Murderer, the police, and the criminals, yet keeps the action moving forward in time were innovative in 1931. Setting and lighting create an aura of mystery that is an essential element of this psychological thriller (see Figure 1.40). The sound is organically integrated into the plot to a degree previously achieved only by René Clair in France. Peter Lorre as the Murderer is outstanding, especially in his final monologue, with his unforgettable cry, *"Ich kann nicht"* ("I can't go on") (Figure 4.3). *M,* in fact, fully satisfies the ultimate touchstone of a film classic: Viewing it is as impressive a cinematic experience today as it was when it first appeared more than 50 years ago.

Lang's last film in Germany until after World War II was *The Crimes of Dr. Mabuse* (*Das Testament des Dr. Mabuse,* 1933), which brings back the mad doctor in another melodrama.

One of the reasons for the success of Lang's German films was that he had such eminent col-

**FIGURE 4.3**

*M,* 1931, directed by Fritz Lang. Franz Becker (Peter Lorre), a murderer of children, confesses his crimes before a jury of criminals.

laborators, among them Erich Pommer (producer), Fritz Arno Wagner and Karl Freund (directors of photography), and Walter Röhrig, Otto Hunte, and Karl Vollbrecht (art directors). The director's most important colleague, however, was Thea von Harbou (1888–1954). She had a reputation as a novelist before she met Lang and later married him in 1921. Each of the director's films from 1920 to 1933 was based on a screenplay by von Harbou, either original, adapted from another source, or derived from her own fiction *(Metropolis, Spies,* and *Die Frau im Mond).* She also collaborated with Carl Dreyer, Joe May, and F. W. Murnau. With such a record of achievement, she was the only screenwriter in Germany in the twenties to challenge the preeminence of Carl Mayer.

In the late twenties, von Harbou and Lang formed divergent attitudes toward the National Socialists. While *M* was being made, she became a member of the Nazi party. After Lang fled Germany, the two were divorced in 1934. Von Harbou went on to direct films and write screenplays that were approved by the Nazi authorities. After the war, she returned to fiction.

For today's audiences, Lang's tendencies toward melodrama and metaphysical pretentiousness undermine the effectiveness of the narrative dimension of his silent films. Yet his characters are not entirely caricatures. If the worst exaggerations are ig-

nored, Dr. Mabuse is an intriguing Lucifer of crime, and Rotwang in *Metropolis* is not without his fascinating aspects, especially when a viewer is aware of certain motivations omitted from the English version. And there is the striking figure of Death in *Destiny,* as well as the touching devotion of the young woman. Yet melodrama and epic situations did allow Lang to preserve a distance between himself and his material, and most of his films suffer from the director's aloofness and manipulation rather than involvement in feelings.

Post–World War II critics have been uneasy also about the recurrent theme of the operation of "blind destiny" in the fate of the characters in Lang's early major films. Like a twentieth-century Thomas Hardy, the director demonstrates over and over again that no matter what choices people make, they are trapped in an inexorable destiny. This is perhaps the inevitable vision of an artist who said repeatedly in interviews that we are all the children of Cain. None of us, therefore, is free of guilt, and one misstep is all that is necessary to drive an individual down a slippery road into a personal abyss of crime and retribution.

Whatever Lang's deficiencies in projecting genuine emotions through his characters and his pessimism about human fate, he was a cinematic craftsman with few peers in the silent and early sound years. He controlled a film's structure so that shots, scenes, and sequences flowed ingeniously from one into the other. This control is evident in his adroit handling of groups or masses of people. By working entirely in studios and paying meticulous attention to details of setting, he was able to relate architecture to characters. We get the impression that his actors are living in rather than merely passing through an environment. Moreover, he used camera-editing dynamics, lighting, and, later, sound to generate atmosphere *(Stimmung)* in his scenes. In his early years Lang was attracted to Expressionism; by the time he directed *M,* he had left behind many of the tenets of the movement but had distilled its techniques into devices (such as forms of chiaroscuro and dreams) that he incorporated into his style.

In 1933 the director left Germany in protest against the censorship exerted by Joseph Goebbels, the Nazi propaganda minister, and out of fear it would soon be discovered that his mother had been Jewish. He directed *Liliom* (1934) for Erich Pommer, who was now working in France. This fantasy did not suit Lang's style, and the result was one of the director's lesser works. Metro-Goldwyn-Mayer hired him, and he arrived in Hollywood in 1934. He was to live and work there, with the exception of a few years spent in Germany after World War II, for the rest of his life.

The first two films Lang made in the United States are similar in subject. In *Fury* (1936), the victim of a lynch mob escapes and avenges himself. *You Only Live Once* (1937) describes how a man framed for murder actually becomes a murderer and is finally killed by the police. The melodramatic plots and the themes of the roles of fate and guilt in the lives of human beings relate these films to the director's previous work. Such connections are more difficult to trace in the 20 films that followed, the most successful of which include *The Return of Frank James* (1940), *Western Union* (1941), *Ministry of Fear* (1944), *The Woman in the Window* (1944), *Scarlet Street* (1945), *An American Guerrilla in the Philippines* (1950), *Rancho Notorious* (1952), *Clash by Night* (1952), and *While the City Sleeps* (1956). Lang's last two films were made in Germany: *Der Tiger von Eschnapur* (1958–1959), in two parts, and *Die tausend Augen des Dr. Mabuse* (1960). They added little to his reputation.

Lang's American films have been a source of controversy. Peter Bogdanovich, who wrote a book on this period of the director's career, and others praise them highly. Most critics, on the other hand, while admiring their intelligence and craftsmanship, find that they lacked the brilliance of his German works. Lang's own comments through the years suggest that he was never completely at home working for studios that placed the highest premium on commercial success. Perhaps there is more truth than fiction in the presentation of Lang in Jean-Luc Godard's *Contempt* (*Le Mépris,* 1963). Lang plays himself as a director who preserves an inner integrity and sensible pragmatism about the project at hand as he contends with an egotistical, ruthless producer.

Friedrich Wilhelm Murnau (1888–1931) is without doubt one of the greatest directors of the silent era. After working as an actor and assistant director in the theater under the supervision of Max Reinhardt, Murnau directed his first motion picture in 1919; unfortunately, of the 13 films he made before 1924, 9 have been lost. But even the titles of some of these early works indicate a fascination with the demonic and the mysterious: *Satanas* (1919), *Janus-Faced* (*Der Januskopf,* 1920, an adaptation of Stevenson's *The Strange Case of Dr. Jekyll and Mr. Hyde*), *Haunted Castle* (*Schloß Vogelöd,* 1921), and *Phantom* (1922). His most important work of this period is *Nosferatu* (1922), based on Bram Stoker's *Dracula.* In this classic horror film, the director makes masterful use of Expressionistic techniques to underscore a grotesque plot with latent sexual implications.

*The Last Laugh* (*Der Letzte Mann,* 1924) represents a shift for Murnau from Caligarism to a blend of the approaches of *Kammerspielfilme* and cinematic Expressionism. The plot deals with the travails of a doorman at a luxury hotel (superbly played by Emil Jannings) (see Figure 1.46) who is demoted to a washroom attendant, resulting in his being ostracized by his proletarian family and friends. A fantasy epilogue is delightful, but it constitutes a radical, disconcerting shift in tone from tragedy to comedy. The work is a *Kammerspielfilm* in its complete absence of titles, its lower-class hero, its implied social criticism in the contrast between the lives of the wealthy in the hotel and the poor in the slums, the lack of proper names for characters, and the simple, narrow scope of the dramatic situation. Subordinate but impressive are the elements of Expressionism: dramatic lighting, a stylized backdrop representing a tenement, and a subjective camera (hallucinations, distorted perceptions, and a dream) (Figure 4.4). Also important is a more extensive and innovative use than in any previous drama of the moving camera: The doorman is followed wherever he goes.

After *The Last Laugh,* Murnau directed two adaptations of classics—*Tartüff* (1925) and *Faust* (1926). He was persuaded by William Fox to journey to Hollywood in 1926. Three films resulted from this association before Murnau became disillusioned by the studio system. Sound was awkwardly added to both *Four Devils* (1928) and *City Girl* (or *Our Daily Bread,* 1929). The director's first motion picture in the United States, however, stands out as an unforgettable drama. The screenplay for *Sunrise* (1927) was by Carl Mayer, based on a Hermann Sudermann story. It cen-

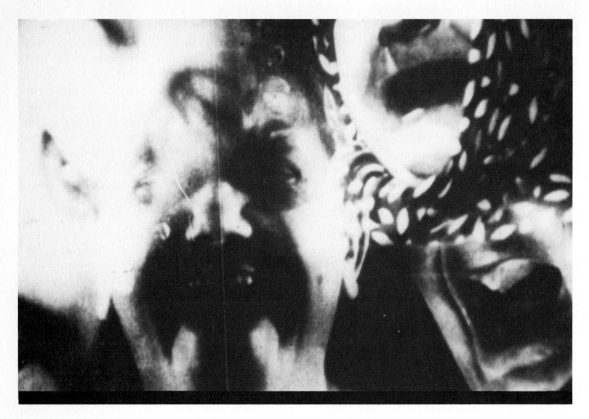

**FIGURE 4.4**

*The Last Laugh,* 1924, directed by F. W. Murnau. The Doorman (Emil Jannings) has been demoted to washroom attendant. In an Expressionistic shot, he imagines that his neighbors are laughing at him.

ters on a love triangle involving the Man (a farmer), the Woman from the City, and the Wife. Murnau took advantage of Expressionistic techniques to add a mythic dimension to the plot. The Man experiences an archetypal journey in which he is ensnared by a modern version of *la belle dame sans merci* but finally comes to appreciate the Christian virtues, personified by the Wife, of pure love and the security of the home. There is a juxtaposition of realistic scenes and mysterious, dreamlike ones—magnificently realized—for example, when the farmer meets the temptress in the woods under a full moon (Figure 4.5), in the dance hall of an entertainment park, and the trip back on a lake.

Murnau's last film was *Tabu* (1931) made in

association with Robert Flaherty on a South Pacific island.* Just before its premiere, the director was killed, at the age of 43, in an automobile accident.

Georg Wilhelm Pabst (1885–1967) was born in Austria and, like Murnau, first acted and directed in the theater. The film that established his reputation, his third, was *Joyless Street* (*Die Freudlose Gasse,* 1925). It contains the characteristics that remained with him during his creative period of less than a decade. The melodramatic plot set in Vienna highlights the effects of a collapsed economy on middle- and lower-class families, a situation taken advantage of by storekeepers, especially a villainous butcher, and by a procuress. Vehement social criticism is evident throughout. With a few exceptions—such as *Secrets of the Soul* (*Geheimnisse einer Seele,* 1926), an exploration of the dream world—this is the main thematic intention of Pabst. Even the erotic *Pandora's*

*p. 352

**FIGURE 4.5**

*Sunrise,* 1927, directed by F. W. Murnau. The Man (George O'Brien) secretly meets the Woman from the City (Margaret Livingston) at night in the light of a full moon. The director imbues the scene with a mythic aura of primordial passion reminiscent of the imagery in the works of Edvard Munch, an Expressionistic painter.

**FIGURE 4.6**

*Joyless Street,* 1925, directed by G. W. Pabst. Greta Garbo plays the role of Greta Rumfort. Although her family lives in poverty, she resists the temptations and moral corruption of post–World War I Vienna.

*Box* (*Die Büchse der Pandora,* 1928), based on Frank Wedekind's play, is transformed by the director into a demonstration of the decadence of bourgeois and upper-class German life.

*Joyless Street* also illustrates how his *Kammerspiel* approach is enlivened by chiaroscuro lighting and sets that reveal the influence of Expressionism. More personal is a fluency of camera-editing dynamics comparable to that of Murnau. Pabst's gift for choosing and bringing out the best in actresses resulted in one of Asta Neilson's finest performances and an impressive one by a relatively unknown actress named Greta Garbo (Figure 4.6). The same Svengalian power operates on Edith Jehanne in *The Love of Jeanne Ney* (*Die Liebe der Jeanne Ney,* 1927), another of the director's outstanding silent films.

*Westfront 1918* (1930), an antiwar drama, was Pabst's first sound motion picture. *The Threepenny Opera* (*Die Dreigroschenoper,* 1931) is an exceptional musical derived from the Brecht-Weill play.* The unity of the proletariat is emphasized in *Comradeship* (*Kameradschaft,* 1931). With his leftist political convictions, it was inevitable that Pabst would

have to leave Germany when the Nazi party came to power. He worked in France and for a brief period in Hollywood, but he seemed to have lost his vitality. Although after 1945 he directed a dozen films in Austria, Italy, and Germany, he matched his former achievements only in *The Trial* (*Der Prozeß,* 1947), an attack on anti-Semitism.

With Hitler at the helm of the German state, the country's great film industry degenerated, and its activities were confined to escapist entertainment and propaganda.

### USSR

In Russia during the twenties, other momentous advances in cinema were in the making. The prerevolutionary film industry was active, but it released undistinguished productions, with such exceptions as the motion pictures made by the eminent stage director and theorist V. E. Meyerhold. All this was changed by the Bolshevik Revolution of 1917 and the civil war (1918–1920) that followed it.

Like so many other activities in the country at that time, the early years of film production and study in the Soviet Union were confused and fervent. By the early twenties, certain characteristics had emerged that were to influence the Russian motion picture in-

*p. 442

dustry to our time. As soon as it gained power, the Soviet government encouraged and completely controlled film production, convinced that motion pictures were the most effective means of propaganda. An indication of how vital the state considered film to its cause was the establishment in 1919, amid civil war and economic chaos, of a national film school. The Institute of Cinematography (VGIK) in Moscow was the first such institute in the world. Facilities during its initial years were woefully inadequate. Only antiquated equipment was at hand, money was scarce, foreign films for study were unobtainable because of the Allied blockade, and, most detrimental, little film stock was available. The consequence was an emphasis by teachers on theory, and no country in the world during the twenties produced more writing on film theory by practicing filmmakers than the USSR.

Fortunately for the students at VGIK, they had inspired teachers. The most prominent of these was Lev Kuleshov (1899–1970). He began directing and writing about cinema just before the Revolution and was a prime organizer of VGIK. The best known of the films he directed—in the twenties and early thirties until his aesthetic concerns were condemned by the state—was *The Death Ray* (*Lucksmerti,* 1925). It was Kuleshov who explored and propagated through his classes and his own work the concept of dynamic montage.

In Chapter 1, *montage* was defined as a form of creative editing. The Russians' views differed from, say, Griffith's editing of *Intolerance* (one of the few contemporary films available for study at VGIK) in developing a coherent, comprehensive theory and advocating it as a principal means of cinematic expression. Kuleshov demonstrated in his class experiments that an audience's reactions to an individual shot were influenced by the shots that preceded and followed it; that is, a cinematic narrative is constructed on the basis of a juxtaposition of related shots. Kuleshov and his associates went further. By imaginative editing and the introduction of images unrelated to but associatively connected with the narrative, they were able to generate feelings and ideas in a viewer that would not have existed without such creative editing. In short, a series of shots became more than a sum of its parts.

Kuleshov believed that *dynamic montage* serves three functions. The first is to further the narrative. An example is crosscutting during a chase sequence. Griffith was already a master of this type of montage when he directed *Intolerance.*

The creating or manipulating of the viewer's emotional responses is the second function. This concept is based on the premise that the elements of a shot (such as distance, angle, and movement) have emotional connotations. When these elements are juxtaposed appropriately with the same elements in the shots that follow, new feelings are elicited from an audience or nascent ones aroused by a single shot are developed. For instance, in Pudovkin's *Mother,* a clash between two opposing groups is anticipated and underscored when strikers move consistently from left to right and the police, in separate shots, from right to left.

The third function of dynamic montage is to instill an intellectual response in an audience—that is, to bring into being through associations of images an idea that is not inherent in the narrative dimension. A famous example appears in *Strike,* Eisenstein's first feature. Cossacks mercilessly attack a group of strikers. Cut to shots of animals being slaughtered. The idea is created in the mind of the viewer that the troops act like butchers killing animals.

Ideally, all three functions of dynamic montage operate simultaneously during a scene. According to Kuleshov and his followers, the attempt to attain this ideal through editing is the foundation of the art of cinema.

In Chapter 1, the characteristics of montage are compared to those of the *mise-en-scène* approach.* In the "Background" section of the essay on *October* in Chapter 5,† the matrix of dynamic montage, particularly Karl Marx's dialectic materialism, is discussed, as is Eisenstein's complex and sophisticated interpretation of the theories of his teacher, Kuleshov.

Practically all the major directors of the silent era of Soviet cinema used dynamic montage extensively. There is a problem of terminology related to this fact that has not yet been resolved by film histori-

---

*pp. 37–41
†pp. 224–225

ans. As pointed out in Chapter 1, the term *montage* is often applied to any creative editing at any time and in any country. In these pages, the Russians' elevation of montage from a method of editing to a fundamental principle of filmmaking, with ramifications in content as well as style, has been indicated by adding the adjective *dynamic*. An inevitable question arises: Since there were interrelations among the directors and similarities in the form and feeling of their films derived from a mutual commitment to dynamic montage, should not this approach also be considered a movement? Most historians of cinema feel the answer to this question is no; however, to preserve a consistency with Realism and Expressionism, the designation will be used in this book as applying to a movement as well as an approach to filmmaking. Dynamic Montage applies to Soviet directors from approximately 1918 to the end of the silent era, when socialist realism became predominant. Its characteristics include an emphasis on dynamic montage to produce epic films in support of the communist system with proletarians or farmers as heroes or the proletariat itself as a composite hero.

The editing techniques of the movement profoundly influenced filmmakers in other countries. The themes and propagandistic bias were less exportable. The concept of an epic, Marxist vision of history, however, did inspire Renoir in his *La Marseillaise,* Bertolucci in *1900,* many Eastern European directors (Jancsó, for example), and others. The theme of proletarians and their problems under economically and politically oppressive systems encouraged a cinema of social criticism in many countries, especially British and American documentaries of the thirties, the movement of Neorealism in Italy during the late forties and the fifties, and the early films of such British New Wave directors as Karel Reisz, Tony Richardson, and Lindsay Anderson.

During the silent era, the most significant Soviet directors were Sergei Eisenstein, Dziga Vertov, V. I. Pudovkin, and Alexander Dovzhenko. Eisenstein's life and work are surveyed in Chapter 5.* The contributions of Vertov are summarized in Chapter 7.†

*pp. 221–226
†pp. 342–343

Vsevolod Ilarionvich Pudovkin (1893–1953) directed his first fiction feature, *Mother (Mat),* in 1926. This was the initial film of a trilogy on what he called "crises of conscience," in which individuals are torn between reactionary and revolutionary forces. In *Mother,* based on a Maxim Gorky novel, the title character wavers between commitment to her husband, a strikebreaker, and her son, a Bolshevik; in the end, she joins her son, and the two are killed in a clash with the police (Figure 4.7). The other two works in the trilogy are *The End of St. Petersburg (Konyets Sankt-Peterburga,* 1927) and *Storm Over Asia* or *The Heir to Genghis Khan (Potomok Chingis-Khan,* 1928). Pudovkin's sound films, such as *A Simple Case (Prostoi sluchai,* 1932) and *Deserter* (1933), are interesting, but they are not up to the quality of his silent works.

**FIGURE 4.7**

*Mother,* 1926, directed by V. I. Pudovkin. Pelageya Vlasova (Vera Baranovskaya) is converted to Communism. At the end of the film, she picks up a banner near the body of her son and faces a charge of mounted police.

Illness resulting from an automobile accident kept the director in retirement between 1934 and 1938. When he returned to filmmaking, his style was in conflict with the precepts of socialist realism, and he was forced to confine himself to undistinguished historical re-creations. His last film, *The Harvest* or *The Return of Vassili Bortnikov (Vozvrashchenie Vassiliya Bortnikova,* 1953), contains at least some of the imaginativeness of his early dramas.

Pudovkin prepared detailed, carefully structured screenplays and dominated his actors. His style differed from that of Eisenstein in his emphasis on well-developed, individual characters gripped by inner conflicts caused by political issues. Another contrast with Eisenstein was the form and accent of his dynamic montage. His editing was primarily in the service of the narrative. Even in his intellectual and emotional types of dynamic montage, he favored the third element of the Marxian dialectic ("thesis, antithesis, synthesis"), whereas his famous colleague stressed conflict between thesis and antithesis. In short, he was more humanistic in his dramas than Eisenstein.

Pudovkin was always interested in acting and performed in his own and others' films. His lectures on film acting delivered in Moscow in 1926 constitute the first incisive treatise on the subject. Also important were his comments on that occasion on filmmaking. His *Film Technique and Film Acting* (published in London in 1929) is a classic of film theory comparable to Eisenstein's *Film Sense* and *Film Form*.

Alexander Dovzhenko (1894–1956), born in the Ukraine, was at his best when the settings of his works were his native area. His most famous silent films are *Arsenal* (1929) and *Earth* (*Zemlya,* 1930). His thirties sound features—*Ivan* (1932), *Frontier* (*Aerograd,* 1935), and *Shchors* (1939)—are passionate dramas, and they demonstrate that unlike Pudovkin, he was capable of successfully making the transition from silent to sound filmmaking. During World War II, Dovzhenko directed or supervised outstanding documentaries.* Before his death, he began but left unfinished *Poem of the Sea* (*Poema o more,* 1958), on events in a Ukrainian village before, during, and after the war; it was completed by Dovzhenko's wife, Yulia Soltseva.

He was as devoted as other Russian film directors of his time to support of the communist system. He differed from his contemporaries, however, in an equal commitment to the land and to the people who live close to nature. Dovzhenko's work has a bardic, lyric quality not to be found in the city-oriented films of Eisenstein, Pudovkin, and Vertov.

*p. 338

Other notable Soviet directors of the silent era are Ivan Perestiani, Abram Room, Yuli Raisman, and Nicholai Ekk.

### FRANCE

French filmmakers of the silent era were preoccupied with the *grandeur* of their country's history, realism, and experimental techniques; at times these three tendencies conflicted with each other.

The most exciting and innovative director of the period was Abel Gance (1889–1981). The first distinctive film he directed was *La Folie du Docteur Tube* (1915), a fantasy containing startling effects. After completing four additional dramas, he achieved a popular success with *J'accuse* (*I Accuse,* 1919), an antiwar film that included documentary footage of trench warfare and ended with a spectacular sequence on a split screen of dead soldiers rising up from the battlefield. *La Roue* (1922) employed creative editing that paralleled the approach of dynamic montage being developed in Russia at the time.

Gance's masterwork is *Napoléon* (1927). Two years in the making, the epic is 4 hours long and includes practically every cinematic technique known at the time and a few that were new (such as a final sequence using three screens that anticipated Cinerama). In addition to the concluding sequence, two others—a snowball fight at a military school involving the adolescent Napoleon and crosscutting between the Corsican alone on a boat in a storm and a near riot in the French Assembly—are breathtaking in their dramatic power and visual imaginativeness. Thanks to the tireless efforts of Kevin Brownlow, the British historian and director, the film was recently reconstructed from various edited prints and presented in practically its original form. If Gance had directed only *Napoléon,* there would still be justification for ranking him as an equal of the finest directors of the silent era, including Griffith, Eisenstein, Murnau, and Dreyer.

The director never again had the opportunity to match the scope and verve of this epic. For the rest of his career, he was to alternate between experimental shorts, such as those that make up *Magirama* (1956), and historical spectacles (for example, *Un grand amour de Beethoven,* 1936; *The Tower of*

*Lust, La Tour de Nesle,* 1954, his first color film; *Austerlitz,* 1960; and *Cyrano et D'Artagnan,* 1964). The recent revival of interest in Gance's work will doubtless intensify with the screenings of *Napoléon.*

No French director of the silent era was comparable in stature to Gance. Louis Feuillade, before his death in 1925, made immensely popular series on the master criminal Fantômas, on a gang of criminals *(Les Vampires),* and on the superhero Judex. Far more realistic were the early efforts of Jean Epstein on life in the city (such as *Coeur fidèle,* 1923) and in the country (for example, *La Belle Nivernaise,* 1923). Before returning to a semidocumentary style in a cycle of films on the life of Breton fishermen, beginning with *Finis terrae* (1928), he explored the capabilities of cinema by using such techniques as slow motion to create mystery and to represent abnormal states of mind in *The Fall of the House of Usher (La Chute de la Maison Usher,* 1928) and other works.

Two outstanding directors who began their careers in the twenties were Jean Renoir* and Jacques Feyder (1887–1948). Feyder's first major success was *L'Atlantide* (1921), and he continued to direct outstanding silent films, including *Crainquebille* (1923) and *Thérèse Raquin* (1928, an adaptation of Zola's novel and made in Berlin). After an unproductive period in Hollywood, he returned to France in the mid-thirties. Here he created his best-known work, *Carnival in Flanders (La Kermesse héroïque,* 1935). Set in seventeenth-century Flanders, it is a superb farce graced by the hallmarks of Feyder's style: fluent camera movement, a sureness of tone derived from painstaking attention to details of setting and costume, and an ability to draw convincing and robust characterizations from his actors. Feyder continued to direct films until the late forties, but the quality of his work declined after *Carnival in Flanders.*

The avant-garde narrative film, most often consisting of short works, flourished in France during the twenties. The principle inspiration for this activity was *Surrealism.* This movement had its origins in Dadaism. During World War I, Tristan Tzara and Hans Arp —later joined by painters Francis Picabia and Marcel Duchamp, writers Paul Eluard and Louis Aragon, and

others—insisted on a rejection of tradition and rationalism in favor of a conscious madness as a protest against what they considered the destruction of civilized life by the war. In 1924, André Breton issued his *Manifeste du surréalisme,* and the precepts of the earlier movement were made more coherent, politically oriented, and intellectually respectable.

Breton and his followers drew not only on the principles of Dadaism but also on the French Symbolist poets' advocacy of derangement of the senses and on the theories of Freud. They asserted that only by extracting images and symbols from the unconscious and joining them by the "logic" of the dream world could a "superrealism" be created and the individual be freed of religious and societal restrictions. Surface reality might be maintained; however, the juxtaposition of its elements would be determined by an unfettered imagination rather than an artificial construct of the intellect.

Breton was supported in his efforts by such painters as Max Ernst, Giorgio di Chirico, and Salvador Dali, the poets Eluard and Aragon, and the theater of Antonin Artaud. Although Breton continued to propagate his ideas until his death in 1966, Surrealism ceased to exist as a vital movement after the early thirties.

The ability of cinema to present a concrete reality, yet at the same time fragment and reconstruct it so that a dreamlike ambiance could be created, appealed greatly to the Surrealists. The first genuine manifestation of this movement in cinema is generally considered to be Germaine Dulac's *The Seashell and the Clergyman (La Coquille et le Clergyman,* 1928). The quintessential Surrealistic film, however, is Luis Buñuel and Salvador Dali's *Un Chien Andalou (The Andalusian Dog,* 1928) (Figure 4.8). Another collaboration between the two artists in the same style was the sound film *The Age of Gold (L'Age d'Or,* 1930). Other uncompromising contributors to the movement were Man Ray in the twenties and Jacques Brunius in the thirties.

The influence of Surrealism is immediately evident in certain works of Jean Cocteau and Georges Franju in France and Hans Richter in Germany. More indirect influences can be discerned in films that contain lengthy dream sequences or a reality suffused

*pp. 122–125

**FIGURE 4.8**

**FIGURE 4.8**

*Un Chien Andalou,* 1928, directed by Luis Buñuel. In this classic Surrealistic work, a young man (Pierre Batcheff) contemplates, like a dreamworld Hamlet, ants crawling in and out of his hand.

with irrational overtones. Examples of films with surrealistic effects include the horror and monster films of James Whale, Bergman's *Wild Strawberries* and *Persona,* and Fellini's *8 ½* and *City of Women.* The major director who more than any other remained loyal to the tenets of Surrealism is Luis Buñuel.*

Not all French avant-garde filmmakers during the twenties were committed to Surrealism, even if surrealistic devices appeared in their works. Louis Delluc was one of the earliest to experiment with innovative techniques, particularly the use of superimposition. One of his most striking works is *Fièvre* (1921). Marcel L'Herbier began with conventional films; soon he incorporated fantastic elements into his narratives, as in *The Late Mattia Pascal* (*Feu Mathias Pascal,* 1925, based on Luigi Pirandello's novel). Before turning to comedy, René Clair made the delightful and absurd short *Entr'acte* (1924). Also belonging in this category of semisurrealistic but definitely avant-garde French cinema are some of the works of Jean Epstein.

### SCANDINAVIA

Only since the 1960s have the accomplishments of major Scandinavian directors of the teens and twen-

ties been given the recognition they deserve. One director, however, was so towering a figure that his films always have been admired and respected, though more by filmmakers and critics than by the general public. Carl Theodor Dreyer (1889–1968) worked in Denmark for a decade as a screenwriter before making his directing debut with *The President* (*Praesidenten,* 1919). During the next 8 years, he was responsible for seven films, including *Leaves From Satan's Book* (*Blade of Satans Bog,* 1919), *The Parson's Widow* (*Prästanken,* 1920), *Michaël* (1924, made in Germany), and *The Bride of Glomsdale* (*Glomsdalsbruden,* 1925).

In 1928 he created his first indisputable masterpiece. *The Passion of Joan of Arc* (*La Passion de Jeanne d'Arc,* 1928, made in France) (Figure 4.9) is a drama of such austere beauty and concentrated emotional intensity that it cannot be compared to any motion picture that preceded it. Falconetti's performance as Joan is unforgettable. The film was a critical success but a financial failure, a pattern that was to haunt Dreyer throughout the remainder of his career. He was to direct only five additional features in the next four decades: *Vampyr* (1931), *Day of Wrath* (*Vredens Dag,* 1943) (Figure 4.10), *Tva Människor* (1945, not released during the director's lifetime),

**FIGURE 4.9**

*The Passion of Joan of Arc,* 1928, directed by Carl Dreyer. Joan is interrogated at her trial. Maria Falconetti as Joan gives a magnificent performance in her first and last appearance on the screen.

*pp. 162–165

**FIGURE 4.10** ─────────

*Day of Wrath,* 1943, directed by Carl Dreyer. At her husband's wake, Anne Pedersson (Lisbeth Movin) confesses she had wished he was dead so that she could marry her stepson. The young woman is aware of what this confession means: Like her mother, she will be burned at the stake for being a witch.

*Ordet* (1955) [see Figures 1.33 and 1.41(b)], and *Gertrud* (1964). During the forties and fifties, Dreyer made 11 shorts, wrote many penetrating essays on cinema, and planned three projects that never were realized: an epic entitled *Jesus,* a version of *Media* in color, and an adaptation of Faulkner's *Light in August.*

Dreyer's work is the epitome of classicism in cinema. He demonstrated to a degree achieved by no other contemporary director that the adage "less can be more" applies to film as well as other arts. He carefully structured the narrative dimension of each drama so that overt action was kept to a minimum. What interested him was earnest feeling, especially as revealed by the human face. Dreyer is the peerless master of the close-up. Objects and gestures assume symbolic proportions because they are focused on so insistently in contexts that allow them slowly to accrue an aura of mystery and subtle overtones. Practically all his films are veined with a counterpoising of objective reality and subjective emotions, of the presence of groups of human beings and the inner loneliness of characters. His women especially suffer but endure, and they are determined, even at the cost of flaunting conventions and social restrictions, to live by their inner convictions of what is life-enhancing. Dreyer was as uncompromising in his art as these fictional women in their lives. Because of both his integrity and his genius, his contribution to the artistic heritage of cinema is an enduring one.

Dreyer and his Scandinavian colleagues did not band together in a self-conscious movement, but much as the Expressionists and Surrealists, they were exploring in their own ways the capabilities of film to reveal the repressed and conflicting desires of human beings. In Sweden, Mauritz Stiller (1883–1928) first gained fame for such epics as *Sir Arne's Treasure* (*Herr Arnes Pengar,* 1919) and lavish productions (for example, *Erotikon,* 1920), yet will be remembered most for the psychological perceptiveness and artistry in two stories of frustrated passion, *Johan* (1921) and *The Saga of Gösta Berling* (*Gösta Berlings Saga,* 1924, which featured Greta Garbo in her first major role). He died in 1928 after an unsuccessful period in Hollywood.

Stiller's countryman and close friend Victor Sjöström (Anglicized as Seastrom) (1879–1960) was a more prolific director for a longer span of time. He began his career in motion pictures as an actor and ended it with a remarkable performance as Isak Borg in Bergman's *Wild Strawberries.* Between 1912 and 1923, he directed more than 40 feature films. His earliest works, such as *Ingeborg Holm* (1913), were preoccupied with social problems. He soon found his true métier in stories of farmers and fishermen in a close contact with nature that bordered on the mystical. His style at times could be ponderous and self-conscious, but at his best he suffused his films with a lyric sensitivity to the beauty and awesomeness of nature. Often the boundaries between reality and illusion were blurred. This approach, made vivid by experiments with cinematic techniques, is evident in one of his most esteemed works, *The Phantom Chariot* (*Körkarlen,* 1920). Among the finest of the director's tales of unsophisticated people contending with and surviving dark forces within themselves and nature are *A Man There Was* (*Terje Vigen,* 1917, based on a poem by Ibsen), *The Girl From the Stormy Craft* (*Tösen fran Stormytorpet,* 1917), and *The Outlaw and His Wife* (*Berg-Ejvind och hans hustric,* 1918).

From 1923 to 1928, Sjöström resided in Hollywood. He was more successful than Stiller in the nine films he directed in the United States, including at least two outstanding works, *The Scarlet Letter* (1926) and *The Wind* (1928). After returning to Sweden, he directed one more drama, then stopped making films,

with the exception of a British production, *Under the Robe* (1937).

After Dreyer, the leading Danish director of the silent period was Benjamin Christensen. His *Witchcraft Through the Ages* (*Häxan,* 1922) is a bizarre, haunting film. He was never again to equal this remarkable work during a filmmaking career that brought him to Germany and Hollywood (where he made *Seven Footsteps to Satan,* 1929).

## OTHER COUNTRIES

Motion picture production in other European countries before sound was less impressive. In England, after the tentative efforts of such men as Cecil Hepworth, only two directors created notable films during the twenties: Graham Cutts, who specialized in thrillers (for example, *The Passionate Adventure,* 1924) and melodramas (such as *The Rat,* 1925, the first in a series), and George Pearson (who made *Squibs,* 1921, and *Reveille,* 1924, among others). Alfred Hitchcock made his debut as a director in 1925 and released nine silent features. Only *The Lodger* (1926) is memorable, and he did not demonstrate fully his unique talents until sound was available. Like Hitchcock, Anthony Asquith will be considered later in this survey; he directed two silent dramas.

Italy early in the history of film production built a reputation for creating historical epics, such as *The Last Days of Pompeii* (*Gli Ultimi Giorni di Pompei,* 1908) and *Quo Vadis?* (1912). One director emerged as a master of this genre. Giovanni Pastrone's most remarkable work is *Cabiria* (1914), on the Second Punic War. A subordinate trend was an emphasis on realistic content and style, exemplified by Febo Mari's *Cenere* (1916, starring the great actress Eleonora Duse). During the twenties and thirties the country's film industry was blighted by fascist censorship.

Austria established a thriving industry after World War I that specialized in adaptations of stage productions and historical spectacles, but the country produced little of particular worth aside from some of the later silent films of Robert Wiene. In Eastern Europe and Spain, the output of motion pictures was small; however, a group of filmmakers in each country gained experience that laid the foundations for less parochial sound films.

## FROM THE ADVENT
## OF SOUND
## TO THE END
## OF WORLD WAR II

### U.S.A.

Although synchronized sound processes for motion pictures were developed in Germany and France, the first practical ones were patented in the United States. After early experiments, a sound-on-disk system called Vitaphone was introduced by Warner Bros. and was first used in *The Jazz Singer* (1927), in which Al Jolson sang songs and spoke two lines of dialogue. The following year Warners released *Lights of New York,* the first all-talking feature film. After a couple of years of apprehension and chaos during which sound tracks were awkwardly added to silent films in progress, Hollywood adjusted to this revolution in motion picture production. By the beginning of the new decade, all new films made in the United States were with sound. Disks were replaced in the early thirties by more dependable and sensitive *optical sound* (the sound track is on the print itself, activated by a photocell).

The studios were ready to take advantage of what was virtually a new medium, and their mode of operation came to be called the *studio system.* Eight companies located in Hollywood monopolized commercial motion picture production in the United States. The "Big Five" were MGM, RKO, Fox, Paramount, and Warner Bros. A notch below in facilities and financial resources were United Artists, Columbia, and Universal. With the exception of United Artists, each operated an entire physical plant. Most of them also owned the theaters in which their products were exhibited. This meant that even the most mediocre production had a guaranteed outlet.

The studio system was organized into a pyramid of power. At the pinnacle were company presidents, for example, Louis B. Mayer, Adolph Zukor, Harry Cohn, Carl Laemmle, Jack Warner. Abetted by their vice-presidents in charge of production (such as Irving Thalberg and David O. Selznick before he became an independent producer), they asserted absolute authority over what films were produced. These self-appointed oracles insisted that audiences wanted to be entertained and to be able—for 3 hours at a double

feature—to dream of riches, adventure, and love beyond their reach. Films could be "serious" as well as entertaining, but they must not challenge existing prejudices and conventions. As Samuel Goldwyn declared, "When I want to deliver a message, I'll send it by Western Union." Criticism of the American way of life was permissible only in the guise of farce or in wisecracks. Aside from obvious evils, such as chain gangs and lynchings, the corrupt individual, not the social system, was always at fault.

Company heads and their vice-presidents not only determined what movies were to be made and at what budgets but also how they were to be created. This authority was maintained by departmentalizing film production, limiting the responsibility of each individual involved, and deciding which employees were assigned to each project. Furthermore, each stage of a major production had to be approved through steps up the hierarchy of a studio, with final decisions made by the upper echelon.

Another characteristic of the studio system was the attention paid to stars. The movie companies publicized them, gently stroked their egos, and tailored films to fit their screen images. But there were iron hands in those velvet gloves. Studios made and broke stars. Contracts restricted actors and actresses to working for one company; exceptions had to be approved. A star was pressured to appear in as many motion pictures a year as possible and suspended if an assigned role was rejected. A studio kept tight reins on its stars because they were essential to the system. The individuality lacking in the majority of screenplays and directing styles was supplied by the personae of the stars.

The studio system was a prescription for film mediocrity, and that was the caliber of most of the 450 to 500 motion pictures released each year by the industry in the thirties and forties. The mainstays of the studios were genre films and series (for example, the Andy Hardy series). Comedies, musicals, Westerns, gangster films, swashbucklers, thrillers, horror films, biographical pictures—these and other types were the staple fare of moviegoers during these two decades. Motion picture companies preferred genre films because most of them conformed to formulae of plot and characterization, with differences supplied by stars and production values. These areas were also easiest for the studio system to exploit. The best of the genre films could be the equals of most dramas, but the majority of them were second- and third-rate entertainments.

Yet each year the major movie companies released at least a few intelligent, stimulating dramas; witty, satirical comedies; exhilarating musicals; and outstanding works in other genres. One of the reasons was the incomparable production facilities and technicians available in Hollywood. More important, there were always a few people employed by the studios who were artists as well as craftsmen. They were capable of working within the limitations imposed by the studio system, yet, when opportunities permitted, could add individual qualities of style, imagination, and vitality. Directors like John Ford, Ernst Lubitsch, and Alfred Hitchcock and such screenwriters as Ben Hecht, Dalton Trumbo, and Billy Wilder were so consistently successful at the box office that they could manipulate the studios instead of being manipulated by them.

Another element that helped to transform hackneyed concepts into impressive motion picture experiences was the stars. The plot vehicles that carried them might creak with clichés and bump over improbable situations, but Greta Garbo, Katharine Hepburn, Bette Davis, Clark Gable, Spencer Tracy, and Humphrey Bogart—to name only a half dozen—could breathe life into shallow roles by the sheer vividness of their personalities. It did not matter that Gary Cooper or James Cagney, Alice Faye or Myrna Loy projected the same screen persona with only minor variations in different films. Audiences responded to their presence more than their acting skills.

From the advent of sound to the end of World War II, a plethora of efficient directors were working in Hollywood. But only a few cinematic artists of the first rank were productive during those years: Chaplin, Ford, Hawks, Lubitsch, Welles, and, in the opinion of some critics, Sternberg. Of these, two devoted themselves primarily to the genre of comedy. Charles Chaplin's post-1928 films are discussed later.* The achievements of Ernst Lubitsch are surveyed in Chap-

ter 6, along with the work of Frank Capra, Leo McCarey, and others. John Ford turned from Westerns to dramas between the late twenties and 1939.*

Howard Hawks (1896–1977) was astonishingly versatile. He directed distinguished Westerns,† comedies,‡ gangster films (such as *Scarface,* 1932, and *The Big Sleep,* 1946), biographical films (for example, *Viva Villa!,* 1934, and *Sergeant York,* 1941), adventure films (for instance, *The Dawn Patrol,* 1930, and *Only Angels Have Wings,* 1939), and sundry other types, including a musical (*Gentlemen Prefer Blondes,* 1953). With an economy of means and unobtrusive techniques, he was able to mold a distinctive style. He paid particular attention to the structure of a film while putting a premium on pithy dialogue and fast-paced action. The interrelationships of characters interested him more than the psychology of individual ones.

His most pervasive theme was how a man must prove himself in a struggle against a hostile environment or against other men by having inner strength and professional skills (whether with a gun, a racing car, or an airplane), discovering in the process that he requires the support of his friends. Women tend to be prizes worthy of being fought for, on the edge of the inner circle of male camaraderie. In the director's comedies, on the other hand, females are active participants in the battle of the sexes, all the more so because they have independent, strong personalities. Hawks's range, perceptive understanding of the American character, and incisive style earned him during four decades of filmmaking the esteem of both audiences and critics throughout the Western world.

The silent films of Josef von Sternberg (1894–1969) were noted earlier.§ His first sound film, *The Blue Angel (Der Blaue Engel,* 1930), was made in Berlin under the auspices of UFA. The story of the downfall of a high school teacher through his involvement with a cabaret singer, starring Emil Jannings (Figure 4.11) and Marlene Dietrich, is a classic. At Paramount, Sternberg directed a series of very popular

---

*p. 405
†p. 394
‡p. 273
§p. 101

films between 1930 and 1935: *Morocco* (1930), *Dishonored* (1931), *Shanghai Express* (1932), *Blonde Venus* (1932), *The Scarlet Empress* (1934), and *The Devil Is a Woman* (1935). Each one starred Marlene Dietrich. Sternberg created for her in these films an exotic, erotic world filled with contrasts of light and dark that symbolized the many ambiguities in the roles she played. Usually at least one sequence is bizarre, a procession or a stage presentation. In fact, the six films are permeated by a mystery that gives the melodramatic plots a mythic aura. Dietrich assumes the proportions of half eternal temptress holding men in thrall and half the type of woman who would sacrifice everything for love.

───────
**FIGURE 4.11**

*The Blue Angel,* 1930, directed by Josef von Sternberg. Prof. Immanuel Rath (Emil Jannings) gives up social position and the teaching profession to marry the café singer Lola-Lola (Marlene Dietrich). His final and fatal humiliation is to perform as a pathetic clown on stage in his hometown.

Reality and myth intermingled in Sternberg's own career. An arrogant, immensely promising filmmaker with a style as distinctive and provocative as any director in Hollywood meets in his middle years a beautiful actress. For 5 years, with the exception of one film (*An American Tragedy,* 1931), he devotes his creative efforts to the actress, producing his finest work and making her an international star. After they part, the quality of his directing falls precipi-

tously, and he completes only one outstanding motion picture (*The Shanghai Gesture,* 1941) in two decades. He gives up filmmaking after 1953.

In the early forties there appeared on the Hollywood scene a genius who within an astonishingly few years was recognized as being in the forefront of American directors. Orson Welles (1915–) was an *enfant terrible* of the theater and radio as actor-director even before he traveled to the West Coast. At 26, he completed his first feature film, *Citizen Kane* (1941) (see Figures 1.11 and 1.36). The critics who participated in the British Film Institute's international, once-a-decade polls for 1962, 1972, and 1982 (published in the magazine *Sight and Sound*) rated this film the greatest motion picture ever made. With the help of Herman J. Mankiewicz as screenwriter and Gregg Toland as director of photography, Welles not only directed but also starred in this masterpiece. Although *Citizen Kane* barely returned RKO's investment—due primarily to a crusade against the film conducted by newspaper magnate William Randolph Hearst, who rightly saw the title character as a thinly disguised portrait of himself—it profoundly influenced filmmakers in the United States and abroad.

Welles released *The Magnificent Ambersons* (based on a Booth Tarkington novel) the next year. It is almost as remarkable a work as *Citizen Kane,* less exciting in its narrative dimension but in many ways more subtle and disciplined in its cinematic techniques [Figure 4.12; see also Figures 1.41(f) and 1.45]. After floundering for a few years, he directed and starred in the superior mystery thriller, *The Lady From Shanghai* (1947) (Figure 4.13). Having affronted Hollywood studio heads with his independence and originality, Welles spent most of his time from the early fifties until the late seventies in Europe. Some of his fifties and sixties films are no more than perfunctory in execution; others are uneven but memorable (for example, *Mr. Arkadin,* 1955; *Touch of Evil,* 1957; and *The Trial,* 1963). His adaptations from Shakespeare include *Macbeth* (1948), *Othello* (1951), and *Falstaff* or *Chimes at Midnight* (1966). *Falstaff* is the one work that is comparable to the best of his early films. His most recent effort, *F for Fake* (1976), is a fascinating discourse on the relationships between illusion and reality.

**FIGURE 4.12**

*The Magnificent Ambersons,* 1942, directed by Orson Welles. George Amberson (Tim Holt) and Lucy Morgan (Anne Baxter) become acquainted at a party given in the Amberson mansion. Welles makes effective use of deep-focus cinematography throughout this sequence.

The director's theatrical background probably inspired his emphasis on a *mise-en-scène* approach and his exploration of ways of expanding the potentials of deep-focus shots. The Expressionist filmmakers as well as the theater influenced his dramatic manipulation of chiaroscuro lighting. Sometimes it is not sufficiently recognized that Welles (who for 4 years worked in radio) has been also innovative in his uses of sound.

In his finest films, Welles often achieved startling effects by condensing and rearranging the normal sequence of events. In many respects, he anticipated

**FIGURE 4.13**

*The Lady From Shanghai,* 1947, directed by Orson Welles. In the brilliant concluding sequence of this thriller, the three main characters—Michael O'Hara (Welles), Elsa Bannister (Rita Hayworth), and Arthur Bannister (Everett Sloane)—confront each other, two of them with guns, in a hall of mirrors at an amusement park.

the nonlinear plots developed in the sixties by such European directors as Antonioni, Godard, and Resnais. He also tended toward melodramatic plots. This preference affected the tone of his dramas. An intense, relentlessly dramatic, larger-than-life ambiance is a hallmark of his style. This quality of inflation can verge unintentionally on the grotesque, especially in his later films, such as *Macbeth*.

It is ultimately the boldness and imaginativeness of Welles's films that make viewing them such rewarding cinematic experiences. Film historians have repeatedly blamed Hollywood for the fact that the director did not continue to create dramas of the caliber of his 1940s works. Perhaps the fault lay as much in his own nature as in the narrow-mindedness and shortsightedness of American producers. In any case, Welles has earned his place in what Andrew Sarris designated as the "Pantheon" of American directors.[3]

Several other distinguished Hollywood directors did most of their best work during this period. King Vidor specialized in king-sized dramas and was often bold in coming to grips with contemporary social problems; among his finest motion pictures, in addition to his major silent dramas,* are *Hallelujah!*† (1929), *Our Daily Bread* (1934), *Stella Dallas* (1937), *Northwest Passage* (1940), *Duel in the Sun*‡ (1946), *The Fountainhead* (1949), and *War and Peace* (1955). Rouben Mamoulian was a master not only of the musical genre§ but also of drama, including *Applause* (1929), *Dr. Jekyll and Mr. Hyde* (1932), *Queen Christina* (1934), *Becky Sharp* (1935), and *Blood and Sand* (1941). Lewis Milestone created carefully constructed, realistic works, among them *All Quiet on the Western Front* (1930), *The Front Page* (1931), *Rain* (1933), *Of Mice and Men* (1939), *Arch of Triumph* (1948), and *Les Miserables* (1952). Mervyn LeRoy revealed his expert craftsmanship in such films as *Little Caesar* (1930), *I Am a Fugitive From a Chain Gang* (1932), *Random Harvest* (1942), and *Quo Vadis?* (1951). William Wellman is most famous for *Public Enemy* (1931), *A Star Is Born* (1937), and *The Ox-Bow Incident* (1943). George Cukor, in addition to his sophisticated comedies,* gave us *David Copperfield* (1934), *Camille* (1936), *Gaslight* (1944), *A Star Is Born* (1954), and others.

During the twenties, many foreign directors were persuaded to come to Hollywood, including Ernst Lubitsch, F. W. Murnau, Paul Leni, Maurice Tourneur, Paul Fejös, Mauritz Stiller, and Victor Sjöström. Michael Curtiz is usually thought of as an American director, but he actually began his film career in Hungary and Germany and did not come to the United States until 1928. In addition to his most famous film, *Casablanca* (1943), he directed, among many others, *Angels With Dirty Faces* (1938), *The Sea Hawk* (1940), *Yankee Doodle Dandy* (1942), and *Mildred Pierce* (1945). William Dieterle emigrated to Hollywood from Germany after two decades of being a prominent film actor and director. His reputation as a dependable American director rests on his biography films (for example, *The Story of Louis Pasteur,* 1935, and *Juarez,* 1939), musicals, and melodramas.

The most eminent director to immigrate to Hollywood in the thirties was Fritz Lang; his American films were noted earlier.† The thrillers Alfred Hitchcock made in this country are listed later in this survey.‡ Although both Billy Wilder and Otto Preminger (both born in Austria) settled in Hollywood in the thirties, their most important work appeared in the late forties and fifties. During the war, some directors, for example, German-born Robert Siodmak and Douglas Sirk (who was born in Denmark but established his career as a filmmaker in Germany), emigrated to the United States. Others, most prominently Frenchmen Jean Renoir, René Clair, and Julien Duvivier, remained only briefly; they had difficulty in adjusting to the studio system.

---

## FRANCE

The 1930s was a period of rejuvenation and impressive achievements in the French motion picture industry. The first impetus was the advent of sound. Almost

---

*p. 101
†p. 441
‡pp. 397, 399
§pp. 441, 445, 449

*pp. 127–128
†p. 279
‡p. 107

as soon as sound processes were available, two major directors demonstrated a full appreciation of the potentials of this new element of presentation: René Clair (whose contributions to cinema are delineated elsewhere in this book*) and Jean Renoir, who is discussed later.

The second significant characteristic of French cinema during the thirties was the efforts of filmmakers to graft to a realistic approach various nonrealistic elements. At its best, this method offered a fusion of concrete settings and verisimilitude in characterization and situation with either fantasy (as in the comedies of Clair), symbolic overtones (as in the dramas of Renoir), or scenes and sequences that borrowed from Surrealism a dreamlike aura without the extremes of irrationality typical of that experimental movement (as in the films of Jean Vigo†).

The term *poetic realism* has been coined to describe this approach to filmmaking. Although there is little evidence that the directors involved consciously adhered to a set of tenets, their works exhibit sufficient similarities, shared premises, and a cross-fertilization of ideas and techniques to label Poetic Realism a movement. If considered as such, the movement manifested itself in France from the early thirties to the outbreak of World War II. Of the four leading figures—Clair, Vigo, Renoir, and Marcel Carné—only Renoir continued to mine the lode of Poetic Realism after World War II. This movement, however, had considerable influence on the development of Italian Neorealism, especially through the enthusiasm for this type of French film expressed by Visconti and Rossellini, and on the development of *Film Noir* in the United States.

Between 1924 and 1971, Jean Renoir (1894–1979) directed more than three dozen films. They include cinematic bagatelles, noble failures, interesting but flawed works, and some of the most impressive motion pictures ever to appear on the screen.

His sharp visual eye came to him naturally, for he was the second son of the great Impressionist painter Pierre Auguste Renoir. He has described his relationship with his father in autobiographies *(Renoir,*

My Father* and *My Life and My Films)*. After World War I, in which he served as a cavalry officer and an aerial reconnaissance pilot, he and his wife devoted themselves to ceramics. In the early twenties, he decided to become a filmmaker. After writing scripts, producing, and acting, he directed his first feature, *La Fille de l'eau* (1924). Of the nine silent films Renoir directed between 1924 and 1931, the most successful were *Nana* (1926, an adaptation of the Zola novel), *La Petite Marchande d'allumettes* (1928, based on a Hans Christian Andersen tale), and a delightful satire of army life, *Tire-au-flanc* (1928).

Renoir's first sound motion picture was the inconsequential *On purge bébé* (1931). In his next work, however, he developed the skill that he was to sustain throughout his career of incorporating creatively natural sounds and background music into the fiber of his films. *La Chienne* (1931) stars Michel Simon as a cashier who not only escapes the noose of a drab existence by means of painting and a prostitute but also escapes punishment for murdering the prostitute. It is also noteworthy for the director's first experiments in deep focus.

Of Renoir's other sound films of the thirties, four are based on famous literary works of the nineteenth or early twentieth century: *Madame Bovary* (1934, from Flaubert's novel), *A Day in the Country* (*Une partie de campagne,* from a story by Maupassant; unfinished in 1936 but edited and released as a 35-minute short in 1946), *The Lower Depths* (*Les Bas-Fonds,* 1936, from the Gorky play), and *The Human Beast* (*La Bête humaine,* 1938, from the Zola novel). *A Day in the Country* is a lovely film that captures in black and white the glow of summer light characteristic of the Impressionist painters.

Two other of his works are basically realistic and done in a tightly controlled style. *Night at the Crossroads* (*La Nuit de carrefour,* 1932) is based on a Georges Simenon Inspector Maigret novel. *Toni* (1934) also involves violence and murder but is richer in texture and more subtle in characterization. With its use of nonprofessional actors and authentic settings and its emphasis on the details of lower-class life, the film is often considered a precursor of Neorealism.

In the mid-thirties, politics and social consciousness became significant elements in Renoir's

---

*pp. 269, 442
†p. 270

films. The screenplay for *The Crime of Monsieur Lange* (*Le Crime de Monsieur Lange,* 1935) was the result of a collaboration between the director and the politically leftist screenwriter Jacques Prévert. The theme of the film is that workers have the right to rebel against an oppressive employer, even to the point of killing him. Prévert's sparkling dialogue and Renoir's superb cinematic techniques rather than the propagandistic message make the film memorable. Two other works are evidence of the director's political preoccupations: *People of France* (*La Vie est à nous,* 1936, commissioned by the French Communist party) and *La Marseillaise* (1938), with a setting of the French Revolution.

Three films stand out as Renoir's masterworks of the thirties and perhaps of his entire career. *Boudu Saved From Drowning* (*Boudu sauvé des eaux,* 1932) was the director's first important sound comedy. It is commented on elsewhere in this book.*

---

**FIGURE 4.14**

*Grand Illusion,* 1937, directed by Jean Renoir. Commandant von Rauffenstein (Erich von Stroheim) feels a kinship to a fellow aristocrat and professional soldier, Captain de Boeldieu (Pierre Fresnay). The German officer sincerely regrets having to shoot the Frenchman and mourns his death.

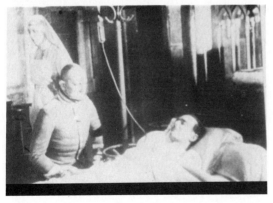

*Grand Illusion* (*La Grande Illusion,* 1937) includes in its outstanding cast Erich von Stroheim, Jean Gabin, Pierre Fresnay, and Marcel Dalio. This story of three

---

Frenchmen imprisoned with their comrades in a German fortress during World War I and the escape of two of them is rich in psychological insights into human nature and the problems of class conflicts (Figure 4.14).

*The Rules of the Game* (*La Règle du jeu,* 1939) is considered by many discriminating students of cinema as the masterpiece of Renoir's many masterful works. In the British Film Institute's once-a-decade poll of critics to list the ten greatest motion pictures ever made (published in *Sight and Sound* in 1952, 1962, 1972, and 1982), *The Rules of the Game* is one of only two films to appear all four times (the other is Eisenstein's *The Battleship Potemkin*).

The essential relationships of the complex plot are established in the first third of *The Rules of the Game*, which takes place in Paris. The aviator Jurieu is in love with Christine, the wife of the Marquis Robert de la Chesnaye. Intimately involved in this love triangle are Geneviève, Robert's mistress, and Octave (played by Jean Renoir), the impoverished friend of everyone, especially Christine and Jurieu. At a weekend gathering at La Colinière, the de la Chesnaye country château, others, including servants and aristocrats, are drawn into Jurieu's obsessive love and the situation ultimately is resolved (Figure 4.15 and see Figure 1.37).

---

**FIGURE 4.15**

*The Rules of the Game,* 1939, directed by Jean Renoir. At the de la Chesnayes' chateau, the guests frolic and talk to each other before retiring to their bedrooms. In the thirties, Renoir, well before Welles, explored the potentials of deep-focus photography.

No capsule synopsis of plot can suggest the richness of this astonishing film. The major theme centers on a universal contrast. On the one hand, there are people, especially in the upper class, who are committed to a rigid, basically sterile code of manners, but one that preserves honor, dignity, and grace (see Figure 1.37). On the other hand, there are individuals who heed the demands of genuine emotions, yet are disruptive of social order and can hurt, even destroy, other people. Interwoven into this central theme are a dozen minor themes. As with any work of art of the highest order, *The Rules of the Game* is true to its time and place settings, yet it simultaneously transcends time and space in its insights into human nature.

Renoir spent most of the forties in the United States. The films he made in this country are uneven in quality. *Swamp Water* (1941), *This Land Is Mine* (1943), and *The Woman on the Beach* (1947) are faulty in concept and execution. Two works, however, possess some of the virtues of his best thirties films. In *The Southerner* (1945), Renoir returns to the semidocumentary style of *Toni* to recount in uncompromising terms the efforts of a poor Southerner to own his own farm. *The Diary of a Chambermaid* (1946, adapted from a novel by Octave Mirbeau) contains social criticism, but the film is intentionally cast in a mode of theatricality that at times complements and at other times conflicts with the realism of characters and setting.

After World War II, Renoir generally left behind the social concerns of his earlier works and either returned to earlier themes in his films or explored new ones while refining or developing new techniques. *The River* (1950, based on Rumer Godden's novel) was made in India. The interrelationship of man and nature, central to *Boudu* and *A Day in the Country,* is given an almost mythic dimension in the film. It is Renoir's first use of color and, as he did with sound, he completely absorbed this new element of presentation into his style. Like *The River, Picnic on the Grass* (*Le Déjeuner sur l'herbe,* 1959) is exquisitely photographed. It is also, within the framework of an absurd plot, the director's most explicit visual paean to the outdoor, healthy, sensual life.

*Experiment in Evil* (*Le Testament du Dr.*

*Cordelier,* 1959) is freely adapted from Stevenson's *Dr. Jekyll and Mr. Hyde* and stars Jean-Louis Barrault. *The Elusive Corporal* (*Le Caporal épinglé,* 1962), a story of prisoners of war, combines questions about the meaning of freedom with the humor, though more delicate and restrained, of the silent *Tire-au-flanc.*

In the fifties and, in one case, early seventies, Renoir developed in certain works a new major theme that had its roots in early films. The connections and contrasts between the theater and life (or art and reality) are examined with artistic skill and vitality in four films: *The Golden Coach* (*La Carosse d'or,* 1952), *French Cancan* (1954), *Paris Does Strange Things* (*Eléna et les hommes,* 1956), and *Le Petit théâtre de Jean Renoir* (1971). Three of these are commented on in Chapter 6, "Comedy."* *Paris Does Strange Things* is a period film set in the same early years of the Third Republic as *French Cancan.* It is a drama involving conspiracies, politics, and spies, but it points to the same conclusion as the comedies: The theater, with its imaginative illusions and satisfying artificiality, is preferable to the grubby, clumsy, haphazard world of politics and emotional intrigues.

In addition to the theme of the interrelationships between the theater and life, several others recur in Renoir's work, including contrasts between the energizing qualities of nature and the stifling atmosphere of city life, conflicts between individual emotional needs and restrictive social mores and class systems, an appreciation of the vitality of women who do not suppress their sensual natures, and an insistence that the borderline between comedy and tragedy is often vague and ambiguous.

Although Renoir was pragmatic and eclectic in taking advantage of every device and approach that would further his intentions, certain techniques are particularly associated with his cinematic style. Sturdy narratives are replete with accurate details of setting, costume, and other elements of presentation. However, Renoir usually imbued this realism with a suggestiveness and a symbolism that are more appropriate to the vision of a poet than to that of a prosaic recorder of reality. It is on this basis that Renoir is considered a founder of Poetic Realism.

---

*p. 269

Since the director was most interested in confrontations between individuals and between them and their environments (physical and social), he favored the *mise-en-scène* approach. Moreover, he was an innovator, even before the proper technology was available, in exploring the potentials of deep focus. His devotion to the *mise-en-scène* approach led to other characteristics of his style: avoidance of point-of-view shots, sparing use of close-ups, and unobtrusive camera movements.

From his earliest films, Renoir was subtle and expressive in his lighting, particularly when shadows were involved. (The last shot of *The Rules of the Game,* which consists of shadows on a wall, is one of the most memorable in the history of French cinema.) This mastery of chiaroscuro extended to color when that element of presentation became popular after World War II.

With the exception of such supreme stylistic classicists as Carl Dreyer and Robert Bresson, the greatest film directors have been those who capture audiences with strong, dramatic narrative dimensions to their films. The styles they developed to communicate their visions of reality, however, may be startling and innovative, immediately recognizable as unique (for example, Bergman, Welles, Godard, and Fellini), or subtle and unobtrusive, requiring close and careful study to appreciate the brilliance of their works (for instance, Hitchcock, Antonioni, Ford, and Satyajit Ray). In the latter category, at the head of any list of masters, should stand the name of Jean Renoir.

Marcel Carné (1909–) directed some of the most memorable dramas of the period. He began his career as a cameraman, then advanced to assistant director to René Clair and Jacques Feyder. In 1936 he completed the film *Jenny,* begun by Feyder. During this production, he met screenwriter Jacques Prévert, and there began their mutually beneficial collaboration. After working together on a minor farce, they created the fine drama *Port of Shadows* (*Quai des brumes,* 1938), which deals with star-crossed lovers (played by Jean Gabin and Michèle Morgan) who have only a brief period of happiness before the man is killed by a jealous gangster.

After the unimpressive *Hôtel du Nord* (1938), Carné's next three films brought his partnership with

Prévert to full fruition. *Le Jour se lève* (1939; rarely referred to by its English title, *Daybreak*) starred Gabin and Arletty, and it was completed just as war broke out in Europe. The style of Poetic Realism is used to tell the story of a worker, beseiged by the police, who recalls his relations with two women and his murder of the seducer of the younger one. *The Devil's Envoys* (*Les Visiteurs du soir,* 1942) and *The Children of Paradise* (*Les Enfants du paradis,* 1945) were made during the Occupation and passed Nazi censorship by taking place in past ages and being, at least overtly, escapist in content. The former is a fantasy of two agents of the Devil who fall in love with their intended victims. *The Children of Paradise* is the quintessence in content of cinematic romanticism, created with exquisite style and unflagging verve. A superb cast headed by Arletty, Jean-Louis Barrault, and Pierre Brasseur evokes the milieu of the theater of nineteenth-century Paris in unfolding the main plot of the love between a famous mime and a beautiful actress (Figure 4.16).

---

**FIGURE 4.16**

*The Children of Paradise,* 1945, directed by Marcel Carné. In a theater in early nineteenth-century Paris appears the great mime Baptiste Deburau (Jean-Louis Barrault) as Pierrot. Here he is chased by a stage policeman.

The collaboration between director and screenwriter ended with a melodrama, *The Gates of the Night* (*Les Portes de la nuit,* 1946). Carné continued to direct films until the early seventies, but inspiration

apparently deserted him. Only one drama, *Thérèse Raquin* (1953), a modernized version of the Zola novel, rises above the routine and conventional.

Aside from *The Children of Paradise,* a perennial favorite of both general audiences and *cinéastes,* Carné's work has been disparaged by postwar critics who value freedom and experimentation in filmmaking on the basis of two characteristics of his style. The first is an oppressive fatalism that haunts his dramas. It seems that in the director's cinematic cosmology, spiteful gods as well as the hypocritical morality of society are determined to destroy the happiness of individuals, especially lovers. Even more reprehensible from the point of view of critics of the sixties and seventies is Carné's almost coldly inflexible craftsmanship. He worked exclusively in studios, and an obvious artificiality of setting and lighting is a hallmark of his style. Although this is the means whereby he adds his brand of "poetry" to his realism, his rigid, meticulous control can restrict and stifle vitality and warmth of expression.

Jacques Prévert (1900–1977) is best known for his collaboration with Carné, but he wrote screenplays for many other directors, including Renoir, Marc Allégret, Jean Grémillon, and his brother Pierre Prévert. He had a genius for writing straightforward but completely effective dialogue. Whenever possible, he instilled social criticism into his work and tended to portray morality as a conflict between personifications of absolute good and evil. At the end of the forties, he stopped writing screenplays for feature fiction films and devoted himself to documentaries and radio programs.

Other notable French directors of this period include Julien Duvivier, who between 1919 and 1967 directed over 60 films; among his more eminent works are *Escape From Yesterday* (*La Bandera,* 1935), *Pépé le Moko* (1936), *Life Dances On* (*Carnet de bal,* 1937), and *Anna Karenina* (1948); Marcel Pagnol, famous for *Angèle,* 1934, and *César,* 1936); Sacha Guitry, who made *Story of a Cheat* (*Le Roman d'un tricheur,* 1936); Marc Allégret (a polished craftsman); Pierre Prévert; Jean Delannoy; Léon Poirier; and Yves Allégret. The activities of Max Ophuls, Jacques Becker, and Claude Autant-Lara, who did their most

estimable work after the war, are discussed in that section of this chapter.

## GREAT BRITAIN

Film production in England thrived during the thirties and World War II, especially under the aegis of Alexander Korda, the foremost producer in his country. With the exception of the documentary,* however, few extraordinary films were released. Three directors emerged as the leading creators of drama: Alfred Hitchcock, Anthony Asquith, and Carol Reed.

The reputation of Alfred Hitchcock (1899–1980) as a master filmmaker began in the mid-fifties, particularly as a result of the unqualified admiration expressed by French writers for *Cahiers du Cinéma.* Even earlier, perceptive critics recognized that his devotion to thrillers was only a means to an end. While he held the attention of audiences—and not so incidentally guaranteed through consistent box office successes the backing of producers—his chief preoccupation was exploring the potentials of his medium. A statement that he repeated in practically every interview succinctly sums up his approach: "I am interested less in stories than in the manner of telling them."

Hitchcock's favorite structural device in his plots was the chase. He was also fond of the "MacGuffin": an object or situation that appears significant but is really a narrative red herring, such as the stolen money in *Marnie.* Preproduction was the most important stage for the director in making a film. He meticulously prepared before shooting. His storyboards were remarkably detailed, his shooting ratio was phenomenally low, and the editing of his films was not quite but almost a mechanical process. Although he would employ introspective actors (such as Montgomery Clift in *I Confess*) and flamboyant ones (for example, Laurence Olivier in *Rebecca* and Tallulah Bankhead in *Lifeboat*), he preferred, as he pointed out himself, malleable actors who would accept his tyrannical direction (Tippi Hedren, Grace Kelly, Teresa Wright, James Stewart, and Cary Grant).

The ultimate sources of the director's impres-

---

*pp. 330–332, 339–340

sive style were his appreciation of the role played by each component of a film and how it could be integrated with the others. He also took delight in devising challenging settings, situations, and approaches within the limitations of a popular genre. Other directors have had as sensitive an eye for composition or have been as imaginative in the use of natural sounds and background music. Few, however, have possessed Hitchcock's gift for structuring scenes and sequences, especially for the purpose of suspense, with an almost flawless precision and sureness that is awesome. His boldness in experimenting with unusual devices (for example, the confinements of place setting in *Lifeboat* and time in *Rope,* the artificial backdrops in *Marnie,* and fettering his hero to a wheelchair in *Rear Window*) was that of a professional so confident of his abilities that he purposely set himself restrictions to overcome.

Hitchcock was an *auteur* director who imposed his vision of reality on his works. There is, in fact, a "Hitchcockian world"—as consistent and coherent as those created by, say, Bergman, Antonioni, and Dreyer. In most of the director's thrillers, an ordinary person, through no fault of his own, is suddenly trapped in a dangerous situation that threatens his life. Sometimes the source of the danger is not identified until the middle or the end of the film; it is usually external, but it may be internal, as in *Marnie* (Figure 4.17); or it may even be inexplicable, as in *The Birds.* Because we identify—and are meant to identify—with the ordinary individual imperiled, the director encourages us to be suspicious of the securities and systems that supposedly safeguard our existence. There is, then, an existential dimension to his cinematic world.

Whatever the threat, a character in a Hitchcock thriller must draw upon resources, sometimes previously unsuspected, to meet the challenge. With only a few exceptions, the director's films are essentially psychological thrillers, for they depend on revelations of character if a viewer is fully to understand events. The motivations of the villains (for instance, Charlie Oakley in *Shadow of a Doubt,* Bruno Anthony in *Strangers on a Train,* and Norman Bates in *Psycho*) are frequently more intriguing than those of actual or possible victims, and the villains may be related

**FIGURE 4.17**

*Marnie,* 1964, directed by Alfred Hitchcock (color). At the end of the film, Marnie relives a traumatic childhood experience. Hitchcock takes advantage of expressionistic distortion to convey the intense emotions felt by the young woman.

emotionally to or even identified with their victims. Most of Hitchcock's "heroes" have serious flaws of character, but their determination, ingenuity, courage, and good luck help them to survive.

After a training period in the early twenties as an art director, screenwriter, and assistant director, Hitchcock made his debut as a director with *The Pleasure Garden* (1925), made in Germany, where he was introduced to the techniques of Expressionism. The influence of those techniques are evident in *The Lodger* (1926), his only impressive silent film. He recognized that sound could significantly increase the effectiveness of his thrillers, and he demonstrated this in *Blackmail* (1929). Among the outstanding films he directed in the thirties were *The Man Who Knew Too Much* (1934; a second version appeared in 1956), *The Thirty-Nine Steps* (1934), *Secret Agent* (1936), *Sabotage* (1936, an adaptation of a Joseph Conrad novel), and *The Lady Vanishes* (1938) (Figure 4.18). In 1939 he left for Hollywood, and his "British period" ended.

In the United States, he continued to be prolific and steadfast in his approach to filmmaking. From 1940, when *Rebecca* was released, until 1976, when *Family Plot* appeared, he directed almost a film a

**FIGURE 4.18**

*The Lady Vanishes,* 1938, directed by Alfred Hitchcock. During tea on a transcontinental train, Miss Froy (Dame May Whitty) writes her name on a dusty window for Iris Henderson (Margaret Lockwood). The action proves important later in this spy intrigue when Miss Froy vanishes.

year, a total of 30 in 3 ½ decades. Each one was a thriller, although the borders of the genre must be pushed out somewhat to include *Lifeboat* (1943) and *Under Capricorn* (1949).

Every enthusiast of Hitchcock's works has a list of favorite American films. Here is one such list: *Shadow of a Doubt* (1943), *Notorious* (1946), *Rope* (1948), *Strangers on a Train* (1954), *Rear Window* (1954), *Vertigo* (1958), *North by Northwest* (1959) (see Figures 1.18 and 1.35), *Psycho* (1960), *The Birds* (1963), and *Marnie* (1964). Now that critics have finally come to realize how acute were Hitchcock's observations on the sources of fears and insecurities in modern society and how inimitable was his style, Hitchcock's place is assured near the top of the honor roll of modern directors.

Anthony Asquith (1902–1968), after a brief apprenticeship in silent films, soon established himself as a thorough professional who could transform stories of English life and stage plays into convincing cinematic experiences. Asquith was particularly adept at adaptations of the plays of George Bernard Shaw, including not only a famous version of *Pygmalion* (1938) but also *The Doctor's Dilemma* (1959) and *The Millionairess* (1960). His adaptation of Oscar

Wilde's *The Importance of Being Earnest* (1952) is a minor masterpiece. The director's association with playwright Terence Rattigan was most successful. Not only did he create film versions of the playwright's *The Winslow Boy* (1948) and *The Browning Version* (1951), but the two collaborated on what is generally considered one of the finest films released in Great Britain in the forties, *The Way to the Stars* (1945). During the sixties, Asquith's work lost its vitality and distinctiveness.

Carol Reed (1906–1976) from the beginning of his directing career in the mid-thirties demonstrated an exceptional ability to convey the milieus of time and place settings and make intelligent, faithful, visually exciting adaptations of novels. Among his memorable feature films before and during the war were *Bank Holiday* (1938), the powerful *The Stars Look Down* (1939), and *Kipps* (1941). His first drama after the war was the striking *Odd Man Out* (1947), reminiscent of John Ford's *The Informer.* Reed's collaboration with Graham Greene resulted in *The Fallen Idol* (1948), *The Third Man* (1949), and *Our Man in Havana* (1959). In the view of many critics, *Outcast of the Islands* (1951) is the most successful adaptation of a Joseph Conrad novel. Reed's films after the mid-fifties were respectable but on the whole disappointing—with the possible exception of the musical *Oliver!* (1968).

Michael Powell (1905–) was in the late seventies the subject of renewed interest and critical acclaim. Although the films he directed in the thirties, such as *Edge of the World* (1937), attracted favorable attention, his full potential was not realized until he founded Archer Films (1942–1956) with Emeric Pressburger. The two shared directing and producing credits; however, the latest film scholarship indicates that Powell was primarily responsible for the cinematic techniques that distinguished their best work.

Among the films released by Powell and Pressburger are *One of Our Aircraft Is Missing* (1942), *The Life and Death of Colonel Blimp* (1943), *A Canterbury Tale* (1944), *I Know Where I'm Going* (1945), *A Matter of Life and Death* or *Stairway to Heaven* (1946), *Black Narcissus* (1947), *The Red Shoes* (1948), *Gone to Earth* (1950), and *The Tales of Hoffman* (1951). Most of these dramas are melodramatic to one degree or another, yet when spectacle does not overwhelm the narrative dimension, as happens in *The Tales of Hoffman,* they contain psychologically penetrating portrayals of individuals, especially those gripped by evil or perversity. There is also a mystic strain in Powell's work that appears, for example, in *I Know Where I'm Going, Black Narcissus,* and *Gone to Earth.* His visuals were rarely perfunctory, his use of sound was imaginative, and his expressive manipulation of color (especially in *Black Narcissus* and the two ballet films, *The Red Shoes* and *The Tales of Hoffman*) was unsurpassed by any contemporary. After the dissolution of his partnership with Pressburger, his films, with the exception of the extraordinary *Peeping Tom* (1960), have been generally mediocre. He still remains, however, one of the most intriguing British directors.

Other notable British directors during this period were Victor Saville (best known for his work in the genre of the musical,* but he also did thrillers and dramas), Zoltan Korda, Thorold Dickinson, and Herbert Wilcox.

---

### OTHER COUNTRIES

In Germany, the first few years of sound-film production resulted in outstanding works by two masters of the twenties, Fritz Lang† and G. W. Pabst.‡ There were also Josef von Sternberg's *The Blue Angel,* Leontine Sagan's *Girls in Uniform* (*Mädchen in Uniform,* 1931), Gerhard Lamprecht's *Emil and the Detectives* (*Emil und die Detektive,* 1931), Max Ophuls's *Liebelei* (1932), as well as interesting films by Paul Czinner, Piel Julzi, Erik Charell, Richard Oswald, Victor Travas, and others.

In 1933, however, Hitler became chancellor of Germany. Almost immediately, Goebbels began his domination of the motion picture industry through censorship and unofficial control of UFA. Until the end of World War II, German and Austrian cinema produced propaganda films (both documentary and fiction), anti-Semitic works (for example, the infamous *Jud Süß* and *Der ewige Jude,* both made in 1940),

and escapist fare. Aside from the documentaries of Leni Riefenstahl and individual works by Veit Harlan, Gustav Ucicky, and Helmut Käutner, these productions were predominantly mediocre.

In Italy, the iron fist of a dictatorship did not press down as forcefully on the film industry as in Germany, but what prevailed under fascist censorship was heroic spectaculars, propaganda works, and social comedies ("white telephone" films). A few directors were able to work within the system and still make notable motion pictures. The most important was Alessandro Blasetti. He combined a versatility of style and a sensitivity to visual values with a tendency toward realism that to some degree anticipated the approach of Neorealism. Among his more eminent films were *Sun* (*Sole,* 1929), *1860* (1933), *The Old Guard* (*Vecchia Guardia,* 1935), *La Corona di Ferro* (1941), and most popular of all, the charming, realistic *Four Steps in the Clouds* (*Quattro Passi fra le Nuvole,* 1942). Blasetti's efforts after World War II were less distinctive, confined mainly to routine comedies and spectaculars.

Other notable Italian directors of the period include Mario Camerini, best known for his bittersweet comedies of the thirties, such as *Men Are Such Rascals* (*Gli Uomini, che Mascazone,* 1932); Mario Soldati, famous for *Picolo Mondo Antico* (1940); and Carmine Gallone and Goffredo Alessandrini, both of whom hewed in their films to the fascist propaganda line.

In retrospect, three of the most important developments in Italy during this decade were the establishment, under the direction of Blasetti, of the Centro Sperimentale di Cinematografia (one of the finest film schools in Europe at the time); the existence of cosmopolitan, intellectual film journals (for example, *Cinema* and *Bianco e Nero*); and the founding of the Venice Film Festival (in 1932). Opportunities for expert professional training and the ambiance of a genuine interest in film in Italy provided a fertile ground for the talents of the great directors who emerged in the country after World War II.

The Russian film industry was also restricted by a dictatorship. The sound films of Eisenstein* and Ver-

---

tov* are examined elsewhere in this volume, and those of Pudovkin and Dovzhenko were mentioned earlier in this survey. Most of the other prominent films of the 1930s were dramas on the Revolution and the civil war, such as Nikolai Ekk's *Road to Life* (*Putyovkha v zhizn,* 1931). A major achievement of the decade was the trilogy on the life of Maxim Gorky directed by Mark Donskoy: *The Childhood of Gorky* (*Detstvo Gorkovo,* 1938), *My Apprenticeship* (*V lyudkyakl,* 1939), and *My Universities* (*Moi universiteti,* 1940). Another famous trilogy had the comprehensive title *Maxim* (1935, 1937, and 1939), directed by Grigori Kozinstsev and Leonid Trauberg.

Other notable Russian directors of the thirties are Sergei Vasiliev and Georgi Vasiliev, who collaborated on many films, including *A Personal Matter* (*Lichnoe delo,* 1932) and *Chapayev* (1934); Alexander Zarki and Josif Heifitz, who collaborated or *Baltic Deputy* (*Deputat Baltiki,* 1937); Lev Arnstam; Yuli Raizman; Mikhail Romm; Friedrich Ermler; Sergei Gerassimov; and Alexei Kapler.

Films produced in other European countries were often worthwhile, but for various reasons these films were, with few exceptions, not exported beyond their borders.

## FROM THE END OF THE FORTIES TO THE END OF THE SIXTIES

### ITALY

After the end of the war in Europe, immediately and unexpectedly, Italy presented to the world a new and provocative film movement. The primary impetus for the development of Neorealism was the poverty, instability, and political conflicts that surfaced in the wake of World War II. Fascism had cultivated illusions about Italy's power and well-being. The shattering of those illusions led many Italian artists to feel it was necessary that their countrymen face, clearly and concretely, the truth of their situation and the realities of the recent past and of the present. This ambition manifested itself in literature as well as cinema, but the

latter also drew inspiration from the medium itself, particularly the Realism of Griffith and Stroheim, the concern with the common man of the German "street films" and Soviet directors of the twenties, and the Poetic Realism of French films of the thirties.

Luchino Visconti's *Ossessione* (1942) and Alessandro Blasetti's *Four Steps in the Clouds* (1942) were influential forerunners of Neorealism. Even before the end of the war, Rossellini had begun work on *Open City* (1945). Dramas in the late forties by Visconti, Vittorio De Sica, Alberto Lattuada, Pietro Germi, and others soon made it clear that a significant movement was emerging. Neorealism had, however, only a short period of triumph. By the early fifties, postwar prosperity in Italy had taken hold, and social criticism lost some of its relevance. Although foreign audiences and critics were enthusiastic about Neorealist films, Italian audiences were generally indifferent, preferring entertainment to art. Moreover, the government, attempting to present a positive image of the country to foreign investors and tourists, was inimical to uncompromising portrayals of poverty and other disruptive aftereffects of war. Official opposition gained a stranglehold on Neorealist filmmakers by passing the Andreotti Law in 1949. This legislation bestowed on its sponsor the power to censor Italian films and to prohibit the exporting of works that promulgated an "erroneous" impression of contemporary Italian life. By the mid-fifties, only a few genuine Neorealist dramas were being released, and most Italian filmmakers had turned to other approaches.

A simplistic definition of Neorealism is an effort on the part of its supporters to go further than previous forms of realism in the direction of the documentary. That is, while creating fictional works, Neorealists preserved as close as possible a correspondence between what was recorded by the camera and what appeared on the screen. More specific characteristics were identified by Cesare Zavattini, screenwriter and chief theorist of the movement. His remarks in "Some Ideas on the Cinema,"[4] based on a recorded interview, constitute the most explicit manifesto of the tenets of the movement: Attention is centered on the experiences of the common man and his everyday life; ordinary events rather than extraordinary ones are the basis of a plot; emphasis is on the influence of environment on

*pp. 342–343

human emotions and actions, especially pressures derived from unjust social forces; social criticism is overt or implied; the cast consists of many—preferably entirely—nonprofessional actors; shooting is done on location; technical paraphernalia, such as special lighting and makeup, is kept to a minimum; esthetic considerations are given minimal attention; and editing is as unobtrusive as possible.

Naturally, not every director involved in the movement adhered to every one of these principles. What Neorealism essentially demonstrated was that cinema could produce fiction films that seemed to be close facsimiles of objective reality with overtones of social criticism, yet allowed filmmakers opportunities for creativity. The influence of the movement is discernible to one degree or another in most motion pictures released after the end of World War II outside of Italy that were realistic in style, including Hollywood's social-conscience films of the fifties and sixties, the work of the British New Wave,* and the early films of Satyajit Ray in India.

Robert Rossellini (1906–1976)—after working in the thirties as an editor and screenwriter, then as a director of documentaries, shorts, and four feature films—brought international attention to this new development in Italian filmmaking with *Open City* (*Roma, Città Aperta,* 1945). Its story of the resistance of members of the underground to German occupation forces is a powerful, poignant drama and features a superb performance by Anna Magnani (Figure 4.19). The film is often considered the first of a trilogy of Neorealist war dramas, the other two being *Paisan* (*Paisà,* 1946, consisting of six episodes during the Allied invasion of Italy) and *Germany, Year Zero* (*Germania, Anno Zero,* 1947). Although still practicing his sparse, realist style, the director turned to religious themes in *The Miracle* (*Il Miracolo,* 1948, starring Anna Magnani) and *Flowers of St. Francis* (*Francesco, Giullare di Dio,* 1949).

*Stromboli* (1949) marked the beginning of a new stage in the director's oeuvre. His intimate relationship with Ingrid Bergman led to a series of films starring the actress: *Europa 51* (1952), *The Lonely Woman* (*Viaggio in Italia,* 1953), *Joan at the Stake*

**FIGURE 4.19**

*Open City,* 1945, directed by Roberto Rossellini. As with every aspect of this film, the death of Pina (Anna Magnani) is depicted with uncompromising realism.

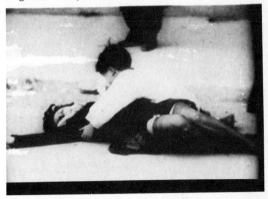

(*Giovanna d'Arco al Rogo,* 1954), and *Fear* (*La Paura,* 1954). These works lack the intensity and uncompromising honesty of the Neorealist trilogy, but they are more carefully structured, are more fluent in style, and demonstrate an increased delicacy and compassion in dealing with human suffering.

In the late fifties, Rossellini's involvement in filmmaking was minimal. Then, in quick succession, he made a documentary on India* and three fiction films: *Il Generale della Rovere* (1959), *Era Note a Roma* (1960), and *Viva L'Italia* (1960, a historical romance). In the sixties and seventies, Rossellini devoted most of his energies to making a series of television documentaries on crucial moments in the history of Western civilization.† His last drama, *Anno Uno* (1974), has not yet been released in the United States.

In practically all of Rossellini's work there is, more than with most directors, a tension between his preoccupation with cinematic style (the artist molding his material to fit his vision) and his desire to allow the powerful emotions of his characters free rein. A viewer is aware that these films were created not only by an artist who was conscious of the ambiguities and ironies of human existence but also by a man who thought deeply about the role and influences of his medium on our culture. Aside from Pasolini and Antonioni, Rossellini was probably the most intellectual of the post–World War II Italian directors. In his teaching at the Centro Sperimentale di Cinematografia and lectures in many countries, he explored the meaning and uses of film from a humanistic perspective. He insisted that a major function of cinema is to educate viewers: to make them more tolerant of the passions and inadequacies of their fellow human beings and more appreciative of the sources and potency of the values of Western civilization.

The works of Vittorio De Sica and the contributions of Cesare Zavattini to Neorealism are discussed in Chapter 5.*

Luchino Visconti (1906–1976) was throughout his life a nonconformist who confounded the expectations of his countrymen. The scion of one of the most ancient noble families in Italy, he attacked the decadence of Italian aristocrats and concerned himself with the problems of the poor; he was a Marxist who refused to become a member of the Communist party; he was a Christian who rejected the Catholic church. After studying music in his youth, he turned to the theater and opera as a director and set designer.

The first solo effort by Visconti as a director was *Ossessione* (1942), based on the novel *The Postman Always Rings Twice* by James Cain. *La Terra Trema* (1948) was even more impressive and influential in encouraging Italian directors to turn to Neorealism. It was derived from a novel by Giovanni Verga dealing with a family of fishermen exploited by businessmen. Visconti's most significant dramas of the fifties were *Bellissima* (1951), *Senso* (1953), and *The White Nights* (*Le Notti Bianche,* 1957, based on a story by Dostoevski). *Rocco and His Brothers* (*Rocco e i suoi Fratelli,* 1960) is one of the director's finest films. For all its melodramatic effects, the drama is an intense depiction of the disintegration of a southern peasant family when they move to the industrial city of Milan. *The Leopard* (*Il Gallopardo,* 1962) followed, an impressive historical pageant in the time of the Risorgimento.

Visconti's world-view grew darker and more pessimistic and his approach more stylized and symbolic in *The Stranger* (*Lo Straniero,* 1967, an adapta-

tion of Albert Camus's novella), *The Damned* (*La Caduti degli Dei,* 1969, a vivid portrayal of decadence, moral corruption, and sexual perversity in Nazi Germany), and *Death in Venice* (*Morte a Venezia,* 1971, based on Thomas Mann's novella) (Figure 4.20). The last major films of the director, including *Ludwig* (1972) and *Conversation Piece* (*Grupo di Famiglia in un Interno,* 1976), convey an ambiance of world-weariness and moral indecisiveness.

---

**FIGURE 4.20**

*Death in Venice,* 1971, directed by Luchino Visconti (color). In the final sequence, the renowned composer Gustave von Aschenbach (Dirk Bogarde) sits on a beach in plague-ridden Venice, his hair dye and makeup melting in the hot sun. Just before he dies, he reaches out toward the boy he loves, who embodies for him youth, beauty, and art.

A clue to the characteristics of Visconti's cinematic style lies in the fact that in Italy he was admired as much for his opera and theater productions as his screen works. As a film director, he was attracted to plots containing intense dramas that verge on and often cross into the province of melodrama. Place settings and background music are vital components of his films. For these reasons, he was the most "operatic" of contemporary directors. On the other hand, his social criticism was focused and unmelodramatic. Visconti was less interested in demonstrating how negative forces in modern society denigrate individuals than in how these forces encourage weakness in his characters. He was particularly fascinated by the ways in which obsessions with love, power, or money

---

*pp. 236–238

overcome an individual's moral values and common-sense. Thus his characters are more often victims of themselves than of adverse conditions. Characters straining to grasp what is beyond their reach in situations delineated by the director with remarkable vigor and boldness make Visconti's finest works uniquely exhilarating yet also emotionally draining cinematic experiences.

Federico Fellini (1920–) has made some of the most personal and startling commercial films of our time. He directed his first work, *The White Sheik* (*Lo Sceicco Bianco*), in 1952. It was followed by *I Vittelloni* (1953, recounting the experiences of five middle-class young men living in a small town), *La Strada* (1954, on the relationship between a crude itinerant circus strongman and a slow-witted but kind and sensitive peasant girl), *The Swindlers* (*Il Bidone*, 1955), *The Nights of Cabiria* (*Le Notti di Cabiria*, 1956, the story of a vulnerable prostitute with a gift for surviving misfortune; Giulietta Masina starred in both this drama and *La Strada*).

All of these films of the fifties are fundamentally Neorealist in approach, yet each one contains elements of personal expressiveness, fantasy, and assertive manipulation of the components of cinema that deviate from the tenets of this movement. Fellini moved into a new stage in his career with *La Dolce Vita* (1960). Marcello Mastroianni and Anita Ekberg star in this surging, vibrant, at times grandiloquent kaleidoscopic view of contemporary high society in Rome (Figure 4.21). The director's next feature was *8 ½* (*Otto e Mezzo*, 1963), which many critics assert is his masterwork. Reality, daydreams, dreams, memories, and numerous symbolic figures and actions blend to reveal the conflicts of Guido Anselmi (Marcello Mastroianni), a film director (obviously based on Fellini himself), as he struggles with creative impotence, confused relations with the women in his life, and an inability to reconcile the past and the present (Figure 4.22).

*Juliet of the Spirits* (*Giulietta degli Spiriti*, 1965) is similar to *8 ½* in consisting of a journey into the inner world of an individual, but this time the subject is a woman (played by Giulietta Masina). The tendency in Fellini's style toward panoramic views of a society peopled with grotesque figures and decadent

**FIGURE 4.21**

*La Dolce Vita,* 1960, directed by Federico Fellini. Sylvia (Anita Ekberg) and Marcello (Marcello Mastroianni) stand in the Trevi Fountain in Rome. It is night, when the water is turned off. One of the characteristics of Fellini's style is his telling use of striking physical settings.

**FIGURE 4.22**

*8 ½,* 1963, directed by Federico Fellini. Throughout the film, the director Guido Anselmi (Marcello Mastroianni)—obviously modeled on Fellini himself—periodically dreams of Claudia (Claudia Cardinale), an ideal woman, a source of inspiration and love. Here she sets a table for him in the middle of an old piazza.

events, demonstrated in *La Dolce Vita,* was given free rein in *Fellini Satyricon* (1969). Loosely based on Petronius's picaresque account of the underside of first-century Roman society, the film is intentionally shocking and extravagant in every respect. For 5 years after the completion of *Satyricon,* the director retreated from exotic and erotic pageantry to short, autobiographic cinematic remembrances of Italian things past: *The Clowns (I Clowns,* 1970, a television production), *Roma* (1972), and *Amarcord* (1974).

He returned again to the style of *La Dolce Vita* with *Fellini's Casanova* (1976). This fantasy on the life of the eighteenth-century sexual athlete and prodigious writer of memoirs (played by Donald Sutherland) is as vivid as its predecessors, but the tone of this epic is sour. *Orchestra Rehearsal* (1979, made for television) is an amusing and telling fable on the conflict between authority and freedom. Fellini released *City of Women* in 1981 and *And the Ship Sails On* in 1983.

Energy and imaginativeness are the hallmarks of Fellini's style, and a viewer is never bored by his films. His spontaneity, intensity, and insistence that, like Terence, he counts nothing human as foreign to him result in memorable but uneven motion pictures. Although through the brilliance and boldness of his cinematic imagination he brings milieus and character types to life, he can also be self-indulgent and diffuse and even on occasion slip from earthiness into vulgarity.

There is a strain of concern with social injustice in Fellini's films; however, of greater interest to him is examining the ramifications of the emotional and spiritual malaise of our time. There is frequently a tension in his work between an uncompromising presentation of reality and a reaching out by his characters for transcendental values. The problem is that these values, to be found in love, art, and religion, are usually illusory. In a Fellinian world, loneliness is a condition from which a human being can be distracted but not easily freed. The ambiguity of a symbolic rather than actual resolution of problems with which Fellini so often ends his dramas is the best he can offer. Still, as made most explicit in *8 ½,* the director's struggles with himself result in the victories of his films, and we participate in the satisfaction of these triumphs of vitality, art, and hope over passivity, commercialism, and pessimism every time we view one of his works.

Michelangelo Antonioni (1912–) shares with Fellini a disillusionment with modern society, especially in its attitudes toward male-female relationships. Their styles, however, are radically different. Antonioni's approach is humorless, implicitly moralistic, and he rarely suggests hope for his characters, symbolic or otherwise. He has made significant contributions to the post–World War II development of the nonlinear plot in the service of deeper psychological insights into human nature. His films are visually exquisite, crafted to a refinement upon which no moment of clumsiness is allowed to intrude. Antonioni is a poet of human nerve endings exposed to and rasped by failure, frustration, and despair.

Elements of presentation play a vital role in Antonioni's works. He is a master of color and the expressive use of natural sounds. Settings are never simply backdrops for actors, but rather touchstones for the emotional states of characters. His feelings about today's cities and industries are ambivalent. On the one hand, he abhors the dehumanizing, unadorned efficiency of modern architecture. Frequently, he will contrast contemporary structures with the human scale and artistic decoration of Renaissance palaces and churches or the hectic impersonality of urban life with the serenity derived from intimate contact with nature. On the other hand, he is fascinated by the energy, purity of abstract design, and clear exposure of structural material to be found in skyscrapers and industrial plants.

Antonioni began his career in cinema as a critic and screenwriter. In the mid-forties, he turned to documentaries and short fiction films. These early works were predominantly Neorealist in tone, as were his feature-length fiction dramas of the fifties: *Cronaca di in Amore* (1950), *I Vinti* (1952), *La Signora senza Camelie* (1953), *Le Amiche* (*The Girl Friends,* 1955), and *Il Grido* (*The Cry,* 1957).

With a remarkable realization of intentions and mastery of an innovative style, the director suddenly created *L'Avventura* (1960), a pivotal work for understanding what critics mean by *modernism* in commercial cinema. The story, Antonioni's own, describes a trip taken by a group of nouveau riche but spiritually sterile characters to a barren island off Sicily. On the island, a young woman, Anna, disappears. Claudia (Monica Vitti), Anna's friend, and Sandro (Gabriele

Ferzetti), Anna's fiancé, return to the mainland in search of her. The two become lovers. Preoccupied with their relationship, they forget about Anna (we are never told what actually happened to her). At a party, the weak Sandro, filled with self-contempt because he has given up his dream of being an artistic architect and instead is a designer of mundane housing projects, betrays Claudia with an expensive prostitute. At the end the two remain together more out of desperation and fear of loneliness than mutual love and respect (Figure 4.23).

**FIGURE 4.23**

*L'Avventura*, 1960, directed by Michelangelo Antonioni. In the final shot of the film, Claudia (Monica Vitti) and Sandro (Gabriele Ferzetti) achieve a tentative, ambiguous reconciliation. The ruin behind them symbolizes both their relationship and the degeneration of values in contemporary society.

*La Notte* (*The Night,* 1960, which deals with a day and night in the lives of an unhappy, estranged couple, played by Jeanne Moreau and Marcello Mastroianni) and *The Eclipse* (*L'Eclisse,* 1962, about a tentative, uncertain love affair between a stockbroker and an intelligent but insecure young woman [Figure 4.24]) are sometimes considered to constitute a trilogy with *L'Avventura*. *The Red Desert* (*Il Deserto Rosso,* 1964) is a disconcerting film about the nervous breakdown of Giuliana (Vitti) as she reaches out in vain for help from her husband, son, and lover (Richard Harris). The expressionistic use of color in the drama is superbly effective, as in Antonioni's next film, *Blow-Up* (1966, made in England). It incisively depicts ''mod'' London in the sixties, and through the story of an egocentric photographer who accidentally witnesses a murder, it explores the relationship of the artist to his society. *Zabriskie Point* (1969, made in the United States) is another attempt on the part of the

director to capture the ambiance of rebellious youth in a rebellious decade. Unfortunately, even some brilliant sequences cannot compensate for a haphazard narrative development and unsubstantial characterizations. *The Passenger* (1975, starring Jack Nicholson) is a stylistic tour de force, including a penultimate single tracking shot of 7 minutes' duration that is phenomenal. The director's oblique, fragmented approach, however, obscures rather than subtly reveals, as his sixties dramas do, who characters are and why they act as they do.

**FIGURE 4.24**

*The Eclipse,* 1962, directed by Michelangelo Antonioni. Vittoria (Monica Vitti) and Piero (Alain Delon) meet at the stock exchange in Rome where Piero works as a broker. They have an inconclusive affair that reveals the strengths and weaknesses of each one's character.

Antonioni has not released an impressive major motion picture since 1975. (*The Mystery of Oberwald* [*Il Mistero di Oberwald,* 1980] is far from impressive.) This is a loss to the art of cinema, for few directors today have his gift for combining technical mastery and a remarkable sensitivity to visual values with insights, made concrete and vivid, into the spiritual ills of the post–World War II era.

Pier Paolo Pasolini (1922–1975) was one of the most versatile artists to emerge from postwar Italy. He was a writer of fiction, poetry, and screenplays, a political essayist, a painter, an actor, an important contributor to the development of the Italian school of cine-semiology,* and, of course, a film director. Three concerns appear and intertwine in his dramas: an unswerving commitment to Marxist politics, an unorthodox attitude toward the Christian religion, and a preoccupation with the ways in which sex influences the actions of human beings.

His earliest works, from *Accattone* (1961) to *The Gospel According to St. Matthew* (*Il Vangelo Secondo Matteo,* 1964) and *The Hawks and the Sparrows* (*Uccellacci e Uccellini,* 1966), deal with social and political problems, even in his life of Christ. With *Teorema* (1968), Pasolini entered the provinces of surrealism and myth. The story involves a mysterious (perhaps divine) stranger who arouses and satisfies the emotional and sexual needs of both female and male members of a bourgeois household (Figure 4.25). His interest in myth resulted in controversial versions of *Oedipus Rex* (*Edipo Re,* 1967), *Media* (1970), *The Decameron* (*Il Decamerone,* 1971), *The Canterbury Tales* (*I Racconti di Canterbury,* 1972), and *Soló* or *The 120 Days of Sodom* (1976, derived from the Marquis De Sade's novel).

**FIGURE 4.25**

*Teorema,* 1968, directed by Pier Paolo Pasolini (color). After a visit from a stranger (Terence Stamp), the life of each member of a pampered, emotionally sterile family is radically changed. The father, Paolo (Massimo Girotti), finds himself in a surrealistic scene naked on a desert, and he howls with frustration at the emptiness of his life.

*p. 91

Pasolini's insistence on shocking or at least disquieting his audiences has not endeared him to all viewers, but even his detractors admit that he was a film director of immense talent and imaginativeness. He influenced many contemporary filmmakers. Marco Bellocchio, for example, has developed the special mixture in his mentor's work of sexual perversity, sadism, and social criticism in *Fists in His Pocket* (*I Pugni in Tasca,* 1966), a thoroughly unpleasant film, and *China Is Near* (*La Cina è Vicina,* 1969).

The true heir apparent to the cinematic territory staked out by Pasolini, however, is Bernardo Bertolucci. The major works of his oeuvre to date are *Before the Revolution* (*Prima dello Revoluzione,* 1964), *The Spider's Strategy* (*Strategia del Ragno,* 1970, perhaps his most organically integrated work), *The Conformist* (*Il Conformista,* 1970, an adaptation of Alberto Moravia's novel), *Last Tango in Paris* (1973), *1900* (1976), and *La Luna* (1979). *1900* illustrates both the weaknesses and the strengths of the director. It is a 4-hour epic (one-fourth was deleted in the version released in the United States) that is diffuse in sections, too didactic in its Marxism, and often stereotyped in its characterizations. Yet there are striking scenes, the connection made between sexuality and political views is convincing, and the counterpoising of the lives of ordinary individuals with momentous historical events is not unworthy of the tradition begun by Griffith and the great Russian directors.

Neorealism did not fade away after the midfifties. At least two directors have demonstrated that the movement still has validity. Ermanno Olmi's depictions of life among white-collar workers and peasants are done with an understanding and a sympathy for their problems that rivals the compassion of De Sica. He is typically Neorealist in his objectivity and dependence primarily on nonprofessional actors, but he adds a poetic dimension to his style that was achieved only by Visconti among the earlier generation of supporters of the movement. His outstanding films include *Time Stood Still* (*Il Tempo si è Fermato,* 1959), *Il Posto* (*The Job* or *The Sound of Trumpets,* 1961) (Figure 4.26), *The Fiancés* (*I Fidanzati,* 1962), *One Fine Day* (*Un Certo Giorno,* 1969), *The Scavengers* (*I Recuperanti,* 1970), and *The Tree of Wooden Clogs* (*L'Albero degli Zoccoli,* 1980).

**FIGURE 4.26**

*Il Posto,* 1961, directed by Ermanno Olmi. In this Neorealistic film, Domenico (Sandro Panzeri), a young man from an impoverished working-class family, obtains a post in an impersonal, bureaucratic industrial firm. Here he is reprimanded by his supervisor and forced to move back in a row of desks, thus being demoted in the hierarchy of the office.

Francesco Rosi has combined melodramatic plots, usually centering on crimes and criminals, with the style of Neorealism and an acute social consciousness. The relation of the individual to authority, the latter often impersonal and oppressive, is the major theme in *Salvatore Giuliano* (1962), *Hands Over the City* (*Le Mani sulla Città,* 1963), *The Moment of Truth* (*Il Momento della Verità,* 1964), *The Mattei Affair* (1972), and *Illustrious Corpses* (1977).

As indicated earlier in this survey, Alessandro Blasetti and Mario Camerini continued to direct films until the late sixties. Giuseppe De Santis was a distinguished creator of Neorealist dramas in the late forties, but the quality of his work declined in the fifties. During a fecund period of 4 years he released *The Tragic Hunt* (*Caccia Tragica,* 1947), *Bitter Rice* (*Riso Amaro,* 1949), *No Peace Among the Olives* (*Non C'è Pace tra gli Ulivi,* 1950), and *Rome, Eleven O'Clock* (*Roma, Ore Il,* 1951). Three other prominent Neorealist filmmakers were Luigi Zampa (for example, *To Live in Peace, Vivere in Pace,* 1946), Alberto Lattuada (for instance, *Without Pity, Senza Pietà,* 1948), and Carlo Lizzani (for example, *Chronicle of Poor Lovers, Cronache di Poveri Amanti,* 1954).

Gillo Pontecorvo is renowned for his superb *The Battle of Algiers* (*La Battaglia di Algiers,* 1965), a fiction film that has all the surface characteristics of a documentary on the struggle of the Algerians for independence. While not being too one-sided, the director's sympathies are obviously with the insurgents. His other feature films, including *Kapò* (1960) and *Burn!* (*Queimada!,* 1970), possess little of the conviction and drama of his most famous work. Renato Castellani was a member of the Neorealist movement (as demonstrated in *Two Cents of Hope, Due Soldi di Speranza,* 1952) but is best known for directing the British production of *Romeo and Juliet* (1954). Mario Monicelli has made numerous films, most of them comedies,* but he also has directed a few worthwhile dramas, such as the superb *The Organizer* (*I Compagni,* 1963). Elio Petri has forged an individual style for his incisive works of social criticism from a leftist point of view, for example, *The Assassin* (*L'Assassino,* 1960), *A Quiet Day in the Country* (*Un Tranquillo Posto di Campagna,* 1968), *Investigation of a Citizen Above Suspicion* (*Indagine su un Cittadino al di sopra di Ogni Sospetto,* 1970), and *Lulu the Tool* (*La Classe Operaio va in Paradiso,* 1971). Other notable Italian directors of this period include Valerio Zurlini, Mauro Bolognini, Francesco Maselli, and Antonio Pietrangeli.

Since the Italian government's shortsighted rejection of Neorealist cinema, state support has been more generous and adventurous through the agencies of the Italnoleggio Cinematografico for film and RAI for television. The latter has been a significant influence in sustaining the vitality of Italian cinema.

### FRANCE

The French motion picture industry quickly recovered from the debilitating effects of war conditions and the German occupation. Unlike Italy, however, a creative cinematic movement did not emerge in this country until the late fifties. Before the appearance of the New Wave filmmakers, there were three categories of directors: veterans of the thirties who were still productive, individualistic and independent directors who

operated basically on the outskirts of the commercial film industry, and newcomers who did not make their debuts as directors until after World War II.

Aside from the unique Jean Renoir, who never faltered in his 45-year career, the major figures of the thirties (including Marcel Carné, René Clair, Marcel Pagnol, Sacha Guitry, Julien Duvivier, and Marc Allégret) continued to be active in the forties and after, but they had passed their prime as directors. Three others had established reputations before World War II; however, generally their finest work was released after 1945. Becker and Autant-Lara were no more than noteworthy in their achievements; Max Ophuls became in his last years a master filmmaker.

Jacques Becker revealed his special talent for authentic, panoramic depictions of different segments of French society in *It Happened at the Inn* (*Goupi Mains-Rouges,* 1943), *Antoine et Antoinette* (1947), *Honor Among Thieves* (*Touchez pas au grisbi,* 1954), and *Night Watch* (*La Trou,* 1960), among other films. His most famous work is *Casque d'or* (*Golden Helmet,* 1952); exquisitely photographed, it deals with violence and love among apache dancers at the end of the nineteenth century.

Claude Autant-Lara's first international success was *Devil in the Flesh* (*Le Diable au corps,* 1947, based on the Raymond Radiguet novel). His later work was uneven, but at his best he could combine telling satire of middle-class hypocrisy with penetrating psychological portrayals of human beings reacting to emotional stress. Among his outstanding dramas are *Keep an Eye on Amelia* (*Occupe-toi d'Amélie,* 1949), *The Red Inn* (*L'Auberge rouge,* 1951), and *Thou Shalt Not Kill* (*Non Uccidere,* 1961, an Italian production).

Max Ophuls (1902–1957) was born in Germany and made films there, in the Netherlands, and in the United States, as well as in France. However, he did his finest work in his adopted home and is usually categorized as a French director. After more than a decade in the German theater, he made his first film in 1930. By the late forties, he had established a reputation as a rather conventional director with a distinctive, theatrical style and a highly developed sense of irony. Most notable of the films of these two decades were *The Bartered Bride* (*Die Verkaufte*

*Braut,* 1932), *Liebelei* (1933), *La Tendre Ennemie* (1936), and—among those he directed in Hollywood —*Letter From an Unknown Woman* (1948) and *The Reckless Moment* (1949).

To this point the oeuvre of Ophuls would have earned him mention in histories of motion pictures as an interesting but minor director. Then unexpectedly, while in France, he experienced a burst of creative energy that resulted in four splendid films made in a period of 5 years and that lifted him to the rank of major filmmaker. *La Ronde* (1950) is described later in this volume.* *Le Plaisir* (1951) contains adaptations of three Maupassant stories linked by a narrator. *The Earrings of Madame de France* (*Madame de . . .,* 1953) is another narrative "round" in which a pair of earrings passes through many hands before returning to their original owner.

*Lola Montès* (1955) is considered by many critics to be Ophuls's masterpiece. Derived from a novel loosely based on the life of the nineteenth-century courtesan who was a lover of Liszt and mistress of the king of Bavaria, the film opens with the humiliation of Montès as a circus attraction and recounts her life in a series of flashbacks. Although there are weaknesses in the drama (especially in the first released version, which was mutilated by its producer), such as the phlegmatic performance by Martine Carol in the title role, the film's expressive use of color and sound, resourceful manipulation of Cinemascope space, and resplendent settings make it a film advanced for its time and still impressive today.

Ophuls developed a fluent style characterized by ingenious tracking and crane shots. Using decor as a touchstone of character and social conditions was one of his fortes, and he did so with a sensitivity comparable to that of Renoir and later Antonioni. The theme he made his own was the bittersweetness of a relationship between a man and woman in which love and sex are two sides of a coin whose value is often unappreciated by those, usually men, who casually hand it on to others. His women are typically romantic creatures, and for that very reason victims of their illusions.

*p. 276

For all his professionalism and experience, Ophuls, with his foreign background and ironic vision of the interflow between reality and illusion, remained outside the mainstream of commercial French filmmaking. Another, very different type of outsider was Jean Cocteau (1889–1963). He was a man of prodigious energy and astonishing versatility. As a poet, novelist, playwright, essayist, painter, actor, creator of books for ballets, screenwriter, and film director, he was always in the vanguard of new movements in the arts. His ambition was to shock the bourgeoisie, and he succeeded so well that even when in his sixties, he was considered an *enfant terrible*.

Cocteau's first film, *The Blood of a Poet* (*Le Sang d'un poète,* 1930), is a classic of Surrealism, though the leaders of that disputatious movement refused to admit that he was a member of their group. He did not return to cinema until 1939, when he turned to screenwriting. During the next three decades, he wrote eight screenplays for works directed by Robert Bresson, Jean-Pierre Melville, Georges Franju, and others, as well as those for his own films.

The second film he directed was *Beauty and the Beast* (*La Belle et la Bête,* 1946), a fable on the relations between reality and illusion, between the provinces of the conscious and the unconscious. The special effects in this film are spectacular, and it is a lovely fantasy (see Figures 1.2, 1.10, 1.31, and 1.43). Although he also directed *The Eagle with Two Heads* (*L'Aigle à deux têtes,* 1947) and *Intimate Relations* (*Les Parents terribles,* 1948), both adaptations of his own stage plays, his third and fourth major works were released in the fifties. In *Orpheus* (*Orphée,* 1950), Cocteau added to a modern version of the Greek myth a reciprocal love between the poet (played by Jean Marais, who starred in all of the director's films) and a messenger of death, the Princess (Maria Casarès). *The Testament of Orpheus* (*Le Testament d'Orphée,* 1959) is a combination of the subjectivity and Surrealistic style of *The Blood of a Poet* and the characters and mythic overtones of *Orpheus*. It is a strange, intriguing film, autobiographical, almost plotless, and impossible to summarize.

Throughout all of Cocteau's art, in other media as well as cinema, certain themes recur. Most prominent is the question of how we, and especially the "poets" among us, can reconcile the demands of commonplace reality with the fascination of the inner world of dreams and hallucinations. He often suggested, as in *Beauty and the Beast,* that the region of the unconscious is the source of a type of truth about human nature inaccessible in everyday life. In the tradition of the Romantics, death and its meaning obsessed him, and, like Keats, he was "half in love with easeful Death." Love is also romantic in his works, truly realized when it transcends the physical, is committed to self-sacrifice, and does not fear—even welcomes—death as the culmination of passion. These themes and Cocteau's bold, imaginative special effects make him one of cinema's leading fantasts.

If Cocteau's films personify the romantic approach to filmmaking at its best, then at the other end of the cinematic spectrum is the classicism of a contemporary, Robert Bresson (1907–). He became involved with cinema in the mid-thirties but did not make his first feature until 1943. In *The Ladies of the Bois de Boulogne* (*Les Dames du Bois de Boulogne,* 1945), his first major work, a woman spurned attempts to revenge herself on her ex-lover by arranging his marriage to a prostitute. Her revenge is frustrated, however, by the prostitute's devotion to her husband and his forgiveness.

Bresson's style had completely matured when he directed his third film. *Diary of a Country Priest* (*Le Journal d'un curé de campagne,* 1950), a faithful adaptation of Georges Bernanos's novel, is a work of cinematic art of the highest order. A shy, saintly young man struggles not only with his dying body but also

---

**FIGURE 4.27**

*Diary of a Country Priest,* 1950, directed by Robert Bresson. A young country priest (Claude Laydu) must bear the consequences of his simple, sincere, selfless religious fervor (symbolized by the cross, which repeatedly appears in shots and is also the last image in the film).

with his doubts about his worthiness to be a parish priest and his inability to establish genuine contact with his parishioners (Figure 4.27). Six years passed before the filmmaker released another film. In *A Man Escaped* (*Un condamné à mort s'est échappé,* 1956), a French lieutenant condemned to death by the Gestapo escapes from one of their prisons. He is able to do so only when he trusts a young man who becomes his cellmate and might be an informer. *Pickpocket* (1957) tells of a thief who steals almost instinctively until he is reformed by the love of a woman. Bresson completed three additional black-and-white dramas during the sixties: *The Trial of Joan of Arc* (*Le Procès de Jeanne d'Arc,* 1962, as austere a version of the trial as that by Dreyer), *Au hasard, Balthasar* (1966), and *Mouchette* (1966).

The director's major theme of the labyrinthine ways that can lead to spiritual regeneration has continued to preoccupy him in his color films to date, but his approach and views have changed somewhat. Bresson's visual style has become less spare and severe; on the other hand, he has been more pessimistic, placing greater emphasis than in his previous works on the forces of sterility that contaminate the potentials in human beings for redemption. This dark vision manifests itself in *A Gentle Creature* (*Une Femme douce,* 1969), *Four Nights of a Dreamer* (*Quatre nuits d'un rêveur,* 1971), *Lancelot of the Lake* (*Lancelot du Lac,* 1974), *The Devil Probably* (*Le Diable probablement,* 1977), and *L'Argent* (1983).

While adhering to the principles of classic filmmaking in the tradition of Carl Dreyer, Bresson fashioned a personal, uncompromising style. He avoids cinematic embellishments so that a small emphasis of imagery or sound suddenly glows with significance. His camera-editing dynamics and elements of presentation never call attention to themselves; the meaning of an action or object seems to come from within itself. Nonprofessional actors predominate in Bresson's dramas, minimizing the effects of an actor's interpretation of a role. Plots contain ellipses in development, and they are a minor rather than major component of his dramas. Climaxes are unassertive and are sometimes recognizable as such only in retrospect. The psychological motivations of his characters

are dealt with obliquely, if at all; therefore, there is a minimum of antecedent action presented.

This reduction of the components of the narrative film to the barest fundamentals requires a viewer to focus on Bresson's essential subject: his characters' spiritual states. Gradually, indirectly and through symbolic acts, we gain insights into the psyche—or, as the director would have it, the "soul"—of his fictional individuals. And there, buried beneath flesh, words, and overt actions, are intense conflicts between good and evil, creativity and sterility, damnation and redemption, the benevolent hound of heaven and the destructive dogs of materialism. Bresson's films are too grave, unadorned, and subtle to be widely popular, but to a sympathetic, sensitive viewer, they are as rewarding as they are demanding.

Although Ophuls, Cocteau, and Bresson may have contributed to the art of film, the French motion picture industry after World War II depended for profits and large audiences on the less adventurous filmmakers of the older generation. New directors did emerge in the late forties and the fifties, but most of them were limited in imagination and skill. A few, however, established individual styles within the restrictions of established practices. René Clement's ability to point up realistic details that create convincing milieus in his dramas and his instinctive sympathy for the downtrodden and outcasts of society are evident in *The Battle of the Rails* (*La Bataille du rail,* 1945), *Forbidden Games* (*Jeux interdits,* 1952), and *Gervaise* (1956, the most dramatic of the cinematic adaptations of Zola's novel *L'Assommoir*), among other works. Henri-Georges Clouzot is most effective in directing gripping psychological thrillers such as *Jenny Lamour* (*Quai des Orfèvres,* 1947), *The Wages of Fear* (*Le Salaire de la peur,* 1953), and *Les Diaboliques* (*The Fiends,* 1955). Jean-Pierre Melville, who died in 1973, with his refined, controlled style, was drawn to studies of introverted people, as in *The Strange Ones* (*Les Enfants terribles,* 1949, an adaptation of a Jean Cocteau novel) and *Leon Morin, Priest* (*Léon Morin, prêtre,* 1961). He was also inspired, as in *Second Breath* (*Le Deuxième souffle,* 1965), by American gangster films. Roger Vadim has wavered between being an exploiter and an artist of cinematic eroticism, evident in *And God Created Woman* (*Et

*Dieu créa la femme,* 1956, starring Brigitte Bardot) and *Dangerous Meetings* (*Les Liaisons dangereuses,* 1960, based on Choderlos de Laclos's classic eighteenth-century novel). Claude Lelouch, the youngest of the group, is best known for his romances, such as *A Man and a Woman* (*Un homme et une femme,* 1965), and his thrillers (for example, *La Bonne Année,* 1973).

While French audiences flocked to movie theaters after the war, serious critics lamented the conventionality of the majority of films being released. They searched in vain for a new, exciting approach comparable to the development of Neorealism in Italy. One group in particular set up a verbal ammunition factory behind the walls of a magazine and from this vantage point bombarded the French motion picture industry with criticism. The magazine was *Cahiers du Cinéma,* and its chief writers were soon to direct their own films. They constituted the main contingent of the New Wave *(Nouvelle Vague),* a movement that revitalized French cinema from the late fifties to the end of the sixties.

It is necessary to distinguish between the cohesiveness in attitude of the leading figures—François Truffaut, Jean-Luc Godard, Claude Chabrol, Eric Rohmer, and Jacques Rivette—as critics and the differences between them as filmmakers. It is even more important to recognize the similarities in certain principles but even greater diversity between the *Cahiers du Cinéma* group and other directors categorized by journalists and critics as part of the New Wave, in particular Alain Resnais, Agnès Varda, Louis Malle, and Georges Franju.

*Cahiers du Cinéma* began publication in 1951. The policy *(politique des auteurs)* advocated by its staff was described earlier in this book as the *auteur* theory.\* In sum, they criticized the conventionality and artificiality of contemporary French films, praised the commercial genre productions of Hollywood, and advocated that the director be the dominant figure in the creation of a film. Their exemplary *auteur* directors included, among the French, Jean Renoir, Jean Vigo, Abel Gance, and Robert Bresson; among the

Europeans, Roberto Rossellini; and among the Americans, Alfred Hitchcock and Orson Welles.

When these critics came to make their own films, they shared, in addition to their friendship, other similarities. Trauffaut, Godard, and Chabrol were under 30 when they made their first feature films; Rivette was 31, and Rohmer was 36. They had as their professional father image the gentle and generous André Bazin, one of the founders of their magazine. They submerged themselves in motion pictures of the past, spending whole days and evenings at the Cinémathèque Française (under the directorship of Henri Langlois, another of the group's heroes). They defied the standard route of becoming a director (working one's way up the industry hierarchy from a specialization to assistant director to director) by first being critics, then directing shorts or documentaries, and finally creating feature films financed by private sources and government subsidies.

Although the films the five produced were disparate in style and subject matter, they all adhered to certain techniques and tendencies to one degree or another. They insisted on the dominance of the director and either wrote or collaborated on their screenplays, usually original ones. On-location shooting was preferred to studio settings, and the role of the art director was minimized. They approved of improvisation and spontaneity, especially if hand-held cameras were used. They did not hesitate to experiment with new techniques, even if it meant breaking what conventional directors considered cardinal rules of filmmaking.

In the area of content, the five also shared certain ideas. They were preoccupied with the nature of reality in what they perceived as an unstable, fragmented, relativistic contemporary world. They felt that the multifaceted theme of the relations of illusion and reality often required nonlinear, elliptical types of film structures, an ignoring of the traditional separations between the genres, and a subjectivism on the part of both filmmakers and characters that revealed the instinctive nature of human beings without necessarily depending on overt character motivation.

The manifestation of these themes and techniques in individual works and the differences in approach of members of the *Cahiers du Cinéma* group

---

\*pp. 90–91

can best be examined by dealing with each director separately. The works and style of François Truffaut are summarized in Chapter 5 in the "Background" section of the pages devoted to *The 400 Blows*.

Jean-Luc Godard (1930–) is surely the most innovative, provocative, influential, imaginative, and uncompromising of the New Wave filmmakers, as well as the most self-indulgent and exasperating. While still a critic, he made a few short films. His first feature was *Breathless* (*A bout de souffle*, 1959). Audiences were shocked by the undisciplined and cynical main character who existed in an unstable world in which the unexpected and inexplicable were commonplace. Michel Poiccard (Jean-Paul Belmondo) is a car thief and murderer of a policeman who attempts to persuade an American student living in Paris (Jean Seberg) to leave the country with him. She betrays him to the police, and he is killed.

During the sixties, Godard, with phenomenal energy and boldness, challenged what had previously been considered the limitations of commercial cinema. *Le Petit Soldat* (1960) deals with a secret agent who is working against the French military in Algiers but has difficulty distinguishing between friends and enemies. *A Woman Is a Woman* (*Une femme est une femme*, 1961) is a comedy with songs and dances in which a young woman entrances and mystifies her husband and their male friend. *My Life to Live* (*Vivre sa vie*, 1962) (Figure 4.28) consists of 12 episodes in

**FIGURE 4.28**

*My Life to Live,* 1962, directed by Jean-Luc Godard. Anna Karina plays Nana, a French prostitute who sells her body but not her integrity.

the life of a prostitute. In *Les Carbiniers* (1963), the director experiments with ways of counterpoising reality and illusion in a fable about two soldiers in a ridiculous war.

*Contempt* (*Le Mépris,* 1963) is one of the director's more conventional dramas, the story of a love triangle that develops during the making of a film version of *The Odyssey*. *Band of Outsiders* (*Bande à part,* 1964) is a pseudogangster film in which three amateur criminals find even death less real than their relationships and the games they play together. More serious in tone is *The Married Woman* (*Un femme mariée,* 1964). A researcher in contemporary mores finds her attitudes toward her husband and her lover contaminated by the commercialism she writes about in which everything, including human beings, becomes an object.

Under the guise of science fiction, *Alphaville* (1965) is a telling comment on modern conformity done in the style of a comic book story or "B" movie (its original title was "Tarzan versus IBM"). *Pierrot le fou* (1965) returns to the present to describe the experiences of a middle-aged man who leaves his wife for an attractive young woman involved with criminals. *Masculin-féminin* (1966) examines the attitudes and actions of a group of young people, "the children of Marx and Coca-Cola." *Made in U.S.A.* (1966), in its fragmented, oblique way, deals with violence and assassination. A plot of sorts consists of the efforts of a young woman to track down the murderer of her lover. *Two or Three Things I Know About Her* (*Deux ou trois choses que je sais d'elle,* 1966), like *My Life to Live,* uses prostitution as a symbol of the debasement of human feelings encouraged by a capitalist society. *La Chinoise* (1967) concerns the members of a Maoist cell who argue about everything they feel and do, including murder.

*Weekend* (1967) is a culmination and summary of the director's increasingly antirealistic style. It is a controversial film, yet not since *Breathless* had Godard so completely and brilliantly fused form and feeling. A couple's weekend drive degenerates narratively into a series of fantastic episodes held together only thematically and by the presence of one or both of the characters (Figure 4.29).Godard demonstrates in the film an obviously honest anguish about a conflict that is a recurring theme in his works: how to reconcile centuries of culture with necessary revolutionary change that must ignore if not destroy that culture.

---

### FIGURE 4.29

*Weekend,* 1967, directed by Jean-Luc Godard. One of the highlights of this cinematic denouncement of the capitalistic society of modern France is a weekend traffic jam (described in one of the titles that punctuate the narrative as "this travesty of civilisation"). In a marvelous single parallel tracking shot that lasts for 10 minutes, we follow one car as it crawls along a highway of accidents and stalled or halted cars, amid a cacophony of blaring horns, sirens, and shouting voices.

Even from these thumbnail sketches of Godard's major pre-1968 films, it is evident that he is a critic of Western society. He has always advocated rebellion, often along Marxist lines, against the crass values of our cultures and the injustices of our political systems. Yet for all his didactic, propagandist intentions, he possesses an impressive gift for creating three-dimensional characterizations of outsiders and individualists who attempt to find, usually unsuccessfully, fulfilling meaning in love, political commitment, or simply rebellion for its own sake. His women (often played during the decade by Anna Karina, his wife at the time) are particularly memorable.

The director's chief influence on contemporary filmmakers and his essential significance lie in his genius for devising viable, innovative cinematic approaches and techniques. He experimented with non-linear plots, undercutting of the illusion of a film as a self-contained entity, intermingling of genres, incor-

porating elements of popular culture into works of art, ignoring conventional principles of continuity and logical development of a dramatic structure, using the hand-held camera without concern for refinements of balanced composition, and manipulating color expressionistically. By means of these devices and many others, Godard imposed a subjective vision of reality on his material and conducted what amounted to a public debate with himself on the role of cinema as a social, psychological, and political interpreter of our world. That he failed as often as he succeeded, that he bored, bewildered, and irritated portions of his audiences as often as he inspired and awed them, is often the fate of an iconoclastic and bold innovator.

*Weekend* was the director's last film in the sixties that retained a clear correlation between means and ends. After 1967, his work became increasingly fragmented and undramatic, as in *Le Gai Savoir* (1968) and *One Plus One* (1968). With *Pravda* (1969), he closely associated himself with the Dziga Vertov group, devoted to making polemic documentaries supporting revolutionary change. This is the approach taken in *Wind from the East* (*Le Vent d'est,* 1969), *Vladimir et Rosa* (1970), and *One P.M.* (1970). Even the fiction films *Tout va bien* (1972) and *Numéro Deux* (1974) are propaganda encapsulated in experiments with images and sound. During the seventies, most of Godard's energy was devoted to radical short films for European television and for sympathetic groups. With *Every Man for Himself* (*Sauve qui peut,* 1980), he apparently returned to commercial-feature filmmaking, though without compromising his individualistic style or critical attitudes toward today's values.

It is not necessary to be a fervent admirer of all of Godard's films or to agree completely with his interpretation of what is wrong with our society to recognize that he, like Bergman, Antonioni, and a few other living directors, has forced us to revise our premises about the capabilities and functions of contemporary narrative cinema.

Claude Chabrol (1930–) began his directing career a year earlier than his colleagues on *Cashiers du Cinéma* with two features. *Le Beau Serge* and *The Cousins (Les Cousins),* both completed in 1958, are powerful films. After making predominantly routine motion pictures during most of the sixties, he again attempted to go beyond the ordinary. The most striking films of this period were *The Girl Friends* (*Les Biches*, 1968), *The Unfaithful Wife* (*La Femme infidèle*, 1968), *The Butcher* (*Le Boucher*, 1969), and *Just Before Midnight* (*Juste avant la nuit*, 1970). In the seventies, the director continued to be prolific, but his work was uneven. *Nada* (1973) and *Violette Nozière* (1978) are among the best of his recent efforts.

Chabrol's favorite genre is the psychological thriller. Although inspired by Hitchcock, he adds an eroticism to his thrillers not to be found in the work of the master of the genre. Chabrol's films generally follow a consistent pattern. The director chooses a closed society, such as a village, and conveys the texture of that society through attention to selected details and an appreciation of the small but telling attitudes and actions of the main characters. Violence hovers in the air as strong emotions frustrated by social restrictions seek expression. The duality of human nature fascinates Chabrol, and he underscores this ambivalence by pairing characters who on the surface are direct opposites but soon reveal that such appearances are deceptive. When his material is suitable, the director is completely convincing in disclosing the dangerous antisocial desires that can grip apparently ordinary people.

Eric Rohmer (1920–) was not only a critic for *Cahiers du Cinéma* but also, after the death of André Bazin, its chief editor from 1958 to 1963. Compared to his colleagues, his development as a filmmaker has been slow and careful. After his first feature, *The Sign of Leo* (*Le Signe du Lion*, 1959), he did not commercially release another one until 1966. He conceived the idea of six "moral tales" *(contes moraux)*. The first two were shot in 16mm, and they were not distributed. The other four were *La Collectionneuse* (1966), *My Night at Maud's* (*Ma nuit chez Maud*, 1969) (Figure 4.30), *Claire's Knee* (*Le Genou de Claire*, 1970), and *Chloë in the Afternoon* (*L'Amour l'apres-midi*, 1972) (Figure 4.30).

The theme the tales share is erotic temptation. In the four feature films, a man who is committed elsewhere emotionally and morally resists the temptation offered by a beautiful, free-spirited woman to stray from the path of virtue. Unlike most other New

**FIGURE 4.30**

*My Night at Maud's,* 1969, directed by Eric Rohmer (color). Jean-Louis (Jean-Louis Trintignant)—regardless of his Catholic background, commitment to Françoise, and strict views on morality—is tempted to have an affair with the beautiful, intelligent, and sexually available Maud (Françoise Fabian).

Wave directors, Rohmer shuns melodrama, though he does have a predilection for unusual accidents that further his plots. The distinguishing quality of his characters is that they talk fluently and at length about their ideas and feelings. Language in these dramas can disguise as well as reveal. One of the fascinations of watching and listening to these films is to attempt to penetrate beneath first impressions of motives, words, and actions to what is psychologically and morally valid about each major character. The visual style of these tales is delicate, subtle, and restrained; in fact, Rohmer is the most "classical" of all the major *Nouvelle Vague* filmmakers. He has an admirable ability of avoiding visual clichés even when his characters do nothing but converse.

During the remainder of the seventies, Rohmer made only two other films. *The Marquise of O* (1976, based on a novella by Heinrich von Kleist) and *Perceval* (1978, a version of Chrétien de Troyes's twelfth-century epic) are different in subject matter and approach from his moral tales. Although not departures from the director's preoccupation with moral dilemmas, the two dramas are more slow-paced, stately, and mannered than their predecessors. They are, however, marvelous realizations of the attitudes and milieus of past ages.

Jacques Rivette (1928–) of all the major talents of the *Cahiers du Cinéma* group has had the greatest difficulty in finding an audience and financing for his films. The reasons are self-evident. His severely intellectual, uncompromising, complex works make great demands on audiences. There are rewards, however, for viewers who have the patience and stamina to sit through his dramas, for his inimitable cinematic constructs yield insights into how individuals' fantasies and paranoia can destroy their capability for contentment in life.

*Paris nous appartient* (1960) is Rivette's first feature film. *La Religieuse* (1965) was banned in France for its alleged anticlericalism. *L'Amour fou* (1968), over 4 hours in length, counterpoints actors rehearsing classical dramas with their real-life relationships. *Out One: Spectre* (1972) was originally a 12-hour television film reduced to 4 ½ hours for theater distribution. *Celine and Julie Go Boating* (*Céline et Julie vont en bateau,* 1974) is atypical in the humor it contains, and while far from conventional, it is the most accessible for most viewers of the director's feature films to date.

One of the writers for *Cashiers du Cinéma* from its earliest days was unusual in that he devoted his filmmaking career to the documentary rather than to drama. The works of Chris Marker are noted in Chapter 7.* He should be mentioned here because both his writings and his experiments in the documentary on the relationship between image and sound and his exploration of both subjective and *cinéma verité* approaches to the reconstructing of reality influenced Godard, Truffaut, and other contemporaries.

Of filmmakers associated with the *Nouvelle Vague* (at least in the minds of critics), who were not writers for *Cahiers du Cinéma,* the most prominent is Alain Resnais. His themes and style are summarized in the "Background" section of the essay on *Night and Fog* in Chapter 7. Agnès Varda (1928–) shares with Resnais, who edited her first feature film, meticulous craftsmanship, an ability to create striking visuals, and a willingness to experiment with nonlinear narratives. These qualities are evident in *La Point courte* (1955), *Opéra Mouffe* (1958), and *Cléo de 5 à 7*

*pp. 336–337, 347

(1961). *Le Bonheur* (1965) (Figure 4.31) is a fascinating work. The director, an avowed feminist, tells with complete detachment the story of a young carpenter who is equally devoted to his wife and his mistress. The irony of the film lies in the fact that events conspire to assure the happiness of this egocentric man. Varda's other features include *Les Créatures* (1966), *Lion's Love* (1969, made in the United States), and *One Sings, the Other Doesn't* (1977).

---

**FIGURE 4.31**

*Le Bonheur,* 1965, directed by Agnes Varda (color). With a visual grace that is typical of the director's cinematography, the young carpenter François (Jean-Claude Drouot) and his mistress Emilie (Marie-France Boyer) are shown in bed together in her apartment.

Louis Malle (1932–) is one of the most eclectic and versatile of the modern French directors. His range of subject matter, his ability to shift abruptly from one genre mode to another, and his adaptable style are quite remarkable. Within a decade after directing his first feature in 1957, he released an erotic love story starring Jeanne Moreau that had French censors up in arms but brought international fame to both director and star (*The Lovers, Les Amants,* 1958); a satirical comedy based on a novel by Raymond Queneau that while deliberately chaotic in structure, even surrealistic, is also a serious commentary on the frustrations and stresses imposed on anyone living in a big city (*Zazie dans le Métro,* 1960); a portrayal of a movie star, played by Brigitte Bardot

(*A Very Private Affair, Vie privée,* 1961); an uncompromisingly realistic study of the last days of an alcoholic (*The Fire Within, Le Feu follet,* 1963); and a spectacle-comedy, starring Moreau and Bardot, with the incongruous setting of a Mexican revolution (*Viva Maria!,* 1965). He also directed, at the end of the sixties, a series of documentaries on India.

Malle's dramas of the seventies include *Murmur of the Heart* (*Le Souffle au coeur,* 1971); *Lacombe, Lucien* (1973), a controversial film on the emotional needs that impel a young French laborer to become a collaborator during the German occupation; and *Black Moon* (1975), an impressive if somewhat pretentious surrealistic fantasy of the strange adventures of a young woman during a civil war between men and women. His latest dramas have been made in the United States, including *Pretty Baby* (1978) and *Atlantic City* (1981).

Alain Robbe-Grillet was one of the leading novelists in the *Nouveau Roman* movement. He became associated with the New Wave filmmakers first by writing the screenplay for *Last Year at Marienbad* and later by directing his own films. The work with which he made his debut as a director—*The Immortal One* (*L'Immortelle,* 1962)—still remains his most striking. In *Trans-Europ-Express* (1966), *The Man Who Lies* (*L'Homme qui ment,* 1968), *Le Jeu avec le feu* (1974), and others, he continued to experiment with nonlinear narratives, projections on the screen of the subjective worlds of characters, and strange relationships between mysterious men and women. Henri Colpi was a distinguished editor of works by Resnais and other *Nouvelle Vague* filmmakers before directing *Une aussi longue absence* (1961), *Codine* (1962), and other feature films.

Georges Franju, like Jean-Pierre Melville, Jacques Demy, and Roger Vadim, has only a tenuous connection to the New Wave movement. After establishing himself as an innovative director of documentaries,* he made his first feature in 1958 at the age of 46. His fiction films include *The Keepers* (*La Tête contre les murs,* 1958), *Thérèse Desqueroux* (1962, derived from François Mauriac's novel), *Judex* (1963, a modern version of the Robin Hood character invented by Louis Feuillade in 1916), *Thomas L'Imposteur* (1965, adapted by Jean Cocteau from his own novel), *The Demise of Father Mouret* (*La Faute de l'Abbé Mouret,* 1970, based on Emile Zola's novel), and *Le Dernier Mélodrame* (1978). Although Franju can create straightforward dramas, he is most interesting when combining illusion and reality in a single work, in the tradition of Jean Vigo.

Other directors influenced to some degree by the themes and techniques of the rebels of the period include Alexandre Astruc, who made *A Life* (*Une Vie,* 1958) and *Shadow of Adultery* (*La Proie pour l'ombre,* 1960); Serge Bourguignon, director of *Sundays and Cybele* (*Les Dimanches de Ville-d'Avray,* 1962) and others; Jacques Doniol-Valcroze, a cofounder of *Cahiers du Cinéma,* best known for *A Question of Rape* (*La Viol,* 1967); Jacques Rozier; Alain Jessua; and Michel Deville.

The late fifties and the sixties constitute one of the most exciting periods in the history of French cinema. Only in the thirties were dramas of a comparable quality and boldness released in impressive numbers. Moreover, there were outstanding achievements in other genres, such as comedy (for example, the works of Jacques Tati) and the documentary. The majority of major directors of the decade continued to be active during the seventies, and others, such as Costa-Gavras and Marguerite Duras, joined their ranks (see "The Seventies" in this chapter).

---

U.S.A.

The American film industry ended the thirties in fine fettle, with high profits and high attendance. Even the quality of the studios' productions was striking, as demonstrated by the Academy Award winners of 1939 (including *Gone With the Wind, Goodbye, Mr. Chips, Stagecoach, The Wizard of Oz, Mr. Smith Goes to Washington,* and *Wuthering Heights*). These favorable conditions continued during the war years, and after the war, Hollywood still prospered. In 1947 receipts reached the unprecedented level of almost $1.7 billion, a sum that was to remain unequaled until the inflation-bloated mid-seventies. Attendance ran to a weekly average of 90 million, a record surpassed only in 1929 and never again even approached. By

*p. 336

the end of the forties, however, the arch of triumph began to descend.

Unwelcome publicity resulted from the House Committee on Un-American Activities investigation of Hollywood in 1947. Antitrust laws passed in 1950 required that the studios give up their control over exhibiting motion pictures. This meant the end of guaranteed bookings for inexpensive genre films. By 1954, for example, production of "B" Westerns had ended. In 1944, some 401 feature films were released in the United States; in 1954, the number dropped to 253. To studio executives, however, their true nemesis was the rise of the medium of television. In 1952, there were 18 million television sets in use; audiences were increasingly staying at home, enjoying free entertainment rather than paying at the box office. More insidious and in the end most destructive to the absolute dominance of the studios over the industry was the rise of the independent producer. His authority in all aspects of production relegated a studio to the roles of renter of facilities, distributor, and financial backer.

Under the pressure of rapidly decreasing revenues, Hollywood reacted in the fifties with hysteria and prophecies of doom, then practical countermeasures. Technical novelties unavailable on "the box" were ballyhooed: wide-screen systems, 3-D, and Technicolor. When denying TV access to their backlog of films did not stop falling attendance at movie theaters, the studios capitulated. Networks were allowed to bid on thousands of films in large blocks, and sound stages were rented to TV production units. Studios merged, staffs were drastically reduced, exclusive contracts with filmmakers and actors were canceled, and schools for potential stars that each studio had maintained were disbanded.

In the sixties, the film industry reached its nadir as a profit-making business. This is made evident by some statistics. In 1955, 254 motion pictures were produced in the United States and 138 imported; in 1965, 153 originated in the United States and 299 were imported. Average weekly attendance in 1957 was 45 million; in 1967 it was 17.8 million. Before 1958, none of the major seven companies showed financial losses; between 1958 and 1969, six of these studios (the exception was Universal) in individual years lost substantial sums.[5] Matters improved considerably during the seventies, but by then the industry had undergone many metamorphoses, and its essential character had changed radically from the heyday of the thirties and forties.

After World War II, the major directors who had established their reputations before 1945 and were discussed in the preceding section continued, with one exception, to be active during the fifties and, in some cases, into the sixties. They included Orson Welles, Howard Hawks, John Ford, King Vidor, Lewis Milestone, Mervyn Le Roy, William Wellman, George Cukor, W. S. Van Dyke, George Stevens, Fritz Lang, Michael Curtiz, and William Dieterle. The exception was Josef von Sternberg. His last important film was *The Shanghai Gesture* (1941); he directed three more motion pictures between 1950 and 1953, two of them refashioned by others, and then retired.

Two veteran European filmmakers began the American periods of their careers in the beginning of the forties and quickly rose to the top rank of Hollywood directors. Alfred Hitchcock came to the United States in 1939, and *Rebecca* was released in 1940. Within a decade, he had joined John Ford and Howard Hawks in a triumvirate of the most consistently successful directors in Hollywood whose experience went back to the silent era. The major themes and techniques of Hitchcock's works made on both sides of the Atlantic were discussed earlier.* Billy Wilder was an eminent screenwriter both in Europe and the United States before his solo directing debut in 1942. He is best known for his comedies of the fifties, which are surveyed in Chapter 6.† Previously, however, he had directed a series of films, including *Double Indemnity* (1944), *The Lost Weekend* (1945), *Sunset Boulevard* (1950), and *Ace in the Hole* (1951), considered part of the *Film Noir* movement in the United States.

The term *film noir* was invented by *Cahiers du Cinéma* critics in the 1950s during their extensive and enthusiastic studies of Hollywood genre films. They discerned in certain films that were released just after World War II dealing with crime, violence, and moral

---

*pp. 126–128
†pp. 279–280

degeneracy similarities in cinematic style and attitudes toward society. It is debatable whether or not these films constitute a genuine movement. However, their directors did influence one another, and the films did share distinct characteristics. On this basis, the films will be treated here as a movement, and we will capitalize *Film Noir.*

The "dark" half of the appellation referred to a vision of society as inherently corrupt, with lust for power, money, and sex as typical as the impurities that contaminate the rivers that run through big cities. Characters who survived this sordidness did so because of a tough stubbornness, a shrewd cynicism about human nature, a loyalty to friends and clients, and an uncompromising professionalism. There was a focus in these films on the gray area between good and evil. The context of this movement, in short, was the American Dream, with its advocacy of individualism, pragmatism, and aggressiveness, turned nightmare.

Plots were complex (which increased the opportunities for ambiguity in characterization) and melodramatic (which held the attention of audiences while they were being exposed to pessimistic attitudes toward society and human nature). It was, however, the cinematic style that was most distinctive; in fact, there are critics who maintain that *Film Noir* can only be characterized in terms of this style. Static, lengthy long shots were favored, yet when the camera did move, it was restless, probing and sweeping in a baroque manner. Chiaroscuro was pervasive. Every effort was made to convey palpably the tone and texture of a place setting, especially nightlife in a big city. Even the homes of the wealthy conveyed an ambiance of seediness buried under a blanket of expensive objects, like the sickly odor of decadence masked by expensive perfume.

Cinematic influences on the movement include American crime films of the thirties (which were less morally ambiguous, less cynical in world-view, less convoluted in plots, and less elaborate in cinematography), the dramatic lighting and preoccupation with intense emotions of German Expressionism, French Poetic Realism (particularly the murder dramas of Marcel Carné), and the contemporaneous works of Italian Neorealists.

In view of the importance of the brooding quality and stylized approach of Expressionism to this American movement, it is not surprising that three contributors should have emigrated from Germany to Hollywood. The most prominent was Fritz Lang, who anticipated the style of *Film Noir* in his first two American dramas, *Fury* (1936) and *You Only Live Once* (1937), and helped to develop it in *The Woman in the Window* (1944) and *Scarlet Street* (1945). Robert Siodmak, who came to the United States in 1940, directed *The Killers* (1946, based on Ernest Hemingway's short story) and *Cry of the City* (1948). Edgar Ulmer learned quickly in the mid-thirties how to make distinctive films with very low budgets. His contributions to *Film Noir* include *Bluebeard* (1944) and *Detour* (1946).

Although other films in addition to ones by Lang and Siodmak anticipated the style of *Film Noir,* such as John Huston's *The Maltese Falcon* (1941), the movement flourished only from 1945 to 1950. Among the works in this style that appeared during that half decade were Edward Dmytryk's *Murder My Sweet* (1944) and *Cornered* (1945), Robert Montgomery's *Lady in the Lake* (1946), Tay Garnett's *The Postman Always Rings Twice* (1946), Hawks's *The Big Sleep* (1946), Anthony Mann's *T-Men* (1947), Edmund Goulding's *Nightmare Alley* (1947), Henry Hathaway's *Kiss of Death* (1947), Raoul Walsh's *White Heat* (1949), Robert Wise's *The Set-Up* (1949), Rudolph Maté's *D.O.A.* (1949), Nicholas Ray's *They Live by Night* (1949) and *In a Lonely Place* (1950), Huston's *The Asphalt Jungle* (1950), Jules Dassin's *Night and the City* (1950), and the aforementioned films by Wilder, Lang, Siodmak, and Ulmer.

After 1950, echoes of the *Film Noir* approach were evident in some motion pictures, including Russell Rouse's *The Thief* (1952), Robert Aldrich's *Kiss Me Deadly* (1955), Hubert Cornfield's *Plunder Road* (1957), and Samuel Fuller's *Verboten!* (1958). French filmmakers were also influenced by this movement, directly in the cases of Jean-Pierre Melville and Henri-Georges Clouzot and indirectly, by way of parody, in certain works by Godard, Truffaut, and Malle.

Four directors who made their first successful films in the forties and rose to particular eminence were John Huston, Elia Kazan, Joseph Mankiewicz, and Otto Preminger. In the opinion of many critics, the most individual and creative of the four is John Huston (1906–). After an adventurous youth, Huston became an outstanding screenwriter (for example, *Jezebel, Dr. Erlich's Magic Bullet, High Sierra,* and *Sergeant York*). He has taken advantage of this experience by writing many of the screenplays for his own films.

Huston's debut as a director was a remarkable one. *The Maltese Falcon* (1941) is a classic of the detective genre. The performances of Humphrey Bogart (as Sam Spade), Mary Astor, Sidney Greenstreet, and Peter Lorre are part of the treasured memories of any movie buff (Figure 4.32). After two more conventional dramas, Huston entered the U.S. Army. The documentaries he created are among the finest directed by an American during World War II.*

---

**FIGURE 4.32**

*The Maltese Falcon,* 1941, directed by John Huston. The four principals (left to right, Humphrey Bogart as Sam Spade, Peter Lorre as Joel Cairo, Mary Astor as Brigid O'Shaughnessy, and Sidney Greenstreet as Kasper Gutman) at the apparent denouement, when the falcon is found, but this is only the beginning of the end.

The director returned to fiction filmmaking with the superb *The Treasure of the Sierra Madre* (1948), a terse study of greed and the instinct for survival cast in the form of a modern Western. The thrillers *Key*

*Largo* (1948) and *We Were Strangers* (1949) were followed by three provocative dramas: *The Asphalt Jungle* (1950), a notable contribution to *Film Noir; The Red Badge of Courage* (1951); and *The African Queen* (1951).

From 1952 to 1960, Huston's work was generally mediocre. The seven motion pictures of this period range from the competent *Moulin Rouge* (1952) and *Moby Dick* (1956) to the disastrous *The Roots of Heaven* (1958). He recovered his stride with *The Misfits* (1961), a modern Western. Since then, Huston's directing activities have been uneven. He could descend to the level of the merely perfunctory in the Italian production *La Bibia* (*The Bible: In the Beginning,* 1966) and rise to the high seriousness of *Freud* (1962), *Reflections in a Golden Eye* (1967), *Fat City* (1972), and *Wise Blood* (1979).

Huston is phenomenally versatile. He is equally masterful in creating the excitement of the adventure spectacular *The Man Who Would Be King* (1975), the humor of the parody *Beat the Devil* (1953), the brooding quality of *The Asphalt Jungle,* the stark realism of *Fat City,* the mythic dimension of *The Red Badge of Courage,* and the moral chiaroscuro of *Reflections in a Golden Eye.* This is not to say that there is no consistency in themes and techniques in his oeuvre. Huston is obviously attracted by plots in which individuals have their lives or security threatened and who learn that the struggle against adversity is a vitalizing experience in itself. His insights into characters are direct, unencumbered by overtones of psychological complexities. The director's style is never less than professional and is characterized by unflagging vigor, integration of every aspect of filmmaking, and attention to the composition and significance of individual shots.

Elia Kazan (1909–) was known as an outstanding director in the theater during the thirties and forties. *A Tree Grows in Brooklyn* (1945) was his first commercial feature film. During the 24 years of his filmmaking career (he has not directed a motion picture since 1969), Kazan created psychological dramas that center on the conflict between an individual and a hostile environment, as in *A Streetcar Named Desire* (1952) (Figure 4.33) and *Baby Doll* (1956)—both derived from plays by Tennessee Williams—*East of*

---

*p. 339

*Eden* (1955), *Splendor in the Grass* (1961), and adaptations of his own novels (*America, America,* 1964, and *The Arrangement,* 1969).

---

**FIGURE 4.33**

*A Streetcar Named Desire,* 1951, directed by Elia Kazan. The conflict between Blanche Dubois (Vivien Leigh) and her brother-in-law Stanley Kowalski (Marlon Brando) only overtly involves money. The two are diametrically opposite in their personalities and values.

He is associated primarily, however, with dramas that deal with specific social themes, including *Gentleman's Agreement* (1947, on anti-Semitism), *Pinky* (1949, on racism), *Panic in the Streets* (1950, on the ineffectualism of government bureaucracies), *Viva Zapata!* (1952, on the betrayal of political ideals), *Man on a Tightrope* (1952, on the threat of communism), and *A Face in the Crowd* (1957, on demagoguery in a democracy). His most controversial and celebrated film is *On the Waterfront* (1954). It is the story of a has-been fighter, Terry Malloy (played superlatively by Marlon Brando), who informs on his boss, a gangster, by testifying before a state committee investigating corruption on the New York waterfront. The film is a thinly disguised defense by the director of his cooperation with the Committee on Un-American Activities during its investigation of communist influence in Hollywood, and the film was denounced by contemporary liberals.

One of Kazan's major contributions to Hollywood filmmaking was to encourage a new style of acting—exemplified in his work by the performances of Marlon Brando, James Dean, and Rod Steiger—that was based on the "Method acting" developed in the Group Theatre and Actors Studio. Kazan never achieved a unique visual style as a screen director, hampered as he was by a tendency toward obvious melodrama and dependency on theatrical effects not fully assimilated into cinematic techniques. He was responsible, however, for a series of films that dramatically and vigorously chronicled two decades of changing American attitudes and prejudices.

Joseph Mankiewicz (1909–) entered the motion picture industry as a screenwriter in the thirties with the assistance of his older brother Herman. He also was active as a producer between 1936 and 1944. When he turned to directing, he was usually screenwriter and producer of his own films.

Between *Dragonwyck* (1946) and *Sleuth* (1972), his last film, Mankiewicz directed many very popular motion pictures, including *The Late George Apley* (1947), *The Ghost and Mrs. Muir* (1947), *Julius Caesar* (1953), *The Barefoot Contessa* (1954), *Guys and Dolls* (1955), *The Quiet American* (1958), and *Suddenly Last Summer* (1959). The qualities that made Mankiewicz a noteworthy director are best illustrated in *All About Eve* (1950, starring Bette Davis in one of her best roles) and *A Letter to Three Wives* (1949). Both are caustic comedies on the insecurities that fester beneath the facades presented by theater stars and married couples. Along with the team of Billy Wilder and Charles Brackett, Mankiewicz wrote the wittiest, most sophisticated dialogue that issued from the American screen in the late forties and early fifties. He was consistently conventional in his cinematic style, but in this as well as every other aspect of his films he demonstrated intelligence, the attribute most often accorded him by critics.

Otto Preminger (1906–) prompts strong reactions from his colleagues, critics, and viewers. For some, he is an opportunist and a shrewd businessman whose chief gift is for publicizing his own flamboyant personality. To others, he has boldly challenged the taboos of Hollywood and is able to invest even mediocre material with personal élan. There is no question that he has an individual directorial style; characteristics of this style are a certain *tristesse* that permeates even his comedies, a distrust of moral certitudes, a fluency of camera-editing dynamics, and a preference for the *mise-en-scène* approach to that of montage. Although he is too impatient and cost-conscious to be an impeccable craftsman, he rarely falls below the standards of a professional equally adept in many genres.

After a career as a stage director and actor in Austria and Germany, Preminger emigrated to the United States in 1935. He directed his first motion picture in Hollywood a year later but did not attract attention until he released the sophisticated murder mystery *Laura* (1944). Since the mid-forties, he has directed and, in most cases, produced over 30 films. His most distinguished work is probably *The Man With the Golden Arm* (1956), a fine drama on drug addiction based on the Nelson Algren novel and starring Frank Sinatra. With this film and the earlier *The Moon Is Blue* (1954), he defied Hollywood's Production Code, and he was a leading figure in efforts to liberalize that code. To his credit, he has never hesitated to challenge the industry's sub-rosa and stated taboos, especially in the areas of race (such as using all-black casts for *Carmen Jones,* 1954, and *Porgy and Bess,* 1959) and sex (for example, *Forever Amber,* 1947, and *Bonjour tristesse,* 1957). It is not, however, the quality of individual motion pictures that is most impressive about the director's oeuvre but the number of notable, often exciting, and usually commercially successful films for which he has been responsible, including *Daisy Kenyon* (1947), *Angel Face* (1952), *Saint Joan* (1957), *Anatomy of a Murder* (1958), *Exodus* (1960), *The Cardinal* (1963), *Bunny Lake Is Missing* (1965), and *Tell Me That You Love Me, Junie Moon* (1969).

Veterans like Ford, Hawks, and Hitchcock and relative newcomers to directing who established imposing records for making commercial successes, such as Huston, Wilder, Kazan, Mankiewicz, and Preminger, have received the lion's share of public acclaim. There has been since World War II, however, a group of new directors whose talents are often no less than their more eminent contemporaries, yet for various reasons they have been relegated to the second echelon of prominence. Fortunately, since the mid-sixties many of these directors less well known to the general public have received the critical attention they deserve.

Nicholas Ray, who died in 1979, was at his best when portraying rebels and alienated individuals, especially adolescents, who became involved in violent situations. This empathy vitalized his most popular work, *Rebel Without a Cause* (1955, starring James Dean). His style was personal: striking, fast-paced, even at times frenetic, and very sensitive to the inherent mood of a film. Among his outstanding works are *Knock on Any Door* (1948), *They Live by Night* (1949), *In a Lonely Place* (1950), *On Dangerous Ground* (1950), *Johnny Guitar* (1954), and *The Savage Innocents* (1959). Don Siegel shares Ray's interest in rebels and outcasts, though he is preoccupied particularly with criminals, hard-boiled detectives, and tough Western heroes. His realistic, driving approach to the conflicts of the individual and authority is evident, among others, in *The Verdict* (1946), *Invasion of the Body Snatchers* (1956), *Baby-Face Nelson* (1957), *The Killers* (1964, based on Ernest Hemingway's story and one of Siegel's finest films), *Madigan* (1968), *Coogan's Bluff* (1968), *Dirty Harry* (1971), *The Shootist* (1976), and *Escape From Alcatraz* (1979).

Samuel Fuller has been admired for his lean, tight, emphatically visual style. In common with many directors who began their careers in the forties and were established by the fifties, he is attracted to plots involving outsiders in violent situations. Fuller is less concerned with social and political problems than in their effects on individuals, as in the Westerns *I Shot Jesse James* (1949) and *Run of the Arrow* (1957); the war films *The Steel Helmet* (1950), *Fixed Bayonets* (1951), and *The Big Red One* (1979); the political films *China Gate* (1957) and *Verboten!* (1958); and the crime films *Pickup on South Street* (1952, perhaps Fuller's finest work), *Underworld USA* (1961), and *The Naked Kiss* (1964).

Joseph Losey is one of the most intriguing contemporary American-trained directors (like Richard Lester, most of his best work has been done in Great Britain). His early Hollywood films, such as *The Boy With Green Hair* (1948), *The Lawless* (1949), a remake of *M* (1950), and *The Big Night* (1951), dealt with specific problems in the guise of thrillers, and they were photographed in a hyperbolic style. A confrontation with the Un-American Activities Committee led to his being blacklisted in the United States and to his self-imposed exile in England.

After directing a series of films in Italy and Great Britain (for example, *Time Without Pity,* 1956), Losey became associated with Harold Pinter, the distinguished British playwright. Pinter wrote the screenplays for *The Servant* (1963, an adaptation) (Figure 4.34), *Accident* (1967, an original scenario), and *The Go-Between* (1971, an adaptation). They are among

**FIGURE 4.34**

*The Servant,* 1963, directed by Joseph Losey. The servant Barrett (Dirk Bogarde), with the help of Vera (Sarah Miles), gains control of the household of his master in this perceptive study of the dynamics of psychological power and class conflict.

the most memorable of the director's films, in which social and emotional situations are the means to the end of commenting pessimistically yet insightfully on the destructiveness and cruelty that can emerge from intimate human relationships. Other noteworthy works directed by Losey include *Eva* (1962, starring Jeanne Moreau), *Secret Ceremony* (1968), *Figures in a Landscape* (1970), *A Doll's House* (1973, an adaptation of Ibsen's play, starring Jane Fonda), *The Romantic Englishwoman* (1975), *Mr. Klein* (1976), and *Don Giovanni* (1979, an adaptation of the Mozart opera).

Fred Zinnemann is an honest, conscientious director who can also at times be a bit pedestrian. He

is an expert filmmaker who does not reach beyond his grasp. Among his most popular films are *The Seventh Cross* (1944), *The Search* (1947), *The Men* (1950), *High Noon* (1952, probably his most artistic work), *From Here to Eternity* (1955), *The Sundowners* (1960), *A Man for All Seasons* (1966), *The Day of the Jackal* (1973), and *Julia* (1977). Robert Rossen, after being an outstanding screenwriter, directed his first film in the late forties. *Body and Soul* (1947) and *All the King's Men* (1949) demonstrate his moralistic, liberal stance with a basically realistic style. After a slack period in the fifties, his work evidenced a new vitality with *The Hustler* (1961) and *Lilith* (1964, his last film, completed 2 years before his death). In the forties, Robert Wise* turned from editing to directing, and Douglas Sirk began his American career. Among the latter's finest films, often underrated, are *Summer Storm* (1946), *Magnificent Obsession* (1954), *Written on the Wind* (1957), and *The Tarnished Angels* (1958).

Hollywood during the fifties was preoccupied with financial problems, and retrenchment was the order of the day; this was a difficult time for novice talent. With the exception of Stanley Kubrick, the new directors who rose to prominence during the decade were often more than competent and definitely professional, but they lacked unique visions of reality. An example is Robert Brooks, who has specialized in faithful, perceptive adaptations of fiction and stage plays, such as *The Blackboard Jungle* (1955), *Cat on a Hot Tin Roof* (1958), *Elmer Gantry* (1960), *Lord Jim* (1965), *In Cold Blood* (1967), and *Looking for Mr. Goodbar* (1977). The same craftsmanship has distinguished the work of Stanley Kramer. He has devoted himself particularly to dramas of social criticism (for example, *The Defiant Ones,* 1958; *Inherit the Wind,* 1960; *Judgment at Nurenberg,* 1961; and *Guess Who's Coming to Dinner?,* 1961).

Another group of screen directors who emerged in the fifties shared a new characteristic: Each had received at least some training in television. Martin Ritt has among his credits such popular films as *Edge of the City* (1956), *The Long Hot Summer* (1958, adapted from two stories by William Faulkner),

*Hud* (1963), *The Outrage* (1964), *The Spy Who Came In From the Cold* (1965), and *Norma Rae* (1979). Robert Aldrich is attracted to plots of violence; among other films, he has directed three first-rate Westerns (*Apache,* 1954; *Vera Cruz,* 1954; and *Ulzana's Raid,* 1972), *Kiss Me Deadly* (1955), *The Big Knife* (1955), *What Ever Happened to Baby Jane?* (1962), *The Dirty Dozen* (1967), *The Killing of Sister George* (1968), and *The Longest Yard* (1974). Robert Mulligan is best known for *Fear Strikes Out* (1957), *To Kill a Mockingbird* (1962), *Daisy Clover* (1966), *Summer of '42* (1971), and *Same Time, Next Year* (1978).

Sidney Lumet's range encompasses social problems (for example, *Twelve Angry Men,* 1956; *The Pawnbroker,* 1964; *Dog Day Afternoon,* 1975; and *Network,* 1976), adventure stories (for instance, *The Anderson Tapes,* 1971; *Serpico,* 1974; and *Murder on the Orient Express,* 1974), and less commercial works, including an adaptation of a Chekhov play, *The Sea Gull* (1968), and of a Broadway play, *Equus* (1977). John Frankenheimer has a talent for making thrillers, such as *The Young Stranger* (1957), *Birdman of Alcatraz* (1962), *The Manchurian Candidate* (1962), *Seven Days in May* (1964), *The French Connection II* (1975), and *Black Sunday* (1977).

Of this group of directors trained in television, the most adventurous and artistic is Arthur Penn (1922–). He made an auspicious debut with *The Left-Handed Gun* (1958), a baroque Western centering on a neurotic antihero. He returned to the genre with the successful *Little Big Man* (1970) and the less successful *The Missouri Breaks* (1976). *The Miracle Worker* (1962) is a laudable adaptation of the Broadway play. One of the few commercial surrealistic works made in Hollywood is the idiosyncratic yet fascinating *Mickey One* (1964) (Figure 4.35). *Bonnie and Clyde* was a sensation in 1967, and few gangster films that followed it have escaped its influence. *Alice's Restaurant* (1969) caught with good humor and sympathy the spirit of youth in the sixties.

Penn has an acute sensitivity to the ambiance of a period, whether it is the Old West, the thirties, or the sixties. Violence is usually a component of his works, but always as a touchstone of characters and the conflicts of an age. He can be straightforward in his direct-

**FIGURE 4.35**

*Mickey One,* 1965, directed by Arthur Penn. When the nightclub comic Mickey (Warren Beatty) attempts to escape from syndicate mobsters, he finds himself in a Kafkaesque world in which unidentifiable powers continually threaten him. The director makes impressive use of expressionistic shadows, as in this shot of Mickey doing a routine on stage.

ing, as for *The Miracle Worker;* on the other hand, he is also capable of a distinctive style that includes an emphasis on visual symbolism and daring camera-editing dynamics.

Roger Corman is a category unto himself. Since the establishment of his production company in 1953, he has released numerous inexpensive, sensationalistic genre films. In the more than three dozen motion pictures that he has directed himself, he has demonstrated an ability that amounts to genius for creating striking works within extraordinary restrictions of time and costs. Most memorable are his adaptations of stories by Edgar Allan Poe, including *The House of Usher* (1961), *The Pit and the Pendulum* (1962), and, probably his outstanding achievement to date, *The Masque of the Red Death* (1964). He has also specialized in gangster films (for example, *The St. Valentine's Day Massacre,* 1967, and *Bloody Mama,* 1970) and contemporary themes (for instance, *The Intruder,* 1961, on race relations; *The Wild Angels,* 1966, on teenage violence; and *The Trip,* 1967, on the effects of hallucinatory drugs). He deserves credit for the opportunities he has given through his production company to young directors; among the young men hired by Corman who later became eminent are

Peter Bogdanovich, Francis Ford Coppola, and Martin Scorsese.

The most individualistic and remarkable director to release his first feature film in the fifties was Stanley Kubrick (1928–). His first two features (*Fear and Desire,* 1953, and *Killer's Kiss,* 1955), both thrillers, received only nominal critical attention. Far more successful was the stirring and vivid *Paths of Glory* (1958), based on an actual French army trial during World War I. Although Kubrick is listed as director of *Spartacus* (1960), about a rebellion of Roman slaves, he has repudiated his contribution, maintaining that he was forced to submit to the dictates of the producer-star, Kirk Douglas. The director had complete control during the filming of *Lolita* (1962), but this adaptation does not do justice to the trenchant wit, satire, and subtle psychological overtones of Vladimir Nabokov's novel, and it offers only minor compensations for the lack of these qualities. *Lolita* was made in Great Britain, and Kubrick has continued to work in that country even when using American financing, actors, and crews.

*Dr. Strangelove, or How I Learned to Stop Worrying and Love the Bomb* (1963), is the first of the expensive, elaborate productions with which Kubrick has come to be associated. This landmark comedy on the most portentous of subjects, the end of the world, is discussed in Chapter 6.* *2001: A Space Odyssey* (1968) is considered by many critics as Kubrick's masterpiece (although others prefer *A Clockwork Orange*). Based on a screenplay (derived from a short story, "The Sentinel") by science fiction writer Arthur C. Clarke (with Kubrick credited as coauthor), *2001* is an epic of the development of man and his technology (see Figure 1.27). Less than half of the 141-minute film contains dialogue, and characterization is—intentionally, one assumes—relatively flat; in fact, the most interesting "character" in *2001* is HAL, the computer. Man finally triumphs over machine in this tale of the first contact of the human race with aliens, but Kubrick offers an implicit warning that we should proceed cautiously in our inevitably increasing dependency on advanced technology.

Most of the 3 years and over $10 million spent on the project were consumed in creating the special effects. No motion picture before it had depended so heavily on advanced cinematic technology for its effects. In this respect, as well as many others, it is the prototype of the science fiction films that have been so popular since the late seventies.

*A Clockwork Orange* (1971) also takes place in the future. It is, however, a more negative vision than *2001,* one in which totalitarianism has joined with technology to control the individual. As in Anthony Burgess's novel, which the drama follows faithfully, Alex, a hoodlum, reacts against the drabness of his society by committing cruel crimes until he is conditioned against violence. In both novel and film, the pivotal question of whether or not individual freedom should be preserved at any cost is fudged somewhat by presenting the chief character as an engaging monster who is more appealing in his vitality than his victims. There can be few reservations, however, about Kubrick's techniques. His camera-editing dynamics and superb use of color and sound made *A Clockwork Orange* one of the most impressive dramas of the seventies (Figure 4.36).

The director's recent films are intriguing more for their form than for their feeling. *Barry Lyndon*

**FIGURE 4.36**

*A Clockwork Orange,* 1971, directed by Stanley Kubrick (color). The first image of the film shows Alex (Malcolm McDowell) ready in costume and makeup for a romp of violence in the streets of London in the future. His cold, cruel eyes staring directly at the camera are as chilling as his later brutal acts.

(1975), adapted from William Thackeray's nineteenth-century novel, is shallow in characterization and, for all its surface action, often tedious. On the other hand, the photography is exquisite, and time and place settings are rendered with style and grace (Figure 4.37). *The Shining* (1979) is a sophisticated horror film that achieves its intention of frightening viewers but is less effective if one scrutinizes the motivations of major characters and the awkward alternating of occurrences that are mysterious but to some degree explicable with those that are purely supernatural.

---

**FIGURE 4.37**

*Barry Lyndon,* 1975, directed by Stanley Kubrick (color). Whatever the weaknesses of the narrative dimension of this picaresque tale, its cinematography is superb. Especially striking is the use of candlelight as key lighting, inspired by the paintings of Georges de la Tour. In this shot, Lyndon (Ryan O'Neal) assists the cardsharp Chevalier de Balibari (Patrick Magee).

Practically all of Kubrick's films center on threats to individual freedom and integrity from societal forces, such as technology, totalitarianism, and bureaucratic authoritarianism, or inner compulsions and weaknesses (as in *Lolita* and *Barry Lyndon*). He tends toward a romantic, expressive style that is tightly controlled to achieve just the effects he desires. By devoting approximately 3 years to each major production, he is able to indulge his obsession with details and to achieve nuances of composition, lighting, and color. In Kubrick's late-seventies films, these techniques and technical preoccupations became ends in

themselves instead of integral supports to the narrative dimension of each film. On the other hand, he is too daring and innovative a director not to surprise us in the future by moving in new, unpredictable directions.

The sixties was a turbulent decade in American history, and Hollywood was reeling from the lowest profit and attendance figures in its history. A few, but not many, outstanding directors began their careers in this decade. One of the most exciting was Sam Peckinpah; his works are discussed in Chapter 8. Robert Altman actually directed two films in the late fifties and three in the sixties, but he did not have a major success until 1970, so his considerable accomplishments will be reviewed in the "Seventies" section of this chapter. The same is true for Francis Ford Coppola, who directed his first feature film in 1961. Roman Polanski's "American period" will be examined later in this section.*

Mike Nichols was a cabaret performer in partnership with Elaine May and a director of Broadway plays before he turned to cinema. His first film was a fine adaptation of Edward Albee's *Who's Afraid of Virginia Woolf?* (1966). His next two motion pictures were social comedies (*The Graduate,* 1967, and *Catch-22,* 1970).† *Carnal Knowledge* (1971) follows the lives of two college roommates in the late forties into the disillusionment and shallowness of their middle age. *The Day of the Dolphin* (1973) and *The Fortune* (1975) are perfunctory works. *Silkwood* (1983) is at least a serious, competent drama. Nichols's experience in the theater has helped him to draw vigorous performances from his actors and to pace individual sequences admirably. Like Elia Kazan, from a similar background, Nichols's cinematic techniques can be overwrought and flashy rather than incisive and sharply focused.

George Roy Hill worked in the theater and television before directing two adaptations of Broadway successes (*Period of Adjustment,* 1962, and *Toys in the Attic,* 1963), a charming Peter Sellers comedy (*The World of Henry Orient,* 1964), and an above-average musical (*Thoroughly Modern Millie,* 1967). His area of particular expertise, however, is fast-

---

*p. 170
†p. 281

paced, carefully structured adventure films with sensitively rendered period atmosphere. The best of these star Robert Redford and Paul Newman either together or separately. Both actors appeared in the realistic Western *Butch Cassidy and the Sundance Kid* (1969) and in *The Sting* (1973), an immensely popular comedy on two 1930s con men. Redford was a 1920s barnstorming pilot in *The Great Waldo Pepper* (1975), and Newman was a contemporary hockey player in *Slap Shot* (1977). One of Hill's most impressive films, a venture into fantasy, *Slaughterhouse Five* (1972, an adaptation of Kurt Vonnegut's novel), was underrated when it was released.

A development of the sixties was an attempt to incorporate into narrative fiction the techniques of *cinéma verité*.* John Cassavetes is a leading practitioner of this style . In *Shadows* (1960), *Faces* (1968), *Husbands* (1970), *A Woman Under the Influence* (1974), *The Killing of a Chinese Bookie* (1976), and *Opening Night* (1977), his eye is an unblinking and indiscriminate camera. His encouragement of improvisation on the part of his actors and few concessions to esthetic considerations have resulted in uneven works and mundane footage that practically any other director would have eliminated, as well as some very intense moments in the personal relationships of his characters. Andy Warhol, a leader of the American Pop Art movement, carried this approach to its logical conclusion. In *My Hustler* (1965), *The Chelsea Girls* (1966, the most striking of his works), *Blue Movie* (1969), and many others, he recorded—literally, for camera movement and editing were minimal—the experiences (with a blurred distinction between fiction and reality) of unconventional, at times grotesque "underground" people. After 1968, Paul Morrissey, Warhol's close associate, directed *Flesh* (1968), *Trash* (1970), *Heat* (1972), *Andy Warhol's Dracula* (1974), and others.

A few, chiefly young filmmakers responded directly to the counterculture of the sixties. Brian De Palma directed *Greetings* (1968) and two other features before turning to horror films.† Jim McBride was responsible for the low-budget *David Holzman's Diary* (1967). *Putney Swope* (1966) attracted more attention than the other films of Robert Downey. Haskell Wexler, one of Hollywood's best cinematographers, directed the controversial but often beautifully photographed *Medium Cool* (1969). The most popular of this type of film was *Easy Rider* (1969), directed by Dennis Hopper. With a rock soundtrack, this story of the odyssey of two motorcyclists revealed dramatically Middle America's resentment toward iconoclastic youth.

Other notable directors who began making films in this decade were Frank Perry, none of whose subsequent works was as telling as *David and Lisa* (1962) and *Diary of a Mad Housewife* (1970); Sydney Pollack (*This Property Is Condemned,* 1966; *They Shoot Horses, Don't They?,* 1969; *Jeremiah Johnson,* 1972; *The Way We Were,* 1973; *The Electric Horseman,* 1979; and others); William Friedkin; Norman Jewison; Franklin Schaffner; Mark Rydell; and Gordon Parks.

The sixties ended with Hollywood attempting to grapple with new production methods and new social attitudes. The stage was set for young directors capable of unconventional ideas, approaches, and subject matter to revitalize the American film industry.

---

## GREAT BRITAIN

After the war ended, Great Britain's film industry could look back with satisfaction on its superb accomplishments in the genre of the war documentary.* It also looked forward to a resurgence of activity in the postwar era but was confronted by two problems: financing and the predominance of American motion pictures in the English theaters. The government came to the aid of the nation's filmmakers. The Cinematograph Films Act of 1947 required that 45 percent of all motion pictures released in the country be of British origin and that 75 percent of the profits made in England by American companies be spent in British studios. In 1948 the National Film Finance Corporation was set up to grant loans to independent producers. In 1952 The British Film Institute (established in the early thirties and sponsor of *Sight and Sound* magazine) was given a showplace for its film holdings—the Film Theatre of London, a counterpart to France's Cinémathèque Française. Only in the area of film schools was the government shortsighted; The National Film School was not founded until 1971.

The first fruits of this support were the "little comedies" of the late forties and early fifties.* Meanwhile, studios were active, especially Alexander Korda's British Lion. Anthony Asquith, Carol Reed, and the Powell-Pressburger team continued to be productive (see the preceding section of this survey). Attracting international attention during this period were the film versions of three Shakespeare plays directed by and starring Laurence Olivier: *Henry V* (1945), *Hamlet* (1948), and *Richard III* (1956).

Two major directors who came to prominence in the mid-fifties were David Lean (1908–) and Basil Dearden. Lean was a highly respected editor in the thirties before he served as codirector with Noël Coward on the patriotic film *In Which We Serve* (1942). Coward wrote the screenplays for the director's next three films: *This Happy Breed* (1943), *Blithe Spirit* (1944), and the touching *Brief Encounter* (1945). Lean then turned to the nineteenth century and created two extraordinary adaptations of novels by Dickens: *Great Expectations* (1946) and *Oliver Twist* (1947). For the next decade, his films were rather commonplace, with the exception of *The Sound Barrier* (1952). All these films were intelligent, straightforwardly made motion pictures, enhanced by occasionally brilliant sequences (this is especially true of *Great Expectations*).

Lean moved toward works of broader scope and greater spectacle with *The Bridge on the River Kwai* (1957), a powerful World War II story that featured an unforgettable performance by Alec Guinness. His last three films before his retirement were large-budget epics with immense casts and striking visual effects, though at times slow-paced and even tedious: *Lawrence of Arabia* (1962), *Doctor Zhivago* (1964), and *Ryan's Daughter* (1970).

In complete contrast to the later films of Lean is the oeuvre of Basil Dearden (who died in an automobile accident in 1971). These works are almost

entirely low-budget, and they usually deal with social problems in a semidocumentary style. Of the 38 films Dearden directed or codirected between 1941 and 1970, two are particularly outstanding: *Sapphire* (1959), on race relations in England, and *Victim* (1961), one of the most honest and sympathetic studies of homosexuality to appear on the screen.

In the fifties, a literary movement developed in Great Britain that was to have important repercussions on England's cinema. What the "Angry Young Men" —including playwright John Osborne; novelists Kingsley Amis, John Braine, and Alan Sillitoe; and critic Colin Wilson—shared was working-class or middle-class backgrounds, resentment of what they considered British snobbery and hypocrisy, and disillusionment with the tradition values of their society. By the early sixties, the literary movement had lost impetus, but its manifestations in film were just beginning to crest.

The spirit of dissent that inspired the Angry Young Men of England in the fifties also resulted in the Free Cinema movement in the film documentary.* Three leaders of the group were Karel Reisz, Tony Richardson, and Lindsay Anderson. When these directors turned to fiction features, they began with adaptations of works by contributors to the literary movement: Reisz's *Saturday Night and Sunday Morning* (1960, an adaptation of an Alan Sillitoe novel); Richardson's *Look Back in Anger* (1959) and *The Entertainer* (1960), both versions of plays by John Osborne; and Anderson's *This Sporting Life* (1963, based on a novel by David Storey). In addition, Jack Clayton directed *Room at the Top* (1958), which was derived from a John Braine novel.

As adaptations, these dramas contained the subject matter and themes of the Angry Young Men movement. The film directors, however, were also rebels in their own medium. They applied to the making of fiction films the principles of Free Cinema: a focus on ordinary people in ordinary situations, a commitment to social responsibility, an assertion of the personal vision of the director, a loosening of the commercial restrictions of the industry, greater spontaneity in shooting and editing, and a preference for

*p. 277

*p. 344

location rather than studio production. They encouraged in their actors an intense, immediate, natural style.

This British film movement of the sixties (it had lost cohesion and purposefulness by the end of the decade) has been variously labeled, but the term *British New Wave* is the least awkward. Each major director of the movement went on to other concerns and styles. Yet each retained the individuality, spontaneity, and verve that was characteristic of them as a group.

Tony Richardson (1928–) has been the most prolific of the British New Wave filmmakers. After directing *Look Back in Anger* and *The Entertainer* and making an excursion to Hollywood for *Sanctuary* (1960, based on William Faulkner's novel), he made two of his best films *A Taste of Honey* (1961, an adaptation of Shelagh Delaney's play) and *The Loneliness of the Long Distance Runner* (1962) (Figure 4.38), based on the novella by Alan Sillitoe. He departed from the subject matter and approach of the British New Wave with a rollicking version of Henry Fielding's *Tom Jones* (1963).

Since the early sixties, Richardson has confined himself either to large, expensive productions (for example, *The Loved One,* 1964; *The Charge of the Light Brigade,* 1968; and *Joseph Andrews,* 1977) or

**FIGURE 4.38**

*The Loneliness of the Long Distance Runner,* 1962, directed by Tony Richardson. Tom Courtenay (number 14 in this shot) plays a Borstal (reform school) boy who will sacrifice anything, even winning a long-distance race, to flaunt his defiance of the establishment.

to adaptations of dramas (such as *Hamlet,* 1969, with Nicol Williamson in the title role, and *A Delicate Balance,* 1973, based on Edward Albee's play). Although always competent and an exceptional director of actors, Richardson has never developed a distinctive cinematic style, and his films tend to have the static quality of photographed stage plays.

Karel Reisz (1926–) is more sensitive to cinematic values and more adventurous in his filmmaking than Richardson. He made his debut as a director of feature films in 1960 with the remarkable *Saturday Night and Sunday Morning,* often extolled as the finest motion picture to emerge from the British New Wave. His inadequate remake of *Night Must Fall* appeared in 1964. Reisz used his considerable talents to better advantage in *Morgan: A Suitable Case for Treatment* (1966), a witty satire on the pretentiousness and hypocrisy of contemporary English society. *Isadora* (1967) is an intriguing if diffuse meditation on the life of Isadora Duncan, with Vanessa Redgrave outstanding in the title role.

During the seventies, Reisz spent a good deal of time making commercial and nonfiction films. He did complete two features: *The Gambler* (1975) and *Dog Soldiers* (or *Who'll Stop the Rain?,* 1978). Although Reisz has a vigorous, vivid, though somewhat mannered style, his chief weakness since his 1960 film is an apparent lack of interest in founding his techniques on coherently developed narratives and in achieving depth of characterization.

Lindsay Anderson (1923–) devoted himself to documentaries and film criticism during the fifties before making his first feature film, *This Sporting Life,* in 1963. His next major work was *If . . .* (1968) (Figure 4.39). This story of a rebellion led by four youngsters against the senior students and faculty of an English private school was inspired—in its plot and its mingling of elements of realism and surrealism—by Jean Vigo's *Zero for Conduct,* and it is a worthy homage to its predecessor. The themes of rebellion against the false values of society and preservation of the rights of the individual that underlie *If . . .* also are central to Anderson's later films: *O Lucky Man!* (1973), a fable in the tradition of Voltaire's *Candide, In Celebration* (1975, based on a David Storey play), and *Britannia Hospital* (1981).

**FIGURE 4.39**

*If . . . ,* 1968, directed by Lindsay Anderson (color). Violence erupts as three students and a girl rebel against the dogmatic authorities at a British public (that is, private) school. The title is significant, for the concluding sequence, in contrast to the preceding realism, is surrealistic.

Although like Tony Richardson, Anderson has been active in the theater, his style is definitely visually oriented. He has never made an uninteresting or perfunctory film, and the critical attention he has received is a reflection of the position he holds as probably the most esteemed British film director of his generation.

Jack Clayton was not involved in the Free Cinema movement; he became a director by working his way up through the industry's hierarchy. His first feature, however, was an adaptation—a year before Richardson's *Look Back in Anger*—of a novel by a leading representative of the Angry Young Men. *Room at the Top* (1958) is based on John Braine's story of an ambitious clerk who finally marries his employer's daughter after having an affair and being responsible for the death of an older, married woman who fell in love with him. In his next two films, Clayton left realism behind to explore internal states of consciousness. *The Innocents* (1961), an adaptation of Henry James's ghost story "The Turn of the Screw," combines psychological insights and all the components of cinema to create an eerie atmosphere. *The Pumpkin Eater* (1964), adapted by Harold Pinter from a contemporary novel, is a probing story of the breakdown of a marriage and a woman's mental stability.

The director's later films have been, by comparison, disappointing, including *Our Mother's House* (1967) and *The Great Gatsby* (1974, a glittering but unsubstantial version of F. Scott Fitzgerald's novel).

Members of the British New Wave may have been chiefly responsible for the excitement that English releases aroused during the late fifties and sixties in sophisticated moviegoers throughout the Western world, but other directors also made significant contributions. Among these were three foreigners who settled or worked for an extended period of time in Great Britain. From the United States came Joseph Losey* and Richard Lester.† Roman Polanski's English films are surveyed later in this section.‡ The James Bond phenomenon began in 1962 with *Dr. No* and has continued to the present to entertain audiences and help to fill the coffers of the British film industry.

Clive Donner is best known for his comedies,§ but he also directed an adaptation of Harold Pinter's *The Caretaker* (1963). Jack Cardiff, once an outstanding director of photography, has been responsible for directing quite a few mediocre films, but at least two are noteworthy: *Sons and Lovers* (1960, a respectable adaptation of D. H. Lawrence's novel) and *Young Cassidy* (1964, based on the early life of the playwright Sean O'Casey). Bryan Forbes became a director after a career as an actor and screenwriter, and he writes the scripts for his own films. He has a gift for taking sensitive subjects and dealing with them delicately yet forthrightly, as in *Whistle Down the Wind* (1961), *The L-Shaped Room* (1962), *Seance on a Wet Afternoon* (1964), and *King Rat* (1965). In his works of the seventies, such as *The Stepford Wives* (1975), he has shown more concern with commercial values than with those of intelligent drama.

John Schlesinger was a TV director and documentary filmmaker before he released his first feature, *A Kind of Loving* (1962). *Billy Liar* (1963, adapted from Keith Waterhouse's novel) was a comic contribution to the list of urban, working-class films created by members of the British New Wave. It was, how-

*pp. 152–153
†p. 453
‡pp. 170
§p. 278

ever, with *Darling* (1965) that Schlesinger's reputation as a first-rate director was established. *Far From the Madding Crowd* (1967) was a lovely but far from subtle version of Thomas Hardy's novel.

A trip to Hollywood by Schlesinger resulted in *Midnight Cowboy* (1969, starring Dustin Hoffman and Jon Voight), a devastating portrayal of the sordid life of two New York City hustlers and the death of one of them. Two years later, back in England, the director completed *Sunday, Bloody Sunday* (1971), an absorbing drama of a bisexual *ménage à trois.* Among Schlesinger's fortes are an ability to elicit expressive performances from his actors, an acute awareness of what constitutes the dominant tone of a film, and a facility for tightly structuring a plot through painstaking editing. These talents are less evident in expensive, expansive productions, such as *Far From the Madding Crowd* and *The Day of the Locust* (1975), or melodramas (for example, *Marathon Man,* 1976).

Peter Brook is a famous stage director who has also ventured into filmmaking. Although he has used sources other than the theater (for example, *Lord of the Flies,* 1963, based on William Golding's novel), he is primarily known for adaptations from his unconventional staging of plays. It is with a theater director's eye that he has filmed, for example, *Marat-Sade* (1966, based on Peter Weiss's drama) and *King Lear* (1971, starring Paul Scofield).

One of the most controversial, imaginative, and self-indulgent directors in the history of British cinema appeared on the cinematic scene in the sixties. Ken Russell (1927–) first attracted attention with a series of cinebiographies of artists, mostly composers, mostly made for television. *Prokofiev* (1961), *The Debussy Film* (1965), *Isadora Duncan* (1966), *Dante's Inferno* (1967, on the Victorian poet Dante Gabriel Rossetti), and *Dance of the Seven Veils* (1970, on Richard Strauss) are interesting and strange, but two on British composers—*Elgar* (1962) and *A Song of Summer* (1968, on Frederick Delius)—are considered by discriminating viewers as minor masterpieces.

After his first feature film, an inconsequential comedy, and a bland thriller (*Billion Dollar Brain,* 1967), Russell directed a distinguished version of D. H. Lawrence's *Women in Love* (1969). The *Music*

*Lovers* (1970) centered more on the sexual problems of Tchaikovsky than the Russian's musical achievements (Figure 4.40). *The Devils* (1971) is based loosely on Aldous Huxley's study of a seventeenth-century incident among Ursuline nuns, *The Devils of Loudun.* The director's intertwining in this work of religious mysticism and sexual perversity is audacious, extravagant, and at times in questionable taste. After the musical *The Boy Friend,*\* Russell returned to the subject of artists in *Savage Messiah* (1972, on the sculptor Gaudier-Brzeska) and *Mahler* (1974).

---

**FIGURE 4.40**

*The Music Lovers,* 1970, directed by Ken Russell (color). Tchaikovsky (Richard Chamberlain), the great Russian composer, is a homosexual. In a dream, he attempts to escape the clutching hands of women.

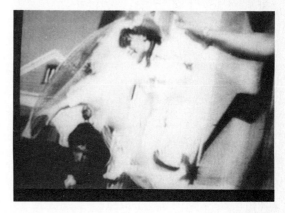

Russell's next film was a film adaptation of a rock ''opera'' ideally suited to his lavish approach and fanciful imagination—*Tommy* (1975).† *Lisztomania* (1975) is the least successful of his films, an incoherent, weird cinematic pastiche. *Valentino* (1977) is less bizarre, but equally unfocused in its plot. In *Altered States* (1979), a science fiction work, the director wisely allowed the special effects to determine the tone.

When Russell restrains his impulses toward excess, as in *Women in Love,* or deals with a subject that requires a phantasmagoric approach, such as

---

\*p. 453
†p. 460

*Tommy,* he can create memorable motion pictures. The problem is that his elaborate, pyrotechnic techniques are often out of proportion to the dramatic requirements of a sequence or even a whole film. This is one way of defining farce, and at his worst the director is unintentionally and inappropriately farcical, as in *Lisztomania.* Within the cocoon of personal visions and prodigal style that Russell has spun around himself is a brilliant, dramatically forceful, and psychologically penetrating director struggling to be born.

Other notable British directors of the fifties and sixties include Ronald Neame (*The Horse's Mouth,* 1959; *Tunes of Glory,* 1960; *The Prime of Miss Jean Brodie,* 1969; and others), Anthony Harvey (best known for *The Lion in Winter,* 1968), Peter Glenville (for example, *Becket,* 1964), Guy Hamilton (*An Inspector Calls,* 1954; *Funeral in Berlin,* 1966; four James Bond films; and others), Peter Yates, Roy Baker, Ken Hughes, Wolf Rilla, Guy Green, Leslie Norman, and Lewis Gilbert. A few young directors made their first feature films in the middle or late sixties, including Kenneth Loach, Desmond Davis, and Peter Watkins; their work will be considered in the "Seventies" section of this chapter.

OTHER COUNTRIES

The Spanish film industry after World War II continued to stultify under the restrictions of the Franco dictatorship. Few motion pictures were exported beyond the country's borders and Spanish-speaking countries in South America. Exceptions were the works of Juan Antonio Bardem (for example, *Death of a Cyclist, Muerte de un Ciclista,* 1953) and Luis G. Berlanga. In the sixties, a group of younger directors, including Miguel Picazo, Francisco Regueiro, and Basilio M. Patino, came to the fore. The most eminent of this group is Carlos Saura, who directed *The Hunt* (*La Caza,* 1965) and *The Honeycomb* (*La Madriguera,* 1969).* With the death of Francisco Franco in 1975, the potentials of the industry increased tremendously.

One Spanish director, who made practically all of his films outside of his homeland, should be included on any list of the most significant filmmakers

of our time. Luis Buñuel (1900–1983) was born into a prosperous bourgeois family and educated in a Jesuit school. After attending the University of Madrid, where he joined a coterie of restless, avant-garde youths (led by Federico Garcia Lorca, Rafael Alberti, and Salvador Dali), he traveled to Paris in 1925. There he became interested in cinema, studied at the Académie du Cinéma, and worked as an assistant to Jean Epstein and other filmmakers.

His first major work was the result of a collaboration with his friend Dali. *Un Chien Andalou* (1928) is a landmark in the movement of cinematic Surrealism* and caused a sensation when it was released. *The Age of Gold* (*L'Age d'Or,* 1930), also made with Dali, was attacked vehemently for what its critics considered licentiousness, sadism, and anticlericalism. Buñuel returned to his homeland to direct *Land Without Bread* (*Las Hurdes,* 1932),† a powerful documentary on an impoverished area of northern Spain.

The next decade and a half were fallow, difficult years for Buñuel. From 1938 to the end of World War II he lived in the United States. In 1945, he traveled to Mexico and directed films there until the mid-fifties. Buñuel's "Mexican period" was a rich one. While working on an average of one or two motion pictures a year with minuscule production budgets, he developed his unique style, a combination of uncompromising realism in the service of social criticism and elements of Surrealism that appeared particularly in the dreams of characters and erotic obsessions that can dominate the life of an individual. Of the 13 films he released in Mexico between 1945 and 1955, the most memorable are *The Young and the Damned* (*Los Olvidados,* 1950, a study of violence, depravity, and betrayal among juveniles in Mexico City), *Subida al Cielo* (1951), *El Bruto* (1953), *Robinson Crusoe* (1952), and *The Criminal Life of Archibaldo de la Cruz* (*Ensayo de un Crimen,* 1955). The most intriguing of the Mexican films is *This Strange Passion* (*El,* 1952), in which a wealthy aristocrat marries the fiancée of a friend and is driven to madness by his obsession with the possibility of her infidelity.

In the mid-fifties, Buñuel was invited to France

*p. 192

*pp. 113–114
†p. 336

to direct two films, *Cela s'appelle l'aurore* (1955) and *Evil Eden* (*La Mort en ce Jardin,* 1956). He returned to Mexico to make *Nazarin* (1958). *Republic of Sin* (*La Fièvre monte à El Pao,* 1959) and *The Young One* (1960) followed.

These works had established Buñuel as a director of intense, provocative, low-budget dramas but hardly a figure of major significance. Then in his sixties, when most filmmakers would be thinking about retiring, he began his mature period and created, one after another, films that startled and entranced both audiences and critics. *Viridiana* (1961, made in Spain) was the first of these masterworks. A beautiful young woman, who had intended to become a nun, takes over her uncle's estate after he had attempted to rape her and then committed suicide. Her efforts to establish a religious home for beggars results in disaster. The disillusioned Viridiana joins the uncle's illegitimate son and his mistress in a *ménage à trois.* The elements in the drama of antireligion, eroticism, and a cynical view of the poor outraged the Spanish authorities. They banned the work and expelled Buñuel.

*The Exterminating Angel* (*El Angel Exterminador,* 1962) is set in Mexico. The symbolic pattern the director develops to suggest modern society is a party in the room of a mansion that for some inexplicable reason the host and his guests cannot leave. As the days go by, the true characters beneath the social masks of these prisoners are revealed. After the spell is broken, the same form of incarceration is inflicted on people in a cathedral where a celebration mass is taking place.

*Diary of a Chambermaid* (*Le Journal d'une femme de chambre,* 1964) is a study of evil and selfishness among the French upper class. In *Simon of the Desert* (*Simon del Desierto,* 1965) (Figure 4.41), made in Mexico, the director returns to a more obvious Surrealistic approach, but with a good deal of

**FIGURE 4.41**

*Simon of the Desert,* 1965, directed by Luis Buñuel. The relentlessly saintly Simon (Claudio Brook) has a vision in which simultaneously he is at the top of his column and is resting on the lap of his mother.

humor included. *Belle de jour* (1967) (Figure 4.42) stars Catherine Deneuve as a doctor's wife who expiates her guilt feelings about sex by having masochistic hallucinations and becoming a part-time prostitute in a brothel.

**FIGURE 4.42**

*Belle de jour,* 1967, directed by Luis Buñuel (color). Séverine (Catherine Deneuve) talks to Madame Anaïs (Geneviève Page), who runs the exclusive brothel where she works during the day.

Two tramps on a journey in *The Milky Way* (*La Voie lactée,* 1968) meet and argue with representatives of various Christian sects. Buñuel's ironic approach is a means of ridiculing the dogmas of Christianity that are rigid and inconsistent. In *Tristana* (1970), the title character (Deneuve) is seduced by her guardian, an elderly man, Don Lope. After an affair with an artist, she returns to Don Lope with vengeance in her heart. *The Discreet Charm of the Bourgeoisie* (*Le Charme discret de la bourgeoisie,* 1972) is similar in theme to *The Exterminating Angel.* Six upper-middle-class friends attempt but never succeed in sharing a dinner together. The events that repeatedly interfere with their plans are wryly ludicrous. Buñuel is masterful in holding together the strands of his plot and in satirizing the inadequacies and hypocrisies of a comfortable bourgeoisie.

*The Phantom of Liberty* (*Le Fantôme de la liberté,* 1974) consists of a series of incidents that by reversing conventional attitudes (for example, defecating is a public event and eating is a private one)

demonstrates how irrational are the premises underlying the mores that society insists are necessary if Western culture is to survive. Buñuel's last film was *That Obscure Object of Desire* (*Cet obscur objet du désir,* 1977). A middle-aged man becomes obsessed with seducing a beautiful but evasive young woman (played by two actresses, though there is no logical reason why one rather than the other appears in a sequence).

Buñuel's cinematic techniques are basically conventional. A viewer is rarely awed or startled by his camera-editing dynamics in themselves. He can even be careless, as in *Simon of the Desert,* in the way he shoots and edits scenes. His greatness lies, however, in the boldness of the contents of his works and the means by which he manipulates his medium to challenge the complacencies and pieties of his audiences.

The important roles in his films of dreams, hallucinations, seemingly irrational actions of characters, and apparently illogical juxtapositions of shots and scenes have led to a minimizing of the fact that the director's dramas are grounded in realism. Not only is everyday reality photographed with an attempt to create a sense of verisimilitude in all elements of presentation, but this approach is also extended to footage that is nonrealistic in content. More than most filmmakers, he adheres to the principle of poetry advocated by Marianne Moore: "imaginary gardens with real toads in them."

Two interrelated major themes pervade practically all of Buñuel's oeuvre. The first is a belief that the individual should have total freedom. Like the existentialists, he insists that people cannot have dignity and self-respect unless they shape their own destiny to meet the needs of their inner nature. The enemies of freedom are all institutions, systems, and codes that restrict the self-expression of the individual. For Buñuel the embodiment of dictatorial forces of conformity is bourgeois morality:

I am opposed to conventional morality, traditional fantasies, sentimentalism, all the moral trash of society. Bourgeois morality is, for me, amoral because it is based on extremely unjust institutions: religion, nationalism, the family, and other pillows of society.[6]

The director's second major theme is a distrust of the efficaciousness of reason. The keystone of bourgeois Apollonian forces is a faith in reason and material objects as sources of security and social unity. From Buñuel's commitment to Surrealism is derived a means of attacking this premise. In his films, irrationality emerges repeatedly, like erupting lava forcing its way through crevices in a thin shell of rock. Of all human sensibilities, the one that confounds logic the most is the sexual, and the director is preoccupied with eroticism. Buñuel has chosen as his special province the sexual obsession, from the relatively minor form of a shoe fetish, which appears frequently in his films (for example, *El* and *Viridiana*), to that of a man gripped beyond reason by desire for a specific woman (the central theme of *That Obscure Object of Desire*). Like sex—and in Buñuel's view intimately connected to it—religious belief cannot be organized and codified. In film after film, he attacks not piety but the efforts of the Roman Catholic church to command how individuals should feel toward others and to place dogma between the individual and "the Other."

Throughout his life, Buñuel preserved an admirable integrity without being inflexible, as when he casts his Surrealistic tenets into narratives that are sufficiently comprehensible to hold the attention of most audiences. Yet he never compromises his vision of the human condition. With the persistence of an intellectual gadfly, he insists that dreams and hallucinations are living realities, impulses are coded messages sent to us by our unconscious, and social rules and regulations, uncritically accepted, can turn into cankers that devour the dignity and freedom of an individual.

The German film industry did not recover quickly from the devastations of war. Moreover, it was divided into two separate centers of production. The facilities of UFA were in the Russian zone, and the East Germans used these studios as a basis for the state-owned DEFA (*Deutsche Film Aktien Gesellschaft*). In the beginning there was fervent activity in the areas of both fiction and documentaries (for example, the compilations of Andrew and Annelie Thorndike*). By the

*p. 341

late forties, however, control of DEFA was in the hands of officials of the USSR, and rigid censorship resulted in the release of only heavy-handed propaganda films and mediocre entertainments. Aside from the work of a few outstanding directors, such as Konrad Wolf, who made *Stars* (*Sterne,* 1958) and *Professor Mamlock* (1961), the German Democratic Republic has contributed little to the cinema of Europe since the 1950s.

One striking talent did emerge during the brief flourishing of creativity in the early years of DEFA. Wolfgang Staudte was responsible for the first postwar German film to attract international attention, *Murderers Are Among Us* (*Die Mörder sind unter Uns,* 1946). *Rotation* (1949) and *The Underdog* (*Der Untertan,* 1951), are also forceful portrayals of the Nazi and denazification periods. In 1955, Staudte moved to West Germany, where he continued to direct films. These have been less successful than his earlier works.

In the German Federal Republic, it took some time for production facilities to be set up and to compete with American motion pictures. West German films tended to be sentimental and to avoid dealing directly with contemporary problems. Escapist fare predominated during the fifties, but a few dramas were honest in confronting Germany's immediate past and present.

Of the 17 motion pictures directed by Helmut Käutner during this decade, two are particularly impressive. *The Last Bridge* (*Die Letzte Brücke,* 1954), a war film set in Yugoslavia, and *The Devil's General* (*Des Teufels General,* 1955), the story of an anti-Nazi Luftwaffe general. Also noteworthy were R. A. Stemmle's *Berlin Ballad* (*Berliner Ballade,* 1948), Kurt Hoffmann's *Felix Krull* (1957), and the actor Bernard Wicki's *The Bridge* (*Die Brücke,* 1959).

The economic recovery of West Germany was in full swing by the early sixties. Affluence encouraged the government to offer grants and loans to filmmakers and to establish the Film Institute of Berlin in 1968. Television, as in most European countries, both sponsored and became a significant outlet for new works. The desired results were achieved. By the late sixties, there was a remarkable revival of commercial and avant-garde filmmaking. Notable among this new generation of directors were Edgar Reitz, Peter and Ulrich Schamoni, Will Tremper, and Roger Fritz; the most prominent were Kluge, Straub, and Schlöndorff.

Alexander Kluge (1932–) developed an individual style in which there is an interplay between documentary footage and staged fictional scenes. Symbolism and fragmented characterizations are also characteristic of his nonlinear narratives with provocative titles, such as *Yesterday Girl* (*Abschied von Gestern,* 1966), his first feature; *Artists at the Top of the Big Top—Disoriented* (*Artisten in der Zirkuskuppel—Ratlos,* 1968); and *Occasional Work of a Female Slave* (*Gelegenheitsarbeit einer Sklavin,* 1975).

Jean-Marie Straub (1933–), a Frenchman who settled in Germany in 1958, has earned the admiration of moviegoers and critics who are responsive to new forms of filmic expression. Influenced by the concepts of the dramatist Bertolt Brecht, Straub casts his Marxist ideology in forms that consciously undermine the cinematic illusion of fiction and, in the Brechtian sense, alienate audiences. He often uses nonprofessional actors, experiments with the relationship between sound and images, and prefers austere, minimal camera-editing dynamics in which the *mise-en-scène* approach predominates. Among his most striking films are *Unreconciled* (*Nicht Versöhnt,* 1965), *The Chronicle of Anna Magdalena Bach* (*Chronik der Anna Magdalena Bach,* 1967), *Othon* (1972), *History Lessons* (*Geschichtsunterricht,* 1973), and *Moses and Aaron* (1975, a faithful rendering of Arnold Schönberg's opera).

Volker Schlöndorff (1939–) is more conventional in his filmmaking than Kluge and Straub. His linear narratives are developed carefully through fluent, elegant cinematic techniques. His favorite theme is the conflict between authority and the individual, as in *Young Torless* (*Der junge Törless,* 1966) and *Michael Kohlhass* (1969, based on a story by Heinrich von Kleist). Other Schlöndorff works include *A Degree of Murder* (*Mord und Totschlag,* 1967), *The Sudden Fortune of the Poor People of Kombach* (*Der plötzliche Reichtum der armen Leute von Kombach,* 1971), *The Tin Drum* (*Die Blechtrommel,* 1979)(Figure 4.43), and *Circle of Deceit* (1981).

These West German directors, like their counterparts somewhat earlier in France and Great Britain,

## FIGURE 4.43

*The Tin Drum,* 1979, directed by Volker Schlöndorff (color). Oskar (David Bennent) has willed that he cease growing, so he has the mind and emotions of a youth in the body of a child. Here he beats his precious drum and emits his glass-shattering cry as he watches the window of the room where his mother is sleeping with his father's best friend.

attempted to infuse new life into the motion picture industry of their homeland. They not only succeeded in their own works but also constitute the spearhead of the *Neue Kino* movement that flourished in the seventies. The leaders of the next stage in the movement, especially Fassbinder, Herzog, and Wenders, will be discussed in the "Seventies" section of this chapter.

Austria made tentative efforts to rebuild its film industry after the war. G. W. Pabst returned to directing in this country, but the results were generally mediocre. Helmut Käutner's *The Last Bridge,* although with German stars, was made in Austria. Generally, however, the Austrian film industry has been moribund since the late fifties; its production facilities have been taken over almost entirely by German television units.

Russian filmmaking, after a few years of decline, became reactivated in the postwar era. Although authoritarian state control of the industry tended to stifle the innovative and imaginative qualities of screenwriters and directors, the Soviet Union did export some notable motion pictures to the West in the fifties and sixties.

Aside from the final works of Eisenstein, Pudovkin, and Dovzhenko and the powerful documentaries of the war years, little of genuine significance appeared until the "thaw" that followed the death of Joseph Stalin in 1953. The most prominent of the new young directors was Grigori Chukrai (1921–). His two tales of wartime romance were acclaimed both in Russia and abroad. *The Forty-First* (*Sorok pervyi,* 1956), his second feature, takes place during the Revolution; *Ballad of a Soldier* (*Ballada o soldate,* 1959) is a World War II story. Among his later films are *Clear Skies* (*Christoie nebo,* 1961) and *There Was an Old Man and an Old Woman* (*Zhilibyli starik so starukhoi,* 1965). Another World War II love story, *The Cranes Are Flying* (*Letyat zhuravli,* 1957, directed by Mikhail Kalantazov), lyric in style and heartwarming in content, was extremely popular in the West. It won the Cannes Festival Award for Best Film in 1958, the first Soviet film to be so honored.

Sergei Bondarchuk, a leading actor in the forties and fifties, turned to directing in 1959 with *Destiny of a Man* (*Sudba cheloveka*), an adaptation of a Mikhail Sholokhov novel. Most of his later films have been large-scale spectacles created with intelligence and verve, such as the four-part *War and Peace* (*Voina i mir,* 1964–1967) and *Waterloo* (1970). Also grandiose, in the best sense of the term, are the adaptations of classic literary works by the veteran director Grigori Kozintsev: *Don Quixote* (1957), *Hamlet* (1964), and *King Lear* (*Karoli Lir,* 1970). One of the most visually poetic and dramatically expressive Russian films of the sixties was *Shadows of Our Forgotten Ancestors* (*Teni zabytykh predkov,* 1964, on pre-Revolution Georgian peasant life), directed by Sergei Paradjanov, whose filmmaking career was curtailed by troubles with the authorities.

Other noteworthy Russian directors of this period include Josif Heifitz (who made the delightful *Lady With a Little Dog, Dama s sobatchkoi,* 1960), Marlen Khutsiev (*I Am Twenty, Mne dvadtsat let,* 1963), Samson Samsonov, Ivan Pyriev, Mark Donskoi, Yuri Yekelchik, and Sergei Yutkevich. Although younger directors, such as Andrei Tarkovsky and Andrei Konchalovsky-Mikhailov, began directing motion pictures in the sixties, their work has been associated in the West with their later films, commented on in the "Seventies" section of this chapter.

Scandinavian filmmaking during the first dec-

ade and a half of the sound era was unimpressive to audiences outside Sweden, Denmark, Norway, and Finland. The only exceptions were the sound films of Carl Dreyer* and Benjamin Christensen and, to a lesser degree, the works of the Swedish director Gustaf Molander (for example, *Intermezzo,* 1936). In the mid-forties, however, there was a cinematic renascence in Sweden. Two men were primarily responsible for this resurgence: Carl Anders Dymling, through his reorganization of Svensk Filmindustri, the major company of the country, and the director Alf Sjöberg (1903–1980).

Sjöberg made his debut as a film director with the powerful *The Strongest One* (*Den starkaste,* 1929) but confined himself to the theater during the thirties. He returned to cinema in 1940 and directed five striking films known only in his homeland before *Torment* (*Hets,* 1944, with a screenplay by Ingmar Bergman) made him famous abroad. He continued to direct impressive films, such as *Only a Mother* (*Bara en mor,* 1949) and *Barabbas* (1953), but most memorable are his adaptations of Strindberg plays, including *Miss Julie* (*Fröken Julie,* 1951)(Figure 4.44)—a superb work, *Karin Mansdotter* (1954), and *The Father* (*Fadern,* 1969).

---

**FIGURE 4.44**

*Miss Julie,* 1951, directed by Alf Sjöberg. In this excellent adaptation of the Strindberg play, the past becomes a reality in the present. Here the young Julie (Anita Bjork) recalls her mother (Märta Dorff) holding her when she was a child.

---

*pp. 114–115

The central figure of postwar Scandinavian filmmaking is, of course, Ingmar Bergman.* Bergman's most respected contemporary during the fifties was Arne Mattsson. This prolific director is known in Sweden for thrillers, but his greatest international success was *One Summer of Happiness (Hon dansade en sommar,* 1951).

The second stage of the renewal of the Swedish film industry was prompted by the establishment of the Svenska Filminstitutet in 1963 and its policy of encouraging new directors. Bo Widerberg's *Elvira Madigan* (1967) is an exquisitely photographed romance. Less famous, but equally satisfying and more substantial among his works, are *Raven's End (Kvarteret Korpen,* 1963), *Love 65 (Kärlek 65,* 1965), and *Adalen 31* (1969). Vilgot Sjöman has made many films of uneven quality but was commercially successful with his erotic *I Am Curious—Yellow (Jag är nyfiken—gul,* 1967) and *I Am Curious—Blue (Jag är nyfiken—blä,* 1968). Mai Zetterling was a major actress before her directing debut on a feature film, *Loving Couples (Alskande par,* 1964). Her feminist views, permeating intense but rather humorless, even dour works, also characterize such films as *Night Games (Nattlek,* 1966) and *The Girls (Flickorna,* 1968). Jörn Donner, eminent critic as well as filmmaker, was born in Finland and returned there in the late sixties. In Sweden, however, he made four trenchant, penetrating portrayals of Swedish mores, including *A Sunday in September (En söndag i september,* 1963).

Of the younger generation of directors, the best known—and the finest Swedish director since Bergman, according to some critics—is Jan Troell. His first feature was *Here's Your Life (Här har du ditt liv,* 1966, almost 3 hours in screening time), an epic with a World War I setting. *Who Saw Him Die? (Ole dole doff,* 1968) followed. His films had little success abroad until the release of *The Emigrants* (1971) and *The New Land* (1973), which constitute an unforgettable saga of a Swedish family's experiences in settling in Minnesota during the nineteenth century. What makes Troell's films so memorable, in addition to his exciting cinematic techniques, is his gentle and sympathetic yet clear-eyed vision of how ordinary people are capable of heroism when challenged by adverse circumstances. Notable Swedish directors of this period also include Jonas Cornell, Kjell Grede, Jarl Kulle, and Jan Halldoff.

The dramas made in other Scandinavian countries have generally attracted little notice beyond their borders. Denmark's creativity in the documentary genre has not extended to fiction films, although Henning Carlsen's *Hunger (Sult,* 1966) was acclaimed in other countries. In Finland, Edvin Laine's lengthy *The Unknown Soldier (Tuntematon sotilas,* 1955) was admired by foreign critics. Jörn Donner, after working in Sweden, became the leader of a group of Finnish directors, including Ailo Mäkinen, Risto Jarva, and Mikko Niskanen. None of them, however, has gained the stature of Donner himself for such works as *Black on White (Mustaa valkoisella,* 1968). Norway too developed a new generation of filmmakers in the sixties whose motion pictures still are relatively unknown outside of Scandinavia.

The countries of Eastern Europe endured Nazi occupation and then experienced complete state control of all aspects of cinema, as well as oppressive censorship by officials responsive to dictates from the Soviet Union. In light of the fate of East German filmmaking,* it is surprising that motion picture industries of considerable significance emerged after World War II in Poland, Czechoslovakia, and Hungary. The reasons for this phenomenon differ from country to country, depending on how authoritarian the Communist party has been in a specific country and the degree of a nation's exposure to the culture and cinema of Western democracies.

Most of these countries, however, have followed a similar pattern. After a slow reconstruction of facilities, establishment of film schools, and the death of Stalin in 1953, a loosening of the restrictions of censorship and radical changes in life-styles resulted in the development of exciting new cinema and the appearance of gifted filmmakers. These propitious conditions lasted until the end of the sixties, when demonstrations and riots in Poland and uprisings in Czechoslovakia led to the return of a stringent censorship that vitiated the vitality of the cinema in most countries of Eastern Europe. Not until recent years has there been evidence of a resurgence of the vigor of the fifties and sixties.

In Poland during the 1930s, few films were more than conventional and provincial, but a group of modernistic and adventurous filmmakers, led by Aleksander Ford, Wanda Jakubowska, Jerzy Bossak, and Jerzy Toeplitz, formed a film society, START, that laid the foundations for a more advanced Polish cinema. After the war, this group, working with extremely limited production facilities, created motion pictures that were admired throughout the Western world. Among these works, most of them dealing with the war, were Ford's *Border Street* (*Ulica Graniczna,* 1948), *Chopin's Youth* (*Mlodosc Chopina,* 1952), and *Five Boys From Barska Street* (*Piatka z ulicy Barskiej,* 1953); Bossak's *The Flood* (*Powodz,* 1946); and Jakubowska's *The Last Stage* (*Ostatni etap,* 1948). Even more influential than these vivid films was the establishment by Jerzy Toeplitz in 1948 of the Lodz Film School (which was later moved to Warsaw). It is recognized as one of the finest national motion picture production training centers in the world.

A new generation of directors, all graduates of the Lodz Film School, came to the fore in the late fifties, including Jerzy Has, Stanislaw Rozewicz, and Tadeusz Chmielewski. Three directors, however, assumed leadership of what has come to be called the *Polish film school.*

Andrzej Wajda (1926–) is the best known outside of Poland's boundaries. He has an intensely dramatic style that comes close to the edge of melodrama, yet can be extremely effective (as in the last sequences of *Ashes and Diamonds* [Figure 4.45]). The director's major theme is the conflicts of pre–World War II traditions and the new communist system. Wajda made a spectacular debut as a director of feature films with a trilogy that is worthy of comparison with the war films of Rossellini and De Sica: *A Generation* (*Pokolenie,* 1955), *Kanal* (1956), and *Ashes and Diamonds* (*Popiól i diament,* 1958). His motion pictures of the sixties and seventies have ranged from additional war films, such as *Innocent Sorcerers* (*Niewinni czarodzieji,* 1960) and *Samson* (1961), to penetrating psychological studies, including

*Siberian Lady Macbeth* (*Sibirska Ledi Magbet,* 1962), *Everything for Sale* (*Wszystko na sprzedaz,* 1968), *The Birch Wood* (*Brzezina,* 1971), and *Man of Marble* (1977). The last work and *Man of Iron* (1981) were in support of the Solidarity movement in Poland.

---

**FIGURE 4.45**

*Ashes and Diamonds,* 1958, directed by Andrzey Wajda. Maciek (Zbigniew Cybulski) is an assassin for a rightist group contending for power with the ruling supporters of Communism. In the end, he is shot and dies alone in agony.

Andrzej Munk died in a car accident at the age of 40 in 1961. After a decade of making documentaries, his five feature films were widely acclaimed for their ironic, bold probing of social issues and their imaginative style, especially *Man on the Track* (*Czlowiek na torze,* 1957) and *Eroica* (1958). Jerzy Kamalerowicz (1922–) does not possess as individualistic a style as Wajda and Munk, but he has a flair for creating suspense and for exploring the manifestations of societal and psychological tensions in a state-controlled society, as demonstrated in *A Night of Remembrance* (*Celuloza,* 1954), *Night Train* (*Pociag,* 1959), *Mother Joan of the Angels* (*Matka Joanna od Aniolow,* 1961), and *Death of the President* (1978).

Consideration of the Polish film school group would be incomplete without noting the contribution of the actor Zbigniew Cybulski. He appeared in many films of the late fifties and sixties, and his performances in those directed by Wajda and Munk helped to make these motion pictures popular. His untimely death in 1967 in a train accident at only 40 was viewed as a national tragedy in his country.

Practically all the directors who came to prominence in the fifties were born in the 1920s. The next generation, all born in the thirties, were too young to experience World War II as adults, and their chief concerns have been more social and psychological than political. Jerzy Skolimowski is among the most talented. His dramas on rebellious Polish youth include *Walkover* (1965), his first fiction film, and *Barrier* (1966). *Hands Up!* (1967) was banned in Poland, and in the seventies most of his films have been made abroad, such as *Deep End* (1970), *King, Queen, Knave* (1972), and *The Shout* (1978). *The Shout* especially illustrates the surrealistic strain that often surfaces in his work. Walerian Borowczyk was a respected animator in his homeland before he left for Paris in the late fifties, where he has directed allegorical, semisurrealistic dramas with erotic overtones, such as *Goto* (1969) and *Immoral Tales* (*Contes immoraux*, 1974).

Roman Polanski (1933–) is the most internationally famous of the Polish directors who came to the forefront in the sixties because of the success of the films he has made in Great Britain and the United States. After graduating from the Lodz Film School, his first feature—and the only one he was to direct in Poland—was highly praised in his country and abroad. Although *The Knife in the Water* (*Noz w wodzie,* 1962) (Figure 4.46) does reflect the director's preoccupation with sexuality, it does not contain the surrealistic element that appeared in his next three dramas, produced in Great Britain: *Repulsion* (1965), *Cul-de-sac* (1966), and *The Dance of the Vampires* (1967).

The first film he made in Hollywood gave additional evidence of his obsession with the bizarre. *Rosemary's Baby* (1968) is a tale of satanism set in contemporary New York. The director returned to England to create a piquant version of Shakespeare's *Macbeth* (1971) and the less successful *What?* (1972). In Hollywood, he made *Chinatown* (1974); it takes place in the thirties and evokes the tone of Humphrey Bogart's Sam Spade and Philip Marlowe detective films. In *The Tenant* (1976), he returned to the

**FIGURE 4.46**

*Knife in the Water,* 1962, directed by Roman Polanski. Andrzej (Leon Niemczyk, left), his wife Christine (Jolanta Umecka), and a hitchhiker (Zygmunt Malanowicz) take a boat trip together. At the end of the film, the husband and wife are forced to reconsider their relationship.

supernatural as a source of menacing evil. *Tess* (1979, an adaptation of a Thomas Hardy novel) is stylistically the most conventional of the director's works; its dramatic structure is flawed, but it contains lovely cinematography.

Polanski's reputation rests primarily on his dramas of terror and suspense, often leavened with dark humor. He lifts these works above the level of most thrillers through his ability to counterpoise without strain a commonplace environment and manifestations of frightening mysteries that have their source either in the minds of characters or in a preternatural dimension of existence. The omnipresent erotic overtones are never cheap or exploitative; rather they are means of revealing hidden depths in his characters. His cinematic style is expert and in passages can be visually exciting, but his areas of particular mastery are pacing and tone. On the other hand, his pessimistic vision of continually threatening forces is frequently projected on the screen with too obvious a manipulation of events to achieve terrifying climaxes and without the subtlety, gracefulness, and objectivity that characterized Hitchcock's portrayals of an equally insecure world.

Czechoslovakia's film industry did not come of age until the advent of sound; its silent films, with the exception of the late-twenties works of Gustav Machaty, were generally undistinguished. The construction in 1932 of the Barrandov Studios, the most advanced in central Europe during the thirties, was a major impetus. The directors, in addition to Machaty, who contributed to a thriving industry included Martin Frič, Otakar Vavra, and Karel Lamac.

After the war, the Czech film industry was nationalized. A film school, FAMU, was established in Prague in 1945. The first evidence of a revival of filmmaking was the animated works of Jiři Trnka and Karel Zeman. Another development of the late forties was the emergence of a separate Slovak cinema.

Although the fortunes of the Czech film industry fluctuated in unison with the tightening and loosening of state control, they generally prospered from 1945 to the uprisings of August, 1968. Not many Czech films, however, aside from animated ones, have been widely circulated beyond its borders. Few moviegoers in the West are acquainted with the works of such directors as Ivan Passer, Evald Schorm, Alfred Radok, Hynek Bocan, the Slovak Juraj Jakubisko, and Vera Chytilová.

Jan Kadar is better known because of the extensive distribution in the West of *Shop on Main Street* (*Obchod na korze*, 1965), one of the many motion pictures on which he collaborated with Elmar Klos. This powerful though flawed story of anti-Semitism was the first Czech motion picture to win an Academy Award in the category of foreign films. After the invasion of his country in 1968, Kadar emigrated to Hollywood. *The Angel Levine* (1970) is one of the films he directed in America. Jiří Menzel has had a fate similar to Kadar's with regard to his reputation in the United States. Although he directed half a dozen films popular in his homeland during the sixties, he is recognized outside Czechoslovakia almost exclusively for *Closely Watched Trains* (*Ostre sledovane vlaky*, 1966), a comedy with serious overtones that also won an Academy Award.

Milos Forman (1932–) is familiar to American audiences for his recent work in this country, but in the 1960s he was an outstanding Czech filmmaker. After studying at FAMU and working as a screenwriter

and assistant director, he completed his first feature, *Peter and Pavla* (*Cerny Petr*) in 1963. *The Loves of a Blonde* (*Lasky jedne plavovlasky*) followed in 1966. The most remarkable film of Forman's Czech period is *The Fireman's Ball* (*Hori ma panenko*, 1967). All these works share the characteristics of a semidocumentary tone, the use of nonprofessional actors, a humor that is wry and sometimes surrealistic, and, most impressive, sharp, penetrating revelations of the ways in which a nation's mores and conventions influence the lives of ordinary people.

In 1968 Forman left Czechoslovakia and eventually arrived at Hollywood. *Taking Off* (1971) was his first American film. *One Flew Over the Cuckoo's Nest* (1975) was tremendously successful. His adaptation of the rock musical *Hair* (1978) did not receive the acclaim it deserved, and *Ragtime* (1981) received more attention than it deserved.

Hungary released few notable works before World War II. In the fifties and sixties, such directors as Karoly Makk, Felix Mariassy, Andras Kovacs, Istvan Szabo, and Istvan Gaal were productive. Most eminent by far, however, has been Miklos Jancsó (1921–). He is a master of visual effects. His carefully constructed works feature extremely lengthy shots and a cinematic choreographing of images equaled by few directors of our time. From the rugged landscape of their homeland emerge individuals and groups that often assume through the director's unique style and emotional intensity a larger-than-life, mythic dimension. In the Jancsó world, life is hard and sudden death and cruelty prevalent. Heroes do come forth, however, especially from peasant stock; they use authority wisely in the service of patriotic causes and derive their strength from the rituals and symbols of community unity.

After devoting himself to documentaries, Jancsó made his first feature film in 1958. He was an accomplished filmmaker when he completed *The Round-Up* (*Szegenylegenyek*, 1965), which is often considered his masterwork. His most outstanding works include *The Red and the White* (*Csillagosok, Kantonak*, 1967), *Silence and Cry* (*Csend es kialtas*, 1968), and *Agnus Dei* (*Egi Barany*, 1970). His productions of the seventies, though worthy, are generally not up to the level of those of the sixties.

Other Central and Eastern European nations have produced respectable cinema, but few directors have established international reputations in Rumania and Bulgaria. Yugoslavia has a fragmented film industry spread out among various ethnic groups. The Serbian Dusan Makavajev, however, has become known for his erotic, unstructured, often grotesque works (such as *WR—Mysteries of the Organism,* 1971).

Switzerland's film industry was practically nonexistent until the sixties and did not develop a character of its own until the emergence of Alain Tanner and Claude Goretta in the seventies (dealt with in the "Seventies" section of this chapter). Greece's cinema was inconsequential until after World War II. Noteworthy in the fifties were the motion pictures directed by Nikos Koundouros. Michael Cacoyannis made outstanding films in that decade (for example, *Stella,* 1955) but is especially important for his cinematic adaptations of ancient Greek tragedies, including *Elektra* (1961) and *The Trojan Women* (1971). He also directed the very successful *Zorba the Greek* (1965). The film, as with Jules Dassin's *Never on Sunday* (*Pote tin Kyriaki,* 1959), was supported by American financing.

This survey is unfortunately too brief to allow consideration of the development of film industries during the postwar era in Central and South America, Africa, and elsewhere. It is impossible, however, to ignore the productions of an Asian nation that have greatly influenced directors in Europe and the United States. In 1951 the grand prize at the Venice Film Festival was awarded to the Japanese film *Rashomon* (directed by Akira Kurosawa). Since that auspicious event, it has been recognized that the best Japanese films constitute a remarkable contribution to the history of cinema.

Japan had a thriving film industry during the four decades preceding World War II. The early silent motion pictures were not exportable because of certain practices derived from the country's contemporary theater. The two most limiting from the point of view of Western audiences were the use of *benshi* (speakers in a theater who narrated as a film was being screened) and *oyama* (female impersonators). On the other hand, the two major categories of subject matter established in those years have prevailed to the present: *jidai-geki* (period films, especially the seventeenth and eighteenth centuries of the Tokugawa shogunate) and *gendai-geki* (on contemporary life).

After the power of the *benshi* and *oyama* had been broken and a new start was necessitated by the devastating earthquake of 1923, which destroyed the motion picture facilities in Tokyo (the center of film production), a group of directors came to prominence. They modernized the techniques and approaches of Japan's cinema. One of the most highly respected of the group was Minoru Murata, director of *Seisaku's Wife* (*Seisaku no Tsuma,* 1924) and *The Street Juggler* (*Machi no Tejinashi,* 1925), who died in 1937. Many of his colleagues continued to be active after World War II. Heinosuke Gosho's realistic portrayals of people of the middle and lower classes and his deft interweaving of comedy and tragedy have made the dozens of films he directed between 1927 and 1968 extremely popular in Japan. Teinosuke Kinugasa is best known to modern audiences for his lovely *Gate of Hell* (*Jigokumon,* 1953), a melodramatic example of *jidai-geki.* His silent films *A Crazy Page* (*Kurutta Ippeiji,* 1926) and *Crossroads* (*Jujiro,* 1928) were influential in persuading contemporary directors that stylistic approaches of the West, especially expressionism and dynamic montage, could be applied to Japanese subject matter. Among his other notable films are *Before the Dawn* (*Reimei Izen,* 1931), *The 47 Ronin* (*Genroku Chushingura,* 1932), *The Summer Battle of Osaka* (*Osaka Natsu no Jin,* 1937), *Lord for a Night* (*Aru Yo no Tono-sama,* 1946), and *The White Heron* (*Shirasagi,* 1958).

Kenji Mizoguchi (1898–1956) and Yasujiro Ozu are two of the grand masters of Japanese cinema. Mizoguchi developed a style of such visual beauty that in this respect he has had few peers anywhere in the world. The subtlety and elegance of composition he achieved with a generally slow-moving camera and lengthy long shots are astonishing. The few color films completed during his last years demonstrate what can be accomplished with this element of presentation through restraint and refinement. Mizoguchi's meticulously structured screenplays were designed to permit him to create convincing visions of the past and the present in which the tone of each sequence is flawless.

In the more than 80 films Mizoguchi directed, a constant theme is the conflicts between traditional and more progressive values (whether the setting is the eighteenth or the twentieth century). His particular preoccupation was the effects of these conflicts on Japanese women. In fact, his insights into the female psyche are penetrating and universal, and his heroines and temptresses have a vitality that makes them memorable. No one who has seen *Ugetsu Monogatori* (1953), Mizoguchi's masterpiece, is likely to forget the two wives or the sensual demon, Lady Wakasa, of this work, which critics have described as "perfect" and "incomparable" (Figure 4.47). Other outstanding motion pictures by the director include *The Sisters of*

---

**FIGURE 4.47**

*Ugetsu Monogatari,* 1953, directed by Kenji Mizoguchi. This beautiful film is replete with memorable shots. In one of them, the demon Lady Wakasa (Machiko Kyo) takes the potter Genjuro (Masayuki Mori) on a picnic and seduces him.

*Gion (Gion no Shimai,* 1936), *Women of the Night (Yoru no Onnatachi,* 1948), *The Life of O'Haru (Saikaku Ichidai Onna,* 1952), *Gion Festival (Gion Bayashi,* 1953), *Sansho the Bailiff (Sansho Dayu,* 1954), *Chikamatsu Monogatori* (1954), *Yokihi* (1955), and *Street of Shame (Akasen Chitai,* 1956).

Yasujiro Ozu (1903–1963) has been characterized by film critics as the most "Japanese" of those of his countrymen who have become internationally known filmmakers. This quality is apparent in both his subject matter and his style. Most of the director's films deal with middle-class family relationships that are recognizable by people of all nations but manifest themselves in mores and conflicts that are uniquely Japanese. *Mise-en-scène* is his predominant approach, with a minimum of camera movement or even action within the frame. Most of his interior sequences are shot from about 3 feet from the floor, the eye level of the Japanese when sitting without chairs. His sparse, economical style, with an emphasis on

character rather than plot development, is in the classical tradition associated in the West with Carl Dreyer and Robert Bresson.

The most distinguished of Ozu's motion pictures are *Tokyo Story* (*Tokyo Monogatori,* 1953) and *Floating Weeds* (*Ukigusa,* 1959, a remake of a 1934 film with the same title). His 52 other films are increasingly being released outside of his country, particularly *The Chorus of Tokyo* (*Tokyo no Gassho,* 1931), *I Was Born, But . . .* (*Umarete was Mita Keredo,* 1932), *The Only Son* (*Hitori Musuko,* 1936), *The Toda Brothers* (*Toda-ke no Kyodai,* 1941), *Early Spring* (*Soshun,* 1956), *Early Autumn* (*Kohayagawa-ke no Aki,* 1961), and *An Autumn Afternoon* (*Samma no Aji,* 1962).

Two names are closely associated with that of Ozu. Kogo Noda wrote the screenplays for practically all of the director's motion pictures (reminiscent of a similar collaboration between De Sica and Zavattini), and the actor Chishu Ryu appeared in all but two of his films. Continuity and an adherence to tradition were hallmarks of Ozu's life and work. Yet within his self-imposed limitations, he created motion pictures of such dignity and refinement that for a sympathetic Western viewer their slow pace and foreignness become virtues rather than defects.

Other outstanding Japanese directors who began their careers before World War II include Yasujiro Shimazu; Daisuke Ito, known for *Man-Slashing, Horse-Piercing Sword* (*Zanjin Zamba Ken,* 1929); Tomu Uchida (for instance, *The Naked Town* (*Hadaki no Machi,* 1937); Shiro Toyoda; Hiroshi Inagaki, director of *A Sword and the Sumo Ring* (*Ippon-Gatana Dohyoiri,* 1931) and *Samurai* (1954); and Satsuo Yamamoto.

Just before and during World War II, censorship in Japan became oppressive. Propaganda films were given first priority. Most of the country's finest directors who continued to work, such as Ozu, Mizoguchi, and Gosho, either devoted themselves to *jidai-geki* films or intimate family plots without propagandist overtones.

The Occupation period was also a difficult time for filmmakers. The Americans imposed restrictions of their own, and imports from the United States flooded the market. In the name of "democracy," General MacArthur's headquarters disrupted the organizational structure of the motion picture studios and forced the issue of to what degree Japanese culture, including cinema, should and could assimilate Western ideas. After the end of the Occupation in 1952, the Japanese film industry reorganized itself and entered a period of expansion and magnificent accomplishments that lasted for two decades.

Kinugasa, Mizoguchi, Ozu, Gosho, and others continued to create striking films. Mizoguchi, in fact, during the last 6 years of his life (1950–1956) experienced a period of surging creativity and released many of the films for which he is famous. (Coincidentally, Max Ophuls, at almost exactly the same time, 1950–1955, also had a blossoming of his genius just before his death.)

As important as the productivity of the older directors was the emergence of exciting new filmmakers. Some—for example, Kurosawa and Kinoshita—were only a few years younger than, say, Ozu and Mizoguchi, but their careers as directors did not begin until the mid- or late forties. As noted earlier, the international attention given to *Rashomon* in 1951 at the Venice Film Festival brought Japanese films into the mainstream of world cinema and was a spur to the ambitions of the country's filmmakers.

Akira Kurosawa (1910–) is probably the most famous Japanese director. After working as a commercial artist, he entered the film industry in the mid-thirties as an assistant director and screenwriter. His debut as a director of his own film did not occur, however, until 1943 with *Judo Saga* (*Sanshiro Sugata*).

As with his older colleagues, Kurosawa's works fall into the two categories of the historical and the contemporary. During various periods in his career, the director supported himself by releasing many technically proficient but unsubstantial *samurai* films. On the other hand, he was also capable of infusing the genre with art and psychological insights, and many of his contributions to this subcategory of *jidai-geki* are brilliant motion pictures. The setting of these films is medieval Japan, when warriors with their own code of honor called *samurai* or *ronin* served under lords or, if masterless, were swords for hire. The parallel to Westerns is evident, and there has been a good deal of cross-fertilization between the two genres. Kurosawa's films of this type, in fact, have often been transformed into Westerns. The most prominent example is *The Seven Samurai* (*Shichi-nin no Samurai,* 1954), adapted by John Sturges as *The Magnificent Seven* (1960).

Other superior *samurai* films directed by Kurosawa include *The Hidden Fortress* (*Kakushi To-ride no San-Akunin,* 1958), *Yojimbo* (1961), and *Sanjuro* (1962). Most famous is *Rashomon* (1950) (Figure 4.48). This masterpiece is simultaneously a satire on the *samurai* genre and a tour de force of point of view.* More generally in the tradition of the *jidai-geki* are *Throne of Blood* (*Kumonosujo,* 1957), a fascinating version of Shakespeare's *Macbeth,* and the epic *Shadow Warrior* (*Kagemusha,* 1980).

**FIGURE 4.48**

*Rashomon,* 1950, directed by Akira Kurosawa. In one of the numerous flashbacks in this film, a priest (Minoru Chiaki) and a woodcutter (Takashi Shimura) observe the bandit Tajomaru (Toshiro Mifune) give his version at an inquest of the death of a samurai and rape of the warrior's wife.

The director has asserted repeatedly that he prefers those of his films with contemporary settings. *Stray Dogs* (*Nora Inu,* 1949), ostensibly a detective story, is actually an intensely dramatic study of post-war Tokyo. *The Idiot* (*Hakuchi,* 1951) is an adaptation of Dostoevski's novel. The favorite Kurosawa film of many enthusiasts is *Ikiru* (1952) (Figure 4.49). It is

*p. 7

**FIGURE 4.49**

*Ikiru,* 1952, directed by Akira Kurosawa. The dying Kanji Watanabe (Takashi Shimura, right) goes in search of a meaning to his life. Before finding it in helping others, he meets a writer (Yunosuke Ito, left) in a tea shop who recommends that he enjoy physical pleasures while he can.

a very moving account of how an old man, a minor bureaucrat, achieves psychic salvation as he dies of cancer. *The Lower Depths* (*Donzoko,* 1957) is an adaptation of Maxim Gorky's play. An American detective novel is the source of *High and Low* (*Tengoku to Jigoku,* 1963). *Red Beard* (*Aka Hige,* 1965), set in the early nineteenth century, is a somewhat sentimental tale of a doctor who finds contentment only when he devotes himself to poor rather than wealthy patients. *Dodeskaden* (1970), the director's first color motion picture, is a stark story about inhabitants of a Tokyo slum. An old hunter who cherishes his freedom and solitary life in the forests is the subject of *Dersu Uzala* (1976), a Soviet-Japanese coproduction.

A prominent characteristic of Kurosawa's style is the tension between or alternation of rigorous control and explosive vigor. He is painstaking in preparing his scripts and demanding of his actors (even of his favorite star, Toshiro Mifune), as well as other members of the filmmaking team. Generally, he does preliminary editing at the end of each day's shooting, so that he molds the rhythms and tone of a work as he proceeds rather than chiefly in the postproduction stage of filmmaking. This could not be done unless he had clear ideas from the beginning about what he was going to create. On the other hand, he tends to include sequences of violence in his films whenever possible. His use of multiple cameras can result in multiple points of view that undermine a viewer's sense of a secure reality. More than most directors, he alternates *mise-en-scène* and montage approaches within a single work.

Another constant of Kurosawa's style is an instinctive sensitivity to striking visual effects. No matter how harsh the reality he is portraying, he refines his images so that they are distillations of beauty and/or drama. Individual scenes may be fragmented or ambiguous, but he is able to preserve the continuity of sequences by a sure, poetic structuring of pictorial values.

What makes the director's films so impressive, however, is that his technical skills are in the service of an unswerving commitment to humanistic concerns. Most of his works with contemporary settings are protests against social injustices. Attaining a degree of goodness in a selfish society, battling for dignity and justice against human indifference, and preserving individuality in an age of conformity are recurrent themes. His view of human nature may on occasion be sentimental, as in *Red Beard,* but rarely simplistic. His villains often have positive qualities, such as energy and determination, and his heroes are frequently tempted by evil. While his women are not portrayed with the depth and variety to be found in the oeuvre of Mizoguchi, they are usually three-dimensional characters with strong, resilient personalities. In short, Kurosawa shares with other great film directors the ability to project his cinematic realities with a vividness, probity, and intensity that distinguish art from simple entertainment.

Kon Ichikawa (1915–), like Kurosawa, became involved with cinema in the mid-thirties (as an animator), but he did not direct his first feature film until the mid-forties. The motion picture that made his reputation in the West was *The Burmese Harp* (*Biruma no Tategoto,* 1956), a poignant story of a Japanese soldier in Burma who leaves the security and comradeship of his fellow troops at war's end to become a Buddhist priest burying the bodies of the slain. Almost as intense is another pacifistic film, *Fires on the Plain* (*Nobi,* 1959). Ichikawa shares with Luis Buñuel (though without the Spaniard's commitment to Sur-

realism) a fascination with human obsessions, as demonstrated in *Odd Obsession* (*Kaji,* 1959), on a husband's sexual perversity that involves his wife and a lover he arranges for her; *Alone in the Pacific* (*Taiheiyo Hitoribochi,* 1963), which deals with a young man's determination to cross the Pacific alone in a 19-foot boat; and *An Actor's Revenge* (*Yukinojo Henge,* 1963), in which a Kabuki female impersonator becomes obsessed with revenging the murder of his parents. The director's talents are also revealed in his dark comedies and documentaries (for example, *Tokyo Olympiad 1964,* 1965). Although Ichikawa's finest films are intriguing for their passion, irony, and unusual main characters, they are impressive also for their visual beauty and graceful continuity.

Masaki Kobayashi directed his first film in 1952 and went on to make a series of powerful motion pictures of social criticism. This stage of his career reached its climax with *The Human Condition* (*Ningen no Joken,* 1958–1961), a three-part, 9-hour antiwar epic on the Japanese invasion of Manchuria. In the sixties, he turned to period pieces, such as *Harakiri* (*Seppuku,* 1962); a collection of ghost stories based on the writings of Lafcadio Hearn (*Kwaidan,* 1964); a gangster movie, *Inn of Evil* (*Inochi bo ni Furo,* 1971); and other genres. Kaneto Shindo has directed more than two dozen films since 1951, but his reputation in the West is based chiefly on *Children of Hiroshima* (*Genbaku no Ko,* 1952) and *The Island* (*Hadaka no Shima,* 1960), a grim but exquisitely photographed story of the life of a farmer during which not a single word is spoken. Keisuke Kinoshita is a versatile director equally at home in satirical comedies, such as *The Girl I Loved* (*Waga Koiseshi Otome,* 1946); neorealistic works, especially *Twenty-Four Eyes* (*Nijushi no Hitomi,* 1954); and kabuki dramas, notably *Ballad of the Narayama* (*Narayama Bushi-ko,* 1958).

Other eminent directors of this period include Kimisaburo Yoshimura, Yasuzo Masumura, and Hideo Sekigawa.

In the fifties, discriminating Western audiences were impressed by the artistic qualities of a multitude of films being made in Japan. The most popular and financially successful products of the country's motion picture industry, however, were well-crafted and original contributions to the genre of monster films. The leading director of those who devoted themselves to this type of entertainment was Ishiro Honda, with such works as *Godzilla* (1954), *Rodan* (1956), and *King Kong vs. Godzilla* (1962).

By the mid-sixties, the great post–World War II period of Japanese filmmaking had begun to wane. Mizoguchi died in 1956 and Ozu in 1963. Between 1966 and 1980, Kurosawa released only two films. Other directors of this generation, most of them born before World War I, were still productive but in many cases were unresponsive to the needs of radically changing social conditions in their homeland. A new generation of filmmakers, born chiefly in the late twenties and early thirties, came to the fore. While preserving the visual sensitivity of their predecessors, they explored new, bold subject matter and daring experimental techniques.

Hiroshi Teshigahara (1927–) became known in the West for his second feature film, *Woman of the Dunes (Suna no Omna,* 1964), an imaginative allegory concerning a scientist trapped with a woman in a sand pit. *The Face of Another (Tanin no Kao,* 1966) is a provocative study of a man's identity crisis. Nagisa Oshima (1932–) has challenged traditional values in Japanese culture and cinema. In his gangster films, such as *Death by Hanging (Koshikei,* 1968) and *Diary of a Shinjuku (Shinjuku Dorobo Nikki,* 1968), and his uncompromising recording of sexual experiences, especially *In the Realm of the Senses (Ai no Corrida,* 1976) and *The Phantom Love (Ai no Borei,* 1978), he has shocked audiences with his subject matter. His freewheeling style of filmmaking, obviously influenced by Godard, has been imitated by many of his younger contemporaries. Masashiro Shinoda has centered his attention on the problems of Japanese youth in the sixties and seventies in such works as *Double Suicide (Shinju ten no Amijima,* 1969) and *Demon Road (Yashaga,* 1980).

Other significant contemporary Japanese directors include Shohei Imamura, who made *The Insect Woman (Nippon Konchuki,* 1964); Susumu Hani, known for *Inferno of First Love (Hatsukoi Jigoku-hen,* 1968); Yasuzo Masumura; Yoshishige Yoshida; and Sachiko Hidari.

Since the mid-seventies, the Japanese motion picture industry has been undergoing a period of transition. Directors such as Teshigahara and Oshima have set up their own production companies. Japanese studios have struggled not only with the loss of many of their most exciting filmmakers but also with rising costs and decreasing attendance at theaters. Exploitation of violence and sex, as in the *yakuza* genre (a form of gangster film), has been on the increase.

Whatever the future holds for Japanese cinema, it can always look back with pride on its past achievements. No country in the world has produced more visually beautiful works of filmic art. For Western audiences, the finest of Japan's motion pictures have offered visions that are rich and strange but, as with significant dreams, also meaningful and memorable.

The cinematic productions of other Asian countries have not attracted similar international interest, with one exception. In 1956 a special jury prize at the Cannes Film Festival was awarded to the Indian film *Pather Panchali.* Its director was Satyajit Ray (1921–). India possesses one of the most prolific film industries in the world (an average of 350 movies a year), but its releases are too standardized and unsophisticated from a Western perspective to be exportable beyond the Orient. Ray, however, inspired by Italian Neorealism, transcended the limitations of his filmmaking countrymen.

Three of Ray's early films constitute the "Apu trilogy": *Panther Panchali* (1955), *Aparajito* (1956), and *The World of Apu (Apur Sansar,* 1958) (Figure 4.50). Based on an autobiographical novel by the Bengal writer Bibhutti-bhusan Bandapaddhay, they are unforgettable depictions of life among lower- and middle-class Indians. Although none of Ray's subsequent work has been as honest and graceful as the trilogy, he has continued to produce impressive films, including *The Music Room (Jalshagar,* 1958), *Two Daughters (Teen Kanya,* 1961), *Days and Nights in the Forest (Aranyer Din Raatri,* 1970), *Distant Thunder (Ashani Sanket,* 1973), and *The Chess Players (Shatranj ke Kilhari,* 1977).

Ray's style is a type of poetic realism. Slowly and carefully, he reveals the milieus of his characters, who usually are caught between the conventions of the past and the increasing freedom and choices of the present. He explores the most fundamental of human activities: birth and death, growing up, love and mar-

**FIGURE 4.50**

*The World of Apu,* 1959, directed by Satyajit Ray. The young man Apu (Soumitra Chatterji) relaxes by playing a flute in his dismal room. He dreams of leaving his tiresome job as a clerk and becoming a successful writer.

riage, work, and artistic expression. Social and political problems are implied rather than delineated. Ray's style has an eloquent simplicity and is capable of a lyric loveliness that has earned him the respect and admiration of audiences throughout the world.

Other notable post–World War II Indian filmmakers are Raj Kapoor, B. R. Chopra, S. Mukherjee, Bimal Roy, Mrinal Sen, and Salil Chowdhury.

## THE SEVENTIES

It is difficult to make valid generalizations about a decade that has so recently ended. Conditions, movements, individual filmmakers, and films that seemed momentous when they first appeared may lose significance after passing through the filter of time. These pages can offer, therefore, only a tentative listing of the most prominent cinematic currents and personages of the seventies.

A fairly safe assertion is that during this decade the greatest influence on motion picture industries throughout the world was the rise of television to the position of chief purveyor of entertainment and information. This medium has functioned as both sponsor and distributor of motion pictures and even spawned

a unique form, the made-for-TV film. Some cinematic genres, such as the documentary, have had function and form molded by their almost complete dependence for distribution on television.

Government involvement or lack of it has been also of prime importance. State-controlled industries demonstrate most clearly the disadvantages (for example, censorship and bureaucratic rigidity) and the advantages (including job security for filmmakers and relative freedom from the financial insecurities and vagaries of the marketplace) of a system of direct subsidies. Even in a democracy, however, state support can make a difference. The resurgence of cinema in West Germany or Australia, for instance, would have been unlikely without national sponsorship. On the other hand, Hollywood, which has never had direct government subsidies, is, if not prospering, at least not moribund.

Worldwide inflation lessened the opportunities for experimentation and also restricted diversity. In a free-enterprise system, this has meant fewer feature motion pictures released and an increase in producers' demands for popular stars, pretested properties, and uncontroversial subject matter. In a state-controlled industry, limited funds encourage those in charge to use criteria other than the ability of a filmmaker in deciding on opportunities and budgets.

One reason for the high cost of commercial filmmaking is the advances in technology and the development of more sophisticated and expensive equipment, from fantastic new special effects to Steadycams and computerized editing systems. Yet there has been one area of technical regression: For financial reasons, the quality of film stock and developing, and consequently the longevity of commercial color prints, has declined.

Another characteristic of the seventies was the rise in the importance of film schools. Since the fifties, all professional filmmakers in the nations of Eastern Europe have been required to be graduates of state film schools, but until recently this type of background had been less prevalent in other countries. For example, the United States has for the first time a generation of young filmmakers who are, with few exceptions, graduates of film schools or programs. Today's filmmakers are generally knowledgeable about aspects of cinema other than those that are solely technical and utilitarian. It is not necessarily true, however, that they are more imaginative, expert, or dedicated than their predecessors.

A phenomenon of the seventies was a discernible growth in the quantity and quality of films produced in the Third World. It is no longer unusual to see at festivals or read in film magazines about motion pictures from the countries of South America, Africa, and Asia. These films are often made with very restricted budgets and with inadequate equipment, but they can possess admirable vitality and audacity.

Audience receptivity to new subject matter and styles has increased since the sixties when the storms of iconoclasm buffeted most Western nations. The boundaries of permissiveness in regard to sex and eroticism have expanded, especially in the areas of language, nudity, and deviance. The same is true of the prevalence of violence and the ways in which it is depicted on the screen. Moreover, moviegoers have been exposed more than ever before to nonconforming attitudes in politics, morality, and religion. Concomitantly, the styles of cinematic expression have been more various and less rigid, so even films that are intended solely as entertainment may contain, for example, a nonlinear narrative, abrupt changes in tone, and expressive uses of color.

### GERMANY

Not since the twenties has German filmmaking been as much admired as during the late sixties and the seventies. Kluge, Straub, and Schlöndorff laid the foundations for the innovative cinema created by a group of West German directors led by Rainer Werner Fassbinder, Werner Herzog, and Wim Wenders. It is possible to designate this group as a movement, but only if the restrictions in generalizations required by individual styles and themes (as was true of the French *Nouvelle Vague*) are kept in mind. No single descriptive label has found universal acceptance among critics, but *German New Cinema* (*Neue Kino*) has had some currency.

Practically all the members of the German New Cinema are young, born in the forties. As is typical of a new generation, they attacked their predecessors for being too conservative in the subject matter and the

techniques of their works. The former criticism was particularly valid for the Federal Republic of Germany's motion picture industry because of its predominantly escapist film fare of the fifties. These rebels have concentrated their attention on the problems that have surfaced in the wake of West Germany's becoming the most powerful economic state in democratic Europe. Since almost without exception they are leftist in their political orientation, themes involving the misuse of power, social inequalities, and avid materialism preoccupy them.

Although each filmmaker has developed a distinctive cinematic style, as a group they share certain approaches. Their narratives tend to be nonlinear, and the motivations of characters are often obscure or at least mysterious. Responding to the example of Kluge, documentary footage may be interspersed in a work of fiction. A popular genre, such as the melodrama or sentimental romance, may serve as the basis for a drama with more profound implications. Camera-editing dynamics often are dramatic, at times self-consciously so, but there is usually little effort toward esthetic refinement (less true of Herzog and Wenders than Fassbinder). Most of the films of this group are intentionally noncommercial. It is unlikely that these directors' works would have been produced without generous government funding, especially through the commissioning of films by state-sponsored television.

The most prolific and to many viewers most exciting member of the German New Cinema movement was Rainer Werner Fassbinder (1946–1982). After a career as a theater actor, he began directing films in 1969 and continued at an astonishing rate considering contemporary production practices. Between 1969 and 1976, he completed 20 features. It is inevitable that such a prodigious output be uneven in quality.

Fassbinder was driven by a resentment that bordered on hatred of capitalistic middle-class West German society. Marxist dogma, sometimes at the expense of common sense and fairness, underlay his attitudes in all his works. The passion and vitality of the director can be subverted by a tendency toward shock for its own sake and a lack of grace and subtlety in his characterizations and camera-editing dynamics. At his best, however, Fassbinder demonstrated a genuine regard for the humanity of his characters and a gift for communicating through his narratives the feelings and inner conflicts of people trapped in a society that, in his view, was dehumanizing them.

The remarkable range of subjects explored by Fassbinder include apparently unmotivated murder and suicide (*Why Does Herr R. Run Amok?,* 1970), racism (*Ali—Fear Eats the Soul,* 1974), betrayal (*Gods of the Plague,* 1970), female and male homosexuality (*The Bitter Tears of Petra von Kant,* 1972; *Fox,* 1975), the possible illusion of group solidarity (*Beware of the Holy Whore,* 1971), challenging the compromises of a society (*Mother Kusters Goes to Heaven,* 1975), death as the final answer to despairing marriages (*The Merchant of Four Seasons,* 1972; *Effi Briest,* 1974), changes of identity (*Despair,* 1978) (Figure 4.51), and being victimized by romantic illusion (*The Marriage of Maria Braun,* 1979).

### FIGURE 4.51

*Despair,* 1978, directed by Rainer Werner Fassbinder (color). This film is based on a novel by Vladimir Nabokov, but the director is as interested in portraying the moral vacuity of contemporary bourgeois German society as in presenting the identity crisis and psychological aberrations of Hermann Hermann (Dirk Bogarde). In this shot, Hermann is captured by the police after murdering a man he mistakenly thinks is his double.

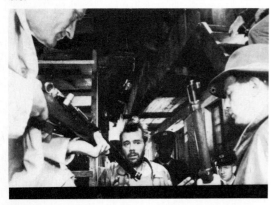

Werner Herzog (1942–), in both his dramas and his documentaries, is as concerned with modern social problems as Fassbinder was, yet he is less doctrinaire and infuses his work with greater symbols and mythic implications. He is also more imaginative and

exciting in his visuals than most other members of his group.

*Even Dwarfs Started Small* (1970) was Herzog's first internationally successful drama. For many critics, the director's masterwork to date is *Aguirre, Wrath of God* (1973), shot in South America and containing many unforgettable scenes. It tells of the self-destructive search for El Dorado by a Spanish conquistador. The misuse of power and the dangers of obsession are two of Herzog's favorite themes. *The Mystery of Kasper Hauser* (1974) was followed by *Heart of Glass* (1976), perhaps the director's loveliest and most delicate drama thus far in his career. *Nosferatu* (1979) was inspired by Murnau's classic, but it is a horror film with its own integrity and a more humanized Prince of Vampires (Figure 4.52). Other

### FIGURE 4.52

*Nosferatu,* 1979, directed by Werner Herzog (color). Klaus Kinski plays the vampire Count Dracula in this modern version of the Bram Stoker novel.

Herzog works include *Fata Morgana* (1971), *Stroszek* (1977), *Wozzeck* (1979, an adaptation of Georg Büchner's early nineteenth-century play), and *Fitzcarraldo* (1981). The director's documentaries (for example, *The Great Ecstacy of the Wood-Sculptor Steiner,* 1975, on a skier) are among the most intriguing made in the seventies.

Wim Wenders (1945–) is preoccupied with all forms of alienation and the disorientation and anxiety it produces. Most of his films involve a journey of some kind; his characters wander in search of contact with other human beings in a society that is cold and committed to an emotionally deadening commercialism and self-interest. The director's style is straightforward and low-key, carefully conceived to achieve the greatest effects from a minimum of camera-editing dynamics and simple elements of presentation. The most popular of his films has been *Kings of the Road* (1976), a picaresque tale of the travels of two men through northern Germany. His first feature, *The Goalie's Anxiety at the Penalty Kick* (1972), was followed by *The Scarlet Letter* (1973, an adaptation of Hawthorne's novel and a departure from his typical style), *Alice in the Cities* (1974), *The American Friend* (1977)(Figure 4.53), and *The Wrong Movement* (1978).

---

**FIGURE 4.53**

*The American Friend,* 1977, directed by Wim Wenders (color). Tom Ripley (Dennis Hopper) watches as Jonathan Zimmermann (Bruno Ganz) dies in a car after committing two murders at the instigation of his American friend.

Hans Jürgen Syberberg is difficult to categorize. Some of his works, such as a 2-hour interview with the former director of the Bayreuth opera and supporter of Hitler (*The Confessions of Winifred Wagner,* 1975), are obviously documentaries. Others are based on historical facts, yet are developed in a manner so freewheeling and subjective as to preclude them from being called documentaries. Perhaps *Ludwig—Requiem for a Virgin King* (1972) and *Our Hitler: A Film From Germany* (1977, 6 hours in its original version and 3 in another) should be labeled fantasies or cinematic meditations on a theme.

Practically all of Syberberg's films are related in one way or another to the origins and ramifications of Germany's support of Hitler and Nazism. There can be no doubt that the director-screenwriter is creative and ingenious in his approaches, such as his use of puppets in *Our Hitler.* For many viewers, however, his work is also pretentious, diffuse, and self-indulgent.

Few other German directors during the seventies have established international reputations. There has not been much opportunity, especially in the United States, to view the dramas of Werner Schroeter, much less those of Uwe Brandner, Peter Fleischmann, Margarethe von Trotta, Ula Stöckl, and Klaus Wyborny. It is obvious, however, that the German New Cinema is a potent movement, and the best directors of this group have demonstrated in their works a vigor, contemporaneity, and stylistic boldness that have fascinated discerning moviegoers throughout the world.

---

### U.S.A.

In the seventies, the earlier generation of master Hollywood directors had either died (for example, John Ford, Alfred Hitchcock, and Howard Hawks) or retired (for instance, King Vidor, Frank Capra, and Rouben Mamoulian). Of those that rose to prominence in the forties, the septuagenarians Billy Wilder (most notably, *Fedora*, 1979) and Otto Preminger (for example, *Rosebud*, 1975, and *The Human Factor*, 1980) directed works that showed a decline in vitality but not in skill. The same holds true for the somewhat younger Vincente Minnelli (for instance, *A Matter of Time*, 1976). Only the apparently indestructible John Huston demonstrated no lessening of élan and versatility.

Most major American directors of the fifties and sixties continued to create outstanding films. The 1970s dramas of many of them—including Stanley Kubrick, Don Siegel, Sidney Lumet, Samuel Fuller, Joseph Losey, Fred Zinnemann, Arthur Penn, Stanley Kramer, and John Frankenheimer—were cited earlier in this chapter. Some, such as Sam Peckinpah, evidenced a marked diminution in the quality of their work. Others moved in new directions. For example, John Cassavetes, without compromising his hallmarks of spontaneity and improvisation in acting and plot development, made films with a more popular appeal than his early dramas (for instance, *Gloria,* 1980). Our chief concern in these pages, however, is the new directors of the seventies.

Robert Altman (1925–) is young neither in experience nor chronological age, but he did not direct a major film until 1970. Once having found himself as an artist, he experienced a 7-year period of remarkable creativity. With the exceptions of Stanley Kubrick (working in England) and Francis Ford Coppola, no living American director released a series of films of such provocativeness and originality. Unfortunately, since 1977 his work has contained only sporadic flashes of the brilliance of his finest motion pictures.

After serving in the Air Force in World War II, Altman learned his craft by making industrial films and then becoming a television director, primarily of episodic shows. His first feature *(The Delinquents)* and his only documentary *(The James Dean Story)* were both released in 1957. For a decade, Altman confined himself to television. In 1968, however, he returned to feature filmmaking with three competent adaptations from novels *(Countdown,* 1968, *Nightmare in Chicago,* 1969, and *That Cold Day in the Park,* 1969).

The director's next work brought him instant fame and an Academy Award nomination for Best Director in 1970. *M*A*S*H* is an irreverent, frenetic antiwar comedy in the lineage of Kubrick's *Dr. Strangelove* and a contribution to the development of the "new wave" in American film comedy.* *Brewster McCloud* (1970) was a little too fantastic and unfocused in its satire to be as popular a comedy as its predecessor. Altman now had the confidence and experience to explore various genres and to realize his very individualistic visions of American society and human nature.

He created two superior Westerns, *McCabe and Mrs. Miller* (1971) and *Buffalo Bill and the Indi-*

ans (1976).* *The Long Goodbye* (1973) and *Thieves Like Us* (1974) are, respectively, a detective film and a gangster film. *California Split* (1974) deals with a couple of compulsive gamblers. Two Altman films are audacious, densely imagistic portrayals of the interior worlds of a young woman having a nervous breakdown *(Images,* 1972) and of three acquaintances on the borderline of insanity *(Three Women,* 1977). Although at times obscure and makeshift in plot structure, both dramas contain haunting sequences. Later films (for instance, *A Wedding* and *Quintet,* both 1978) have been disappointments for most admirers of the director's work.

Altman's masterpiece to date is *Nashville* (1975), one of the most impressive films made in Hollywood during the seventies (Figure 4.54). The setting

---

**FIGURE 4.54**

*Nashville,* 1975, directed by Robert Altman (color). Ronee Blakely and Henry Gibson play two stars of country and western music. Their happy, friendly faces are only facades. She has just recovered from a nervous breakdown and is heading for another one; he is a cynical, brutal man who is using his popularity to further devious political plans.

is the capital of country music. The subject of this panoramic drama with 24 major characters is the dynamics of a representative segment of American society seduced by shallow values and superficial experiences and for whom a form of entertainment and its

---

*pp. 282–283

*pp. 397, 401

stars become a substitute for reality and genuine heroes. The plot may be too obviously manipulated and the characterizations sometimes two-dimensional, but the film contains a multitude of clever, at times masterful visual effects. The sound track is so innovative, particularly in the fragmentation and overlapping of conversations and natural sounds, as to constitute a landmark in the development of new techniques in this element of presentation.

Altman works rapidly, depending a good deal on the improvisation of his actors and his own inspiration. This can lead, on the one hand, to individual works that are inconsistent in quality, careless in craftsmanship, and meandering. On the other hand, at his best Altman achieves an authenticity of tone, an admirable use of unconventional techniques, and provocative characters who convince us that they are gripped by genuine emotions and needs. Perhaps most impressive of Altman's laudable qualities as a director is his ability, similar to that of Peckinpah, for making characters believable as individuals while simultaneously personifying those drives, values, virtues, and faults that are distinctly American.

Of outstanding significance in the seventies was the rise to positions of power in Hollywood of a group of relatively young men (most still under 40 at the end of the decade) who directed some of the most popular and highest-grossing motion pictures of recent years. Francis Ford Coppola, Martin Scorsese, George Lucas, Steven Spielberg, Brian De Palma, Paul Schrader, John Milius, and Michael Cimino are sometimes described collectively as the Young Turks or irreverently, in the title of a recent study, the "Movie Brats."[7]

Their individual works are in most respects very different, but they share similar backgrounds and attitudes toward filmmaking. With the exception of Spielberg, each is a graduate of a film school. All of them are film buffs, knowledgeable about the history of foreign as well as American cinema, and they keep informed about avant-garde styles and technical advances. Each appears determined to make commercially successful films over which he has sufficient control to realize his intentions fully. Certain of these young filmmakers (Coppola, Lucas, Spielberg, Milius, and Schrader) are close friends, and their mutual co-operation on many projects is almost unique in an industry that views cutthroat competition, rivalries, and power strategems as intrinsic to its life-style. Even among the members of this inner circle, however, there is not enough evidence of interrelated influences on their individual films to refer to a cinematic movement.

It is a journalistic cliché to describe Francis Ford Coppola (1939–) as the "godfather" of the Young Turks. He was the first to establish a beachhead in Hollywood, is today one of the most powerful director-producers in the United States, and has been generous in helping those of his friends who are talented. After studying theater in New York and film in California, Coppola became an assistant to Roger Corman, and he directed his first professional feature, *Dementia 13* (1963), under the auspices of the canny producer. Before his next directing assignment, he wrote screenplays, including *This Property Is Condemned* (1966) and *Is Paris Burning?* (1966). Later he was to do scripts for other directors, most notably *Patton* (1970, for which he won an Oscar).

Coppola's first important work was *You're a Big Boy Now* (1967). This low-budget comedy on the sixties generation was overshadowed by another film on the same subject released that year—*The Graduate*. His initial large-budget motion picture was the musical *Finian's Rainbow* (1968). He returned to a more personal style for *The Rain People* (1969).

The film that made Coppola famous was the immensely successful *The Godfather* (1972) (Figure 4.55), followed 3 years later by a sequel. In between, the director created his most incisive and imaginative low-budget drama to date, *The Conversation* (1974). The grandiose and powerful *Apocalypse Now* was released in 1978.

Coppola's vitality is a quality that even his most deprecating critics cannot deny. Without prodigious energy and self-confidence, he could not have accomplished so much so soon (he was only 33 when he directed *The Godfather*). He is not, however, a "rude genius" but a fine craftsman and a thoroughly professional filmmaker. He is particularly imaginative in taking a dramatic situation, usually tending toward the melodramatic, and focusing on revealing details,

**FIGURE 4.55**

The Godfather, 1971, directed by Francis Ford Coppola (color). The males of the Corleone family at the wedding of the Don's daughter: (left to right) Michael (Al Pacino), Don Vito (Marlon Brando), Sonny (James Caan), and Fredo (John Cazale).

while at the same time shifting his perspective enough to add an element of the bizarre or almost hallucinatory. Examples are the concluding sequence of The Conversation and the USO performance at the Vietnamese front in Apocalypse Now. In this respect, the influence of Fellini is evident.

Exploration of the psychology of complex characters is not the director's forte. He is at his best in dealing with the dynamics of a group or of relatively unsophisticated individuals contending with internal or external forces beyond their control. When tone and structure fuse—as in The Godfather, The Godfather—Part II, and The Conversation, Coppola's most impressive works thus far—the result is remarkable cinema. When tone is not supported by a carefully developed plot and clearly delineated characters, even memorable scenes do not coalesce into an organic unity. In the view of at least one critic, this is the source of the essential failure of Apocalypse Now as drama. One for the Heart (1981) has a mundane plot and shallow characterizations that vitiate its striking production values.

Coppola has the potential of becoming one of the most significant American directors if he continues to take advantage of his unique talents. Meanwhile, he is also an important force in the areas of motion pic-

ture production and financing through his company Zoetrope Studios (which, unfortunately, lost its physical plant in 1982). In addition to his efforts on behalf of young American directors, he has been responsible for the revival of Abel Gance's Napoléon and the distribution of films by foreign film artists (for instance, in 1980 he "presented" Jean-Luc Godard's Every Man for Himself and, with George Lucas, Akura Kurosawa's The Shadow Warrior).

Steven Spielberg (1947–) is another Hollywood wunderkind. Although his output is less extensive than Coppola's, he has been equally precocious (he directed his first feature-length drama at the age of 25). After two made-for-television movies, Spielberg directed the popular Sugarland Express (1973), which could be described as a comedy version of Bonnie and Clyde. Jaws (1975) impressed not only audiences but also the industry by earning well over $100 million in total rentals in 2 years. Close Encounters of the Third Kind (1977) was another "blockbuster" and with Lucas's Star Wars initiated a cycle of science fiction releases. Spielberg experienced his first major failure with 1941 (1979), a bloated, extravagant farce, but he resumed a tenor of financial successes with Raiders of the Lost Ark (1981) and E. T. The Extra-Terrestrial (1982).

Each of the director's major films is based on a journey that includes a spectacular climactic sequence. His characters are predominantly identifiable American types caught up in unusual events that test their integrity and self-sufficiency. In this respect, the influence of Hitchcock is discernible. Unlike his predecessor in the thriller genre, Spielberg is fascinated by special effects and is not particularly adept at creating subtleties of characterization. On the other hand, his craftsmanship is admirable, and he has a distinctive talent for controlling and developing the rhythms of individual scenes, sequences, and a whole film.

George Lucas's second feature film was American Graffiti (1973), a perceptive, humorous yet touching portrayal of a night in the lives of high school graduates. The setting is a small California town in the early sixties. Lucas's true interest, however, is obviously in romantic fantasy and the challenges it presents to the medium of cinema, for his first feature was a work of science fiction (*THX-1138*, 1970), and since *American Graffiti* he has committed himself to a series of films on galactic warfare.

Star Wars (1977, produced and directed by Lucas), *The Empire Strikes Back* (1980, produced by Lucas and directed by Irvin Kershner), and *Return of the Jedi* (1983, produced by Lucas and directed by Richard Marquand) are three episodes in a projected nine-part saga. The three episodes are triumphs of special effects, exciting adventure stories with spectacular battles between personifications of unambiguous good and evil, and they contain a sort of mythic effervescence that a particularly immature adolescent might mistake for profundity. Still, these films—and probably the future ones in the series—are robust entertainment. So too is *Raiders of the Lost Ark,* another excursion (though earthbound) into popular culture that Lucas produced and his friend Spielberg directed. Recent interviews suggest that he is more interested in supervising the making of motion pictures through his production company, Lucasfilm, than in directing himself.

John Milius was one of Hollywood's leading screenwriters (for example, Huston's *The Life and Times of Judge Roy Bean,* 1972, and Pollack's *Jeremiah Johnson,* 1972) before turning to directing. All his works to date have been action films invigorated by gusto and sophistication: *Dillinger* (1973, a gangster film), *The Wind and the Lion* (1975, a romantic adventure), and *Big Wednesday* (1978, on surfing). Paul Schrader, like Milius, began as a prominent screenwriter (including Scorsese's *Taxi Driver,* 1976, and De Palma's *Obsession,* 1976). The dramas he has directed are more preoccupied with social problems than those of any other member of the inner circle of Young Turks. *Blue Collar* (1978) deals with three disgruntled workers in an auto factory. *Hard Core* (1978) is an exposé of the film pornography industry. *American Gigolo* (1979) is a realistic depiction of the emotional price paid by a man who rents his body to wealthy women.

Two outstanding young directors who have only tentative connections to Coppola's "family" are Martin Scorsese (1942–) and Brian De Palma. Both are attracted, though from different perspectives, by the dark underside of human nature that is the source of violence and evil. Scorsese has an almost Dostoevskian sensitivity to how a moral weakness in an individual can develop and fester until the person is possessed by an irrational, explosive need that can destroy him and others. The director also captures the ambiance of a specific time and place by focusing on telling details of setting and reactions of characters. This gives authenticity to such documentaries as *Italianamerican* (1974) and *The Last Waltz* (1978, on the farewell concert of The Band). Violence and moral degeneration pervade *Mean Streets* (1973), *Taxi Driver* (1976) (Figure 4.56), and *Raging Bull* (1980, a

**FIGURE 4.56**

*Taxi Driver,* 1976, directed by Martin Scorsese (color). A psychopathic taxi driver, Travis Bickle (Robert De Niro), is determined personally to clean up the human debris that surfaces at night in New York City. Here he drives an unsavory passenger, played by the director himself.

"biopic" on the fighter Jake La Motta). Less typical and interesting are *Alice Doesn't Live Here Anymore* (1974), the musical *New York, New York* (1977),* *The King of Comedy* (1983), and his first two feature films.

For all Scorsese's vigor, skill, and sensibility that can make palpable the fear, hatred, and paranoia of his characters, he tends to depend too much on melo-

---

*p. 459

drama to hold the attention of his audiences and to distract them from weaknesses of characterization, particularly point of view and motivation.

Brian De Palma (1941–) first devoted himself as a director to capturing on film the idealism and confusion of radical youth of the late sixties in such films as *The Wedding Party* (1963), *Greetings* (1968), and *Hi, Mom!* (1970). With *Sisters* (1973), however, he began making sophisticated, commercially successful horror films that are prepared with meticulous care, contain striking effects, and go beyond typical examples of the genre in depth of characterization. Although De Palma has succeeded to some degree at his avowed intention of achieving the brilliance of form characteristic of Hitchcock's thrillers, the director has little of the irony and consistent vision of evil found in the finest works of the master. The psychological horror films of Roman Polanski, to mention another director skilled in the genre, have more substance and subtlety than De Palma's *The Phantom of the Paradise* (1974), *Obsession* (1976), *Carrie* (1976), *The Fury* (1978), *Dressed to Kill* (1980), and *Scarface* (1983).

Many prominent young directors of the seventies have functioned outside the circle of friends and associates that make up the Young Turks. The story of Peter Bogdanovich is a sad one of the rise and decline of an impressive talent. He entered the field of cinema as a writer of excellent books on American film (for example, *The Cinema of Orson Welles* and *Fritz Lang in America*). The documentary *Directed by John Ford* (1971) also revealed his critical acumen. Bogdanovich's second feature (after a low-budget thriller sponsored by Roger Corman) was one of the finest of the decade. *The Last Picture Show* (1971) is a nostalgic yet clear-eyed evocation of a small Texas town in the mid-fifties. He then released two outstanding comedies (*What's Up, Doc?,* 1972, and *Paper Moon,* 1973*). His decline began with an uninspired adaptation of a Henry James novella (*Daisy Miller,* 1974), followed by a surprisingly inept musical (*At Long Last Love,* 1975) and a frenetic and graceless comedy (*Nickelodeon,* 1976). His last film of the seventies, *Saint Jack* (1979), about a sleazy American expatriate

in Singapore, contains a degree of forced vitality but does not herald the resurgence of his talent that admirers of his earlier films have awaited for so long.

There has been no decline in the abilities of Michael Ritchie. Although he has proved himself capable of directing robust comedies (*The Bad News Bears,* 1976, and *Semi-Tough,* 1977) and a sardonic gangster film (*Prime Cut,* 1972), he is at his best in molding semidocumentary, ironic, provocative commentaries on American values, especially competitiveness and materialism. *Downhill Racer* (1969), *The Candidate* (1972), and *Smile* (1975) contain interesting plots, but it is the subtle yet pointed satirical intentions of the director that make them distinctive films.

James Ivory was born and trained in the United States but is often thought of as an Englishman because he has directed so many motion pictures abroad, especially in India, with English casts. No contemporary has quite his sensitivity to the nuances of class conflicts and delicate sensibilities. Moreover, he is a resourceful craftsman with an unostentatious style. His films with Indian settings include *Shakespeare Wallah* (1964), *Autobiography of a Princess (1975),* and *Hullabaloo Over Georgie and Bonnie's Pictures* (1978). *The Wild Party* (1974), *Roseland* (1977), and *The Europeans* (1978, an adaptation of a Henry James novel) take place in the United States. Ivory's films are rarely spectacular and are never "blockbusters" at the box office, but he is consistent in creating intelligent, mature dramas.

Other relatively young directors whose work suggests unusual potential established their reputations in the seventies. Terrence Malick's *Badlands* (1973), his directorial debut, is a vivid story about a latter-day Bonnie and Clyde. He is also responsible for one of the most exquisitely photographed dramas since Kubrick's *Barry Lyndon—Days of Heaven* (1978). Michael Cimino, after working as a screenwriter, directed his first film, *Thunderbolt and Lightfoot,* in 1974. Despite its weaknesses and its supposedly unpopular subject matter, *The Deer Hunter* (1978), on the Vietnam war, was a box office success. *Heaven's Gate,* a $36 million Western prematurely released in 1980, demonstrates the danger of allowing even a superior filmmaker to be self-indulgent. Other notable young directors include John Badham (who made *Saturday Night Fever,* 1977), Walter Hill (for instance, *Hard Times,* 1975, and *The Warriors,* 1979), Alan Parker (*Midnight Express,* 1977), and two novelists turned film directors—Michael Crichton (best known for *Coma,* 1978, and *The Great Train Robbery,* 1979) and Nicholas Meyer (*Time After Time,* 1979).

Certain prominent directors of an older generation (born in the 1930s or earlier) did not become widely known until the late sixties or the seventies. Bob Rafelson perplexed his audiences with unconventional films that intrigued critics but did not do well at the box office, such as *The King of Marvin Gardens* (1972) and *Stay Hungry* (1976). More commercial are the works of John Boorman (including *Deliverance,* 1972, and *Exorcist II,* 1977) and Sidney Furie (such as *The Impress File,* 1965, and *Lady Sings the Blues,* 1972; a change of pace was his *The Boys of Company C,* 1978, one of the best films on the Vietnam war). Hal Ashby was unusual among Hollywood directors of this decade in reaching large audiences with controversial dramas on social problems, including *The Last Detail* (1973), *Shampoo,* 1976, and *Coming Home,* 1978. Robert Benton is a meticulous craftsman with a flair for making heroes of ordinary people in challenging circumstances, as exemplified by the offbeat detective story *The Late Show* (1977) and the phenomenally popular *Kramer vs. Kramer* (1979). Larry Peerce began his directing career with two perceptive dramas (*One Potato, Two Potato,* 1966, and *Goodby Columbus,* 1969), but the quality of his work has since fallen off. Arthur Hiller moved from television to film. He is unusually versatile, equally professional in creating comedies (for example, *Plaza Suite,* 1971), musicals (*Man of La Mancha,* 1972), romances (*Love Story,* 1970), and dramas (for instance, *The Hospital,* 1971, and *The Man in the Glass Booth,* 1975).

A special category of directors who rose to distinction during the seventies includes those who shifted from one area of filmmaking to another. Alan Pakula had been a major producer since the late fifties. Since 1969 he has been an eminent director as well. Among his credits are *The Sterile Cuckoo* (1969), *Klute* (1971), *All the President's Men* (1976), and *Comes a Horseman* (1978). Melvin Frank was a successful screenwriter (usually collaborating with Norman Panama) during the forties and fifties. His specialty is comedy, and when he became a director in 1968, he continued working in this genre, as exemplified by *A Touch of Class* (1973) and *The Prisoner of Second Avenue* (1975). Quite a few actors turned to directing during the seventies. The most prolific has been Clint Eastwood in Westerns (most notably *The Outlaw Josey Wales,* 1976), adventure films, and comedies. Paul Newman has been attracted to serious plots, as in *Rachel, Rachel* (1968) and *The Effect of Gamma Rays on Man-in-the-Moon Marigolds* (1972). Other actors who directed at least one film in the seventies include Robert Redford (*Ordinary People,* 1980), Sylvester Stallone, Peter Fonda, Dennis Hopper, Alan Arkin, Warren Beatty, Gene Wilder, Marty Feldman, Carl Reiner, Jack Nicholson, Burt Reynolds, and George C. Scott.

Two other categories of directors also should be considered separately, but in these cases solely to underline the breakthrough made by black and women filmmakers in Hollywood during the seventies. Before the late sixties, no black director of note was making feature films. The crucial year of change was 1969, when Ossie Davis directed *Cotton Comes to Harlem,* a comedy thriller, and Gordon Parks, Sr., released *The Learning Tree,* an autobiographical study of a black youth growing up in Kansas during the twenties. Davis went on to direct *Kongi's Harvest* (1970) and *Countdown at Kusini* (1974), both made in Africa, as well as *Black Girl* (1972) and *Gordon's War* (1973).

Sidney Poitier contributed as a director as well as actor to the making of motion pictures presenting black attitudes and sensibilities. His credits include *Buck and the Preacher* (1971), *Uptown Saturday Night* (1974), and *Let's Do It Again* (1975). Probably the most radical and militant black drama distributed commercially in the seventies was *Sweet Sweetback's Baadasssss Song* (1971). It was written, produced, and directed by Melvin Van Peebles, who also played the title role. Other notable black filmmakers are Bill Gunn, Michael Schultz (for instance, *Cooley High,* 1975, *Car Wash,* 1976, and *Greased Lightning,* 1977), Bill Crain, Woodie King, Jr., and Mark Warren.

Women directors in the United States before

the seventies were almost as rare as black ones. Feminists have reminded us that Alice Guy-Blaché, a Frenchwoman, directed films in this country from 1913 to 1925, as did Lois Weber at about the same time. Dorothy Arzner is best known for her films of the thirties. Ida Lupino in the late forties shifted from acting to producing and directing. Women did better in the genres of the documentary and the avant-garde film, as evidenced by the work of Helen Grayson in the former area and Maya Deren in the latter.

The woman director who first attracted attention after World War II was Shirley Clarke, with such American neorealistic dramas as *The Connection* (1962), *The Cool World* (1963), and *Portrait of Jason* (1967). Susan Sontag, one of today's most perceptive writers on culture, directed her first film, *Duet for Cannibals,* in 1969 and *Promised Lands* in 1973. Some actresses, following the example of Lupino, have turned to directing: Barbara Loden's sole film to date is *Wanda* (1970); Joan Darling has limited herself also to a single effort (*First Love,* 1977); Elaine May has been more prolific with *A New Leaf* (1971), *The Heartbreak Kid* (1972), and *Mikey and Nicky* (1976). Joan Tewkesbury, a distinguished Hollywood screenwriter, directed her first film (*Old Boyfriends*) in 1979. Two of the most impressive talents of recent years have been Joan Micklin Silver (*Hester Street,* 1974; *Bernice Bobs Her Hair,* 1976; and *Between the Lines,* 1977) and Claudia Weill (for example, *Girlfriends,* 1978, and *It's My Turn,* 1980). There are many other women directors of commercial fiction features, such as Karen Arthur, who are just beginning to build their reputations.

The best American directors of the seventies produced exciting, provocative dramas, as well as, in many cases, timid, perfunctory ones. The "blockbuster" mentality of Hollywood's financial forces has created restraints but has not completely contaminated the integrity of these directors. A more insidious temptation is to rely on the marvelous technical facilities available in Hollywood, especially in the area of special effects, at the expense of a substantial, carefully crafted narrative dimension and imaginative cinematic techniques that allow the realization of the feelings as well as form of the filmmaker's vision. The most recent films of Kubrick, Altman, Peckinpah, Coppola, Spielberg, De Palma, Cimino, and others suggest that glittering surface effects cannot completely compensate for tentative intellectual concepts and shallow emotional insights into human nature. On the other hand, these filmmakers are too talented not to discover new methods of making the ends as important as the means, and that, for them, is the challenge of the eighties.

## ITALY

Many of the great post–World War II Italian directors died during the seventies, including De Sica, Rossellini, Visconti, and Pasolini. Antonioni did not release a feature film between 1975 and 1980. Only Fellini, Olmi, Bertolucci, and Rosi have more or less continued to be prolific. With one exception, no major Italian director has come to the fore in the last decade.

The exception is Lina Wertmuller (1928–). After extensive experience in the theater and television as a writer and director, she completed her first feature, *The Lizards,* in 1962. Two additional films followed, but Wertmuller was not recognized as an outstanding director until *The Seduction of Mimi* (1972). Her fame increased with *Love and Anarchy* (1973), *All Screwed Up* (1974), *Swept Away by a Strange Destiny on an Azure August Sea* (1974), and *Seven Beauties* (1976).

The chief theme of Wertmuller's films is the use and abuse of power. Politics, therefore, plays an important role in her works, manifested in class conflicts and in condemnation of the fascist mentality (as it appears in members of the Fascist party and in such tyrannical organizations as the Mafia). What most interests the director, an avowed feminist, is the attempts of males to dominate females, especially through sex. Moreover, Wertmuller, like Pasolini, Bertolucci, and Liliana Cavani, sees a connection between politics and sex, so that fascists are often sexual sadists and a male chauvinist can be a coward and an opportunist. The latter is exemplified by Pasqualino, a potential mafioso in *Seven Beauties,* who is willing to humiliate himself by using a dogged sexual prowess to survive in a German concentration camp.

This bald summary of the director's multifaceted major theme—much like her own statements in interviews—is simplistic and does not do justice to the complexity and ambiguity of her dramas. For example, in one of her most memorable works, *Swept Away,* the poor sailor who dominates his wealthy mistress on a desert island is a communist. The contemptible Pasqualino in *Seven Beauties* possesses a certain charm, is not completely without a conscience, and does survive to propagate his kind.

Wertmuller writes her own screenplays, and their originality and vitality contribute greatly to her motion pictures. She is also a superior craftsman in her art, though with a tendency to overextend scenes that could be more tightly edited. One of the reasons for the popularity of her films is her gift for combining comedy and drama, so that a work like *Love and Anarchy* can contain hilarious sequences, yet have serious overtones and even a tragic ending. Her comedy sometimes becomes farcical and enters the province of the grotesque, a proneness she may have developed under the guidance of her mentor Fellini (she was assistant director for *8 ½*). Although two of her latest films (*The End of the World in Our Usual Bed in a Night Full of Rain,* 1978, and *Revenge,* 1979) demonstrate a slackening of her imaginativeness and skill, she is a distinctive director who has been praised deservedly (if on occasion extravagantly so, especially in the United States) for her honest, bold examinations of contemporary sociosexual problems.

None of the recent Italian directors has received the acclaim of Wertmuller, but a few have made expressive individual films. The Taviani brothers, Vittorio and Paolo, after releasing documentaries and earlier feature films, became prominent with *Padre Padrone* (1977), *The Meadow* (1979), and *The Night of the Shooting Stars* (1982). In *The Night Porter* (1974) and *Beyond Evil* (1979), Liliana Cavani is preoccupied with the intertwining of sex, violence, and politics. Other notable Italian dramas of the seventies are Dario Argento's *The Bird With the Crystal Plumage* (1970), Marco Leto's *Black Holiday* (1973), Gian Luigi Calderone's *Appassionata* (1974), Ettore Scola's *A Special Day* (1977) and *We All Loved Each Other So Much* (1975), and Franco Brusati's *To Forget Venice* (1980).

## FRANCE

Many of the filmmakers associated with the *Nouvelle Vague* of the sixties became part of the establishment in the seventies. This is not to suggest that Truffaut, Chabrol, Lelouch, Malle, Rohmer, Varda, and others have completely incorporated the conventional into their films. They have continued to experiment, when appropriate, while refining their visions of reality, but they no longer shock audiences. They have become "name directors" whose works are given respectful, if not always enthusiastic, receptions by typical moviegoers in their own country and abroad. Other filmmakers of dramas who came to prominence primarily in the 1970s also made films that received some degree of box office success in addition to critical approval.

One director who has developed a responsive audience for his political films is Constantin Costa-Gavras (1933–). Brought up in France by Russian-Greek parents, he created two thrillers before finding his true métier in 1968 with *Z.* This work began the director's fruitful collaboration with actor Yves Montand and cinematographer Raoul Coutard, which continued during the seventies. *Z* reveals Costa-Gavras's leftist leanings and hatred of totalitarian regimes, his ability to invest a drama with the aura of a documentary, and his gift for maintaining suspense even in a convoluted plot.

*The Confession* (1970) (Figure 4.57) is as passionate in its denunciation of communist totalitarianism as *Z* was of rightist dictatorship. *State of Siege* (1972) marks a shift in the director's perspective, for he cast Montand as a CIA agent captured by South American guerrillas and is evenhanded in presenting the views of both ends of the political spectrum. Later works are *Special Section* (1975), *Clair de Femme* (1979), and *Missing* (1982).

Other new directors who have had at least some popular success include Bertrand Tavernier (for example, *The Clockmaker,* 1974, *Let Joy Reign Supreme,* 1975, and *Spoiled Children,* 1977), Jean Eustache (best known for *The Mother and the Whore,* 1973, which runs 219 minutes), the actor Philippe Noiret (*The Secret,* 1974, a thriller), Claude Miller (for instance, *The Best Way to Walk,* 1976), Michel De-

**FIGURE 4.57**

*The Confession,* 1970, directed by Constantin Costa-Gavras (color). Yves Montand plays the Czecho-slovakian Communist official Stansky who is ousted during a power struggle in his party. He is tortured and interrogated (as in this shot) until he confesses to crimes he did not commit.

ville (*Benjamin,* 1968, and others), Michel Drach (for example, *Les Violins du Bal,* 1973), and Jean-Louis Comolli (*La Cecilia,* 1967).

The proud tradition of the French avant-garde sustained itself in the seventies both in short, radically experimental works and in feature films that appealed to limited audiences, usually were supported by government subsidies, and were mostly seen abroad only at festivals and in big cities. The most successful in finding at least a degree of popular acceptance for his difficult dramas was Resnais. Godard would fit into this category if he had not exiled himself from commercial feature filmmaking during most of the seventies. Bresson is not avant-garde in his techniques—quite the contrary; however, like Resnais and Godard, he has been uncompromising in adhering to his unique cinematic style regardless of the reactions of audiences. More typically avant-garde has been the works of Rivette, Robbe-Grillet, Marker, and Franju (see the preceding section of this chapter). Younger directors who have joined their ranks, such as Luc Moullet and Marin Karmitz, are little known in or outside of France except by *cinéastes.*

The spirit of revolt is not confined to avant-garde cinema, but it is more subdued in the present than the previous generation of French filmmakers.

Young directors who did not turn to situation comedies have made compromises, as has happened in so many of the arts since the radicalism of the sixties. What has come to be labeled as the "second wave" or the "newest wave" is made up principally of new French directors who have incorporated into their styles many of the innovative techniques of their predecessors, yet have also made their motion pictures more accessible than the works of filmmakers who are defiantly avant-garde. Among those who have used this approach are Eduardo De Gregorio (*Serail,* 1977), Luc Bèraud (*Turtle on Its Back,* 1978), and Paul Vecchiali (*The Machine,* 1977, and others). This list is incomplete, however, for it is restricted to male directors.

No country has witnessed the rise to prominence of so many women directors as France during the seventies. To prove this assertion (as was done with contemporary American women directors), they are considered here as a separate category. There had been women directors since the earliest days of French cinema, but with a few exceptions, such as Alice Guy-Blaché and Germaine Dulac, they were not respected as the equals of their male colleagues until Agnes Varda began her career in the mid-fifties. In the late sixties and the seventies, however, women as a group became a discernible force in France's motion picture industry.

Aside from an emphasis on the sensibilities of females and, in some cases, feminist concerns, these women directors have been indistinguishable from male directors in their technical proficiency, imaginativeness, concern with contemporary problems, and range of styles. The leading woman avant-garde filmmaker has been Marguerite Duras (1914–). She was a highly regarded novelist associated with the *Nouveau Roman* of the fifties before turning to screenwriting (for example, she wrote the original screenplay for Resnais's *Hiroshima mon amour*). Duras made her debut as a solo director with *Destroy She Said* (1969). Among her other works are *Women of the Ganges* (1972), *Nathalie Granger* (1974), and *India Song* (1976). Her fragmented, oblique plots, filled with non sequitur scenes of seemingly banal action, have restricted her admirers to a chosen few.

Not many French women directors have followed the obscure trails blazed by Duras. Far more realistic has been the approach of the actress Jeanne Moreau in *Lumiére* (1976) and *The Adolescent* (1979). Also traditional in style but not necessarily subject matter is Diane Kurys's *Peppermint Soda* (1978), a charming story of a youngster growing up in Paris, and the films of Yannick Bellon, Michal Bat-Adam, and Nadine Trintignant.

More interesting from a stylistic point of view are the female members of the "second wave." Chief among them is a director considered by many critics as one of the most provocative working in France today. Chantal Akerman's greatest success of the half dozen feature films she has directed to date is *Jeanne Dielman* (1976), in which Delphine Seyrig gives a remarkable performance as a conventional housewife with the unconventional avocation of prostitution. Appropriate to the dual nature of the title character is a style that alternates between realism and surrealism. Another Akerman film that has caused controversy as well as aroused admiration is *The Meetings of Anna* (1978).

Coline Serreau made an impressive directorial debut with *Why Not!* (1977), the story of a felicitous *ménage à trois*. Nelly Kaplan's *Néa* (1976) also caused a sensation when it was released. The plot of the relationship between an adolescent who writes a popular pornographic novel and an older, promiscuous bookseller is beautifully photographed in a manner that adds allegorical overtones to the story. Other women directors have established reputations in other genres, such as comedy (for example, Nicole de Buron's *Go, Mama, Go,* 1979) and the documentary (for instance, Ariane Mnouchkine's captivating *Molière,* 1977).

### GREAT BRITAIN

British cinema in the seventies was not as innovative and striking as during the sixties, even though the majority of English directors of that period continued to be productive. Some of the most interesting dramas of the seventies released in the country were created by three Americans working in England—Joseph Losey, James Ivory, and Richard Lester. On the other hand, a few directors who began their careers in Great Britain, such as Karel Reisz and John Boorman, be-

came predominantly Hollywood filmmakers. Though the British film industry was not thriving, it was active, and fine new directors did appear.

Nicolas Roeg (1928–) was an eminent cinematographer in the sixties. In 1970 he codirected (with Donald Commell) *Performance,* starring Mick Jagger. His first solo effort, *Walkabout* (1971), on the relationship between an aborigine youngster and two white Australian children lost in the Outback, was quite different in theme and style. *Don't Look Now* (1973), a psychological thriller, is based on a Daphne du Maurier story. *The Man Who Fell to Earth* (1976) is science fiction with implied social and cultural criticisms of our time. A police investigation of an attempted suicide is the means in *Bad Timing* (1980) whereby the director explores a complicated affair between a middle-aged American psychologist residing in Vienna and a neurotic young woman with a rapacious sexual appetite.

As these brief plot summaries of Roeg's films indicate, he is a versatile director. He is particularly fascinated by the involuted psychological needs of characters, usually having a sexual foundation, that reflects the tensions and inadequacies of contemporary society. Roeg's works are always visually expressive and masterful, if sometimes confusing, in their manipulation of nonlinear plots, intermeshing symbols, and abrupt shifts in time and place settings. For many sophisticated moviegoers, he is the most distinctive of recent English directors.

Ken Loach does not have the international reputation of Roeg but is highly regarded in his homeland. He is considered one of the best directors of TV dramas (especially when Tony Garnett is his producer). His feature films include *Kes* (1970), *Family Life* (1971), and *Black Jack* (1979). Loach's approach is typically low-key, realistic, and concerned with social issues, and he reveals a special gift for working with children. Bill Douglas's eminence is based on three autobiographical dramas that trace the growth of Jamie, a Scottish youth brought up in a mining town and finally joining the RAF: *My Childhood* (1972), *My Ain Folk* (1973), and *My Way Home* (1978). Douglas is able to convey the loneliness and confusion of adolescence with an immediacy and poignancy reminiscent of Ermanno Olmi's *Il Posto.*

Other notable new English directors include Derek Jarmon (for example, *The Tempest,* 1979), Ridley Scott (*The Duelists,* 1977; *Alien,* 1979; and others), Franc Roddam (*Quadrophenia,* 1979), Phil Mulloy, Bill Forsyth, James B. Harris, and Karl Francis. A special category consists of actors who also direct, such as Richard Attenborough (from the musical *Oh, What a Lovely War,** 1969, to *Magic,* 1978, and *Gandhi,* 1982) and David Hemmings (*Just a Gigolo,* 1978)

### OTHER COUNTRIES

Spain has experienced the beginning of a resurgence of filmmaking since the passing in the mid-seventies of the Franco regime and its stringent censorship. Carlos Saura built on the reputation he gained during the sixties† with *Cria Cuervos* (1976)—a superb study of a woman (played by Geraldine Chaplin) in 1995 recalling her childhood in Madrid in 1975, *Elisa My Love* (1977), *Blindfolded Eyes* (1978), and others. Juan Antonio Bardem continued to direct films, but none attained the brilliance of *Death of a Cyclist.*

Of the younger filmmakers, two in particular made dramas that met with international acclaim. Victor Erice's *The Spirit of the Beehive* (1973), like Saura's *Cria Cuervos,* is a powerful exploration of childhood. José Luis Borau's *Poachers* (1975) is a trenchant psychological drama with political implications. Other notable Spanish directors of the seventies include Jaime Chavarri, Manual Gutierrez Aragon, and Jaime Camino.

Spanish-language dramas of a high caliber also emerged from Cuba (for example, the works of Humberto Solas and Tomas Gutierrez Alea), Mexico, and South American countries.

In Scandinavia, no one filled the vacuum left by Ingmar Bergman during his exile, self-imposed (1976–1980). Established filmmakers, such as Bo Widerberg in Sweden and Jörn Donner in Finland, continued to be active, and a new generation of relatively unknown Scandinavian directors set to work. A similar situation existed in the Low Countries. The Dutch director Fons

Rademakers received praise for *Max Havelaar* (1978, an adaptation of a nineteenth-century novel). The Belgian director André Delvaux was promoted by critics as an outstanding filmmaker. His dramas blend realism with a type of fantasy that is often surrealistic. Delvaux's first fiction film after having confined himself to documentaries was *The Man Who Had His Hair Cut Short* (1966). To date, he has directed only three other features: *Un Jour, un Train* (1969), *Rendez-vous à Bray* (1971), and *Belle* (1973).

One Greek motion picture of the seventies caused a stir when it was released in Europe. Its director, Theodor Angelopoulos, was proclaimed immediately as a rival to Michael Cocoyannis, Greece's leading filmmaker. *The Traveling Players* (1975) is a lengthy epic (almost 4 hours long) that uses the device of a provincial theater company acting in a pastoral play to present more than a decade (from 1939 to 1952) of Greek political history. The only other notable new Greek director is Nikos Panayotopoulos. His *Idlers of the Fertile Valley* (1978) is both a social criticism of the bourgeoisie and a Pinteresque study of the effects of an "earth mother" type of woman on a family of males. This film and *The Traveling Players* suggested that Greek filmmaking was on the verge of a renaissance.

Yugoslavian cinema was also experiencing its own new wave of filmmakers. Among the leading figures are Krsto Papic (for example, *A Village Production of Hamlet,* 1974), Aleksander Petrovic (director of among other films *The Master and Margarita,* 1972), Dejan Karaklajic (best known for *Beloved Love,* 1977), Goran Paskaljevic, Srdan Karanovic, and Lordan Zafranovic.

Russia's film industry was productive during the decade but was plagued by political censorship. Only a meager number of its motion pictures have been exported to the West, and festivals still provide the main opportunity to view the best of them. One Soviet director, Andrei Tarkovsky (1932–), has been lauded in Europe and the United States, though his works have had a limited circulation in his own country. His first feature film was *Ivan's Childhood* (1962); *Andrei Publex* (1966) was praised at the Cannes Film Festival of 1969. *Solaris* (1972), a science fiction feature con-

*p. 453
†p. 162

taining striking special effects, led to Tarkovsky's being considered by Western critics as the most exciting of contemporary Russian directors. *The Mirror* (1979) added to his reputation. His *The Stalker* (1980) was proclaimed by many who attended the Cannes Film Festival of 1980 as the most significant film screened at that event. *Nostalghia* (1982, made in Italy) has had a less enthusiastic reception.

Andrei Mikhalkov-Konchalovsky is more conventional in style and subject matter than Tarkovsky. After directing his initial feature *(The First Teacher)* in 1965, he made a couple of films that did not meet with the approval of the Russian authorities. He turned then to adaptations of literary works by Turgenev and Chekhov and to epics that underscore his vigorous, poetic style (such as *Siberiade,* 1979). Younger Soviet directors include Nikolai Gubenko (who made *The Orphans,* 1978), Georgi Dameliya (creator of *Autumn Marathon,* 1979), and Nikita Mikhalkov, younger brother of Mikhalkov-Konchalovsky, whose *Slave of Love* (1978) was received with critical enthusiasm when released in the United States.

Most Eastern European film industries recovered slowly from the governmental repression that was instituted after the upheavals at the end of the sixties; in most cases, challenging new directors did not emerge until at least the middle of the seventies. In Poland, one exception was Krzystof Zanussi (1939–), who is viewed in his own country as sharing with Andrzej Wajda the distinction of being the nation's most respected contemporary filmmaker. His second feature, *Family Life* (1971)—the first was *The Structure of Crystals* (1969)—demonstrated conclusively that his interest in metaphysical ideas and moral ambiguity, combined with a gift for bold visual images suggesting symbolic implications, make him an outstanding director. Among his other major works are *Illumination* (1973), *A Woman's Decision* (1975), *Camouflage* (1977), *The Spiral* (1978), and *Constant* (1979). Other prominent young Polish directors (most of them in their thirties) include Feliks Falk (for example, *Chance,* 1979), Wojciech Has (best known for *The Hourglass,* 1974), Grzegorz Krolikiewicz, Krzystof Kieslowski, and Edward Zybroweski.

Hungary's film dramas continued to be dominated in the seventies by Jancsó and Szabo. A few new directors, however, released noteworthy films. Marta Meszaros is one of the few women directors in Eastern Europe to have focused her attention primarily on the female sensibility, as in *Nine Months* (1976), *Two Women* (1978), and *Just Like at Home* (1979). Among other active young filmmakers are Imre Gyongyossy (for example, *A Quite Ordinary Life,* 1977), Pal Gabor (for instance, *Angi Vera,* 1979), Pal Sandor, Istvan Darday, James Rozsa, Karoly Makk, and Ferenc Kosa.

The third major film industry of Eastern Europe, that of Czechoslovakia, has been the slowest to encourage new talent. Aside from Jirí Menzel, few directors have established reputations outside their nation. The situation in Rumania and Bulgaria has been even less promising.

Although few countries in the Western world do not have some heritage of filmmaking, there is, as this survey has demonstrated, an ebb and flow in cinematic creativity. On occasion, for no apparent reason (research usually reveals less obvious causes rooted in special cultural, economic, and political conditions), a country's cinema will suddenly demand international recognition. In the seventies, this is what happened in Switzerland and Australia.

Before World War II, Switzerland's film industry was very modest, and it was almost entirely confined to the German-speaking section of the nation. After the war, such directors as Kurt Früh and Franz Schnyder made a few worthwhile German-language dramas. It was in the sixties that the French-speaking Swiss began producing notable directors, such as Henry Brandt. The present fame of Switzerland's cinema, rests, however, primarily on the works of Alain Tanner (1929–) and Claude Goretta (1929–). While both directors are French in style, the settings and attitudes of their dramas are distinctly Swiss.

Alain Tanner's first important success was *La Salamandre* (1971). *Return From Africa* (1972) and *The Middle of the World* (1974) were followed by the highly acclaimed *Jonah Who Will Be 25 in the Year 2000* (1976), which deals with a group of individualistic couples who interact and spend most of their time talking about politics and eating. After confining himself for a few years to nonfiction works in Super-8 and on videotape, Tanner returned to commercial filmmaking with *Messidor* (1979), a story of two young female hitchhikers who become involved in violence and murder.

It would be simplistic to label Tanner a maker of political dramas, but all his works are concerned with aspects of political and social problems. As with many contemporary filmmakers, he is preoccupied with the question of what happened in the quiescent seventies to young people who were committed to the idealism of the rebellious sixties. However, Tanner shares more the perspective of Resnais than Costa-Gavras in that he is fascinated by the subjectivity of an individual's ideas as well as emotions and by how circumstances and relationships influence what a person believes and how that person acts. The director also, like Godard, explores the interchange between the medium of film and its audiences and experiments with cinematic techniques (for example, the use of an off-screen commentary).

Claude Goretta derives his strengths as a director from a different tradition than his countryman. The chief influence on his work has been Jean Renoir, and his style, more conventional than Tanner's, could be described as an updated poetic realism. His characters usually find themselves confronted with moral dilemmas rather than political ones, and they tend to be more typical than the nonconformists to be found in Tanner's dramas.

*The Lacemaker* (1977) is Goretta's most moving film. It tells poignantly of a young woman whose fragile ego collapses after an unhappy love affair, and she ends up institutionalized. Among his other works are *The Invitation* (1973), *The Wonderful Crook* (1975), *La Dentellière* (1977), and a four-part television series on the life of Jean-Jacques Rousseau, a "docudrama."

If Tanner and Goretta are to be considered harbingers of a new creative stage in Swiss filmmaking, other distinguished directors of the country will have to join them. This has not yet happened.

There is no doubt, however, that Australia, within a single decade, moved to the forefront of countries releasing important films; in fact, in the seventies, this nation challenged if not surpassed the United States and Great Britain in the production of unpretentious, relatively inexpensive, sensitive, and memorable English-language dramas. It is not possible to describe this as a resurgence of cinematic activity because earlier there was practically no national filmmaking of any significance in Australia. The works of Raymond Longford, Charles Chauvel, and Ken G. Hall hardly qualify as significant. The majority of prominent motion pictures made in the country after World War II were financed and directed by foreigners.

What vitalized the Australian film industry, as happened in West Germany, was government support of native filmmakers. In 1970 the Liberal party in power established a film and television school and a corporation that provided a portion of the funds for productions. The terms were not munificent; they confined filmmakers to limited shooting schedules and budgets that rarely surpassed $1.5 million dollars per motion picture, but that was sufficient to inspire the industry. Since 1975, Australian films have won prizes at festivals and have been distributed in most of the major cities of the world.

Of the new directors, the most exciting has been Peter Weir. After *The Cars That Ate Paris* (1974), he released *Picnic at Hanging Rock* (1975), an unforgettable story of an encounter at the turn of the century between young ladies from a finishing school and preternatural forces of nature. *The Last Wave* (1977) continued the director's fascination with myth. *The Plumber* (1978), his last work of the seventies, represented a change of pace. It is a more intimate drama, Pinteresque in structure and dialogue, containing, like his other works, elements of surrealism.

Bruce Beresford's first outstanding film was *The Getting of Wisdom* (1978), a delicate, lovely adaptation of a Henry Handel Richardson novel. *Breaker Morant* (1980), about the trial of three Australian soldiers during the Boer War, was a critical and box office success in the United States and Europe. Fred Schelisi's first feature, *The Devil's Playground* (1976), on students in a Catholic seminary, is a low-key, effective drama. His next work, *The Chant of Jimmie Blacksmith* (1978), caused considerable debate in his homeland. It deals with violence perpetrated by a young aborigine, a sort of Australian Nat Turner. Phillip Noyce's highly praised *Newsfront* (1978) combines actual newsreel footage with a fictional narrative to tell the story of Australian newsreel companies before television.

Other notable Australian directors are Ken Hannam (who made *Sunday Too Far Away,* 1975), Donald Crombie (best known for *Caddie,* 1975), Phillippe Mora (for instance, *Mad Dog Morgan*, 1976), John Duigan (including *The Trespassers*, 1976, and *Mouth to Mouth,* 1978), Tom Jeffrey, Tim Burstall, Gill Armstrong, Michael Thornhill, and Jim Sharman.

This survey of film drama began in 1903 and ends in 1980. The richness of those eight decades could only be suggested within the space available, and the contributions of many countries outside of Europe and the United States have not been covered. Even within these pages, however, the remarkable achievements of this relatively young art and form of entertainment are evident. Cinema has been a major influence on the culture of the twentieth century, and whatever metamorphoses it undergoes, it is likely to remain so in the future. In the "Afterword" of this book, some present-day influences on future developments in the medum are outlined.

# Individual films and movements

# 5

D. W. Griffith's *Broken Blossoms* serves as an example of Realism in the silent era. This film illustrates, with the exception of battle scenes, all the characteristics of the director's themes and techniques, and it is the most tightly structured of Griffith's major works. Film Expressionism reached its epitome early in *The Cabinet of Dr. Caligari.* This film's uncompromising application of Expressionistic camera-editing dynamics and elements of presentation, however, was more admired than imitated by contemporary filmmakers. For all its flaws, *Variety* is an interesting film, and its integrated combination of Expressionistic devices and realistic elements was the approach favored by most of the outstanding German directors of the twenties.

The principles of Dynamic Montage are demonstrated in the analysis of Sergei Eisenstein's *October,* a masterpiece that has not received the attention it deserves. *The Bicycle Thief* is examined as an example of Italian Neorealism, and *The 400 Blows* as typical of the French New Wave.

Each section of this chapter (and those in Part Three) devoted to a specific film is made up of three parts. In the first of these, the background of the principal individuals involved in the creating of a film and of the film itself are considered. Chief attention is usually, though not invariably, centered on the director, including biography, major works, and main themes and techniques. Relevant information on a motion picture—such as critical reception, distribution problems, and variations in rentable prints—conclude this part.

The plot summary for each film is lengthy. I assume that other people share my frustration with a one-paragraph description of the plot of a motion picture that is then analyzed extensively. My summaries do not serve, naturally, as replacements for printed screenplays, but they are the best substitutes possible when screenplays are unavailable to a reader.

A comprehensive analysis of any worthwhile motion picture can be extended without padding for literally dozens of pages. My objective, even in the lengthiest commentaries, is not to exhaust potential discussion of a film. I trust that a reader who has seen or will see a motion picture that I explore can uncover intriguing aspects that I have unintentionally or purposely ignored. My goal in each case is to highlight significant features of a film's narrative dimension, camera-editing dynamics, and elements of presentation. Within this framework there are two emphases. First, I have made every effort to justify generalizations by specific references to a film. Second, form is usually of primary concern, so that the camera-editing dynamics of at least one scene (and typically more) are scrutinized in detail.

One critical apparatus also requires an explanation. Titles of foreign films are in English (unless one is usually designated by its foreign title); however, the first time a title appears, its original form is given in parentheses. This is necessary because the majority of reference books and indexes list films by original titles. To maintain consistency in capitalizing and accenting, the practices of one volume have been followed: Georges Sadoul's *Dictionary of Film Makers.* [1] The date refers to the premieres in the country of origin. Although in some cases filmographies in other sources appeared more accurate and were used, the Sadoul volume again has been the main authority consulted in this respect.

━━━━━━━━
### REALISM

#### *Broken Blossoms*

*That the cinema could be incomparably greater, and that this was to be the basic task of the budding Soviet cinema—these were sketched for us in Griffith's creative work, and found ever new confirmation in his films. Our heightened curiosity of those years in* construction and method *swiftly discerned wherein lay the most powerful affective factors in this great American's films.*

Sergei Eisenstein, 1944[2]

**CAST**

*Lillian Gish (Lucy), Richard Barthelmess (The Chinaman [The Yellow Man]), Donald Crisp (Battling Burrows), Arthur Howard (The Manager), Edward Peil (Evil Eye), George Beranger (The Spying One), and others.*

**CREDITS**

*Director—D. W. Griffith, Screenwriter—D. W. Griffith (based on the short story "The Chink and the Child" by Thomas Burke), Director of Photography—G. W. Bitzer, Special Effects— Henrick Sartov, Technical Adviser—Moon Kwan, Musical Accompaniment—Louis F. Gottschalk and D. W. Griffith.*

1919/United Artists
Black & White/102 minutes (silent, 18 fps)

━━━━━━━━
BACKGROUND

D. W. Griffith (1875–1948) was an experienced film director when he created *Broken Blossoms.* In a few years, producers were to lose confidence in his ability to deliver financially profitable films. In 1919, however, the tall, 44-year-old Southerner with a jutting nose and piercing eyes could look back on a career that though marred by controversy and misunderstanding also included a renown that reached as far as Moscow.

That career began when David Wark Griffith, only son of an old but impoverished Kentucky family, became stage-struck and determined to be an actor and playwright. His success in both professions was minimal. It was in 1907 in New York that Griffith, leading an impecunious existence with his wife, Linda Arvidson, learned that he could earn money as a film actor and a creator of story ideas for the Biograph Company. The following year he accepted an assign-

ment as a director. The first film Griffith directed, *The Adventures of Dollie,* was released on July 14, 1908.

Between 1908 and 1914, he created nearly 500 one- and two-reel films for Biograph, an average of one a week. During this period he not only became a director of the first rank but also revealed a genius for developing cinematic techniques that transformed film from an unsophisticated entertainment to an art form. Although he had predecessors, such as Méliès and Porter, Griffith more than any other director of the pre–World War I period demonstrated that narrative motion pictures did not have to be essentially photographed stage plays. In addition, Griffith attained a unique versatility and adaptability by essaying in these short films every type of narrative from tragedy to farce, from historical spectacles to intimate love stories, in urban and rural settings.

In 1912 Griffith had become increasingly restive under the restrictions imposed by one or two reels (one reel was screened in 12 to 15 minutes at 18 fps). Encouraged by longer films being made in Europe, he completed *Judith of Bethulia* (four reels) in 1913. The board of directors of Biograph, however, convinced that an audience would not sit through more than 30 minutes of film, relieved Griffith of his directing assignments and made him a supervisor of production. "DWG" promptly left Biograph and joined Mutual Film Corp. He took with him his invaluable cameraman, G. W. ("Billy") Bitzer, and most of his finest actors and actresses, including the Gish sisters, Blanche Sweet, Mae Marsh, H. B. Walthall, and Robert Harron.

After experimenting with four features of from five to seven reels, he was ready to create his first indisputable masterpiece. *The Birth of a Nation* (12 reels) had its New York City premiere on March 3, 1915. While gratified by the box office success of the film and the lavish critical praise of its cinematic techniques, spectacular battle scenes, and characterizations, Griffith was shocked by the controversy aroused by his portrayal of Reconstruction blacks and the Ku Klux Klan. He defended himself in a pamphlet titled "The Rise and Fall of Free Speech in America" (1916).

The accusation that he was a bigot influenced

Griffith's choice of subject matter for his next film, *Intolerance* (1916). This colossal, 14-reel film (the longest in the director's oeuvre), with its quartet of stories (modern, Judean, medieval, and Babylonian) and almost $2 million cost, was a financial failure. On the other hand, *Intolerance* profoundly influenced foreign filmmakers, and it is now recognized as a flawed but significant work.

The United States had entered World War I when Griffith, working for Artcraft Pictures, traveled to Great Britain to make a propaganda war film, *Hearts of the World* (1918). Five other features followed, none very impressive.

In 1919, Griffith, Charles Chaplin, Mary Pickford, and Douglas Fairbanks formed United Artists Corp. That same year he began shooting *Broken Blossoms,* and it became his first work under the aegis of United Artists. After two potboilers, the director revealed again his unique abilities in *Way Down East* (1920, United Artists). Although often sentimental and dated even for its day in dealing with prejudice against an illegitimate pregnancy, the film was worthy of "the Master," the appellation applied to Griffith by his admiring staff. The sequence of Lillian Gish's rescue from ice floes can still thrill a modern audience.

Griffith's next important film was *Orphans of the Storm* (1921), a historical spectacle with a French Revolution setting. Like *Way Down East,* the film was a critical and financial success.

Between 1922 and 1931 Griffith directed 12 more features, but he could not again create a film that compared with the best released in the previous decade. The usual reasons given for his decline are that he could not keep up with the times, lost touch with the changing tastes of American motion picture audiences, and ignored advances in cinematic techniques. Whatever the explanation, Griffith's creative energies obviously flagged. There were still brilliant scenes in such films as *America* (1924) and *Abraham Lincoln* (1930), but the verve, visual imagination, and structural control that had characterized his pre-1922 works were missing.

D. W. Griffith's last years were sad ones. Being almost completely ignored by an ungrateful motion picture industry transformed the proud, sensitive man of inviolate integrity into a bitter, quarrelsome person

who drank heavily and isolated himself in a hotel room. After Griffith's death in 1948, a series of retrospectives of his films, primarily in the sixties, and the publication of many critical studies have led to his acceptance as one of the greatest directors in the history of American cinema.

Griffith's most lasting contribution to filmmaking was the techniques he developed in shooting and editing his dramas. These techniques can be described most effectively by referring to examples in a specific film, so this area of Griffith's achievements will be examined in the analysis of *Broken Blossoms.* The remainder of this background section will be devoted to a survey of the narrative dimension of his films.

The plots of Griffith's films and the themes they contain were influenced by the director's background and the types of stories considered appropriate for motion pictures at the time he was creating his shorts and features. He had little formal education, and his cultural tastes were formed in the popular American theater. In the pre–World War I period, stage plays were predominantly sustained by mawkishness and melodrama, featuring elaborate staging but "lacking largeness of spirit," as John Gassner notes.[3] Film plots were even less impressive because they were intended for a relatively unsophisticated audience that demanded spectacle, sentimentality, and stereotypes. Griffith went beyond his contemporaries in the motion picture industry of the teens by dealing with genuine human emotions and existing social problems while refining his narratives, tightening structure, and adding subtleties of motivation. By the twenties, though, his approach seemed decidedly old-fashioned to audiences who were being exposed to the more frank and complex films of Stroheim and Sternberg, the American films of Lubitsch, Sjöström, and Murnau, and foreign works.

It is possible to subsume most of the themes that appear in Griffith's features under the heading of the conflict between idealism and moral corruption. This multifaceted theme emerges from a prototypal plot in the director's longer works: Innocence and goodness, personified by a young woman and her beloved, are threatened by evil forces. These forces may consist of manifestations of lust, violence, hypocrisy, intolerance, or other variations of the cardinal sins. One of the fascinations of Griffith's narratives is observing how in each case he develops the characters involved in this conflict and deals with its implications and resolution.

The young women in the feature films seem cast from one mold and were played principally by three actresses—Lillian Gish, Dorothy Gish, and Mae Marsh. They are physically fragile creatures, sweet, innocent, highly moral, religious, sensitive, sentimental, optimistic, and usually quiet and reserved. They generally have the asexual quality of a pubescent adolescent. Underneath their gentle mien, however, are veins of stamina and determination.

Their beloved are faithful, dogged, upright, chivalrous young men who, for all their heroic deeds, are usually subservient to their women. Like the heroines, these young men appear to have minimal sexual drives, or at least they commit themselves to pure, undemanding love that has marriage as its goal.

The most overt threat to Griffith's damsels is the lust of a villian. Sensuality in general is reprehensible in the director's world unless it is banked, channeled, and sanctified by marriage. Lust is also represented as a manifestation of the more general evil of antagonism between classes and races. For example, in *The Birth of a Nation,* Elsie is desired by Silas Lynch, a mulatto, and Flora by Gus, a black; in *Way Down East,* the country girl Anna is seduced by a wealthy dandy from the city; and Henriette, ostensibly from the lower class, in *Orphans of the Storm* almost falls into the clutches of the Chevalier de Vaudry, an aristocrat.

Violence that results from war, revolution, and their aftermaths also may oppress heroines. Griffith condemns the horror and cruelty of war. The carnage of the American Civil War, the fall of Babylon and the St. Bartholomew's Day Massacre in *Intolerance,* World War I, and the excesses of the Directory during the French Revolution are presented in vivid details. On the other hand, he felt that war might in certain cases be necessary to defend honor and national institutions. He justified World War I in *Hearts of the World* by portraying the Germans as brutes. The American Civil War may have been inevitable, but not the cruelty of Reconstruction, so the Ku Klux Klan, in his view, was correct to rebel against carpetbaggers and "upstart" blacks.

Religious faith is a support to heroine and hero, but organized religion when solidified into prejudice can be a danger. This is evident in "The Judean Story" (the crucifixion of Christ) and "The Medieval Story" in *Intolerance.*

Although Griffith at times may have rationalized the necessity for war and been ambiguous toward institutionalized religion, he was unqualified in his condemnation of rigid social conventions that become self-righteous prejudices and the way poverty not only devitalizes human beings but also leaves them defenseless against sanctimonious do-gooders. His heroines must often contend with one or both negative forces, as in "The Modern Story" in *Intolerance,* when a group of "Uplifters" take away the child of the Dear One because she is poor and her husband is in jail, and as in *Way Down East,* when a New England family casts out Anna, a faithful servant, after discovering that she once had an illegitimate child.

It is ironic that at the same time Griffith so fervently attacked intolerance in many of his films, he was not entirely free of the disease himself, especially in his attitudes toward race. Whatever historical justification the director may have felt he had, his portrayal of blacks in *The Birth of a Nation* is derogatory and offensive. In *Broken Blossoms,* he makes a Chinaman the hero and underscores the absurdity of the Caucasian brute, Battling Burrows, railing against "that Chink." Yet two years later Griffith directed *Dream Street,* a "yellow peril" film in which a Chinaman desires a white woman but is told when he is rejected, "After this, you let white girls alone." Defenders of Griffith point out, however, that racial prejudices were common in the United States during his active years.

Almost as inconsistent as Griffith's attitude toward racial minorities in his films is his treatment of the questions of how virtue can defend itself against evil. He never completely resolved this problem for himself, oscillating throughout his career between two possibilities. On the one hand, he seemed to suggest that a heroine and hero can finally triumph over adversity by remaining faithful to their ideals of goodness and love. The happy endings of "The Modern Story" in *Intolerance, Way Down East,* and *Orphans of the Storm* were achieved by this type of passive resistance. On the other hand, a Griffith hero might resort to violence to defend himself and his beloved. It is on this basis that the director justified the Ku Klux Klan in *The Birth of a Nation.* In *Intolerance* only Jesus accepts his fate without a struggle; the Babylonians and Protestants meet sword with sword, and even the Boy in "The Modern Story" uses his fists against his enemy. In a war film such as *Hearts of the World,* killing the enemy is never questioned as an appropriate response to evil.

It is evident, then, that Griffith felt there were times when goodness must meet violence with violence if it is to survive. The director was never completely comfortable, however, with this type of situation ethics. The ambiguity of his feelings manifests itself most directly in *Broken Blossoms.*

Some critics charge that Griffith's main characters learn little from their harrowing experiences and are essentially the same at the conclusion as at the beginning of the film. To a degree this is true. The director's happy endings foreshadow nothing but continual bliss in the future. To survive, however, these heroines and heroes must overcome their bewilderment and disappointment and recognize that they live in an imperfect world. Although they do not lose their intrinsic virtues, and Griffith is not always explicit about any changes in their views of life, we believe too much in their intelligence, unsophisticated though it may be, not to be assured that from their experiences they have emerged less complacent and are wiser about the ways of the world.

This theme of ideals challenged and tempered, yet essentially preserved is a particularly American one. In this, Griffith, more than any other director of his time, embodied in his work the strengths and weaknesses of this country before the disillusionment of the thirties.

Production of *Broken Blossoms* began in November, 1918, while Griffith was editing *The Girl Who Stayed at Home* (1919) and creating *True Heart Susie* (1919). He completed the latter but suspended shooting on *Broken Blossoms* because he was having difficulties obtaining the cinematic effects he wanted. This careful preparation is not the only evidence that from the beginning Griffith was aware that he was embarking on a major film. He also withdrew the film

from his original schedule as one of his potboilers for Artcraft Films at a high financial cost and chose it as the first he would do for United Artists.

Griffith did the adaptation from Thomas Burke's short story himself. As usual, he worked closely with his director of photography, Billy Bitzer, but also employed experts for special effects and technical assistance. He drew upon his recollections of London and the inspiration of a set of watercolors by the English artist George Baker to evoke the atmosphere of Limehouse, a slum district of London located on the Thames, which is the setting of the film.

Lillian Gish was the director's immediate choice for the role of Lucy. Nor was there any problem in casting Battling Burrows, for Donald Crisp had worked before with Griffith as an actor and assistant director. It was in choosing the actor to play the Chinaman that he hesitated. After rehearsals had begun, Griffith discovered Richard Barthelmess, a college graduate who was only 24 at the time. The director worked closely with his young protégé, even accompanying him on trips to Chinatown in Los Angeles to study Chinese mannerisms. Griffith's concern with the acting in this intimate drama extended to rehearsals. He allotted 6 weeks to preproduction activities, an unusually lengthy period in those days.

The expenditure of time, energy, and money proved worthwhile. *Broken Blossoms* was a fabulous success in every respect. Critics almost unanimously proclaimed it a masterpiece; Griffith received the best reviews of his career. Audiences flocked to the George M. Cohen Theatre in New York, and the film's popularity continued for years.

---

PLOT SUMMARY

The Chinaman (Barthelmess; called "The Yellow Man" in the titles) departs for England to propagate the "message of peace to the barbarous Anglo-Saxons."

Years have passed, and the disillusioned Chinaman now lives in Limehouse, a slum area in London, where he owns a shop. Leaning against a building, he muses on a recent visit to a "scarlet house of sin." Nearby, Battling Burrows (Crisp) recalls with his manager (Howard) his last fight in the ring. Burrows's daughter Lucy (Gish), on the street outside their two rooms, remembers being cautioned by a friend against marriage and by "ladies of the street" against their profession. She joins Burrows and is bullied by him as she serves lunch.

The Chinaman speaks to two ministers. Crosscutting between Lucy and her father follows. After fondling her sole treasures, inherited from her mother, Lucy goes shopping; Burrows enters a pub. Lucy has completed her purchases when she is accosted by Evil Eye (Peil) but is protected by the Chinaman, who has admired her from afar. Meanwhile, the fighter is reprimanded by his manager and leaves the pub in a rage. The Chinaman follows Lucy to her door. When the girl accidentally spills some hot food on her father's hand, he beats her into unconsciousness, then leaves for his training quarters to prepare for a fight. Lucy awakens and, in shock, staggers outside and wanders the streets. Finally, she stumbles against the door of the Chinaman's shop and collapses inside.

The Chinaman discovers her and carries her to his upstairs room. He gives Lucy a robe to wear and hands her ribbons and flowers. Ecstatically, he watches over her as she sleeps.

A friend of Burrows, The Spying One (Beranger), has business in the Chinaman's shop and learns that Lucy is upstairs. He immediately informs her father; Burrows vows revenge. There follows crosscutting between Burrows in the ring and the Chinaman with Lucy, first giving her a doll and then overcoming the temptation to seduce her.

While the Chinaman is out buying flowers for Lucy, Burrows enters the shop, smashes the furniture in the upstairs room, and drags his daughter away. Evil Eye observes what has happened and "gladly bears the news" to the Chinaman, who rushes home. He is in anguish when he finds his beloved gone. He takes a gun out of a chest and runs into the street.

In their apartment, Burrows threatens Lucy with a whip. She escapes into a closet and locks it, but her father smashes in the door with an ax, pulls her out, and beats her on the head with the whip handle. He leaves her on the bed and goes into the next room. While the Chinaman hesitates in the street outside, Lucy forces her mouth into a feeble smile and dies. The Chinaman enters through a window and bends over her. Burrows hears something and comes into the room. The fighter attacks the Chinaman with the ax, but the Chinaman shoots him dead. The Chinaman then picks up Lucy and carries her away.

While the Manager and the Spying One discover the body of the fighter and inform the police of the murder, the Chinaman, in his room, puts Lucy on his bed and covers her with the robe. He then commits suicide with a dagger, smiling and looking toward Lucy during his last moments.

---

ANALYSIS

*The narrative dimension*
Griffith based his screenplay for *Broken Blossoms* on a short story by Thomas Burke, "The Chink and the Child," included in the volume *Limehouse Nights* (1916). Burke wrote melodramatic, sentimental stories that were carefully structured and contained a patina of realism. Our concern here, however, is the changes Griffith made in the original story.

Lucy is 12 in the tale; Griffith advanced her age to 15. Burke relates no incidents in Lucy's past beyond her being left with her father as a child. Griffith adds depth to his film characterization by including two flashbacks in which she is warned against marriage and prostitution. We are thereby made aware of how limited are her options in the future. The loneliness of the youngster is suggested by the scene in which, before shopping, she takes out her secret hoard, consisting of tinfoil and the pathetically small inheritance from her mother. Furthermore, the treasured piece of silk and the ribbon symbolically associate the mother with the Chinaman, for among the gifts he gives Lucy are a silk robe and ribbons for her hair.

She appears to have no friends. Her feelings toward her father are dominated by fear, submissiveness, and physical dependency on the scraps of food and the bed that he supplies. Her relationship with the Chinaman is, as we shall see, more complex, although even with him she is fundamentally passive. Her only drive seems to be to survive. In short, both Burke and Griffith present Lucy as a simple, one-dimensional character. Battling Burrows, on the other hand, is more caricature than character. In both story and film, he is consistently brutal, selfish, and vengeful.

The most developed character in the film is

unquestionably the Chinaman. We are told something of his past and his motivations and, most important, we are able to perceive his inner conflicts. He is, in fact, the only person in the film who struggles with forces within himself. In this respect, Griffith in his scenario has significantly improved on the portrayal in the short story. Burke simply describes a wandering Chinese sailor named Cheng Huan who has the soul of a poet and stays in London because he is too lazy to find a boat to take him back to Shanghai.

Griffith obviously saw an opportunity to bring into the film his favorite theme: the conflict between idealism and moral corruption. He devotes the first sequence of *Broken Blossoms* to presenting the Chinaman as an idealist determined to convert the Western world to the teachings of gentle Buddha. Even his unsuccessful efforts to act as peacemaker between two fighting sailors, a portent of the future, do not slacken his zeal. An unspecified period of time passes between his leaving China at the end of the first sequence and the next time we see him. We learn that "The Yellow Man's youthful dreams came to wreck against the sordid realities of life." In a flashback he appears in "a scarlet house of sin" smoking opium and gambling. He has not completely lost his ideals, however, for he does intervene between the arguing gamblers, an echo in a sordid setting of his encounter with the sailors.

There is an additional reference to the Chinaman's inability to fulfill his dream of being a missionary of peace. A minister introduces the Chinaman to a colleague who will be departing for China "to convert the heathens." The Chinaman's small, pained smile as he wishes the young man well reveals that he appreciates the irony of the situation and still suffers from an awareness of his failure. Christianity is mildly satirized when the older minister hands to the Chinaman a pamphlet; a close-up reveals its title—"Hell." A contrast is forced upon us, a little heavy-handedly, between the message of love advocated by the Chinaman, a Buddist, and the emphasis in Christian doctrine on fear and retribution.

The depth of the Chinaman's commitment to love and nonviolence is tested by his experiences with Lucy and Burrows. We could view Griffith's presentation of the young man's relationship with the girl as simply a romance grounded in the unrealistic conventions of sentimental stage dramas and films popular in the United States during the first two decades of the century. This approach, however, would be unfair to the depth of the characterization of the Chinaman, though not necessarily of Lucy. And here lies a major problem in the plot of the film. The Chinaman's reactions to the girl depend to a large extent on her character, and that character is so limited, even so unbelievable, as to restrict the feelings she arouses in us. This becomes clear if we examine her responses to the man who loves her.

When she collapses on the floor of the Chinaman's shop and he revives her, Lucy is still in shock. She only stares at him when he moves his face toward hers as if to kiss her. A title tells us she feels gratitude for "the first gentleness she has ever known." Upstairs in his room she is showered with gifts, to which she responds with childlike pleasure, especially when given a doll. Only once does the Chinaman make an overt advance after he brings her upstairs. He leans his face to within a few inches of Lucy's. In a reaction shot, a close-up, we see the girl's eyes widen, a perplexed, disturbed look on her face, and she draws back. Turning away, the Chinaman slowly lifts the robe and kisses it instead. There is some indication, then, that Lucy at least senses the feelings of the man whose bed she occupies. Moreover, when accused by her father, she repeatedly cries, " 'Tain't nothin' wrong!" as if knowing what he takes for granted.

It is possible to consider Lucy a calculating, manipulating creature taking advantage of her admirer's love, but there is little evidence to support such an interpretation. We can only conclude that the girl is simpleminded, naive even for a 15-year-old, and that she intuitively but only dimly senses the passion that eddies around her. Lucy is too passive, too limited in feeling to be more than an object of love, a catalyst for the emotions of others—and, given her nature, she is destined to be a victim.

In this relationship, therefore, our attention, beyond sympathy for a passive victim, centers almost entirely on the Chinaman. In both story and film he observes the girl from a distance and discerns, as no one else does, her goodness and beauty. Beyond this starting point, the two versions diverge drastically.

Burke explains Cheng's special perceptiveness only by stating that he was a poet without realizing it and felt things more passionately than other sailors. Griffith, by presenting a lonely, sensitive, gentle man, makes plausible his appreciation of Lucy and, more significant to the plot, his rejection of his sexual desires. There is also the scene in which the girl is threatened by Evil Eye. In protecting her, the Chinaman assumes a role that is in conflict with the impulses he shares with Evil Eye, who can be seen as a projection of the alter ego or dark shadow within the Chinaman's psyche.

Griffith reinforces the image of the Chinaman as protector and savior of a suffering creature by differing from the story in the way in which the two come together. Cheng finds Lucy in the *bagnio* he frequents; she is brought there by an older girl who saw in the child "a possible source of revenue." In *Broken Blossoms,* the beaten Lucy collapses on the floor of the Chinaman's shop. In addition, Cheng's treatment of Lucy in his room is far more physical than that of his counterpart in the film. He kisses "her cheek and lip and little bosom"; "she returned his kisses impetuously, gladly." That, according to the author, was "all their demonstration" during the two days he held her: ". . . his love was a pure and holy thing. Of that we may be sure, for his worst enemies have said it. . . ."[4] As with a number of lines in the book, this quotation is paraphrased on a title card in the film: "His love remains a pure and holy thing—even his worst foe says this."

The Chinaman's hatred of Burrows for what the man has done to his daughter is natural and straightforward. Yet Griffith has made ambiguous the way in which the young lover finally deals with the brute. After the Chinaman returns home and despairs over the loss of Lucy, he decides to follow her. Before he leaves, he slips a gun into his jacket. There is no indication in the acting or title cards as to whether he intends to use the gun for defense or to murder Burrows. In the short story, however, Burke is explicit. Cheng goes to the fighter's home to destroy him. When he finds the beaten body of Lucy, he commits suicide. Burrows arrives home drunk, does not light a candle, and falls asleep. Cheng, however, has left a snake in the bed that kills the fighter.

Griffith presents a confrontation between the man who loves Lucy and her father. The Chinaman does not immediately shoot Burrows; he stands near Lucy's body with a grim smile on his face. This might suggest that he will not kill Lucy's murderer unless he has to. When the fighter lifts an ax to strike the Chinaman, the latter pulls out the gun and fires. Legally, the Chinaman kills in self-defense.

Are we intended to conclude that a disillusioned pacifist has learned that Buddhist forbearance cannot survive in a world in which men like Burrows exist? Or is the Chinaman trying to live up to his ideals until actually attacked and commits suicide not only in sorrow from the death of his beloved but also out of remorse and shame for what he was forced to do? The film provides no clear-cut answer. This is surprising, because Griffith himself brought in the theme of pacificism versus violence. However, ambivalence toward the use of violence when innocence is challenged by evil, as noted in the background section, often appears in Griffith's films. For many viewers, the final sequence of *Broken Blossoms* is dramatically effective but intellectually and morally unsatisfying.

In evaluating the narrative dimension of the film, we can list as one of its prime virtues the tightly structured plot. Few scenes could have been eliminated without vitiating its progressive emotional intensity. This sense of a lean, controlled structure is helped by a unity of action (two characters brought in conflict with a third through a single incident), of time (less than 24 hours), and of place (three main settings: the Burrowses' home, the Chinaman's shop, and the fight ring). Only in one incident, when Lucy falls into the shop, is verisimilitude strained, although we might justify the "accident" by referring to an unconscious need driving the girl to the one person who has ever protected her. Also praiseworthy is the subtlety and sympathy with which the Chinaman is presented.

On the other hand, the caricatured portrayal of Battling Burrows, Lucy's shallow nature, and the sentimentality with which she is presented are weaknesses in the film. Another flaw—one that is characteristic of Griffith's work—is the titles, written by the director. Those that convey dialogue or name a setting are effective enough, but today we cannot help but cringe when such phrasing as the following appears: "In the scarlet house of sin, does he ever hear the temple bells?''; ''The child with tear-aged face . . .''; ''The Spirit of Beauty breaks her blossoms all about his chamber''; ''There he brings rays stolen from the lyric moon . . .''; ''As he smiles goodby to White Blossom, all the tears of the ages rush over his heart.'' Even a contemporary critic who praised *Broken Blossoms* lavishly felt obliged to add: ''. . . the descriptive phrases lean lamely upon crutches of sentimentality.''[5]

The narrative dimension of *Broken Blossoms* has enough vitality to grip modern audiences with a minimal adjustment on their part to the fact that more than half a century has passed since the film was made. To appreciate fully the motion picture's cinematic techniques, however, a viewer today should not only be aware of how they contribute to the success of the drama itself but should also regard them from a historical perspective; that is, recognize the ways in which these techniques were significant in the development of the art of cinema at the time they first appeared. *Broken Blossoms* is useful in this regard because, with the exceptions of panoramic shots for spectacle and the moving camera, it is a paradigm of Griffith's filmic style. In the next 12 years, aside from two sound dramas, he did not initiate any new concepts or devices. The following survey, then, is intended as a summary from a historical perspective of the characteristics of the director's use of camera-editing dynamics and elements of presentation.

*Camera-editing dynamics*
The most prominent components of camera-editing dynamics in *Broken Blossoms* are the shot, transitions, and techniques for continuity between scenes and sequences.

*The shot/* Griffith's innovations in the development of the shot include composition, masking, spatial depth, camera movement and angles, camera distances (close-ups), and subjective shots.

The director had learned the value of carefully composing his shots by the time he made his first feature film. For external settings in *Broken Blossoms,* the relation between individuals, buildings, and streets is worked out with particular consciousness of the harmony or contrast between horizontal and vertical

values, for example, the shot of the Chinaman leaning against a wall at the beginning of the second sequence of the film. Interiors presented for Griffith the same necessity of relating one or two people to a restricted physical area, but a group in a specific setting offered special opportunities for impressive pictorial composition (for instance, the scene that takes place in the ''house of sin''). Griffith employed masking* to emphasize the horizontal or vertical planes of a shot without moving his camera (see Figure 1.4).

Spatial depth was easily achieved in scenes photographed outdoors or in external settings on studio stages, for structures and other background supplied a depth perspective, and people often walked toward and away from the camera. This is evident in the often repeated establishing shot of the street in front of the Chinaman's shop, with the sidewalks converging toward the arch in the background (Figure 5.1).

It was in shooting interior scenes that directors in the early days of cinema restricted themselves to a stable camera during an entire scene and required actors to move on a single plane at a fixed distance from the camera. More than any other director of his time, Griffith increased the possibilities of exploring spatial depth by not only having his actors move toward and away from the camera but also by changing the position and even the angle of the camera between shots. An observant viewer of *Broken Blossoms* notices how imaginatively the director moved both his camera and his actors in the scenes that take place in the Burrowses' home and the Chinaman's upstairs room while preserving the convention of a missing fourth wall.

Although Griffith had no hesitation in his other features in taking advantage of panning, tilting, and tracking, his camera in *Broken Blossoms* is surprisingly still. There are very few panning and tilting shots, and these are usually limited to a few degrees. The director was equally chary of tracking shots; there are only two genuine ones in the entire film (when the Chinaman rides in a rickshaw and later, in his upstairs room, when his eyes narrow and he advances toward Lucy). Another factor contributing to the generally

*p. 15

**FIGURE 5.1**

*Broken Blossoms.* This establishing shot of the street in front of the Chinaman's shop appears 24 times during the film with variations in lighting to indicate changes in time settings.

static quality of individual shots is that most of them are at eye level. Perhaps he felt that more camera movement and different angles would have distracted from the intimacy of his drama.

One of the discoveries Griffith made as his style developed was the dramatic value of close-ups of faces (although strictly speaking, they are more often close shots). The emphasis on individuals and their relationships in the plot of *Broken Blossoms* offered numerous occasions to use this type of shot, and the director took advantage of every one [see Figure 1.8(d)]. It is hard to imagine how the character of Lucy, since she is so passive, and the internal conflicts of the Chinaman could have been conveyed as fully without close-ups.

The director often added a soft focus to his close-ups. The slight blurring particularly graced the features of his gentle, girl-woman stars. That the device was innovative as late as 1919 is demonstrated by a humorous story in a contemporary magazine. A manager of a New Jersey movie theater explains why he is critical of Griffith: " '. . . those close-ups in *Broken Blossoms* were so out-of-focus when I started to run that there print that I had to cut out most of them.' "[6]

Subjective shots are used a few times in the drama, though rarely with notable creativity. We do see Burrows from Lucy's point of view. Another example is when Lucy looks into the window of the Chinaman's shop; there is a cut first to a group of dolls displayed and then to one of them (foreshadowing of the gift of a doll to her by the Chinaman).

*Transitions/* The transitions between shots in *Broken Blossoms* are conventional for the day. The cut predominates. Sometimes a fade-out and a fade-in

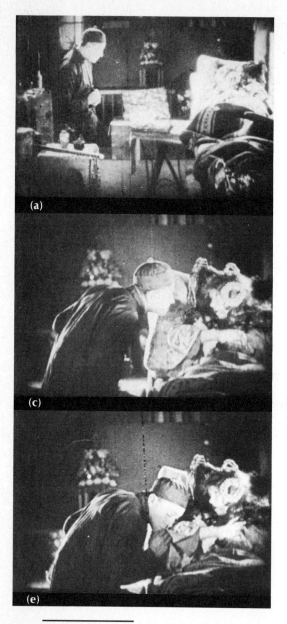

**FIGURE 5.2**

*Broken Blossoms.* Crosscutting between the setting of
the room above the Chinaman's shop where Lucy has
found refuge (a, c, e) and the fight ring where Burrows
battles an opponent (b, d, f).

indicate the end of a scene and a shift to a new scene in a different setting. Griffith seems to have viewed fades as visual exclamation marks. For instance, in the beginning of the scene in which the Chinaman installs Lucy in his upstairs room, fades occur three times between six shots (including titles). An iris-in or iris-out is employed less than a half dozen times (as opposed to the repeated use of the fixed iris, which is not a form of transition). There are no wipes in the film.

All of this suggests that Griffith did not consider transitions as esthetic devices that could help him control the rhythm and tone of his films. There is, however, an exception that appeared in earlier films by the director and was to establish a precedent generally adhered to by future filmmakers: Flashbacks are usually, but not consistently, introduced and concluded by dissolves.

*Techniques for continuity between scenes and sequences/* Of the unifying devices that join together or pervade scenes and sequences in *Broken Blossoms,* the most interesting for a viewer today are flashbacks, crosscutting, symbols, rhythm, and tone.

All the flashbacks in the film that are within the consciousness of a character occur at the beginning of the second sequence. Each one introduces a major preoccupation or aspect of the three main characters that influences his or her actions. The disillusionment of the Chinaman is made evident by the contrast between his recollections of being in a Limehouse brothel and his idealism demonstrated in the opening sequence of the drama. Also in this scene is the bold experiment for 1919 of having a flashback within a flashback: the Chinaman recalling the temple bells in China while still in the "house of sin." Burrows's chief satisfaction in life is physical domination over others, so he fondly remembers a victory in the ring. Lucy's passivity is the result of frustration, for there is no escape from her father. We are made aware of this through two flashbacks in which she is warned against marriage and prostitution.

Although there is parallel editing in the first Limehouse sequence, crosscutting to create suspense and to integrate the two main plot lines—Burrows's revenge and the relationship of the Chinaman and Lucy—dominate the second half of the film. The first

prominent instance of this device illustrates how it can reveal psychological insights into characters by solely visual means. Lucy is in the Chinaman's upstairs room and decides to wait until the next day before leaving her rescuer. Meanwhile, Burrows had sworn revenge against the man who he believes has seduced his daughter.

The sequence consists of six segments in two settings interrelated by crosscutting. The following synopsis gives an overall view of the sequence (*A* refers to the Chinaman's room, *B* to the ring where Burrows is fighting): (1)(A) The Chinaman presents Lucy with a doll (7 shots) [Figure 5.2(a)]. (2)(B) After the usual preliminaries, the fight starts and the end of the first round is reached (24 shots) [Figure 5.2(b)].(3)(A)The Chinaman, with narrowed eyes, moves toward Lucy (4 shots) [Figure 5.2(c)]. (4)(B) Burrows is knocked down but rises [Figure 5.2(d)] to temporarily floor his opponent, and the fight continues (8 shots). (5)(A) The Chinaman resists the temptation to seduce Lucy (5 shots, 1 title) [Figure 5.2(e)]. (6)(B) Burrows wins the fight and leaves to "right his Honor" (10 shots, 1 title) [Figure 5.2(f)].

The purpose of the crosscutting is to counterpoint Burrows's physical conflict with the Chinaman's own internal conflict. Even the stages of the events in each setting are related dramatically. In segment 3, the Chinaman appears gripped by evil intentions; in segment 4, Burrows is knocked down. We see the Chinaman resist temptation in segment 5; then, in segment 6, Burrows wins his fight. Griffith parallels the situations of the two men, for both are engaged in a struggle, but the differences between them are even more important. The fighter is using his physical strength and brutal nature to dominate a person, which is basically the way he bullies Lucy. On the other hand, the Chinaman's victory is over the evil within himself, and this works to the advantage of the girl.

In *Broken Blossoms,* certain objects and actions assume symbolic significance. The ringing of the large bell in the Buddhist temple, presented three times in the film (Figure 5.3), is associated by the Chinaman with his dream of peace and goodwill among men. The large bell in China is in contrast to the smaller one in England used to indicate the beginning and end of the rounds in the fight (brought to our attention by close-ups). We have, therefore, the call to peace versus the call to violence, as the idealism of the Chinaman is opposed to the brutality of Burrows.

---

**FIGURE 5.3**

*Broken Blossoms.* This shot of the ringing of the large bell in the Buddhist temple assumes symbolic significance. It appears at the very beginning of the film, in the flashback when the Chinaman recalls an evening spent in a house of sin, and after the Chinaman kills himself.

Two objects symbolize the relationship between the Chinaman and Lucy. The more apparent is flowers. The very title of the film prepares us to notice flowers. At climactic moments, the title cards are decorated with a drawing of a plum tree in blossom, and we are informed that the Chinaman, when looking at Lucy, thinks of "Oh, lily flowers and plum blossoms!" The girl yearns for flowers and attempts unsuccessfully, while being observed by the Chinaman, to trade tinfoil for them. She is finally given six small blooms in a vase by the man who loves her; the vase is later smashed by Burrows. The Chinaman leaves her to go shopping and purchase additional flowers but is told by Evil Eye that Lucy has been taken away by her father. With intentional irony, Griffith shows us Evil Eye buying a flower and, with a self-satisfied grin, smelling it.

Flowers in the film, as is inherent in the nature of any symbol, evoke a cluster of associations. Lucy is a blossom of innocence and beauty. Both Evil Eye and the Chinaman see her this way. The latter, however, also associates Lucy and flowers with China and his earlier naive hopes. From another perspective, Lucy's, flowers represent the only possibility in her grubby existence of contact with beauty and the emotional warmth she has projected into the image of her mother. The Chinaman gives her not only flowers but also the sympathy and affection that she unconsciously reached out for as she tried to buy a small bouquet.

Similar symbolic overtones are invested in the doll. The love the Chinaman offers Lucy is transferred in her mind to the doll he gives her. To this object she can respond safely and childishly. She clutches it desperately when she is in the closet (Figure 5.4) as Burrows breaks down the door; it is still in her hand when she dies.

---

**FIGURE 5.4**

*Broken Blossoms.* Lucy becomes hysterical in the closet in which she has locked herself as her enraged father smashes through the door. She clings to the doll given to her by the Chinaman.

The rhythm of *Broken Blossoms* is slow compared to the typical pace of a motion picture today. Even by the standard of Griffith's other major works, the film's development is particularly leisurely. The content obviously encouraged the director in establishing a relatively slow rhythm. Another factor, however, should also be taken into consideration by a modern viewer. Not only were images projected at a slower rate in the silent era, but the styles of early directors were based on the assumption that audiences would become confused if not constantly reminded of the relationships between the characters and between the characters and the setting of a scene. Griffith shared this assumption, even though he streamlined his editing of scenes more than most of his American contemporaries in the teens. A characteristic of this approach is the insistent reappearance of master shots; for instance, in *Broken Blossoms,* the one of the street in front of the Chinaman's shop is repeated two dozen times. Griffith was able to achieve emotional tensions and subtleties despite slow-paced editing, as in the brief scene (under 2 minutes) when Lucy is accosted by Evil Eye but protected by the Chinaman.

A special tone is achieved in *Broken Blossoms* through the director's juxtaposing of two approaches to his material. The settings (even though all are studio constructions), much of the action and characterization, and the lighting in some scenes (for instance, high-key for the fight) suggest a realistic approach. On the other hand, the poetic character of the Chinaman, the naiveté of the girl, the scenes with Lucy in his bedroom (including the low-key lighting), and the fog in the last third of the film convey a romantic atmosphere. The two stylistic ambiances blend, complement, and contrast with each other; the result is a tension throughout the film that emotionally reinforces its major themes.

### Elements of presentation

All five major elements are pertinent to *Broken Blossoms:* acting, sets, lighting, color (tinting), and sound (background music).

One of Griffith's contributions to filmic art was his effort to wean his actors and actresses away from the larger-than-life facial expressions and gestures characteristic of the contemporary theater and cinema. Exaggeration that approaches caricature, however, is still evident in the minor characters (for instance, the leering Evil Eye and the snickering Spying One) and particularly in Donald Crisp's interpretation of Battling Burrows.

A repeated seesawing between moments of inspired acting and others of strained reaching out for audience sympathy makes Lillian Gish's performance as Lucy uneven, though on the whole memorable. The manner in which she often clutches her arms around her chest is a perfect expression of her insecurity. In the closet scene near the end of the film, Lucy's hysteria is justified, and the actress rises to the occasion with tour de force acting. On the other hand, the famous gesture of forcing a smile with two fingers is endearing, but it is too much of a good thing when it becomes her final action on her deathbed. At the beginning of the sequence in which Lucy, only half conscious after her father's beating, wanders down streets and into the Chinaman's shop, Gish repeats more than once an excessive, ridiculous movement of twirling her body like a top.

Richard Barthelmess as the Chinaman is the true star of the film. Except in two scenes (in ecstasy when Lucy is asleep in his room and in despair after she has been taken away by her father), his portrayal is admirably restrained. He subtly conveys the sadness, intelligence, and tenderness of a disillusioned idealist who can still commit himself to a final dream of love. In fact, the actor creates one of the most believable and sympathetic male characters in all of Griffith's oeuvre.

Griffith and his coworkers (no art director is listed in the credits) designed sets that marvelously project the atmosphere of an early-twentieth-century London slum. The interiors are realistic in general and in detail. A viewer senses rather than sees their griminess. The outdoor settings are also realistic and prepared with care. There is little of the papier-mâché artificiality evident at the time in so many exterior sets photographed in studios.

Robert M. Henderson points out the extraordinary attention Griffith paid to the lighting and general ambiance of the film, to the extent of hiring, for the first time in his career, a director of special effects (Hendrick Sartov).[7] The results justified the expense and time. There is some extravagance but more truth in Gerald Mast's view that "*Broken Blossoms* remains one of the most beautifully lit films in screen history."[8]

What is most impressive is how the lighting contributes to the emotional tone of a scene. The boxing ring, for example, is starkly, brightly lighted. In contrast, the Chinaman's upstairs room is filled with darkness, shadows, and soft lights. The area of the bed where Lucy reclines, illuminated by candlelight and moonlight, becomes a fairyland of peace, hope, and wishes gratified. A viewer, however, cannot be completely uncritical of the lighting of the room. The use of spotlights in close-ups and two-shots is at times inconsistent and uneven, with Lucy's face fully lighted and the Chinaman's, a couple of feet away, in semi-shadows.

In the last sequences, the lighting of the exteriors is extraordinary for 1919. After the Chinaman leaves Lucy alone, there are repeated shots of the street in front of the shop. Each time we return to this setting, the shadows have lengthened, indicating the approaching evening. With the fall of night, a fog descends on Limehouse. Immense patience and ingenuity must have gone into creating shots of the Chinaman, barely visible in the night and fog, as like an avenging ghost he hurries through the streets intent on helping his beloved.

Although modern viewers can still judge the effectiveness of acting, sets, and lighting, even in a faded print, they cannot fully recapture the experience of the audience when *Broken Blossoms* was premiered because tinting and music are absent.

Griffith had some experience in the tinting of a film, having gone to the expense of adding this method of color to a number of prints of *Intolerance.* It is not quite clear whether *Broken Blossoms* at its premiere was only tinted or whether colored lights were also used. One contemporary reviewer suggests the latter: "Mr. Griffith has added a revolutionary color touch by the use of Chinese blue, thrown, not by the projector or out of the film, but independently, from the projection booth. This is not a tint . . ."[9] In any case, we do know that the Buddist temple scene, for example, had a yellow glow. Other settings and titles had individual colors: gray, brown, orange, gold, and blue. The effect must have been quite startling and was admired by all the reviewers whose comments are still extant.

From the beginning of the century, "silent" films were accompanied by music played on a piano or organ. In deluxe motion picture theaters, orchestras or small instrumental ensembles could be heard. Griffith adhered to this practice for most of his features. *The Birth of a Nation,* for example, was accompanied by excerpts from the works of Wagner, Verdi, Beethoven, Grieg, and other composers, as well as traditional American airs.

A largely original score was composed for *Broken Blossoms* by Louis F. Gottschalk. The main musical theme was suggested by Griffith. Robert M. Henderson, who located a sheet-music copy of the song, notes wryly: "Griffith's idea of music had more of Old Kentucky in it than either of London or China."[10]

When Griffith made *Broken Blossoms,* he intended to create a masterwork, and he succeeded. It is a fluent, intimate drama, but not shallow. In many ways, the director revealed more intensely and clearly than in his other films his humanity and the artistry of his cinematic style.

## EXPRESSIONISM

### Variety (Variété)

Variety *put American movie-goers into a white heat of enthusiasm over film art. It became the most important movie of the day, rivaling* Greed *and* The Cabinet of Dr. Caligari *in the amount of discussion it provoked.*
Lewis Jacobs, 1939[11]

**CAST**
Emil Jannings ("Boss" Huller), Lya de Putti (Berte-Marie), Warwick Ward (Artinelli), Maly Delschaft (The Wife), and others.

**CREDITS**
Director—E. A. Dupont, Screenwriters—E. A. Dupont and Leo Birinsky (based on a novel by Friedrich Hollander), Producer—Erich Pommer, Director of Photography—Karl Freund, Art Director—Oscar Werndorff, and others.

1925/UFA
Black & White/91 minutes (silent, 18 fps)
(American release version)

### BACKGROUND

Ewald André Dupont (1891–1956) directed one memorable film and two or three worth viewing once;

his more than three dozen other motion pictures merely supply material for footnotes in detailed histories of cinema. He began his career in cinema as a critic, turned to screenwriting, and finally became a director in 1917. His first film to attract attention was *The Ancient Law (Das Alte Gesetz,* 1923). *Variety,* unquestionably his finest work, was a fabulous success and brought him international attention.

He settled in England in 1927. Two of the films he made there are of sufficient merit to compensate for their glaring weaknesses. *Moulin Rouge* (1928) has a banal plot centering on a love triangle between a mother, who is a star at the famous dance hall in Montmarte, her daughter, and the daughter's fiancé. What makes the film interesting is the camera-editing dynamics, including a few Expressionistic shots, an outstanding performance by Olga Tschechowa as the mother, an exciting car chase, and, most of all, a verisimilitude in depicting the atmosphere of the Moulin Rouge both behind the footlights and backstage. *Piccadilly* (1929), with a screenplay by Arnold Bennett, is a pleasant but unremarkable murder mystery except for the lighting and realistic sets. Dupont's most ambitious work in Great Britain was *Atlantic* (1929), the first sound film with complete dialogue made in Europe. Its subject, a contemporary *Titanic* sea catastrophe, had possibilities for at least an exciting spectacle, but unfortunately the film's premiere was not a night to remember. Reviews of the day confirm the opinion of Ivan Butler that *Atlantic* was "one of the biggest failures, silent or sound, to be made in Britain."[12]

The discouraged director returned to Germany for a few years, where he made, among other films, *Salto Mortale* (1931), which Lotte H. Eisner maintains in some of its long shots and tracking shots stands as a direct forerunner to Max Ophuls's *Lola Montès.*[13] The motion pictures he directed in Hollywood from 1933 to 1939, such as *Forgotten Faces* (1936) and *Hell's Kitchen* (1939), are known only to television late show viewers. From 1940 to 1949, Dupont was a Hollywood talent agent. In the early fifties, he returned to directing, but only of "B"-level films (for example, *Return to Treasure Island,* 1954).

One of the minor mysteries of the history of cinema is how Dupont could create one outstanding

film, considered a masterpiece in its day, and in his many other motion pictures show only occasional sparks of unusual talent. His best work aside from *Variety* suggests that his forte was an aura of realism within a melodramatic plot (which he often scripted himself). He also knew how to achieve striking effects with his camera, but very rarely did he reach the level of the camera-editing dynamics of *Variety.* On the basis of internal evidence and Dupont's other works, it seems likely that he was strongly influenced by his collaborators, most particularly his cinematographer, Karl Freund, and his producer, Erich Pommer.

Karl Freund was director of photography for F. W. Murnau (for example, *The Last Laugh* and *Tartüff*), Fritz Lang (including *Metropolis*), Carl Dreyer's *Mikaël,* Walther Ruttmann's *Berlin,* Robert Wiene's *Arme Eva,* and various works directed by Paul Wegener, Max Reinhardt, and Paul Czinner. He came to Hollywood in 1930 and served as cameraman for Rouben Mamoulian on *Dr. Jekyll and Mr. Hyde* and *Golden Boy,* Tod Browning's *Dracula,* Sidney Franklin's *The Good Earth,* Fred Zinnemann's *The Seventh Cross,* and John Huston's *Key Largo.* He also worked with John Ford, George Cukor, Clarence Brown, James Whale, Vincente Minnelli, and Jules Dassin. He directed some minor films of his own and turned to television in the fifties.

It is more difficult to fix the contribution of Erich Pommer to *Variety.* This man was as extraordinary a producer as Freund was a cinematographer. While head of his own company, Decla-Bioscop, he released *The Cabinet of Dr. Caligari* (1919). It was through his efforts as production chief from 1923 to 1932 that UFA* became the greatest producer of distinguished films in the world during the silent era. Some of the directors who collaborated with him personally were Murnau, Lang, Dupont, Sternberg, Joe May, Erik Charell, and Wilhelm Thiele. As with so many major German filmmakers, he left his homeland in the early thirties. He worked in Great Britain, Hollywood, Germany (1946–1956), and again in Hollywood, where he died in 1966. His English-language films were not as outstanding as those he supervised in Germany, but he produced the popular *Fire Over*

---

*p. 102

*England* (1937, directed by William K. Howard and starring Laurence Olivier and Vivien Leigh) and lesser works directed by Alfred Hitchcock and Garson Kanin.

No matter what the efforts of the director-screenwriter, producer, and director of photography, *Variety* might not have been so successful if it were not for the fine acting of Emil Jannings. He was considered the greatest character actor in Germany during the silent era, and there are critics who would not limit this accolade to one country. He could play a figure of vitality and ruthless willfulness, such as Henry VIII in Lubitsch's *Anna Boleyn,* Harun-al-Rashid in Leni's *Waxworks,* Mephistopheles in Murnau's *Faust,* or—particularly impressive—a powerful, sensitive man of limited intelligence struck by adversity, such as the Doorman in Murnau's *The Last Laugh,* the title role in Dimitri Buchowtski's *Othello,* and "Boss" Huller in *Variety.* With the exception of Sternberg's *The Blue Angel,* he was less outstanding in sound films. His flirtation with the Nazi regime (he served as production chief of UFA in the early forties) led to his retirement after World War II.

Dupont's film was highly praised in Europe, but it was a triumph, a phenomenon in the United States. As Lewis Jacobs suggests,* it was greeted with wild enthusiasm. Even more important, it had an immediate influence on the cinematic techniques of the more adventurous of Hollywood filmmakers. A modern viewer can best appreciate the response in this country to *Variety* by reading contemporary reviews and being stunned by statements like the following: ". . . this latest product to reach us from German studios surpasses anything in film that has gone before it, at least as far as our knowledge goes."[14] This was written in 1926, only a few years before the end of the silent era in film!

Although *Variety* received critical and popular acclaim, it encountered difficulties with the censors. After its 12-week run at the Rialto Theater in New York, the film was censored in other states. The opening third (the Hamburg sequences) was removed, as were a few other shots (such as Artinelli at his window

after the seduction of Berthe). The ostensible reason was to make Huller more sympathetic to audiences, but there is no question that what really disturbed the censors was Berthe's sensual dance, without which the Hamburg section makes no sense. There are consequently two versions of the film. The original German print is approximately 150 minutes (18 fps) in duration; the edited American release version is 91 minutes (18 fps) long. Unfortunately, only the latter is available today from film rental companies.

## PLOT SUMMARY

Prisoner 28 is brought to the warden's office. It is up to the official to decide whether or not the prisoner is to be released. His decision would be easier, he says, if he hears the circumstances surrounding the crime directly from the criminal, who has remained steadfastly silent. Prisoner 28, whose face we do not see, begins to speak.

(The following paragraph describes material omitted from the American version.)

"Boss" Huller (Jannings) and his wife were once famous trapeze artists. They have been reduced, however, to running a sleazy miniature circus on the Hamburg waterfront. The wife (Delschaft) has become fat, disheveled, and sullen. A disreputable-looking man brings to Huller a beautiful West Indian dancer, Berthe-Marie (de Putti). The rowdy audience goes wild when she does a sensual dance. Huller himself is not immune to her physical charms. Deserting his wife and child, he goes off with Berthe and returns to being an aerialist.

The setting is Berlin. Huller and Berthe are performing their trapeze act at a small carnival. Meanwhile, the Berlin Wintergarten is preparing for the premiere of its spectacular variety show, drawing to the hall acts from all over Europe. The star attraction is the aerialist team, the Artinelli Brothers. When Artinelli (Ward) arrives at the Wintergarten, however, he informs the director that his brother was killed during a performance in London and therefore the act must be canceled.

Artinelli is in the audience on opening night. The manager recommends the next morning that a new team be formed. He says that he has heard of a couple of good trapeze artists at a local carnival and recommends that the two visit them. In front of the trailer, the manager talks to Huller while Artinelli stares at Berthe. After the men leave, Huller indicates that he is reluctant to accept the offer but is persuaded to do so by his wife.

"The Three Artinellis" perform their trapeze act at the Wintergarten; it is a great success. At a party given by Artinelli to celebrate the premiere of the act, the guests perform on a table. Berthe jumps up and does an erotic dance. She falls into the arms of her husband, who throws her to Artinelli. The lights suddenly go out for a few moments. Artinelli kisses Berthe on the cheek, unnoticed by Huller. The following sequence consists of crosscutting between Huller playing cards at a café and Artinelli seducing Berthe.

The three are at breakfast. Artinelli opens an invitation to the Berlin Artists' Spring Fete, but Huller has to attend a meeting that evening and naively suggests that the other two go together. At the fete, an acquaintance of Huller's observes Artinelli and Berthe kissing. A worried and angry Huller awaits his wife's return, but when she enters the room at 4:30 A.M., she reassures him.

Huller once again is playing cards at the café. The young man who was at the fete draws on a table a picture of Artinelli and Berthe embracing and Huller wearing cuckold's horns. Word of the betrayal spreads throughout the room. Huller leaves with the manager and the young man, but having forgotten his wallet, he returns. He notices the drawing and furiously smashes the table.

Huller is profoundly disturbed when he appears for the performance that evening, but he says nothing. He has a vision of intentionally not catching Artinelli and causing the seducer's death. During the actual performance, however, he cannot bring himself to do it, and the act ends without mishap. He leaves word for Berthe that he is visiting a friend and will be home very late. We see him drinking at a bar.

Walking down the hotel corridor, Artinelli and Berthe are obviously inebriated. She finds her room empty, for Huller is waiting for Artinelli. The younger man draws a knife, and the two men struggle. In the next scene, Huller enters his room and washes his hands. When Berthe sees the blood, she screams. He ignores her and leaves their room. When she attempts to stop her husband, Berthe falls down a flight of stairs. He goes outside the hotel, hails a taxi, and directs that he be taken to the nearest police station.

We return to the office of the warden of the prison and learn that Huller is Prisoner 28. The warden is moved by the story and speaks of the mercy of God as greater than His judgment. In the closing shot of the film, the prison doors open to reveal a view of trees and a clear sky.

---

ANALYSIS

Plot is the least significant component of *Variety*. It consists of a traditional love triangle of husband, wife, and lover. Throughout the film, the three remain types rather than individuals. Artinelli is the handsome, elegantly slim, debonair, ruthless, devious, cowardly seducer. Warwick Ward, who plays the role, admirably suggests a combination of decadent sensuality and an almost effeminate, serpentine grace, but, as was true of so many actors in silent motion pictures, he seems unable to free his facial features from stereotypic expressions. The intensity with which he looks at Berthe from the first moment he sees her and the sly, contemptuous narrow-eyed manner in which he observes Huller borders on the ridiculous. The object of his admiration, Berthe, conveys in every scene in which she appears her exotic and erotic nature. She is a selfish, crafty young woman married to an older man who indulges her every whim. Lya de Putti, with her rounded body, superb eyes, and rosebud mouth, has all the physical attributes to play the role of a West Indian seductress who would without compulsion break up a marriage and be unfaithful to her husband. She easily meets the requirements of an undemanding role.

The central character of the film is "Boss" Huller. Rather simple-minded and slow-witted, he does not demand too much of life. He enjoys the glamour of the music hall and has pride in his abilities as a "catcher" on the trapeze. He also has a sensual nature not satisfied by his thick, ungainly Hamburg wife. Gratitude to Berthe for accepting him makes the middle-aged man a slave to the young woman. For all his limitations and weaknesses, however, he has determination and integrity. This is best illustrated at the end of the film when he kills Artinelli and leaves Berthe. He immediately gives himself up to the police and, as we learn during the narrative framework, refuses to defend himself. We sense that he is not only attempting to expiate for committing a murder but also for the sin of leaving his wife and child. Siegfried Kracauer categorizes *Variety* as one of a series of films made in Germany during the twenties that share the common theme of an individual breaking away from social conventions, yet forced in the end to submit to authority.[15] In this interpretation, the God-like warden's forgiving Huller at the end and the last image of the opening doors of the prison are symbolic of salvation. Unfortunately, this theme is vitiated in the censored version of the film, which eliminates the Hamburg episode.

Emil Jannings expresses what little subtlety of feeling can be drawn from such a straightforward, uncomplicated person as Huller. Considering the screen-acting conventions of the time and Jannings's own tendency toward exaggerated facial expressions and broad gestures, his acting is fairly restrained in the film. Only in one type of situation and in one sequence does he present an external image of an emotion, rather than projecting it through the personality of a character: When he is indulging Berthe, his simpering or hangdog expressions are completely artificial. So too is his scowling mask of vengeance when he confronts Artinelli. On the other hand, as in most of Jannings's portrayals, there are wonderful moments for which a viewer is willing to forgive the actor any self-indulgence. An example is when he returns to his room after killing Artinelli and washes his hands. Suddenly, he looks up, as if awakened from a nightmare, bewildered by his surroundings. For a long time he stares at his reflection in the mirror. We can almost hear him thinking: Who is that person? Was it that stranger or I who committed murder?

When we praise *Variety,* it is not for the stale plot or the acting, impressive though the latter may be in the case of Jannings. What makes the film significant are two qualities infused into it by Dupont and Freund. The first can be summed up in the German word

*Stimmung,* translatable as "mood" or "atmosphere." The second consists of means of visually suggesting the subjective emotions of a character.

The film presents both the world of the theater or music hall and the ordinary world of the performers. Dupont depicts the glamour of the former, particularly through chiaroscuro, and spectacular camera-editing dynamics, and the drabness of the latter, especially through realistic settings. To the director's credit, he does not artificially separate the two worlds and the conventionally appropriate cinematic techniques for each; he interrelates them.

The first shots of the carnival in Berlin focus on its glitter and flux [see Figure 1.5(b)]. One striking shot has the camera on a Ferris wheel, so we see the crowd as would a rider. Very soon, however, we become aware of the sleazy side of the carnival as we are introduced to the barkers and their sideshows. A low-angle shot of Huller and Berthe on the trapezes doing their act draws out attention away from the crowd. This is the introduction of a motif developed during the film: The aerialists seem to be in a sphere of their own, which allows a freedom, daring, and interdependence that separates them from the mundane human beings below (an impression proved later to be incorrect). A reinforcement of this sense of isolation is a very high angle shot looking down at the crowd, perhaps a subjective view of Berthe's, who appeared glancing below in the previous shot. The two descend from the heights and enter the crowd. The following scenes of Huller and his wife present another, less elevated reality.

The next theatrical sequence is in a more elegant setting. It is opening night at the Berlin Wintergarten with Artinelli in the audience. Dupont is imaginative in suggesting in brief cinematic time a series of acts. Slow dissolves connect shots of clowns, acrobats, jugglers, and dancers. Three times there is an interesting juxtaposition of two shots to achieve humorous effects: a man balancing a ball on his nose and a seal doing the same; a woman moving her arms and neck in a pseudo-Egyptian dance and a comedian similarly moving his arms and neck; a chorus line kicking their legs and a line of tin soldiers marching. Diversity is attained through cutting to the orchestra and audience. A method of representing the latter includes another unusual device. Twice we see opera glasses pointed at the camera (four in one shot and three in the other). On the two circular glasses of each binocular are reflected in miniature what is happening onstage.

The first appearance of the "Three Artinellis" is a masterful integration of lighting, camera angles, the moving camera, and subjective shots. The opening one is a very high angle, very distant view of the three onstage in the spotlights of the darkened Wintergarten. The camera pans to the left as they proceed, still in the circles of the spotlights, to two ladders and climb up (Huller on one side, Artinelli and Berthe on the other). Twice we see nothing but two beams of light in the darkness. When the lights in the ceiling of the hall are turned on, the audience is visible from above. During the rest of the scene the camera remains at the two extremes of looking down at the audience from above or up at the aerialists from the audience's point of view. The orchestration of these shots splendidly conveys the excitement and movement of the act.

The most distinctive shots are those from above, generally presenting the view of the trapeze artists. In one we watch Huller hanging by his legs, his body foreshortened, and we move back and forth above the audience, as though swinging on the trapeze. There are other shots of this type or ones in which the camera is simply pointed at the audience. It is important to keep in mind, however, for comparison with the next appearance of the Artinellis, that these shots are basically objective in perspective. With one exception, there is no indication from a previous shot that we are seeing through the eyes of a single person. The exception is an undistorted, brief long shot of Artinelli and Berthe that appears to be subjective from the point of view of Huller.

The images of the audience are not of individuals but of groups surveyed in pans. Thus again in contrast to a later sequence devoted to the act in the music hall, there is little visual distraction from the theatricality of the experience. At the end of the act, there is a variation on the binoculars device. As the three take bows, the two men are seen not reflected

in opera glasses but through them. First there is a medium shot of Huller in which his head is clear in a circle and the rest of his upper torso blurred. Artinelli is seen with his head visible in a circle, but the frame is otherwise in darkness. In both cases there are previous shots of women putting opera glasses to their eyes.

After a transition scene, we are at the party given by Artinelli to celebrate the premiere of the new act. The scene has narrative significance: Berthe's performance on the table reminds us of her dance in Hamburg that revealed her sensual nature; during the moment the lights are turned out, Artinelli kisses the young woman, his first physically overt act in the process of seducing her. Our concern here, however, is the tone of the scene. There is a combination of theatricality in the high-angle shots of improvised performances on the table seen through the revolving blades of a ceiling fan and realistic shots of the inebriated performers in a drab room. Just about halfway through the Berlin section of the film, therefore, is a fusion of the two worlds of the theater and the everyday life of the performers. One shot at the end of the scene is notable: A cluster of hats on a rack fills the frame; hands reach in and take away individual hats, like flowers plucked from a bouquet.

Between the two performances of the aerial team that we see on the screen, Huller discovers his wife's infidelity. His personal life thereafter invades his professional one, and we come to share, through individual subjective shots, his feelings of dismay and desire for revenge. The initial manifestation of his emotional instability in the second performance occurs just before the three are to go on the stage. As Huller joins the others, we see Berthe and Artinelli laughing together, and their faces are slightly blurred. A moment later there is a shot of Huller closing his eyes [Figure 5.5(a)], then a slow dissolve to a swarm of swaying lights filling the frame, representing the faces of the audience as seen from above. Next is a medium shot of Artinelli before the camera, surrounded by those lights [Figure 5.5(b)]. Feet leave a platform; a figure is somersaulting; a tumbling body is not caught, falling. The camera seems to be hurtling down toward the floor. After images of Huller and the audience,

FIGURE 5.5

*Variety.* Huller closes his eyes (a) and fantasizes that he is responsible for the death of his rival (c). He imagines the faces of the audience (represented by particles of light) superimposed on the figure of Antinelli (b).

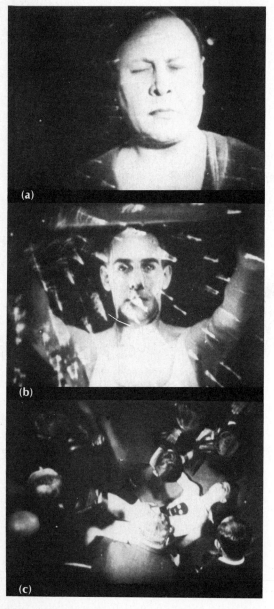

(a)

(b)

(c)

there is a very effective shot, a direct vertical from above, of the twisted body of Artinelli on the floor surrounded by the heads of people [Figure 5.5(c)]. Back to Huller with eyes closed, and our assumption is confirmed: The scene was the man's fantasy, distorted by his emotions.

The actual performance is about to begin. At this point, the death's-head attached to Artinelli's costume falls to the ground. Huller watches out of the corners of his eyes as his wife pins it back on. The obvious symbolic meaning is that she is attaching death to her lover. A condensed repetition of the first performance follows. There are some of the same striking shots, but now our attention is drawn to Huller, as when we see him wiping his forehead as he swings back and forth, sitting on the trapeze. Naturally, we are in suspense to know if he will be responsible for Artinelli's falling to his death. The tension Huller is under is revealed by two subjective shots: One is of the audience below from his point of view [Figure 5.6(a)]; next, the frame is filled with eyes whirling in a circular net of small lights (representative of the audience from above) [Figure 5.6(b)]. This projection of his guilt feelings is too much for him; he allows the act to end without mishap.

The theatricality of the second performance is undermined not only by the personal feelings of one of the aerialists but also by cuts to individuals in the audience, which was not done during the first performance. The most prominent example is intercuts of the manager, who was present when Huller learned of his wife's infidelity: fretting in his seat, having a drink, and finally rushing outside the hall and waiting. There are also shots of a waiter collecting beer mugs, groups of people, and the orchestra. One of the final images of the sequence is the applauding hands of the audience, seen from above, filling the frame.

FIGURE 5.6

*Variety.* (a) A subjective shot from Huller's point of view as he looks down at the audience from a trapeze above. (b) The same view distorted by his feelings of guilt, so that the audience becomes a swarm of accusing eyes.

(a)

(b)

The ordinary world of the performers has little of the glamour of the theatrical one. The office of the warden in the narrative framework is stark in its bareness. The physical settings of the Hamburg scenes are shabby and exude a sleazy atmosphere. The trailer at the Berlin carnival where Huller and Berthe live is crowded, disorderly, and dirty. The aerialist keeps the stub of a cigar in a container over the stove, and he throws out water through the door. The Berlin hotel rooms are plain and dreary.

Dupont could have photographed the scenes in these dull settings in the straightforward, unadorned manner we associate with realism. He chose instead to retain the realistic appearance of the settings but to dramatize the actions and emotions of the characters by means of imaginative camera-editing dynamics.

This approach is best illustrated in the narrative framework. The second shot of the film is from a very high angle, almost vertical, of shadowed walls like the three sides of a pit. At the bottom, a line of white-clad figures, with hands held behind their backs, obviously prisoners, shuffle in a circle around a guard in the center [Figure 5.7(a)]. The oppressive, forlorn atmosphere of the prison is thus wonderfully conveyed in one image. The spirit of this Expressionistic shot (the appropriateness of the adjective will be considered below) is carried on to the next one: Prisoner 28 being led along a corridor that suggests a tunnel leading into darkness [Figure 5.7(b)]. The bare room of the warden, who is God-like in his white beard and piercing eyes, with a cross on the wall half obscured by shadows [Figure 5.7(c)], is a haven after the physical confinement of the previous two shots.

We do not see the face of Prisoner 28 until the last scene, only his massive, broad back. The shots of Huller's back become a motif of *Variety* that a number of critics have maintained is repeated so often as ultimately to "erode the visual power of the image."[16] This is a valid point, but the motif still has the ability to evoke symbolically the guilt for leaving his family and his beloved's betrayal that the man bears with such determined fortitude in the climax near the end of the film. We see only Huller's back and hat during most of the scene in which Artinelli, drunk and frightened, is forced to face him in the bedroom. Later,

**FIGURE 5.7**

*Variety.* Three views of Prisoner 28 before he tells the warden (c) the history of his crime.

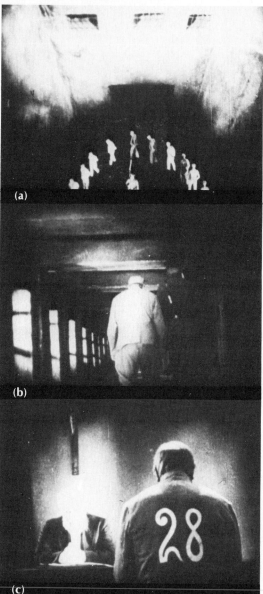

(a)

(b)

(c)

when he leaves Berthe, he walks away from the camera down the corridor.

The back shots, though the most often repeated, are not the only memorable images in the nontheatrical sequences. When Artinelli is ready to spring his trap of seduction, he stands with his ear to his closed door, listening for the approach of Berthe. Next, there is a fixed-iris shot of the young woman outside her door; cut to the seducer, then to a close-up of his ear [Figure 5.8(a)]. Finally, this close-up is superimposed on a shot of Berthe, visible from the waist down, walking along the corridor [Figure 5.8(b); see also Figure 1.6]. This is definitely a clever way to

indicate sound in a silent film. Equally clever is the use in the scene that follows of the curtains and blinds as the means Artinelli devises to persuade Berthe to close the door behind her. What is missing in the truncated version of *Variety* is the ironic touch of Artinelli raising the blinds after the seduction.

Another distinctive shot occurs when Berthe returns home from the Spring Fete and pauses before entering her bedroom to apply lipstick. We see her in the right half of the frame, and in the left half is the circular mirror containing her reflection. A second version of this shot appears when she has left Artinelli (Huller is waiting in his room) and just before she lets herself into the empty bedroom (Figure 5.9).

## FIGURE 5.8

*Variety.* A visual representation of sound in a silent film. Antinelli listens (a) to the footsteps of Berthe in the hallway (b). (The following two shots are illustrated in Figure 1.6.)

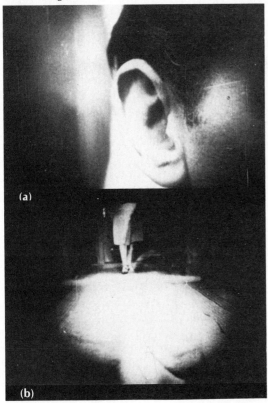

(a)

(b)

## FIGURE 5.9

*Variety.* Berthe looking at her reflection. Mirror shots often appear in Expressionistic films.

The climactic revenge-murder sequence is impressive despite its melodramatic tone and Huller's glaring face: There are additions to the back shots of the avenging husband when Artinelli enters his room; the high-angle one of the seducer crouching at Huller's feet; the final shot of the fight, with only a hand (near the base of the frame) clutching and dropping a knife, the bed of betrayal in the background; the acting of Jannings when he washes his hands; the extreme close-up of Berthe's screaming face; Huller steadfastly walking down the corridor dragging his desperate wife behind him; and the two neatly architectonic shots of the staircase Huller descends and Berthe tumbles down.

Although we feel that we have entered into Huller's not too complicated mind, it is surprising how few important subjective shots there are from his point of view. After the Hamburg sequence, the first occurs in the café where Huller discovers the drawing made by the malicious acquaintance and thereby learns of his wife's infidelity. There is a superimposition of his face on the room whirling in a circle from left to right, then only the room in motion. Next in chronological order are the blurring of his partners' faces, his fantasy of causing the death of Artinelli, and, finally, the two shots while he is on the trapeze.

This detailed survey of the camera-editing dynamics and use of elements of presentation in *Variety* should suggest (as far as words can) why the film is still an exciting viewing experience. What Dupont and his fellow filmmakers did was to take an essentially melodramatic, trite love-triangle story, drape it with a combination of realism and theatricality, and add the glitter of dramatic lighting, unusual camera angles, imaginative use of the moving camera, and remarkable individual shots. How to label the director's approach is an intriguing problem and of some historical significance in indicating the heritage left by the movement of German Expressionism.

Lotte H. Eisner describes the style of *Variety* as "an 'Impressionism' which bears traces of having passed through Expressionist abstraction."[17] Siegfried Kracauer writes that the director "adapted the methods of the expressionist postwar period to the exigencies of the realistic Dawes Plan period."[18] These two eminent authorities, whatever their differences in emphasis, agree that the film contains modified Expressionistic techniques. As indicated earlier in this volume,* the main objective in German Expressionism was to project on the screen the emotional states of characters. This was accomplished through stylized sets and acting, chiaroscuro lighting, subjective shots (often distorted by experiences that result in visual disorientation, such as dreams, drunkenness, and

heightened emotions), as well as other devices. The problem with an unadulterated Expressionistic film, such as *The Cabinet of Dr. Caligari,* is its abstractness and artificiality. This style can be provocative and even moving in an individual film, but large audiences are unlikely to be drawn to one film after another that adhered strictly to the tenets of this movement. Principally for this reason, Expressionistic films per se were produced in quantity for only a few years. The movement's basic ideas and the techniques developed to express them were too serviceable, however, to abandon completely.

What German directors, and later those of other countries, soon realized was that Expressionistic principles and devices in modified forms and used in single scenes could be combined with other modes of representation, even one as diametrically opposite as realism. F. W. Murnau and Fritz Lang recognized the potentials of this approach and by means of it created some of the greatest silent films. Even G. W. Pabst, who is associated with cinematic naturalism, fused Expressionistic and realistic techniques in *Secrets of a Soul* (1926). Such later directors as Vigo, Welles, Bergman, and Fellini owed a debt to German Expressionism in the development of the expressionistic elements in their styles.

By the time Dupont made his first notable film in 1923, Expressionism was already in decline. Following the lead of Murnau (*The Last Laugh* appeared in 1924) and Lang (*Destiny* was released in 1921), he combined in *Variety* realism with bold lighting derived from Expressionistic chiaroscuro, occasional stylized sets (as in the narrative framework portion and the corridors and staircases of the Berlin hotel), distinctive shots that contribute to the *Stimmung* of places and situations, and, although only infrequently, visualizations of the subjective emotions of the main character.

*Variety* is not a cinematic masterpiece, but it is a significant film. Perhaps because it is not as overwhelming as *Sunrise* or *Metropolis,* we can more objectively appreciate how the tenets and techniques of German Expressionism could be adapted to the needs of other movements and thus influence the art of film for decades after the 1920s.

---

*pp. 103–104

━━━━━━━━━

## DYNAMIC MONTAGE

### October or Ten Days That Shook the World
### (Oktyabr)

*The hieroglyphic language of the cinema is capable of
expressing any concept, any idea of class, any political
or tactical slogan, without recourse to the help of a
rather suspect dramatic or psychological past.*
                                    *Sergei Eisenstein*[19]

**CAST**

*Nikandrov (Lenin), Vladimir Popov (Kerensky),
sailors of the Red Navy, soldiers of the Red Army,
and citizens and workers of Leningrad.*

**CREDITS**

*Director, Screenwriter, and Editor*—*S. M.
Eisenstein, from the book Ten Days That Shook
the World* by John Reed, Assistant Director—
Grigori Alexandrov, Director of Photography—
Edvard Tissé, Art Director—Kovriguin, and others.

1928/Sovkino
Black & White/161 minutes (silent, 18 fps) (original)
100 minutes (silent) (U.S.A. version)

BACKGROUND

Sergei Mikhailovich Eisenstein (1898–1948) has been
one of the most influential filmmakers. He attained
this preeminence not only through the motion pictures
he directed but also through his theoretical writings on
film. Any serious student of cinema is familiar with
such works as *The Battleship Potemkin, October,*
and *Ivan the Terrible.* His writings, some of which
were composed nearly half a century ago, have not
become dated; indeed, the more film theory advances
in scope and depth, the more respected are his ideas.

In his youth, Eisenstein first studied engineering,
then architecture. He joined the Red Army in 1918.
After demobilization, he worked as a set designer for
and director of theatrical productions. In 1924 he became dissatisfied with the restrictions of the theater
and turned to cinema.

With little formal preparation in this medium,
he completed his first film in 1925. *Strike (Stachka)*
describes a protest by factory workers in 1912 and its
suppression by the czarist government. The work consists of six parts and was shot entirely on location.

Eisenstein collaborated on this production with two
men who were to be important contributors to most
of his major works: Edvard Tissé as director of photography and Grigori Alexandrov as assistant director.

*The Battleship Potemkin (Bronenosets Pot-
yomkin,* 1925) is a landmark in the history of cinema
and Eisenstein's most complete and balanced expression of his concepts of dynamic montage and epic
film. Although greeted with no more than moderate
enthusiasm by Soviet audiences, *Potemkin* was a sensation when it was released in European countries and
later in the United States. The plot is a celebration of
an episode in an unsuccessful 1905 uprising in which
sailors on the *Potemkin* mutinied against their officers
and were supported by the citizens of Odessa, with
the result that the ship was allowed to pass through a
squadron of vessels sent to intercept it. The fourth of
the five sections of *The Battleship Potemkin* is entitled ''The Odessa Steps.'' It is doubtful if any portion
of any film has been more analyzed than the footage
that constitutes this sequence.

*October* (1927) was the next film the director
completed. He then returned to *The General Line*
(*Generalnaya Linya,* 1929, also titled *Old and New,
Staroye i Novoye*), a production he had interrupted to
work on *October.* The story of a peasant woman's
dedication to a collective farm, *The General Line*
focuses on a heroine who is individualized and humanized. This is a departure from the principle of the
proletariat as a collective hero illustrated in the director's previous works. This film began his problems
with the Russian authorities. It was attacked by Soviet
critics for its ''formalism,'' a code word used at the
time to condemn filmmakers who were considered
overly concerned with esthetics and intellectual ideas.

Before *The General Line* was released, however, Eisenstein, Alexandrov, and Tissé had left Russia
on a tour of Europe and the United States. The government had approved the trip for the purposes of studying new film technology, particularly in the area of
sound. The three travelers were required to pay their
own way from lecture fees and film productions, so
they accepted a commission from a wealthy Frenchman to make a short sound film (*Romance sentimen-
tale,* 1930, 30 minutes). Eisenstein was soon bored by

the project and, leaving Alexandrov and Tissé behind to complete it, he traveled to the United States.

Paramount offered the director a contract, but because of conflicts within the studio and Eisenstein's insistence on having total control over his productions, negotiations were broken off. One of projects suggested by the Russian and for which he even prepared a script was an adaptation of Theodore Dreiser's novel *An American Tragedy*. Through the efforts of admirers of Eisenstein's works, Upton Sinclair, the socialist novelist, offered to sponsor a film on Mexican peasant life with funds supplied by his wealthy wife.

Eisenstein spent 1931 shooting in Mexico with Alexandrov and Tissé, who had joined him. *Que Viva Mexico!* was to consist of a prologue, four related episodes, and an epilogue, and it was intended to capture the spirit of Mexican peasants as they celebrated events related to birth, marriage, death, and religion. After the director had shot almost 150,000 feet of film, which he sent back to Hollywood for processing, and was working on the final episode, Sinclair abruptly canceled their contract. The reasons for this unfortunate turn of events are delineated in a book by Harry M. Geduld and Ronald Gottesman.[20] Eisenstein and his colleagues were forced to return to Russia without ever viewing the developed footage or being allowed to edit it.

Although *Que Viva Mexico!* is consistent with the director's earlier work in its epic scope and brilliant composition of shots, the primitiveness of setting and people appears to have stimulated in him latent sensitivities to the grotesque, the power of ritual (especially in the relationship of man and nature), and the erotic. Material from the film was used (without Eisenstein's permission) in various releases, including *Thunder Over Mexico* (1937) and *Time in the Sun* (1939). It is possible to rent 4 ¼ hours of unedited footage from the Museum of Modern Art in New York.

Eisenstein's reception when he returned to his homeland was not cordial. The Soviet authorities had condemned his activities in North America, and the criticism of *The General Line* still hung over him. For 3 years he worked only on the periphery of film production. In 1935 he was finally permitted to begin his

first sound film. With interruptions because of illness, he labored for 2 years on *Bezhin Meadow* (*Bezhin lug,* 1935–1937), the story of a youngster who is killed by his reactionary father for saving a crop from arsonists. While the film was being edited, however, a committee of Soviet filmmakers denounced Eisenstein. The director accepted the criticism and never completed *Bezhin Meadow*.

As a reward for his compliance, Eisenstein was allowed to make *Alexander Nevsky* (1938), based on the exploits of a thirteenth-century prince. It contains many spectacular sequences, particularly a battle on ice between the Teuton Knights and Nevsky's Russian army, and the background music by Prokofiev is famous, yet the film contains few of the exciting, innovative techniques found in Eisenstein's other works. The director was once again brought in conflict with the authorities. The year after the epic was released, Stalin signed a pact with Hitler. The portrayal of the Teuton Knights as cruel invaders was an embarrassment to the government, and *Alexander Nevsky* was withdrawn from circulation until the Soviet Union joined the Allies in World War II.

Five years passed before Eisenstein received another assignment. In 1943 he began a lengthy film devoted to the life of Ivan the Terrible. Part one of *Ivan Grosny* was completed within the year and released in 1944. It is a splendid pageant with imposing settings, powerful characterizations of the czar and his court, and intriguing camera-editing dynamics in the service of a stylized approach that is reminiscent of silent-film epics. For the first time in his career, Eisenstein focused his attention on a single, complex human being and demonstrated that he was as adept at conveying on the screen subtle psychological insights into a character as in manipulating types and masses of people. He was aided by the superb performance of Nikolai Cherkasov as Ivan (the actor had been admirable also in the less demanding role of Alexander Nevsky). Stalin approved of—and obviously identified with—an interpretation of Ivan as a national hero overcoming all obstacles in the way of his ascent to power, and the Soviet critics, responding to the dictator's cue, praised the film highly.

Part two of *Ivan the Terrible* (*The Boyars'*

*Plot*) was completed in 1946; it deals with the czar's victory over the boyars (members of the aristocracy) and the church. Eisenstein used color for the first time in a lengthy sequence near the end of the epic. While retaining the pageantry and tableau effects in the composition of shots found in part one, he delves even deeper into the inner conflicts that bring the czar close to insanity. This portrayal of a vulnerable leader haunted by the memories of his dead wife and of his crimes did not appeal at all to Stalin. The film was not released to the public until 1958.

Eisenstein made detailed plans for the production of part three, which was to be photographed in color. While engaged in the final editing of part two, however, he suffered a severe heart attack. He was too ill to commence shooting again and died in 1948.

Throughout his career, Eisenstein published essays on film theory. The two most important collections of his writings are *Film Sense* (1942, edited and translated by Jay Leyda) and *Film Form: Essays in Film Theory,* (1949, edited and translated by Jay Leyda). Revised editions of both books appeared subsequently.

Eisenstein's writing style is intense and sometimes abstruse. His essays can offer difficulties for some readers not only because he attempts to communicate feelings as well as ideas but also because of the scope of his vision. Eisenstein's ambition was to create what could be described as a cinematic unified field theory. That is, he wished to establish a comprehensive theory of film based on the most fundamental ways in which people interpret their circumambient universe. For support of his premises, the theorist-director turned not only to cinema but also to psychology, linguistics, anthropology, sociology, literature, art, philosophy, and political science. References to these fields enrich his writings; however, they also convolute his ideas. Another weakness of Eisenstein as theorist was his indefiniteness in categorizing and defining his concepts. More poet than thinker, his discussions of such terms as *overtonal montage* and *dynamization of the subject* suggest rather than explain specific ideas.

No matter how profound his interest in culture and twentieth-century ideas, the central experience of Eisenstein's life, as with most Russians of his generation, was the Revolution. He was completely dedicated to the ideals of communism, even when treated shabbily by narrow-minded governmental bureaucrats. All his films, with the exception of the incomplete *Que Viva Mexico!,* are basically propagandistic in that they support the need for and glorify the existence of the Soviet Union. Historical accuracy and a balanced view of people and history are replaced by a self-serving Soviet interpretation of the recent and ancient past, so that in *October* the events of 1917 can be described without a single reference to Leon Trotsky. No matter how faithful Eisenstein may be to the essential revolutionary and patriotic spirit of the Russian people, his films are factually unreliable as cinematic reconstructions of pre–World War II Russian history.

The genre designation of *epic,* a celebration of a people's heroic tradition, is appropriate to each of Eisenstein's feature films. In the United States and Europe, such epics as *The Birth of a Nation* and Bertolucci's *1900* focus on representative individuals involved in significant historical events. In keeping with the emphasis of Marxism on the role of the proletariat in influencing political change, most of Eisenstein's films have the people as composite heroes. This is true even in *The General Line* and *Bezhin Meadow,* in which ordinary individuals are in the dramatic foreground, and in *Alexander Nevsky,* in which the title character is a rather dimly perceived leader. Only in *Ivan the Terrible* is the individual more central to the action than the masses. Events themselves in which the people participated, therefore, are featured in the director's works. Although there are descriptive title cards in the silent films and expository speeches in the sound ones, this emphasis can offer a problem to non-Russian viewers unfamiliar with the details of Russian history.

Except for *Ivan the Terrible,* Eisenstein depended on two-dimensional types rather than fully developed characters in his narratives. Physical characteristics and personality traits appropriate to a role were important in typecasting. The term Eisenstein originated was *typage.* He felt that by this method of casting an actor could project personality and attitudes from the screen without elaboration in the screenplay or on the part of the director.

Groups are central to a proletarian epic, and Eisenstein was masterful in presenting masses in action on the screen. In such sequences as the attack on the Winter Palace in *October* and the battle on the ice in *Alexander Nevsky,* he balanced overviews of the groups with shots of participating individuals. He was careful to relate shots of crowds to external settings. Like Fritz Lang, his contemporary in Germany, Eisenstein was sensitive to how architecture can help to structure single shots and contribute to the tone of scenes and sequences. Moreover, the Russian director was fascinated by sculpture and architectural decoration, often using them for symbolic purposes, such as the aroused lion in *The Battleship Potemkin* and the metal peacock in *October.*

In photographing interior scenes, Eisenstein demonstrated his ability to manipulate lighting to achieve tonal effects. Although dramatic lighting is to be found in his early films, the culmination of his expressive use of this element of presentation was *Ivan the Terrible.* Eisenstein never had the opportunity to explore the potentials of color. Only in a section of his final work, *Ivan the Terrible, Part Two,* does color appear, and even here the film stock was of poor quality.

The director approached sound warily. He feared—legitimately, for this actually happened in the early years of the sound era—that it would become simply an adjunct to the visuals of a motion picture. On the other hand, he recognized that sound could add a vital new dimension to cinema if properly utilized, as he, Pudovkin, and Alexandrov declared in their famous manifesto, "A Statement on the Sound-Film," in 1928.[21] Eisenstein incorporated sound effectively in his last three works, but not as innovatively as did his contemporary Dziga Vertov. He was fortunate in having the background music for *Alexander Nevsky* and *Ivan the Terrible* composed by Sergei Prokofiev.

Admirable as is Eisenstein's mastery in his films of the components of the narrative dimension and elements of presentation, it was in his exploration of the area of camera-editing dynamics that he made his most significant contributions to cinema. His name is particularly associated with the development of dynamic montage. As noted in Chapter 4,* this form of creative editing and its three levels—narrative, intellectual, and emotional—were codified by Lev Kuleshov before and during World War I. Every major Soviet director was influenced by the theories of this great teacher. More than any of his colleagues, however, Eisenstein molded the meaning of dynamic montage for filmmakers of the Western world.

Essential to Eisenstein's theories is the philosophy of dialectic materialism. Borrowing the term *dialectic* from Immanuel Kant, nineteenth-century philosopher G. W. F. Hegel devised the logical method of proceeding from thesis and antithesis to synthesis. Confining this approach to a reality that was in their view entirely materialistic, Karl Marx and Frederick Engels made it the official philosophy of communism. They argued that progress takes place through a struggle of opposites and that in societies the primary area in which growth emerges from conflict is the economic by means of class struggle.

Eisenstein adapted dialectic materialism to cinema. For him, the basic cell of the organism that is a film is the shot. It may be self-sufficient and static. Generally, however, a shot inherently contains potential connections of content and form with the shots that follow. The director exploits these potentials to create a *synthesis*—a new idea or emotion—that could not exist without a "collision" of two or more shots. Here lies the essence of Eisenstein's brand of dynamic montage:

By what, then is montage characterized and, consequently, its cell—the shot?
By collision. By the conflict of two pieces in opposition to each other. By conflict. By collision.[22]

Every characteristic of a shot can be in conflict with the same characteristic in the next shot: in form, for example, change from a low-angle shot to a high-angle one; from one in low-key lighting to another in high-key lighting; objects moving from left to right within a frame, then from right to left in the next. In content, for instance, there may be a shift from a group shot to one of an individual or a shot of human

---

*p. 110

beings struggling followed by one of a statue. Al-though many characteristics of a shot may attract our attention by their contrast, one is dominant and the others subordinate. The dominant characteristic determines the development of a dialectic.

How a cinematic dialectic progression relates one or more shots to those that follow is illustrated by Lincoln F. Johnson in *Film: Space, Time, Light and Sound* (1974) through an analysis of the "Odessa Steps" sequence from *The Battleship Potemkin*. [23] The following is one of his examples. The dominant characteristic of two shots is soldiers descending the steps firing their rifles; this is a thesis. The next four shots, from a high angle, reveal the surprise and shock of passive women on the steps; this is the antithesis. The synthesis is created in the mind: recognition of oppression.

Eisenstein was aware that his concept of montage functioned in diverse ways, and, therefore, especially in the essay "Methods of Montage" (in *Film Form*), postulated what he termed "the formal categories of montage." *Metric montage* is when "the content within the frame is subordinated to the absolute length of the piece."[24] Naturally, the subject matter of a scene will be influential. For example, in a chase scene dominated by metric montage, regardless of the content of individual shots, fewer frames make up each shot as the pursuer gets closer to the pursued. Eisenstein considered this type of rigid approach as relatively unsophisticated and avoided it as much as possible.

*Rhythmic montage* comes into play when the movement within a frame or a dominant rhythm governing the lines of a static object determine the duration of single shots. An instance of this method is when a dance is shown on the screen and the number of frames of each shot decreases as the dance movement becomes more active and increases as the dance rhythm slows.

*Tonal montage* is dependent on the dominant emotional or dramatic tone manifested in shots. It can be determined by action, lighting, spatial organization, or any other characteristic of a shot. Eisenstein refers to this type of montage as *melodic-emotive* and *emotive vibration*. [25] Among contemporary directors, Ingmar Bergman is particularly skillful in creating a visual emotive vibration; in fact, the whole opening sequence of *Persona* is an instance of complex tonal montage. Another example in this director's work is the shots of moon and clouds, swans on a lake, and the illuminated castle that precede the supper given by Mrs. Armfelt in *Smiles of a Summer Night*.* These shots were included for no other reason than to contribute to the tone of a sequence.

*Overtonal montage* is a means whereby connotative significances within a shot or shots are communicated to a viewer. Any aspect of an image can create overtonal vibrances that are subordinate to the dominant tone, yet should be taken into account. In the "Odessa Steps" sequence, a woman in black wearing a white shawl and pince-nez, later shot in the eye, is featured because of her appearance, age, and authoritativeness. Everything about her suggests that she is middle-class and accustomed to being listened to. Eisenstein's desire to include these associations accounts for the emphasis on the woman in shots whose dominant tonal effect is of threat and oppression.

*Intellectual montage* is a juxtaposition of two or more shots that induces in viewers an idea that is a comment on the action and gives what appears on the screen a significance that would not exist without this type of editing. In many ways, this is the boldest and most startling form of montage. An example occurs in Charles Chaplin's *City Lights:* A crowd of people stream from a subway entrance; the next shot is of a flock of sheep climbing out of the same subway entrance. The idea is not only that people in a crowd act like sheep but also that the main character, Charlie the Tramp, is different, an individual.

The chief value of these five methods of montage is to focus a viewer's attention on some of the principles that may have determined how a filmmaker edits scenes and sequences in a motion picture. It is with this purpose in mind that the methods are referred to in the analysis of *October* that follows.

The attention paid in critical studies of Eisenstein to his theories of dynamic montage have often obscured the fact that he believed firmly in the organic unity of a film. He insisted that a cinematic work of art

*p. 310

is a living re-creation of reality, not a dead facsimile. The quick that vitalizes flickering shadows on a screen is the complete interrelationship and interdependence of every factor that contributes to a viewer's experience of watching, listening, and reacting to a motion picture.

Theory and practice in any art do not always coincide, especially when the artist himself is the theorist. This is particularly true of the cinema, in which many people contribute to the making of a film, and external influences can be considerable. Eisenstein's theories are significant in themselves and help to illuminate his intentions and the rationales of his techniques, but these theories should not be considered as ex cathedra explanations of how specific films were created. As with all great artists, Eisenstein often worked by intuition, and, as with all great films, each of his is more than the sum of intellectual explanations of it.

Eisenstein was working on *The General Line* when the Soviet government decided that the tenth anniversary of the 1917 Revolution should be commemorated by its leading filmmakers. Eisenstein chose *October* as his project. He was given full freedom and cooperation: At his disposal were thousands of members of the army and navy and the citizens of Leningrad (formerly Petrograd). Over 160,000 feet of film were shot on location during 6 months of intense work. By November, 1927, when the celebrations were to take place, the director and his colleagues had produced a version 12,467 feet long.[26]

Unlike *The End of St. Petersburg,* Pudovkin's contribution to the anniversary, *October* was not released in 1927. Trotsky had been expelled from the party that year, and the Soviet officials insisted that history be rewritten. Eisenstein was ordered to delete from his work all images of and references to the once great communist leader. This took 4 months to accomplish (the first public screening of *October* was on March 14, 1928), and the film was shortened by one-fourth, to 9,186 feet. An "original version" reconstituted in Russia in 1967 has not been distributed outside the USSR.

The reaction of Russian critics was adverse, and most of the public was bewildered by the new techniques in the epic. No one denied the power of the crowd sequences and the sincerity of Eisenstein's commitment to the communist cause. To many viewers, however, the narrative lacked coherence. Moreover, *socialist realism* was just beginning to become the official cinematic esthetic, and the charges of "formalism," obscurity, and intellectual arrogance that were to be leveled against *The General Line* were anticipated by many Soviet critics in their criticism of *October.* The film was more favorably received abroad, yet it was generally considered inferior to *The Battleship Potemkin.*

Prints available in the United States today of *October* range widely in length, and they are usually retitled *Ten Days That Shook the World.* Most rental companies offer a print at silent speed of 161 minutes. There is also one of 104 minutes at sound speed (containing background music by Shostakovich, added in the thirties) and another, radically edited version of 50 minutes. Except for the omission of the satirical montage of shots of religious images,* a viewer cannot easily determine what footage has been eliminated in a specific print.

PLOT SUMMARY

Demonstrators rush up stairs and pull down a huge statue of Alexander III, father of the present czar, Nicholas II, and opponent of all political and social reform. A title card informs us that in February, 1917, the czar and his supporters were overthrown; the provisional government takes their place at Petrograd (capital of the Russian Empire from 1703 to 1917). The victory of these "in-betweens" is celebrated by members of the church and the middle class.

Anticipating peace, Russian soldiers fraternize with the Germans. The provisional government, however, does not fulfill its promise of ending the war. Fighting at the front and suffering at home continue.

Lenin arrives at the Finland Railroad Station in Petrograd on April 3 and declares that the Bolsheviks must come into power if the people are to keep the rights for which they fought in overthrowing the czar. In July, a mass demonstration led by the Bolsheviks is ruthlessly suppressed by the government. Among the

*p. 232

incidents shown on the screen are government troops firing into the crowd, a young man being killed, the closing of the Nerva Bridge, and members of a regiment that sided with the workers being disarmed and made prisoners.

Alexander Kerensky is appointed head of the provisional government and installs himself and his staff in the luxurious Winter Palace of the czars. The Napoleonic ambitions of the new chief of state are challenged by another enemy of the people. Kornilov, a general of the old imperial army, marches against the provisional government. He is defeated by soldiers and by citizens of Petrograd led by the Bolsheviks.

The Second Congress of the Soviets is to meet on October 25 in Petrograd to consider whether or not the provisional government should be replaced. The Bolsheviks, guided by Lenin, prepare to seize power. The citizens of the city organize themselves into the Red Guard, and the cruiser *Aurora* anchors on the Neva River near the Winter Palace. Kerensky deserts his post when he realizes that the Cossacks and other troops will not come to his defense.

At the Smolny, the building where the congress is meeting, the Mensheviks and other supporters of the present government unsuccessfully argue against the Bolsheviks. Meanwhile, the Red Guard and marines from the *Aurora* take over the city. At the Winter Palace, barricades are set up by its defenders: young military cadets and the women that make up the "Battalion of Death." The Bolsheviks send an ultimatum of surrender to the officials of the government in the palace. When no response is forthcoming by midnight, they attack and depose the provisional government. Lenin is tumultuously greeted by a congress now in the hands of the Bolsheviks.

### ANALYSIS

Of primary interest in this analysis are the camera-editing dynamics Eisenstein used in *October*. The film is so rich in these techniques, however, that only highlights can be examined in a few pages. An approach that follows the chronological development of the film is the most expedient.

The first image of *October* illustrates a favorite device of the director: a piece of sculpture personify-

ing a group of people, a situation, or an emotion. On a pedestal is a metal eagle with wings outspread, filling the screen. The bird faces camera right. It symbolizes the rebellion of the Russian people against their oppressors. The next four shots are dominated by rhythmic montage. First, a crowd rushes up stairs, generally from the lower right corner of the frame to the upper left; second, the same action moves from the base of the frame toward the top; third, people move from the lower left corner to the upper right; fourth, the first shot is repeated. The impression is of an encompassing movement upward.

The czar's fall is represented by the destruction of a statue of Alexander III. Before it is pulled down, inserts demonstrate the principle of intellectual montage: four shots of a mass of soldiers joyously waving their rifles [Figure 5.10(a)] and three of a thicket of scythes [Figure 5.10(b)]. By juxtaposing these contrived shots with the main action of the scene, Eisenstein has by solely visual means instilled an idea in the minds of viewers: The people welcome the overthrow of the czar. Immediately following these inserts are three repeated views from three different distances of the statue being toppled over [Figure 5.10(c)]. The repetition emphasizes the importance of the action.

Two title cards inform us that the provisional government has assumed power. Often Eisenstein verbally describes an event, then visually dramatizes the significance of what has happened. The establishment of the provisional government results in rejoicing among the bourgeoisie and representatives of the church, identified throughout the film as enemies of the proletariat [see Figure 1.8(c)]. We are reminded of the people by another appearance of the statue of the eagle. In keeping with the director's emphasis on contrast, however, the bird is facing in the opposite direction (camera left) to that of the initial shot of the film.

The commitment of the new rulers to the war is indicated by two shot of diplomats in formal attire. At the front, the soldiers believe peace is at hand. This is first symbolized by rifles with bayonets attached being plunged into the earth. Following is a specific scene of the Russian soldiers fraternizing with the Germans. The cessation of hostility between the soldiers is demonstrated by the sharing of food and an ex-

**FIGURE 5.10**

*October.* An example of intellectual montage. Before a crowd completes the destruction of a statue of Alexander III (c), shots are intercut of rifles and then scythes waved in the air. The idea is implanted in the minds of viewers that soldiers and farmers approve the action of the urban revolutionaries.

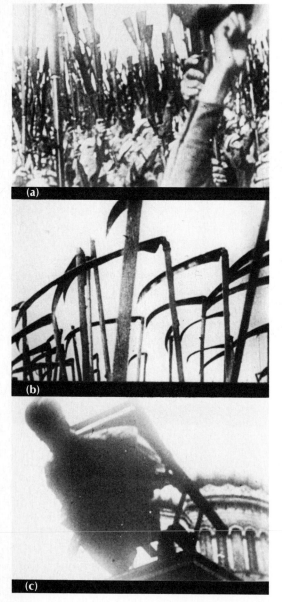

(a)

(b)

(c)

change of helmets. Suddenly, shells explode in their midst, and each side retreats to its own trenches. The war will continue.

A particularly powerful example of intellectual montage occurs in the Russian trenches. A group of soldiers bow their heads as pieces of earth from an exploding shell fall on them. Cut to a close-up of one soldier who looks up. There are three shots of a gun carriage being lowered. Back to the soldier in the trench closing his eyes and bending his head. The gun carriage descends; the group in the trench; the soldier; the gun carriage inexorably descending.

The home front and military front are juxtaposed through parallel editing. Women are standing on a bread line in the snow. The tableau is presented from different distances, and the passage of time is indicated by some women who are upright in early shots but are lying down in the snow while still in line in later ones. This scene is crosscut with shots of soldiers operating the windlass of an artillery piece and of others sleeping in the snow.

The next scene is in contrast to the previous one of the stresses of war. Lenin arrives at the Finland Railroad Station in Petrograd to save Russia. Eisenstein carefully orchestrates the reception and appearance of his hero. Shots of the packed terminal are contrasted with individual group shots. The civilians face camera right; the soldiers face left. Finally, Lenin is shown in a low-angle shot with a transverse banner dramatically filling a third of the area of the frame, then from other angles as he delivers his message of rebellion against the provisional government (Figure 5.11).

The July demonstration against the established authority opens with a high-angle shot of thousands of people massing in the main square of Petrograd. Others surge across the Neva Bridge. Banners play an important role in this sequence as symbols of the unity of the people. The peaceful intention of the demonstration is indicated by shots of the marines, who are supporting the Bolsheviks, removing the bayonets from their rifles and by close shots of those rifles pointed toward the ground. This emphasizes the perfidy of the government, for a few moments later there is a juxtaposing of the barrel of a machine gun

**FIGURE 5·11**

*October.* Lenin arrives at the Finland railroad station in Petrograd and delivers a harangue to the welcoming crowd.

and overhead shots of the demonstrators. Images of the firing of the gun and of the gunner produce the *effect* of superimposition; actually, the separate static shots are each only two frames in length.[27] Views of the crowd dispersing are also remarkable. With smoke wafting in front of the camera lens, the people viewed from a great distance and a very high angle look like ants scurrying to the edges of the frame.

A young man escapes with a rolled-up banner. He pauses for a moment in front of a parapet. There is a subjective shot of what he sees: an officer leaning over a smiling woman who is holding a parasol with one hand and gesticulating with the other. This image is intended to suggest the self-indulgence, even deca-

dence of the bourgeoisie. The officer rises and holds the young man as women hit and stab the Bolshevik with their parasols. Very brief, hectic shots of the murderous women are contrasted to relatively lengthy ones of the officer's lady smiling, her hand at her chin, twirling her parasol. What Eisenstein calls the *"emotional sound* of the piece . . . its dominant"[28] in tonal montage is, in this case, that of violence and hatred.

In this scene, as throughout the film, the director utilizes typage as an instrument of propaganda. The young Bolshevik has honest, virile good looks. The officer has crude features, and his lady friend appears sinister, even witchlike, with her heavy makeup, long nose, and sneering mouth. The matronly maenads are fat, and their faces are distorted with viciousness.

The opening of the Neva Bridge is deservedly one of the most famous passages in *October,* less complex and lengthy but in its own way as striking as

(a)

(b)

(c)

(d)

(e)

(f)

(g)

(h)

the "Odessa Steps" footage in *The Battleship Potemkin*. The bridges are ordered by the authorities to be lifted after the attack on the demonstrators. There are three shots from three different angles and distances of the body of a woman, face down, with her long hair spread out in front of her, at the center of the bridge. Crosscutting begins between the surface of the Neva Bridge and the girders below slowly rising. Bodies lie on the top of the drawbridge as it begins to separate. Two more shots follow of the woman, who is at the edge of the line of separation. People run by from right to left, some still carrying banners as they attempt to escape from the center of the city to their own districts across the river [Figure 5.12(a)]. Following are shots of the woman first from one side and then from the other of the two segments of the bridge. The rising girders appear again [Figure 5.12(b)]. Back to the body of the woman, now entirely on one side [Figure 5.12(c)]. A shot of running feet on the surface of the bridge. A view of a portion of the city from under the bridge. A carriage caught on a pole is on the edge of the left rising segment of the bridge [Figure 5.12(d)]. Two more lengthy shots of the carriage contrast with the previous brief ones. A low-angle shot looking up at the separated portions of the drawbridge; the carcass of a white horse dangling from the carriage is hanging in the air [Figure 5.12(e)]. Another view appears of the separate halves of the bridge. Again we see the horse from below, now in the upper right corner of the frame, followed by shots of the carriage and of the girders. There is an intercut of a scupture with the elongated eyes and stolid features of an Egyptian diety, representing an implacable authority. One side of the bridge, almost horizontal, fills the screen; at the very edge is a minute figure. Another, closer view of the imperious stone face [Figure 5.12(f)]. Back to the previous shot of the bridge. The small figure falls; we realize it is the body of the woman [Figure 5.12(g)]. In succession are shots of the carriage, the white horse, the bridge girders, and the horse dropping. The camera tilts down (this is the first camera movement in the

scene) to follow the animal as it splashes into the water. Next presented are the underside of the structure, a long shot of the separated portions of the drawbridge [Figure 5.12(h)], and a final shot of the girders —now still.

The scene can serve as a touchstone of Eisenstein's genius. In 105 seconds he joined together 42 shots to create a dynamic montage that operates simultaneously on the narrative, intellectual, and emotional levels. There is an overall contrast between the inexorable rising of the bridge (one-third of the shots from below) and the horrifying events on the top. The general is represented by people running; the specific, by the body of the woman, the carriage, and the carcass of the white horse. Four major types of montage are included: rhythmic, tonal, overtonal, and intellectual (the last emerging from the two shots of the statue). Here is dynamic montage at its most intense and most effective.

After a scene of members of the First Machine Gun Regiment, which sided with the workers, as prisoners, Kerensky's entering the Winter Palace is an opportunity for Eisenstein to satirize the new head of the provisional government through intellectual montage. After two preliminary shots of Kerensky and his aides marching through the halls of the palace (first away from and then toward the camera), there is an insert title: "The Dictator." The stages of his climb to fame are indicated by the titles "The Commander-in-chief," "The Minister of the Army and Navy," and "The Prime Minister." In between these titles are shots of Kerensky walking up a staircase, but in each case it is the same staircase and the same action, photographed from various angles at the same pace. With each political advance, he simply proceeds up the same steps. The satirical intent of the director is obvious.

Following a meeting with the obsequious servants of the former czar, Kerensky stands in front of the doors to the private apartments of the deposed emperor, and Eisenstein lets loose another satirical shaft. There are inserts of a metal peacock displaying its feathers as it twirls around.

A series of images of the imprisoned Bolsheviks are shown. Back to Kerensky in a luxurious apartment. His first act in office is to restore the death penalty for

**FIGURE 5.12**

*October.* Images from the magnificent sequence of the opening of the Neva bridge.

desertion, underscoring the threat he represents to the prisoners. He then climbs a narrow flight of stairs within the apartment. What is on the ambitious politician's mind as Eisenstein portrays him is indicated by images of a statuette of Napoleon, toy soldiers dressed in nineteenth-century uniforms, and glasses bearing the imperial seal. The director is relentless in emphasizing that the head of the provisional government is an enemy of the Revolution. We see Kerensky seated at a table putting together a liqueur bottle consisting of four sections and placing on it a top in the shape of the imperial crown.

Another threat to the Revolution materializes. A leader of the conservative faction marches against Petrograd with an army comprised chiefly of the "Wild Division"—Tartar regiments from eastern Russia. Kornilov, a general of the old imperial army, is shown literally as a man on horseback. He proclaims himself a defender of "God and country." The appeal to religion is ridiculed by Eisenstein through intellectual montage as nothing more than another form of authoritative oppression of the people. A series of shots of religious icons are presented. They range from primitive fetishes to Buddhas. Lit from below, these figures look grotesque and frightening. (This footage has been eliminated from practically all prints of *October* available for rental in the United States.)

The true intention of Kornilov is suggested by a repeat of the shot of him on horseback [Figure 5.13(a)], followed by a statue of Napoleon on horseback [Figure 5.13(b)]. Kerensky is again also associated with the French emperor. The two "Napoleons" are in conflict, and the possibility of one's destroying the other is indicated by the director in another bold use of intellectual montage. One of Kornilov's tanks rises high up on a hill. Cut to the statuette of Napoleon in the Winter Palace. The tank moves down; the statuette is shown in pieces.

The general's army advances, represented by shots of tanks, trains, and armored trucks. The Petrograd workers join the soldiers in defending the city. They appear in a series of images in which rhythmic, tonal, and overtonal montage coalesce. In each shot, soldiers and workers are set against a black background as they pull artillery. Personifying the spirit of

## FIGURE 5.13

*October.* By juxtaposing a shot of Kornilov with that of a statue of Napoleon, the director suggests without words the Napoleonic ambitions of the general.

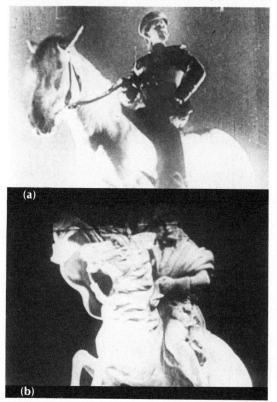

(a)

(b)

the Revolution, they are leaning forward against a wind that blows back their clothes as they move determinedly from right to left in the frame. Interspersed are shots of the prisoners being freed and armed as handbills are prepared for circulation.

Having dealt with the general situation, Eisenstein, in keeping with his typical approach, next focuses on a specific incident. A civilian and a soldier from Petrograd, both armed with handbills, enter a camp of Kornilov's Tartar soldiers. At first they are met with distrust; however, an argument for bread, peace, land, and brotherhood is effective. The scene ends with the first divertissement in the film: The Tartars and the Bolshevik soldier dance together.

Rather anticlimactically in the American version of the film, the defeat of Kornilov is reported in an insert title. Now begin what Eisenstein designated as acts 3 and 4 in his original screenplay.[29] For most of the remainder of the film, there is crosscutting between three locations in Petrograd. At the Winter Palace, the provisional government has its offices and makes its final stand. Outside the palace and in the streets of the central portion of the city, the Bolsheviks have gathered their military strength. The Smolny was an eighteenth-century convent turned into a factory; it is the building used as an assembly hall for the Second Congress of the Soviets. Repeated shifting from one location to another can be confusing to a non-Russian viewer, and this portion of the epic lacks the unity of the first half.

The proletariat of Petrograd organizes itself into the Red Guard. Lenin is shown at a meeting of the Bolshevik Central Committee planning strategy for the congress that will begin on October 25. It is decided that power must be in their hands if they are to overthrow the provisional government and take its place. Approval of this decision by the people is indicated by impressive shots. From a very high angle, the camera views a mass of heads; at the same moment, they turn and look toward the camera. Following this are shots of a mass of rifles waving in the air.

The cruiser *Aurora,* its crew sympathetic to the Bolsheviks, sails up the Neva, anchoring within firing distance of the Winter Palace. The provisional government panics and attempts once again to lift the bridges. Marines from the *Aurora,* however, take control of the bridges so that the workers in the suburbs can once again enter the center of Petrograd. Kerensky calls on the Cossacks for help. Their neutrality is epitomized by the soldier who tells Kerensky on the telephone that the Cossacks are mounting while we see the horses still in their stalls. After the minister of war hangs up the telephone, there are repeated shots of the rear ends of the horses, an unsubtle expression of Eisenstein's view of Kerensky.

The head of the provisional government enters a car with his entourage and proclaims that he is going in search of loyal troops. He then flees, and the immense gates of the Winter Palace close behind him.

Young military cadets enter the Winter Palace to defend it. Joining them is the female "Battalion of Death." There is a contrast between the women soldiers, formidable in battle dress as they march, and a scene, introduced by a brassiere hanging from a holder for billiard sticks, of them undressing and preparing to sleep on the billiard table of Czar Nicholas II.

Delegates arrive at the Smolny for the Congress of the Soviets. At one point there is a scene of Lenin disguised in bandages and dark glasses. The reason for the disguise is that since the July demonstration the leader of the Bolsheviks has been branded an outlaw by the government. Meanwhile, officials of the provisional government meet in the Winter Palace without their chief, represented by an empty chair. Intercut are three shots of Kerensky in his car. One of them includes a view of a small American flag attached to the front of automobile, indicating that it was supplied by the American embassy.

At the Smolny, the congress begins its deliberations. A few faces in the crowd are featured; they will appear repeatedly. The Military Revolutionary Committee is also active. There is crosscutting between close-ups of a map of the city on which crayon marks reveal the deployment of the Red Guard, shots of the *Aurora,* marines from the cruiser landing, troops guarding bridges and buildings, and the Winter Palace being surrounded.

In the election of the Central Executive Committee of the Soviets, the Bolsheviks win over the Mensheviks and the Socialist Revolutionary Bloc, both defenders of the provisional government. At the palace, an ultimatum demanding surrender is sent by two soldiers under a flag of truce, with 20 minutes allowed for consideration. As a device for building suspense, shots of clocks appear periodically. It is now 11:30. At this point, a youngster crawls out from under the legs of a soldier to watch what is happening. This representative of the next generation of Bolsheviks reappears at significant moments in the action that follows.

A Menshevik at the congress attacks the Bolsheviks and pleads for support. An old man sits asleep; this is a human reaction to the speech. Eisenstein then goes a step further and employs intellectual montage. After a shot of the speaker are ones of harps being played. Intercut of the old man rubbing his ear. Rows of harps with fingers flitting over them are superimposed on each other. The old man places his fur hat over his ear. The harps are followed by low-angle shots of a statue of an angel carrying a cross. Another anti-Bolshevik speaks. Now there appears a hand languidly playing a guitar. Eisenstein himself recognized that his attempt to portray the foes of Bolshevism as sentimentalists had gone awry. Years later he described this montage as "lifeless literary symbolism and stylistic mannerism."[30]

Back to the Winter Palace, where some troops of the "Battalion of Death" surrender. Eisenstein dramatizes by the use of visual synecdoche the conflict felt by these women. One of them, a blonde, sits dejectedly staring into space. She looks up at the statue against whose pedestal she is leaning. It is Rodin's *The Kiss.* There is cutting back and forth between the two stone figures and the face of the woman. The director goes no further, but the significance of the scene is made clear by the previous shot of a female soldier surrendering.

Eisenstein was not a humorless man. It is reported that at a party in Hollywood someone asked him if Russians ever laughed. His reply was, "They will when I describe this party." Yet humor appears infrequently in his films. The next scene is the only one in *October* that borders on the comic. The provisional government's Committee on Safety of the Country and the Revolution, led by the major of Petrograd, attempts to cross a bridge and enter the Winter Palace. They are stopped by a giant marine. Most of the shots of the soldier are from a low angle and those of the ancient citizens, ridiculous in their outrage, from a high angle. They quickly retreat when the marine makes a threatening gesture. At the same time, three soldiers surreptitiously enter the palace by way of the cellar. A clock indicates the time is 11:50. Cut to Cossacks in the main court, persuaded by a Bolshevik soldier to maintain their neutrality.

At the congress, moderates still attempt to discourage the Bolsheviks. While the speaker is being shouted down, a messenger arrives to announce that the Twelfth Army is with the radicals. An important element of this army is a battalion of cyclists. Shots of hands applauding at Smolny are alternated with those of spinning bicycle wheels and soldiers waving their

rifles. The congress will no longer appear on the screen until the end of the film so that uninterrupted attention can be paid to the crucial events at the Winter Palace.

Activity at the headquarters of the Red Guard is intensified, signified by feet rushing in and out through the door to its office. The time is now 11:55. The three soldiers who had entered the palace through the cellar are on a balcony overlooking a room in which an official of the provisional government is haranguing cadets who are defending the main council room and is declaring that the ultimatum will be rejected. At 12:00 no reply to the ultimatum has been sent.

A flag goes up the main mast of the *Aurora,* and the ship opens fire on the Winter Palace. The soldiers on the balcony inside throw grenades. Crystal chandeliers tremble from the explosions. A series of images of artillery being loaded and fired is intercut with insert titles: "For peace—," "for bread," "for land."

There are high-angle shots of the courtyard before the gates of the palace as a swarm of Red Guard soldiers race forward (Figure 5.14). A defender fires a machine gun. These shots, resembling those of the machine gunner firing into the crowd during the July demonstration, remind us that the Red Guard has much to avenge.

---

**FIGURE 5.14**

*October.* Eisenstein's genius in visually orchestrating crowd scenes is demonstrated in the attack of Red Guard soldiers on the Winter Palace.

The first barricades are overrun. As always, Eisenstein does not neglect the individual. There are three shots of a wounded soldier waving his comrades on before collapsing. The main gate is reached. As an attacker climbs it, there is a close-up of his foot stepping on the royal crown that is part of the decoration of the gate. The last barrier is passed. The soldiers run through the halls of the palace. They rush up the stairs that Kerensky climbed at the beginning of the film. The battle rages even in the wine cellars and private rooms. A marine stares at the luxury of one of the bedrooms. Cases of military medals are opened, and one of the soldiers cries, "Is this what we fought for?" More shots of the battle.

The next incident was probably prompted by reports that circulated throughout the Western world of the vandalism of the Bolsheviks as they took over palaces and homes. Surrendering cadets, defenders of the provisional government, are searched and found to have stolen silverware and other objects. Meanwhile, the last line of defense, the cadets outside the council room of the government, are overcome. Cut to the wine cellars, where citizens of Petrograd, especially old women, are prevented from stealing bottles by members of the Red Guard and the marines. In a fury of resentment against these tokens of luxury, the soldiers smash the bottles. Intercut are shots of the youngster, who has appeared repeatedly since the ultimatum was delivered to the palace, waving his hat with joy as he alternately stands and sits on a throne. The rhythmic montage (a soldier swinging a rifle over his right shoulder, the boy swinging his hat over his right shoulder) suggests that even though they are in different areas of the palace, the youngster is applauding the actions of the soldiers.

The council of the provisional government prepares to meet the invaders. Their authority, however, is smashed; the doors of the council room are broken down. The provisional government is declared deposed by an ardent, bespectacled young man we have seen before as a leader of the Military Revolutionary Committee. A clock indicates 2:07 A.M. Other clocks fill the screen, showing different times in different areas of Russia. Brief shots follow: the council room again, lights going on in Petrograd, a collection of clocks recording the momentous moment in different parts of the world, the youngster asleep on a throne, spinning clocks, applauding hands.

We are back in Smolny. An insert card with capital letters spells "LENIN!" The leader of the revolution appears on the podium. The final shot is of Lenin speaking.

There are three major problems Eisenstein had to deal with in creating an epic of the people determining their future in a crucial moment of history, and his success in solving each one is debatable. First, there is the insistence in Eisenstein's writings that a dramatic structure can be effective with the proletariat or farmers collectively as a hero. With the exception of *Strike,* no other completed film by the director tests this theory as rigorously as *October.* The main character of this drama is Kerensky, a caricatured villain. The counterbalancing positive personality should have been Lenin, but he appears as no more than a symbol of a leader of the Revolution. Many viewers find this lack of concrete, developed characters a weakness of the film.

The second difficulty Eisenstein had to contend with was the complexity of what happened in Petrograd during the summer and fall of 1917. There is a diffuseness to the plot of *October* not to be found in his other films. He was forced to depend a great deal on explanatory title cards and crosscutting. This element of incoherence is intensified in the truncated American version of the film.

Finally, the director made more extensive use in *October* than in any of his other works of intellectual montage in the service of what he admitted were "purely intellectual aims."[31] These effects are striking, even, as in the case of the Menshevik speaker and images of harps being played, when somewhat strained. The price Eisenstein paid for this intellectual brilliance was to give *October* a quality of dryness, of a type of manipulation of the components of cinema that often appeals more to the minds of viewers than to their feelings.

Whatever its weaknesses, *October* remains a remarkable achievement. The parts may be more impressive than the whole; however, many of those parts are magnificent.

## NEOREALISM

### The Bicycle Thief
### (Ladri di Biciclette)

*[The Bicycle Thief] is one of the first examples of pure cinema. No more actors, no more story, no more sets, which is to say that in the perfect aesthetic illusion of reality there is no more cinema.*
André Bazin, 1949.[32]

### CAST

*Lamberto Maggiorani (Antonio Ricci), Enzo Staiola (Bruno Ricci), Lianella Carell (Maria Ricci), Elena Altieri (Signora Santona, a clairvoyant), Gino Saltamerenda (Biaocco), and others.*

### CREDITS

*Director and Producer—Vittorio De Sica, Screenwriters—Cesare Zavattini, Oreste Biancoli, Suso Cecchi d'Amico, Adolfo Franci, and De Sica (from a novel by Luigi Bartolini), Director of Photography—Carlo Montuori, Editor—Eraldo da Roma, Music—Alessandro Cicognini, Art Director—Antonino Traverso, and others.*

1949/Produzioni De Sica
Black & White/90 minutes

### BACKGROUND

Vittorio De Sica (1901–1974) was one of the three principal founders of the school of Neorealism in postwar Italian cinema. Roberto Rossellini and Luchino Visconti earned the respect of audiences for their uncompromising portrayals of ordinary individuals in real situations, their artistry, and their belief that cinema, if honest and passionate, could affect people's consciences. It was De Sica, however, who touched the hearts of viewers and compelled them through his obvious sincerity and compassion to empathize with the victims of human selfishness and governmental indifference. André Bazin writes: "To explain De Sica, we must go back to the source of his art, namely to his tenderness, his love . . . for his characters."[33]

De Sica's early career as an actor gave little evidence that he would eventually develop into a significant film director. He made his professional stage debut in 1922. A handsome, charming, intelligent young man, he quickly became a popular theater actor in comedies and musicals. By the thirties, he also was a romantic lead in the type of escapist films favored by the fascist government.

In 1940 he had an opportunity to direct a motion picture. His first important work was *The Children Are Watching Us (I Bambini ci Guardino,* 1943). This drama marked his first collaboration with screenwriter Cesare Zavattini, an association that was to last until De Sica's death. The film that established the director's international reputation was *Shoeshine (Sciuscià,* 1946). It is a poignant story of two adolescents in Nazi-occupied Rome whose intimate friendship is converted into antagonism by their stay in a reformatory to the point where one is responsible for the death of the other. In *Shoeshine* emerges the major theme of practically all of De Sica's finest works: the difficulty of innocent people surviving in a morally corrupt, materialistic world.

Three years later the director released *The Bicycle Thief,* followed quickly by the delightful fantasy *Miracle in Milan (Miracolo a Milano,* 1950). Totò, a complete naïf, is helped by the spirit of the eccentric old lady who brought him up in resisting the efforts of a villainous businessman to take over a shantytown located on an oil field. For all its humor and imaginativeness, the film is a provocative satire on the untrammeled ruthlessness of businesses and the indifference of the state to the plight of the poor.

In *Umberto D* (1952), the title character is an aged pensioner whose only satisfactions in life are his dog, his furnished room, and the friendship of a servant girl. Although there are moments of sentimentality, particularly in the last sequence, the film is an expressive portrayal of an old man struggling to preserve his self-respect in a society that evades its responsibilities to the aged.

*Umberto D* ended De Sica's quartet of memorable films of social criticism cast in the mode (even in the case of the fantasy) of Neorealism. These films were acclaimed in foreign countries, but their themes struck too close to home in Italy. After *Shoeshine,* the director had to finance his three other Neorealistic films to a large extent himself. Heavily in debt, De Sica returned to acting and made compromises in his directing during the remainder of the 1950s. He acted in (and sometimes produced) more than three dozen films during this decade. The majority were cinematic fluff, such as *Bread, Love, and Dreams;* however, in at least one work, Rossellini's *Il Generale della Rovere*

(1959), he proved that he was as accomplished an actor in dramatic works as in comedies. He directed only three films during the fifties, each in a different style.

*Stazione Termini* (reedited and retitled *Indiscretion of an American Wife* for the U.S. market, 1953), a lugubrious story, has American stars (including Jennifer Jones and Montgomery Clift) and was backed by Hollywood money. *Il Tetto* (1955) is a slight, charming film with a Neorealistic patina. Though an obvious bid for commercial success, *The Gold of Naples* (*L'Oro di Napoli*, 1954) is a very enjoyable and astute description of lower-class life in Naples and established Sophia Loren as a leading Italian comedienne.

In 1960 De Sica was ready to return to serious filmmaking—with an important difference. He now depended predominantly on stars, studio production facilities and crews, and screenplays adapted from popular literary works. Although the director is usually still as honest in underscoring man's inhumanity to man as he was in his early motion pictures, these films of the sixties lack the spontaneity, immediacy, and rough-hewn but forceful style of Neorealism. It is significant how often war rather than social injustice is the chief oppressive force.

*Two Women* (*La Ciociara*, 1960) is his most important work of the 1960s, though the lesser-known *The Last Judgment* (*Il Giudizio Universale*, 1961) and *The Boom* (*Il Boom*, 1963) are bolder, more subtle films. Adapted from Alberto Moravia's novel of the same title, *Two Women* depicts the experiences of a mother and daughter who near the end of the war leave Rome for the countryside to escape the bombardments and then return to the capital. It was made in Cinemascope and starred Sophia Loren (as the mother, a role that won her an Oscar for Best Actress), Eleanora Brown (the daughter), Jean-Paul Belmondo, and Raf Vallone. Though at moments melodramatic (especially in a climactic rape sequence), contrived, and sentimental, it is overall a powerful drama with effectively realistic scenes of country life in Italy during the war.

*The Condemned of Altona* (*I Sequestrati di Altona*, 1962) is also adapted from an eminent literary work (a Jean-Paul Sartre play). In this case, the material was evidently uncongenial to De Sica's sensibilities, and as a consequence it is a pretentious, meandering, confusing film. On the other hand, *Marriage, Italian Style* (*Matrimonio all 'Italiana*, 1964) is another pleasurable comedy. The director's other films of the sixties are best ignored.

De Sica began the seventies, as he had the sixties, with an outstanding film. *The Garden of the Finzi-Continis* (*Il Giardino dei Finzi-Contini*, 1971) is an adaptation of Giorgio Bassani's novel on the experiences of two wealthy Jewish families in Ferrara on the eve of World War II. The director's lyric use of color and graceful camera-editing dynamics make the film his most visually striking work. On the other hand, a nostalgia for the delicate, self-indulgent life-style of the very wealthy and the discursiveness of some of the sequences are atypical of De Sica's style. It is noteworthy that this was De Sica's first major film for which Zavattini did not write the screenplay.

The director made a couple of inconsequential movies before his final important work. *Brief Vacation* (*Una Breve Vacanza*, 1973) tells of a young woman, encumbered with a dependent husband and family, who is forced to spend time at a tuberculosis sanitarium. She falls in love with a sympathetic doctor but finally returns to her responsibilities. Social criticism is muted; however, the film is a return for De Sica to his earlier unpretentious, Neorealistic approach. It is a fitting swan song for the most compassionate of Italian directors. The director was working on *The Voyage* (*Il Viaggio*, 1974) when he died.

De Sica's style has often been underrated because it is so unobtrusive. The development of a plot is straightforward, without flashbacks or crosscutting; the composition of shots is rarely striking; the point of view is predominantly objective; there are few visual symbols; background music and natural sounds are unexceptional; lighting is entirely natural, without artificial effects; settings, props, and costumes are suitable to the tone, usually bland and even dreary, of a specific film. What a perceptive viewer does notice is the care with which the *mise-en-scène* approach is used and the masterfulness with which nonprofessional actors are directed. It takes a certain type of genius to make the camera so convincingly appear to be recording reality rather than re-creating it.

This summary of the director's style is applicable to his Neorealistic works. When he became more conventional, as in *The Garden of the Finzi-Continis* or *Two Women,* he proved that he could manipulate the artificialities of his medium as efficiently as any Hollywood craftsman. On the other hand, the further he moved away from capturing reality with a warm, intense, yet objective eye, the less distinctive became his work.

It is unfair to discuss De Sica's oeuvre without giving due credit to Cesare Zavattini (1902–). Practically all of the director's 22 films from 1943 to 1969 were based on screenplays written by Zavattini. The only important exception is *The Garden of the Finzi-Continis.* This collaboration between director and screenwriter is one of the most fruitful in the history of cinema, comparable to that between F. W. Murnau and Carl Mayer, Marcel Carné and Jacques Prévert, and Frank Capra and Robert Riskin.

The screenwriter worked with other directors, most notably Alessandro Blasetti (for example, *Four Steps in the Clouds,* 1942), Giuseppe De Santis (*The Tragic Hunt,* 1947, and *Roma, Ore 11,* 1951), and Visconti (*Bellissima,* 1951). He also functioned as the principal theorist of Neorealism, much as Carl Mayer did for Expressionism and the *Kammerspielfilme.* In one of his most influential statements, he advocated the "moral responsibility" of cinema and, in his view, the most important subject matter of the medium:

I want to meet the real protagonist of everyday life . . . Neorealism has perceived that the most irreplaceable experience comes from things happening under our own eyes from material necessity. . . . We must identify ourselves with what we are.[34]

With the passing of Neorealism as a vital movement in the early fifties, Zavattini's approach fell into disfavor. He had to content himself with collaborating whenever possible with De Sica, writing commercial scripts, and devoting himself to painting. Insights into the writer's personality and ideas can be gleaned from his fascinating book, *Sequences from a Cinematic Life.*

The indifference of Italian moviegoers and the opposition of the government to *Shoeshine* made it difficult for De Sica to finance *The Bicycle Thief.*

There were some opportunities, but each would have required major compromises. One offer is amusing in retrospect but probably was not at the time to a desperate director who, after an international success, had to wait 3 years before making his next film. An American producer, according to De Sica, offered him "millions" on the sole condition that Cary Grant play the part of the worker.[35] In the end, De Sica had to produce and to a large degree finance *The Bicycle Thief* himself. He stuck to his principles by using only nonprofessional actors and shooting entirely on location.

The result was again ignored or condemned by Italian audiences and critics but proclaimed everywhere else as a masterpiece. In the United States (where the film's title was translated as *The Bicycle Thief* instead of the more accurate and appropriate *The Bicycle Thieves*), it was chosen Best Foreign Film for 1949 by the New York Film Critics, given a special Oscar at the Academy Awards ceremonies, and named Best Picture (and De Sica Best Director) by the National Board of Review. Not surprising in light of the attitude of the Italian government toward the film, it received no awards at either the Venice or Cannes Film Festival. Perhaps the most prestigious accolade given to *The Bicycle Thief* was its ranking in the *Sight and Sound* 1952 survey of critics' choices of the 10 best films of all time: It was ranked number one. In 1962 it dropped to sixth place, and it did not appear on the list at all in 1972. Rather than drawing cynical conclusions about the amorphous standards by which motion pictures are evaluated and the validity of any ranking at any time of "best" films, it would be kinder to point to the results of the 1952 *Sight and Sound* survey as an indication of the tremendous impression *The Bicycle Thief* made on critics as well as general audiences when it was first released.

### PLOT SUMMARY

In 1946, after months of being out of work, Antonio Ricci, who lives with his family on the outskirts of Rome, is finally offered a job as a poster hanger. Although the position requires a bicycle and he has pawned his own, he accepts.

When he tells his wife Maria about his dilemma, she insists that they pawn their bed sheets. At a municipal pawnshop, they exchange the sheets for their bicycle. The two then proceed to the poster office, where the job is confirmed and Antonio is told to report in the morning. On their way home, Maria asks that they make a stop for a moment to pay 50 lire to Signora Santona, a fortune-teller who prophesied that Antonio would find a job. Antonio gently chides his wife for her gullibility.

It is 6:30 the next morning. Bruno Ricci, a vivacious youngster of about 10, is cleaning his father's bike. Antonio drops Bruno off at a gas station where the boy works and rides away.

A colleague shows Antonio how to put up a poster, then leaves him. As he is awkwardly working, a young man jumps on the bicycle leaning against a wall and rides off on it. An accomplice blocks Antonio as he runs after the thief, and another misdirects the desperate workman and a helpful taxi driver. The thief escapes.

Antonio reports the theft at a police station but receives little help or encouragement. That evening he enters the party headquarters in search of his friend Biaocco, a sanitation worker, who suggests that the next day they search the markets for the bicycle.

Early Sunday morning, Antonio, Bruno, Biaocco, and two other sanitation workers go through the market on Piazza Vittorio. Father and son are next driven to another market at Porta Portese. It is raining when they arrive, and the two find shelter at the side of a building. They are joined by a group of Austrian priests. As the rain stops, Antonio sees the thief talking to an old man. When the fellow again escapes, the two corner the old man on a bridge. He refuses to help them. Father and son follow him into a church that offers food to the poor. During mass, Antonio permits the old man to go for food, and the man slips away.

Outside the church, Bruno makes a remark critical of his father. Antonio loses his temper and slaps the boy. He commands his son to wait at a nearby bridge while he continues to search for the old man. A few minutes later he hears cries that someone is drowning. A terrified Antonio runs back shouting his son's name. He is relieved when he finds Bruno sitting on the steps of the bridge.

In an attempt at reconciliation, he takes his son into a restaurant but is unable to eat. In desperation,

he and Bruno visit the fortune-teller; however, she cannot help them. As they leave Signora Santona's apartment, the thief once again appears. Antonio pursues him into a brothel and drags him out into the street. A crowd of the thief's neighbors surround Antonio and threaten him. Bruno, meanwhile, has gone for a policeman. The thief has or feigns an epileptic seizure. Antonio insists on searching the young man's apartment but can find nothing. The policeman explains that there is really no case against the suspect. Antonio, frustrated and outraged, abruptly leaves, followed by his son.

The two wait for a bus outside a stadium. Antonio spies a bicycle leaning against a wall on an empty street. He directs his son to go home, but Bruno misses the bus. The youngster thus witnesses his father attempting to steal the bicycle and being caught by a crowd. The owner of the bike decides not to bring Antonio to the police station when he sees the tearful Bruno clinging to his father's leg. As father and son walk away, Antonio begins to sob. Bruno grasps his father's hand, and the two disappear into the crowd leaving the stadium.

───────────

ANALYSIS

The setting of *The Bicycle Thief* is Rome soon after the end of World War II. Unemployment is rampant, poverty is widespread, and black markets are flourishing. Antonio Ricci must support himself, his wife, and two children on the insufficient sum he receives from the state; even his older son, Bruno, about 10 years of age, works at a gas station. He is a member of a party, probably Communist, and has a friend, Biaocco, who is a sanitation worker.

That is all we know—or really need to know—about Antonio's past and present. He is typical of thousands of Italian workers at the time, yet emerges in the film as an individual. His character is not complex: a devoted family man, intelligent, responsible, with an innate dignity. Taking care of his family appears to be his only ambition. In short, he is an admirable person, and it is easy to understand why during most of the film his son idolizes him.

Antonio's relationship with his wife Maria is intimate and warm. Although Maria accepts the burdens of poverty, she can be rebellious and has a will of her own. When she prepares to wash the bed sheets before pawning them, she angrily kicks a pail of water; she tells her husband to shut up when he bewails his fate; she knows Antonio does not believe in the clairvoyant, yet she insists on paying the woman. This last incident is significant because it demonstrates not so much her gullibility, encouraged by frustration, but her honesty. The repeated evidence of the integrity of the Ricci family emphasizes how desperate Antonio must be before he can bring himself to steal. Mrs. Ricci appears physically only at the beginning of the film, but her presence is felt throughout as an indestructible source of love and consolation. For this reason, Antonio suffers all the more, even when he is not really responsible, for failing her.

It is conceivable that the major theme of *The Bicycle Thief*—the demoralizing effects of poverty and an indifferent society on the character of a human being—could have emerged from the motion picture without the son Bruno. What would have been lost, however, is the concrete and poignant expression of that theme. Not only is the boy a delightful person in himself, a welcome source of humor in a series of bleak events, but he also plays an important role in our understanding of what is happening to Antonio. The workman is a taciturn individual, so without Bruno we could only guess at his emotions. Antonio's statements and actions in response to his son make us aware, obliquely but definitely, of what he is feeling.

Bruno grew up during the hard times of the war, and we can assume that from those experiences he developed the traits of independence and aggressiveness he demonstrates throughout the film. He holds a full-time job at a gas station; he chides his father for not complaining when a bicycle pedal was dented in the municipal pawnshop; he goes off on his own in pursuing the old man; he pulls his father to the front of the group in the fortune-teller's room; when the thief is caught, he brings a policeman on his own initiative. He reminds us in many respects of two boys in another film directed by De Sica. Giuseppe and Pasquale in *Shoeshine* are also confident and shrewd, street-wise; however, they turn to crime and a path that leads to betrayal and death. Bruno is the other side of the coin: a child of war too, but brought up in

a family that cherishes him and teaches him the values of honesty and independence. Furthermore, he has an ideal in his father.

The boy goes through three stages in his attitude toward his father. In the first, his admiration is unqualified. During the first scene in which Bruno appears, the boy imitates his father. Uncritically and unquestioningly he follows his father's directives as they search for the stolen bicycle. A new stage begins when for the first time the boy doubts his father's wisdom. The old man has escaped from them in the church, and Bruno remarks that his father shouldn't have allowed the man to go for food and thus slip away. Later, when the thief is cornered, we sense that Bruno cannot understand why his father does not press charges against the young man. The final stage is when Bruno witnesses his father stealing the bicycle and being humiliated. From this devastating experience and others that Sunday, the boy has become a sadder but more mature, more realistic person. He may idealize his father less, but perhaps he has learned to love the man more.

Bruno's growing up and the countertheme of Antonio's fall are caused by forces beyond their control. These forces might be called fate. This would be the justification of victims who passively endure adversity or philosophically question what has happened to them as they sit upon dung heaps. De Sica and Zavattini will have none of this, but they are aware that it is tempting for a poor person to blame fate or bad luck for his suffering. So they bring in the clairvoyant while making clear that she is a fraud. That Antonio, a disbeliever, should turn to her for a miracle indicates how completely helpless he feels. And he is quickly disillusioned by the fortune-teller's response. In the vision of reality presented in the motion pictures of De Sica and Zavattini, miracles only occur in Milan in the context of a fable.

The film is based on the assumption that the forces that oppress Antonio are social in origin. A Marxist critical approach, therefore, can be useful in revealing class conflicts if a critic is aware that this perspective need not be in the service of an advocacy of communism. The system—the self-serving bureaucracies it engenders, abetted by the indifference and hypocrisy of its citizens—drives a predominantly good but poor man to steal. The overt purpose of *The Bicycle Thief* is social criticism without a political orientation: The system is wrong, but no alternative is supported, such as revolution, communism, socialism, or a new form of democracy. The closest to any statement of political aims is the assertion by the speaker at party headquarters of the need for public building programs. What the filmmakers have done in this respect, surely a valid function of art, is to expose the problems of men like Antonio Ricci in all their human dimensions without offering concrete solutions.

The plot of *The Bicycle Thief* develops as a series of incidents that concurrently reveal the relationships within the Ricci family and the world in which they live, particularly the forces that frustrate their desire to survive with self-respect. The first quarter of the film leads up to the theft of the bicycle. In the initial scene we are presented with the sad spectacle of healthy men eager to work but unable to find jobs. How can they live? One answer is dramatized by solely visual means when Antonio and Maria go to the municipal pawnshop with their bed sheets to obtain money to redeem the bicycle. In a subjective shot from Antonio's point of view, we see long lines of stored bicycles, then a man climbing up a ladder with their sheets. The camera tilts to reveal floor-to-ceiling shelves stuffed with pawned sheets.

The remainder of the film dramatizes the ramifications for the family of the theft of the bicycle. It is an accident that the thieves spot Antonio's bicycle, for he has not been careless. He had no choice but to leave it against the wall while putting up the poster, and earlier, when he joined his wife at the clairvoyant's apartment, he had asked boys to watch it. What is no accident is the indifference of passersby as he pursues the thief.

At the police station, a description and the number of the bicycle are taken, and a signature is added to the report: A bureaucratic system has fulfilled itself by replacing a human problem with a sheet of paper. The victim is now on his own. If *The Bicycle Thief* were a work of doctrinaire, antiestablishment propaganda, the police would be portrayed as callous brutes

(as Eisenstein and Godard do in their films). De Sica and Zavattini are too realistic for such clichés. The official may be abrupt and unsympathetic, but logically there is little that the police can do, for it is hardly feasible for them to check every bicycle in Rome. Values are relative. For Antonio, the loss of his bicycle is almost a matter of life and death; for the official, as suggested by his remark to the newspaper reporter, it is a minor crime.

At party headquarters, another form of social organization is operating, and it too is ineffectual in helping Antonio. Only through a human one-to-one relationship—friendship, an extension of the family—does he obtain sympathy and practical assistance. The speaker obviously means well in advocating massive public building programs, but he is talking about the problematic future. As with the police station scene, De Sica and Zavattini do not exaggerate or propagandize.

The search for the bicycle begins the next day, a Sunday, at a market. The bins of bicycle parts and rows of frames indicate the enormousness of the task Antonio and his friends have set themselves. It is also a depressing sign of the times that, as is evident from the defensiveness of the shopkeeper painting a frame, most of the bicycles were probably stolen.

On the way to another market, it begins to rain; even nature is working against poor Antonio. He and Bruno run from the sanitation truck to the shelter of a wall. There the youngster looks up with bewilderment at the Austrian priests next to him as they chatter in their own language. André Bazin says of the incident that "it would be difficult to create a more *objectively* anticlerical scene."[36] Perhaps the critic is reading more into the scene than he is drawing out, but one sees his point: The complacent, comfortable mien of those priests is offensive when they are physically juxtaposed against the anguished Antonio.

The thief is recognized as he talks to an old man, but then escapes again. Antonio and Bruno now follow the old man into a church, where an Italian Salvation Army unit is set up. The well-dressed, obviously well-off people who run this operation surely mean well. What they cannot disguise, however, is the self-satisfaction they derive in being charitable. In this society, duty is a substitute for compassion, just as the law replaces justice with legality. The resentment of the filmmakers toward the church and complacent Christians is more explicit, but no more effective, than the scene with the Austrian priests.

No one is allowed to eat until after mass. Even the poor must pay before they are fed. The church follows business procedures: Deposit time at mass and you will receive a dividend of food. It is Antonio, familiar with hunger, who is compassionate and acquiesces to the old man's request that he be allowed to eat before leaving. This gives the crafty creature a chance to escape.

Bruno, in many ways harder and shrewder than his father, voices his view that Antonio made a mistake in trusting the old man. This is the first time he has doubted his father. Antonio, harassed enough without this criticism, slaps the boy. The boy is sullen until his repentant father suggests lunch.

The restaurant scene is touching because of the contrast between the surface gaiety of the expensive milieu and the despair in Antonio's heart as he squanders most of his last lire and makes a pretense of enjoying himself. The arrogant waiter, the singer with the band, the supercilious boy at a nearby table, and Bruno's trouble in eating the mozzarella are reminders that the two are outsiders excluded by poverty from a comfortable life.

Antonio's decision to visit the clairvoyant is the first step in his moral decline, anticipated by his slapping his son. Until this point, he has preserved his integrity and self-respect. By consulting a person he has previously called a fraud, he is betraying his beliefs. This is a short step in the direction of the larger one of stealing a bicycle. Naturally, the clairvoyant is of no help.

On leaving her building, Antonio spies the thief. Perhaps the filmmakers are being ironic in showing a visit to the fortune-teller does lead to finding the thief, though not the bicycle. The appearance of the young man for the second time after stealing the bicycle, however, prompts a more important consideration.

De Sica and Zavattini have adhered to the major tenets of Neorealism as noted in Chapter 4*:

_____

*pp. 130–131

Center attention on the common man in everyday life, feature nonprofessional actors, dispense with any cinematic techniques that distance the camera from the reality it is capturing (for example, studio productions, unnatural lighting, and self-conscious compositions of shots), and emphasize the influence of environment on basic human needs, especially unjust social pressures that debase human dignity. The one element that the filmmakers have violated is to preserve a sense of "life as it is" without imposing on the narrative artificialities that require credulity on the part of viewers. It is within the limits of verisimilitude that Antonio's bicycle be stolen and that he be caught when stealing himself. We can even accept that in a city the size of Rome, he might come across the thief once. When, however, his path accidentally crosses that of the youth twice within a few hours, we feel for the first time (though not the last: It is too convenient that Bruno misses the bus and thus witnesses his father's humiliation) that characters are being manipulated for the purposes of plot rather than what Bazin calls in another context "the necessity of the events."

The thief runs into a house of prostitution, followed by Antonio, while Bruno is forced to wait outside. The existence of the brothel is additional evidence of the corruption of society, for it is legalized (the madame worries about what the commissioner will say if he hears about the dispute, and in the script she is listed as the "Licensee"). Moreover, the thief is well known to the prostitutes, and they defend him. There is here an implied contrast between the youth who spends his ill-gotten gain in a house and Antonio, who would use his money for a home.

In front of the apartment where the thief, whose name we now learn is Alfredo, lives, Antonio is surrounded by hostile neighbors. Two men, whose appearance and manners suggest that they are criminals of some sort, threaten Antonio. Alfredo the thief receives more help from disreputable neighbors than a law-abiding family man from the government. Whether the youth's epileptic seizure is genuine or pretense is not made clear.

Antonio has identified the thief, but that does not mean he can recover his bicycle. His problem becomes evident as he and the policeman brought by Bruno search Alfredo's apartment. It is a depressing place. There may be some truth, though it is doubtful, to the mother's statement that Alfredo has been looking for a job for a long time. These people are even worse off than the Riccis. And without finding the bicycle and with no witness other than himself, Antonio has no case, as the not unsympathetic policeman explains. Of what value would it be to Antonio to bring Alfredo to court? In a sense, both of them are victims of a society that encourages a youth to steal and a man to have to depend on a bicycle to support his family.

The last sequence is the climax of the film, a superb fusion of content and style. Little has been noted in this essay on the motion picture's camera-editing dynamics and elements of presentation because they are so unobtrusive. The stylistic ideal of Neorealim cannot quite be Bazin's "no cinema" but to move as far as possible in that direction. Since the film emphasizes the interrelationship of Antonio and his environment, the basic approach is *mise-en-scène*. If ever a director deserved the title of *metteur-en-scène,* it is De Sica. Repeatedly we see Antonio and Bruno in long, eye-level shots. People often walk behind or in front of them. In recalling *The Bicycle Thief,* a viewer is hard put to remember specific shots; it is scenes that come to mind. There are exceptions: the camera tilting to reveal the shelves of bed sheets in the municipal pawnshop, Antonio and Bruno in the rain at the second market, Bruno whirling around to face the camera just before he is going to urinate, the boy eating the stringy mozzarella, the final images of the film. However, those shots or series of shots are memorable for content rather than composition, striking angles, or lighting. De Sica completely subordinates his ego as a director to the needs of the film.

This does not mean he is incapable of creating esthetically impressive shots that are also dramatically effective. There are at least two outstanding examples. When Antonio hears that a child is drowning and fears it is Bruno, he runs from the stationary camera, disappears into the blackness of a tunnel, centered in the frame, and on the sound track we hear his call of "Bruno!" reverberating in the tunnel. Later he is in the thief's apartment talking to the policeman. They are outlined by an open window. Antonio is in profile from the waist up at the left edge of the window, the policeman is exactly counterpoised at the right edge, and Bruno's head is at the base of the frame between the two. Through the window, across the alley, we see a woman holding a child at her own window and looking directly at the camera.

Although *mise-en-scène* most tellingly presents Antonio as the victim of forces larger than himself, it is through close shots that we apprehend the suffering of the taciturn workman. This distance is also necessary to reveal Bruno's reactions. The usual pattern, as in the scene of the Austrian priests, is a long shot of a setting, a medium shot of a person, and a close-up of Bruno's face as he responds to the person. It is montage, including close shots, that makes the ending of the film so powerful.

The last sequence is built on the principles of contrasts and reactions. After leaving Via Panico, where the thief lives, Antonio and Bruno walk down some streets and enter a piazza. Bruno has trouble keeping up with his father and wears a worried expression as he looks up at Antonio. The latter's glazed eyes see only his own despair and desperation. So oblivious is he to everything around him that he does not notice when Bruno is almost hit by a car as they cross a street.

They stop near a bus stop in front of a stadium, and the tired Bruno sits on a curb. Antonio remains standing, and we observe a conflict develop in him, without a word being spoken, through objective shots of him and subjective ones from his point of view. First we see through Antonio's eyes rows of bicycles guarded by a policeman; a roar from the stadium explains why there are so many at one spot. It is like a feast spread before a starving man, only there is a pane of thick glass between him and it. Antonio walks a short distance and stares in another direction. A subjective shot of an empty street with a bicycle leaning against a wall next to the entrance to a building. A close-up of Antonio's face. The juxtaposition of the two shots in context is an example of how montage can convey an idea solely by dynamic editing, for we realize Antonio is tempted to steal the bicycle. He returns to Bruno and sits down next to his son. [Figure 5.15(a)]

What follows is a series of shots alternating between Antonio and what he sees: the stadium, An-

tonio, racing cyclists on the street, Antonio rising to this feet, the stadium, Antonio, the rows of bicycles, Antonio, people walking in front of the stadium, Antonio checking that the unguarded bicycle is still there. A shot of Bruno anxiously watching his father. Back to Antonio wiping his sweating brow. He sees the game is over, with people coming out of the stadium and riding away on their bicycles. Antonio paces up and down. Finally, he walks to Bruno, gives him some coins, and tells him to take the bus home. Bruno misses it and stands alone.

The camera is at first objective as Antonio steals the bicycle [Figure 5.15(b)], the owner runs out shouting, and men run after the thief. The chase is presented in panoramic shots [Figure 5.15(c)]. It takes us a moment to realize they are subjective from Bruno's point of view. We are made aware of this perspective by a medium shot of the boy's horrified face [Figure 5.15(d)]. Antonio is caught, knocked down, and surrounded by a crowd [Figure 5.15(e)]. He tentatively, wearily raises his arm to defend himself from blows and shoves. The owner of the bicycle is first among the persecutors. A shot of Bruno trying to reach his father and shouting, "Papa . . . papa . . ." He is isolated, then picks up Antonio's hat, which was knocked off his father's head. Tears stream from the boy's eyes as he faces the camera.

Antonio is being pushed toward a police station by a small group of men when Bruno appears, grips his father's legs, and looks defiantly at the men. Antonio, completely passive, looks down at his son. The owner of the bicycle observes the two and relents. He decides to forget the matter and, after thanking the others, walks away. Shouts and insults are heard as Antonio and Bruno leave together. His face tear-stained, Bruno hands the hat to his father, who automatically puts it on.

The camera now leads the two, cutting from one to the other. The series begins with a medium shot of Antonio in the left half of the frame, people walking by in the right half. His lips quiver and he looks down. When he lifts his head, he is crying as he walks [Figure 5.15(f)]. Cut to Bruno, looking up at his father, his child's face tight with anxiety and pity. The camera is still tracking back, leading them. In the next shot, half of Antonio's body is visible from shoulder to thigh, his arm hanging. Bruno stares straight ahead (a delicate touch: He does not look at his father) as he grasps Antonio's hand [Figure 5.15(g)]. The boy's hand is gripped tightly in response. Only then does Bruno glance up, stumble a bit, then look again at his father. Cut to Antonio, tears in his eyes. Close-up of the clasped hands. One more shot of Bruno's anxious face. The last shot of the film: from behind the two, a medium shot. The camera holds as they move away; people come between them and the camera; the two have disappeared into the crowd [Figure 5.15(h)]; fade to black.

There is no need for the film to continue. We know the poverty and degradation the Riccis will have to endure. Antonio will perhaps become a bitter man, and in his shame it may be some time before he will be able to assert authority over his son. Bruno, who in one day took a giant step toward manhood, may be more critical of his father in the years to follow (until he himself has a son he fails), but the love between them, symbolized by the clasped hands, will surely last. And it is an awareness of that love that lightens our concern for the future of the Riccis. They will endure as a family despite the forces of an inimical society and selfish individuals. This is the message that De Sica and Zavattini present with humanity, sensitivity, and an art that scorns artifice. Their reward is the probable survival of *The Bicycle Thief* when more cunning, self-consciously "artistic," and intellectual films are forgotten.

---

**FIGURE 5.15**

*The Bicycle Thief.* Images from the memorable last sequence of the film during which the desperate Antonio himself becomes a bicycle thief.

## THE FRENCH NEW WAVE

### The 400 Blows
### (Les Quatre Cent Coups)

*Truffaut has said of his film that it should be judged not by its technical perfections but by its sincerity; but of course a man's sincerity can only be judged by his technique. It is in fact through the success of his technique that Truffaut catches so much of life's richness.*

*Eric Rhode, 1960[37]*

**CAST**

*Jean-Pierre Léaud (Antoine Doinel), Claire Maurier (Gilberte Doinel), Albert Rémy (Julien Doinel), Patrick Auffay (René Bigey), Guy Decomble ("Little Quiz"), and others.*

**CREDITS**

*Director—François Truffaut, Screenwriters— François Truffaut (original story) and Marcel Moussey (adaptation and dialogue), Producer— Georges Charlot, Director of Photography—Henri Decae, Art Director—Henri Decae, Composer— Jean Constantin, Editor—Marie-Josephe Yoyotte, and others.*

1959/An S.E.D.I.F. and *Les Films du Carrosse* Coproduction
Black & White/98 minutes

---

### BACKGROUND

François Truffaut (1932–) is one of the most significant of the filmmakers who, spawned by *Cahiers du Cinéma,* directed films in France in the late fifties and thereafter and came to be known as members of the New Wave movement. His early years hardly suggest the preparation of a person who would rise to eminence in cinema or, for that matter, any other field. Much has been made by critics of the analogies between many experiences of the young François and those of the fictional Antoine Doinel, beginning with *The 400 Blows.* As the director himself has repeatedly pointed out, however, he used only certain events of his youth in creating the Doinel series of films, and it is more a spiritual than factual cinematic autobiography.

François, like Antoine, had an unhappy childhood. He left school at 14 to work at various jobs and at 17 was sent by his father to a center for juvenile delinquents. More than anyone else, it was André

Bazin, the prominent film critic, who directed the young man's energies into productive channels and who helped him to make a career of his passionate interest in movies. In March, 1953, Truffaut joined the staff of *Cahiers du Cinéma,* established in 1951 by Bazin, Lo Duca, and Jacques Doniol-Valcroze. From January, 1954, when his first article appeared, until 1959 he wrote for the magazine. His violent attacks on such conventional directors as Yves Allégret, Claude Autant-Lara, and René Clement for their well-constructed, "literary" films soon earned him renown as the *enfant terrible* of French film criticism. At the same time, with Jean-Luc Godard, Eric Rohmer, Jacques Rivette, and others, he established the tenets of the *politique des auteurs.* *

Truffaut's debut as a director of feature films occurred in 1959 with *The 400 Blows.* Earlier he had directed the short films *The Mischief Makers (Les Mistons,* 1957) (see Figures 1.7 and 1.20) and *Histoire d'eau* (1958, with Godard). After 1959 he worked feverishly, producing a minimum of a feature film a year. Somehow he also found time to publish a book of interviews with one of his favorite living directors, Alfred Hitchcock.

The subject matter of Truffaut's films is diverse. *Shoot the Piano Player (Tirez sur le pianiste,* 1960) uses the gangster film to make serious comments on the dangers of emotional isolation and fear of commitment to human relations. In *Jules and Jim (Jules et Jim,* 1961) he brilliantly explores the relationships between a woman and two men; it is probably the director's most profound film to date. *Fahrenheit 451* (1966) is science fiction. *The Bride Wore Black (La Mariée était en noir,* 1968) deals with vengance and murder; *Mississippi Mermaid (La Sirène du Mississippi,* 1969) belongs in the genre of melodramatic romance. *The Wild Child (L'Enfant sauvage,* 1970) is based on a historical incident of the early nineteenth century in which a child of nature is civilized by a sympathetic and dedicated teacher. *Day for Night (La Nuit américaine,* 1973) can be described as Truffaut's visual love letter to the art of making films. *The Story of Adele H. (Histoire d'Adèle H.,* 1975) examines the obsessive

---

*p. 142

love of the daughter of Victor Hugo for a worthless army officer. *Small Change* (*L'Argent de poche,* 1976) demonstrates the director's genius for presenting honestly and sensitively the world of children and young people. In *The Man Who Loved Women* (*L'Homme qui aimait les femmes,* 1977), the lead character writes a memoir of his obsessive, romantic, and ultimately masochistic pursuit of women. *The Last Metro* (*Le Dernier métro,* 1980) is a vivid, compelling story of life in a small Parisian theater during World War II. *The Woman Next Door* (*La Femme D'À Côté,* 1981) is another story of obsessive love that ends tragically.

The Antoine Doinel series of five works, all starring Jean-Pierre Léaud, includes *The 400 Blows; Antoine et Colette,* a story of Antoine in love at 16 (part of the anthology film *Love at Twenty, L'Amour à vingt ans,* 1962); *Stolen Kisses* (*Baisers volés,* 1968) in which the hero, after a love affair with an older woman, becomes engaged to Christine Darbon; and *Bed and Board* (*Domicile conjugal,* 1970), which shows the married Antoine tempted by a lovely Japanese woman but ultimately returning to his wife and child. In *Love on the Run* (*L'Amour en fuite,* 1978), which the director maintains is the last in the series, Antoine, now divorced, finally achieves a degree of maturity (brief excerpts from the four earlier films are included as flashbacks).

Truffaut's other films, less successful or less ambitious, are *Soft Skin* (*La Peau douce,* 1964), *Two English Girls* (*Les Deux Anglaises et le continent,* 1971), *Such a Gorgeous Kid Like Me* (1973), *The Green Room* (*La Chambre verte,* 1979), and *Confidentially Yours* (1983).

As befits an advocate of the *auteur* theory, Truffaut's style is individual. His chief characteristic is his marvelous visual eye. Every other cinematic element is subordinated to camera-editing dynamics. He repeatedly experiments with new techniques and willingly admits that he has learned from such contemporaries as Godard and Franju. The foundation of his visual style, however, is derived from an intensive study of older directors, particularly Jean Vigo, Jean Renoir, Marcel Carné, Jean Cocteau, Robert Bresson, the Italian Neorealists, and Alfred Hitchcock. He pays homage to them not only in his writings but also in his films by "echoing" passages in their work, as in a Vigo-inspired scene in *The 400 Blows.* *

His departures from traditional approaches include the generally episodic, nonlinear structure of his films; a lessening of the roles of the independent screenwriter (in every one of his films he wrote the screenplay himself or in collaboration with others) and the set designer (preferring location shooting to studio sets); an avoidance of set speeches; and a predilection for improvisation. Truffaut also does not hesitate to mix cinematic modes (for example, comedy and tragedy in *Jules and Jim*) or transcend the formulae of a specific genre (as in *Shoot the Piano Player,* ostensibly a gangster film). He is often innovative in the use of natural sounds and background music.

Truffaut has appeared in his own films as the teacher Itard in *The Wild Child,* the director Ferrand in *Day for Night,* and a main character in *The Green Room,* so he appreciates the problems facing actors. Those in his films testify to the respect and encouragement he has given them. He was able to draw from Jean Moreau one of her finest performances in *Jules and Jim,* make Jean-Pierre Léaud a star, and demonstrate the versatility of Albert Rémy and Marie Dubois.

Of the many themes that appear in many types of films created by Truffaut, one predominates: the conflict between illusion and reality and the ways people torture themselves by obsessively adhering to an ideal. Usually it is a man fixated on the image of a woman (for example, Jules and Jim, Antoine in every film after *The 400 Blows,* Louis Mahé in *Mississippi Mermaid,* and Bertrand in *The Man Who Loved Women*), but it can be a woman possessed by an impossible love (as Adele H., or Julie Kohler in *The Bride Wore Black*). Maturity is acceptance of innocence lost, however regretfully, and reaching compromises with reality (as for the narrator of *The Mischief Makers* and Victor in *The Wild Child*). This insight into the wonder and fragility of the dreams of youth makes the films of Truffaut that feature youngsters so poignant.

Another important theme in the director's work

is the dangerous repercussions of a fear of emotional commitment to another person, a type of narcissism that leaves the individual withdrawn and self-protective (Jules, Charlie in *Shoot the Piano Player*). There is also the other side of the coin of this theme: a reaching out to the unknown for selfish reasons, regardless of the cost to others. For Truffaut, adultery and casual affairs reveal this insecurity, which demands evidence (especially when youth has faded) that one is still desirable and lovable (for example, Catherine in *Jules and Jim,* Pierre Lachenay in *Soft Skin,* Alphonse in *Day for Night*).

As is true of most of the New Wave directors (with the notable exception of Godard), Truffaut is not obviously politically engaged. Outrage at social injustice and at political repressions of freedom of thought can, however, appear in his work. The former is evident in *The 400 Blows,* the latter in *Fahrenheit 451* and the newsreel of book burning in *Jules and Jim.*

There is a general quality in Truffaut's work that transcends technique and themes and more than any other characteristic distinguishes him from his contemporaries. It is his humanity. Everything at which he points his camera is vested with sympathy. With the exception of bureaucratic systems and societal forces that impersonally and arrogantly restrain human imagination and liberty, there are no villains in his films. Even the captain in *Fahrenheit 451* is misguided rather than evil. The men and women in Truffaut's films are neither gods nor devils; they are simply human beings struggling within their limitations, capable of stupidity and selfishness but also of altruism and tenderness. A viewer comes away from a Truffaut film with the feeling of having shared a vision of human nature that is clear and penetrating and is also founded on tolerance and generosity.

*The 400 Blows* was financed by a government subsidy and loans from the director's father-in-law and friends. The sum finally gathered was only a quarter of the cost of an average feature film in France during the late fifties, so Truffaut had to impose stringent economizing. No studios were used, and the technical crew was kept to a minimum. Little-known actors were employed. The lead role was given to a nonprofessional, Léaud, chosen from literally dozens of applicants given 16mm screen tests. Money was also saved by postsynchronizing the sound. The only luxury Truffaut allowed himself was to photograph the film in Dyaliscope, a French version of Cinemoscope that produced brighter images and allowed for wide-angle shots.

The film was an instant success. It won many prizes, including the Grand Prix at Cannes in 1959, the Catholic O.C.I.C., and the New York Film Critics Circle choice as Best Foreign Film. Reviewers at every point along the critical spectrum praised it. Even other directors—a group not given to generous statements about newcomers—used superlatives; for example, Akira Kurosawa spoke of *The 400 Blows* as "one of the most beautiful films I have ever seen," and Jean Cocteau remarked, "I've never been so moved at the cinema."[38]

Only one shadow darkened Truffaut's euphoria. His mentor died a few months before *The 400 Blows* was released. At the end of the credits appears the following statement in French: "This film is dedicated to the memory of André Bazin."

## PLOT SUMMARY

Under crawling credits appear five shots of buildings along the streets of Paris, with the Eiffel Tower in the background. The first sequence of the film takes place in a classroom. Antoine Doinel (Léaud) is caught passing a pinup and punished by "Little Quiz," his teacher (Decomble). Antoine walks home with his friend René Bigey (Auffay). In the Doinel apartment, the youngster is interrupted while doing his homework by the entrance of his mother, Gilberte (Maurier), an attractive woman in her mid-thirties, who is curt and demanding of her son. Julien (Rémy), his father, arrives home. During dinner the two adults argue about how they will spend Sunday.

The next morning Antoine is persuaded by René not to attend school. They see two movies and spend time in an amusement park. On the way home, they see Gilberte kissing a man who is not her husband. She realizes that her son has observed her. An obnoxious schoolmate, Mauricet, spies on the two truants as they retrieve their briefcases. That night Antoine has dinner alone with his father. When Gilberte finally arrives home, the parents argue and both express resentment toward their son.

The following day Mauricet reveals to the Doinels that their son was absent from school. When Antoine is asked by his teacher for an absence note, he blurts out that his mother died. The Doinels show up at school, and Julien slaps Antoine in front of his schoolmates.

The youngster runs away from home with the help of René. He spends a lonely night wandering the streets of Paris. At school Gilberte arrives and takes her son home. After washing and putting the boy to bed, she has a long talk with him, attempting to win his confidence—and secrecy about seeing her with her lover—as well as promising him a reward if he does well in his French composition class.

Antoine is back at school. The gym teacher takes his pupils for an outing (a sequence inspired by one in Jean Vigo's *Zero for Conduct*). Later, Antoine is impressed by Balzac's *The Search for the Absolute* and writes a composition in class imitating the ending of the novel. A candle lit earlier by the youngster in homage to Balzac causes a fire at home. The family goes to the movies to escape the smoke.

Little Quiz unjustly accuses Antoine of plagiarism. The outraged boy again runs away; he secretly lives in René's apartment. During this time, the two bring a little girl to a puppet show and plan to steal a typewriter from Julien's office. The theft is successful; however, they cannot pawn the typewriter. Antoine insists on returning it and is caught by the night watchman.

Julien drags his son to a police station, where Antoine is booked for theft and vagrancy. A police official recommends to Julien that his son be sent to an observation center for juvenile delinquents. Antoine is treated like a criminal that night and the following morning. During a conversation between Gilberte and a judge, she reveals that Julien is Antoine's stepfather.

At the Observation Center for Delinquent Minors, Antoine is interviewed by a psychologist. Gilberte visits him and cruelly announces that she and her husband will have nothing further to do with him. René is not allowed to visit his friend. During a soccer game, the rejected Antoine escapes under a fence and evades his pursuer. He runs to the ocean nearby. At the edge of the water, he turns and faces the camera in a freeze frame.

## ANALYSIS

As the plot of *The 400 Blows* unfolds, we observe the external and internal forces that have molded Antoine Doinel into an unhappy, frustrated adolescent. Truffaut does not, however, present his film in a conventional, literal manner; rather he invests a series of realistic incidents with symbolic overtones. To appreciate the director's approach, we must recognize that he is not only presenting one boy's rejection by his parents but also the fundamental meaning and effects of such a rejection for any youth.

Most people would agree that an adolescent's basic psychic need is a balance of, on the one hand, paternal authority tempered by fairness and tolerance and, on the other hand, genuine maternal solicitude made tolerable by respect for an emerging independent individual. An artist can give us insights, on both conscious and subconscious levels, into the dynamics of a young person's relation of self with a paternal-maternal emotional center. This can be done not only by presenting concrete situations between the character and his parents (or substitutes for them) but also by using masculine and feminine symbols. This is one interpretation of the major theme of *The 400 Blows*.

The film opens with five moving shots, connected by dissolves, of the fronts of buildings facing streets of Paris. During this footage of less than 3 minutes, a crawling title moving vertically presents the credits. Theme music we come to associate with Antoine emanates from the sound track.

These shots do more than indicate the setting and provide an opportunity for the credits. We notice that in each one, usually over the top of the buildings, the Eiffel Tower is visible in the background. In the first two shots the camera is moving from left to right, in the next two from right to left. It is as if we were circling the Eiffel Tower, though never getting closer, as it stands dominant, authoritative, phallic in the center. Finally, in the last shot the camera moves down a boulevard, directly toward the tower and presenting the clearest view of it, but only for a few seconds before a fade to black.

The Eiffel Tower can be considered as representing a type of masculine authority never reached. The tower also symbolizes Paris. Most of the film takes place in the city, and Antoine spends as much time wandering its streets as he does at school or at home. In fact, it is a kind of foster home for him. We see the city bustling with people during the day, bright with electric lights and window displays at night, still and majestic in repose in early morning light—a vital, living presence that envelops the young man. Yet Paris rejects him as his stepfather and his teachers do. Perhaps Antoine senses early that this will happen, for even while in the city, he dreams of an alternative.

He confides to his friend René that he would love to see the ocean. At the end of the film he realizes his dream. The sea is traditionally associated with the feminine, particularly the mother, with salvation, peace, and ultimately death. *The 400 Blows* opens, then, with a symbol of paternal authority and closes with one of maternal succor. Tower and sea are quintessential representations of two psychic poles, separate yet interrelated, that appear in various metamorphoses throughout the film.

The dominant masculine authority in Antoine's life should be his father. The significant weakness of Julien Doinel is not that he is a stepfather but that he is an inadequate parent. He is a good-natured person who attempts to plaster over emotional crevices in the family relationships with jokes. On the other hand, Julien is a coward. He cannot face directly the infidelity of his wife or the responsibility of his wayward stepson. He deals with problems either by losing his temper or by escaping. His chief and seemingly only pleasure is his motor club, through which he can physically as well as emotionally depart from home and city. When Antoine becomes too much of a problem, Julien hands the boy over to the authorities and completely deserts him, even after Antoine has sent him a personal letter from the reformatory.

In his silent, perceptive way, Antoine watches his stepfather and understands. He can reach out to the man only obliquely, but Julien does not have the moral character to respond except superficially and with clichés on good behavior and the need for ambition. The young man receives from his father only shallow affection without masculine authority.

In school, Antoine is subjected to authority without affection. Little Quiz is a mean, petty tyrant who takes Antoine's independence and René's self-confidence as personal affronts. The schoolteacher is figuratively the grandson of Prof. Rath in *The Blue Angel* and the son of "Caligari" in *Torment* in his insensitivity to the problems and needs of growing boys.

Other characters in the film reflect in a minor key the same type of inability of Little Quiz and Julien Doinel to offer Antoine a source of paternal strength. The supervisor in the reformatory who slaps Antoine is a Little Quiz who reveals his sadism in a more overt, physical manner than the schoolteacher. René's father, M. Bigey, resembles Julien Doinel in his weakness, selfishness, and lack of a genuine emotional relationship with his son. Bigey's passion is racing horses, and in the storage room of his apartment is a life-size wooden horse. It is surely an intentional irony on the part of the director to associate the ineffectual M. Bigey with this effigy of a horse, one of the most virile of animals, used by artists of all ages to symbolize male potency.

Not only do all manifestations of the paternal in Antoine's world fail him, but he is equally disappointed in the maternal. His mother is a frustrated, egocentric, devious woman. Gilberte did not want Antoine and was only dissuaded by her mother from having an abortion. We assume that she married Julien out of desperation. Now she feels trapped in a cramped apartment that she neglects, with a son who is a burden and a husband who earns an inadequate salary. A combination of frustration and egotism has encouraged self-pity in her, as is clear when she tells Antoine that she is used to being condemned and all her life has been surrounded by imbeciles.

As with every other major character in the film, she has a means of escape. In her case, it is extramarital affairs. Such affairs are inevitable because she is a manipulator of men (we never see her with a woman) and aware that her only power lies in the sensuality she exudes. Since Gilberte uses her sensuality as a weapon, a means to an end, there is an air of vulgarity about her that coarsens the set of her no-longer-young features. At times of stress, her eyes narrow and the muscles around her mouth tighten into an expression of pouting sullenness. It comes as no surprise that she would use her sexuality to influence her son.

A boy of Antoine's age is at the edge of the awakening of sex: vulnerable, uncertain, curious, embarrassed by his preoccupation. It is a pinup that first gets Antoine into trouble at school; his schoolmates react with silly gestures at suggestive lines in the poem "The Hare"; although René and Antoine speak little about sex, the first movie they go to while playing hooky is *The White Slave* (next they see an adventure film); during the interview with the psychologist, we learn of the young man's futile efforts to lose his virginity. We realize, therefore, that one of the problems Antoine is confronting is his adolescent sexual drives.

His mother attempts to take advantage of this vulnerability when she wants him to be silent about seeing her kissing her lover on the street. She takes him home the morning after he has stayed away all night. She gives him a bath, kisses him, and insists that he rest in his parents' bed. While he lies in bed naked, she rattles on about her problems with her parents, a diary she kept, and her puppy love for a young shepherd. She promises him 1000 francs if he does well in his next composition. Her last statement is that he mustn't tell his father, supposedly about the money, but actually referring to her infidelity.

Gilberte is, however, so crude and transparent in her approach that her son—evident in close shots of his face and his general constraint—is fully aware of her duplicity. And we sense that it is the deception and insincere expressions of understanding and love that hurt Antoine more than the infidelity. It is understandable why early in the film he said impulsively that his mother had died. Actually, she has, as far as his emotional needs are concerned.

Only two other females have roles of any consequence in the film. René's mother is preoccupied with her drinking, social affairs, and avoidance of her husband. Like Gilberte, she seems indifferent to the duty of a mother to her son, though financial security and a large house allow each member of the Bigey

family to lead an independent life. The other woman with whom Antoine comes in contact is the psychologist at the reformatory. During the interview she establishes a rapport with the young man, but her probing is motivated by professional concern, symbolized by the question-and-answer format.

There is an alternative for Antoine to family and school—complete independence and freedom. How is this possible in our society, however, for a boy of 13? Too many prison doors would have to be unlocked, and the keys are not within reach. Furthermore, for all his stoicism and resourcefulness, Antoine is still a boy: insecure, vulnerable, shyly responsive to kindness. For these reasons, he alternates throughout the film between, on the one hand, accepting a circle of physical security and emotional deprivation and, on the other hand, breaking the ties that bind him.

Faced with an unhappy home and tyrannical teachers, Antoine follows the example of the adults around him and tries to escape. He turns to Balzac and attempts to make the virile, intense writer his patron saint. The result is that he almost burns down the apartment and is thrown out of school. He is a truant from school and goes with René to an amusement park, but the two apparently find their chief pleasure in films (two in one day and another the next night). The only time he is happy with his parents is when they all go to a motion picture.

Twice Antoine attempts to evade home and school by running away. The first time, after being slapped by his father in front of his classmates, he wanders at night, cold, hungry, and lonely (Figure 5.16). On the second occasion, after being expelled from school, he steals a typewriter from his father's office but is honest enough to attempt to return it when he cannot pawn it. Ironically, he is caught when bringing it back. These two escapades, both failures, prove to Antoine—and to us—that he cannot at his age survive alone and free, even in a big city.

The theft of the typewriter and Julien Doinel's weakness of character lead to Antoine's being transferred from an emotional prison to one that is both physical and emotional. In the last third of the film— the young man in the hands of the Paris police and then at the Observation Center for Delinquent Minors

FIGURE 5.16

*The 400 Blows.* A lonely Antoine wanders through the streets of Paris at night.

—the walls of Antoine's world close in even more around him until he makes one last, desperate attempt to escape (the last sequence). Both human beings and the system, out of weakness, selfishness, and indifference, seem to conspire to crush the boy's spirit.

At the police station, Antoine's statement is taken down by a bored and cynical detective. In the detention room, he is placed in a cage with an Algerian criminal. A small concession to his age is made: The tired and dispirited youngster is moved into a smaller cage when three prostitutes are brought in. In the van that takes the prisoner from the police station, Antoine's face, tears in his eyes, reveals with poignant understatement what he is suffering. He spends the night in a dark cell. Although the youngster demonstrates grit as he rejects coffee and smokes a hand-rolled cigarette, close shots of his face at night and in the morning show his fear and bewilderment. A police photographer takes mug shots of Antoine, roughly shoving his face into position. All this is done to a boy in his early teens whose "crime" has been to run away from home and return a typewriter he had stolen. Antoine's ordeal is a paradigm not only of the plight of minors in the hands of the law but, more generally, of all injustice that results when a bureaucratic system of legal authority has the power to transform a human being into a name and number on a file card.

The first scene in the observation center includes a pointed visual commentary on the relationship of adults and children. As a group of boys in dark uniforms line up, a guard places three little girls, apparently the daughters of employees of the center, into a cage. We are reminded of the cage at the police station in which Antoine was restrained. The guards obviously feel that their offspring might be contaminated by any contact with reformatory boys. What Truffaut is underlining through this incident is a major theme of his film: Adults manipulate children, supposedly for their own good, on the basis of adults' premises and prejudices without considering the special perspectives and needs of youngsters.

Antoine had a certain liberty of action at home and in school but reached out, to no avail, for authority tempered with love. The point is that he did reach out for help; it is those on whom he depended that failed him. This situation repeats itself at the observation center. He has lost all freedom and is subjected to an arbitrary authority. On the other hand, there is the possibility of buoys that he can grip to keep him afloat during his incarceration: his friendship with René, his parents, and the help the institution may give him. Yet one at a time, each of these potential forms of love is denied him.

René is not allowed to visit Antoine because he does not have a pass. Mme Doinel arrives, but not to encourage and console her son. In a very unmaternal display of selfishness, she severs all ties between Antoine and his parents.

The scene with the female psychologist is remarkable. It consists of seven shots connected by dissolves. The camera is completely stable, unvarying in presenting medium shots of Antoine (at a table, from the chest up), against a gray background of a wall, the youngster looking either directly at or a little to the right of the lens (Figure 5.17). We never see the psychologist, only hear in a voice-over her questions and leading comments.

Although Antoine is cooperative, we are aware that he is being interrogated. The visuals of the scene inevitably remind us of the "mug shots" taken when he was arrested. From one point of view, the psychologist is a part of the bureaucratic police system

FIGURE 5.17

*The 400 Blows.* Antoine is interviewed by a psychologist.

attempting to characterize and pigeonhole the youngster. A viewer of the film gains pertinent information about Antoine's background and attitudes, such as his lying and stealing, his mother's cruelty and desire for an abortion, insights into his stepfather's weakness, and his attempt to lose his virginity. Yet no evidence is presented that the cross-examination is helping Antoine with his problems. There is perhaps a therapeutic value in his speaking freely about himself, and with time the psychologist might be able to direct him toward what society considers a healthy adjustment to reality. In the context of *The 400 Blows,* however, this experience is to Antoine only another futile attempt on the part of adults to manipulate and bully him.

When the observation center becomes for the youngster an oppressive authority without love or freedom, he runs away. As the inmate who ran away and was recaptured remarks, liberty is worth any punishment. Antoine escapes to the ocean. This last hope, however, is another blind alley rather than a source of salvation.

In *The 400 Blows,* Truffaut created a powerful film that saddens us as we sympathize with Antoine's frustrations, yet also exhilarates us, as does any work of art that fully realizes through an individual style the potentials of its medium of expression. It is not astonishing that a young director of 27 should break with the standard formulae for commercial filmmaking of his day; however, it is phenomenal that he should demonstrate such a sure mastery of a new approach in his first feature film. The innovations of Truffaut's style in the film include most of the characteristics discussed under "Background," but the ones most pertinent to *The 400 Blows* are the departures from the conventional development of plot, elimination of artificial studio sets, a psychology of character that emerges from silence and action rather than set speeches, and, most important, a projection on the screen of the vision of the director that is expressed primarily through the visuals.

The structure of the film is not as nonlinear as some of the director's later works, but there are scenes and motifs that are not justified, a violation of the classic rules of dramaturgy. The most obvious example is a scene in which Antoine and René accompany a small girl to a puppet show. There is no explanation of the identity of the child—we have not seen her before, nor do we see her again—or why the two boys go to a show for children. There is also the question as to who took the *Guide Michelin,* about which Julien Doinel repeatedly inquires. There are explanations for both mysteries, but one must go outside the film proper for them. The girl appears in an incident in the original scenario[39] that was omitted in the finished film (incidentally, Truffaut uses the situation in a later film, *Small Change*). The same holds true for the guide. In a rejected scene, Antoine and René convert the pages of the *Guide Michelin* into ammunition for a peashooter.[40] Although C. G. Crisp informs us that at least the latter scene was restored by the director in a 1967 revision of *The 400 Blows,*[41] the relevant point here is that Truffaut could be so unconcerned about tight, logical narrative development as to release his film without justifying every scene and motif.

Another area in which the director can be cavalier by the standards of more conventional contemporary filmmakers is the indication of physical time. During the first two-thirds of the film, we have little difficulty following the sequence of days and nights. At the observation center, however, there is a blurring of time; we have no idea how long Antoine has been at the reformatory before he escapes. The period must have been brief, because when the youngster wanders the streets of Paris at night, there are Christmas greetings in a store window, and when the boys march to the soccer field from which Antoine runs away, they pass a Christmas tree. This general loss of clear temporal sequence can be explained as indicating Antoine's dissociation from reality while he is imprisoned at the center.

The realism that permeates the film is especially evident in the settings. The Doinels' apartment, the classrooms, and the jail have none of the artificiality of studio sets. It is obvious that these scenes were shot on location. Passersby even glance momentarily at the camera.

Truffaut is also innovative in creating the reality of his characters. Dialogue takes second place to the expressions of an actor and camera-editing dynamics in exposing the emotions of a character. In fact, there is often an inverse proportion between the depth and complexity of feelings of an individual and his verbal expressions. In *The 400 Blows,* the most obvious characters, the adult Doinels and Little Quiz, speak the most. Antoine, on the other hand, says surprisingly little, though our attention is focused principally on him. The only exception is the encounter with the psychologist. At most crucial moments, when the youngster feels deeply, we gain insights into these feelings not through the few words he speaks but from his expressions as the camera tracks into close and medium shots of him: when he is in "The Rotor" at the amusement park, as he wanders the streets of Paris at night, while his parents argue about him, as his mother attempts to seduce and bribe him into remaining silent about her affair, during his experiences in the jail and in the police van, and during his escape to the sea.

This approach could not succeed without an expressive actor with screen presence in the role of Antoine, so Truffaut was fortunate in discovering Jean-Pierre Léaud. The other actors, in lesser roles, are also outstanding, especially Albert Rémy as the father. Perhaps only Patrick Auffay as René is a bit too cold and suave for a youngster of 13.

Of all the admirable characteristics of *The 400 Blows,* the most memorable are the camera-editing dynamics. In this area Truffaut reveals his precocious masterfulness and demonstrates by example what he meant when he criticized post–World War II French films as being more literary than visual. Earlier we examined in detail two scenes: screen action under the credits and the interview with the psychologist. Other individual scenes and shots illustrate noteworthy cinematic techniques.

Antoine and his family are at dinner in two scenes. In both cases Truffaut indicates visually the divisiveness in the family by never including the three persons together in a single shot. Instead, he uses a series of one- and two-shots. In the single scene in which there is genuine unity among them, we see them together: leaving the movie theater, in a car, and entering their apartment building.

A few times during the film, Truffaut uses a pan to transverse time as well as space. While playing hooky, the two boys are seen at the right edge of the frame after leaving a motion picture theater. There is a swish pan to the left—a blur of black and white—and we find Antoine and René in a different setting, entering another theater. A variation of this technique occurs in the final sequence.

There is a wonderful fluidity in the scenes of Antoine wandering the streets of Paris at night, and within a few minutes we feel his isolation and loneliness. The views of the audience of children in the scene of the puppet show are delightful. The director combines shots of a few of the children with pans and intercuts of the puppets. One of the most moving passages in *The 400 Blows* shows Antoine at the police station, in the police van, and in jail. During the four scenes that follow his interview with the detective, Antoine remains almost entirely silent (he speaks only one sentence, to the Algerian in the cage). The emphasis is on the visuals and background music. A shot-by-shot analysis of the sequence would demonstrate with what brilliance, especially in the discreet use of subjective shots, Truffaut creates a combination of tone and rhythm that, without dialogue, forces a viewer to share the suffering and bewilderment of the youngster.

The scene in the amusement park in which Antoine rides in "The Rotor" has been acclaimed as a tour de force of camera-editing dynamics. Antoine enters the ride with two men and a woman. As speed builds up, the riders are pressed against the wall by centrifugal force. The boy, pinned to the wall, is able to work his way upside down, then attempts but cannot push himself away from the wall. When "The Rotor" slows down, Antoine and the others slide to the floor and stagger as they walk out. A viewer of the film both watches the youngster and shares in his reactions. This is accomplished through three types of angle shots: high-angle ones looking down on the

youngster and the three others in "The Rotor" [Figure 5.18(a)]; low-angle shots of the observers above, presumably from Antoine's point of view [Figure 5.18(b)]; and eye-level or slightly tilted-up shots from within "The Rotor" of Antoine either whirling by or appearing to be stationary so we can observe him [Figures 5.18(c) and 5.18(d)].

This ride constitutes an exciting few minutes of film, but it also can be considered as having symbolic overtones. Antoine is trapped in "The Rotor" as he is in the circumstance of his life. The force of events and his own choices destine him to futile motion. When he looks outside his own ego, the external world appears incomprehensible or blurred. He does not help matters by stubbornly insisting on his own nonconformist perspective, seeing things, so to speak, upside down. René watches and encourages him but is essentially an outsider, part of the external world, not imprisoned as

**FIGURE 5.18**

*The 400 Blows.* Three different angles used in "The Rotor" sequence: high (a), low (b), and eye-level (c, d); (b) is a subjective shot from Antoine's point of view.

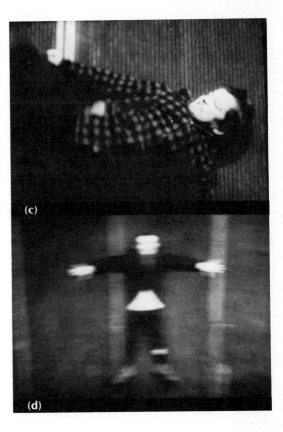

is Antoine. "The Rotor" eventually stops, and the youngster escapes. Perhaps Truffaut is slyly offering us a hope for Antoine not presented in this film but realized in the later works in the Doinel series.

Another particularly memorable scene is the final one of the film. Antoine has slipped under the fence surrounding the soccer field and eluded the pursuing guard. We see him running away from under a bridge where he has hidden momentarily. Three lengthy shots follow with dissolves as transitions. The first is approximately 1 ½ minutes in duration. The camera moves parallel to Antoine as he trots along a road toward the right, passing trees, farmhouses, and a car. The youngster is seen full length, in profile, generally in the center of the frame, although at times closer to the right edge (see Figure 1.26). On the sound track we hear the musical theme associated with him throughout the film.

This shot can be compared esthetically to onomatopoeia in poetry (the sound of a word suggests its meaning); that is, extended movement on the screen provides kinesthetic clues that allow the physically passive viewer to feel the action and thus the emotions or "meaning" associated with its context. In the case of Antoine trotting, the shot is lengthy enough for a viewer to sense physiologically the act of running and to understand the youngster's situation, to share his exhilaration in escaping as well as purposefulness in heading unhesitantly in one direction.

Shot 2 begins with Antoine in the distance coming down a hill. The camera then slowly revolves to the left, revealing a river or inlet, two boats, a jetty,

**FIGURE 5.19**

*The 400 Blows.* Images from the last moments of the film. The final shot (d) is a freeze frame. It was unusual in 1959 for this device to appear in a dramatic narrative.

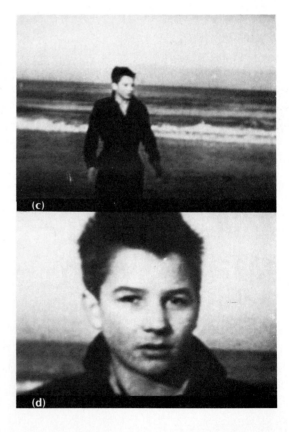

bushes, and eventually a glimpse of the sea. The pan ends on land, with Antoine at the base of the frame, his back to the camera. For a moment he hesitates, looks around, and continues running. We assume now that his objective is to reach the sea, and we recall his statement to René that he would love to see the ocean.

Our assumption is confirmed in the next shot (of just over a minute in duration). We observe Antoine at the top of a wooden staircase leading to sand. He quickly descends, moves parallel to the camera [Figure 5.19(a)], then passes and leads it. We hear the sound of waves and see first the edge of the water line, then the ocean in the background, as the youngster splashes up to his ankles [Figure 5.19(b)]. He stops and looks down as he takes a few steps to the right [Figure 5.19(c)]. He stares directly at the camera. A track-in to a medium shot ends with a 5-second freeze frame [Figure 5.19(d)]. The superimposition of "Fine" is followed by a fade to black.

The ocean was designated earlier in this essay as a symbol of the mother Antoine seeks after his natural mother has failed him. He reaches the ocean in the final shots of the film. We cannot know what he had hoped for; he probably did not know himself, reaching out in his desperation for any solace, no matter how intangible, for his loneliness and frustra-

tion. We can conjecture that as he hesitates at the edge of the water, he considers the possibility of death, a violent entrance into a warm womb where there will be peace in endless rocking. When he turns his back on the ocean, he has rejected it and death. The inevitable question in his mind is, What next?

By means of a freeze frame of Antoine looking directly at the camera, Truffaut breaks through the usually inviolate wall between the reality of the characters on the screen and that of an audience. The implied question, What next?, is posed not only by Antoine to himself but is forced upon each viewer. Few individuals in the audience can help but feel that image of the unhappy youth as an accusation. The unspoken question leads to others that go beyond one adolescent: To what degree are selfish parents and society in general responsible for the Antoines of this world? When is society going to deal intelligently and compassionately with rejected youngsters who cannot conform to our inflexible parental and societal structures? The director thus makes the "Fine" that appears over Antoine's image an irony, for while our observation of a few weeks in young Doinel's life does end, we continue long after leaving the theater to be haunted by the significance of an adolescent's experiences that transcends a specific time and specific place.

PART THREE

# film genres

Part Three is devoted to four genres:* comedy, documentary, Western, and musical. Although the
scheme of each chapter is adjusted to accommodate
individual subject matter, there is a basic format. The
chapter opens with a prefatory note. In it I explain
briefly the emphases of the background section and
justify my choices of films to examine. A survey of
the characteristics and history of the genre follows.
The pages on characteristics are intended to be primarily objective and practical, but I have included
views that are personal and theoretical. My hope is
that readers will apply the criteria developed both to
films discussed in the chapters and to others within
the genre with an awareness that exceptions prove
a rule and that definitions and categories are a means
to judgment, not judgments themselves. Whenever
possible, I have drawn illustrations from motion pictures explored later in the chapter.

The history of a genre encompassed in 50 or
so pages is inevitably incomplete. I have attempted
to balance, on the one hand, a focus on more significant individual filmmakers and works, with summaries of the distinguishing traits of a period, movement,
or style, and, on the other hand, lists of typical or
lesser-known directors and films. This material
should enable a reader to appreciate the historical
matrix from which a filmmaker and film emerge and
should also suggest possibilities for further viewing
and research.

The analysis of each film follows the tripartite division indicated in the introductory note to
Chapter 5.

---

*pp. 88–89

# Comedy

## 6

The survey of the characteristics of film comedy that opens Chapter 6 is based on the premise that this cinematic genre can best be approached through an understanding of the basic traits of the comic imagination regardless of medium. Although the examples I offer to illustrate generalizations are drawn from the cinema, the subject matter of these pages is the impetuses, functions, and categories of this particular mode of people's reactions to the human condition. The history section encompasses the highlights of film comedy from the silent era to the end of the seventies.

Charles Chaplin's *The Gold Rush* represents silent comedy. In contrast, *Smiles of a Summer Night* contains impressive visuals but is preeminently a situation sound comedy, depending for many of its most striking scenes on dialogue, natural sounds, and background music. It is especially through language that the irony of the director is communicated to an audience.

The "new wave" of American film comedy of the seventies is an exciting and vital contemporary movement in cinema. *The Producers* may at first seem an eccentric selection as an example of this movement. It is, however, in my opinion, the most coherent and carefully structured of the early works of Mel Brooks and Woody Allen. Moreover, the very audacity of its plot and characterizations reveals forcefully the essential quality of this type of comedy: to challenge, even outrage, audiences.

## SURVEY OF CHARACTERISTICS AND HISTORY

How to define clearly and comprehensively the comic imagination, regardless of medium, has baffled thinkers from Aristotle to Bergson and Freud. Even when writers confine themselves to cinema, the results have been stimulating rather than convincing. Books by the perceptive critics Raymond Durgnat and Gerald Mast demonstrate more than anything else how immense are the problems involved in exploring film comedy. It is impossible in the few pages devoted here to the subject to do more than offer some tentative ideas that might provoke readers into turning to more expansive writings (see the bibliography at the end of this volume) and to forming conclusions of their own.

Because terminology and approach are particularly important in considering this subject, it is necessary to begin with some expediencies. Although comedy and humor are often differentiated, the two will be synonymous in these pages. Distinctions between the enjoyment from comedy that is solely entertainment and that from comic art will be ignored. Although they are interrelated, it is useful for purposes of analysis to explore separately two points of view: that of audiences, their reactions, and the sources of those reactions, and that of the creator of a work and the techniques utilized to form a comic context. In both cases, key words (in italics) are touchstones for considering a few basic concepts.

*Comedy* is defined in *The American Heritage Dictionary* as a "play, motion picture, or other work that is humorous in its treatment of theme and character and has a happy ending." We will return later to possible interpretations of the expression "happy ending." Anything humorous is amusing and pleasurable and usually prompts a laugh or smile; however, we rarely if ever respond to a film, which unfolds in time, continually in this way. We label a motion picture comic, therefore, if we feel its predominant tone is one of humor. A Charlie the Tramp feature may contain moments of pathos, yet the overall effect is one of pleasure.

We are already in the middle of our first problem: Are there objective criteria for determining the pleasure derived from humor in a film comedy, or is such a determination completely subjective? The answer is that both factors operate simultaneously. We know from our experiences that background, psychological and physical makeup, and state of mind at a specific time will affect when or to what degree a person will consider a character or situation humorous. On the other hand, an individual's reactions are not completely subjective, for members of an audience in a particular theater at a particular time usually laugh and smile together. There are forces that encourage us to share a common view of what is comic.

*Social conditioning* is one such force. There can be no other explanation of why a film will be greeted in one country with unrestrained laughter and in another with stony silence or why an audience in 1975 is amused by a motion picture lauded as a tragedy in 1915. And the more personal the subject matter of a comedy, the greater the distinction between audience reactions. An interesting treatise could be written on responses of viewers from different countries to film comedies that center on sexual mores.

One of the means by which social cohesion is promoted in a culture is by *"sets"*; that is, even before experiencing a work, an individual is prepared psychologically to react in a specific manner. In the case of motion pictures, most people, as they enter a theater, have some idea of the approach that will be taken in a specific film from reviews, the title, posters outside, and associations with an actor or director. These "sets" are often reinforced by *clues* communicated by a filmmaker to indicate his approach. An audience must of course be able to recognize the significance of these clues, or they are ineffectual. One way this is done is through background music. The epitome of a contrast between visuals and sound that demonstrates a comic intention occurs at the end of Stanley Kubrick's *Dr. Strangelove:* While the earth is being destroyed on the screen, the audience hears on the sound track a chorus singing the popular tune "We'll Meet Again." Usually clues are given in the opening sequence. A viewer is not likely to be prepared for a tragedy when in the first scene of Vittorio De Sica's *Miracle in Milan* a baby is found in a cabbage patch.

Once we have identified a film as a comedy, we are secure from fear for the safety of the main charac-

ters. We may be thrilled by Harold Lloyd hanging from a skyscraper clock or the Marx Brothers on a battlefield, yet we are sure our heroes will *survive.* Amusement cannot exist if through identification with a character we share genuine terror. This does not mean a comic character cannot feel physical fear or emotional pain, but an audience must be confident that a physical threat will not result in death or mutilation, that emotional suffering will be compensated by gain, or that a tragic event is so exaggerated or understated that viewers are distracted from reality. An example of each of the three methods of reassuring us that a situation is comic: In Mel Brooks's *The Producers,* an explosion destroys a theater, yet in the next scene we are not surprised to see the three dynamiters on trial, albeit in bandages; in Bergman's *Smiles of a Summer Night,* Fredrik suffers when he loses his young wife to his son but is consoled by his former mistress; Woody Allen's *Bananas* opens with an assassination, yet media coverage is so exaggerated (Howard Cosell playing himself is a clue to humor) that we are distracted from remembering that the assassinated president was a human being.

In the light of these comments, it should be clear why citing a "happy ending" as a characteristic of comedy is too indefinite to be of much value. A character who survives (or at least copes with death, as at the ending of Allen's *Love and Death*) may not be happy, may even be sad, but takes a positive view of the future.

Reference was made to an audience's identifying with a comic character. Comedy requires a special relationship of a viewer to a character. This relationship may be described as consisting of both identification and distance. *Identification* means that we feel some empathy for a character on the screen and the difficulties in which that character is entangled. Without this empathy, we are unconcerned with the fate of the character. For this reason, as Walt Disney knew from the beginning of his career, an animal, real or animated, can only be a source of humor if it is anthropomorphized. The reverse of this process also holds true. The closer a human being is to a machine, the less the potential for humor. In Mack Sennett's films, for instance, the effectiveness of the comedy is limited because the director manipulates his characters as though they were suicidal machines.

Closely related to identification is *recognition*. Humor requires comprehension on the part of viewers of what is intended as funny before reaction is possible. A line of dialogue may be hilarious, but it will be greeted with silence by an audience if it is in a foreign language and there are no subtitles. The same difficulty exists for situations, actions, and even gestures. The less dependent the subject matter of a comedy and its means of expression are on culturally oriented subtleties, the more universal it will be. We made a foray into this area of comedy in defining social conditioning and clues. Our cultural milieu, then, can limit our ability to recognize fully what is intended as humorous and what is not. A Tati comedy, for instance, with its clever gibes at the dangers of mechanization, is unlikely to be appreciated by a rural audience in an undeveloped country that has little contact with a big city.

Identification based on recognition, however, is one side of this particular equation for comedy. A viewer who identifies too closely will lose the perspective necessary to laugh at what others consider humorous: the pain, embarrassment, or problems will be too immediate and real. On the simplest level, a fat man with his leg in a cast is not going to be amused when Oliver Hardy slips on a banana peel. What a viewer must also have in addition to identification is a counterbalancing *distance* from the comic situation. Only with a degree of objectivity can we smile at traits we recognize in ourselves or safely reveal the aggressive tendencies that often underlie laughing at others.

We have been examining a few of the sources of individuals' reactions to comedy in an audience. Now we can turn to the other side of the coin: devices or techniques a creator uses to convey that his approach is comic. One such device is clues, considered earlier from the perspective of the audience. Another, perhaps the most significant, is *exaggeration*.

To exaggerate is to magnify, to enlarge, to distort through emphasis. These defining phrases assume a norm upon which exaggeration builds. Once again we find ourselves in the foggy province of the subjective. We must postulate, therefore, that an audience at a particular moment in a particular place shares a view through social conditioning within a culture of what is more or less normal. Departure from the norm through enlargement is most often in the form of a reaction on the part of an actor to a situation or statement but may be obvious from appearance (an example is a clown's costume) or movement (as in the crouched stride of Groucho Marx). It is easiest to appreciate how this device functions in a situation, for the difference between one that is humorous and one that is not may lie solely in the exaggerated reaction of the actor. For instance, in Mel Brooks's *The Producers,* when the timid Leo meets the domineering Max, the former is frightened. There is nothing funny about a person's being bullied. We laugh, however, when Leo collapses, trembling and moaning, and pulls out his piece of "security blanket" to rub against his cheek. There is a wide range of comic exaggeration: from the hysterical antics of Leo to a restrained double take to the simple raising of an eyebrow.

The converse of exaggeration can be equally effective for purposes of comedy. *Understatement* is related to irony (discussed later) and results when something is intentionally represented as less than is in reality. In Bergman's *Smiles of a Summer Night,* Desirée is furious when she recalls how she has been taken advantage of by Fredrik. He states that he too has suffered. She replies, "You've suffered! From *what?* Tight shoes?"

Many other devices encourage a person to view a situation, character, or action with amusement. A few of the more commonly used are *incongruity* (inappropriate or illogical, as when Buster Keaton in *The Navigator* sets up a men-at-work sign before repairing a ship underwater in a diving suit); *paradox* (seemingly a contradiction, actually suggesting a truth; for example, Algernon's remark in *The Importance of Being Earnest* about a woman recently widowed: "I hear her hair has turned quite gold from grief"); *surprise* (the unexpected, what we would never conceive of doing under normal circumstance, as when a starving Charlie in *The Gold Rush* pretends that the shoelaces he is eating are spaghetti); *irony* (one thing is said or done and its opposite is intended or happens; for instance, when Max and Leo in *The Producers* present the worst play they can find in order to cheat their backers and it turns out to be a hit); and *wit* (cleverly or ingeniously expressed, as when Fredrik in *Smiles of a Summer Night* remarks to his son: "If you're thrown, mount again before you become frightened. That rule can be applied both to love and horseback riding."[1]).

The definitions obviously overlap. Furthermore, it must be kept in mind that none of these devices, including exaggeration and understatement, are intrinsically comic. They are contributing factors to humor only in the context of comedy, which is created when a specific type of reaction to the human condition is expressed. One way of apprehending the fundamental assumptions underlying this attitude toward existence is to compare certain aspects of comedy and tragedy.

Comedy and tragedy have one source in common: an individual's discontent with fate, whether perceived as determined by "the Other," insentient circumstances, or a person's own nature. Tragedy results when people resist forces that humble them, restrict their freedom of choice, and ultimately destroy them; comedy requires that people accept their fate, however ruefully, and survive. The latter, then, teaches us the value of pragmatism, of common sense, of a realistic view of human capabilities. Humor is the admonishing rod warning us of the futility of tilting against windmills.

Comedy is usually less gripping than tragedy, but it is more difficult to analyze. For one thing, it includes a wider range of forms and can appear as solely entertainment as well as art. Moreover, unlike tragedy, comedy presents two types of characters, related but dissimilar. First there is the object of ridicule toward whom we believe ourselves superior and at whom we feel justified in directing aggressive impulses. There is also the comic hero, beset by problems and often floundering in foolish ways, yet who arouses our compassion and also our admiration of the ways he deals with and survives an inimical fate. In addition to moral judgment, our attitude toward each type is influenced to a large degree by the proportions of distance and identification in our reactions to a character. In the object of ridicule we recognize

negative qualities of our own, such as hypocrisy or pretentiousness but feel sufficiently distant to countenance attacks on him. The hero too must be distant enough for us to laugh at him without feeling threatened; however, predominantly we identify with him, for we approve of his flexibility and ability to endure under stress.

Comedy might not exist if the world we live in were entirely governed by what man conceives of as the laws of logic. Perhaps this is why utopias devised by thinkers from Plato to B. F. Skinner are such humorless places. As it is, our existence is permeated with unexpected events and irrational human responses to which an individual adapts, resists, or escapes through insanity (in which state one can believe that the universe conforms to a private logic). Comedy reminds us of the limitations of reason and the necessity of accepting absurdity with good grace or taking the consequences. A person who is rigid physically, emotionally, or in both ways lives by the principle that what should be or appears to be according to the rules of logic actually exists. We are amused by Margaret Dumont (whatever the name she assumes in a film) because she is convinced that people say what they mean and act according to a code of social decorum. She simply cannot adjust to the anarchistic antics of the Marx Brothers. Such inflexible individuals become the objects in a comedy of good-natured satire, as in the case of Dumont, or ridicule, as happens with villains in the Marx Brothers' films.

Paradoxically, while comedy insists on the limitations of rationality, it also commends honesty and realistic appraisals of situations. Hypocrites, snobs, bullies, egotists—all subjects of comic ridicule—are not honest with themselves or realistic about their qualities. On the other hand, the comic hero is both, which is the reason a Woody Allen character can be self-deprecating when perceiving his own delusions or ineptitude. If a comic hero loses this objectivity, he becomes an object of pity (incongruous with humor) rather than admiration. Comedy, therefore, not only supports flexibility as opposed to rigidity but also objectivity and honesty in contrast to illusions and self-delusions.

It is a short, perhaps inevitable, step from these

remarks to the assertion that comedy serves some type of social or moral function. This is a controversal subject bristling with touchy questions. In a brief survey, it is more expedient—and safer—simply to suggest the ideas of two philosophers who exemplify this conviction.

Henri Bergson argues that in "laughter we always find an unavowed intention to humiliate, and consequently to correct our neighbour, if not in his will, at least in his deed."[2] What must be corrected, he suggests, is a lack of flexibility in dealing with a situation because "mechanical inelasticity" is disruptive of social order. The main function of comedy, in this view, is to encourage adaptability that leads the deviator back to the norm. That norm is usually determined by the patterns of a culture. One could go further than Bergson and note that even within a culture there will be disagreement as to what needs correction and how to achieve it. Emile de Antonio's *Milhouse: A White Comedy* (1971), for example, might prompt a liberal audience to laughter but enrage one of conservative Republicans.

American philosopher James K. Feibleman takes a related stance with a different emphasis. For him,

the categories of actuality are always what they have to be and seldom what they ought to be. . . . Thus comedy ridicules new customs, new institutions, for being insufficiently inclusive; [and] makes fun of old ones which have outlived their usefulness and have come to stand in the way of further progress.[3]

Comedy, Feibleman maintains, reconciles us to actuality and serves as a touchstone of the practicality and usefulness of attitudes and beliefs.

A difficulty confronting a philosopher or critic examining the function or any aspect of comedy is the lack of preciseness in terminology. This is particularly evident in attempts to define categories or forms of comedy. Even Siegfried Kracauer, with his German passion for categorizing, avoids dealing with this dilemma in *Theory of Film.* In *The Comic Mind,* Gerald Mast refers to three "traditions": dialogue (comedy through talk), clown (built around a central comic performer or performers), and irony (complex structural conception).

Another approach that can be useful is derived from certain distinctions. The first of these would be between a film comedy that emphasizes a character and one that focuses primarily on a situation. The former contains a subdivision that is more common in motion pictures than in any other medium. A persona comedian is one who is recognizable from earlier films to an audience as soon as he or she appears on the screen. A set of personality traits and types of reactions are assumed by a viewer without the need to establish them within the framework of a specific film, although the name and experiences of the persona comedian may differ from work to work. Chaplin's Charlie and most of the silent clowns are obvious examples, but the term is also applicable to, among others, W. C. Fields, the Marx Brothers, and Jacques Tati.

A second distinction is based on the degree of exaggeration in a film comedy. At one extreme is slapstick, "screwball comedy," and farce (if this last is allowed as a form of comedy and not considered a separate genre), in which character and situations are largely incredible. At the other end of this scale of exaggeration are realistic comedies, such as those directed by Jean Renoir. Between realism and farce, above or below a middle ground, could be placed fantasy and romantic comedy in the area of the less believable and the works of Tati in that of the more believable.

A final distinction is possible between types of ridicule or satire, a component, as we have seen, of most comedy. The broadest forms are burlesque and parody (as in the films of Mel Brooks); more subtle is ironic comedy (an example would be *Smiles of a Summer Night*). The "screwball comedies" of Frank Capra are closer to burlesque, while the comedies of Preston Sturges and Billy Wilder are nearer to irony.

As these examples suggest, evaluating degree is essential, and all three types of distinctions could be applied to a single film. What is definitely not intended is for these distinctions—or, for that matter, the characteristics of comedy examined earlier—to become intellectual procrustean beds or to encourage futile exercises in labeling in the manner of Polonius' speech to Hamlet about the abilities of the players.

It is not often that the debut of a film genre can be pinpointed. In the case of comedy, however, historians agree that the first intentional comic action on a screen was Louis and Auguste Lumière's *L'Arroseur arrosé* (1895). Loosely translated as "the watered waterer," this half-minute shot shows a trick played on a gardener who is watering plants with a hose. A mischievous boy steps on the hose so that the water stops. The gardener looks into the hose spigot; the boy removes his foot; the water splashes on the gardener's face; the gardener grabs the boy and spanks him. (Decades later, Truffaut repeats this scene, with updating, in *The Mischief Makers*, 1957.)

Until the end of the century and a few years beyond, comedy in motion pictures consisted of this type of one-shot, visual rendering of a simple joke. The only advance was the appearance in more than one film of the same character. An example in the United States was the Edison Company's Happy Hooligan, a disreputable tramp who was constantly getting into trouble; in France there was Alphonse and Gaston.

Georges Méliès initiated the concept of a comic story told in a series of shots and including special effects. Others followed suit and developed more sophisticated cinematic techniques, especially building on the genuine narrative that appeared in Edwin Porter's *The Great Train Robbery* (1903). Porter was less innovative when he made his own comic film, *Dream of a Rarebit Fiend* (1906), depending a great deal on the trick photography of Méliès. Meanwhile, humorous animated shorts were released by Emile Cohl.

In 1905 the first comic screen actor to gain an international reputation made his debut. Max Linder (1883–1925) prompted laughter from the ludicrous situations in which the elegantly dressed, handsome sophisticate found himself. However, he did not create a versatile comic persona and did not learn until after the approach had become commonplace to use the camera as a means of achieving humorous effects. The best introduction to his work is the compilation film *Laugh With Max Linder* (*En Compagnie de Max Linder*, 1963).

Other clowns, such as John Bunny in the United States and Charles Prince and André Deed in France,

became well known. But it was a producer-director who moved film comedy to its next stage. Mack Sennett (1880–1960) worked with D. W. Griffith at Biograph from 1908 to 1912 as an actor and director. He learned much from "the Master" about dramatic construction, camera placement, editing, and the use of crosscutting to create suspense. Griffith himself made comedies at Biograph, but the genre was not his forte. Sennett developed a style of fast-paced rhythmic action that was to influence practically all Hollywood comedy of the silent era. The freedom and energy of his films compensated for ridiculous plots and flat characters. He elevated machines, especially automobiles, to the level of human beings and simultaneously reduced his actors and actresses to machines out of control. His anarchy was not completely unfocused, for he was clever in satirizing social and intellectual pretentiousness. The chase became a hallmark of his films.

The most successful of Sennett's comedies were created under the aegis of his Keystone Studio from 1912 to 1915. During this period originated the Keystone Kops, the Sennett Bathing Girls, and the first comedy feature, *Tillie's Punctured Romance* (1914). From mid-decade to the early twenties, Keystone was controlled by other companies, and the products of the studio became more restrained and sane. A decline in the quality of Sennett's work began in the twenties and reached its nadir with the innovation of sound. He retired in 1935.

The roster of actors who worked at one time or another with Sennett included every major clown of the silent period, with the exception of Buster Keaton. Only two other producers competed to any degree with the first genius of film comedy. Hal Roach was responsible for cultivating the talents of Harold Lloyd, Laurel and Hardy, Our Gang, and Charley Chase. He continued his career into the early fifties. Al Christie was a prolific producer (over 800 films by the early twenties) and is associated particularly with Larry Semon, a popular twenties comedian of bizarre appearance.

Missing in the Sennett comedies was a central character with whom the audience could identify, a three-dimensional human being who experienced genuine emotions, had motivations that were more than crude and tentative, and was involved in plots that bore a resemblance to reality. From approximately the mid-teens to the end of the silent era, especially with the advent of feature-length comedies, certain actors created specific personae and individual styles. Among the most popular were Roscoe "Fatty" Arbuckle, Mabel Normand, Ben Turpin, Billy Bevan, Charley Chase, Laurel and Hardy, Larry Semon, Snub Pollard, and Mack Swain. This list does not include the four silent clowns who even in their day were recognized as far superior to any of their peers: Charles Chaplin, Buster Keaton, Harold Lloyd, and Harry Langdon.

Chaplin remains, as he was called in the twenties, "the King of Comedy." The depth and range, emotional power, and wit of his films have never been equaled.* Chaplin's closest rival was Buster Keaton (1895–1966), and since the mid-sixties there has been a critical revival of interest in his work. Keaton created the persona of an attractive, athletic, stolid, sensible man who repeatedly finds himself in situations beyond his control. He "muddles through," however, with luck and a determination to do what is required of him. Machines and people constantly frustrate and amaze him because they do not operate properly, whereas his flexible body and logical mind always do. This does not mean that Buster is immune to illusions. His love affairs are just that, but, unlike Charlie, he is clear-sighted about the inadequacies of the women to whom he is attracted. He is as vulnerable as Charlie and as ingenious in escaping traps. The difference, however, is that the Tramp wears his heart on his sleeve and reacts physically to every strong emotion that grips him, whereas "the Great Stone Face," as Keaton was called, accepts and perseveres, revealing his feelings with an economy that is all the more effective because it is subtle.

Economy also enters into the structure of Keaton's films. Every humorous routine is justified by the context of a scene. In the films he directed, he demonstrated an appreciation of the ways in which camera-editing dynamics can contribute to comedy, and

fluency, versatility, and control are evident in his cinematic techniques.

Keaton's shorts before 1920 are a distillation of his comic approach. It was in his silent features, however, that he revealed his genius for structure and characterization. His most popular features of the twenties were *Sherlock Junior* (1924), *The Navigator* (1924), *Go West* (1925), *The General* (1926, generally considered his masterpiece) (Figure 6.1), *Steamboat Bill, Jr.* (1928), and *The Cameraman* (1928). During the thirties, conflicts with his studio, MGM, and personal problems led to his being relegated to shorts and small parts. In the sixties he had a brief comeback before his death, most notably in the silent *Film* (1965, with a scenario by Samuel Beckett).

**FIGURE 6.1**

*The General,* 1926, directed by Buster Keaton. During the Civil War, a young Southern railroad engineer rides behind Union Army lines to rescue his girlfriend. At one point, the barrel of a small cannon on his train that he is firing slides down and points directly at him.

Harold Lloyd (1893–1971) was almost as impressive as Chaplin and Keaton in conceiving individual gags; on the other hand, he was unable to unify and develop feature-length comedies without becoming repetitious and uninspired. For this reason his most uniformly satisfying works are two compilation films, *Harold Lloyd's World of Comedy* and *The Funny Side of Life* (both 1963). He usually played a clean-

*pp. 285–288

cut, collegiate American youth consumed with the desire to be a success by middle-class standards but having few of the abilities, a sort of comically inept Horatio Alger hero. Lloyd's persona, however, lacked the vulnerability and exuberance of Chaplin's and the banked vitality and ingenuity of Keaton's.

His most successful silent film is *The Freshman* (1925) (Figure 6.2), followed at some distance by *Grandma's Boy* (1922), *Safety Last* (1923), and *Why Worry?* (1923). Lloyd, like Chaplin and unlike Keaton and Langdon, survived the introduction of sound. Though less popular than his silent works, such films as *Movie Crazy* (1932) and *Mad Wednesday* or *The Sins of Harold Diddlebock* (1947, directed by Preston Sturges) are respectable efforts.

**FIGURE 6.2**

*The Freshman,* 1925, directed by Fred Newmeyer. More through accident and grit than ability, Harold Lloyd wins the big game for his college.

The last and least of the quadruplet of master silent clowns was Harry Langdon (1884–1944). He projected a passive, childish creature who attracted catastrophes like a magnet does iron and to which he responded with agonizingly slow awareness. To those who found Langdon appealing, this asexual adult with the appearance of an overgrown baby, who means well but is a born victim, could be both whimsically comic and poignant. James Agee, an admirer, wrote that "Langdon had one queerly toned, unique little reed. But out of it he could get incredible melodies."[4]

Others found him a cinematic Johnny One-Note, pathetic rather than appealing, only intermittently capable of subtlety within his limited range.

Langdon's outstanding films are *Tramp, Tramp, Tramp* (1926) (Figure 6.3), *The Strong Man* (1926) and *Long Pants* (1927), the last two directed by Frank Capra. His sound films were financial and critical failures.

**FIGURE 6.3**

*Tramp, Tramp, Tramp,* 1926, directed by Harry Edwards. Harry Langdon enters a transcontinental walking race to win the prize money for his ailing father and the hand of the sponsor's daughter (Joan Crawford); the latter is beckoning to him in this shot.

The clowns were the finest expression of American silent comedy. Naturally, other types of comedy were produced, from versions of operettas (such as Erich von Stroheim's *The Merry Widow*) to social-situation comedies (for example, Cecil B. De Mille's *Male and Female,* 1919). Only one director of stature who did not also act emerged in the genre; the silent films Ernest Lubitsch made in the United States will be mentioned when we consider his sound motion pictures.

The Europeans were unable to develop personae comedians who achieved renown outside of individual countries. In France, however, satirical situation comedies appeared. The most notable directors using this approach were René Clair and Jean Renoir, both of whom created even more important sound films.

Gerald Mast has perceptively distinguished between silent and sound comedy. He describes the former as "a medium whose only tools were movement, rhythm, and physical objects and surfaces."[5] Silent films were, in his view, as much ballet as realistic dramas. On the other hand, sound comedy is structured, not physical. "It is *written* comedy. Perhaps a better term might be conceived, or shaped, or planned, or constructed."[6] Ultimately, sound comedy is more realistic in contributing not only synchronized dialogue but also natural sounds. Very generally, sound comedy has attempted to create the impression of a recognizable world in which exaggeration is confined to the verbal rather than the physical and in which the whole is more important than any individual scene. Losses in exuberance, fantasy, and visual rhythms have been compensated for by the potentials for greater intellectuality, subtlety, verisimilitude, and depth of characterization.

Many directors and actors were unable to adjust to the demands of sound. Others resisted but eventually came to terms with this new element of presentation. René Clair (1898–1981) fit into the latter category. He had had a great success with *An Italian Straw Hat* (*Un Chapeau de paille d'Italie,* 1927). This delightful comedy is so effective pictorially that words and sounds are superfluous. It comes as a surprise, therefore, that Clair a few years later should make five films (*Sous les toits de Paris,* 1930; *Le Million,* 1931; *A nous la liberté,* 1931; *Quatorze juillet,* 1932; and *Le Dernier Milliardaire,* 1934) that completely integrated sound with visuals. *A nous la liberté* is the best known of the quintet.

This film and its two predecessors are often classified as musicals, so they are considered in the chapter on that genre.* Clair went on to make films in Britain (such as *The Ghost Goes West,* 1935), the United States (for example, *I Married a Witch,* 1942), and, after the war, in France again (including *Beauties of the Night, Les Belles de nuit,* 1952). None of these comedies, unfortunately, has the vitality and imagination of the earlier works.

Clair's sound comedies have been criticized as being too artificial and ingenuous. At his best, however, as in *A nous la liberté* and *Le Million,* his satires of the bourgeoisie have bite, his control of all aspects of his medium is impressive, and, when not carried away by idealism, he is capable of self-irony even while conveying his convictions that male friendship, contact with nature, and less role playing between male and female are necessary antidotes to the mechanization and materialism of modern life.

Jean Renoir* directed only one notable silent comedy, *Tire-au-flanc* (1928), a satire on army life and upper-middle-class pretentiousness. In many of his sound films, ironic humor with dark overtones appears, such as *A Day in the Country, The Rules of the Game,* and *Picnic on the Grass.* Four of his most memorable works are as close to complete comedies as Renoir wanted to achieve. In *Baudu Saved From Drowning* (1932), Michel Simon plays an anarchistic primitive who imposes himself on a bourgeois family. It is a hilarious film, admirably directed, filled with sharp barbs for those who prefer possessions and pretensions to the natural and spontaneous. *The Golden Coach* (1953) is set in eighteenth-century Peru. Freely based on a Prosper Mérimée story, it centers on the life of Camilla, a famous actress pursued by three very different lovers, who lose out to the only rival capable of receiving the actress's depth of passion—the theater. The film is visually enchanting in its *commedia dell'arte* style, alternately funny and moving, and illuminated by the intense performance of Anna Magnani. *French Cancan* (1954), set in Montmarte in the 1880s, describes the founding of the famous Moulin Rouge. Beneath a surface of loveliness, vitality, and gaiety runs a vein of sadness, even bitterness, at the inventiveness of human beings in finding ways of hurting people who love them. *The Petite Theater of Jean Renoir* (1971), made for television, is the director's farewell to cinema. Appropriately, it contains his chief characteristics when creating comedy: warmth, imagination, satire, and the ability to convince viewers that comedy is not carefree but a defense against being oppressed by the serious business of living.

Acclaim as well as controversy accompanied

Jean Renoir and René Clair throughout their careers. Recognition was much slower in coming to Jean Vigo (1905–1934), and then only after his death. He created two feature films and a documentary* during his brief lifetime. The first comedy, *Zero for Conduct* (*Zéro de conduite,* 1933), is a superb fusion of realism and surrealism, innovative directing, and insights into the loneliness and wonder of the world of adolescents. The plot deals with the rebellion of a group of students against a tyrannical principal and narrow-minded teachers. Many of the sequences—for example, the opening one in which two boys meet on a train bringing them back to school after a vacation—are completely accurate portrayals of youngsters. On the other hand, fantasy is used repeatedly to supply a dimension of emotional expressiveness beyond the range of realism. A scene in which the students form a procession after taking over a dormitory at night haunts the memory of anyone who has seen it.

Vigo's second film, *L'Atalante* (1934), was, to its detriment, reedited and a sentimental song added before it was released on the day the director was buried. Still, Vigo's humanity and cinematic genius come through in this comic romance of the travels on a barge of its captain, his bride, and an eccentric but lovable mate (Michel Simon).

Of the other French sound comedies produced before World War II, only Marcel Carné's farce *Bizarre, Bizarre* (*Drôle de drame,* 1937), with a cast including Jean-Louis Barrault, Michel Simon, and Louis Jouvet, and Jacques Feyder's *Carnival in Flanders* (1935)* need be mentioned. Film comedies in other Western countries, with one exception, were either too provincial to be of much interest outside their borders or were basically musicals, such as Gracie Fields's films in England. The exception, of course, was the United States.

Of the quartet of American clowns, Chaplin alone was able to sustain his reputation after the advent of sound. Some lesser figures adapted to the new medium, although their best work usually had appeared in the twenties; the most notable example is the team of Laurel and Hardy. On the other hand,

sound was the making of at least one popular persona comedian of the thirties. W. C. Fields (1879–1946) had had only moderate success in silent films, but his fame was secured when he was able to give voice to his rage at nagging wives, nasty children, and a fate that continually frustrated his dreams of wealth, seducible women, and an endless supply of liquor and card games. The plots of Fields's films are illogical and nonlinear, for their purpose is not to develop a coherent theme but to present situations in which the screenwriter-star can throw darts tipped with venomous satire at provincial American life, the complacent rich, the self-righteous defenders of moral values, and the myth of American idealism. At his best Fields demonstrates not only his misanthropy and critical eye but also impeccable timing in delivering lines and superb mastery of verbal inflections in *Million Dollar Legs* (1932), *You Can't Cheat an Honest Man* (1939), *The Bank Dick* (1940), *My Little Chickadee* (1940), and *Never Give a Sucker an Even Break* (1941). Another facet of his acting abilities was apparent when he played Humpty Dumpty in *Alice in Wonderland* (1933) and Micawber in *David Copperfield* (1934).

In *My Little Chickadee,* Fields costarred with one of the few women on the American screen who could upstage him (Figure 6.4). Mae West (1892–

---

FIGURE 6.4

*My Little Chickadee,* 1940, directed by Edward Cline. Cuthbert J. Twillie (W. C. Fields) tries his seductive wiles on the voluptuous and wealthy Flower Belle Lee (Mae West).

---

1980), after being a star on Broadway in *Sex* (1926) and *Diamond Lil* (1929), brought to film comedy of the thirties a gust of forthright sexuality. Her risqué dialogue (she wrote her own scripts), ripe figure in flamboyant costumes, and frank appreciation of male virility offended the prudish. The wit and physical presence of the woman, who makes most of our contemporary sex goddesses seem anemic, tongue-tied mannequins by comparison, enlivened *She Done Him Wrong* (1933, an adaptation of *Diamond Lil*), *Belle of the Nineties* (1934), *Go West, Young Man* (1936), and *My Little Chickadee,* among other films. She published an appropriately entitled autobiography, *Goodness Had Nothing to Do with It,* in 1959 and appeared in *Myra Breckinridge* in 1970.

For all the success of Fields and West, the most popular personae comics of the period were a zany group called the Marx Brothers. They started as a vaudeville team of five brothers and went on to Broadway musicals. At the time they began making films, Gummo left, and then there were four. Their first motion pictures, for Paramount, were adaptations of two of their stage musicals and filmed in New York: *The Cocoanuts* (1929) and *Animal Crackers* (1930). When they moved to Hollywood, they starred in three of their best films: *Monkey Business* (1931) (Figure 6.5), in which they exploded in the world of high society; *Horse Feathers* (1932), set on a college campus; and *Duck Soup* (1933), which takes place in the mythical kingdom of Freedonia. They shifted to MGM for their next films. Zeppo, the straight man of the group, left, and then there were three.

The three Marx Brothers were more constricted at MGM, and both romantic stories and big production numbers were added to their comedies. They survived in good form in *A Night at the Opera* (1935) and *A Day at the Races* (1937), but a decline in their comic inventiveness became evident in *Room Service* (1938), *At the Circus* (1939), *Go West* (1940), and the films that followed in the forties. They split up as a team in 1949.

The primary appeal of the Marx Brothers lies in their ability to get away with anarchy. They enter situations in which there is some semblance of sanity —a party, a football game, a government, an opera— and when they are through, everything is in a sham-

FIGURE 6.5

*Monkey Business,* 1931, directed by Norman Z. McLeod. The Marx Brothers (front row: Zeppo, Groucho, Harpo, and, at the far right, Chico) become involved with gangsters and a kidnapping when they stow away on an ocean liner.

bles, hastily pasted together only so that the film can end. Yet we in the audience, supposedly logical, law-abiding individuals, laugh at and applaud such crazy mayhem. Perhaps we envy the superabundant freedom and unrestrained self-expression of these madmen, or it may be that the Margaret Dumonts of the world are so sure of their privileges and others are so confident that logic and proper manners are the lubricants of a well-functioning society that we feel they deserve devastating debunking. Whatever the reasons, these irresponsible comics struck a responsive chord in American moviegoers enduring the restrictive burdens of first an economic depression and then a world war.

The brothers combined the advantages of both silent and sound comedy. Groucho (1895–1977) was visually humorous with wire-frame eyeglasses, rolling eyes, mustache, cigar, and crouched stride, but he was even more effective in his arrogant, non sequitur wisecracks. Chico (1891–1961) also depended on speech: a vaguely Italian-American accent to justify outrageous puns and the delivery of statements that contain an echo of common sense, yet somehow go beyond logic to the irrational. Harpo (1893–1964) was half silent clown in a wild wig who communicated with his body and a horn and half satyr who used his muteness to advantage to prove that where women and food were concerned, he was not so dumb. For almost two decades these brothers delighted motion picture audiences as lunatics in china shops called Hollywood sets.

Other well-known personae comedians of the thirties and early forties in the United States were Will Rogers, Joe E. Brown, Jack Benny, Jimmy Durante, Ole Olsen and Chick Johnson, Bob Hope, and the Ritz Brothers (Al, Jim, and Harry). Most of them, however, either went on to greater success after World War II or did not dominate a series of films. In situation comedies appeared actors and actresses who turned also to other genres but showed a flair for comedy; some were teamed together in more than one film. Among the most admired were Marie Dressler and Wallace Beery; Katharine Hepburn and Cary Grant or Spencer Tracy, particularly in Howard Hawks films; Jean Arthur and Gary Cooper or James Stewart in Frank Capra films; Myrna Loy and William Powell in the Thin Man series; Jean Harlow and Clark Gable; Carole Lombard, Claudette Colbert, Irene Dunne, Rosalind Russell, and Lucille Ball.

Situation comedies do not depend primarily on the antics of a single actor whose persona evoked set responses in an audience but on the attitudes and ideas, often in conflict, of many characters. They are usually associated, therefore, more with directors than actors. In the United States during the thirties, two directors, Ernst Lubitsch and Frank Capra, more than any of their colleagues, produced scintillating comedies that required viewers to listen as well as look.

Ernst Lubitsch (1892–1947) began making films in Germany in 1911 and soon became renowned for the stylishness of his visual effects, ability to draw the best from his actors, and wit when he turned his hand to satirical comedies. His historical romances, such as *Madame Dubarry* (*Passion* in the U.S., 1919), and his comedies, for instance, *The Oyster Princess* (*Die Austernprinzessin,* 1919), attracted the attention of Hollywood. He came to the United States in 1922, along with one of his major stars, Pola Negri.

After a false start with *Rosita* (1923), starring Mary Pickford, he was successful in bringing European sophistication to American comedy, most notably in *The Marriage Circle* (1924), *Forbidden Paradise* (1924), *Lady Windermere's Fan* (1925), and *The Student Prince* (1927). Critics began referring to "the Lubitsch touch." This term often meant whatever a critic was praising in the director's work. More specifically, it referred to Lubitsch's ability to present details —a gesture, an action, the way an object is handled —to indicate an emotional state or situation. For example, a good deal is suggested about a marriage silently when a man enters an elevator with his wife but does not remove his hat until an attractive woman steps in two floors below.

Sound allowed Lubitsch additional opportunities for wit, irony, and satire. He began with musicals,* but soon turned to situation comedy. In 1932 he released one of his very best, *Trouble in Paradise,* starring Herbert Marshall and Miriam Hopkins as jewel thieves who fall in love during the process of robbing a rich widow (Kay Francis). Other comedies included *Bluebeard's Eighth Wife* (1938), *Ninotchka* (1939, starring Greta Garbo), *To Be or Not to Be* (1942), *Heaven Can Wait* (1943), and *Cluny Brown* (1946). Although he directed such dramas as *The Man I Killed* (1932) and *Angel* (1937), he was most comfortable with comedies.

Lubitsch's technical skill, especially the integration of setting and dramatic action, and his Svengali influence over the actresses with whom he worked drew the approval of other professionals. To the general American audiences, however, he was associated with an adroitness in slyly deflating, with consummate style, our romantic illusions about love, heroism, and class.

A contemporary of Lubitsch in the thirties mined a vein of more intrinsically American comedy. Frank Capra (1897–) began his career in motion pictures as a gagwriter for Mack Sennett and went on to become a screenwriter for and director of Harry Langdon films. His first sound films, including *Ladies of Leisure* (1930) and *Platinum Blonde* (1931), were competent but not outstanding. A breakthrough occurred in 1932 when he teamed with Robert Riskin, the screenwriter, to create *American Madness.* Riskin

---

*p. 441

was responsible for the scripts of all of the director's best thirties films and 1941's *Meet John Doe*. Capra's idealism and sentimentality, as well as his knack for visually highlighting comic scenes, led to the phenomenal popularity of *It Happened One Night* (1934), *Mr. Deeds Goes to Town* (1936), *Mr. Smith Goes to Washington* (1939), *You Can't Take It With You* (1938), and *Meet John Doe* (1941).

During World War II, Capra supervised and in some instances directed individual films for the "Why We Fight" series (1942–1945).* His later films—*It's a Wonderful Life* (1946) (Figure 6.6), *State of the Nation* (1948), *A Hole in the Head* (1959), and *A Pocketful of Miracles* (1961)—were respectfully received but out of tune with the cynical attitudes of postwar audiences.

---

**FIGURE 6.6**

*It's a Wonderful Life,* 1946, directed by Frank Capra. George Bailey (James Stewart) returns to his family after contemplating suicide. With the help of an angel and a visit to the future, he has learned that whatever one's problems, family and friends can make life wonderful.

A term has been applied to certain films of the thirties, especially those directed by Frank Capra, that is clumsy but used too often by critics to ignore. *"Screwball comedy"* contains eccentric characters in ludicrous situations; the humor is broad and the action

fast-paced. Gregory La Cava's *My Man Godfrey* (1936) and Howard Hawks's *Bringing Up Baby* would also fit into this category. World War II is generally considered to have brought about the demise of screwball comedy, with occasional resurrections, as in Peter Bogdanovich's *What's Up, Doc?* (1972).

Whatever label is applied to Capra's thirties comedies, most of them share the premise that America's problems can be solved by optimism, integrity, sincerity, and fairness; as this list suggests, a degree of naiveté also helps. Capra was not blind to the faults of our system or those of human nature. He simply had confidence in homespun, small-town virtues and the power of a good man fighting for a worthy cause to rally people around him and win in the end against overwhelming obstacles.

The director's thirties films would appear today outdated and simplistic in their optimism were it not for his sure sense of comic pacing, an ability to laugh affectionately at the ingenuousness and awkwardness of his heroes, and a gift for distinctive characterization, especially of eccentrics. He was also fortunate in being able to cast as his main male characters Gary Cooper *(Mr. Deeds Goes to Town, Meet John Doe)* and James Stewart *(Mr. Smith Goes to Washington, You Can't Take It With You, It's a Wonderful Life)*. They could make believable, at least for an hour and a half, Capra's shy, innocent, honest heroes.

Although Chaplin, Lubitsch, and Capra were the major directors of comedies in the thirties in the United States, others were outstanding. The versatile Howard Hawks was a distinguished creator of comedies as well as motion pictures in many other genres.* His distinctive, taut wit and sharp, direct style, especially when dealing with the battle of the sexes, are apparent in *Twentieth Century* (1934), *Bringing Up Baby* (1938), *His Girl Friday* (1940), *Ball of Fire* (1941), and *I Was a Male War Bride* (1949). Leo McCarey (1898–1969) directed many of the silent shorts of Laurel and Hardy and Charley Chase. In the thirties he demonstrated his professionalism and appreciation of boisterous humor in *The Kid From Spain* (1932, with Eddie Cantor), *Duck Soup* (1933, the

---

*pp. 338–339

*p. 118

Marx Brothers), and films starring W. C. Fields, Harold Lloyd, and Mae West. *Ruggles of Red Gap* (1935, starring Charles Laughton) is a movie classic, and probably McCarey's best film is *The Awful Truth* (1937, with Cary Grant and Irene Dunne). Although he never lost his adroitness as a director, in later years his humor became flaccid, as in *My Favorite Wife* (1940), or inane, as in *Rally Round the Flag, Boys!* (1958). Other sound comedies that were successes before and during World War II include *The Front Page* (1931, directed by Lewis Milestone), *Bombshell* (1933, Victor Fleming), *The Thin Man* (1934, W. S. Van Dyke), *My Man Godfrey* (1936, Gregory La Cava), *Nothing Sacred* (1937, William Wellman), *Topper* (1938, Norman Z. McLeod), and *Holiday* (1938, George Cukor).

A convenient dividing line between two types of comedy that appeared in the United States is the end of World War II, thus extending the spirit of the thirties to the middle of the forties. Certain films and the work of at least one director, however, have been traditionally labeled by film historians as of the forties. These motion pictures are usually tougher and more satirical than typical comedies of the thirties but do not express the disillusionment of the fifties. Actually released during the forties and falling under this heading, in addition to Howard Hawks's films, would be George Cukor's *The Philadelphia Story* (1940), Garson Kanin's *Tom, Dick, and Harry* (1941), George Stevens's *Woman of the Year* (1942, the first of nine films in which Katherine Hepburn and Spencer Tracy costarred), Rouben Mamoulian's *Rings on Her Fingers* (1942), Joseph Mankiewicz's *The Late George Apley* and *The Ghost of Mrs. Muir* (both 1947), Joseph Losey's *The Boy With Green Hair* (1948), and Walter Lang's *Sitting Pretty* (1948, memorable for the performance of Clifton Webb as Mr. Belvedere). It was the films of Preston Sturges, however, that most typified the qualities associated with the decade.

Preston Sturges (1898–1959) first attracted attention as a successful Broadway playwright. In 1930 he joined Paramount Pictures as a screenwriter and was recognized as one of the finest in Hollywood during the thirties. He persuaded his studio to allow him to direct as well as write the screenplay for *The*

*Great McGinty* (1940) and in the same year *Christmas in July*. During the forties he wrote the scripts for and directed, among others, *The Lady Eve* (1941), *Sullivan's Travels* (1941), *The Palm Beach Story* (1942), *The Miracle of Morgan's Creek* (1943), *Hail the Conquering Hero* (1944), and *Mad Wednesday* or *The Sin of Harold Diddlebock* (1947, with Harold Lloyd). His few fifties films were definitely not of the caliber of his earlier works.

*Sullivan's Travels* (Figure 6.7) illustrates Sturges's strengths and weaknesses. A director of popular escapist movies (Joel McCrea) decides to do a "significant" film to be titled *Oh Brother, Where Art Thou?* His attempts to research poverty (accompanied by a trailer, butler, and girlfriend, Veronica Lake) are unsuccessful. Through an accident and a case of amnesia, he is actually arrested and imprisoned in a chain gang. In prison he learns that simple entertainment is also significant. When eventually he is released and restored to his former position, he is content to continue to make comedies.

The dialogue is crisp and natural. The satire of Hollywood and condescending, ineffectual efforts of intellectuals to help the poor, who rarely have the virtues of Ma Joad, is realistic and cuts deep. The tone

**FIGURE 6.7**

*Sullivan's Travels,* 1941, directed by Preston Sturges. John L. Sullivan (Joel McCrea, first row, second from right) has learned from his recent experiences and will return to directing comedies. Veronica Lake has her hand on McCrea's shoulder.

becomes almost tragic in the second half of the film (Sturges's humor always has a dark side to it), but all turns out well at the end. This is a problem in this film and most of Sturges's other works. What the director's savage eye sees is palliated by rationalizations, conventional clichés, and "positive" endings. Sturges had the ability to write original screenplays; was effective, at times imaginative, in his directing; appreciated how a sound track could comment ironically on the visuals; and knew how to draw outstanding performances from even mediocre actors. What he lacked was the courage to face and to express honestly and completely in comic terms his rueful vision of human nature and American society.

Film comedy in all countries of the Western world underwent radical changes after World War II. It became more cynical and satirical; many taboos, especially those involving sex and language, slowly disappeared; narrative structure became more unconventional and experimental; costs mounted rapidly; and by the end of the fifties, color was demanded by audiences.

In France, the most welcome postwar event in film comedy was the emergence of a comedian who for the first time in two decades could be compared to the great silent clowns of the American screen. Jacques Tati (1908–1982) began his theatrical career giving performances in cabarets, specializing in mime. In the thirties he directed and acted in two motion picture shorts and played subordinate roles in other films. He created his first feature, *Jour de fête*, in 1947. A meticulous craftsman, he took 4 to 6 years to make a feature-length film; he released only five works in the following 2½ decades: *Mr. Hulot's Holiday* (*Les Vacances de Monsieur Hulot*, 1951), *My Uncle* (*Mon Oncle*, 1958), *Playtime* (1967), *Traffic* (*Traffic*, 1971), and *Parade* (1974, for television).

Mr. Hulot became Tati's persona: a tall, long-legged, somewhat awkward individual with a loping stride, who on the surface accepts rules and regulations, yet instinctively remains a nonconformist. He is the personification of passive resistance. In his own way, unaware of the commotion he leaves in his wake, he steadfastly pursues a goal (enjoying a vacation, supervising a section of a plastics factory, meet-

ing a corporation official, delivering a camping car). Inevitably we find ourselves approving of this strange, likable hero without strongly identifying with him or understanding his motives. Instead of him, we focus our attention on the situations in which he finds himself.

Continually the filmmaker (who was responsible for all major aspects of his productions, from screenplay to editing) is subtly commenting on what is presented on the screen. What makes Tati so fascinating is that he entertains us and implies his point of view not through the narrative but through other cinematic dimensions. His plots appear (until a film has been seen more than once) rambling and even aimless, and dialogue is kept to a minimum. Tati's primary means of comic expression is the visuals and nonverbal sounds and music. As with all film comedians, he creates self-contained jokes—for example, in *Mr. Hulot's Holiday*, the hero's bizarre tennis style. This type of humorous physical act or situation unfolds in a quiet, leisurely manner that does not disguise for a perceptive viewer how very carefully it has been planned.

It is, however, in being satirical that Tati is visually most effective—and sly. The house in *My Uncle*, the office building in *Playtime* (Figure 6.8), and the

**FIGURE 6.8**

*Playtime*, 1967, directed by Jacques Tati (color). Mr. Hulot (Tati) loses his way in a large, modern office building. During his wanderings, he finds himself looking down at a labyrinth of workers' cubicles.

camper in *Traffic* are marvels of technology, impressive until we realize that the people who live and work in them have become as mechanical as their environment. What better symbol can there be of the worst aspects of our modern cities than the cars, buses, and trucks in *Playtime* driving around in a circle?

Tati's use of sounds synchronized to his visuals is incomparable. It is not an exaggeration to state that no previous director of comedies has integrated sound into his films with greater variety and startling brilliance. Whether it is jazz background music or the noise of traffic, sound not only sets a mood but also comments, often ironically, on what is happening. Words become superfluous when the sound track can convey the attitudes and feelings of the director more immediately and universally.

Pierre Étaix shares with Tati an emphasis on nonverbal humor in an age of sound films. It may have been inculcated in him by his early experiences as a circus clown (he appeared later in Fellini's *The Clowns*) and a mime in music halls. His best-known film is *Yoyo* (1965), although *Le Grand amour* (1969) also has been praised highly. Étaix has his own style, which takes advantage of his small, trim body to create stylish, clever scenes. He has little, however, of the cinematic resourcefulness and depth of Tati.

It is a small irony Tati might have devised that the outstanding French situation film comedy after World War II should have been directed by a man born in Germany and adapted from an Austrian play. Max Ophuls, most famous for his dramas,* directed *La Ronde,* based on Arthur Schnitzler's *Reigen,* in 1950. The cast is fabulous, including Anton Walbrook, Simone Signoret, Simone Simon, Danielle Darrieux, Jean-Louis Barrault, Isa Miranda, and Gérard Philipe. The film consists of 10 connected episodes, each having as its subject a type of love. All the stories are entrancing but also touching as we are reminded how often sexual desire and love (two sides of the same coin in the film) are experiences shared by two people in which one will eventually be hurt.

Aside from Tati's first three features, *La Ronde,* and the works of Jean Renoir noted earlier, no French comedies were exceptional successes during the for-

ties and fifties. This situation brightened in the sixties. Although the New Wave filmmakers confined themselves generally to dramas, they produced a few comedies, none completely carefree: François Truffaut's *Stolen Kisses* (1960) and *Bed and Board* (1970), Jean-Luc Godard's *A Woman Is a Woman* (1961), and Louis Malle's *Viva Maria!* (1965). Also deserving mention are the comedies of Philippe De Broca, particularly *Playing at Love* (*Les Jeux de l'amour,* 1960), *That Man From Rio* (*L'Homme de Rio,* 1964), and *King of Hearts* (*Le Roi de coeur,* 1966); the first film of Jacques Demy, *Lola* (1961); and Alain Jessua's *Comic Strip Hero* (*Jeu de massacre,* 1967).

Italy before World War II had a rather undistinguished motion picture history until the movement of Neorealism. Italian comedy, however, has not always been as exportable as its dramas. A prime example is the work of Eduardo De Filippo, an outstanding figure of Italian theater as a playwright and actor. His portrayals of Neapolitan life are parochial only in the dialect used, not in their plots and characterizations. Yet of the many films he directed and appeared in, only *Neapolitan Millionaire* (*Napoli Milionaria,* 1950) attracted an audience outside Italy. In this film, De Filippo featured, in addition to himself, Totò, Italy's favorite clown.

The seriousness of Neorealism was not conducive to humor; however, one of its masters, Vittorio De Sica, created a warm fantasy comedy in *Miracle in Milan,* as well as more realistic comedies, such as *The Gold of Naples* and *Marriage, Italian Style.* * De Sica acted with and directed Sophia Loren and Gina Lollabrigida; these two and Anna Magnani (who was capable of doing any type of role, from tragedy to farce) have been Italy's favorite film comediennes.

Federico Fellini's first film as sole director was *The White Sheik* (*Lo Sceicco Bianco,* 1952), starring Alberto Sordi and Giulietta Masina, a farce on the conflict between the illusion and reality of a cartoon character as experienced by a naive admirer. Comic in subject but not in tone is Fellini's *The Clowns* (*I Clowns,* 1970), and there are many humorous incidents in his *Amarcord* (1974).

Of the postwar Italian directors associated pri-

---

*pp. 138–139

*p. 237

marily with comedy, two stand out. Pietro Germi (1914–) began making films in the style of Neorealism, but in the early sixties he directed a series of comedies centering on Italian mores, particularly attitudes toward sex. *Divorce, Italian Style* (*Divorzio all'Italiana,* 1961, starring Marcello Mastroianni) was popular in Europe and the United States, as to a lesser degree were *Seduced and Abandoned* (*Sedotta e Abbandonata,* 1963) and *The Birds, the Bees, and the Italians* (*Signor e Signori,* 1965).

Mario Monicelli (1915–) also made his reputation as a Neorealist and then turned to lighter fare. His humor often has dark overtones, and his satire is invariably sharp-edged. His best-known comedy, *The Big Deal on Madonna Street* (*I Soliti Ignoti,* 1958), included in its cast Totò, Marcello Mastroianni, and Vittorio Gassman. His next work, *The Great War* (*La Grande Guerra,* 1959), starred Alberto Sordi. Other Monicelli comedies include *Casanova '70* (1965), *L'Armata Brancaleone* (1965, a hilarious burlesque on costume epics), and *Brancaleone alle Crociate* (1971).

Other successful Italian comedies of this period are Luigi Comencini's first two in the "Bread and Love" series, *Bread, Love, and Dreams* (*Pane, Amore e Fantasia,* 1953) and *Bread, Love, and Jealousy* (*Pane, Amore e Gelosia,* 1954); the last of that series, directed by Dino Risi, *Bread, Love . . .* (*Pane, Amore . . . ,* 1955), as well as Risi's *Poor but Handsome* (*Poveri ma Belli,* 1956) and *Love and Larceny* (*Il Mattatore,* 1959); Franco Brusati's *Tenderly* (1968); and Marco Ferreri's black comedies, including *El Pisito* (1957), *El Cochecito* (*The Wheelchair,* 1959), and *La Grande Bouffe* (1973).

Great Britain's comedies during the thirties and World War II, as indicated earlier, did not hold much interest for audiences in other countries. A giant step toward international popularity was taken when the Ealing Studios initiated a series of comedies that were characterized by extraordinary events occurring in realistic lower- and middle-class settings. Although often referred to as "little comedies," there was nothing little about the talent involved. Michael Balcon, head of production at Ealing from 1938 until the company was dissolved in 1955, was the guiding spirit of this new type of domestic comedy. He was abetted in his efforts by a team of resourceful screenwriters, directors, and actors. The most prominent Ealing writers were T. E. B. Clarke, Robert Hamer, John Dighton, and William Rose; Alexander Mackendrick was the most remarkable of the directors, closely followed by Charles Crichton, Henry Cornelius, and Robert Hamer. It was in Ealing films that Alec Guinness demonstrated that his impressive abilities as a screen actor encompassed comedy as well as drama. Other fine players in these films were Stanley Holloway, Margaret Rutherford, Terry-Thomas, Wilfrid Hyde-White, Joan Greenwood, and Peter Sellers.

Among the most distinctive of the Ealing films were *Whisky Galore* (1949, titled *Tight Little Island* in the United States, directed by Alexander Mackendrick), *Passport to Pimlico* (1949), *Kind Hearts and Coronets* (1949, with Alec Guinness and Joan Greenwood), *The Lavender Hill Mob* (1951), *The Man in the White Suit* (1951, directed by Alexander Mackendrick, again starring Alec Guinness and Joan Greenwood), and *The Ladykillers* (1955, directed by Mackendrick, with Guinness and Peter Sellers).

Other directors not associated with Ealing Studios also produced films of social criticism that depended on a balance of broad comedy and realism. Most prominent were the Boulting twins, John and Roy, who alternated in their collaborations as director and producer. *I'm All Right, Jack* (1959) was the most successful. Peter Sellers, who gave a striking performance as a dictatorial shop steward, had to compete with the formidable Margaret Rutherford, as well as Ian Carmichael and Terry-Thomas. Other Boulting comedies included *Brother-in-Law* (1957) and *The Family Way* (1966). In the category of "little comedies" also belongs *Last Holiday* (1950), *Genevieve* (1953), and Anthony Kimmins's *The Captain's Paradise* (1953), starring the indefatigable Guinness.

Although Britain's "little comedies" were successful at home and abroad, other types were produced after World War II. These can generally be divided into the more conventional ones of the forties and fifties and an original approach that first fully manifested itself in the sixties in the work of Richard Lester. Typical of the former are the adaptations of modern classic comedies by Anthony Asquith, best known for his dramas. In 1938 he had directed Bernard Shaw's

*Pygmalion.* He went on to do two other Shaw plays, *The Doctor's Dilemma* (1958) and *The Millionairess* (1960, with Peter Sellers in one of his finest roles). Asquith's *The Importance of Being Earnest* (1952) is a cinematically mundane but faithful rendering of Oscar Wilde's delightful farce. *The Yellow Rolls Royce* (1964) is fun, but an unworthy swan song for one of Great Britain's most important directors. Even more than Asquith, Gabriel Pascal is associated with transforming Bernard Shaw's plays into films; in fact, this was his sole major achievement as a filmmaker. After producing Asquith's *Pygmalion,* he went on to produce and direct two other Shaw comedies—*Major Barbara* (1941) and *Caesar and Cleopatra* (1945)— as well as produce and not direct *Androcles and the Lion* (1953). Any production with which Pascal was connected, with the exception of *Pygmalion,* is unimaginative and generally static but possesses an impressive pageantry that should not be denigrated.

Other notable English comedies of the forties and fifties include David Lean's *Blithe Spirit* (1945), an adaptation of the Noël Coward play; Mario Zampi's *Laughter in Paradise* (1951, a showpiece of the talents of Alastair Sim, a consistently fine comedy actor) and *The Naked Truth* (1957, starring Peter Sellers); Ronald Neame's *The Horse's Mouth* (1958), a fainthearted version of the Joyce Carey novel, starring —yes—Alec Guinness; *Knave of Hearts* (1954, directed by René Clément and featuring Gérard Philipe); Robert Day's *The Green Man* (1956); and Basil Dearden's *The League of Gentlemen* (1960).

In 1963 Tony Richardson's version of *Tom Jones* (with a script by John Osborne) burst upon the screen with lusty, rollicking, even vulgar vitality. Less important than whether the motion picture was faithful to the intentions of Henry Fielding was the sense that a new, iconoclastic, improvising, driving spirit had emerged in English film comedy. Richard Lester, born in the United States, confirmed the impression that the Angry Young Men of the fifties had found in the sixties a better medium than fiction or the theater to communicate their satirical view of the foibles and inanities of postwar England—and no rules of form or style were going to restrain their self-expression. Lester's two Beatles musicals, *A Hard Day's Night*

(1964) and *Help!* (1965),* were less improvised than appeared on the surface. There was no question, however, that the director would use his camera in any way he saw fit, no matter how bizarre it looked on the screen, and the last thing he was going to worry about was adhering to criteria of a conventional plot. *The Knack* (1965) is wonderfully zany fun, if somewhat self-indulgent, as are most of Lester's films. Clive Donner's contribution to his country's comedies includes *What's New, Pussycat?* (1967) and *Here We Go Round the Mulberry Bush* (1967). In Karel Reisz's *Morgan . . . A Suitable Case for Treatment* (1966), the main character literally "goes ape."

European countries other than France, Italy, and Great Britain have of course produced their own comedies. They have usually been ignored in the United States, with a few exceptions, such as two Czech films, *Closely Watched Trains* (1966, directed by Jiří Menzel) and Milos Forman's *The Fireman's Ball* (1967). Ingmar Bergman of Sweden transcends any neat generalizations. His comedies are discussed elsewhere in this chapter, especially the marvelous *Smiles of a Summer Night* (1955).

The United States has remained the comedy capital of the world. No other nation has produced more internationally accepted films in this genre, either before or since World War II. Only in the area of the persona comedian has American film humor deteriorated. There have been no adequate substitutes for Chaplin, Keaton, and Lloyd in the silent era and Fields, West, and the Marx Brothers in the thirties. The most popular clowns of the forties were the slapstick team of Abbott and Costello. More sophisticated and stylish was the humor of Danny Kaye, whose best film was *The Secret Life of Walter Mitty* (1947, directed by Norman Z. McLeod). Red Skelton also had a following in the forties and early fifties.

The most difficult comedian of this period to evaluate is Jerry Lewis (1926–). From 1949 to 1956 he was teamed with Dean Martin in 16 films. Lewis has continued on his own to the present. A number of his post–Dean Martin comedies have been directed by others, particularly Frank Tashlin, but since 1960, with

------

*p. 453

*The Bellboy,* he has been his own director and often screenwriter and producer as well. *The Nutty Professor* (1963) is one of the more successful of this group.

How does one judge a film clown with obvious gifts, creative in constructing comic situations, and who knows more about the technical aspects of filmmaking than most directors, yet seems to have no intuitive feeling for the value of restraint? Lewis's mugging and purposeful lack of physical coordination are outrageous. He has created the persona of a perennial adolescent who appears to have fits of delirium tremens whenever confronted by a problem he cannot handle or by an attractive woman. One might dismiss him casually as a comic who has never fulfilled his potentials if he did not have such a fanatic following and, more surprising, received extravagant praise from certain European film critics, who refer to him as a modern Chaplin and an *auteur* director. For some of us, however, "the problem of Jerry Lewis" (the phrase Gerald Mast and other critics have used in discussing the actor-director) is no more than a minor question mark in the history of contemporary film comedy until Lewis produces works of more substance, balance, and depth.

Bob Hope and Jack Benny were not typical film clowns, for their humor depended almost entirely on expertly timed verbal comments and a limited set of facial expressions. In the forties, however, both were prominent film stars. Hope appeared in the "Road" series (from *Road to Singapore,* 1940, to *Road to Bali,* 1952) with Bing Crosby (a low-key comedian in his own right) and Dorothy Lamour. Bob Hope also appeared in a delightful burlesque of the Western, *The Paleface* (1948). Benny was less active; his most successful films were *Charley's Aunt* (1941) and *To Be or Not to Be* (1942, directed by Ernest Lubitsch). Both Hope and Benny acted in motion pictures only sporadically during the fifties and after.

It is not difficult to account for the dearth of comedians whose personalities are more important than the plots of their films. Television has provided through variety shows and situation comedies more flexible and profitable formats than either cinema or the theater. It is likely that such persona comedians as Milton Berle, Sid Caesar, Jackie Gleason, Lucille Ball,

Carol Burnett, and Dick Van Dyke would have appeared more frequently in motion pictures if television did not exist.

American directors who had made their reputations in comedy during the thirties and continued to work in the forties and beyond include Frank Capra, Howard Hawks, and George Stevens. We have already considered the forties films of Preston Sturges. René Clair created a few undistinguished comedies during his brief stay in Hollywood from 1939 to 1947. George Cukor equaled the success of *The Philadelphia Story* with *Born Yesterday* (1950). He also directed two of the best of the Hepburn-Tracy collaborations, *Adam's Rib* (1949) and *Pat and Mike* (1952).

Most of the popular stars of the thirties appeared in situation comedies in the forties and fifties. New ones also became prominent during these two decades. Marilyn Monroe, a sensational star in the fifties, was most natural and effective in comedies. Audrey Hepburn, Doris Day, and Shirley MacLaine were equally successful in musicals and straight comedies. Other outstanding comediennes included Judy Holliday, Betty Hutton, Veronica Lake, Dorothy Lamour, Jayne Mansfield, and Celeste Holm. Of the male actors, Jack Lemmon and William Holden became top stars. Rex Harrison, David Niven, and George Sanders added an English accent to the American comedies in which they appeared. Other notable comedians were Brian Donlevy, Paul Douglas, Tony Curtis, Rock Hudson, Robert Cummings, Keenan Wynn, Eddie Albert, Fred MacMurray, Clifton Webb, Peter Lawford, Andy Griffith, and Jack Carson.

As Preston Sturges was the outstanding director of American comedies in the forties, Billy Wilder (1906–) was in the fifties. Wilder established a reputation in Germany in the late twenties as a fluent and prolific screenwriter. With the advent of the Third Reich, he left Germany and settled in Hollywood as a screenwriter. Among his credits (as coscreenwriter) are Lubitsch's *Ninotchka* (1939) and Hawks's *Ball of Fire* (1941). His first directing assignment was *The Major and the Minor* (1942); his coauthor on the script was Charles Brackett, with whom he collaborated on most of his forties films. There followed a series of relentlessly realistic, polished dramas that caused Wilder to be regarded as a leading Hollywood director.*

In 1950 he revealed another facet of his talent. *Sunset Boulevard* is a unique combination of cynical humor and tragedy. The Wilder-Brackett screenplay and Wilder's directing skill drew an exciting performance from Gloria Swanson as a former screen star living on past glories who destroys a vacillating screenwriter (William Holden). Comedy predominated—never sunny, but with less tragic overtones—in the films that followed: *Ace in the Hole* (1951), *Stalag 17* (1953), *Sabrina* (1954), and *The Seven-Year Itch* (1955).

The Wilder-Brackett collaboration ended with *Sunset Boulevard.* In 1957 the director found another outstanding screenwriter in I. A. L. Diamond. The two joined forces for *Love in the Afternoon* (1957), *Some Like It Hot* (1959), *The Apartment* (1960) (Figure 6.9), *One, Two, Three* (1961), *Irma La Douce* (1963), *The Fortune Cookie* (1966), *Avanti!* (1972), and others. The films after *The Apartment,* while always expertly directed, are somewhat mechanical in their humor and lack the sharp satirical focus of the earlier works.

Wilder has few peers in his ability to use humor, particularly in the form of witty, ironic dialogue, to thinly disguise a mocking, even bitter view of human nature. Corruption flourishes in a Wilder film, not only as personified by ruthless men and women who take advantage of wealth and power for selfish ends but also in the way weak people deceive themselves into believing that a step up the ladder of success compensates for sacrificing integrity and self-respect. Self-deception is often symbolized in the director's films by the characters' ambiguity of identity or disguises. Wilder satirizes not only people's fear of being themselves but also the stereotypes, especially those derived from motion pictures, that become personality masks. *Some Like It Hot* includes parodies of gangster films, a romantic hero like Cary Grant, and Hollywood fantasies in which money is the solution to all problems.

*p. 148

## FIGURE 6.9

*The Apartment,* 1960, directed by Billy Wilder. C. C. Baxter (Jack Lemmon) is promoted, and he moves his personal effects to a private office. The key to his success is the apartment he lends to company executives for their liaisons.

Wilder is an outstanding director in his own right, but from a broader perspective he stands as a transition figure between, on the one hand, the irony and concern with setting of Lubitsch and the moral preoccupations of Capra and Sturges during the thirties and forties and, on the other hand, the fast-paced, verbal-oriented, unrestrained satires and farces of Woody Allen and Mel Brooks in the late sixties.

In addition to Wilder's films, a number of other successful comedies were released during this decade: *Father of the Bride* (1950) and *The Reluctant Debutante* (1958), both directed by Vincente Minelli; Walter Lang's *Cheaper by the Dozen* (1950); *Harvey* (1950, directed by Henry Koster); *The Quiet Man* (1952, John Ford); *The Moon Is Blue* (1953, Otto Preminger); *How to Marry a Millionaire* (1953, Jean Negulesco); *Roman Holiday* (1953, William Wyler); *Mister Roberts* (1955, directed by John Ford and Mervyn LeRoy); *Around the World in 80 Days* (1956, Michael Anderson); *The Solid Gold Cadillac* (1956) and *Bell, Book & Candle* (1958), both directed by Richard Quine; *Will Success Spoil Rock Hunter?* (1957, Frank Tashlin); and *Auntie Mame* (1958, Morton Da Costa). *Pillow Talk* (1959, directed by Michael

Gordon) was the first in a series of popular comedies starring Doris Day and Rock Hudson.

Stanley Kubrick's *Dr. Strangelove: Or, How I Learned to Stop Worrying and Love the Bomb* opened in 1963. Previous forms of satire—the oblique approaches of the silent clowns, the barbs of W. C. Fields, the irony of Lubitsch, the farce of the Marx Brothers, the sentimental chiding of Capra, the anger of Sturges, the savage but restrained thrusts of Wilder —had not prepared audiences for Kubrick's explosive cynicism. A psychotic general (Sterling Hayden) activates the system that sends United States planes to attack Russia with atomic bombs. The Russians, however, have just installed a doomsday machine that will destroy the world if a bomb is dropped on their country. All the efforts of a sensible president, a reasonable British military attaché, a mad former Nazi scientist (all three roles played by Peter Sellers), and a brutal Army general (George C. Scott) cannot stop one of the planes from reaching its destination.

The screenplay by Kubrick, Terry Southern, and Peter George is merciless in revealing the narrow-mindedness, prejudice, and simple insanity that can pervade our society when power is concentrated in the hands of scientists, military leaders, and politicians. A subtheme is the way sex has become in our time the touchstone of existence (even machines "copulate," as in the opening scene) and, when shorn of reason and humanity, leads to death (the psychotic general destroys the world because he has become impotent, and the bomb that activates the doomsday machine is manifestly phallic).

*Dr. Strangelove* anticipates by a few years a "new wave" in American film comedy. The turbulence of the sixties—assassinations of prominent political figures, demonstrations against the Vietnam War, racial conflicts, dissent on campuses, moral and social traditions challenged by young people—influenced a number of comedies that appeared during the second half of the decade. Mike Nichols's *The Graduate* (1967) defined with vigor and irony what was meant by an expression popular at the time, "the generation gap." Although not as audacious as *Dr. Strangelove,* the story of Ben Braddock's initiation into sex by Mrs. Robinson and into love by her daughter continued to

expand the limits of what were permissible subjects for satire and to accustom audiences to surprising, bold scenes, such as the concluding one in the church. A few years later, Nichols was not fully able in *Catch-22* (1970) to transfer to the screen the cynicism and extravagance of Joseph Heller's remarkable World War II novel.

A contrast to the satirical comedy of Kubrick and Nichols were the superior light entertainments of Blake Edwards. He would be admirable if he had directed only Audrey Hepburn in *Breakfast at Tiffany's* (1961) and initiated the Inspector Clouseau (Peter Sellers) series (*The Pink Panther,* 1959; *A Shot in the Dark,* 1964; and so on), but he was also responsible for *Operation Petticoat* (1959), *The Great Race* (1965), *"10"* (1979), *S.O.B.* (1981), and *Victor/Victoria* (1982).

Successful comedies were created by directors associated with other genres. Among those who took leave from making musicals were Charles Walters (*Please Don't Eat the Daisies,* 1960), Gene Kelly (*Gigot,* 1962, a tour de force for Jackie Gleason), and Stanley Donen (*Charade,* 1963, an Audrey Hepburn–Cary Grant vehicle). Stanley Kramer radically changed pace by moving from his typical film of social consciousness to *It's a Mad, Mad, Mad, Mad World* (1963). Although at his best in dramas and adventure stories, George Roy Hill showed a talent for comedy early in his career as a film director with *The World of Henry Orient* (1964, starring Peter Sellers). A decade later he made the immensely popular *The Sting* (1973), a story of two con men, played with élan by Paul Newman and Robert Redford. William Wyler is a veteran who has made every type of film, including comedies, since the mid-twenties. In the sixties he did not repeat the success of *Roman Holiday,* but *How to Steal a Million* (1966) did star Audrey Hepburn, this time teamed with Peter O'Toole rather than Gregory Peck. Francis Ford Coppola's only comedy until the eighties was *You're a Big Boy Now* (1966).

Other popular comedies of the sixties not previously noted include *Under the Yum Yum Tree* (1963, directed by David Swift); *How to Murder Your Wife* (1964) and *Lord Love a Duck* (1965), both directed by George Axelrod; *Those Magnificent Men in Their*

*Flying Machines* (1965, Ken Annakin); the caustic *The Loved One* (1965, Tony Richardson); *The Russians Are Coming, the Russians Are Coming* (1967, Norman Jewison), *The Flim Flam Man* (1967, Irvin Kershner); and *Putney Swope* (1969, Robert Downey).

It would be unfair in surveying the fifties and sixties not to mention Neil Simon, who has been a consistent source of plots for hit comedies. With a rare exception (for instance, *The Goodbye Girl,* 1977), Simon's films have been adaptations of his stage plays. A list of the most successful, however, is impressive: *Come Blow Your Horn* (1963), *Barefoot in the Park* (1967), *The Odd Couple* (1968), *Plaza Suite* (1971), and *The Sunshine Boys* (1975). One characteristic all these adaptations share is that they depend for their humor and characterization on Simon's scintillating dialogue, so as films they are for the most part usually static.

The "new wave" in American film comedy that was the most significant force in the genre during the seventies and built upon the exaggerated satire and new freedoms in subject matter and expression initiated by Kubrick and Nichols first manifested itself a couple of years before the end of the sixties. In 1968 and 1969 two films appeared that marked the debuts of two directors whose later works have been among the most popular of recent years. Mel Brooks's *The Producers* (1968) and other works of the director are discussed later in this chapter.* In brief, the significance of this film to post–World War II American comedy is its daring subject matter, its perversion of conventional standards of morality, and an ability to perpetrate outrageous farce with a vitality that had not been evident since the Marx Brothers. The other film was Woody Allen's *Take the Money and Run* (1969). Although it attracted some attention, only a few perceptive viewers would have been willing at the time to prophesy that its director-actor-screenwriter would in a few years become the most exciting talent devoted to film comedy.

Woody Allen (1935–) began as a gagwriter for television shows, then moved on to comedy acts in Greenwich Village clubs and throughout the country.

In the mid-sixties he was the screenwriter for a successful comedy, *What's New, Pussycat?* (1965, directed by Clive Donner). A year later he wrote a play for Broadway, *Don't Drink the Water,* and put together ("directed" might be overstating the case) *What's Up, Tiger Lily?* (1966), a film in which a ridiculous new sound track in English replaces the original of a Japanese melodrama.

*Take the Money and Run* was Allen's first genuine feature (Figure 6.10). In it, Virgil Starkwell (played by Allen) is an incredibly inept bank robber. *Bananas* (1971) concerns the adventures of Fielding Mellish (Allen), a reluctant and incredibly inept revolutionary. After acting in but not directing a film version of his second stage play, *Play It Again, Sam* (1972, directed by Herbert Ross), Allen wrote, directed, and starred in *Everything You Always Wanted to Know About Sex —But Were Afraid to Ask* (1972) and *Sleeper* (1973). All these films share certain characteristics besides being very funny. The main character is consistently an intellectual, manic-depressive, accident-prone, likable nebbish. This persona depends for comic effects more on verbal than visual humor. The films are inventive, combining wild fantasy with realistic satirical touches. Allen has no hesitation in adapting the conventions of cinematic genres to his own purposes,

**FIGURE 6.10**

*Take the Money and Run,* 1969, directed by Woody Allen (color). By means of a cake of soap carved into the shape of a gun and blackened with shoe polish, Viril Starkwell (Allen) attempts one night to escape from jail. All goes well until he steps outside with his hostages—into the rain.

such as that of the pseudodocumentary crime film in *Take the Money and Run* or science fiction in *Sleeper*. His satire is sharply focused, especially in dealing with relations between the sexes, parents, intellectual pretentiousness, and the importance of the mass media in contemporary life. The chief weakness of these films is that the parts are more important than the whole. Allen's gift for the non sequitur extends from a conversation to a scene to a sequence. The result is a certain meandering and incoherence.

*Love and Death* (1975) marked the beginning of a new stage in Allen's career. This burlesque of nineteenth-century Russian novels demonstrates that he had matured as a screenwriter and director. Situations and characters are still delightfully ridiculous, but there is a continuity in plot development and a greater variety and subtlety in characterization. It is, moreover, Allen's most visually striking film. Allusions to classic fiction and motion pictures, always present in his films, appear with greater style and sophistication than in his earlier works.

The promise of *Love and Death* was fulfilled in *Annie Hall* (1977), Allen's finest film to date. The humanity, control, and expressiveness in this work make viewing it both funny and moving. The plot centers on the love affair between Alvy Singer (Allen) and Annie Hall (Diane Keaton, the female star of his three previous films); it tells poignantly how two mature individuals can be attracted to each other and still separate. Allen finally succeeded in doing what he had attempted in previous films and novelists like Saul Bellow, Philip Roth, and Bernard Malamud had accomplished in fiction: universalizing the intellectual New York Jew. After an excursion into drama (*Interiors*, 1978), Allen returned to his forte in *Manhattan* (1979) and *Stardust Memories* (1980). The latter is more caustic than any of the director's previous works, and it demonstrates that America's reigning genius of film comedy has the potential of exploring new avenues of humor (as he does in *Zelig*, 1983).

Peter Bogdanovich* turned to comedy after *The Last Picture Show* (1971). *What's Up, Doc?* (1972), *Paper Moon* (1973), and *Nickelodeon* (1976) proved that he appreciated the spirit of screwball comedy of the thirties and could balance sentiment and zany humor. However, *Nickelodeon* was more frantic than funny, and since then Bogdanovich has not directed a comedy.

Paul Mazursky came to prominence with *Bob & Carol & Ted & Alice* (1969, with Elliot Gould and Natalie Wood), a caustic satire on contemporary sexual mores. He went on to *Alex in Wonderland* (1970, starring Donald Sutherland), *Blume in Love* (1973, starring George Segal and Susan Anspach), the touching *Harry and Tonto* (1974, starring Art Carney), *Next Stop, Greenwich Village* (1976), and the bittersweet *An Unmarried Woman* (1978, with Jill Clayburgh and Alan Bates). Mazursky has a bold, individual style that is particularly effective in dealing with eccentric and obsessed people. He is not afraid of being sentimental and extravagant, qualities not always appreciated by sophisticated audiences. In *An Unmarried Woman*, however, more drama than comedy, he has controlled his free-wheeling imagination and created a substantial and sharply focused portrayal of a lonely woman who finds the inner strength to be truly independent. *Willie and Phil* (1980) is in the same serio-comic mode, but too tentative in characterization to be impressive as either drama or comedy.

Elaine May has devoted herself exclusively to comedy, yet with decreasing coherence and wit, in *A New Leaf* (1971), *The Heartbreak Kid* (1972), and *Mickey and Nicky* (1976). Carl Reiner has demonstrated his ability to produce boisterous humor with a minimum of subtlety in *Enter Laughing* (1967), *Where's Poppa?* (1970), *Oh, God* (1977), and *The One and Only* (1978). The work of Ted Kotcheff is more structured that that of May and more sophisticated than the comedies of Reiner, as is evident in *The Apprenticeship of Duddy Kravitz* (1974) and *Fun With Dick and Jane* (1978).

Three directors of comedies during the seventies better known for their efforts in other genres are Robert Altman (*M\*A\*S\*H*, 1970, and *Brewster McCloud*, 1970), Michael Ritchie (*The Bad News Bears*, 1976, and *Semi-Tough*, 1977), and British filmmaker Peter Yates, who has now apparently settled in Hollywood (where he made such films as *For Pete's Sake*, 1974, and *Mother, Jugs and Speed*, 1976).

*p. 186

As in earlier decades, American comedy in the seventies continued to be diverse in content and style. Two extremes would be the farcical *Animal House* (1978, directed by a team of *National Lampoon* alumni) and the witty *A Touch of Class* (1973, directed by Melvin Frank). The subgenre of social commentary in the mode of humor has flourished in the films of directors already noted, as well as in *Little Murders* (1971, directed by Alan Arkin), *Up the Sandbox* (1972, directed by Irvin Kershner), and *Car Wash* (1976, directed by Michael Schultz). Parody has been a weapon in the hands of filmmakers other than Brooks and Allen. Victims of this form of satire include the detective film (Robert Benton's *The Late Show,* 1977), the Western (Howard Zieff's *Hearts of the West,* 1975, and Robert Aldrich's *The Frisco Kid,* 1979), the horror film (Stan Dragoti's *Love at First Bite,* 1978), and the disaster film (*Airplane!,* 1979). A special category that has been long overdue in finding supportive audiences consists of comedies directed by black filmmakers and featuring black actors (for instance, Ossie Davis's *Cotton Comes to Harlem,* 1969, and Sidney Poitier's *Let's Do It Again,* 1975). Then, of course, there are humorous motion pictures that defy easy categorization, such as, among many possible examples, *Harry and Walter Go to New York* (1976, directed by Mark Rydell), *Rafferty and the Gold Dust Twins* (1976, directed by Dick Richards), *House Calls* (1978, directed by Howard Zieff), and *The Great Train Robbery* (1979, directed by Michael Crichton).

As in other decades, sixties and seventies film comedies produced stars. Among the male stars, the most prominent have been Walter Matthau, Woody Allen, Elliot Gould, and Mel Brooks (who as a director provided opportunities for displays of the special talents of Gene Wilder and Marty Feldman). Richard Pryor, Godfrey Cambridge, and Bill Cosby are among leading black comedians. Other male actors have not confined themselves to comedies but have been outstanding in the ones in which they appeared: Robert Redford, Alan Arkin, Peter O'Toole, George Segal, Ryan O'Neal, Donald Sutherland, Richard Benjamin, and Richard Dreyfuss. Some television personalities have been equally personable in films, including Art Carney, Jonathan Winters, James Garner, Tony Randall, and the inimitable George Burns.

A surprising number of the leading comediennes since the early sixties originally made their reputations in musicals. The most obvious examples are Barbra Streisand and Julie Andrews, but others include Natalie Wood, Leslie Caron, Barbara Harris, Polly Bergen, and Carolyn Jones. Jane Fonda does not conform to this pattern—or any other derived from the motion picture industry. Tatum O'Neal is also exceptional, more for her youth than for nonconformity. Diane Keaton and Louise Lasser came to prominence in Woody Allen's films, as did Madeline Kahn and, to a lesser extent, Cloris Leachman in Mel Brooks's comedies.

The film comedies of Great Britain were not exported with much success during the seventies, although certain actors, such as Dudley Moore and Peter Cook, became popular with American audiences. A significant success was a series of films produced by an ensemble of British comedians known collectively as Monty Python. Their zany, irreverent, often shocking motion pictures include *And Now for Something Completely Different* (1971), *Monty Python and the Holy Grail* (1975), *Jabberwocky* (1977), and *Monty Python's Life of Brian* (1979).

European comedies have fared somewhat better in the United States than those from England, especially if we stretch the definition of the genre to include the works of Luis Buñuel* and Lina Wertmuller.† Tati was France's master of wit, but this country's filmmakers have developed a type of satirical domestic comedy reminiscent of Great Britain's "little comedies" of the fifties (with an emphasis, however, on sex not found in their more staid predecessors). Among the most internationally popular of them are *Cousin, Cousine* (1975), *Get Out Your Handkerchiefs* (1978), *La Cage aux Folles* (1978), and *Peppermint Soda* (1978). Italian filmmakers have updated the tradition of Monicelli and Comencini with such works as *La Grande Bouffe* (1973) and *Bread and Chocolate* (1978).

---

*pp. 162–165
†pp. 188–189

Comedy is the hardiest of film genres. Unlike the musical and the Western, its future looks bright. As noted at the beginning of this survey, comedy is imbued with the principle of adaptability, and as a film genre it will surely, as always, be flexible in adjusting to changing times.

# SILENT COMEDY

## The Gold Rush

*[Charles Chaplin] was the first man
to give the silent language a soul.*
James Agee, 1946[7]

### CAST

*Charles Chaplin (The Lone Prospector [Charlie]), Mack Swain (Big Jim MacKay), Georgia Hale (Georgia), Tim Murray (Black Larsen), Malcolm White (Jack Cameron), Henry Bergman (Hank Curtis), and others.*

### CREDITS

*Director, Screenwriter, and Producer—Charles Chaplin, Associate Director—Charles Reisner, Directors of Photography—R. H. Totheroh and Jack Wilson, and others.*

1925/United Artists
Black & White/85 minutes (with background music)

### BACKGROUND

Charles Spencer Chaplin (1889–1977) attained the unique distinction of becoming the most famous actor in the history of motion pictures. He did this primarily by creating a persona, Charlie the Tramp, who captivated audiences throughout the world.

Chaplin was born in the slums of Lambeth, London. While he was still a youngster, his alcoholic father died and his mother had a nervous breakdown. After spending a few years in an orphanage, he became a music hall performer. By the age of 17 he had joined the famous Fred Karno Company as a comedian and pantomimist and toured England, the Continent, and the United States. His hard childhood was to haunt the man, and his music hall experiences would supply material to the mature artist.

In 1913 Mack Sennett asked Chaplin to join the Keystone Studio. During 1914 he appeared in 34 one- and two-reelers and one feature film, *Tillie's Punctured Romance*. In addition to learning about film comedy from Sennett (a debt he always acknowledged), he developed the tramp figure and soon was writing and directing his own films.

Charlie the Tramp was so popular that in 1915 Chaplin was able to leave Keystone and to join the Essanay Company. His creator gave Charlie greater depth of character, range, and sensitivity in the 13 two-reel films (plus a one-reeler and the four-reel *Carmen*) made for this company. Chaplin discovered Edna Purviance, the actress he was to use in over 30 of his films until 1923, and hired Rollie Totheroh, who was to be his cameraman in all the Charlie films. The best of the Essanay films are *A Night Out* (costarring Ben Turpin), *The Champion, The Tramp,* and *A Night in the Show* (all made in 1915).

Chaplin continued his rise up the ladder of fame, artistic development, and financial success by moving to the Mutual Company in 1916. Eric Campbell joined Edna Purviance as a favored actor. Among the 12 two-reelers created for Mutual were 4 of his finest short films: *One A.M.* (1916), *The Pawnshop* (1916), *Easy Street* (1917), and *The Immigrant* (1917).

From 1918 to 1922 Chaplin, now the most celebrated and imitated star in Hollywood, worked for the First National Film Company with a contract to make eight films for a salary of $1 million. He could afford in 1917 to build a small studio of his own, which increased his sense of independence. Chaplin now expanded the length of his films to three reels (*A Dog's Life,* 1918; *Shoulder Arms,* 1918; *Sunnyside,* 1919) and four reels (*The Pilgrim,* 1923). He also created his first feature film, *The Kid* (1921). This story of the love between the Tramp and an adopted youngster (played by Jackie Coogan) was a resounding success and demonstrated to the world that a Hollywood film could be both comic and moving.

When his contract with First National expired, Chaplin was able to work under the aegis of the United Artists Company, which he had founded with D. W. Griffith, Mary Pickford, and Douglas Fairbanks in 1919. He was to stay with this company from 1923 until he left the United States in 1952. After a melodrama, *A Woman of Paris* (1923), about a country girl who loses her true love when she becomes the mistress of a wealthy Parisian (Chaplin wrote and directed the film but only played a walk-on role), he went on to create the other great Charlie features. After *The Gold Rush* (1925) appeared *The Circus* (1928), Chaplin's last completely silent film. Charlie accidentally becomes a star clown in a small circus and falls in love with an equestrienne, but she loves a handsome tightrope walker. The Tramp nobly arranges for the two young people to marry, and he leaves the circus. In *City Lights* (1931), Charlie willingly goes to jail so that the blind girl he loves can afford an operation that restores her sight. In the last scene, she discovers that the benefactor she imagined as wealthy and suave is a shabby tramp. *Modern Times* (1936) is a satire on industrialism and modern society in general in which Charlie finds a soul mate in a lovely, vivacious orphan (played by Paulette Goddard). Of course, each plot is merely a vehicle for incomparable scenes of humor and for revelations of the complex character of Charlie.

Whatever Chaplin's achievements in film after 1936, his most enduring accomplishment unquestionably is his portrayal of the Tramp. Although he appeared in more than two dozen shorts and five feature films, Charlie retained basic characteristics no matter what the setting or plot. To appreciate why the Tramp became a legend of American culture and the most famous fictional figure born in Hollywood requires an understanding of the most salient of these characteristics. Many of them only suggested here will be elaborated upon in the analysis of *The Gold Rush.*

Charlie's costume signals an important ambiguity in his status and personality. The bowler, cane, tie, jacket, and other habiliments in themselves proclaim a gentleman. This impression is reinforced by his polite manners, especially when dealing with women. On the other hand, his clothes are ill-fitting and worn, his shoes oversized, and his wallet usually empty. He is, then, a tramp, but of a special sort: a gentleman tramp who will retain his dignity and innocent pretensions under all circumstances. For instance, the first thing he does after being knocked down is to recover his cane and hat. Because he is an unusual type for

which there is no conventional niche in American society and because he cherishes his freedom of movement and choices, Charlie is a perennial outsider. In most of his films, he is a catalyst influencing the lives of others while he remains unchanged.

His first priority after preserving his self-respect and freedom is to survive. This is no easy task, for he is threatened continually by disaster. Luck sometimes favors him, but usually this comic Job is beset by one adversity after another. Perhaps the gods enjoy testing him because he meets each challenge with such vitality and imaginativeness. He is physically agile and resilient; he is mentally clever and especially ingenious in extricating himself from dangerous situations; he retains his good-naturedness and aplomb under circumstances that would make any normal mortal aghast.

Aside from fate itself, the natural enemies of Charlie are burly policemen, bullies of any breed, the arrogant wealthy, and sanctimonious do-gooders. Since courage and boldness are two of his traits, he does not avoid confrontations, though he may run away to fight again another day.

People who try to take advantage of the intrepid Tramp usually end up regretting having met him, but Charlie is often less successful in his encounters with unfriendly inanimate objects. He is imaginative enough to recognize, as do primitives and children, that every object in the universe possesses a spirit, a will of its own. Hammers, folding chairs, ladders, waxed floors—these are a few examples of objects with malignant intentions toward Charlie and with which he battles.

With his verve and determination, it would seem that the Tramp, no matter how oppressed by a cosmic conspiracy, would be able to survive with a certain equanimity. There are, however, chinks in his emotional armor. He is vulnerable to the helpless, children, and attractive women. The last, to make matters worse, he tends to idealize and to read love into any smile or expression of gratitude. Over and over again, his heart is broken before he tips his hat, swings his cane, and jauntily walks down an open road to new adventures.

If this thumbnail character sketch of Charlie appears to be written about a living person, it is because he has assumed a life of his own. Like other great comic characters of fiction and drama, such as Don Quixote, Falstaff, Uncle Toby, and Samuel Pickwick, the Tramp is more vivid and real to us than most human beings we meet at cocktail parties.

The films of the twenties and early thirties confirmed the evidence of *The Kid* that Chaplin could structure a feature film without becoming repetitious and diffuse, weaknesses his contemporaries Harold Lloyd and Harry Langdon were not able to overcome. He was also able to meet the challenge of the advent of sound. Wisely, he would not allow Charlie to speak, but he demonstrated that he understood the potentials of this new element of presentation by creating his own background music, effectively using natural sounds for comedy, and devising a nonsense song for the Tramp in *Modern Times* (Figure 6.11). Ultimately,

however, Charlie could not survive the demand in the thirties for spoken dialogue and an audience that became restive in the presence of his special blend of independence, sentiment, and satire; his last appearance was in *Modern Times*.

In the forties and early fifties Chaplin released three films. *The Great Dictator* (1940) is a satire on Hitler and the Third Reich. In *Monsieur Verdoux* (1947), a dapper little man maintains that in a society that countenances a world war and the cruelty of a depression, he is justified in bigamously marrying and then murdering wealthy women in order to support his crippled wife and his son. *Limelight* (1952) is

FIGURE 6.11

*Modern Times*, 1936. In the Tramp's last feature, Charlie does a song (a pastiche of foreign languages) and dance before a supper-club audience.

about a forgotten music hall comedian who restores hope in a paralyzed dancer (Claire Bloom) and helps her to become a star. In the final sequence, he is triumphant at a benefit show and dies.

Each of these non-Charlie works is memorable. Without the ballast of the Tramp's character, however, the films show an uncertainty on the director's part in conveying his social criticism and alternating sentiment and sentimentality. Perhaps Chaplin was preoccupied with his offscreen problems. The failure of three of his four marriages, sex scandals, refusal to become an American citizen, charges of tax evasion, and support of the Soviet Union during World War II —all gave him bad press, and the American people became increasingly critical of him. Anti-Chaplin feelings reached a climax when he was threatened in the late forties with a subpoena to appear before the House Committee on Un-American Activities.

He left the United States permanently in 1952 and settled in Switzerland with his fourth wife, née Oona O'Neill, and his children. In England he made *A King in New York* (1957) and *A Countess From Hong Kong* (1967). There are in both works, especially the former, occasional flashes of genius, but generally they are products of the end of a great filmmaker's career.

Chaplin lived his last years in comfort and honor. *My Autobiography* (1965) was a best-seller. Hollywood, which had turned its back on him in the forties, recanted and greeted him with open arms at the 1972 Academy Awards ceremony. He was knighted 2 years before his death in 1977.

After Chaplin completed *A Woman of Paris,* in 1923, he was ready to make his first comedy for United Artists. He determined it would be, as he notes in his autobiography, "an epic! The greatest!"[8] The germ of an idea came while looking with Douglas Fairbanks at stereoscopic views of the Klondike. One view of the Chilkoot Pass, with a caption "describing the trials and hardships endured in surmounting it,"[9] stimulated his imagination. The second source of inspiration was a strange one and led him to reflections on the relationship between tragedy in life and comedy in art (". . . it is paradoxical that tragedy stimulates the spirit of ridicule, because ridicule, I suppose, is an

attitude of defiance . . ."[10]). Chaplin read a book about the Donner party, a group of pioneers stranded in the Sierra Nevada who in desperation resorted to cannibalism. The most concrete manifestation of the filmmaker's reading is the scene in *The Gold Rush* between Charlie and Big Jim in the snowbound cabin when the latter is prepared to eat his companion.

Chaplin was so committed to making *The Gold Rush* an outstanding film that he devoted more than a year in preparing it and spent $800,000, an enormous sum for a comedy in the mid-twenties. Another unusual feature of its production was some location shooting, actually near where the Donner party was trapped.

The investment of effort and money paid off richly. *The Gold Rush* was tremendously popular; it is estimated that the film grossed over $7 million worldwide. More significant, it gave the filmmaker the confidence to go on to the other Charlie masterpieces that followed.

In 1942 Chaplin composed his own musical score for the film.

PLOT SUMMARY

In a prologue, a crowd of men, including Charlie (Chaplin), climb in a long line up a mountain to the Chilkoot Pass, which leads to the Alaskan gold fields.

Crosscutting between Charlie walking and sliding along a trail and Big Jim MacKay (Swain) discovering gold on his claim. Title: "Then Came a Storm."

Black Larsen (Murray) is inside his cabin burning posters announcing that he is wanted for murder when Charlie, caught in the storm, enters but is not welcomed. Big Jim blows in and, after being threatened by Larsen, disarms the murderer. "And Three Men Were Hungry," so they decide to cut cards to see who will go in search of help. Larsen loses and leaves.

Crosscutting between Larsen and the two occupants of the cabin. Larsen happens upon two lawmen who are pursuing him. He kills both and steals their sled. At the cabin, Charlie and Big Jim are hungry enough to eat the former's shoe. Larsen discovers Big Jim's claim. Meanwhile, Big Jim hallucinates from hunger and sees Charlie as a rooster. He recuperates, but the next morning he attacks Charlie. As they wrestle, a bear enters. It is promptly shot by Charlie, and the famine is over. The storm ends, and the two men go their separate ways.

When Big Jim returns to his mine, he finds Black Larsen. During a struggle, Big Jim is knocked unconscious by the murderer. As Larsen attempts to escape, he is destroyed by an avalanche. Big Jim awakens; still dazed, he stumbles away from his mine.

In town, we are introduced to the lovely Georgia (Hale), a dance hall hostess, as she refuses to ride with Jack Cameron (White), "A Ladies Man." Charlie has arrived and pawns his prospecting equipment. At the Monte Carlo Dance Hall, Georgia looks at some photographs of herself; she throws one of them on the floor. Charlie enters and is attracted to Georgia. He spies the photograph and picks it up under the suspicious eyes of a tall, grimy man. To prove her independence of Jack, Georgia invites the tramp to dance with her. He does very well until a dog to which he has inadvertently tied himself with a cord drags him away, but he is rewarded with a rose from Georgia. Later, in protecting Georgia, Charlie gets into a fight with Jack.

Charlie tricks Hank Curtis (Bergman) into giving him breakfast by pretending he is frozen stiff. (A brief insert of Big Jim wandering in the snow.) The tramp becomes caretaker of Curtis's cabin. Georgia and three female friends happen by, and Charlie invites them in. She discovers the photograph and rose under Charlie's pillow. After flirting with him, she accepts on behalf of herself and friends an invitation from her admirer to dinner on New Year's Eve. Charlie begs, borrows, and shovels snow to earn money for the dinner.

It is New Year's Eve. A crowd, including Georgia and Jack, is in the dance hall. Meanwhile, Charlie has completed preparations for the dinner. He falls asleep and dreams that his guests have arrived. He entertains them with the "Oceana Roll," in which two rolls and two forks are transformed by the magic of pantomime into the feet and legs of a dancer. It is 12:00. Crosscutting between a celebration at the dance hall and Charlie awakening and realizing he has been forgotten. While he goes to the dance hall in search of Georgia, she, Jack, and some friends invade the cabin. When she sees the preparations for the dinner, her conscience is stricken. Jack attempts to kiss her, but she slaps him.

On New Year's Day, Big Jim appears at the recorder's office in the town, but he cannot remember the location of his mine. At the dance hall, a contrite Georgia writes to Jack a letter of apology for slapping him and a declaration of love. The cad laughs and has the unaddressed letter given to Charlie, who has just entered. The tramp assumes it is intended for him and, overjoyed, frantically searches the hall for his beloved. Big Jim sees his friend and offers to share his potential wealth with Charlie if the tramp leads him to the cabin, from which he is sure he can locate his claim. Before Charlie is dragged away, he embraces an astonished Georgia and promises to make his fortune for her sake.

Charlie and Jim arrive at the cabin. During the night a storm moves the structure across the plain of snow to the edge of a cliff. After the two men escape from the teetering cabin, Jim discovers that they are in front of his claim.

In an epilogue, Big Jim and Charlie, now multimillionaires surrounded by newspapermen, are leaving on a ship for home. Georgia is also aboard. Through an accident, Charlie is mistaken for a stowaway; Georgia offers to pay his passage. All problems are resolved, and the two kiss as a photographer takes their picture.

## ANALYSIS

Of all the Charlie feature films, *The Gold Rush* is the most carefully structured. This quality is achieved through the director-screenwriter's use of certain unifying devices. There is, first of all, a circular plot development with a counterpoint of two settings: Charlie arrives at the Klondike, has adventures in the wilderness, stays in town, returns to the wilderness, and leaves the Klondike. Within each setting there are also parallel situations. In the wilderness, a storm occurs during the opening sequence and another appears when the tramp returns. In town, we first see Charlie entering the Monte Carlo Dance Hall, the climax of his stay in the community is when he goes to the dance hall in search of Georgia, and the last scene takes place in the dance hall. Furthermore, unity of time is preserved. Although we are not quite sure how much time elapses between sequences, all events after Charlie enters the Klondike lead to a climactic New Year's Eve and then away from that crucial night to his departure from Alaska.

Without these devices, we would be more aware of the film's two separate plots (corresponding to the settings), which are interdependent rather than fully integrated. In fact, the two settings constitute two different worlds, each in its own way challenging the physical and emotional mettle of the tramp-prospector. It is Charlie's personality and reactions, rather than the plot, that relate the events in the different settings.

The frozen wilderness of the Klondike appears to be governed by unpredictable and, from a human point of view, capricious forces of nature: A sudden storm can draw strangers together in a shelter; an unexpected avalanche can kill a murderer. Perhaps Chaplin is suggesting that whatever or whoever controls nature is a combination of moralist and sadist with a dark sense of humor. If *nature* is expanded to encompass all of life, this would be a fairly accurate formulation of the religious attitude that emerges from Chaplin's films.

Happenings in the wilderness are not only unpredictable but also often unbelievable. As with all the silent clowns, Chaplin had no hesitation in indulging in his films in the most fantastic events, such as having workers caught in gigantic machines, yet emerging unscathed. In the wilderness section of *The Gold Rush*, he ignored the laws of probability more frequently than in any of his other films. Only a statistician adding exponents to a million could calculate the possibility that Larsen would happen upon Jim's strike and later be destroyed by an avalanche or, even more outrageous, that in the second wilderness sequence a cabin could be pushed by a storm miles from its original site, stop next to Jim's gold mine, and teeter at the edge of a cliff—without awakening the two men in the wandering cabin! We can accept these implausibilities for two reasons. First, they are not intended to be taken seriously. The director is laughing with us, not attempting to fool us, so we tolerate these events in the same spirit as we do the obvious papier-mâché rocks, the models for special effects, and the inappropriate outfit Charlie wears in bitter cold.

Second, and even more important, these elements of fantasy are confined to external physical occurrences and do not affect characterization and human reactions. In this respect, Chaplin's films differ from those directed by Mack Sennett. There is nothing unbelievable in the main function in the film of the wilderness: a testing ground of the stamina, courage, ingenuity, and instinct for survival of people who challenge nature. The goal is gold and the wealth it can bring, but only the strongest—and not necessarily physically strongest—achieve that reward. Chaplin makes this point on the survival of the fittest in the prologue of the film. It opens with a line of men trudging through the Chilkoot Pass. Four of the seven shots that make up the sequence are panoramic ones, emphasizing the smallness of the prospective prospectors as opposed to the vastness of the snow and hugeness of the boulders. The odds are against man in his struggle with nature. In the fifth shot, a man carrying a sled on his back falls to the side. Even more significant than this evidence that there are those who will not pass what a title card calls "A Test of Man's Endurance" is the way the others callously ignore him. We see that in the frozen wastes of the Klondike, nature is not the only enemy; there is also the selfishness and greed of man.

There are only three main characters in the wilderness sequences. They have survived this far, but the means vary and reveal the nature of each one. Black Larsen is a completely evil person; he is one of the few unmitigated villains in Chaplin's films. Through murder and theft, he endures. Retribution comes to Larsen through an improbable accident of nature; the title before the avalanche that states "The North, A Law to Itself" is a flimsy justification. His death, therefore, can only be considered as a fantastic event necessary to meet the requirements of the story.

Big Jim MacKay, in contrast, is basically a fair, likable person: He fulfills his promise to share his wealth with Charlie and appears genuinely glad that he has not shot his friend during hallucinations induced by starvation. His good-fellowship, however, has limitations: When he first enters the cabin, he grabs a bone out of Charlie's hand; friendship does not prevent him from attempting to eat the tramp when hunger becomes unbearable; in the rocking cabin at the edge of the precipice, Jim clambers over the smaller man to safety. We find in Jim, therefore, that combination of goodwill and selfishness that is typical of the majority of Chaplin's secondary film characters.

The center of our attention, naturally, is Charlie. What is most significant in the wilderness is that he handles himself so well in a hostile environment of nature and man. His ingenuity, imagination, and adaptability stand him in good stead, as does his ability to recognize exactly what forces oppose him and to realize they are external to himself. He can deal successfully with the potential destructiveness of nature and the avarice of man only by keeping his inner resources intact.

The situation changes when he enters the town. Although dangers continue to threaten him, accidents, unlikely but plausible, replace the fantastic events of the wilderness. Hunger and money are still problems, but he can handle them by exerting cleverness and energy, as when he tricks Hank Curtis into supplying him with breakfast or when he shovels snow to be able to afford the New Year's Eve dinner. More difficult to face is loneliness in a crowd and the suspiciousness of his fellow human beings, though he is obviously accustomed to being ignored and distrusted. We observe this in the scene in which he first enters the Monte Carlo Dance Hall. In a very expressive shot, he stands in silhouette, his back to the camera, watching the dancers. Later, he reassures rather than confronts the tall, grimy man who watches Charlie closely as the tramp attempts to obtain the photograph discarded by Georgia.

The chief danger in the town, however, originates within Charlie. His Achilles' heel is his idealization of women and his belief that female physical beauty is concomitant with purity and goodness of heart. In short, Charlie is completely naive about women. As if this were not enough vulnerability, he also believes that as a gentleman (one of the paradoxes in the Charlie films is that the Tramp is intrinsically more of a gentleman than those of a higher social plane), it is his duty to assist people who are defenseless or in distress. The combination of these two susceptibilities often leads Charlie to convince himself that an attractive young woman needs his help even when this is not the case.

The tramp-prospector creates such a delusion after he enters the town. From the moment he sees Georgia in the dance hall, he is attracted to her. His love might have remained a forlorn desire if not for a series of accidents. He overhears Georgia complain that she is bored and wishes there were someone worthwhile who would take her away from the dance hall. (Her remarks are conveyed by means of a title card.) So, Charlie obviously concludes, the maiden is not only lovely but also in distress. When she asks him to dance with her, he is ecstatic, not knowing that Georgia only chose the disreputable-looking tramp to prove to Jack Cameron that she is independent. Charlie needs no further evidence of her interest in him to appoint himself her knight errant. Unknown to her, this Don Quixote defends his Doncinella from the conceited and aggressive Jack.

Another series of accidents results in Georgia's discovering his secret admiration and cruelly making a dinner appointment for New Year's Eve that she has no intention of keeping. Even when she does not appear on the night that he has prepared for with great sacrifice and care, he is discouraged but loyally retains his love. It is a nasty trick played on him by Jack—the vengeful bully has delivered to Charlie a note intended for himself in which Georgia declares her contrition and love—that revives the little man's hopes. He returns to the wilderness to gain a fortune for his beloved.

There can be no doubt even from this brief synopsis of the relationship of the tramp and the dance hall hostess that all the romantic interest is on Charlie's part. The situation could not be otherwise unless Chaplin brought fantasy into the town as well as the wilderness sequences. Georgia is very attractive, but she is also a hard-bitten, shallow, selfish young woman. Her most appealing personality trait is her sense of independence, although often it seems simply to be a ploy to attract the handsome, free-spending Jack. On the other hand, she has the grace to feel guilty about deluding Charlie after seeing how important the dinner was to him. In the last sequence, she also is willing to buy the tramp a ticket under the impression that he is a stowaway. On the whole, however, she does not have the sensitivity to appreciate the special virtues of Charlie hidden beneath his unprepossessing appearance.

The town is no less cruel than the wilderness. People ignore or laugh at Charlie in the dance hall; the tall, grimy man is suspicious of him; the other "hostesses" join Georgia in tricking the tramp; Jack bullies him; Big Jim is overjoyed at seeing him because he is needed. Only Hank Curtis shows compassion by feeding Charlie and allowing him to live in the cabin—the exception that proves the rule. There is, however, a difference in the way in which Charlie reacts to life in the two settings. In the wilderness he is pragmatic, the secret of his adaptability. Even when he pretends that a boiled shoe is a turkey, he has the practical goal of making the inedible palatable. Charlie accepts that he is a wanderer, a tramp, a survivor who is free and independent. In a world in which every man is primarily for himself, he establishes no ties that can sap his self-sufficiency and inner dignity.

In the town, Charlie is assailed by forces he did not have to contend with in the wilderness. In the process, he loses his ability to judge himself and others shrewdly and realistically. Not only is his dignity and self-assurance threatened, but, since he wishes to marry Georgia, so is the precious freedom that he boldly advertises to the world through his tramp costume. The town, therefore, represents a stability, an oasis of civilization, primitive though it may be, a place of camaraderie and social ties (indicated by the New Year's Eve celebrations at the dance hall) that could entrap the basically anarchistic Charlie.

The conflict between wilderness and town is a basic theme not only in The Gold Rush but also in most of Chaplin's Charlie films. The Tramp is free, an independent spirit, an adventurer who has learned to survive in the wilderness. That wilderness exists wherever man lives by greed and selfishness, whether on the ice plains of Alaska or the streets of a big city. Love tempts the Tramp to betray his true nature, to become a part of "civilization," to accept Apollonian forces that would bind and restrict him. Fortunately, in most Charlie films, shorts, and features, he loses his loved one or resists the temptation and in the last scene walks jauntily away from the camera, alone (with the exception of Modern Times, in which he is accompanied by a kindred spirit, the Gamin), along a dusty road into the unknown and new adventures. That closing shot reassures and exhilarates viewers, for in all of us is the desire to escape responsibilities and restrictions. Charlie is ourselves in a distorting mirror; that is why we simultaneously admire and pity him.

Charlie's commitment to freedom explains in large part not only his universal appeal but also what makes him so intrinsically American. Until the last few decades, as long as there was even a vestige of a frontier, no conflict so characterized our nation as that between the song of the open road or call of the wild and the need for roots in a community and the mixed blessings of "civilization." In this respect, Charlie is a comic, urban version of the hero of the classic Western who in the end rides into the sunset and who also has a dual appeal.

If this interpretation of the significance of Charlie has validity, then the last sequence of The Gold Rush is a transgression against all that precedes it. We simply do not believe in such a contrived happy ending. Chaplin has departed from his own principle of confining the fantastic to external events that challenge but do not affect the nature of Charlie. There is, therefore, a measure of truth in the last words (title card) of the film. The photographer is taking a picture of the millionaire-tramp and Georgia. The two kiss and the photographer remarks, "Oh, You've Spoiled the Picture." Even if we can accept the unlikely possibility that Georgia had not heard of Charlie and Jim's good fortune, the idea of a wealthy, married Charlie is incongruous with everything we associate with the Tramp.

Although the last sequence does violence to the integrity of the narrative dimension, it contains a number of humorous exchanges between Charlie and Big Jim that are superb. This is a problem that inevitably arises whenever one examines the structure of Chaplin's Charlie films—or, for that matter, those of most of the other silent clowns. It is evident that when there

is a conflict for the director-producer-writer-actor between structural coherence and a comic turn, the latter is given priority. Ideally, a scene should reveal the
nature and emotions of a comic character at the same
time it is funny, but this is not always the case in
Chaplin films. The difference is illustrated by the two
most famous scenes in *The Gold Rush.* In the cabin,
Charlie boils his shoe and shares it with Jim. We laugh
at the relish with which the starving tramp eats sole
and laces, while we recognize that his imagination is
helping him to survive (Figure 6.12). On the other
hand, the "Oceana Roll" incident on New Year's Eve
serves no functional purpose, although it is an utterly
delightful piece of pantomime. It is to Chaplin's credit
that he admitted the superfluity of the interlude and
almost wished that he had not included it.[11]

**FIGURE 6.12**

*The Gold Rush.* If a boiled shoe can serve as a turkey
and a shoestring as spaghetti, then a nail can be a
wishbone.

Chaplin is concerned with developing the character of his persona not only through comedy but also
through moments of sentiment. This type of situation
differs from the comic not only in content but also the
style in which it is presented. While comedy can
occur under any set of conditions involving the inanimate as well as the animate, pathos emerges primarily
when the Tramp is exposed to loneliness and a love
that can alleviate that isolation. Chaplin himself recog-

nized the difficulty of combining the two modes, usually kept separate, for at times he undercuts a moment
of sentiment with sudden humor. An example is the
scene in *City Lights* in which he first meets the flower
girl: He has just discovered that she is blind and sits
down to admire her; a moment later, she unintentionally throws a pail of water on him.

In silent films, humor is derived from body
movement, usually the collision of the comic hero
with people and things that frustrate his needs and
will. Chaplin knew that sentiment is most effective
when a character is quiescent. In those incidents in
which Charlie is most emotionally affected and the
audience most moved, the Tramp is still, often with
the camera close enough to him to reveal his facial
expression. The epitome of this approach is the last
shot of *City Lights:* a close-up of Charlie's face with
a half smile on his lips but fear and pain in his eyes as
he divines the profound disappointment of the flower
girl when she discovers that the idealized hero who
was responsible for restoring her sight is a frail, disreputable tramp. In *The Gold Rush,* there are three
touching moments. When Charlie first enters the
dance hall, we see him in a long shot in the crowded
dance hall, his back to the camera, leaning on his cane
[Figure 6.13(a)]. The image conveys as words never
could the loneliness of that small, isolated figure. On
New Year's Eve there is a medium shot, with Charlie's
face in profile, as from the door of his cabin he listens
to the New Year's Eve celebrations at the dance hall
and has to admit to himself that all his efforts, hopes,
and dreams are for nothing and his beloved has forgotten him [Figure 6.13(b)]. Later in the same sequence, he is silhouetted against a lighted window,
shoulders hunched, hands in his pocket, as he looks
into the Monte Carlo Dance Hall searching in vain for
Georgia [Figure 6.13(c)].

To use the nouns *sentiment* and *pathos* to indicate the quality in these moments may in some cases
be overly generous. The two shots on New Year's Eve
described in the preceding paragraph come perilously
close to the borderline between sentiment and sentimentality. In other films, such as *The Kid* and *The
Circus,* Charlie does on occasion slip from displaying
emotions appropriate to the circumstances to reacting

**FIGURE 6.13**

*The Gold Rush.* Charlie as a loner and rejected suitor. (a) He visits the dance hall for the first time. (b) He must admit to himself that Georgia will not come to his New Year's Eve dinner. (c) He looks through the window of the dance hall in search of his beloved.

excessively to a situation and thereby becoming affected and manipulative. Admittedly, the terms *appropriate* and *excessively* are subjective; one viewer's pathos is another's bathos. There can be little argument, however, with the assertion that Charlie's idealization of women does make him susceptible to sentimentality. Whether this is the case in *The Gold Rush* is, again, a matter of individual criteria of the justifiable limits of emotional display.

The camera-editing dynamics utilized by Chaplin are influenced by his emphasis on individual scenes in which Charlie is the center of attention. It is doubtful if any major director contemporaneous with Chaplin was more conservative in his techniques. This is evident in *The Gold Rush.* He favored the stationary camera to the degree of being reluctant to tilt and pan within a shot (there are only two genuine pans in the whole of the film) or changing angles within a scene. Tracking is rare. His transitions are almost entirely cuts and fades in and out, with a few rapid dissolves, especially between scenes. There are four uses of an iris in the film (see Figure 1.13).

Close shots are reserved, though not invariably, for Charlie's moments of deepest emotions. Most of *The Gold Rush* consists of lengthy long shots with occasional cuts when necessary to briefer medium shots. An exception is the "Oceana Roll" turn, which is a lengthy medium shot. Occasionally, Chaplin does experiment, as in three instances in this film. During Big Jim's hallucination, a superimposition allows Charlie's metamorphosis into a rooster; the letters on the title cards enlarge progressively as Big Jim sees the tramp and shouts, "The Cabin," three times, and the process is repeated when a few minutes later Charlie calls out Georgia's name; and the images of Big Jim and Charlie on the floor are tilted in relation to the frame when the cabin rocks on the end of a cliff (Figure 6.14).

Chaplin is as conservative in sets and lighting as in camera-editing dynamics. The only unconventional use of lighting occurs in the "Oceana Roll" scene: The background is blacked out, and spots highlight Charlie's face and hands (Figure 6.15). The town sets are realistic; however, in the wilderness the rock formations consist of poorly disguised papier-mâché, and the cabin blown in the storm and perched on the

FIGURE 6.14

*The Gold Rush.* In a cabin tilted toward the edge of a cliff over an abyss, Charlie and Big Jim attempt to crawl to safety.

cliff is an obvious model. Although we would like to think that Chaplin was consciously emphasizing through his sets the fantasy element in the wilderness sequences, the suspicion does arise that as producer he was simply saving money.

FIGURE 6.15

*The Gold Rush.* Charlie performs the "Oceana Roll," a pantomime in which two rolls become the feet of a dancer.

There is a justification for Chaplin's conservative filmmaking techniques. During intimate moments, he moves his camera close to Charlie and keeps him still. Generally, however, the audience is most interested in Charlie's comic antics, during which his whole body reacts to a specific setting, other people, and things in that setting. The most effective way for viewers to enjoy what is happening is for the camera to be stable and far enough from the action to reveal Charlie at full length, where he is moving, and the reactions of others. Naturally, Chaplin had to cut away from his master shots for purposes of elucidation, for emphasis, and to avoid visual monotony. We can recognize, however, why he so insistently favored the *mise-en-scène* approach of stable, lengthy long shots.

Chaplin's immediate goal in his Charlie films was to entertain; however, his ultimate intention was to create through his persona a vision of reality that would also move his audiences. He succeeded because the Tramp becomes a three-dimensional character with such an abundance of energy that he imbues with life the two-dimensional screen on which he exists. Charlie died in the mid-thirties. Perhaps it is just as well, for his innocence, instinctive goodness, and gaiety might appear incongruous in a world that engendered concentration camps, atomic bombs, and genetic engineering. On the other hand, when we no longer respond to his love of freedom and individuality, his verve and vulnerability, his dignity and adaptability, we will know that the forces of materialism and mechanism have infected our psyches and that we have diminished as human beings.

## SITUATION COMEDY

### Smiles of a Summer Night (Sommarnattens Leende)

*One of my strongest cards . . . is that I never argue with my own intuition. I let it take the decisions. . . . But then, after one has decided something intuitively, it's necessary to follow it up intellectually. Intuition reaches far out into the dark. Afterwards one must try to go on foot to the spot where intuition's javelin has landed, using one's common sense.*
*Ingmar Bergman, 1970*[12]

**CAST**

*Gunnar Björnstrand (Fredrik Egerman), Eva Dahlbeck (Desirée Armfeldt), Ulla Jacobsson (Anne Egerman), Jarl Kulle (Count Malcolm), Margit Carlquist (Charlotte Malcolm), Harriet Andersson (Petra, the maid), Björn Bjelvenstam (Henrik Egerman), Ake Fridell (Frid, the groom), Naima Wifstrand (Mrs. Armfeldt), Gull Natorp (Malla, Desirée's maid), and others.*

**CREDITS**

*Director and Screenwriter—Ingmar Bergman, Producer—Allan Ekelund, Director of Photography —Gunnar Fischer, Art Director—P. A. Lundgren, Composer—Erik Nordgren, Editor—Oscar Rosander, and others.*

1955/Svensk Filmindustri
Black & White/108 minutes

### BACKGROUND

Ingmar Bergman was born in Uppsala, Sweden, on July 14, 1918, the son of a Lutheran clergyman. By the time he entered college in 1937, he had decided to become a playwright and theater director. At the University of Stockholm, Bergman majored in literature and art. While still an undergraduate, he was actively engaged in amateur theater productions and had his first personal contact with filmmakers.

He began writing plays in the early forties. In 1944 he became director of the Hälsingborg City Theater. It was also in this year that he wrote his first screenplay. So impressed were officials at Svensk Filmindustri, Sweden's leading motion picture production company, that he was apprenticed to the prominent director Alf Sjöberg. The film Sjöberg directed based on Bergman's script, *Torment (Hets,* 1944), was an immediate success. Within 2 years the brilliant apprentice was allowed to begin his own motion picture, *Crisis* (1946).

The three major activities of Bergman's professional career thus were established early. He became one of the most respected directors of theater and opera productions in Sweden. From 1952 to 1958, he was director of the Malmö City Theater. In the sixties he was appointed to the most coveted position in the theater world of his country, chief director of the Royal Dramatic Theater in Stockholm (1963–1966). His productions have been acclaimed for their imaginativeness, carefully controlled dramatic pacing, and outstanding performances elicited from the actors involved.

After *Torment,* Bergman continued occasionally to write screenplays for other directors, including *Woman Without a Face* (1947) and *Eva* (1948), both directed by Gustaf Molander; *While the City Sleeps* (1950), directed by Lars-Eric Kjellgren; and *The Pleasure Garden* (1961), directed by Alf Kjellin. Bergman wrote theater plays during the forties, most of the earlier ones one act in length. Bergman's chief efforts as a writer, however, have centered on the screenplays for his own films. With the exception of four motion pictures *(Night Is My Future, Three Strange Loves, This Can't Happen Here,* and *The Virgin Spring),* he has written the screenplays (occasionally with a collaborator, and the majority are original) for the 41 feature films that he has directed thus far.

Bergman's international fame is based on his work as a film director. From 1945 to 1953, he experimented with various techniques and struggled toward an individual style. The films of this period are *Crisis (Kris,* 1946), *It Rains on Our Love (Det Regnar pa var Kärlek,* 1946), *A Ship to India (Skepp till Indialand,* 1947), *Music in Darkness (Musik i Mörker,* 1947), *Port of Call (Hamnstadt,* 1948), *The Devils' Wanton* or *Prison (Fängelse,* 1949), *Three Strange Loves* or *Thirst (Törst,* 1949), *To Joy (Till Glädje,* 1949), *This Can't Happen Here* or *High Tension (Sant Händer inte Här,* 1950), *Summer Interlude* or *Illicit Interlude (Sommarlek,* 1951), *Secrets of Women* or *Waiting Women (Kvinnors Väntan,* 1952), *Monika* or *Summer With Monika (Sommaren med Monika,* 1952). With the exception of *It Can't Happen Here,* a political film, they deal primarily with disappointed, lonely men and women, frequently adolescents, who attempt to find solace in intimacy between them.

*Summer Interlude* and *Monika* are the two most interesting of these 12 motion pictures. In the former, a ballet dancer, through recollections of her love affair with a young man who dies accidentally, comes to terms with her feelings of fear and guilt and accepts the love of a current admirer. In *Monika,* two young people spend an exciting summer traveling on a boat together, marry, and then separate. The title

character is played by Harriet Andersson, who thereafter frequently appeared in the director's films.

In *The Naked Night* or *Sawdust and Tinsel (Gycklarnas Afton,* 1953), Bergman for the first time demonstrated the characteristics of his style that were to make him a unique film artist. An aging owner and ringmaster of a small traveling circus is torn between the temptations of returning to a quiet existence with the wife and child he had left and of remaining with the circus and his young mistress Anne (Harriet Andersson). He is humiliated during a performance by an actor who has seduced Anne, but he stays with the circus. Humiliation and forgiveness are also the themes of a remarkable sequence at the beginning of the film, a flashback, involving the clown Frost and the clown's wife, Alma. Although harshly dealt with by Swedish critics, *The Naked Night* was the beginning of a new stage in Bergman's filmmaking career.

*A Lesson in Love (En Lektion i Kärlek,* 1954) and *Dreams* or *Journey Into Autumn (Kvinnodröm,* 1955) are less unique and in many ways represent a sliding back to the more conventional style of his pre-1953 works. *Smiles of a Summer Night* (1955), discussed in Chapter 6, is a bittersweet comedy, a masterpiece of this genre. The film attracted a good deal of favorable attention in Sweden and abroad, but it was the director's next motion picture, awarded the jury's special prize at the 1957 Cannes Film Festival, that established his international reputation. *The Seventh Seal (Det Sjunde Inseglet,* 1956) describes how in plague-ravaged fourteenth-century Sweden a knight (Max von Sydow) plays a game of chess with Death (see Figure 1.32) that extends his life. On their journey, the knight and his squire (Gunnar Björnstrand) meet various people, including a family of actors, Jof, Mia (Bibi Andersson), and their son Mikael. The knight is able to save this family, but in the end Death catches up with him and his companions. The striking visual effects, especially in sequences of a procession of flagellants and the burning of a witch, as well as interesting characterizations and outstanding acting, impressed audiences so that they ignored the fuzziness of the philosophical premises of the film.

*Wild Strawberries (Smultronstället,* 1957), Bergman's next drama, is ranked by many critics as one of the director's two most completely realized works (the other is *Persona*). Isak Borg, a 78-year-old doctor, during a one-day trip from Stockholm to Lund, also goes on an inner journey into his psyche by means of dreams and a reverie (see Figures 1.28 and 1.30). At the end of the film, he comes to a better understanding of himself and finds the courage to reach out to others. Bergman manipulates his medium with consummate artistry and takes full advantage of the outstanding performances by Victor Sjöström (the eminent Swedish director who portrayed Borg), Bibi Andersson, and Ingrid Thulin. Here is one of those singular films that becomes more meaningful the more often it is seen.

After a straightforward study of a group of women in the maternity ward of a hospital, *Brink of Life* (*Nära Livet,* 1958), the director once again created a world replete with mystery, religious overtones, and unusual characters. In *The Magician* or *The Face* (*Ansiktet,* 1958), Max von Sydow plays a mesmerist whose powers challenge the rationalism of a medical doctor (Gunnar Björnstrand). A climactic sequence in an attic where an autopsy has just been performed haunts the memory of any receptive viewer. The ending leaves unanswered the question of whether the mesmerist, whose middle name is Emanuel, is saint or charlatan.

*The Virgin Spring* (*Jungfrukällen,* 1959) is Bergman's only major film for which he did not write his own screenplay. It is based on a fourteenth-century legend of a virgin who is raped and killed by three shepherds; in time, the murderers are dispatched by the young woman's father (Max von Sydow). When her body is found, a spring miraculously gushes from the earth. Tone and action development are more impressive than portrayals of the chief characters.

After making a pleasant comedy, *The Devil's Eye* (*Djävulens Öga*), Bergman's preoccupation with religious questions, which dominated his works of the second half of the fifties, reached a culmination in a trilogy of "chamber films" (a limited number of characters in restricted time and place settings). *Through a Glass Darkly* (*Sasom i en Spegel,* 1961) is a devastating drama of the escape of a young woman (Harriet Anderson) into insanity from the complications of her

relationships with her novelist father (Gunnar Björnstrand), husband (Max von Sydow), and brother. In the chilling climax, she has a vision of God as a grotesque spider. In *Winter Light* (*Nattsvardsgästerna,* 1962), the pastor Tomas has lost his faith, is unable to help a parishioner who eventually commits suicide, and rejects the woman, Märta, who loves him. He does ask the woman, however, to join him as he celebrates Mass in an empty church at the end of the film. The acting of Ingrid Thulin (Märta) and Gunnar Björnstrand (Tomas) is unforgettable; in fact, a scene in a schoolroom in which Tomas cruelly tells Märta why he does not love her is one of the most affecting in all of Bergman's films. *The Silence* (*Tystnaden,* 1963) has as its setting an enormous, baroque hotel in a foreign country. Anna (Gunnel Lindblom) is a selfish sensualist who hates her ill sister Ester (Ingrid Thulin). She finally leaves Ester to die alone (see Figure 1.38) except for an aged hotel waiter. The only hope for the future is that Ester has passed on a message of the need for communication between human beings to Anna's young son. This is Bergman's bleakest film, a nihilistic vision of the world in which God is silent.

After the completion of this trilogy, Bergman's obsession with "the God question" no longer haunted him; as he put it, "the problem doesn't exist any more."[13] In his next period, he would concentrate his attention on the psyche of the female. He also would go further in exploring ways in which the illusion of reality on the screen is disrupted by reminders of film as artifact, as artificial construct into which viewers cannot comfortably lose themselves. As usual before a major effort, he relaxed by creating an undemanding work. *All These Women* or *Now About These Women* (*For atte inte Tala om Alla Dessa Kvinnor,* 1964) is a farce that demonstrates Bergman is not immune to failure.

After a serious illness in 1965, Bergman made *Persona* (1966). It is probably the director's greatest work to date and one of the most fascinating and provocative films of the post–World War II era. Elisabeth Vogler (Liv Ullmann), a famous actress, suddenly refuses to speak. She and a nurse, Alma (Bibi Andersson), settle in a beach house. The two women go through complicated stages in their relationship from friendship to an intimacy that alternates and at times fuses love and hate before they separate at the end. This plot summary is as inadequate as characterizing Picasso's *Guernica* as a visual protest against the bombing of a defenseless town; in both cases, the significance of the work of art lies in the boldness of its execution. Hallucinations, dreams, flashbacks, lengthy monologues, close-ups [see Figure 1.41(e)], startling juxtapositions and superimpositions of images —these are the components of a film masterfully combined by Bergman to explore the personalities of two women and to suggest that ultimately, on the deepest level of their psyches, they are one. Most innovative of all, however, is the director's creation of a prelude of brief images related by tonal association rather than the connective tissue of a narrative and his disruptions of the illusion of a screen reality. Two remarkable instances of the latter are actual disintegration of the image on the screen at a climactic moment and an intercutting of shots of Bergman and his production crew into the last minutes of the film.

Bergman's next feature was a return to the negativism of *The Silence*. In *Hour of the Wolf* (*Vargtimmen,* 1968), not even the support of his healthy, loving wife (Liv Ullmann) can save the artist Johan Borg (Max von Sydow) from insanity. The too tentative psychological foundation of the film is compensated for by visually brilliant sequences that project Johan's hallucinations directly on the screen [see Figure 1.41(c)]. *Shame* (*Skammen,* 1968) preserves this pessimistic mood as an already unsteady marriage (the couple is again portrayed by Ullmann and von Sydow) collapses under the pressures of a war in the future. The powerful final sequence presents a boat of refugees on water contaminated by radioactive material. *The Rite* (*Riten,* 1969) was made for television. Although an enactment of the ritual itself is effective, the film is generally obscure, and the development of characters is unnecessarily ambiguous. *Passion of Anna (En passion),* released the same year, is an intriguing story of the interrelations of four individuals on an island. The dangers of self-deception, emotional isolation, and violence threaten the lives of the characters played by Liv Ullmann, Bibi Andersson, Max von Sydow, and Erland Josephson. This is Bergman's

first successful color film. It also contains some memorable cinematic innovations. Two of the most striking are the device of having the actors step out of character and, directly facing the camera, discuss the roles they are playing, and the dream of Anna that begins at the end of the earlier *Shame*.

The *Faro Document* (*Faaroedokument,* 1970) is the director's first documentary (it was revised and new material was added in 1979). It deals with sheep breeding on the island of Faro, where Bergman made so many of his films. *The Touch* (*Beroringen,* 1970) is also unique in that the director uses a non-Scandinavian actor in a major role. Elliott Gould stars in this story of a married woman (Bibi Andersson) who falls in love—for reasons that are never clear—with a selfish, immature American archaeologist. Bergman's next film, *Cries and Whispers* (*Viskningar och Rop,* 1973) is far more successful. A dying woman, attended by her two sisters and a loving servant who in fantasy resurrects her, is finally able to reconcile herself to her past and the certainty of death. There are tour de force performances by Harriet Andersson, Ingrid Thulin, and Liv Ullmann. Although Bergman had worked with color earlier, he had not before *Cries and Whispers* made this element of presentation so expressive and integral a component of a drama.

*Scenes From a Marriage* (*Scener ur ett Äktenskap,* 1974) was originally made as six episodes for television presentation, then shortened for distribution in motion picture theaters. The breakup of the seemingly ideal marriage between Marianne (Liv Ullmann) and Johan (Erland Josephson) is depicted with an attention to detail and verisimilitude that has impressed and disturbed audiences throughout the Western world. *Face to Face* (*Ansikte mot Ansikte,* 1975) once again features a "night sea journey" of an individual into the world of the unconscious. Dr. Jenny Isaakson endures hallucinations, dreams, rape, and an attempted suicide before she is ready, with the help of an understanding, homosexual psychiatrist (Erland Josephson), to face the truth about herself and come to terms with the pressures of her life. Liv Ullmann's acting as Jenny is superb.

After releasing in 1976 a lovely film version of Mozart's *The Magic Flute,* Bergman had a confrontation with the tax bureau of the Swedish government and left his homeland. This severing of himself from his psychic roots had a detrimental effect on the director's work. *The Serpent's Egg* (1977) was made in Munich. This story of post–World War I Germany in which a mad scientist's murders anticipate the public violence of Nazism is one of Bergman's least convincing stories. *Autumn Sonata* (1978) is a return—a regression rather than advance for the director—to the psychologically penetrating style, within restrictions in time and place settings, of the "chamber films" of the early sixties. Ingrid Bergman and Liv Ullmann give outstanding performances as a mother and daughter who cannot bridge the chasm of selfish needs and misunderstandings that separate them. *From the Life of the Marionettes* (1980) is another dark vision of a marriage that fails. After returning to Sweden in the beginning of the eighties, Bergman declared that he would direct his final feature film. *Fanny and Alexander* (1983), filled with vitality and masterfully executed, is a magnificent family chronicle that contains many of his most characteristic themes and techniques.

In 3½ decades as a director-screenwriter, Bergman has been one of the most innovative of contemporary commercial filmmakers in exploring the potentials of his medium. His screenplays supply the frameworks of his films, and he constructs them with care. There is usually a clear, linear plot on the level of physical time, even if enclosed by a narrative frame (as in *Wild Strawberries* and *Hour of the Wolf*). Bergman occasionally depends on the device of an unidentified, inconsistently used narrator (for instance, *Persona* and *Passion of Anna*) that has disturbed some critics.

Bergman's chief aim as a screenwriter and director is to create opportunities to delve deeply into the psyche of each major character. To this end, he will insert the visual projections of dreams, reveries, hallucinations, and memories with which his films are particularly associated. Yet powerful as these subjective images may be, Bergman also writes with the flair of a dramatist whose language can serve to make both emotions and ideas vivid and expressive.

Whatever his skills as a screenwriter, Bergman

is preeminently a master of camera-editing dynamics. He composes his shots with a discerning eye for creating simultaneously dramatic and esthetic effects, and he is often ingenious and surprising in the transitions he devises between shots.

In projecting dreams and hallucinations on the screen, as well as memories through flashbacks, Bergman eschews obvious special effects. Sometimes he will make use of a textural device, such as bleaching a sequence (for example, a flashback in *The Naked Night* and a hallucination in *Hour of the Wolf*) or have costumes and setting in stark white (for instance, the fantasy luncheon in *Wild Strawberries*). He prefers, however, that the action within footage declare that a scene or sequence is illusory or a memory. Occasionally, as in a major sequence in *Persona,* it takes time for a viewer to realize that a subjective experience is being presented.

One has the impression at times that Bergman would like to bring his camera closer and closer until he actually enters the psyche of a character. Since this is impossible, he depends a great deal on close shots and close-ups. He is so confident of the expressiveness of his actors and his language that he will hold one shot on an individual who speaks for 2, 3, even 5 minutes, as in *Passion of Anna* when Anna describes her accident. This static device may slow the pace of a film, but what is revealed about a character is so fascinating that only the most impatient viewer can object.

Through his remarkable ability to create tone and manipulate rhythms, Bergman can evoke an ambiance of intangible feelings and mysterious conflicts that is a fertile ground for symbolic meanings. This can be strikingly effective, as in the director's finest films, if the narrative dimension has established a stratum to which symbols are firmly attached, rooted in character and action. Sometimes, however, Bergman presents passages that are provocative but so ambiguous that the viewer feels that the significance of a scene is to be found not within the context of a film but only in the subconscious of its creator. This type of hiatus between the filmmaker as human being and the filmmaker as artist occurs, for instance, in sections of *Hour of the Wolf* and *The Rite.*

Sound is an important component of all of Bergman's dramas. The background music is most impressive when the director draws from the works of classical composers, such as in *The Devil's Eye* (Scarlatti), *Through a Glass Darkly* (Bach), and *Cries and Whispers* (Chopin and Bach). The scores for almost half of his films are by Erik Nordgren, a competent but not particularly imaginative composer. This faint praise is inadequate, however, for the scores by Lars-Johan Werle; his eerie, modernistic background music is a distinct contribution to *Persona* and *Hour of the Wolf.*

Bergman uses natural sounds so appropriately and subtly that his originality in this area is often not fully appreciated. This is especially true of his inclusion of nonrealistic natural sounds, such as the abnormally loud ticking of a clock in more than one film, the heartbeat in *Wild Strawberries,* and a booming sound near the end of *Passion of Anna.*

Expressionistic chiaroscuro is a forte of the director, especially when Sven Nykvist is his cinematographer. Since so many of his characters enter into the underworld of the unconscious, the symbolic contrast of light and dark is meaningful. Dark woods often personify the dangers to which a character is exposed by going beyond the rational. Bergman turned to color later than most post–World War II directors. He may have been deterred by the disastrous results of his initial essay in *All These Women* (1964). In *Passion of Anna* (1969), he used distinctive though low-key color for the first time. Although this element of presentation plays a significant role in such dramas as *Cries and Whispers* and *Face to Face,* Bergman has not been as consistently innovative in his expressionistic manipulation of color as Antonioni, Visconti, Godard, and others.

Place settings also are an essential element of the unique visions embodied in the director's films. Nature assumes the proportions of a character in many of his dramas, such as the seacoast in *Summer Interlude* and *Monika;* the woods in *The Seventh Seal, Wild Strawberries, The Magician,* and *The Virgin Spring;* the bleak landscape of Faro in the "island films." Interiors may be simply realistic or project a symbolic dimension (for example, the summer house in *Wild Strawberries,* the attics in *The Magician* and *Through a Glass Darkly,* the church in *Winter Light,* the hotel in *The Silence* [Figure 6.16], and the castle in *Hour of the Wolf*).

FIGURE 6.16

*The Silence,* 1963. The youngster Johan (Jörgen Lindström) wanders the halls of a hotel, the main setting of the film. The almost empty, baroque structure symbolizes a world in which traditional values are gone and God is silent.

No matter what religious, political, philosophical, or social concepts underlie Bergman's films, always central to his dramas are human beings. In his major films, events are important primarily for what they reveal about characters' feelings. When the director loses touch with this essential source of his strength as an artist, other considerations dominate (as happened in *All These Women, The Serpent's Egg,* and, to some extent, *The Virgin Spring*); the vitality of a work seeps away, and the film becomes artificial. For this reason, Bergman depends on the resources of superior actors.

From the beginning of his career, he needed and found a group of extraordinary actors. In fact, no other director since World War II has had more consistently outstanding performers appear in his dramas. A mere listing of the major members of his "repertory" group evokes in a viewer familiar with Bergman's films memories of performances that are among the most intense and moving of our time: Liv Ullmann, Bibi Andersson, Ingrid Thulin, Harriet Andersson, Gunnel Lindblom, Eva Dahlbeck, Max von Sydow, Gunnar Björnstrand, and Erland Josephson.

The director's "family" extends beyond his actors to other members of the filmmaking team. Allan Ekelund has been his producer for the majority of his films. Either Gunnar Fischer or Sven Nykvist has served as director of photography for three-fourths of the director's oeuvre to date. The names Nils Svenwall and P. A. Lundgren (art directors), Erik Nordgren (composer), and Oscar Rosander and Ulla Ryghe (editors) are familiar to anyone who pays attention to the credit listings for the director's motion pictures.

A useful approach to Bergman's themes is to deal with them under three comprehensive and interdependent headings: the individual and binding forces larger than the self, the individual and other human beings (including the family), and the individual and self. There is a justification for basing an examination of the vision of reality that emerges from Bergman's films on the major categories of relationships described in Chapter 1 of this book.* A predominant characteristic of the director's productions is his preoccupation with the dynamics of relationships, particularly conflicts, rather than syntheses and resolutions of human dilemmas.

As with many significant twentieth-century artists, Bergman is concerned with one of the crucial questions of our age: Can the individual find emotional and intellectual supports outside the self when the usual binding forces beyond the family—particularly nature, religion, and community—appear to have lost their mythic power to reconcile oneself to death, suffering, and frustration? The individual who confronts this question either attempts to reestablish connections with binding forces or, as the existentialists suggest, accepts an absurd universe and fashions with courage, commitment, and independence one's own values that allow the individual to live with dignity and good faith. Bergman is drawn to both positions and often projects his own inner conflict into contrasting characters in the same film. So the mystic Albert Emanuel Vogler in The Magician is challenged by the

dedicated rationalist Dr. Vergerus. Another version of this conflict is the male, reaching for what is transcendental, opposed by the female who willingly settles for the solace of love between two people, as in Winter Light and Hour of the Wolf.

Nature is one form of binding force that transcends the individual. In his poetry, Wordsworth described the benefits of intimate contact with nature as threefold: a mystic insight into the meaning of existence, a moral influence, and a healing of emotional wounds. None of Bergman's characters find in nature "the philosophic mind" and "faith that looks through death."[14] The most they gain is a stoic acceptance that a person's travail and death are washed away by the eternal rhythms of nature. This idea manifests itself repeatedly in The Seventh Seal, beginning with a shot in the first sequence consisting of a superimposition of rolling waves over the chessboard between the Knight and Death (see Figure 1.32). The character who cannot see beyond his own egocentricity turns his back on nature, as does Isak Borg during a luncheon in Wild Strawberries.

Bergman even more emphatically rejects the concept of the moral superiority of the "natural man." The farmers in his "island films," unsophisticated characters (for instance, Anne and Harry in Monika), and peasants in his historical works are generally as unhappy and selfish as city dwellers. Some exceptions are a few of the characters in The Virgin Spring, Jof and Mia in The Seventh Seal (who are not typical in being actors), and Vogler's "grandmother" in The Magician (a gypsy with occult powers).

What the director-screenwriter does affirm is the healing powers of nature, particularly through the use of appropriate symbols. One version of this theme is human love flourishing in a natural setting that later is blighted in the city (for example, in Summer Interlude and Monika). The salvation of an individual or reconciliation of a couple is associated with nature, as in the endings of The Seventh Seal, Wild Strawberries, The Virgin Spring, and Scenes From a Marriage. In each of these films, a major transformation symbol in the last sequence is water. A more personal symbol derived from nature is wild strawberries (in Summer Interlude, The Seventh Seal, Wild Strawberries, and Shame). This fruit is endowed by the artist with overtones of innocence, memory, peace, love, and female sexuality.

Wrestling with the shadow of God is the predominant theme of the films from *The Seventh Seal* (1957) to *The Silence* (1963). Religion plays a role in works before and after this group, but it is central to Bergman's motion pictures of the late fifties and early sixties. Four questions insistently appear, directly or obliquely, in these films, all of them implicit in the lamentations of that arch religious questioner, Job. If God does exist, why does He not reveal Himself concretely? If God does exist, how can He allow human beings to suffer and to destroy each other? If God does not exist, can life have meaning? What can substitute for the succoring power of the deity? Bergman has no convincing answers to these questions, but he does come to some tentative conclusions through his characters.

The seeker for God must endure loneliness and frustration, and by his search he may be made indifferent to others (as the Knight in *The Seventh Seal*) or even cruel (as Tomas in *Winter Light*). If the pursuit of God by these hounds of earth is never completely successful, at the best ending in ambiguity *(The Magician, The Virgin Spring, Cries and Whispers)*, there can be compensations along the way. Tomas learns at the conclusion of *Winter Light* that there is a measure of power in the very ritual of the Mass. The most important consequence in most of the "God quest" films is the revelation of the significance of love between human beings.

There are very few major characters in Bergman's motion pictures for whom God is a palpable, bright presence: Jof in *The Seventh Seal,* the vicar in *The Devil's Eye,* and Anna in *Cries and Whispers.* What these characters share is their basic simplicity. They are not heroes or intellectuals; belief seems to have come to them as an act of grace.

After the mid-sixties, Bergman left behind his preoccupation with questions of God's existence. The proximity of death, as in the earlier works, still forces his characters to face the meaning of their lives. Now, however, it is in a human relationship or an inner integrity that a degree of salvation is to be found.

The community has rarely been a positive, dependable binding force in the director's work. In the majority of his films, it is indifferent or dangerous to the individual. The latter potential in the form of community violence that can reach its most destructive manifestation in war appears frequently enough in Bergman's oeuvre to constitute a major theme.

In his films of the forties and fifties, war is very much subordinated, with a few exceptions (such as the trite *This Can't Happen Here*), to emotional and religious problems. Violence is individual (as in *The Naked Night* and *The Virgin Spring*), abstract (for example, *The Devil's Wanton*), or natural (for instance, the plague in *The Seventh Seal*). After 1960, beginning with the "chamber films," war intrudes obliquely but with terrifying implications. Jonas in *Winter Light* commits suicide after being obsessed with the possibility of the Chinese possessing atomic bombs. In *The Silence,* the tank that appears in the street at night is a superb image of the mechanical inhumanity of modern war and revolution. National or international violence experienced secondhand, especially through television, plays a role in several post-1960 films, including *Persona* and *Passion of Anna.* The most explicit of Bergman's films on the ramifications of war is *Shame.* The lives of Eva and Jan are blighted and their integrity stained by an invasion of their island. Significantly, considering the nature symbols noted earlier, they grew strawberries before the war, and they die aimlessly afloat in polluted waters.

With the failure of or at least inadequate potentials for fulfillment from nature, God, and the community, Bergman's characters usually turn to human relations, particularly those between man and woman. There is one consistent theme in all of the director's major films: a condemnation of individuals who are so self-centered or fearful that they cannot relate honestly to others. The result is that they either use other people or withdraw into themselves. An obvious example is Isak Borg in *Wild Strawberries,* but the same emotional disease afflicts David in *Through a Glass Darkly,* Tomas in *Winter Light,* Anna in *The Silence,* Elisabeth in *Persona,* Anna and Andreas in *Passion of Anna,* David in *The Touch,* Karin and Maria in *Cries and Whispers,* and others. Bergman's censure wavers a bit when he deals with two special types of egocentrics: With those obsessed by the search for God, he is indulgent, more so in the case of the Knight in *The*

*Seventh Seal* than the pastor in *Winter Light.* Bergman clearly also appreciates the need of artists to be
selfish to some degree if they are to create. In the end,
however, he cannot approve of people who only take,
even if for the sake of art, and give little of themselves
in return. His most devastating portrayal of the egocentric artist is the writer David in *Through a Glass
Darkly.*

Whatever their professions or positions in society, the majority of Bergman's characters are lonely
and vulnerable. Some, such as Anna in *The Silence,*
never make the effort to go beyond the walls of their
inner isolation. Most struggle, however, in E. M.
Forster's famous expression, to "only connect" with
another human being.

In the director's world, it is the men who most
frequently are insecure and lost. One reason is that
they can use their professional activities as an excuse
for not confronting their psychic needs. Exceptions
are the artists, pastors, and doctors, for example, for
whom personal and public realities interfuse, usually
to the detriment of both. Sometimes they wish only for
security and a family, like Harry in *Monika* and Martin
in *Through a Glass Darkly.* More often they want both
love and adventure, especially as they reach the crisis
stage of middle age. This is the situation of Albert
Johansson in *The Naked Night,* Dr. Erneman in *A
Lesson in Love,* and Johan in *Scenes From a Marriage.*
At times they fail because they mistake superficial
needs, such as the sexual, for the more profound satisfactions of genuine love and commitment. Or they are
so involved in their own self-centered, confused, subjective desires that they cannot go beyond themselves
without help (two extremes are Johan in *Hour of the
Wolf* and Andreas in *Passion of Anna*).

Help is available from those women who,
drawing upon powers of intuition and sensation, can
lead a male to psychic health. They may fail, as Alma
does with Johan in *Hour of the Wolf.* They may be
rather unsophisticated, like Mia, who is responsible
for the only moment of peace the Knight experiences
in *The Seventh Seal.* A woman may have problems of
her own, yet could through her love be of benefit to
an unhappy man if he did not reject her. This occurs
in *Dreams, Winter Light,* and *The Touch.* More successful are the Saras and Marianne in *Wild Strawber-*

*ries,* Desirée in *Smiles of a Summer Night,* and Marianne in *A Lesson in Love.*

The majority of these female characters are
stronger, more honest, and more sympathetic than the
men. They are frequently mature, perceptive, independent human beings for whom love of a man is a
fulfillment that does not lessen their individuality. This
is not always the case: Anna in *The Silence* is as selfish
and misguided as Dr. Vergerus in *The Magician,* and
Anna is as confused and insecure as Andreas in *Passion of Anna.* Yet on the whole, Bergman has created
a crowded cinematic gallery of memorable, admirable
women.

In the mid-sixties, as Bergman turned from a
preoccupation with the "God quest," his characterizations of women became more central and gained
greater depth. Whereas in his earlier films, his strong
women—for instance, Marianne in *A Lesson in Love,*
Desirée in *Smiles of a Summer Night,* Mia in *The
Seventh Seal,* Marianne in *Wild Strawberries,* Manda
in *The Magician,* and Britt-Marie in *The Devil's Eye*
—seem to have attained their maturity before each
film opens, now the director leads us into the struggles
of women to come to terms with themselves and others. There were predecessors in Marta (*Summer Interlude*), Anne *(Monika),* and others, but nowhere
previously do we find an exploration of the female
psyche so rich in subtlety and ambiguity as in *Persona.*
*The Touch, Cries and Whispers, Scenes From a Mar-
riage,* and *Face to Face* have in common that among
their main characters are women unsure of themselves and dependent on others. They are capable,
however, of discovering inner powers that enable
them to develop into human beings who may not find
an amorphous happiness in the end but gain something more enduring: a confidence that they can survive (or die) with some degree of independence and
dignity.

As Bergman's vision of women becomes more
complex after the mid-sixties, so does his portrayal of
the family. He has always been too conscious of the
conflicts between generations and the psychological
undercurrents that affect the relationships of parents
and children, and those between parents to idealize
the family. In his pre-*Persona* films, however, this
awareness can represent a potential source of emo-

tional strength and support (manifested most unambiguously with symbolic overtones in Jof, Mia, and their child in *The Seventh Seal*). A warmth also permeates the parent-child relationships in *The Virgin Spring* and *The Devil's Eye*. In other works, the mother, with children or expecting one, is usually supportive of the vitality of the family, while the man is the disrupter, the wanderer tempted by the unknown. In *The Naked Night*, Albert could not endure domesticity and working in a shop, even if his wife would accept him, and so returns to Anne and the circus. In *A Lesson in Love* and *Smiles of a Summer Night*, a determined woman draws a man she loves back to the fold of the family. Marianne's insistence in *Wild Strawberries* that she have her unborn child contributes to Isak's progress toward psychic transformation. This pattern is not without exception; for example, Anna in *The Silence* is a mother but also a destroyer of love.

The only early film in which a mother deserts her child and family, yet is not dealt with completely unsympathetically by Bergman is Anne in *Monika*. This film anticipates a change in the director's portrayal of women that begins with *Persona*, in which Elisabeth essentially rejects her son as she withdraws into herself. Anna in *Passion of Anna*, although she cannot admit it to herself, has killed her son as well as her husband in what is ostensibly an accident. The main female characters in *The Touch*, *Scenes From a Marriage*, and *Face to Face* are concerned more with their emotional problems than with their children. In concentrating on the inner conflicts of the female, Bergman has shifted his perspective from women who function chiefly as unifiers of the family and healers of the emotional wounds of their men to those seeking first of all self-knowledge and psychic integrity.

This is not as radical a change for the director as may appear on first view. Many of his characters embark on journeys into the world of the unconscious. In his work before the mid-sixties, they were predominantly men; thereafter, the emphasis shifts to women. One of the tenets of Bergman's psychology as it appears in his films is that a human being cannot connect honestly and completely with another person unless the individual first confronts the conflicts and needs of the inner self and comes to terms with them.

To paraphrase Socrates, the unexamined psyche is a dangerous one. This is essentially a platitudinous concept in an age in which the principles of psychoanalysis are understood by anyone with even the slightest pretense to sophistication. It is the insight with which Bergman applies this concept to individual characters and the cinematic techniques he uses to express the world of the unconscious on the screen that make this aspect of his works so exciting.

C. G. Jung, the depth psychologist, offers an intellectual framework for comprehending the process and meaning of a confrontation with the inner self. In addition to many other theories, Jung asserts that when an individual ignores the needs of the unconscious, a pressure of destructive psychic energy builds up. There are people who refuse to face the consequences of this pressure. They either have nervous breakdowns or create thick defensive walls around their emotions that they can preserve only by being selfish, uncompromising, and egocentric.

Another group heeds a force in the unconscious that is creative (a concept that places Jung in opposition to Freud's vision of the makeup of the psyche). The power of the creative unconscious is not directed toward affirming forms of societal morality but toward a balancing of the four major functions of the psyche—thinking, intuition, feeling, and sensation—that enables the individual to be fulfilled personally and in relations with others. The energy of the creative portion of the unconscious is usually made concrete and brought into consciousness, especially for males, as projections of the *anima* (or soul) in the form of female images. These female *imagoes* prompt the individual to face the dangers of a "night sea journey," a trip into the personal and collective unconscious in which the person is forced to confront, primarily through dreams, the truths of the past and present. The weak can be destroyed by this horrendous experience. People who survive are transformed or psychically "reborn." The external world has not changed, but their vision of it has, and they now have the courage to attempt to establish honest and beneficial connections with others.

Without maintaining that Bergman was directly influenced by Jung's writings (a question too complex to examine here), it is possible to apply the concepts of the depth psychologist to the director's films to gain a better understanding of the psychological dynamics that govern certain characters. Dr. Vergerus in *The Magician* and Anna in *The Silence* are examples of individuals who deny the truth about themselves. Other characters make tentative efforts that involve memories and endure, with some degree of honesty, profound experiences that shake their complacency or defenses. Yet because they do not go deeply enough into themselves, their gains are temporary or ambiguous. In this category belong Albert in *The Naked Night,* the Knight in *The Seventh Seal,* Tomas in *Winter Light,* Anna and Andreas in *Passion of Anna,* and several others. Less fortunate is Johan *(Hour of the Wolf),* who is destroyed by his "night sea journey." Karin *(Through a Glass Darkly)* has another mental breakdown preceding her final vision of God. Dr. Abramsson, the emotionally cramped bureaucrat, cannot survive a potent, mysterious ceremony in *The Rite.*

On the other hand, a measure of self-knowledge is gained by and benefits Isak Borg *(Wild Strawberries)* by means of dreams (Figure 6.17); Elisabeth and Alma *(Persona)* through their complex relationship, dreams, and memories (Figure 6.18); Marta *(Summer Interlude)* by the aid of relived memories;

### FIGURE 6.18

*Persona,* 1966. Early in the film, Alma (Bibi Andersson) confides in Elisabeth (Liv Ullmann, facing the camera). Their physical proximity in the shot and similarity in clothes anticipate a later fusion of their identities.

Agnes *(Cries and Whispers)* by virtue of memories and hallucinations; and Jenny Isaakson *(Face to Face)* primarily through dreams (Figure 6.19). Not inner experiences projected on the screen but intense emotional contacts are the agencies that enable Karin in *The Touch* and Marianne in *Scenes From a Marriage* to struggle to new psychic balances.

### FIGURE 6.17

*Wild Strawberries,* 1957. Isak Borg (Victor Sjöström), in the last and most significant of his dreams, is forced by the Sara of his youth (Bibi Andersson) to confront himself and face the truth about his past.

### FIGURE 6.19

*Face to Face,* 1975 (color). Jenny Isaksson (Liv Ullmann) dreams that she sees herself laid out in a coffin.

We have only superficially examined a few themes in Bergman's films. These works are too complex and diverse to be boiled down in the cauldron of a critical mind into easy generalizations, especially when the different cinematic techniques the director uses in each film are ignored. Moreover, any statements about the oeuvre of a living director must of necessity be incomplete and tentative. Whatever he accomplishes in the future, however, Bergman has already established himself for many of us as a great motion picture director and one of the most stimulating artists of our century.

*Smiles of a Summer Night* (1955) was Bergman's second comedy (preceded by *A Lesson in Love,* 1954). While writing the screenplay, he was directing Franz Lehar's *The Merry Widow* and Molière's *Don Juan* at the Malmö City Theater, and the influence of operettas and stylized comedy is evident in the film. *Smiles of a Summer Night* was shot in 55 days and cost $150,000, considered in Sweden at the time a major investment.[15] The film won the Jury Prize at the Cannes Festival, was acclaimed, and went on to international fame.

With two exceptions—Ulla Jacobsson as Anne and Björn Bjelvenstam as Henrik—every major actor and actress in the film had appeared in earlier of the director's works and were to appear again. In the very small role of an actress on the stage with Desirée, Bibi Andersson made her debut in a Bergman film. Every chief member of the production staff, including Gunnar Fischer (director of photography), Erik Nordgren (composer), P. A. Lundgren (art director), and Oscar Rosander (editor), had also worked with Bergman on one or more of his previous motion pictures.

### PLOT SUMMARY

The setting is a provincial town in Sweden; the time is late spring, 1901. Fredrik Egerman (Björnstrand), a successful lawyer, is in his office working. A subordinate brings in two tickets to a play that evening starring Desirée Armfeldt. After Fredrik leaves, two of his clerks gossip, and we learn that Desirée was Fredrik's mistress for 2 years after his first wife died, but they separated, and later he married a young woman of 17.

Before returning home, Fredrik picks up photographs of Anne, his lovely wife. When he enters his house, he is greeted by Petra (Andersson), the pert maid. Henrik (Bjelvenstam), his son from his first marriage, home from the university where the young man is studying theology, is reading to Anne (Jacobsson). After Fredrik gives the theater tickets to a delighted Anne, he suggests a nap. While asleep, Fredrik caresses his wife but calls out the name of Desirée; Anne is hurt and bewildered.

In the theater we see the voluptuous, sophisticated Desirée (Dahlbeck) on stage. Anne asks Fredrik to take her home. A disheveled Petra answers the door. Henrik confesses to his father that he was a failure sexually with Petra and is desperately unhappy. Later, Fredrik furtively leaves the house.

He appears backstage at the theater, where he is enthusiastically welcomed by Desirée, who has not seen him for years. In her dressing room, he tells his former mistress that his present wife is still a virgin after 2 years of marriage and asks for advice. Desirée is not pleased with this role but invites him to her apartment for a glass of wine.

With Malla (Natorp), Desirée's maid, leading the way, the three walk through the streets at night while the actress sings a song. Just before entering the apartment, Fredrik falls into a puddle of water. Inside, he changes into a robe, nightshirt, and nightcap. A boy of 4 walks through the room. He is Fredrik, Desirée's son, of whose existence the elder Fredrik was unaware. She refuses to say whether or not he is the father. An argument between the two is interrupted by the appearance of Count Malcolm (Kulle), an arrogant military man who is Desirée's present lover. He forces Fredrik to leave without changing into his street clothes; they are given to him in the hallway by Malla.

The next morning Desirée persuades her mother, Mrs. Armfeldt (Wifstrand), to give a party for the Egermans and the Malcolms. The shrewd old lady suspects that her daughter is concocting a plot, a conjecture that Desirée does not deny. Later, Count Malcolm informs his wife Charlotte (Carlquist), an elegant, imperious young woman and a friend of Anne Egerman, of Mrs. Armfeldt's invitation and tells her about the events of the previous night.

That same morning, Fredrik is in his study. Charlotte visits a bored Anne. The countess describes Fredrik's nocturnal adventure and delivers a speech in which she expresses her resentment of all men, yet ends with a declaration that she still loves her husband. Fredrik enters and asks his wife about Mrs. Armfeldt's invitation; after a moment's hesitation, she accepts.

It is the afternoon of Mrs. Armfeldt's dinner party. Petra and Frid (Fridell), the Armfeldts' coachman, are attracted to each other. In the room Henrik will occupy, Frid shows Petra how a lever operates a mechanism that brings in a bed through a sliding panel from the adjacent room, where Anne and Fredrik will sleep.

The Malcolms arrive. Desirée carries Charlotte off to a room upstairs, where she suggest a plan whereby the countess will win back her husband and the actress can have Fredrick to herself.

At the elegant dinner, Mrs. Armfeldt serves a special wine after Count Malcolm has been manipulated into betting that his wife cannot seduce Fredrik. Each drinks a glass of the wine. Henrik smashes his goblet and launches into a condemnation of all of them. When he lowers his head into his arms, Anne consoles him, and Fredrik realizes his wife loves his son. Henrik finally staggers away. Anne excuses herself and leaves with Petra. After the others go to the yellow pavilion for coffee, Charlotte tempts the distraught Fredrik.

While the guests are in the pavilion listening to Desirée singing, Henrik decides to commit suicide. He botches the job but accidentally falls against the lever that brings in the bed bearing Anne. The two declare their love for each other.

Frid explains to Petra as they lie on a haystack that the first smile of the summer night is for lovers. Henrik comes to fetch the coachman. With the help of Frid and Petra, the young lovers elope. As they leave, they are observed by a silent, suffering Fredrik.

The summer smiles for the second time, Frid declares to Petra, for fools like themselves. The third smile of the summer night is for the sad and lonely. Cut to Desirée as from her bedroom she watches Fredrik and Charlotte entering the pavilion together. She alerts Malcolm, who marches into the pavilion and insists that he and Fredrik play Russian roulette. The gun fires in Fredrik's hand, but the bullet is a blank. When the count leaves, his wife demands his love for winning the wager on her ability to seduce Fredrik. He agrees that he will be faithful—in his fashion. Meanwhile, Desirée consoles Fredrik, and we know that she too has won.

Petra and Frid, who has agreed to marry her, run off in the morning light to breakfast.

---

ANALYSIS

*Smiles of a Summer Night* is a bittersweet comedy on the subject of love: the joy and suffering, exhilaration and despair, selfishness and altruism that it can evoke.

One of the secrets of the film's success is the brilliance with which Bergman, by means of contrast and parallelism, paradox and irony, encourages in each viewer a balance between distance and identification. Robin Wood compares *Smiles of a Summer Night* to Mozart's operas.[16] The reference to this composer is appropriate, particularly from one point of view: Mozart, to a greater degree than most other composers, has the ability to lay bare the intricate form of a musical piece, yet at the same time include themes that are delicate, poignant expressions of human sentiment. Bergman achieves cinematically the same type of balance.

Balance, however, does not preclude tension. In Mozart's music there is stress between the confines of structure and the pressure of emotions to express themselves explosively. So too in *Smiles of a Summer Night,* Bergman sets up tensions between, on the one hand, an artificial manipulation of plot and relationships and the need of human beings for stability and, on the other hand, instinctive, indecorous desires. By contrasting these two multifaceted forces, favoring first one and then the other, the director-screenwriter captures the ambiguity of love and life.

The chief means used in the film to manipulate characters is accident: Fredrik happens to talk in his sleep just before he and Anne go to a play starring Desirée; the actress's son walks through the room while Fredrik is present; Malcolm unexpectedly returns the one night in years that Fredrik visits Desirée; Henrik fails in his suicide attempt and accidentally falls against the mechanism that brings into his room the bed containing Anne. Desirée just happens to look out the window at the moment Charlotte and Fredrik enter the pavilion.

Chance as well as human design (especially on the part of Desirée) leads to repeated changes in the relationships and couplings of the characters: Fredrik and Anne, Fredrik and Charlotte, Fredrik and Desirée; Desirée and Malcolm, Desirée and Fredrik; Malcolm and Desirée, Malcolm and Charlotte; Henrik and Petra, Henrik and Anne; and so on. There is, however, a circular quality to these changes. In the end, Fredrik returns to Desirée and Malcolm to Charlotte.

Yet within this intricate, artificial plot structure, emotions flame up, smolder, or are extinguished. Feelings can become so exaggerated at times that domestic comedy turns into farce, as in the first encounter between Fredrik and Malcolm (when the former wishes to avoid his rival and Desirée says that they are not on the stage, he remarks, "But it's farce all the same"), Henrik's attempted suicide, and the game of Russian roulette in the pavilion.

Another aspect of the interplay of neat artificial structure and untidy emotions is the manner in which Bergman makes each of his characters completely individual, yet also joins them together into groups that are invested with mythic significance. These categories correspond, perhaps a bit too obviously, to the three smiles of the summer night and contrasting attitudes toward love. The mythic dimension exists because nature and man, the universal and the individual, become two sides of the same psychic coin.

One group is composed of a quadruplet of characters. Fredrik, Desirée, Malcolm, and Charlotte have had enough experience of love to respect its dangers as well as its gratifications, and they are therefore generally cautious, usually ironic, and often cynical when confronted by it. But these sophisticated, worldly people cannot always control their feelings. Fredrik has a passion for Anne that deep within himself he knows is hopeless, and Charlotte confesses to Anne that she both hates and loves her husband. The quadruplet is among "the sad, the depressed, the sleepless, the confused, the frightened, the lonely" on whom the summer night smiles for the third time.

Love can no longer be for them innocent, spontaneous, vigorous, concerned only with itself and so unmixed with baser matters. All four are emotionally old. It is not solely a matter of physical age, for Charlotte is only a few years senior to Anne. Love simply demands more than they can give; they have made of it a means rather than an end. They are intelligent enough, however, to know this. They remember what love can mean and suffer because they can never again bathe in its full splendor. In the conversation between Fredrik and Henrik after the former returns early from the theater, the son ironically remarks that it must be wonderful at Fredrik's mature age to know what it means to love. The father's response: "It's terrible, my son, and almost more than one can bear."

The second summer night smile is for "the simpletons, the incorrigibles." As Frid admits, it applies to Petra and himself. Theirs is a love that is natural, good-natured, unabashedly physical. It is earthy and uncomplicated, and, appropriately, nature is its setting in contrast to the indoor intimacy of the others. Although the two enjoy existence, and Frid at the end of the film can declare, "This is the life—there's none better," they are the least interesting of the major characters. We like them, approve of their physical vitality, and enjoy their humor, but they are what they appear to be and are not personally engaged in any conflict that involves us in the drama of their lives.

Young lovers evoke the first smile of the summer night. The adjective *young* is essential, for this type of romantic love demands innocence, unsureness, selfishness, commitment, and a seriousness of which only youth is capable without appearing ridiculous. Anne and Henrik, unlike the elders, do not know who they are or what they feel. Anne believes that she loves Fredrik as a husband, but really her feelings are those appropriate to a father. She tries to be a mother to Henrik, yet wants, though refusing to admit it to herself, to be his lover. She pretends to be a mature woman and mistress of the house; in reality, she plays with a dollhouse, giggles with her maid, and refuses to wear her hair up. She wanders and waits until destiny (and romantic writers insist there is always a special one for lovers) helps her to fulfill herself.

Henrik is incredibly awkward, confused, and

whiny, even for a 19-year-old. He is, in fact, the only character in the film who is drawn in too broad strokes. His emotional confusion extends to every aspect of his life. He is studying for the ministry, yet, contrary to the advice of Martin Luther, wants the birds of sexuality to nest in his hair. He cannot understand his feelings toward Anne beyond jealousy of his father. He alternates between antagonism and pathetic appeals for pity and understanding in his relationships with his father and Petra. The only constants in his feelings are unhappiness, for reasons he cannot consciously fathom, and an instinctive confidence that love can offer more than what his elders and Petra have exacted from it.

Once Henrik and Anne reveal their love to each other, they act with decisiveness and without regard to the pain they will cause Fredrik. They have endured the punishment of being true lovers; now they insist on the reward. The two are unconcerned about the future.

It is possible to diagram the plot structure of *Smiles of a Summer Night* as a triangle: The two older couples form one point of the base, Frid and Petra the other, and Henrik and Anne the pinnacle. To complete this analogy, the triangle should be enclosed by a circle. Mrs. Armfeldt encompasses all three worlds, has known all forms of love, yet is beyond them. As the old lady says to her daughter, she is both tired of people and can't stop loving them. In the scene in the bedroom, in a white nightgown and surrounded by white, she is a ghostly figure. This unearthly aura clings to her even as, again dressed in white, she presides at the dinner table. She sees all, knows all, is distant and involved, and with one gesture precipitates the resolution of conflicts. We recognize Mrs. Armfeldt from dreams, art, and the theories of C. G. Jung as a manifestation of the archetype of the mother figure in a benevolent form of the good witch of myth.

Halfway through the film occurs the crucial sequence, a superb example of cinematic art, toward which all previous action leads and from which all subsequent action flows: the supper at Mrs. Armfeldt's castle. The relationships of the characters have reached a point of stasis. Fredrik, Anne, and Henrik are in the same situation as at the opening of the film,

Malcolm and Charlotte are still apart, Petra and Frid have not yet come together, Desirée has left Malcolm and has plans for Fredrik. The dinner takes place in early summer, but the magic of Midsummer Eve is in the air.

The sequence opens with a tripartite visual motif, twice repeated, used to indicate the passage of time: a shot of the moon and clouds, another of swans on a lake, and finally a long shot of the castle lit up and reflected in a pond. Cut to the hands of a servant opening a bottle of wine. The close-up prepares us for the important role it will play in the action that follows. A track back reveals each male servant appreciating the aroma of the bottle of wine he carries. We see a magnificently set table in a high-angle long shot and hear classical music in the background. On one long side of the table sits Mrs. Armfeldt, with Frid behind her, and on the other side are the guests in evening clothes and gowns. The servants are ranged behind the guests. As the wine is served, a series of two-shots reveal the seating arrangement (from left to right): Charlotte, Fredrik, Anne, Henrik, Desirée, Malcolm.

An animated discussion is going on. The question is whether a man or a woman dominates an *affaire d'amour.* To the disgust of Henrik, love is spoken of in terms of strategies and battles. Surely Desirée initiated the subject, for it is part of her plan, and Malcolm falls neatly into the trap by accepting a bet proposed by his wife that she could seduce Fredrik in less than 15 minutes. Malcolm lifts his glass to seal the wager, followed by the others; however, before they drink, Mrs. Armfeldt speaks.

She is facing the camera on eye level and addressing it directly as she describes the very special wine [Figure 6.20(a)].. One drop of milk from the breast of a young mother (cut to Anne and Henrik, then back to the old lady) has been placed in each cask. (It is amusing to discover that the English subtitle ends there, but the screenplay indicates that also added is a drop of ''seed'' from a young stallion.) She continues: ''This sap gives the wine a special exciting power. Everyone who drinks of it does so at his own risk.'' A trill on a harp is heard as, after another two-shot of Anne and Henrik, we see Mrs. Armfeldt drink. A medium one-shot of each of the others, separated by dissolves, in the following sequence: Desirée, Malcolm, Anne (who whispers, "I drink to my love"), Charlotte ("My success"), Fredrik ("Anne"), Henrik. The young man, however, hesitates, then, without putting the glass to his lips, sets it down and looks defiantly toward the camera (his hostess). Cut to the old lady, staring at the camera (Henrik), who after wiping her lips with a finger, licks it. Back to Henrik as he suddenly drinks deeply, but ends by smashing the glass on a saucer.

These few minutes are imbued with the preternatural. We are aware that something strange and mysterious is happening. Each guest at the table gives in to the potency of this wine consecrated, as we know from the legend, to sexuality. And the wine has been offered by the old lady as a priestess might to celebrate the power of Dionysus, creator of wine and god of passion. Only Henrik resists; however, after a gesture by Mrs. Armfeldt, he too succumbs. That gesture is haunting. It is obscene, fascinating, frightening, and, in the context of the scene, magical. Yet why does the good witch require Henrik to drink? The answer lies in what follows.

Henrik makes a complete fool of himself, attacks everyone, especially his father, and smashes another glass. In utter despair, he puts his head down in his arms on the table. In the understated climax of the film, Anne places her hand on the young man's shoulder and says, "Henrik, calm yourself" [Figure 6.20(b)]. Her voice is surprisingly serene, firm, and almost disembodied, as though the comfort she gives could not be expressed in words, only a touch, and she alone could and had the right to give such comfort. Cut to a tight close-up of Fredrik's face, shocked and wide-eyed [Figure 6.20(c)]. The viewer's disconcertedness, brought about by an abrupt shift from long shot to close-up, is increased by a jarring blare of the orchestra, like an exclamation mark. Fredrik understands, as does everyone at the table except the young man as surely as if it had been proclaimed in a fervent declaration, that Anne loves Henrik. This fine cinematic moment is marred, at least for one viewer, only by the too obvious musical underlining, but then Erik Nordgren's scores for Bergman's films are rarely characterized by subtlety.

A three-shot of Henrik, Anne, and Frederik, then a cut to Mrs. Armfeldt. From the objectivity of her venerable age tempered by the compassion that still clings to her, she sums up in a generalization the sympathy all feel for Fredrik but cannot express directly: "Why is youth so terribly pitiless? And who has given it leave to be?" The imperceptive Henrik continues in his impetuous, egocentric ways. He rises in reaction to a comment by Malcolm and moves threateningly toward the soldier (once again there is that overemphatic blare of the orchestra). He is deflated by meeting in Malcolm an impenetrable, steely egotism even greater than his own. Moving to the end of the table, his back to the camera, his arms outspread, Christ-like, Henrik makes a choked apology [Figure 6.20(d)], then staggers out of the room.

Anne rises and calls after him. The camera shifts position to the other end of the room. The young woman runs toward the camera, stops at a medium distance, and appears on the verge of fainting. Her husband slowly comes up behind her. They are joined by Petra, who helps Anne to leave. Fredrik takes a step in the direction in which Anne and Petra have gone, then stops, his face half in shadows. Mrs. Armfeldt announces that coffee will be served in the yellow pavilion. After an exchange between Desirée and Charlotte and a scene between Charlotte and Fredrik, the sequence ends.

The rest of the film consists of a series of incidents that finally result in an appropriate pairing of characters: Henrik and Anne, Fredrik and Desirée, Malcolm and Charlotte, Frid and Petra. Although not quite inevitable, for accident does contribute, the denouement is unsurprising once Anne has inadvertently revealed her love for her stepson. And that revelation can be seen, in some mysterious way, as a direct consequence of Henrik's drinking the wine served by Mrs. Armfeldt. The old lady, after appearing passively in the pavilion, disappears from the film. She has served her purpose. Or has her purpose been served and her spell set in motion forces toward consequences that she intended from the beginning?

In spite of the ineffable mystery that suffuses the supper sequence, *Smiles of a Summer Night* is enclosed in a casing of language. All the older characters

**FIGURE 6.20**

*Smiles of a Summer Night.* Significant moments during the dinner at Ryarps Castle. (a) Mrs. Armfeldt speaks about the special wine they will be drinking. (b) Anne calms the distraught Henrik. (c) Fredrik suddenly realizes that his young wife is in love with his son. (d) Henrik apologizes to the group for his disruptive behavior.

(d)

are fluent and often witty. Between bouts of lovemaking, Frid reveals a sensitivity to images, and Petra is rarely at a loss for words. Henrik and Anne, however, are ineloquent, a trait epitomized by the exchange when they finally verbalize their love, which consists of two phrases repeated by each one: "I love you" and "I've loved you all the time." Naturally, lovers act, not speak, and it is only poets dreaming of or recalling love who put splendid language on their lips.

Bergman's dialogue operates on two levels, the specific and the general. This supports the director's attempt to make his characters simultaneously distinctive and representative. For example, Desirée on the stage describes how women can manipulate men by appealing to their hearts, minds, and sex; at Mrs. Armfeldt's dinner, male-female affairs are referred to in terms of warfare; even Henrik speaks of sin as an abstract entity.

Dialogue is also used, of course, for the more conventional purpose of revealing personality. This is effectively done with the main character, Fredrik. He speaks extremely well, not an unusual quality in a successful lawyer. In his first encounter with Malcolm, he wins the verbal skirmish, though losing the battle by having to leave in a nightshirt. He can be ironic and even a bit condescending in talking to his son, but he suggests his concern. He conveys to Desirée in her dressing room his feelings toward Anne, while still flirting with the actress, as when watching her in the bath, he remarks, "The years have given your body

the perfection which perfection itself lacks." At Desirée's apartment, he verbally fences with her about the past, lunging as well as parrying. (The director underscores this conflict visually at one point by using 15 reverse-angle shots in succession.)

On the other hand, Bergman is too fine a cinematic artist not to take full advantage of his camera and the skills of his actors to communicate the feelings of characters by nonverbal means. In the case of Fredrik, what is most memorable about him is not his fluency but his silent moments of doubt and pain. During Charlotte's visit to his home, he returns to his study and takes from his wallet the photographs of Anne. He arranges them, touching them with a finger, then after a moment must wipe his misted-over pince-nez. At Mrs. Armfeldt's dinner party, the expression on his face when he realizes that his wife loves his son and when he looks after his wife leaving the room fully convey his anguish without words. We share Fredrik's pain as, hidden and silent, he watches Henrik and Anne running away together, and later he picks up the veil she has dropped. When playing Russian roulette with Malcolm, the count refers to Anne's elopement. Fredrik stares, then his face hardens, as though he had closed a door against hope and a will to live. He lifts the pistol to his forehead.

Toward none of the other characters do we feel as sympathetic as to Fredrik. Anne is too childish, Henrik too self-indulgent. Malcolm and Charlotte rarely allow their shields of aristocratic self-confidence to slip. Petra and Frid need no sympathy, for they reveal no inner conflicts. Desirée is self-sufficient, tough, and pragmatic. Only where her son is concerned is she vulnerable. Her eyes flash, and she slaps Fredrik when he questions her fitness as a mother. There is also the scene when she is taking curtain calls. The curtain falls for the last time, and alone on the stage, Desirée's body sags a bit, as though she no longer has the strength to continue the pretense. This subtle action gives us an insight into the effort a no-longer-young woman must now put into her acting and helps us to understand why she would want to settle down with a family.

Bergman takes full advantage not only of his fine actors (with the exception of Björn Bjelvenstam as

Henrik) to project emotions but also of settings and inanimate objects. In the former category is the exquisite scene in which Desirée sings a song as she walks to her apartment with Fredrik and Malla. We can well appreciate why Fredrik is fascinated by the beautiful, intelligent woman when she can create an ambiance of such charm and spontaneity. The camera contributes to the mood in just two shots: a panoramic one as the three pass a pond, then a tracking shot of them walking along a pavement (Figure 6.21), the camera finally tilting down to their reflection in the

water on the street and tilting up as the shot ends. We have already considered the dinner sequence and noted the three shots (twice repeated) of sky, swans, and house. There is a wonderful *mise-en-scène,* conveying elegance and restraint, in the pavilion where Desirée sings and accompanies herself on a harp. Final among many possible examples is the last shot of the film, in which Petra and Frid, in a setting of high grass, a windmill, and the sky, run and sing as swelling, joyous music is heard on the sound track (Figure 6.22).

Inanimate objects are sometimes made symbolic by means of Bergman's deft handling. The photographs of Anna represent Fredrik's image of his wife. He views them with pride and possessiveness when he receives them from the photographer. The

---

**FIGURE 6.21**

*Smiles of a Summer Night.* In a charming scene, Desirée sings to Fredrik and Malla as the three walk from the theater to her apartment.

FIGURE 6.22

*Smiles of a Summer Night.* The summer night has ended. Frid and Petra, now engaged, run back to the castle in the clear, serene light of early morning.

next time we see them is in his study, where he touches them with affection mixed with doubt. In the pavilion, Desirée puts them in her pocket, indicating that she is now in charge of the relationship. Another example is the wooden figurines in the tower clock. As with the sky-swans-house sequence of shots, these caricatures, moving in a circle, indicate the passage of time, and they appear twice. They symbolize the characters, like all of us, trapped in a circle of time. The second time the figures appear, we are reminded of the transience of any dance of love, for at the end appears the figure of death. The revolver used in the Russian roulette also assumes symbolic proportions as Malcolm holds it in his hand near the cheek of his wife when he promises to be faithful—in his fashion. It is, as Malcolm himself, a danger to Charlotte, but then we recall that the revolver is empty.

Under the spell of Bergman's potent blend of the realistic and the preternatural, the individual and the mythic, age and youth, bitterness and sweetness, many viewers would have no hesitation in ranking *Smiles of a Summer Night* with the great ironic comedies in any medium: the films of Jean Renoir and Jean Vigo, the novels of Vladimir Nabokov and Anthony Burgess, the dramas of Molière and Shaw, and the operas of Mozart and Rossini.

## AMERICAN "NEW WAVE" COMEDY

### The Producers

*My movies are about people and how they love and hate each other, how they deal with each other, but mostly how they need each other.*
Mel Brooks, 1977[17]

**CAST**

*Zero Mostel (Max Bialystock), Gene Wilder (Leo Bloom), Dick Shawn (Lorenzo St. DuBois [L.S.D.]), Kenneth Mars (Franz Liebkind), Christopher Hewett (Roger De Bris), Estelle Winwood ("Hold me, touch me"), Lee Meredith (Ulla), and others.*

**CREDITS**

*Director and Screenwriter—Mel Brooks, Producer —Sidney Glazier, Director of Photography— Joseph Coffey, Art Director—Charles Rosen, Composer—John Morris, Editor—Ralph Rosenblum, and others.*

*1967/A Joseph Levine–Sidney Glazier Production Embassy Pictures/Color/88 minutes*

BACKGROUND

Mel Brooks (born Melvyn Kaminsky in 1926) had two types of experiences before he established himself in Hollywood that influenced the film comedies he created there. First there was his Jewish-American background. There have been many patterns in the fabric of Jewish-American humor, but two are particularly significant because they have been adapted by writers and filmmakers. The most prominent has been elaborated upon by such Jewish-American novelists as Saul Bellow and Philip Roth and by Woody Allen in his films. It involves the intellectual who is a self-made victim yet survives; a brilliant individual when it comes to ideas but a nebbish in dealing with practical and emotional problems. The comedy lies in his self-awareness and wit. He prevails, as did his forefathers, though primarily because he makes jokes about his ineptitude and mistakes. Among his pseudonyms are Portnoy, Herzog, Virgil Starkwell, and Alvy Singer. Mel Brooks uses aspects of this mode of humor, but his true commitment is to an older tradition based on the Jewish immigrant's cynicism about fate and human nature. It takes the form of broad satire of pieties derived from community mores and institutions. Brooks's shrewd, skeptical, farcical humor has an orientation that bears the stamp of someone brought up in a Jewish-American heritage.

The second important influence on Brooks's film comedy is the decade (1949–1958) he spent as a gagwriter for Sid Caesar. Comedy for the television variety shows popular in the fifties was broad, fast-paced, and dependent on verbal gags. The format of brief segments required a swift development of characters and situations with little subtlety. Yet since the skits centered on "personalities" (for example, Sid Caesar), they had to be inventive to sustain audience interest. When Brooks made his first films, he adapted many of these techniques to motion picures.

On the other hand, he also reacted against his television experience. Instead of adhering to the group approach typical of TV, he dominates his films by writing or collaborating on the screenplays, directing, producing, and acting in them. Furthermore, he deals with many subjects, especially in the areas of sex and race, in ways impossible on standard television.

In the sixties, he collaborated with a feature actor on Sid Caesar's show in creating a series of phonograph records. The first was entitled *2,000 Years with Carl Reiner and Mel Brooks* (1960) and presented the impressions of a Jewish storekeeper with astonishing longevity. Brooks generally failed in his attempts to write for the theater (for example, collaborating on the short-lived *Shinbone Alley*, 1957). He did better in devising ideas and working on scripts for film comedies.

His first public success in motion pictures was the cartoon short *The Critic* (1963). Ernest Pinoff was responsible for the animation, while Brooks conceived, wrote, and narrated the reactions to a modern art show of a spiritual descendant of the 2,000-Year-Old-Man; he doesn't understand what he sees but suspects that most of it is "dirty." *The Critic* won an Academy Award in its category. Brooks returned to television by collaborating with Buck Henry, the well-known screenwriter, on the popular series "Get Smart."

The times were propitious for a new type of irreverent, satirical film comedy, and Brooks finally found his true métier.* He completed *The Producers* in 1968, and from then on he has devoted himself almost entirely to motion pictures. In 1969, Woody Allen released his first feature, *Take the Money and Run.* Although a decade younger than Brooks and with a more intellectual approach, Allen shared the same Jewish-American background and television experience (for a much briefer period).

*The Twelve Chairs* (1970) was Brooks's second feature film. He wrote and directed it himself, as well as playing a bit part as an ex-serf. The picturesque plot, set in the Soviet Union, describes the efforts of three men to recover jewels secreted in one of a set of chairs dispersed throughout Russia. *Blazing Saddles* (1974) is a parody of classic Westerns and has a plot of sorts: a black sheriff (Cleavon Little) rescues a segregated frontier town hardly worth saving with the aid of the Waco Kid (Gene Wilder), a regenerated gunfighter, and a resurrected Frenchy (Marlene Dietrich) from *Destry Rides Again* (played by Madeline Kahn). The villains are a corrupt governor (Mel Brooks), attorney general (Harvey Korman), and assorted killers. The screenplay for this outrageous and hilarious film was written by Brooks and four collaborators, including Richard Pryor.

*Young Frankenstein* (1975) is an affectionate satire of James Whale's 1931 monster film and was written by Brooks and Gene Wilder. The latter stars as the grandson of the Baron, who brings the monster back to life. Featured are Madeline Kahn, Marty Feldman, Peter Boyle, and Gene Hackman.

*Silent Movie* (1976) is a development of the bold idea of presenting a silent film about the making of a silent movie. Unfortunately, Brooks's comic talent is not entirely visual. His attempts to make up for the loss of dialogue underscore one of his major weaknesses, a tendency to exploit frantic, even mindless, action. Equally serious a defect is the shallowness of characterization that cannot be compensated for by the acting skills of Brooks himself, Sid Caesar, Marty Feldman, Dom De Luise, and a number of stars in

*p. 282

guest appearances. In the opinion of some critics, this is the weakest of Brooks's comedies to date.

The director regained his momentum in his next film, *High Anxiety* (1977). This "psycho-comedy" is a delightful takeoff on Alfred Hitchcock dramas. The ridiculous plot is simply a vehicle for delivering parodies of individual scenes and techniques from *Spellbound, Psycho, Vertigo, The Birds,* and half a dozen other of the master's thrillers. Within the director's free-wheeling style, it is the most controlled and sharply focused of his four parodies of film genres. Brooks not only produced, directed, wrote (with three collaborators), and starred in the film but also composed and sang the title song. *The History of the World, Part I* (1981) is a disjointed, often very funny, at times offensive, imaginative farce. In short, it is typical Brooks when he is not at his best.

Mel Brooks's comedy is so broad and direct that his intentions and methods appear obvious. Behind the facade of farce and frenetic energy, however, he has serious things to say about serious subjects. To do so, he must attract our attention and then hold it. He attains his first objective by basing each of his works on an intriguing idea, and to date none of his plots has been routine or unimaginative. His films are filled with incidents and action, usually two or more people attempting to fulfill an objective (as in *The Producers, The Twelve Chairs, Young Frankenstein,* and *Silent Movie*) or a battle in many stages between forces of good and evil (*Blazing Saddles* and *High Anxiety*). So much happens in his films that viewers often are unaware that overall structuring is one of Brooks's fortes.

Characterization is another matter. His characters are consistently interesting and varied, the heroes more than the villains, but usually shallow. What they do is more important than who they are. Brooks takes stereotypes, exaggerates them, places them in bizarre situations, and depends a great deal on his actors' breathing life into his creations.

This does not mean that Brooks's characters function only as tools of the plot and vehicles for farcical situations. In their larger-than-life forms, his people reveal hidden ambitions, desires, and strengths that we often ignore because we dismiss them as merely stereotypes. A frightened, cautious accountant really wants "everything"; a black man in the racially prejudiced nineteenth-century West risks his life to become an admired and respected hero; a famous psychiatrist has a debilitating neurosis of his own. We laugh at these characters but also like and understand them, for they are really projections of facets of our own needs and insecurities. Moreover, Brooks's creations are vulnerable, and, as the epigraph suggests, they depend on each other. There is not one of the director's films in which friendship and love do not play important roles.

Having attracted our attention and drawn us into a film by means of an unusual, exciting plot and characters with whom we can identify to some degree, Brooks holds our interest and protects us from overinvolvement detrimental to comedy by distancing us from these events and characters. He does this primarily through gags and routines, shock, and exaggeration. The writer-director's experience in television is revealed in his profuse use of one-liners and comic turns. While this humor entertains us, it can also be disembodied, like jokes in a jokebook, because it is not directly derived from situation and character. In addition, Brooks's films are so replete with verbal and visual gags that inevitably some are more effective than others. A viewer has not the time to savor the best when the worst is given equal prominence.

Brooks repeatedly surprises and shocks us. This technique not only intrigues us but also can force us to recognize how often we sweep unpleasant truths about human nature and social institutions under the carpet of propriety. The trouble is that the director does not always distinguish between shock solely for effect and shock with satirical bite. Two somewhat similar incidents illustrate the difference. In the first scene in *High Anxiety,* Thorndyke is led to a men's toilet by a supposed Federal Agent who turns out to be a flasher. In *Young Frankenstein,* the Baron's sexually frigid fiancée is kidnapped by the monster. She responds after the creature unzips his pants (off-camera) by beginning a lusty rendition of "Ah, Sweet Mystery of Life." The first situation is amusing but purposeless, unless it serves to demonstrate Thorndyke's gullibility. The second is a comment on female sexual repressions and fantasies, as well as a barb directed at the euphemisms for passion in film operettas. At his best, Brooks is a sharp-eyed satirist who jolts us into an awareness of our hypocrisies and pretensions.

Exaggeration is at the heart of his type of comedy. It is the foundation of his humor and satire. Unfortunately, as with everything Brooks does in his films, he often lacks restraint and descends to sheer silliness. An example is the sequence in the governor's office in *Blazing Saddles.* On the other hand, when he's good, he's very, very good, as in L.S.D.'s audition in *The Producers.*

Although Brooks's cinematic techniques are generally conventional, he is capable of striking shots and transitions, as noted in the analysis of *The Producers.* He also knows how to use the camera to create visual humor; he may not be as brilliant as Woody Allen in this respect, but he is often more effective in taking advantage of recorded natural sounds and music.

One underlying theme in Brooks's oeuvre to date is of particular interest. All of his major characters are dreamers who sustain themselves in an absurd world by illusions. One of the chief sources of illusions in the contemporary world, especially in America, is movies from Hollywood, "the dream factory." Brooks has taken as his special province to demonstrate how we are hypnotized by the silver screen into confusing illusion and reality. Hollywood stereotypes can become a substitute for the immediate experiencing of people and events. After his first two motion pictures, his next four were parodies of film genres (Western, monster, thriller) and a form (silent). Each one is self-contained, but additionally pleasurable if a viewer recognizes allusions to a specific film or genre clichés.

Brooks invests his allusions with humor through new contexts, exaggeration, and imagination. So in *High Anxiety,* Thorndyke is attacked by birds—not with their beaks and claws, as in Hitchcock's *The Birds,* but with their excrement. (It is likely that the director was familiar with the short *The Dove,* 1968, directed by George Coe and Anthony Lover, a parody of Ingmar Bergman films in which this device appears.) Brooks, however, goes further in undercutting the confusion of "reel life" with real life. At the end

of *Blazing Saddles,* a fight bursts from the film proper into the studio set of another film. The nineteenth century fuses with the twentieth. In the last scene, the sheriff and the Waco Kid ride into the sunset in search of new adventure, not on horses, but in an automobile. In *High Anxiety,* the camera moves toward a window. Instead of a flash of lightning (as in *Citizen Kane*) or stop-motion (as in Murnau's *The Last Laugh*) allowing the camera to pass smoothly through the glass, it crashes into it, startling the characters in the room. In the last scene, the tracking camera knocks a hole in the wall of a set, and we hear on the sound track a desperate voice commanding the crew to pull back and "maybe no one will notice." This technique is a means, pioneered by Bertolt Brecht in the theater, of denying an audience the easy comfort of being simply observers distanced from action on the screen, able to consider a film as a dream in which responsibilities do not begin (to negate Delmore Schwartz's title of a short story in which memories are presented as images on a movie screen). This is a weighty interpretation of one of Brooks's intentions, but even with his many excesses and occasionally questionable taste, his films are funny (sufficient justification for their popularity) and, as in the most effective comedy, have serious implications.

The origin of *The Producers* is a song title, "Springtime for Hitler," that Brooks conceived in the early sixties. Unable to develop the idea as a novel or play, he finally made it into a screenplay. With Joseph E. Levine and Sidney Glazier as backers and Glazier as producer, Brooks wrote and directed the film, as well as composed the songs "Springtime for Hitler" and "Prisoners of Love."

Brooks was fortunate in having Zero Mostel and Gene Wilder play his two main characters; it is hard to imagine what the film would have been like with other actors. Zero Mostel, an exuberant personality, was until his death principally a theater actor in both dramas (for example, *Ulysses in Nighttown*) and musicals (for instance, *Fiddler on the Roof*). He appeared occasionally in films, usually as a gangster (*Panic in the Streets, Murder, Inc.*), but also as one of the stars of *A Funny Thing Happened on the Way to the Forum* (1966). Gene Wilder first attracted attention in a small role in *Bonnie and Clyde* (1967).

After *The Producers,* he starred in *Quackser Fortune Has a Cousin in the Bronx* (1970), *Start the Revolution Without Me* (1970), *Willy Wonka and the Chocolate Factory* (1971), and in one of the episodes in Woody Allen's *Everything You Always Wanted to Know About Sex—But Were Afraid to Ask* (1972). He played the Waco Kid in *Blazing Saddles* and the title role in *Young Frankenstein.* He has also tried his hand at directing film comedy. A deft comedian, he usually portrays bewildered young men taken advantage of by others. Wilder is one of a group of actors who have appeared repeatedly in Brooks's films; they include Madeline Kahn, Dom De Luise, Marty Feldman, Harvey Korman, and Cloris Leachman.

*The Producers* caused controversy when it appeared but was financially successful, especially on college campuses. Although made for under $1 million, it reportedly earned $5 million in 3 years. The imaginativeness of the plot was recognized even by Hollywood, which gave Brooks an Academy Award for best original screenplay.

---

### PLOT SUMMARY

Max Bialystock (Mostel), once a famous theatrical producer, has fallen on hard times. He survives in New York City by having affairs with rich old ladies who are willing to invest in his nonexistent plays. Between the credits, we see Max earning an investment check from one of his clients, the oversexed sexagenarian "Hold me, touch me" (Winwood). After she leaves and her check is appropriated by the landlord, a nervous, timid bookkeeper (Wilder) from Max's accounting agency enters the office to check the books.

As he works, Leo Bloom makes a discovery and casually mentions it. If a play is a failure, the investors would not expect their money back and the government would not check. The producer could pocket anything over what the play costs; this surplus could be a substantial sum if there was enough money invested. The unscrupulous Max reacts with alacrity to the scheme. After the two spend a day together that ends in the evening at the Lincoln Center fountain, Leo decides to leave his gray little life and join Max.

The two read through stacks of plays until they find "Springtime for Hitler: A Gay Romp with Adolf and Eva at Berchtesgaden." They agree that this idiotic paean of praise to Hitler could last no more than one night on Broadway. They sign a contract with its author, Franz Liebkind (Mars), a fanatical Nazi who lives alone, keeps pigeons, and somehow has escaped being committed to an insane asylum. Max goes on alone to the next stage of the scheme: persuading his little old ladies to invest in his new play. Finally, an exhausted Max has sold 25,000 percent of his play, and his safe is full of money.

The two are now ensconced in an expensively appointed office. The senior producer continues to drive himself, however, by hiring Roger De Bris (Hewett), "the worst director that ever lived." Roger's incredible incompetence is almost as startling as his flaunted homosexuality.

Casting for the role of Hitler bogs down until Lorenzo St. Du Bois, or L.S.D. (Shawn), accidentally wanders into the theater and sings "Love Power." His ludicrous strutting and singing are just what Max has been looking for.

The premiere of *Springtime for Hitler.* At first things go according to plan. The audience is open-mouthed with astonishment and dismay as they watch the chorus dressed as Nazi soldiers singing and dancing in praise of Hitler and Germany against a backdrop of swastikas and an immense picture of the Führer. A jubilant Max and Leo retire to the bar across the street to celebrate. What they miss is the appearance of L.S.D. He is so ridiculous that the audience, about to leave en masse, assumes the musical is a farcical satire. Max and Leo are happily drinking when the bar is invaded by members of the musical's audience during intermission. To the horror of the producers, they learn that *Springtime for Hitler* is a great success, a solid hit!

The two return to their office. A furious Franz arrives. He has enough sense to recognize that his beloved Führer was ridiculed, not glorified. First he tries to shoot Max and Leo, but calms down when Max comes up with a solution to their problem: blow up the theater. With Franz in charge of the explosives, the result is predictable. They dynamite the theater—but while they are inside.

The three are on trial (Franz is swathed in bandages). The jury finds them "incredibly guilty." Leo, with the moral support of the old ladies, makes an impassioned defense of Max. To no avail, for the next scene is in prison where the irrepressible Max is directing a prison musical. Leo is giving receipts amounting to well over 100 percent to investors—including the warden.

### ANALYSIS

One can easily imagine the scene. It is 1966, and Mel Brooks is in a producer's office trying to sell the idea for his first feature film. "You see, Max, we have this has-been theatrical producer who survives by seducing old ladies and persuading them to invest in his nonexistent plays. A neurotic bookkeeper happens by and gives the producer the idea of how to make money on a flop. They finally find a musical guaranteed, they think, to fail called 'Springtime for Hitler,' written by a Nazi nut who wants to glorify Hitler. The two hire a homosexual director, a stoned rock singer called L.S.D. . . . Now wait a minute, Max, you're not seeing the comic possibilities, like a chorus line of beautiful girls dressed as storm troopers (Figure 6.23). The picture even has a moral ending—of sorts."

Max, after swallowing his second Alka-Seltzer and turning alternately red and purple, shouts, "Seducing old ladies . . . homosexual director . . . 'Spring-

### FIGURE 6.23

*The Producers.* Among the many bizarre moments in *Springtime for Hitler* is a chorus line dressed as Nazi storm troopers.

time for Hitler' . . . You're crazy! It's outrageous, it's indecent, it's . . . it's un-American!"

What Max has missed is that the film is intentionally outrageous and irreverent. It also is as zany, improbable, and satirical as a Marx Brothers film. What is different is the subject matter. The sixties was a decade of iconoclasm, with a counterculture attacking traditional American values and a hypocrisy that could keep this country involved in Vietnam. Comedy film writers looked around and asked themselves, Is anything sacred? The obvious answer was no, especially after the Hays Office had retreated in the fifties from its stringent standards of language and forbidden subjects. Brooks's *The Producers* and Allen's *Take the Money and Run* tested the new tolerance of bourgeois standards of permissible subject matter.

*The Producers* is, of course, a farce, leavened with generous portions of verbal wit, surprising eccentric characters, and satirical thrusts at the theater, Nazism, rich old ladies, secretaries, homosexuals, prisons, and any other subject that happened to come into view. It is all flagrant and impossible, yet not completely divorced from reality. Seeds of truth are by the magic of Brooks's imagination cultivated into grotesque blooms whose prototypes we recognize in the gardens of the psyche. Yet they are so exaggerated that we are not made uncomfortable and can laugh at the foibles, selfishness, and ridiculousness of these caricatures. A minor example: New Yorkers know the necessity of locking their doors. When, however, Max visits one of his rich clients, prudence is carried to a ludicrous extreme as he waits while what seems to be dozens of locks, bolts, and bars are unfastened.

The film is carefully structured. It develops neatly in six stages: the conception of the swindle, the overcoming of Leo's scruples, the preparations for the play, the play itself, the aftermath of its success, and the epilogue in prison. The problem is that for all its careful structuring, Brooks has limited himself to one comic premise (producing a play guaranteed to fail) that is exhaustively milked rather than having attempted the wider range and depth inherent in the works of, say, Billy Wilder or Jacques Tati.

Farce is one of the most difficult forms of drama in which to act. The actor must quickly establish a characterization with such style and vigor that the audience is immediately fascinated and does not have time to consider what is plausible. The theater maxim "Hook an audience in the first 10 minutes and they'll stay still for anything" applies especially to farce. Zero Mostel is a master at this. His personality is so powerful and extraverted, accompanied by the appropriate physique, that an audience is instantly overwhelmed and pliable. In *The Producers,* even before the credits are finished, we suspect what kind of person Max Bialystock is, and a few scenes later our suspicions are confirmed. He is completely unscrupulous, resentful of a fate that has not given him what he considers his true deserts, lecherous, a cajoler if that suits his purpose, otherwise a bully (see Figures 1.15 and 1.17); most important, he is a survivor that no adversity can completely defeat. He is not, however, a disagreeable character. His vitality is commendable under any circumstances. Also admirable are his intelligence and self-knowledge. His asides and rolling eyes reveal that he knows exactly what he is doing and what it looks like to others. In this regard, he is completely honest. He may halfheartedly justify himself, as he does to Leo; however, he obviously learned early that verve and nerve will get him further quicker than honesty and scruples. The Yiddish word *chutzpah* might have been invented just for him. His spicy nature has been slyly indicated by Brooks in Max's surname. A *bialy* is a round Jewish roll sprinkled with onion flakes that originated in the Polish city of Bialystok.

Max's primary concern is always himself and his advantage, but there is no question that he develops an affection for Leo, even a fatherly interest in helping the bookkeeper to become, as he puts it, a butterfly instead of a cocoon. Fortunately, the transformation fits into Max's designs; altruism is hardly one of his characteristics.

And Leo needs help. As Max accurately states, the young man "lives in a gray little room, going to a gray little job, leading a gray little life." Everything frightens him. When he feels too threatened, he escapes into hysteria and regresses into childhood. Then this adult Linus must caress his security blanket. When he comes out of a pornographic movie (entitled *War and Piece*), he is sucking his thumb. Just as Max is the

archetype of the exploiter, Leo is the eternal victim. As his name, Leopold Bloom, suggests, if he married, it would be to a Molly who makes him a cuckold as he walked through the streets of New York instead of Dublin.

He does, however, have potentials. Leo is intelligent, affectionate, and loyal. As with many shy, frightened people, he has a secret awareness that, as he says at the Lincoln Center fountain, he works for people he is smarter than, better than. Also typical of lonely, repressed individuals, his dreams of what he wants as "his share" are derived from the movies (a major theme, as noted earlier, in Brooks's works). At the fountain, he shouts, "I want everything I've ever seen in the movies."

Max, therefore, does not have too much of a task in corrupting Leo, but he does it with diabolical finesse. First he establishes an intimacy ("Call me Max. You know I don't let just anybody call me Max, only those people I like"). Then he introduces the rewards of escape from a gray life, starting at the level of the childlike bookkeeper with a balloon and merry-go-round and proceeding to relaxing in a rowboat when Leo should return to his office. Before going to a pornographic movie, they rise above the city. At the top of the Empire State Building, Max becomes truly diabolical, a combination of Mephistopheles and Satan. The position of the corrupter, over Leo's shoulder, and the lighting that flattens Max's leering face make it clear that Brooks is parodying Satan tempting Christ on the mountaintop (Figure 6.24). In contrast to the conclusion of the biblical incident, Max-Satan is triumphant.

The failure of the plans for embezzlement leads to a jail term for Leo, but he has gained a kingdom, an emotional rather than a material one. At the trial, he expresses his gratitude to Max. He begins his speech to the judge with a description of the producer that suggests with friends like Leo, Max doesn't need enemies. Soon, however, he makes an impassioned defense of this "wonderful man" (sentimental music coming up on the sound track) who hurt no one—surely not Leo or the old ladies. The two examples of what Max has done for him—called him Leo and sang with him—are hardly impressive, but we understand

**FIGURE 6.24**

*The Producers.* Max, as an overweight Satan, tempts an easily tempted Leo at the top of the Empire State Building.

Leo's intent. The butterfly has emerged from the cocoon, albeit a bit frayed and with wings that will soon be decorated with prison stripes.

The secondary characters are less humanized than Max and Leo, more flat caricatures, yet delightful grotesques. Franz Liebkind is a fanatic so divorced from reality that we cannot identify him with blitzkriegs and concentration camps. Irony is the weapon Brooks uses against him, beginning with his name. *Liebkind* can be loosely translated as "little darling." His arrogance, cowardice, ineptitude, and stupidity prevent him from posing a threat. Like the actors who audition for the role of Hitler, he is such a burlesque that we associate him more with the soldiers of an operetta Nazidonia than the storm troopers of Germany. Only his complete isolation from other human beings and his devotion to pigeons soften our feelings toward him. Brooks, however, undercuts this impulse. The scene on the roof immediately brings to mind another loner who communes with pigeons: Terry Malloy (Marlon Brando) in *On the Waterfront.* So ridiculous is the implied comparison that Franz is deflated to a shadowy figure wearing a helmet that could hardly frighten children.

The role of L.S.D. is a tour de force of comic acting on the part of Dick Shawn (Figure 6.25). He is the ultimate spaced-out flower child of the sixties, a travesty of a stereotype, a vaudeville burlesque of a cliché. The same is true of the homosexual director Roger De Bris and his private secretary, as well as Ulla, the Swedish secretary, the "conciurge," "Hold me, touch me," and the other old ladies. Brooks's satire pricks a little, but it tickles more. Although this type of exaggeration allows him to play with risqué subjects and types of people with impunity, it confines the cogency and effectiveness of that satire.

As a director, Brooks does not experiment boldly with the medium of film to achieve comical effects. He can, however, be unconventional in his cinematic techniques. A specific example is the scenes in Central Park. The opening panoramic shot of the park ends with use of a zoom lens that brings us to Max and Leo walking along a path. Swish pans to the left are transitions between the scenes. A more general characteristic of Brooks's cinematic style is a fondness for high-angle shots, often direct verticals, for comic effect: Leo hiding behind a post outside Max's office at the beginning of the film, the two reading scripts and in the small elevator that goes to De Bris's upstairs apartment, a production number of the play.

Allusions, both through words and images, is another device that Brooks uses extensively. We have already noted that the names of characters are not casually chosen. One of the scripts that Max reads begins: "Gregor Samsa woke up one morning to find he had been transformed into a giant cockroach." Allusions to Kafka's *The Metamorphosis,* Joyce's *Ulysses* (Leo's name), Goethe's *Faust,* and the Bible (the corrupting of Leo by Max) are a minority, however, compared to allusions to motion pictures. This is not surprising in a director who later created four parodies of film genres and forms. Although there is a reference in *The Producers* to a specific film, *On the Waterfront,* most of Brooks's film parodies are of style and situation.

When Max is forced to play the game "The Countess and the Chauffeur" with "Hold me, touch me," his name, Rudolpho, reminds us of how often the plots of Valentino films centered on love between a male commoner and a female aristocrat. (Later Max

**FIGURE 6.25**

*The Producers.* L.S.D., a weird bloom of the flower-children generation, does not realize it, but he is auditioning for *Springtime for Hitler.*

**FIGURE 6.26**

*The Producers.* A Busby Berkeley technique is parodied: The chorus in *Springtime for Hitler* forms a revolving swastika.

has his revenge by naming the chauffeur of his Rolls-Royce Rudolpho.) The panning shots of the skyline of New York during the corrupting of Leo constitute a film cliché. In the presentation of *Springtime for Hitler,* there is a shot of the chorus dressed as storm troopers forming the shape of a revolving swastika (Figure 6.26). The angle is a direct vertical and, unlike the other shots of the play, could not be seen by a theater audience; it is a film-musical perspective. Anyone who has seen a thirties Hollywood musical would recognize the allusion to the style of Busby Berkeley.

Of all the scenes in the film, the one that ridicules most brilliantly a stock Hollywood situation takes place at the Lincoln Center fountain. It begins with the fountain silhouetted at night [Figure 6.27(a)]. The camera is so far away that we can barely make out the minute figures of Max and Leo at the center sitting on the edge of the fountain. We can, however, distinctly hear their voices. As Leo agrees that he leads a gray life and deserves better, the camera holds, but a tinkling melody is heard on the sound track that rises in volume as the young man becomes more excited. When he says that he wants everything he has ever seen in the movies, we can just make him out standing at the edge of the fountain. As he shouts, ''I'll do it!'' water spurts up and the music cascades from the sound track [Figure 6.27(b)]. He runs along the rim of the fountain [Figure 6.27(c)]. Cut to a low-angle medium shot of him with the jets of water behind him. In the next shot, the same setting, we see Max in silhouette as he spreads out his arms. A moment later he swings one arm like an orchestra conductor ending a piece, and, as if in response, there is an abrupt fade to black. That gesture ends not only the scene but also the sequence in which Max has effectively played out the role of the Great Manipulator, Mephistopheles, trapping a white-collar Faust in his net. Mel Brooks is also devilishly clever in molding the rhythms and tone of the three shots of the scene into a parody of the pomposity and artificiality of the climax of a Hollywood ''B'' movie.

There are admirers of *The Producers* that consider it a minor classic. This is perhaps too generous an evaluation, although it is a hilarious, vigorous, witty comedy within its limitations. The film, however, will always have a certain historical significance as one of the first of a new wave of American film comedy—iconoclastic, irreverent, satirical, wildly inventive, unconventionally structured—that developed in the 1970s.

**FIGURE 6.27**

*The Producers.* Shots from the scene at the fountain in New York's Lincoln Center. In a stereotyped Hollywood setting and situation, Leo declares, ''I want everything I've seen in the movies.''

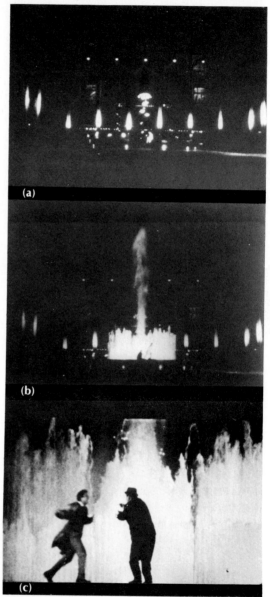

# Documentary

## 7

After a discussion of the characteristics of the documentary, with an emphasis on its relationship to actuality, 5 categories and the work of 20 major filmmakers are considered.

The four films selected for analysis illustrate three categories of the documentary. Robert Flaherty's *Man of Aran* is an example of a work in which material is manipulated consciously to portray an aspect of the relationship of man and nature. At the other end of the spectrum of documentary approaches to reality is the *cinéma verité* style of Frederic Wiseman's *Titicut Follies*. Both Leni Riefenstahl's *Triumph of the Will* and Alain Resnais's *Night and Fog* are brilliant, overt political propaganda documentaries that dramatize a similar subject from diametrically opposite points of view. A comparison of the two films demonstrates clearly that a documentary is a "creative treatment" rather than a photographic recording of actuality.

### SURVEY OF CHARACTERISTICS AND HISTORY

The World Union of Documentary defined the documentary film in 1948 as

all methods of recording on celluloid any aspect of reality interpreted either by factual shooting or by sincere and justifiable reconstruction, so as to appeal either to reason or emotion . . .[1]

The chief virtue of this description is comprehensiveness. As a working definition, however, it is as useful as an ax is for carving a wood sculpture. A more sensible approach is to apply these characteristics to the nonfiction (or factual) film and consider the documentary as a special genre within this broader category. Based on "factual shooting" or "justifiable reconstruction," the nonfiction film includes, in addition to the documentary, the newsreel (record of current events), the travelogue (description of a place, often for purposes of promotion and advertising), the educational or training film (to teach an audience how to do or understand something), and the process film (to describe how an object or procedure is constructed).

Richard Meran Barsam offers a helpful distinction between other nonfiction films and the documentary on the basis that the former is generally concerned with only the facts and the documentary with facts and opinion.[2] The word *opinion* is perhaps too vague. The genuine documentary contains, to one degree or another, a filmmaker's interpretation of objective reality, a distinct vision of the significance or meaning of what is presented on the screen. John Grierson emphasizes that aspect of the documentary in his definition: "a creative treatment of actuality."[3] The two components of this description supply the bases for examining fundamentals of the genre.

The term *actuality* ("objective reality," although there are semanticists who make a distinction between *reality* and *actuality*) suggests that the documentary has as its subject matter events as they occur with the original participants and without manipulation on the part of the filmmaker. In some styles, particularly *cinéma verité,* this is the goal strived for, though rarely achieved. In general, however, many allowances, exceptions, and compromises must be made.

Three restrictions especially preclude the documentary's completely capture of actuality. First, it is not always feasible for the camera to be present at every stage in the unfolding of an event. Second, the presence of the camera and crew can influence the action of human participants. Finally, and most important, every camera movement involves choices that highlight one element of an event and exclude others.

The possibilities for such manipulation increase during editing. This creativity, a refashioning of reality, differentiates other forms of the nonfiction film from the documentary. On the other hand, the documentary shares a "creative treatment" of a subject, at least in principle, with the fiction film. The most obvious point of contact between the two types of motion pictures is the narrative dimension: The documentary very often contains a story that involves human beings. A crucial question, then, is, How can we be sure that one film is a documentary and another is fiction unless we are told so and believe the filmmakers?

The answer is that we cannot be sure from internal evidence. No cinematic technique is exclusive to the nonfiction film. Furthermore, there is no objective criterion by which to know that a person has actually lived or is living through an experience and is not simply an actor. It is conceivable that a filmmaker could deceive us intentionally by presenting a fiction film as a documentary. This is, however, an extreme and uncommon situation. Of greater interest is the problem of how much leeway directors and their collaborators have in a "sincere and justifiable reconstruction" of events that honestly attempts to capture actuality on film. We will soon discover that the prerogatives of creative treatment give filmmakers a wider mandate to manipulate objective reality than most viewers of documentaries realize.

The many choices a director makes in a specific film usually form a pattern. This pattern reveals the filmmaker's intention or interpretation of objective reality. It is mostly conscious on his part, but it could be unconscious. In analyzing aspects of the narrative dimension, camera-editing dynamics, and elements of presentation in a documentary (or, for that matter, of any genre), we attempt to determine the meaning and ramifications of a director's choices. For instance, when Leni Riefenstahl in *Triumph of the Will* presents Hitler in low-angle shots, she is aggrandizing her subject. The dramatic music in the final storm sequence in Flaherty's *Man of Aran* and the absence of background music in Wiseman's *Titicut Follies* mold our feelings as we view the film.

The interpretation of actuality permeating a film, therefore, generally corresponds to a director's own feelings about the subject. There is the possibility

that the filmmaker accepts the intention of his sponsor even though he disagrees with it. Predominantly, however, a director believes in his interpretation and wishes to persuade his audience of its validity. As soon as we use the word *persuade,* we enter the province of propaganda and its role in documentary filmmaking.

Philip Dunne, an American director, is emphatic on this point: "In the broadest sense, the documentary is almost always an instrument of propaganda."[4] The qualifying phrase "in the broadest sense" is significant. Since the majority of directors have a specific intention in making a documentary, Dunne is correct in his assertion. On the other hand, there is another connotation to the word *propaganda:* a very assertive, manipulative treatment of objective reality. It is useful, therefore, to designate the latter "overt propaganda" to distinguish it from the less obvious propaganda intrinsic in most documentaries. And it follows that the more overt the propaganda in a documentary, the more subjective the attitude of a filmmaker toward the subject.

This element of subjectivity offers us a means of comparing the ways in which directors interpret actuality. We can postulate an imaginary scale for the documentary between the most objective approach possible in the genre and the most subjective and place a film somewhere on the scale according to how subjective the director is *in general* in the creative treatment of his material. Naturally, even within an approach that emphasizes either subjectivity or objectivity, there will also be gradations of degree.

The area of making a documentary in which subjectivity can most emphatically assert itself is that of reconstruction. Not all documentaries contain events that occurred prior to shooting or ones arranged in order to dramatize the director's intention, but many do. Alain Resnais's *Night and Fog* is entirely made up of both types of reconstruction. Robert Flaherty in most of his major films—including *Man of Aran,* discussed later in this chapter—persuaded his subjects to perform actions that had long ago passed out of their cultures.

What we have noted as true of the documentary as a whole in relation to fiction applies also to reconstruction on any scale. On internal evidence, it is very difficult to discern whether a scene or sequence has been reconstructed completely, in part, or not at all. Moreover, there is no way a viewer can distinguish in a specific film between a reconstruction that is "sincere and justifiable" and one that is insincere and unjustifiable. It should be clear now, for the point has been repeated a number of times, how essential is integrity in a documentary filmmaker and how necessary are equal measures of faith and skepticism in an audience.

Although the documentary employs all the cinematic techniques available to other genres, one device of the narrative dimension is more prominent in the documentary than in other types of motion pictures. Many documentaries (in fact, most nonfiction films) include a commentary or title cards. A verbal commentary can function in one of two ways, with various combinations possible. It may be solely descriptive, an adjunct to the visuals, supplying information necessary to understand what is happening on the screen. The title cards and commentaries in the films of Robert Flaherty generally fall into this category. Or the commentary may be interpretive as well as descriptive, conveying directly the attitude of the director toward the material. An example would be *Night and Fog.*

Once again we can refer to our objective-subjective scale. The less verbal commentary, the more easily viewers can come to their own conclusions, although other means may be used to manipulate their reactions. An overtly propagandistic documentary, for instance, is likely to employ a commentary that attempts blatantly to persuade an audience to accept the director's interpretation of actuality. A similar range exists in an interview. Questions asked off- or onscreen may simply encourage the subject to reveal himself or herself, or they may be more probing and manipulative.

Many other aspects of the documentary will be touched upon throughout this survey and in its concluding paragraphs: technical developments, problems of financing and distsribution, and the influence of television and videotape on the forms and functions of the documentary. Equally provocative are problems of morality related to the genre (some of which are considered in the analyses of individual documen-

taries following this survey). A few examples: What rights does a sponsor have in determining the intention of a film? Should a filmmaker be concerned with the source of his financing? Can a filmmaker endanger the lives of subjects to reconstruct a dramatic moment? Does a director have carte blanche in invading the privacy of his subjects, even with their permission? These and other moral dilemmas are inherent in the creating of many documentaries, and they should not be ignored by either filmmakers or their audiences.

The history of the documentary has its origins in the earliest motion pictures (Louis Lumière's avowed goal was "to record life as it happens"), reconstructions of historical events (for instance, Georges Méliès's *L'Affaire Dreyfus,* 1899), the birth of newsreels and travelogues, World War I propaganda films, and the realism manifested in the dramas of Griffith, Stroheim, and others. After the documentary emerged as a distinct genre in the early twenties, however, it developed in multiple ways with respect to subject matter, approach, and style. Tracing this development in chronological order by nations can be confusing, especially since so many major documentary filmmakers worked in different countries. The following survey of the history of the documentary, therefore, is divided into five topical categories.

Nature and man, social commentary, political propaganda and war, *cinéma vérité* or direct cinema, and esthetics and art are headings that do mix subject matter and approaches. That is, documentaries that deal with nature and man, war, and art are predominantly devoted to specific subjects that can be expressed by various means. Social commentary, political propaganda, *cinéma vérité,* and esthetics, on the other hand, are chiefly documentary approaches or styles that within certain limitations can be utilized regardless of subject matter. The five headings, however, are useful as a schema for organizing a historical survey of a very diverse cinematic genre.

One type of documentary is not discussed: the complete reconstruction of an event of an earlier age. The exclusion is due to restrictions of space rather than because many critics insist that this type of motion picture is not a genuine documentary, even though the characters portrayed by actors actually lived and the events presented are as authentic as historical research allows.

The leading practioner of this approach was Roberto Rossellini. In a series of films for Italian and French television (averaging an hour each), he chose significant moments in history as subjects. The most famous are *The Rise to Power of Louis XIV* (*La Prise de pouvoir par Louis XIV,* 1966), *Acts of the Apostles* (*Gli Atti degli Apostoli,* 1968, five episodes), and *Socrate* (1970). Englishman Peter Watkins used a similar method in presenting the defeat of Prince Charles in 1746 in *Culloden* (1964) and French director Ariane Mnouckine in *Molière* (1977). Television has been aware of the appeal of this type of documentary, or "docudrama," as evident from its series "You Are There" (1954–1957, 1971–1972) and, more recently, biographies in which professional actors play such personages as Martin Luther King, Jr., John Kennedy, Robert Kennedy, and Richard Nixon. Another form of documentary historical reconstruction consists of compilations (usually still photographs) instead of a narrative drama. Examples include Esther Shub's works on the Romanov dynasty,* Colin Low and Wolf Koenig's *City of Gold* (1957) on the Klondike gold rush, and Donald Hyatt's *The Real West* (1961) and *End of the Trail* (1965).

## NATURE AND MAN

One of the earliest forms of motion picture to become popular was travelogues, for they had the ability to introduce people to foreign places, especially exotic ones, with a greater intensity and immediacy than newspapers and books. During the first two decades of this century, however, they were usually undramatic, unstructured, unimaginative combinations of images of places and people, presented with awkwardly written title cards. A typical example is American George C. Hale's *Tours and Scenes of the World,* a hit at the St. Louis Exposition of 1904. Far more exciting were records of expeditions. A sensation in 1912 was footage of Robert Scott's voyage to the South Pole photographed by a member of the explorer's party, Herbert Ponting. Less adventurous but almost as exotic was Charles Urban's *Delhi Durbar*

*p. 337

(1911), a 2½-hour record in Kinemacolor (red and green only) of celebrations in India of the coronation of King George V.

A film was released in 1922 that demonstrated that the travelogue approach could be the basis of a genuine documentary. *Nanook of the North* and Robert Flaherty's other works are examined elsewhere in this chapter, but in sum what the "father of the documentary" did in his first motion picture was to go beyond the picturesqueness of the travelogue to create a narrative that dramatized both a primitive setting and the people who lived in it.

During the twenties, Flaherty was not alone in contributing to the tradition of nature and the natural man in cinema, though few films were as outstanding as *Nanook of the North* and *Moana* (1925). Merian C. Cooper and Ernest B. Shoedsack shot two fascinating feature-length documentaries. In *Grass* (1925), they accompanied nomadic tribes in Iran across plains and mountains in search of fresh pasturelands. *Chang* (1927) is devoted to the life of a Thai family living in the jungles and exposed to predatory animals and rampaging herds of elephants. Both films contain many striking scenes, but the title cards are on the level of mundane travelogues.

More substantial were the documentaries of three Frenchman. Léon Poirier's *Black Cruise* (*Croisière noire,* 1926) depicts an automobile trip down the continent of Africa. Jean Epstein abandoned for a time his avant-garde cinematic experiments in 1929 to direct a film on Breton fishermen, *Finis terrae*. He returned to this setting to create *Gold From the Sea* (*L'Or des mers,* 1932, with sound). Georges Rouquier's first film, *Vendanges* (1929), set in the opposite end of France, is a poetic visual record of a grape harvest.

In post-Revolutionary Russia, even documentaries that dealt with nature and man had political overtones. Dziga Vertov, to whom we will return repeatedly in this survey, pointed the way for his colleagues. *A Sixth of the World* (1926) is a panoramic view of the Soviet Union that emphasizes geographic diversity and not so incidentally praises the accomplishments of the new regime. Victor Turin's *Turksib* (1929) attracted international attention. The building of the Turkistan-Siberia railroad provides the narrative structure for remarkable scenes of the land and people of Soviet Central Asia and Siberia. Other notable Russian films that fit into this category are Mikhail Kalatozov's *Salt for Svanetia* (*Sol Svanetia*, 1930) and *Spring* (*Vesnoy*, 1930) by Mikhail Kaufman.

During the thirties, documentaries of social commentary were the predominant mode in the Western world. Even the tradition of nature and man was influenced, so that often films of this type were infused with social and political significance. Furthermore, sound was now available and added a vital new dimension to these documentaries.

Robert Flaherty continued to march to his own tune and finished *Man of Aran* in 1934. The American had been brought to England by John Grierson, who insisted that the documentary was most true to its primary function when revealing social conditions and problems. It was inevitable that films made under Grierson's auspices should be more concerned with man and machines than man and nature. One film for which he served as producer combined both themes. Basil Wright's *The Song of Ceylon* (1934) is divided into four sections. The first two are devoted to the land and religion of Ceylon; the last two center on "the voice of commerce."

In the United States during this decade, there was the same mixture of descriptions of nature with moral earnestness, as in Pare Lorentz's *The Plow That Broke the Plains* (1936) and *The River* (1937), both discussed later as examples of documentaries of social commentary. This approach characterized the major American rural documentaries of the period, including Flaherty's *The Land* (1942).

Henri Storck has been Belgium's leading documentary filmmaker. His films of social commentary and on art and artists will be considered under those headings; however, some of his activities should be mentioned here. *Images of Ostende* (1929) and *Idylle à la plage* (1931, with sound added in 1932) are lovely short works on the seacoast of northwestern Belgium. Storck also acted as editor of *Easter Island* (*L'Ile de Pâques*, 1935, directed by John Ferno) and producer of *Lords of the Forest* (*Les Seigneurs de la forêt*, 1959, directed by Heinz Sielmann and Henry Brandt), set in the Belgian Congo. In France during the German occupation, Georges Rouquier began *Far-*

*rebique* (1946). It describes in detail the life of a French peasant family, encompassing three generations, during the four seasons of a year. The real subject of *Farrebique* is the land and the peasants' harmony with nature, though it is far from a pastoral idyll.

If Flaherty could be said to have a spiritual son, it would be Arne Sucksdorff (1917–). His first works were shorts made during World War II and a few years after in the countryside of his native Sweden. The very titles of some of them indicate their subject matter: *An August Rhapsody* (*En Augustirapsodi*, 1939), *A Summer's Tale* (*Em sommarsaga*, 1941), *The Gull* (*Trut*, 1944), and *Shadows on the Snow* (*Skuggor over Snon*, 1945). His initial feature film was widely acclaimed. *The Great Adventure* (*Det Stora Äventyret*, 1953) (Figure 7.1) tells of how a boy on a farm saves a baby otter from being killed and, with the help of his young brother, hides it from his parents. Other features directed by Sucksdorff include *The Flute and the Arrow* (*En Djungelsaga*, 1957), on life in a primitive village in India, and *The Boy in the Tree* (*Pojken i Trädet*, 1961), a return to the setting of the Swedish countryside.

**FIGURE 7.1**

*The Great Adventure*, 1953, directed by Arne Sucksdorff. The director's marvelous close shots of nature and animals contributed to making this film a favorite among adults and young people.

Bert Haanstra, a Dutch director, shares with Sucksdorff a sensitivity to the protean character of nature in *Panta Rhei* (1951, Greek for "everything flows") and *The Changing Earth* (*Aardolie,* 1953). He has an intuitive feeling for animals (revealed, for instance, in *Ape and Super-Ape, Bij de beesten af,* 1972) and brilliantly conveyed the spectacle and danger of insects on the rampage in *The Rival World* (*Stijd zonder einden,* 1955).

Robert Rossellini's *India* (1958) is a remarkable work that has not received the attention it deserves. Social protest is muted, atypical of most documentaries made about this country by foreigners (for example, Louis Malle's *Calcutta,* 1969). What preoccupies Rossellini is the connection between man and animals and man and nature in four episodes: a marriage, a laborer leaving a dam that he has worked on for years, an old man attempting to save a tiger from hunters, and the pathetic experiences of a monkey after it has lost its master.

Among directors not previously mentioned who have devoted themselves in part or principally to exploring the ramifications of close contact between man and nature are Herman van der Horst, Gösta Werner, Max Anderson, Thomas Stobart, Paul Zils, and Peter Gimbel. To this list should be added the names of Jacques-Yves Cousteau, with his very successful sea documentaries beginning with the feature *The Silent World* (*Le Monde du silence,* 1956), and Thor Heyerdahl for his *Kon-Tiki* (1951). The wildlife films produced by Walt Disney Studio, such as *Seal Island* (1948) and *The Living Desert* (1953), can be entertaining and informative when they do not strain for humor and too obviously anthropomorphize animal life.

The anthropological or, more narrow in scope, ethnographic film is a subdivision of the nature-and-man category that developed significantly after World War II. This type of film is distinct from the documentaries of Flaherty and Sucksdorff in not attempting to manipulate or reconstruct events to achieve dramatic effects, and structure is usually supplied by a commentary. The purpose is to record aspects of the culture of a primitive or semiprimitive group.

Outstanding anthropological films include the works of Paul Fejos, a Hollywood director who turned to documentaries in the mid-thirties (for instance, *Dance Contest in Esira,* 1936), John Marshall's *The Hunters* (1958, describing a giraffe hunt in southern Africa), and Robert Gardiner's *Dead Birds* (1963, on ritual warfare in New Guinea). Jean Rouch began his filmmaking career with conventional documentaries in Africa (such as *Les Fils de l'eau,* 1955, a compilation of five of his shorts), then explored the possibilities of *cinéma verité* (considered later in this survey under that heading).

Many other filmmakers have focused their attention on the relationship of nature and man, and surely others will continue to do so in years to come. The resurgence since the mid-sixties of the ecological movement has acted as an impetus. Although the number of places on the earth where man lives in close contact with nature are shrinking, oceans have become a new frontier that filmmakers are not neglecting. And only earthbound parochialism limits our association of nature with our planet. The ultimate frontier is space, and it is likely that directors of the future will extend the cinematic tradition that Robert Flaherty initiated to worlds beyond Spaceship Earth.

---

SOCIAL COMMENTARY

This category can be divided into three subdivisions. (1) A documentary of *social description* has as its primary purpose to present to an audience social conditions, particularly how an environment and institutions affect the lives of people. Any criticism of these conditions is oblique, implied rather than stated. An example of a film of this type is Basil Wright's *The Song of Ceylon.* (2) In a documentary of *social criticism,* the director is less objective and his intention is to make audiences conscious that something is wrong in their society and should be remedied. The message, for example, of Willard Van Dyke and Ralph Steiner's *The City* is that city planning is too often haphazard and neglects human needs. (3) When a director is angry about a situation and wishes to induce outrage in his audience and even provoke them to action, he creates a documentary of *social protest.* Joris Ivens and Henri Storck's *Borinage* is an instance of this type of overt propaganda.

As with the lines of demarcation between categories, the distinctions between the subdivisions of documentaries of social commentary are often blurred. The only criterion for characterizing a documentary as belonging in one category or subdivision rather than another—recognizing that arbitrariness may play a role—is to judge the predominant intention of the director from the film itself.

In the twenties most documentary filmmakers (with the exception, at least to a degree, of those in the Soviet Union) were preoccupied with traveling to exotic settings or exploring the esthetic potentials of the new genre. The troubles of the thirties—an economic depression, rise of Nazism in Germany, wars in Spain and China, purges in the Soviet Union—turned the attention of people, including filmmakers, to the deficiencies of conventional economic and social systems and encouraged political agitation.

In no country did documentary filmmakers respond to these doubts with greater expertise and brilliance than in Great Britain, and to a large extent this was due to the efforts of one man. John Grierson (1898–1972) was an organizer, a director of men rather than films, an expert in public relations, a proselytizer for the cause of the documentary, a critic and theoretician. He is associated with his activities in England and Canada, but his influence extended to all countries where motion pictures were made and studied.

Grierson spent 3 years (1924–1926) in the United States on a Rockefeller Fellowship. While here he wrote a review of Flaherty's *Moana* in which the term *documentary* was first applied in English to a specific type of nonfiction film.[5] On returning to Great Britain in 1927, he persuaded a branch of the government, the Empire Marketing Board (EMB), to establish a film unit with himself as "films officer." The purpose of the EMB was to promote the marketing of food supplies in the British Empire, but Grierson expanded his mandate to include all aspects of British life, especially the conditions of the working class. During its existence from 1928 to 1933, the EMB Film Unit made over 100 documentaries. Of these, Grierson directed alone only *Drifters* (1929) and *The Fishing Banks of Skye* (1933) and codirected two others.

After the EMB was dissolved, its film unit was taken over by the General Post Office (GPO); Grierson was again in charge. With the outbreak of World War II, another organizational change occurred. The GPO Film Unit was incorporated into the Ministry of Information and its title changed to the Crown Film Unit (1940–1951). Grierson was not involved in the last metamorphosis of his unit, having resigned in 1937.

The new setting for Grierson's talent was Canada, where as film commissioner (1938–1945) he set up the National Film Board and encouraged such filmmakers as Norman McLaren and Stuart Legg. After 1945 he was involved in various organizations and directed a Scottish television program devoted to documentaries. In his last years, he taught film at McGill University in Canada.

Whatever his later achievements, Grierson's peak as a molder of the form and function of the documentary came in the thirties. During this decade he developed his theory of the genre as an expression of "social responsibility." In his essay "First Principles of Documentary," he states that the documentary should "photograph the living scene and the living story," that "the original (or native) actor, and the original (or native) scene, are better guides to a screen interpretation of the modern world" than studio recreations, and that "the raw can be finer (more real in the philosophical sense) than the actual article."[6] The documentary, therefore, can disseminate information about the contemporary world and influence viewers to work to improve the conditions in their environment. Grierson made no bones about considering the genre as "a pulpit, and [using] it as a propagandist."[7]

He was not always consistent in his views, particularly when discussing the role of esthetic values in the documentary of social commentary. Often he argues that art, especially self-conscious art, can undermine the immediacy of a re-creation of an objective reality ("documentary was from the beginning an 'anti-aesthetic' movement"[8]). On the other hand, his own definition of the documentary was a *"creative treatment of actuality"* (italics added), and he commented, "We had always the good sense to use the aesthetes."[9] A phrase in "First Principles of Documentary" to some degree reconciles this apparent contradiction. He maintains that "beauty will come in good time to inhabit the statement which is honest and lucid and deeply felt and which fulfills the best ends of citizenship."[10] In other words, a documentary is a work of art when the art is a by-product of the best efforts of a filmmaking team, not a goal in itself. Grierson's ideas are developed in *Grierson on Documentary,* one of the most influential books on the genre.

Grierson was fortunate in seeing his theories implemented by others. In fact, the young British directors he cultivated, cajoled, taught, and bullied constitute the spine of what has come to be called the "Grierson school" of the documentary.

Basil Wright (1907–) began working with Grierson in 1928. His best-known work, *The Song of Ceylon* (1934), was described earlier. With Harry Watt, Wright codirected *Night Mail* (1936), an account of the nightly journey of a mail train from London to Glasgow. W. H. Auden's verse, Benjamin Britten's music, and the evocative natural sounds supervised by Alberto Cavalcanti contribute to making this 24-minute documentary a minor classic. In 1937 Wright formed the Realist Film Unit and under its auspices directed *Children in School* (1937). UNESCO supported *World Without End* (1953, codirected by Paul Rotha). Among his other works are *O'er Hill and Dale* (1931), *Waters of Time* (1951), and *A Place for Gold* (1961). Although always aware of the social implications of his subjects, Wright is one of the most lyric in style of Grierson's protégés.

Edgar Anstey joined the EMB Film Unit in 1931. His uncompromising documentaries of social protest include *Housing Problems* (1935, with Arthur Elton) and *Enough to Eat* (1936). Harry Watt directed a number of documentaries on his own (such as *North Sea,* 1938, and *Target for Tonight,* 1941) but was most successful in collaboration with Wright, Anstey, and Humphrey Jennings. Paul Rotha worked with Grierson for only a short period of time but is identified with the producer-director's approach. Although active as a documentary filmmaker (for instance, *Shipyard,* 1933, *World of Plenty,* 1943, and *Land of Promise,* 1946), he is equally well known as a writer (for example, *Documentary Film,* 1936, revised in 1939 and 1952).

Other prominent directors of the Grierson school include Arthur Elton, Stuart Legg, John Taylor, and Evelyn Spice. The Grierson tradition has lost a good deal of its impetus since World War II, but it is still evident in various ways in the works of Karel Reisz, Thorold Dickinson, Paul Dickson, Bill Lauder, and Denis Mitchell.

In the United States, the Depression was felt more deeply and widely than in Great Britain. It gave rise to documentaries of social criticism and protest that were similar in style to those made in England but different in origin, sponsorship, and, naturally, subject matter. Most major American filmmakers in the twenties, with the notable exception of Flaherty, were drawn to Hollywood. Visual social criticism did have a heritage, however, in the related field of still photography that dated back to the beginning of the century and found expression in the works of Alfred Stieglitz, Jacob Riis, Lewis Hine, and Walker Evans, among others.

It was natural, therefore, that when the Film and Photo Leagues was organized in 1930 to do something about the economic and political crises of the day, the most prominent members, particularly in the New York branch, were still photographers with a left-wing political orientation. The group produced only a few newsreels and one feature (*Hunger,* 1933, on the National Hunger March of 1932), but it was very influential.

The National Film and Photo League (as it was eventually called) encouraged the formation and lay the groundwork for a still photography unit of the federal government's Resettlement Administration (RA). Supported by this unit, Walker Evans, Arthur Rothstein, Dorothea Lange, Ben Shahn, and others traveled throughout the country photographing migrant workers, dust-storm victims, and other manifestations of a devastated rural America. The director of this agency, Rexford Guy Tugwell, sought to extend these activities to films. The person he selected to head this new unit was an unlikely but fortunate choice.

Pare Lorentz (1905–) was a journalist and film critic who had never directed a motion picture. He was so personable and self-confident, however, that he was capable of persuading anyone that he could do anything. His first project for RA, on the subject of efforts at conservation to counter the dust storms in the Midwest, had the ridiculously small budget of $6,000 for a 30-minute film (the final cost was approximately $20,000). After shooting was completed, Lorentz, although with no experience whatsoever, did his own editing and wrote the commentary. *The Plow That Broke the Plains* premiered in 1936. Audiences were very enthusiastic, and critics described it as the finest American documentary since Flaherty's films in the twenties.

When Rexford Tugwell, now with the Department of Agriculture, suggested a film on the Mississippi River, Lorentz boldly began the new project. With Willard Van Dyke, Floyd Crosby, and Stacey Woodard as cameramen, he directed *The River* (1937) (Figure 7.2). The documentary evokes the history and majesty of the great river as it illustrates the problems of flood control.

---

**FIGURE 7.2**

*The River,* 1937, directed by Pare Lorentz. Interspersed among panoramic views of the mighty Mississippi River are scenes that document the need for more flood-control projects.

So popular was the film that the Roosevelt administration established the United States Film Service in 1938, with Lorentz in charge. He directed *The Fight for Life* (1941), a somewhat theatrical but gripping depiction of the problems faced by doctors and nurses working in a maternity clinic in a Chicago slum area. Lorentz also initiated under the sponsorship of other agencies Joris Ivens's *The Power and the Land* (1940) and Robert Flaherty's *The Land* (1942). He was beginning a film of his own on unemployment when in

1940 Congress withdrew appropriations. The U.S. Film Service had proved too successful in being controversial and provocative.

During the war, Lorentz produced training films for the U.S. Air Corps and then was chief of one of its overseas divisions. After withdrawing from government service, he became a private film consultant and to date has not directed another motion picture.

With the government having proven unreliable and overly cautious, American documentary filmmakers either established their own groups or sought financial support elsewhere. Paul Strand, Leo Hurwitz, and others set up Frontier Films in 1936. This politically left-wing group was responsible for *The Heart of Spain* (1937) and *China Strikes Back* (1938).* One of its most effective films was *Native Land* (1942, directed by Strand and Hurwitz, with a commentary spoken by Paul Robeson), an account using professional actors of anti-union and anti-civil rights activities in America. Another outstanding product of Frontier Films was *People of the Cumberland* (1937, directed by Ralph Steiner and Sidney Meyers), on unionization in Appalachia.

In addition to Lorentz, a number of directors of documentaries of social commentary became prominent in the thirties. Paul Strand began as a major American still photographer and returned to this field after 1948. He was a founder of Frontier Films, a cameraman on *The Plow That Broke the Plains,* and codirector of *The Heart of Spain, China Strikes Back, People of the Cumberland,* and *Native Land.* He also was producer, screenwriter, and cameraman for *The Wave (Los Redes,* 1935, directed by Fred Zinnemann and Emilio Muriel), a documentary sponsored by the Mexican government on fishermen striking against their exploitative employers. Leo Hurwitz was, with Strand, a committed political polemicist. He initiated his career as a director with *Hunger* (1932) and *Scottsboro* (1934) and went on to make, among other documentaries, *Strange Victory* (1949), on racial prejudice in the United States, and *Verdict for Tomorrow* (1961), dealing with the Eichmann trial. Other directors include Herbert Kline, who was responsible

---

*p. 338

for a number of antifascist films as well as *The Forgotten Village* (1941, from a script by John Steinbeck, on the abysmal medical conditions in an Indian village in Mexico), Ralph Steiner, Sidney Meyers, and Louis de Rochemont.

Willard Van Dyke (1906–) began as a still photographer and was peripherally involved with Frontier Films. His directing skill in motion pictures came to the fore principally in the forties. He and Ralph Steiner were disillusioned by the radical politics of the members of Frontier Films and in 1939 set up their own rival group, American Documentary Films. Dedicated as much to the art of liberal politics as to the documentary, this organization was short-lived, but it did sponsor one classic. *The City* (1939, codirected by Van Dyke and Steiner, with a musical score by Aaron Copland) summarizes in 43 minutes the evolution of American cities from the New England town and the mistakes in planning or lack of planning that led to overcrowded conditions and slums; the film ends with a vision of an ideal city.

During the next three decades Van Dyke directed or collaborated on more than 50 documentaries whose vividness, careful structuring, and liberal social consciousness that disdained unrealistic extremes made him a major figure in the history of the American documentary. Among his best-known films

**FIGURE 7.3**

*Valley Town,* 1940, directed by Willard Van Dyke. A typical Middle American steel town must face the problems of automation. The fine score composed by Marc Blitzstein demonstrates how background music can add to the effectiveness of a documentary.

are *Valley Town* (1940) (Figure 7.3). *The Children Must Learn* (1940), *The Bridge* (1942, codirected by Ben Maddow), *Steeltown* (1943), *San Francisco* (1945), *Journey Into Medicine* (1947), *Cabos blancos* (1954), *Land of White Alice* (1959), and *Depressed Area* (1963). From 1965 to 1973, Van Dyke was director of the department of film at the Museum of Modern Art in New York. Now in his seventies, he is a vigorous film teacher and lecturer.

After World War II, the tradition of social criticism and protest was kept alive in the works of Irving Jacoby (for instance, *The Pale Horseman,* 1946), George Stoney (for example, *All My Babies,* 1953), Alexander Hammid, and Ben Maddow, among others. Especially noteworthy are the works of Sidney Meyers and Lionel Rogosin. Meyers was writer, editor, and codirector of documentaries for Frontier Films. In 1948 he directed and produced *The Quiet One,* a poignant story of a Harlem black youth. *The Savage Eye* (1960, directed by Meyers, Ben Maddow, and Joseph Strick) is a fiction film with a documentary approach. Lionel Rogosin's *On the Bowery* (1955) is a stark presentation of the underside of New York life. *Come Back, Africa* (1959) was clandestinely shot by Rogosin and describes the terrible conditions and bitter resentment of the inhabitants of the native areas of Johannesburg, South Africa.

Documentaries in America during the sixties and seventies have been dominated by the *cinéma verité* approach, but, as we shall see, direct cinema is essentially a documentary style and does not preclude the possibility of overt objectivity with latent social commentary. Two issues during these decades aroused fervor and encouraged documentaries: Vietnam and civil rights. Documentaries on the former are noted under the heading "Political Propaganda and War." Among those on the civil rights movement that especially attracted attention were *Crisis: Behind a Presidential Commitment* (1963, directed by Richard Leacock and others), *The Angry Voices of Watts* (1966, Stuart Schulberg), *A Time for Burning* (1966, William Jersey), *Still a Brother* (1969, William Greaves), and *The Battle of East St. Louis* (1970, Perry Wolff).

So many American filmmakers during the sixties and seventies created documentaries that fit into the category of social description, criticism, and protest that even a lengthy list of their names would be incomplete and a short one unfairly exclusive. Among the best-known such directors are Arthur Barron, Emile de Antonio, Peter Davis, Harold Becker, and Martin Carr. Special mention should be made of Barbara Kopple's *Harlan County* (1976), a compelling account of a mine workers' strike, and the films of an increasing number of other women directors, such as Julia Riechart (for example, *Union Maids,* 1976, codirected by Jim Klein) and Amalie Rothschild.

Non-English-language documentaries of social commentary have often lacked the universality to circulate beyond a specific country and therefore have not been available in the United States. The most prominent exception is the work of Joris Ivens (1898–). Born in the Netherlands, Ivens' first films were impressive experiments in cinematic rhythm and design.* In 1929 Ivens was invited to the Soviet Union by V. I. Pudovkin. He remained a year, then returned in 1932 to direct *Song of Heroes (Komsomol),* which describes in detail the construction of a blast furnace. His experiences in Russia made doctrinal his youthful sympathy for oppressed workers in the Netherlands and Germany. Since the early thirties, one of the consistent characteristics of his work has been a commitment to leftist politics.

In 1933 Ivens joined forces with Henri Storck to create a documentary on a strike of miners in a district of Belgium. *Borinage (Misère au Borinage)* was shot clandestinely and reveals, with moving directness, police oppression and the illegal tactics employed by the mine owners. Influenced by what he had seen in Borinage, Ivens returned home to complete *New Earth (Nieuwe gronden,* 1934), an indictment of a capitalistic economy in which wheat could be dumped into the sea to maintain market prices.

Now Ivens began the travels that were to bring him to many countries around the world as filmmaker and passionate critic of the wrongs he observed. He went to Spain during its civil war and directed *The Spanish Earth* (1937), sponsored by Contemporary Historians, a group of American liberals. The commentary was written by Ernest Hemingway, and the

background music is by Virgil Thomson and Marc Blitzstein. The film deals with a village near Madrid that lays plans to irrigate land confiscated from landowners while enduring bombings and fighting Franco's insurgents (Figure 7.4).

FIGURE 7.4

*The Spanish Earth,* 1937, directed by Joris Ivens. The setting is the Spanish Civil War. In this shot, a Republican soldier fires on the enemy during the defense of Madrid.

Ivens next journeyed to the East and the Chinese-Japanese war. *The Four Hundred Million* (1939) is a pro-Chinese film emphasizing the atrocities perpetrated against civilians by the Japanese soldiers. While not as stirring as *The Spanish Earth,* it is a very effective propaganda documentary.

With the outbreak of war in Europe, Ivens was invited to the United States by Pare Lorentz. He directed *Power and the Land* (1940) for the Department of Agriculture on the changes rural electrification brought to American farmers. After Pearl Harbor, Ivens turned to war documentaries. *Our Russian Front* (codirected by Lewis Milestone) appeared in 1941 and *Action Stations!* (for the Canadian government) in 1942. *Know Your Enemy: Japan* (completed in 1944), however, was considered ideologically unacceptable by the U.S. War Department and was not distributed. In 1944 Ivens was appointed film commissioner for Indonesia by the Dutch government. Almost immediately he came in conflict with the authorities and resigned his post to make *Indonesia Calling* (1946), a documentary account of a dock strike.

During the next decade he worked in Poland, Russia, and East Germany. Among the films he directed were *The First Years* (*Pierwsze Lata,* 1949), *The Song of the Rivers* (*Das Lied der Ströme,* 1954), and *The Wild Rose* (*Die Windrose,* 1956). Ivens returned to the style of his youth to make *The Seine Meets Paris* (*La Seine a rencontré Paris,* 1957), an exquisite evocation of Paris as seen from barges on the Seine River, the charming *The Little Circus* (*Le Petit Chapiteau,* 1963), . . . *A Valparaiso* (1963, on the Chilean port), and *Le Mistral* (1965, which describes the winds' effects on the people of southern France).

In the late sixties and after, Ivens directed documentaries on the conflicts in Vietnam and Laos that condemned American participation. The two that caused the most stir were *17th Parallel* (*17e Parallèle,* 1967) and *The People and Their Guns* (*Le Peuple et ses fusils,* 1970), both made under French auspices, though the latter was banned by the French government. More recently, Ivens completed a 12-film series on the People's Republic of China that premiered in France in 1976. His compelling autobiography, *The Camera and I,* was published in 1969.

Ivens is a master of every aspect of the documentary, but the vividness of his visuals and the masterfulness of his editing stand out. One does not have to agree with his politics to admire his magnificent artistry. To ignore his subject matter and point of view, however, is to strip his work of one of its most important components: a genuine concern about people, especially those burdened by oppressive social and political conditions. Although he is not always accurate and objective in discerning the causes of such oppression, Ivens's cinematic eye is unblinking in recording the physical and emotional suffering or heroism of people struggling to survive, yet maintaining their dignity and hope for a better future.

Like Ivens, Belgian Henri Storck has worked in diverse areas of the documentary. One of his major interests is social problems in his native land. He first suggested to Ivens that they codirect *Borinage.* A few years later he directed alone *Les Maisons de la misère* (1938), a powerful study of a slum and the need for new housing. After the war, Storck created *Au Car-*

*refours de la vie* (1949), a United Nations–sponsored documentary on juvenile delinquency.

Luis Buñuel is famous for his fiction films, but he made one documentary that has few equals in its uncompromising portrayal of extreme poverty. *Land Without Bread* (*Las Hurdes,* 1932) has its setting in a region of Spain, Las Hurdes, where for many people simple survival required that they debase themselves to such an extent that the film has the quality of a living nightmare. To drive home his outrage, the director contrasts the squalor of the poor with the ostentatious wealth of the church and adds the irony of a neutral commentary.

Georges Franju, as with Buñuel, is better known for his fiction films than his documentaries, in which, again like Buñuel, he uses the technique of an almost impersonal commentary accompanying contrasting images. In *Blood of the Beasts* (*Le Sang des bêtes,* 1949), a visit to a slaughterhouse in Paris becomes, through the juxtaposition of images, symbolic of the violence in man that manifests itself in war and crime. In *Hôtel des Invalides* (1952), we follow a group of schoolchildren through the famous military museum and veterans' home and are made to feel the discrepancy between the proclaimed glory of war and its actual costs to human beings.

Chris Marker began his career as a journalist and writer and in fact has continued to write commentaries for documentaries made by other directors. The first film he directed was *Olympia 52* (1952), on the Olympic games at Helsinki. Soon, however, he turned to a type of film closer to his concerns, ones of social protest. *Sunday in Peking* (*Dimanche à Pékin,* 1955), *Letter From Siberia* (*Lettre de Sibérie,* 1957), and *Cuba Si!* (1961) are, as the titles suggest, geographically widespread and leftist in political stance. *Description of a Combat* (1960) is set in Israel. *Le Joli mai* (1963) is of particular interest for its *cinéma verité* style.*

In 1967 Marker formed the Société pour le Lancement des Oeuvres Nouvelles (SLON). The purpose of the organization has been to coordinate the efforts of politically leftist directors in creating social protest documentaries. Its first film was *Loin du Viet-*

---

*p. 347

nam (1967). The director has increasingly devoted himself to SLON. He was codirector of *La Sixième Face du Pentagone* (1968), concerning the peace march on Washington, and *La Bataille des dix millions* (1970), which deals with the problems involved in harvesting a Cuban sugar crop.

Some Yugoslavian filmmakers, such as Dušan Makavejev and Krsto Papić, have created documentaries of social satire and protest within the restrictions imposed by their government. The same holds true for Jerzy Bossak in Poland and Kurt Goldberger in Czechoslovakia.

Two influences today on documentaries of social description, criticism, and protest are television as a distribution outlet and the improvement in the quality and decrease in the cost of videotape equipment. Perhaps an anticipation of the future in the United States and other democracies is offered by Canada. In 1967 the National Film Board sponsored Challenge for Change. Under the supervision of John Kemeny and with the help of American George Stoney, documentaries on problems in the nation were screened on cable television. Soon the professional filmmakers became only advisers to members of the audience who made their own videotapes and films. Similar but private and far more limited groups already exist in New York and Boston.

## POLITICAL PROPAGANDA AND WAR

The potential of motion pictures to influence audiences' political attitudes, especially during war, was recognized early in the medium's history. Some of the first reconstructed "newsreels," such as J. Stuart Blackton's *Tearing Down the Spanish Flag* (1898) at the time of the Spanish-American War, were made with this purpose in mind. It was not until World War I, however, that feature-length propaganda films, such as the British *The Battle of the Somme* (1916, directed by Geoffrey Malins and J. B. McDowell), appeared.

The genuine propaganda documentary had its origins in Russia in the twenties. Lenin's famous statement, "Of all the arts, for us film is the most important," indicated the Soviet view that motion pictures should be a handmaiden of the state. In fact, the dramas of most of the major Russian film directors of

the twenties, including Eisenstein, Pudovkin, and Dovzhenko, reflected support of the state to one degree or another.

Most of the works of Dziga Vertov, Russia's greatest documentary filmmaker, have political overtones. These films will be considered when Vertov's career is summarized under the heading "*Cinéma Verité*, or Direct Cinema." Other prominent silent documentaries by Soviet directors include the compilations of Esther Shub—for instance, *The Fall of the Romanov Dynasty* (*Podeniye dinasti Romanovikh*, 1927), based on, among other sources, home movies made of Nicholas II and his family; Mikhail Kaufman, Vertov's brother, directed a number of significant documentaries, notably *Moscow* (*Moskva*, 1927); and Yakov Blyokh's *Shanghai Document* (*Shanghaisky document*, 1928) is a description of the Chinese city with an emphasis on the Communist insurrection of 1927.

Films supporting the Communist party were made outside Russia. With the exception of Jean Renoir's semidocumentary *Life Belongs to Us* (*La Vie est à nous*, 1936), however, they are of interest only to historians. What did galvanize Communist and liberal filmmakers was the Spanish Civil War (1936–1939).

One young Russian director, Roman Karmen (1906–1978), established his reputation during this war and was eventually to gain international renown for his vivid cinematic records of other wars throughout the world. A year in China during the Japanese invasion of that country resulted in *In China* (1941) and other films. He was the USSR's most famous documentary filmmaker at the front during World War II. The best of the footage he accumulated, especially on the siege of Leningrad, appeared in *The Great Patriotic War* (*Velikaya Otechestvennaya*, 1965). Later he directed *Judgment of the People* (*Sud narodoy*, 1947, on the Nuremberg trials). The settings of his postwar documentaries include India, Vietnam, and Cuba.

The chief value of Karmen's films is their immediacy rather than structure or esthetic finesse. He often risked his life to photograph events as they were happening, and a viewer of his work has the sense of being present as history is being made.

Joris Ivens's war documentaries of the thirties

have already been considered. Karmen and Ivens, however, were not the only directors to make important propaganda documentataries during this period. *Heart of Spain* (1937, directed by Herbert Kline and Geza Karpathi) is outstanding. Mention should be made of a compilation film created 2½ decades after the events in Spain: Frédéric Rossif's *To Die in Madrid* (*Mourir à Madrid,* 1965). From the Chinese-Japanese War came Henry Dunham's *China Strikes Back* (1937).

All the post–World War I documentaries noted so far were politically left-wing. The extreme right, however, was not completely quiescent in its filmmaking. Whatever vitality the Italian motion picture industry had in its early years was smothered by Fascism. The German studios, on the other hand, still had enough vigor to produce a director whose documentaries in support of the Nazi regime were of such power and beauty that they drew reluctant admiration even from ardent anti-Nazis. The life and works of Leni Riefenstahl are discussed later in this chapter. No one remotely comparable to Riefenstahl emerged in Germany during the thirties. Nor did any of the supporters of Franco create documentaries from the rightist point of view that could challenge *The Spanish Earth* and *Heart of Spain.*

World War II prompted the governments of the participants to set up documentary units to produce overt propaganda films. The number of such documentaries released between 1939 and 1945 was immense; the quality, with a few exceptions, was less impressive.

In Germany, Riefenstahl was out of favor and produced no documentaries during the war. Walter Ruttmann's oeuvre will be surveyed under the heading "Esthetics and Art." His most successful war documentary was *German Tanks* (1940). Franz Hippler was a dedicated Nazi responsible for, among others, *The Eternal Jew* (*Der ewige Jude,* 1940, including excerpts from fiction films) and *Victory in the West* (*Sieg im Westen,* 1941). Hans Bertram's *Baptism of Fire* (*Feuertaufe,* 1940) was another effective propaganda documentary from the Axis point of view; it describes the invasion and defeat of Poland.

Most of the Italian and Japanese war documen-

taries were obvious and mediocre. One of the latter, however, *Sunk Instantly* (*Gochin,* 1943), most of it shot from within a submarine and through its periscope, is reportedly of interest.

Among the Allies, the French produced no striking war documentaries. Fascinating footage was shot by Danish underground members and smuggled into England. After the war, this material was compiled by Theodor Christensen into the feature *Your Freedom Is at Stake* (*Det Gælder din frihed,* 1946).

The Russians, on the other hand, were very active. Mention was made earlier of the World War II documentaries of Roman Karmen. A great director of fiction films of the late twenties and thirties, Alexander Dovzhenko, turned to documentaries during the war. Two of his finest are *Liberation* (*Osvobozhdeniye,* 1940) and *The Fight for Our Soviet Ukraine* (*Bitva zu nasha Sovietskaya Ukrainu,* 1943). Other important Russian war documentaries include Leonid Varlamov and Ilya Kopalin's *The Defeat of the German Armies Near Moscow* (*Razgrom nemetskikh voisk pod Moskvoi,* 1942), Varlamov's *Stalingrad* (1943), and Yuli Raizman's *Berlin* (1945). Two unusual films are *Day of War* (*Den Voiny,* 1942, compiled by Mikhail Slutsky), which consists of footage shot during one day throughout Russia by dozens of cameramen, and *Cameraman at the Front* (*Frontovoj Kino-operator,* 1946), a postwar compilation of the work of Vladimir Sushinsky, including his own dying moments photographed by a colleague.

In the United States, immediately after Pearl Harbor, Frank Capra, known for his thirties comedies, was given an assignment by the U.S. War Department to organize a documentary film unit. This unit produced the series "Why We Fight," which consists of seven feature-length films: *Prelude to War* (1942), *The Nazis Strike* (1942), *Divide and Conquer* (1943), *The Battle of Britain* (1943), *The Battle of Russia* (1944), *The Battle of China* (1944), and *War Comes to America* (1945).

These are compilation films, drawn entirely from existing documentaries (including those made by the enemy) and newsreels. Although at times simplistic, they are excellently done. The propaganda is not strident, but the implied question of the title of the series is answered intelligently and with evident sincerity. The films are technically as well made as any that were released during the war, fully integrating visuals, narrative, and music.

In addition to the "Why We Fight" series, Capra's U.S. War Department Documentary Film Unit released *Tunisian Victory* (1943), *Know Your Ally: Britain* (1944), *Two Down, One to Go* (1945), as well as Joris Ivens's *Know Your Enemy: Japan* (1945), noted earlier as not released by the government.

Capra's group was only one of many that produced war documentaries, either under government auspices or through other sources. Time-Life, Inc., in its "March of Time" series, created one of the earliest: Louis de Rochemont's *The Ramparts We Watch* (1940). After Pearl Harbor, three Hollywood masters of fiction films directed documentaries. John Ford's *Battle of Midway* (1942) has been criticized as overly sentimental, but it was popular. William Wyler's *Memphis Belle* (1943) is a technicolor film on flying fortresses and their missions.

It was left to John Huston to direct two of the finest documentaries to come out of World War II. His first effort, *Report From the Aleutians* (1943), an account in color of the activities of an isolated bomber squadron, is competent but not remarkable. *The Battle of San Pietro* (completed 1944), however, is a masterpiece of the genre. It deals with a campaign in the Italian hills and the devastating effects of the battle on both soldiers and civilians. Here is combat photography at its best, yet projecting sympathy for the victims of carnage. The film was not released until 1945 because Washington officials felt that depiction of the horror and doubt engendered by war was not appropriate in a propaganda documentary. In *Let There Be Light* (completed ca. 1945), Huston turned to the home front and the rehabilitation ward of an army hospital. Whereas his previous film conveyed the pity of war, this one centered on the waste of war. Again Huston came up against resistance from officials unhappy at the thought of the public's being exposed to the truth about the realities of combat. The film was banned until the late seventies.

Other outstanding American combat documentaries include Garson Kanin's *Ring of Steel* (1942) and

*Fellow Americans* (1942), Samuel Spewack's *The World at War* (1943), Darryl F. Zanuck's *At the Front in North Africa* (1943), *The Liberation of Rome* (1944), *The Battle for the Marianas* (1944), *Fury in the Pacific* (1945), *To the Shores of Iwo Jima* (1945), and Carol Reed and Garson Kanin's *The True Glory* (1945, an Anglo-American collaboration). There was also *The Negro Soldier* (1942), commendable in praising the contributions of blacks to the defense of America throughout its history but riddled with stereotypes and dishonest in totally ignoring the fact of segregation in the United States armed forces.

The home front was also a subject of documentaries, intended either as cautionary (for example, Walt Disney's cartoon *Out of the Frying Pan Into the Firing Line,* 1944, on saving fat scraps) or morale-building (such as *War Town,* 1943, on defense workers, and *America's Hidden Weapon,* 1944, on farmers). *Toscanini: Hymn of the Nations* (1945, directed by Alexander Hammid) was made in celebration of the liberation of Italy and was popular in both the United States and Europe.

A final category consists of films dealing with the ramifications of the war at home and abroad. The finest was Huston's *Let There Be Light.* Helen Grayson's *The Cummington Story* (1945) describes the effect of a group of war refugees on a small Connecticut town. Twenty-five years after the event, a compilation film was composed by Paul Ronder on the atomic bombings of Japan, *Hiroshima-Nagasaki: August 1945.*

When Great Britain entered World War II, a group of documentary filmmakers had for almost a decade been trained by John Grierson, and this is probably a major reason why of all the countries involved, England released as a whole the most impressive war documentaries. Even among this crew of outstanding directors, one stands out from his contemporaries. Humphrey Jennings (1907–1950) developed a personal, inspired, poetic style that makes his works unique. In 1934 he joined Grierson's G.P.O. Film Unit and directed or codirected short documentaries. It was the war, however, that sparked his genius.

In his early war documentaries, he groped for

an individual approach. First he collaborated with others (for example, *The First Days,* 1939, and *London Can Take It,* 1940, both with Harry Watt), then directed on his own. In *Spring Offensive* (1940), on farming, and *The Heart of Britain* (1941), on the war's effects on people in northern industrial towns, he was able to record significant shots of simple individuals and mold from them a pattern that conveyed the spirit of a group of people at a specific time and place.

Four films are the products of Jennings's artistic maturity. *Words for Battle* (1941) combines excerpts from great poems and prose of the past with the sounds and images of the present. In *Listen to Britain* (1942) there is no commentary, only 20 minutes of songs, classical music, natural sounds, and snatches of conversation to accompany marvelous footage of Britons living their everyday lives in wartime with pride and dignity. *Fires Were Started* (1943) (Figure 7.5) is Jennings's only feature-length war documentary. It depicts the activities of a unit of the National Fire Service during a day and night of the London blitz. With brilliant simplicity the director weaves a visual and auditory tapestry of "terrible beauty." One understands why Georges Sadoul praised the film as "perhaps the crowning achievement of the British documentary school."[11] *A Diary for Timothy* (1945) has a passionate, though a bit overwrought, commentary by E. M.

---

**FIGURE 7.5**

*Fires Were Started,* 1943, directed by Humphrey Jennings. Home defenses during the London blitzes of World War II are recorded with verve and artistry.

Forster, read by John Gielgud. The film does not possess the dramatic intensity of *Fires Were Started* or the grandeur of *Words for Battle,* but it has a poignant elegiac tone all its own.

Peace appeared to bank the fire in Jennings. His postwar documentaries, such as *The Cumberland Story* (1947) and *Dim Little Island* (1949), are basically conventional. He died when he accidentally fell from a cliff while shooting a film in Greece.

There were other outstanding British filmmakers of World War II documentaries. Most of the directors who had worked under Grierson in the thirties, mentioned earlier, continued to be active: Harry Watt (*Squadron 992,* 1939, and *Christmas Under Fire,* 1941, among others), Arthur Elton (for example, *Airscrew,* 1940), Basil Wright (*The Battle for Freedom,* 1942), and Paul Rotha (for instance, *Soviet Village,* 1944, and *Total War in Britain,* 1945). Two directors not associated directly with Grierson contributed noteworthily to the war effort; both are better known for their fiction features. Roy Boulting's *Desert Victory* (1943), one of the best combat films made for the British government, is an exciting account of the triumph over Rommel's forces in North Africa. He followed this stirring film with *Tunisian Victory* (1944, with Frank Capra) and *Burma Victory* (1945, with David Macdonald). Carol Reed directed *The Way Ahead* (1943) and *The True Glory* (1945, codirected by Garson Kanin).

In addition to those already listed, among the more interesting British war documentaries were David Macdonald's *Men of the Lightship* (1940), J. B. Holmes's *Merchant Seamen* (1941) and *Coastal Command* (1942), Thorold Dickinson's *The Next of Kin* (1942), Len Lye's *Cameramen at War* (1944, a compilation), Pat Jackson's *Western Approaches* (1944), and John Eldridge's *Our Country* (1945).

After World War II ended, numerous documentaries on concentration camps and the Nuremberg trials appeared. The majority depended on footage and photographs from Nazi archives. One of the most moving is *Le Retour* (1946), directed by the famous still photographer Henri Cartier-Bresson. The Nuremberg trials was the subject of *Judgment of the People,* directed by Roman Karmen (noted earlier). Archival material was the basis of *Requiem for 500,000* (1963), by the Polish directors Jerzy Bossak and Waclaw Kaimierczak. The most famous of these films is Alain Resnais's *Night and Fog,* analyzed later in this chapter.

No one mined the Nazi archives more assiduously than Andrew Thorndike and his wife Annelie. Based in East Germany, they presented a definite Communist bias in their films. Their most distinctive work appears in the two films that make up the "The Archives Testify" series (more were intended but never completed): *Holiday on Sylt (Urlaub auf Sylt,* 1957) and *Operation Teutonic Sword (Unternehmen Teutonenschwert,* 1958). In the 1960s they created more conventional propaganda documentaries.

No documentaries made on the subject of World War II and its aftermath have been more controversial or acclaimed than those fashioned by Marcel Ophuls (1927–). The son of Max Ophuls was an assistant to his father and other prominent directors before making two dramas of his own. He found his true métier, however, when he turned to the documentary. His first important work was *Munich, or the Hundred-Year Peace (Munich, ou la paix pour cent ans,* 1967), which describes the events leading to World War II. *The Sorrow and the Pity (Le Chagrin et la pitié,* 1967, 4½ hours) consists of newsreels, documentary footage, and interviews with participants on both sides of the German occupation of France. Ophuls presents a mosaic of heroes and cowards, resisters and collaborators, that is as dramatic as any fiction film.

*A Sense of Loss* (1973) deals with the conflict in Northern Ireland. Ophuls's next effort was another mammoth documentary. *The Memory of Justice* (1976, 4½ hours) is in the same format as *The Sorrow and the Pity,* but its scope is broader, including Vietnam and other conflicts of the last three decades as well as World War II. Ophuls remarked that the purpose of this documentary was to prove the impossibility yet necessity of judging both oppressor and oppressed.

Although since the mid-fifties there have been wars and conflicts in Korea, the Near East, India, and elsewhere, none has been as lengthy or more documented than the struggles in Vietnam. Roman Karmen's *Vietnam* (1954) deals with the French involvement. By the sixties the United States had become increasingly committed to South Vietnam. The most striking documentaries of this period were either anti-American or critical of how the United States was conducting the war. The films of Joris Ivens and Chris Marker have already been mentioned. Cuban director Santiago Alvarez made *Hanoi, Tuesday the 13th (Hanoi, Martes Trece,* 1967), among others. *Pilots in Pyjamas (Piloten in Pyjama,* 1967) was directed by East Germans Walter Heynowski and Gerhard Scheumann. Poland contributed *Fire (Ogien,* 1969), by Andrzej Brzozowski, who also directed several other films on the war. Even allies and neutrals focused on the "ugly Americans." British director Felix Greene shot *Inside North Vietnam* (1968); Michael Rubbo from Canada directed *Sad Song of Yellow Skin* (1970). There were many others.

The official American view of the war was not well presented. The Department of Defense documentary *Why Vietnam?* (1965) was so one-sided and overtly propagandistic as to be denounced even by supporters of the war. By the early seventies the war had become so unpopular that Emile de Antonio's *In the Year of the Pig* (1969) and Joseph Strick's *Interview with My Lai Veterans* (1971) were shown in theaters, and the influential *The Selling of the Pentagon* (1971) appeared on television. Strident antiwar sentiment was expressed in *Hearts and Minds* (1974), a combination of interviews, special footage, and excerpts from newsreels directed by Peter Davis, who had written and produced *The Selling of the Pentagon.* Although one-sided and often crudely obvious in its propaganda, it is an extremely effective work.

Political propaganda documentaries attempt to persuade audiences that one system is superior to another, and there is little doubt this type of film will be made as long as political rivalry exists. Most war documentaries try to to justify mass death and devastation to one degree or another. Many of the very best of them, however—those directed by Ivens, Huston, and Jennings, for example—condemn the very subject they re-create. Here is the true justification for molding art from man's self-destructive tendencies.

## CINÉMA VERITÉ, OR DIRECT CINEMA

The French term *cinéma verité* was first applied by Jean Rouch and Edgar Morin to describe their approach in *Chronicle of a Summer* (1961). It indicates a prime inspiration, for the expression is a translation of "Kino-Pravda" ("film-truth"), the title Dziga Vertov gave to a series of documentaries. To understand the origin of this style, therefore, one must be acquainted with the work of the great filmmaker.

Dziga Vertov (1896–1954) was the pseudonym Denis Kaufman adopted in his student days (a practice not followed by his brothers Mikhail and Boris). After being a medical student and poet, he turned to film production during the Russian Revolution. In 1920 Vertov became chief editor of a government newsreel *Film-Weekly (Kino-Nedelya)* that was circulated throughout the country. He also put together lengthy compilation films, including *History of the Civil War (Istoriya grazhdenskoi voini,* 1921).

In the early twenties he developed his theories on a new type of nonfiction film that he christened *kino-eye* (in Russian, *kino-glaz*—literally "film-eye," but it has become a convention in English not to translate *kino*). Fundamental to this new approach was the intention, as Vertov described it in a lecture in 1929:

. . . to place in cinema production a new emphasis of the "unplayed" film over the play-film, to substitute the document for mise-en-scene, to break out of the proscenium of the theatre and to enter the arena of life itself.[12]

The kino-eye, then, captures real people in real situations. Equally crucial was the next step of re-creating this material through editing by using every technique of cinema in the service of instilling a sensory experience of immediacy in audiences:

*Kino-eye* avails itself of all the current means of recording: ultra-high speed, microcinematography, reverse motion, multiple exposure, foreshortening, etc., and does not consider these tricks, but as normal techniques of which wide use must be made.[13]

In one respect, these two steps can be contradictory. The first guarantees an appearance of authenticity and encourages the filmmaker to be as objective as possible. The second, however, leaves the esthetic door ajar, and the director may impose his own intention and personality on his material. This is what happened in the case of Vertov. Especially his feature-length films bear the mark of his style, not just generally in approach, but also in camera-editing dynamics.

The initial concrete manifestation of the director's theories was the *Kino-Pravda* series. It consisted of 23 visual journals that were released from 1922 to 1925. Each one dealt with a collection of current events ranging in subject matter from an important trial to the planting of crops. *Kino-Pravda* was not simply lengthy newsreels. Vertov searched for what he considered of true significance in everyday life as opposed to the topicality of newsreels, and his editing transformed his material.

The first feature Vertov directed in accordance with his new approach was *Kino-Glaz* (1924), a miscellanea of Moscow scenes. More national in perspective was *Stride, Soviet!* (*Shagai, Soviet!,* 1926), followed by *A Sixth of the World* (*Shestaya chast mira,* 1926) and *The Eleventh Year* (*Odinnadtsati,* 1928). All three national films proclaimed the achievements of the Soviet Union. In 1929 he completed his last silent film and the one generally regarded as his masterwork, *The Man With a Movie Camera (Chelovek s kinoapparatom).* It is a combination of propaganda, social commentary, and exploration of the esthetic potentials of cinema. Practically every cinematic device imaginable is used, from animation to what amount to zoom shots. Reality and illusion fuse as people being photographed react to the camera and, at the end, camera and tripod literally take a bow. *The Man With a Movie Camera* is a fantastic, unique documentary, a cornucopia of cinema ideas that filmmakers have drawn upon for decades since its release (Figure 7.6).

The next film Vertov directed, *Enthusiasm (Entuziazm,* 1931), is an account of the life of coal miners in the Don basin (the subtitle is *Symphony of the Don Basin*). As experimental as *The Man With a Movie Camera* is in camera-editing dynamics, *Enthusiasm* is in orchestrating natural sounds and music with visuals.

Difficulties, however, were developing for Vertov. His work was denounced as insufficiently didac-

**FIGURE 7.6**

*The Man With a Movie Camera,* 1929, directed by Dziga Vertov. An example of one special effect that appears in this cornucopia of cinematic devices.

tic. *Three Songs of Lenin* (*Tri pesni o Leninye,* 1934) is in praise of the Soviet leader. *Lullaby* (*Kolibelnaya,* 1937), on the women of Russia, was the director's last feature-length documentary and received little distribution. Vertov continued to make a few short works but was generally consigned by the government to editing newsreels. He died ignored in his native land; however, his reputation in the Western world has increased with each passing decade.

Although the influence of Vertov's ideas and techniques was widespread, his approach did not generate a genuine movement until the late fifties and early sixties with the development of *cinéma verité* (in English-speaking countries, the term *direct cinema*

is usually a synonym). This mode of documentary appeared almost independently in England, United States, and France.

Basically *cinéma verité* is a style or method of filmmaking that is not dependent on subject matter; it could conceivably be applied to any subject. Although *cinéma verité,* direct cinema, or uncontrolled documentary includes many variations, certain principles make it a distinct style.

The keystone concept is to present as close a simulation of reality as is possible in the medium. To this end, anything that stands between the camera and subject, such as scripts, sets, and special lighting, is eliminated or minimized. Crews are small. Featured players are not professional actors, nor are they told what to say or to do by the director. Action is unstructured and spontaneous, and the director does not alter the situation being witnessed.

In postproduction, the editing should not distort

the sequence, rhythm, or tone of what is recorded by the rearranging of shots, crosscutting, or other molding editing devices. Even highlighting moments of suspense is considered an undesirable manipulating of material. Only natural sounds are included, and no background music is added. Recorded dialogue fulfills all the functions of a commentary.

This is a formula for making an unadulterated direct-cinema documentary. As we will see in reviewing films actually made in the style, this ideal is rarely achieved, and many directors would disagree with certain elements as criteria of stylistic purity. One can go further and question the validity of a number of premises and ramifications of a *cinéma verité* documentary. Some, such as whether the mere presence of a camera, no matter how unobtrusive, affects the reactions of subjects, are dealt with in the essay on Wiseman's *Titicut Follies* in this chapter. Moreover, in summarizing earlier the characteristics of the documentary, the point was made that it is virtually impossible for a filmmaker to be completely objective. The processes of shooting and editing preclude this possibility; therefore, a direct-cinema director attempts to be as objective *as possible,* no more.

The first cohesive movement that can be designated genuine, though not fully developed, direct cinema arose in Great Britain. A group of young filmmakers presented a series of six programs at London's National Film Theatre from 1956 to 1959. The title they gave the series was "Free Cinema." Foreign documentaries were included, such as Rogosin's *On the Bowery* and Franju's *Blood of the Beasts,* but what really caused the audiences to sit up and take notice was the young directors' own work.

Although many filmmakers presented their documentaries, the two who attracted the most attention were Lindsay Anderson and Karel Reisz. Anderson was an outspoken critic before making documentaries in 1948. His first outstanding success was *Thursday's Children* (1954, codirected by Guy Brenton), a moving but conventional film on deaf children. *O Dreamland* (1954), a realistic portrayal of people at a seaside amusement park, and *Every Day Except Christmas* (1957), on the Covent Garden market, were in a different style. Karel Reisz also began as a

film critic. His first documentary, shown at the "Free Cinema" series, was *Momma Don't Allow* (1955, codirected by Tony Richardson), on the members of a jazz club. *We Are the Lambeth Boys* (1958) is a penetrating study of a working-class boys' club. What differentiated these documentaries and others shown at the "Free Cinema" series from their predecessors was their spontaneity, concern with everyday rather than exceptional events, disdain for "arty" effects, and an effort on the part of their directors to avoid imposing upon an audience their own interpretations of the significance of the actuality they presented.

Anderson and Reisz went on to make fiction films, but the spirit of direct cinema has been kept alive in England by such directors as John Fletcher, Denis Mitchell, Kenneth Loach, Richard Cawston, and, most recently, Roger Graef. Most of these directors' documentaries have been sponsored by or at least shown on BBC-TV.

While the "Free Cinema" series was being presented, *cinéma verité* was developing along different lines in the United States. Richard Leacock (1921–) more than any other American filmmaker was responsible for refining and promoting this style. In the early fifties, after working as a cameraman and director, he met Robert Drew, an editor for *Life* who was becoming involved in documentaries for television. They established Drew Associates in 1958 under the sponsorship of Time-Life, Inc.

The collaboration between producer and director lasted until 1963. During those 5 years Drew Associates not only innovated many of the techniques of direct cinema but also provided training for such future prominent directors as D. A. Pennebaker, Albert Maysles, Gregory Shuker, and James Lipscomb. The first problem Drew and Leacock faced—and solved— was to obtain portable, versatile equipment without cumbersome connecting cables between sound recorder and camera. The early films, such as *Bullfight at Malaga* (1958), were tentative, experimental efforts.

*Primary* (1960) was the initial breakthrough. The subject is the John Kennedy–Hubert Humphrey Democratic primary contest in Wisconsin in 1960; the style of shooting and editing prompted a group of professional filmmakers that year to grant the work an award, describing it as a "revolutionary step." The participants *seem* unaware of the presence of the crew; people cross in front of the camera as if it did not exist; the lighting is entirely natural, including haphazard shadows and dim images; the synchronized sound (a good deal of footage was shot without sound) makes no adjustment for the position of a speaker, and extraneous noises are included; many of the shots are lengthy (a famous one is a tracking shot of Kennedy entering a building and going on stage that has only one cut during its 4-minute duration [Figure 7.7]).

**FIGURE 7.7** ━━━━━━━

*Primary,* 1960, directed by Richard Leacock and others. John F. Kennedy is surrounded by supporters on his way to deliver a speech during the 1960 Democratic primary in Wisconsin.

This documentary is not, however, an example of pure direct cinema. Leacock and his cameramen were not completely indifferent to climaxes and revealing details. Nor was the editing a perfunctory matter of providing transitions between exposed footage when the shooting ratio was between 10 and 20 to 1 and the film cost more than $200,000.[14] Furthermore, one scene of the film is repeated, an artificial editing device.

Drew Associates was responsible for 18 documentaries after *Primary,* for most of which Leacock was chief filmmaker. Among the more interesting were *Yanki No!* (1960, on United States–South American relations), *The Children Were Watching* (1960, school integration in the South), *Eddie* (1961, a racer in the Indianapolis 500), *David* (1961, an ex-addict living at Synanon House), *Jane* (1962, Jane Fonda rehearsing for a play), *The Chair* (1962, the successful attempt to save Paul Crump from the electric chair), and *Crisis: Behind a Presidential Commitment* (1963, Attorney General Robert Kennedy directing the integration of the University of Alabama). Most of these documentaries are based on what Stephen Mamber calls a "crisis structure": a dramatic moment involving a contest of some sort which reveals the characters of the participants and the context of their struggles.[15]

Leacock left Drew Associates to work with Donn Pennebaker, a partnership that lasted for 7 years. The two directors generally worked independently but helped each other. Among the films Leacock directed in the sixties were *Happy Mother's Day* (1963) and *A Stravinsky Portrait* (1964). He was relatively inactive as a director during the seventies.

Donn Alan Pennebaker (1930–) was involved in numerous Drew Associates productions, including *Primary, David, Jane,* and *The Chair.* He has made films on many subjects but is particularly associated with documentaries on musicians and the theater. Bob Dylan's 1965 concert tour in Great Britain is the subject of *Don't Look Back* (1966). Probably Pennebaker's most famous work is *Monterey Pop* (1968), which presented the performances of the leading singers at a rock festival. *Keep on Rockin'* (1970) is limited to four performers at another festival. *Lambert and Co.* (1964) and *Original Cast Album: Company!* (1970) are based on recording sessions.

In many respects, Pennebaker is a more orthodox direct-camera filmmaker than Leacock. He does not search for a crisis situation, and his editing is relatively unobtrusive. The excellence of his work lies especially in his sensitivity to music and sounds in general and an ability to put a frame around objects that appears casual, yet requires an acute visual eye. The filmmaker continues to work at his own company in New York City.

Albert Maysles (1933–) and his brother David (1931–) have carved out for themselves a special area of direct cinema: documentary studies of unusual individuals in the form of interviews. The two have made documentaries, however, in which the event is more important than the celebrities involved. *Gimme Shelter* (1970) is a controversial film centering on the Rolling Stones' concert at Altamont, California, during which a man in the audience was stabbed to death. *What's Happening! The Beatles in the U.S.A.* (1964) is an account of the rock singers' first tour in America.

More typical of the Maysles brothers' work are *Showman* (1962, on the producer Joseph Levine), *Meet Marlon Brando* (1965), *Salesman* (1969), and *Grey Gardens* (1975, on Edith and Edie Beale). *Salesman* in particular illustrates the positive and negative qualities of their approach. Unlike the other Maysles films, the salesmen we observe have no claim to fame for accomplishments or family connections. The four Bible salesmen in Florida (with opening scenes in Boston and flashforwards to a sales meeting in Chicago) are ordinary men trying to earn a living. Our interest is soon focused, however, on the least successful of the group, Paul Brennan. As so often with direct-cinema documentaries, we are surprised at how natural people appear to act with a camera present; however, we begin to sense that the filmmakers do structure their material. Each salesman is introduced by his name and nickname superimposed on his image; the flashforwards to the sales meeting are dramatically inserted when Paul, conscious of his poor sales record, is on a train to Chicago; the sequence of his failures is so neat as to be suspect. This is not necessarily a criticism of a very effective documentary; it simply indicates that the film is closer in style to that of Leacock than the more objective approach of Pennebaker.

Whether dealing with the famous, those glancingly touched by fame, or ordinary people, the Maysles brothers have extended the range of direct cinema by concentrating on individual human beings, not chiefly manifestations of social problems or attitudes. They are an adventurous filmmaking team that has surprised and provoked audiences in the past and are likely to do so in the future.

The last of major American *cinéma verité* directors is Frederick Wiseman. His activities are discussed separately later in this chapter. Other prominent directors who work primarily in this style include Gregory Shuker, William Jersey, and James Lipscomb. Many documentary filmmakers have used the techniques and tone of direct cinema but have rejected objectivity in favor of overt social criticism, such as Emile de Antonio, Barbara Kopple, and Cinda Firestone. A relatively recent innovation is documentaries made entirely on videotape, for example, those directed by Michael Shamberg and David Cort.

Canadian filmmaking has been in advance of the United States in at least one respect: the support given to new and unconventional filmmakers through Canada's National Film Board. Films made for the Challenge for Change project, noted earlier, were often in the *cinéma verité* style. The Québec school, devoted to French-language documentaries on French-Canadian subjects, are exciting, particularly the work of Michel Brault and Pierre Perrault. The best-known Canadian director of direct cinema is Allan King. Of the many films he has made, two especially have received international acclaim. *Warrendale* (1968) deals with emotionally disturbed children at a center in Ontario where a special "holding" technique is used to comfort them. *A Married Couple* (1969) is an account of the day-to-day activities of a couple, the Edwardses. In both films, as in all his work, King demonstrates empathy with his subjects and a prime intention to use the unstructured approach of direct cinema to reveal their emotions.

In France, another mode of *cinéma verité* was initiated by Jean Rouch (1917–). His experience in making ethnographic documentaries* and the inspiration of the work of Georges Rouquier† had taught him the value of shooting film without preconceptions and with minimal editing. In *Treichville* (*Moi, un noir*, 1958) and *La Pyramide humaine* (1961) he experimented in Africa with having the camera not only observe and be led by his subjects but also encourage them to reveal their attitudes and feelings. When he

---

*p. 330
†p. 329

returned to France, Rouch decided to try this approach on Parisians. He enlisted the help of the sociologist Edgar Morin as codirector. The product of their efforts was the fascinating, innovative, influential *Chronicle of a Summer* (*Chronique d'un été,* 1961) (Figure 7.8).

In the summer of 1960 the two directors and their crew stopped people on the streets and asked them, "Are you happy?" A few of these individuals, including workers, artists, and students, were then interviewed at length, separately and in groups. We follow them to their homes, at work, at a picnic, and at dinners. The major participants were then shown the footage, and their comments were recorded. The interviewer (Morin) repeatedly appears on the screen, encouraging and prodding them. In the last scene, Rouch and Morin discuss what they have tried to do and to what degree they have succeeded. The basic premise of the film is that the camera can act as a triggering device that allows subjects to release their memories and emotions. According to Rouch, they begin by acting but end by creating their own psychodramas recorded on film. Some people, obviously, will react in this fashion, and others will not.

This film's spontaneity and unpremeditated structure are characteristic of *cinéma verité,* but what

### FIGURE 7.8

*Chronicle of a Summer,* 1961, directed by Jean Rouch. Marceline, one of the interviewees, recalls her experiences in a German concentration camp and her relationship with her father while walking down a Paris street.

of the objectivity central to this style? In Rouch's approach, the subject and the filmmakers collaborate in discovering insights into a situation or a human being. Rouch and his colleagues, however, are being objective in a significant way. They do not have preconceived premises or ideas that are illustrated by their documentaries, as is evident in those made by more traditional directors.

During the sixties and seventies Rouch divided his efforts between returning to anthropological documentaries in Africa and experiments in carrying the *cinéma verité* style into fiction (as in *La Punition,* 1962, and *Petit à petit,* 1970). Nothing he has done to date, however, has had the vitality and impact of *Chronicle of a Summer.*

Chris Marker is often included in lists of notable French *cinéma verité* filmmakers. His personal, overtly propagandistic approach,* however, is not in this style, except in one film. *The Lovely May* (*Le Joli mai,* 1963), inspired by *Chronicle of a Summer,* consists of interviews with a wide range of Parisians in May, 1962. An interviewer (Marker himself) is heard but not seen on camera, and there is a commentary. Although the interviews are spontaneous, a sense of irony imposed by the commentary prevails, and for this reason some *cinéma verité* proponents criticized the film as essentially subjective.

Other French directors whose documentaries have been considered as basically *cinéma verité* include Mario Ruspoli (for example, *Regards sur le folie,* 1961, on life in a psychiatric hospital), François Reichenbach, and Jean Herman. Some critics include certain of the works of Georges Franju.†

Direct cinema has also been a mode of documentary expression in other countries. The Russian Grigori Chukrai, best known for his dramas, used the device of interviews to evoke the battle of Stalingrad in *Memory* (*Pamat,* 1969). In Japan, the documentaries of Noriaki Tsuchimoto (most notably *Minamata,* 1971, on the horrendous effects of mercury pollution from a factory) are in this style.

*Cinéma verité* has been and is likely to be for

---

*pp. 336–337
†pp. 336

some time to come a vital force in the contemporary documentary. As mentioned earlier, the extensive availability of videotape equipment has increased the popularity of direct cinema. Concomitant with this popularity, however, are two dangers. On the one hand, merely recording actuality may be considered sufficient without the essential component of ''creative treatment,'' and, on the other hand, a superficial appearance of spontaneity and immediacy can be a veneer for overt propaganda. Genuine *cinéma verité* does not fall between the stools of a personal stylistic statement and relative objectivity; it spans them.

### ESTHETICS AND ART

Every documentary filmmaker is concerned with how he expresses his intentions—that is, the most imaginative and concentrated means of communicating the emotions inherent in a situation. Although in the work of the finest directors, means and ends are fused, esthetic values in documentaries are usually subordinated to subject matter. There is, however, a category of this genre in which the filmmaker's primary concern, regardless of the subject of his film, is design, pattern, structure, and other aspects of form.

Painters such as Fernand Léger, Moholy-Nagy, and Hans Richter discussed and exploited the potentials of cinema to produce motion art. They soon realized that representational subjects interfered with exploration of the esthetic values of the medium, so they created the genre of abstract film. Certain artists preferred to retain actuality (and thus more easily hold the attention of audiences), yet still give chief emphasis to form. Although there were pioneers before him, no one was more influential in developing this new type of documentary than Walther Ruttmann (1887–1941).

After studying painting and architecture and being a professional poster designer, Ruttmann turned to filmmaking. His earliest works, such as the ''Opus'' series (1921–1924), were abstract. Ruttmann's initial documentary was *Berlin: The Symphony of a Great City (Berlin: die Sinfonie der Großstadt,* 1927). This 78-minute film consists of images of the city on a spring day from dawn to midnight (Figure 7.9). The people in the film are generally undifferentiated masses, more shapes and patterns than human beings. They are photographed with as much concern for formal qualities as buildings and streets. Even a dramatic moment, the suicide of a woman, is treated as merely an incident among many that make up the rhythms of the city. Ruttmann's intention was to create a visual symphony, and he succeeded.

### FIGURE 7.9

*Berlin: The Symphony of a Great City,* 1927, directed by Walther Ruttmann. The ordinary and the unusual are repeatedly juxtaposed in this archetypal cinematic portrait of a city.

The acclaim awarded *Berlin* encouraged the director to continue with this approach, now adding the dimension of sound. *World Melody (Melodie der Welt,* 1929) is a compilation film, made up of material supplied by a shipping line of human activities throughout the world. Ruttmann returned to the format of *Berlin* to capture on film the rhythms of other German cities: *Düsseldorf* (1935), *Stuttgart* (1935), and *Hamburg* (1938).

Although Ruttmann had a reputation in the 1920s as a liberal in politics, he became in the early thirties a fervent supporter of Hitler and the Third Reich. During World War II he directed Nazi propaganda films, most notably *Deutsche Panzer* (1940), an account of the German army's conquest of France. He was working on a documentary at the Russian front when he was killed.

The term *city symphony* has been applied to a documentary that focuses on a day in the life of a specific city. Ruttmann's *Berlin* was not the first, only the most famous. In the United States, there had been Julius Jaenzon's *New York 1911* and *Mannahatta* (1921), directed by Charles Sheeler and Paul Strand. The year *Berlin* was released (1927), Mikhail Kaufman created *Moscow (Moskva).* Vertov's *The Man With a Movie Camera,* described earlier, while more humanistic than Ruttmann's films, demonstrates Vertov's concern with formal values and in this respect was even bolder and more innovative.

A year before *Berlin* was completed, a city symphony was released that brought to prominence a filmmaker who was to influence advances in the documentary significantly. Alberto Cavalcanti (1897–) was born in Rio de Janeiro but educated in Switzerland. He entered the French film industry as a set designer. After making his directing debut in 1926 with *Le Train sans yeux,* he created in the same year *Only the Hours (Rien que les heures).*

This documentary is often compared with *Berlin* because of the many similarities and differences between them. Both present a city from morning until night and are impressive examples of visual poetry in motion. They contrast, however, in two respects. In evoking Paris, Cavalcanti is looser, more impressionistic than the director of *Berlin.* It is not too farfetched to compare the style of the Brazilian filmmaker to free verse as opposed to Ruttmann's rhymed stanzas. Cavalcanti does not disdain cinematographic bravura, as in conveying visually the feeling of an amusement park ride. He even dares a Vertovian effect: An editor's hand appears on the screen to tear up a freeze frame. A good deal of superimposition is used, and a distorted clock indicates the hours of the day.

Cavalcanti's striking film techniques do not distract from his intention to make a social comment. He is protesting the differences between the life-styles of the wealthy and the poor. The director underscores his point of view by means of two devices. The first is to individualize certain people of the lower class who appear on the screen, for example, a prostitute (she is seen in the beginning, middle, and end of the film) and especially a female newspaper seller who is murdered. The other device is contrast through juxtaposition or superimposition of images. We see a poor man eating in the street; cut to a patron of an elegant restaurant. Superimposed on a steak on a plate is an image of beef hanging in a slaughterhouse.

Cavalcanti turned to fiction in the late 1920s and early 1930s. Most of these films deal with characters from the lower strata of society, but the director's artistry adds a glow of beauty to his realism. *En rade* (1927) is one of the best of the group. The director is often credited with being a forerunner of French Poetic Realism associated with many of the thirties films of Renoir and Marcel Carné.

In 1933 Grierson invited Cavalcanti to join the G.P.O. Film Unit. Under British auspices, the Brazilian directed a number of documentaries, including *Coalface* (1936), *Line to Tcherva Hut* (1936), *We Live in Two Worlds* (1937), and *Men of the Alps* (1939). Worthwhile as these films are, Cavalcanti's chief function at G.P.O. was as a producer (for example, Watt's *North Sea* and Jennings's *Spare Time*) and as an innovator in the use of sound in documentaries (for instance, *Night Mail*). During the forties he joined the Ealing Studios, where he again directed dramas and served as a mentor for such young directors as Basil Dearden and Charles Crichton.

Cavalcanti returned to Brazil in 1950 to encourage an incipient film industry and to direct both fiction films and documentaries. Among the latter was *Song of the Sea (O Canto do mar,* 1954), a visual and auditory evocation of a town the director lived in as a boy. Since the mid-fifties he has made motion pictures in many countries in Europe, directed plays, and lectured on cinema.

Cavalcanti was not the only director working in France who created a city symphony that combined esthetic values and social criticism. Before Jean Vigo made his two unique comedies,* he directed *A propos de Nice* (1930). The young man (he was 25 when he made the film) described the work as *"pont de rue documenté"* ("a type of social documentary"). As with Cavalcanti in *Only the Hours,* Vigo is criticizing the pretentiousness and arrogance of the

---

*p. 270

wealthy, although he is more vehement than his predecessor. Also in imitation of the Brazilian, he uses juxtaposition of images as a means of satire, such as when two doll figures in evening clothes on a chessboard are swept away by a croupier's rake and the next shot, with parallel directional cutting, is of a streetcleaner sweeping away garbage.

City symphonies have continued to be made. A few later examples are Arne Sucksdorff's *Rhythm of a City (Manniskor i Stad,* 1947, on Stockholm), John Eldridge's *Waverly Steps* (1949, on Edinburgh), Andrzej Munk's *A Walk in the Old City (Spacerek staromiejski,* 1955, on Warsaw), and Francis Thompson's *N.Y., N.Y.* (1958).

There is no limit to the subjects of documentaries that can supply excuses for a director who is concentrating primarily on esthetically satisfying cinematic forms and patterns. In 1928 Joris Ivens confined himself to a railroad bridge in Rotterdam in creating *The Bridge (Der Brug).* His *Rain (Regen,* 1929, codirected by Mannus Franken) is a 15-minute cinematic gem that simply presents a rain shower in Amsterdam (Figure 7.10). Coincidentally, the same year that *Rain* was made, Ralph Steiner in the United States produced *$H_2O$,* consisting of a montage of water images. Ivens continued this approach in *Industrial Symphony* (1931, also known by the name of its sponsor, Philips Radio) on a factory in the Netherlands.

---

**FIGURE 7.10**

*Rain,* 1928, directed by Joris Ivens and Mannus Franken. Even a gutter becomes a thing of beauty when photographed by a master filmmaker.

Although John Grierson is associated with documentaries of social commentary, it was under his auspices (in fact, he was the cameraman) that an 11-minute film was made that is a model of the fusion of visuals and sound without a spoken commentary. *Granton Trawler* (1934, directed by Edgar Anstey) presents a trawler operating off the coast of Scotland. In *Glass* (1958), directed by Bert Haanstra, the traditional methods of glassblowing are contrasted to an automated assembly-line system. Shots of glassblowers at work are exquisite, with carefully synchronized sound.

This list of esthetic documentaries could be extended to include dozens of other titles. Most devoted directors have indulged themselves, especially in their youth, in the pleasure of what Jay Chapman described in reference to Cavalcanti as *"joie de cinématographie."*[16] These directors have retained their credentials as documentary filmmakers by not deserting reality, as those who create abstract films, but rather transforming it. The genre would be impoverished if it did not allow within its boundaries (as some *cinéma verité* purists have advocated) films that primarily give viewers esthetic pleasure and allowed filmmakers to express their "joy in cinematography."

A special category of this type of film is too important to ignore even in a brief survey. Literally hundreds of documentaries emphasize pattern and design because these qualities are inherent in their subject matter—that is, films of works of visual art. The most consistently outstanding documentaries in this category have resulted from the collaboration between the Italians Luciano Emmer and Enrico Gras. Among their many works are *The Drama of Christ (Il Dramma di Cristo,* 1948, on Giotto's frescoes in Padua), *The Legend of St. Ursula (La Leggenda di Sant'Orsola,* 1949, on Carpaccio's paintings in the Accademia, Venice), *Piero Della Francesca* (1949), *Goya* (1950), *Leonardo da Vinci* (1952), and *Picasso* (1954).

A very selected list of documentaries on the visual arts includes Curt Oertel's *Michelangelo* (1939, titled *The Titan* when released in the United States in 1940 in a version produced by Robert Flaherty); Henri Storck's *Le Monde de Paul Delvaux* (1946) and *Rubens* (1948); those by Alain Resnais (for example *Van*

*Gogh,* 1948; *Gauguin,* 1950; and the superb *Guernica,* 1950); Paul Haesaerts's *De Renoir à Picasso* and *Visite à Picasso* (both 1950); Roger Leenhardt's *The Norman Conquest of England* (*La Conquête de l'Angleterre,* 1955, on the Bayeux tapestry); Bert Haanstra's *Rembrandt, Painter of Men* (1956); Henri Georges Clouzot's feature-length *The Picasso Mystery* (*Le Mystère Picasso,* 1956); Basil Wright's *Stained Glass at Fairford* (1956); and Herb Golden's *Homage to Rodin* (1968).

Documentaries on musicians usually do not result in impressive visual works. An exception is the television films directed by Ken Russell, including *Prokofiev* (1961), *Elgar* (1962), and the delicate *A Song of Summer* (1968, on the last years of Delius).

Since the 1950s the documentary has undergone changes and been subject to pressures that are molding not only its present but also its future. The chief influence has been the role of television as sponsor and outlet. It is a rare documentary that can recoup its costs without being shown on the small screen. There is simply not a sufficient audience for documentaries in commercial motion picture theaters. This situation has affected the length, form, and tone of the genre. For example, films of social criticism have a much harder time being presented today than, say, in the thirties. One hopeful sign in the United States is increasing opportunities offered by public and cable television.

Government support of documentaries is a tradition in Europe but not in the United States. In this country, foundations have filled the role of federal and state sponsorship. During the last few years, however, the National Endowment for the Arts and state councils for the arts have increased their recognition of and budgets for filmmakers. Another source of support in the United States is college campuses. It is possible for a documentary to survive without TV as an outlet by being screened on campuses, especially if the director accompanies the film and lectures on it. Yet another route is for a work to attract attention by winning a prize at one of the dozens of festivals and competitions that are held each year or be included in lists offered by nonprofit distribution organizations.

The predominant gauge for documentaries is still 16mm, but technical advances in Super-8 are persuading some filmmakers to convert to it. Videotape is also being used more extensively, especially for a *cinéma verité* approach.

The documentary will surely remain a viable, vital film genre, for no other has such a unique combination of being grounded in actuality but open to the molding treatment of creativity.

## NATURE AND MAN

### Man of Aran

*Flaherty's films are not just moving pictures. They are experiences, similar in a geographical sense to visiting Paris or Rome or seeing the dawn rise over the Sinai desert. Flaherty is a country, which having once seen one never forgets.*
*Arthur Calder-Marshall, 1963*[17]

**CAST**
*Colman "Tiger" King (Man of Aran), Maggie Dirrane (Wife), Michael Dillane (Son), and others.*

**CREDITS**
*Director—Robert Flaherty, Screenwriters—Robert and Frances Flaherty, Producer—Michael Balcon, Composer—John Greenwood, Editor—John Goldman, and others.*

1934/Gaumont-British Corp.
Black & White/76 minutes

### BACKGROUND

No director of documentaries is better known to the general public than Robert Flaherty. Although not as innovative as Dziga Vertov or as brilliant as Joris Ivens, his name has become a legend associated with making films in exotic places and having a fierce determination to be independent and to realize his visions at any cost. The truth of his life and accomplishments may be less impressive than his legend, but few would argue with the assertion that he was a great filmmaker, led a fascinating life, and deserves the title of "father of the documentary."

Robert Flaherty (1884–1951) was born in Iron Mountain, Michigan. While still a youngster, he accompanied his father into Canada in search of gold. Between 1910 and 1916 he was commissioned to explore the Hudson Bay area and search for minerals by Sir William Mackenzie, an entrepreneur responsible for opening up much of subarctic Canada. During the expeditions, he kept a diary that reveals how completely absorbed he was in the northern lands and their people. From this record he later drew a travel book, *My Eskimo Friends* (1923), and two inconsequential novels. After his second expedition, Sir William suggested that he take a motion picture camera with him; he did so after 2 weeks of instruction in New York on its use. From 1913 to 1916 he shot footage of the Innuit Eskimos. Unfortunately, while packing the edited negative, a cigarette he carelessly left on a table ignited the film. Flaherty consoled himself by insisting that he had not been satisfied with what he had done. Another important event occurred during those 6 years. In 1914 he married Frances J. Hubbard. She was to be a steadfast supporter throughout his life and assisted him in creating practically all his documentaries.

Flaherty was determined to return to the north and shoot the film he envisioned. The opportunity finally came when in 1920 he persuaded the president of Revillon Frères, a fur-trading company, to subsidize him. For 2 years Flaherty stayed in the area of northeastern Hudson Bay collecting footage. The final result was *Nanook of the North* (1922). In this documentary we follow Nanook, a master hunter, and his family in their perpetual search for food (Figure 7.11). The film, released by Pathé in the United States, was a revelation for contemporary audiences. With a few exceptions, all previous motion pictures of foreign lands were travelogues, not documentaries: They recorded but did not dramatize actuality. *Nanook of the North* did only fairly well in the United States, but in the capitals of Europe it was proclaimed a masterpiece.

Jesse Lasky at Paramount Pictures was sufficiently impressed to commission Flaherty to make "another *Nanook*." The director and his wife spent almost 2 years in the Samoan Islands to create *Moana* (1926). Instead of a struggle with nature, as in *Nanook of the North,* there is harmony. The climax of the documentary are Moana's initiation into manhood by the painful ceremony of tattooing and his romance with a lovely islander. Although the film was highly

## FIGURE 7.11

*Nanook of the North,* 1922. Nanook needs only a hole in the ice and a harpoon when fishing.

praised by critics, it was only moderately successful at the box office.

Flaherty occupied himself in 1926 with two shorts: *The Pottery Maker* for the Metropolitan Museum of Art and *The Twenty-Four Dollar Island,* a privately sponsored film about Manhattan. Both turned out to be cinematic bagatelles. The director's next chance to work on a major film came from an unexpected source. F. W. Murnau, the great German filmmaker, persuaded Flaherty to join him on a fiction film set in the South Seas. Flaherty wanted to do a pseudodocumentary and Murnau a romance involving a taboo love affair between a pearl fisherman and a priestess. The credits for *Tabu* (1931) list Flaherty as codirector, coscreenwriter, and codirector of photography (with Floyd Crosby). Murnau's concept and style, however, dominated the work.

John Grierson, head of the Film Division of Britain's Empire Marketing Board, hired Flaherty in 1931. The American's first assignment was to direct a documentary on industrial craftsmanship. In his usual extravagant manner, Flaherty in a period of months shot thousands of feet of film. He used no script, however, and for all the brilliance of individual scenes, the material lacked thematic development. The desperate Grierson added footage and edited the conglomeration. Unable to market the feature, he took out 20 minutes of the footage and titled the result *Industrial Britain* (1931). Flaherty's cinematic genius is evident here and there, but, as with *Tabu,* the overall vision of the film is that of another person.

An even more important ramification of Flaherty's association with Grierson was the financing of *Man of Aran* (1934) by Gaumont-British Film Company.

A year later the director's association with the British film industry continued, but in a new setting. Alexander Korda, executive director of London Film Productions, sent Flaherty to India to direct a commercial drama based on a Rudyard Kipling story of the relationship between a youngster and an elephant. The filmmaker spent most of 1935 and half of 1936 on location. He was unaccustomed, however, to big production methods, ignored a carefully prepared script, did not integrate synchronized sound recording with his visuals, and was self-indulgent in accumulating footage. Korda was unsympathetic to his director's sensitive, documentary approach. Most of the film was reshot, using artificial studio effects, and was completely reedited. The final version of *Elephant Boy* (1936) contains only a few of Flaherty's scenes intact, and it is a muted echo of his original concept and style.

The director's next assignment was in the United States. Pare Lorentz, in charge of the short-lived United States Film Service, asked him to make a documentary on the plight of Western farmers and the efforts of the Department of Agriculture to help them. *The Land* (1941) was a controversial film. The government refused to circulate the 42-minute feature in the United States and abroad, supposedly because the war and reduced unemployment had made the film obsolescent. The validity of this censorship is debatable, but even the director's most fervent admirers admit that *The Land* was not one of his greatest achievements.

From 1940 to 1945 Flaherty worked on various projects, including an assignment for Frank Capra's War Department Film Division, but no film worthy of notice resulted. Then he was given a final chance to produce another major work. The Standard Oil Company asked Flaherty to make a documentary describ-ing the difficulties of drilling for oil. Once again, the director and his coworkers, including his wife, spent 2 years on the project. Although a scenario was approved by Standard Oil, Flaherty adhered to his typically tentative, searching, comprehensive shooting practices. Restraining influences, however, were the presence of Richard Leacock as cameraman and Helen van Dongen as editor. The latter forced the director to make choices, to mold a narrative dimension. The final print is the most coherent and structured of all Flaherty's feature films, yet each scene carries the imprint of his unique style.

*Louisiana Story* (1948) is often referred to as the director's finest film. There is a marvelous fusion of mood and concrete details in telling the story of the successful attempt of a crew's search for oil as seen through the eyes of a youngster who has lived in the Louisiana bayous all his life (Figure 7.12). Adding significantly to the dramatic and esthetic effectiveness of the documentary is the superb background music by Virgil Thomson, who was awarded a Pulitzer prize for his score (the first time this prize was bestowed on music composed specifically for a film).

The director lived for 3 years after the premiere of *Louisiana Story,* during which he was not involved in any notable motion picture activities.

**FIGURE 7.12**

*Louisiana Story,* 1948. Alexander Napoleon Ulysses Latour (Joseph Boudreaux) explores the vicinity of his home, an area of the swamplands of Louisiana. Soon he will confront and adjust to a crew of outsiders drilling for oil.

Flaherty's four major films *(Nanook of the North, Moana, Man of Aran,* and *Louisiana Story)* are classics. On the other hand, his uncompromising stands against commercial pressures, haphazard methods of creating a film, and stubborn insistence on having his own way restricted his opportunities. For all his genius in being able to dramatize the lives of unsophisticated people and to capture with an imaginative eye the interrelationship between human beings and the physical world they inhabit, he never fully understood how a documentary could be structured through judicious editing or how sound can increase the effectiveness of visuals.

In addition to limitations in Flaherty's production methods and style, criticism of his work usually centers on two concepts fundamental to his intentions. In capturing the elemental life-style of his subjects, the director generally ignored cultural influences. Many contemporary critics felt his lack of social consciousness was a significant defect.

Flaherty also was attacked by those who believed that any radical rearrangement of reality for dramatic effect or any staging of events was a violation of the essential purpose of the documentary. He did not hesitate in *Nanook of the North* to portray the Eskimos as living more primitively than they actually did or arranging for the hunting of seals with a harpoon, whereas for years the Eskimos had used guns. At the time *Moana* was shot, ritual tattooing had not been practiced for decades. As noted later, the same kind of manipulation was imposed on the men of Aran hunting sharks. The events of *Louisiana Story* were completely arranged for the camera. In fact, Helen van Dongen calls the film "a fable" and goes so far as to declare, "To me Flaherty is *not* a documentarian; he makes it all up."[18]

Flaherty was an independent, prickly individual who made his films his own way regardless of contemporary styles and principles. Yet he created a world of his own that is large and significant enough to absorb limitations, contradictions, and deficiencies without lessening the impact of the artist's vision of man and nature.

Through the efforts of John Grierson, Flaherty was introduced early in 1931 to Michael Balcon, pro-

duction chief of Gaumont-British, the largest motion picture studio in England. He outlined to the producer his plans for making a film about the Aran Islands, located off the coast of Ireland. Balcon agreed to the project, giving the director a free hand and a budget of £10,000 (approximately $50,000).

Robert and Frances Flaherty arrived at the Aran Islands in the fall of 1931 and remained there until the fall of 1933. They were joined by Pat Mullen, a native who had traveled in the United States and was later to become a writer. He published an account of his experiences with the Flahertys titled *Man of Aran* (1935); it is a fascinating record of the shooting of the film and offers insights into the personality of Flaherty at work.

Everyone involved in the project had a hard time. Flaherty was a man possessed: demanding, irritable, given to displays of violent temper. Although fairly early he had decided that the film was to be primarily from the point of view of the boy, he slowly and secretly felt his way to a structure for the material. As usual, he was profligate in shooting. For a film that finally consisted of less than 3,000 feet, he exposed 200,000 feet of stock.[19] In defense of the director, shooting from a motorboat in heavy seas was difficult. During the final storm scenes, the waves striking cliffs rose to a height of 400 feet above sea level.

The final storm sequence was the most arduous to photograph. Three men in a boat during an appropriate storm had to wait at sea until Flaherty signaled that enough sunlight was available. The journey in was very dangerous. To the consternation of the crew and the other islanders, the men came within a hair's breadth of drowning. Yet for all of Flaherty's genuine concern, he did not forget to keep his camera going.

After a good deal of advance publicity, *Man of Aran* had its premiere on April 25, 1934, in London. The film was popular enough with audiences, but the English critics were less enthusiastic. While all agreed that the photography of the film was magnificent, its director was attacked for ignoring economic, social, and religious problems of the Aran Islands and falsifying through the shark hunt the inhabitants' way of life. On the other hand, *Man of Aran* was generally acclaimed in other countries, including the United

States. It was awarded the Grand Prix at the Venice Film Festival of 1934.

George Stoney, influenced in his own work by Flaherty, directed a fascinating documentary, *Man of Aran: How the Myth Was Made* (1978).

### SUMMARY OF EVENTS

After the credits, a title card informs us of the location of the Aran Islands off the west coast of Ireland, the bareness of the rocky land buffeted by "the most gigantic seas in the world," and the determination of the islanders to survive a struggle with sea and land that has no respite.

The film opens with a scene of a youngster catching a small crab. The setting shifts to the inside of a house, where a woman rocks a cradle and looks out a window. Eventually a visual counterpoint is established between a boat on the water struggling to reach shore and the boy and his mother anxiously watching. The two groups come together when the boat lands in a turmoil of waves and spray and is dragged onto the strand.

The next section of the film is devoted to "the land upon which the Man of Aran depends for sustenance." The woman leaves her baby in a protected area among rocks and goes to collect seaweed. Meanwhile, the Man of Aran breaks up boulders. The couple finally plant furrows of potatoes in a base of pieces of stones covered by seaweed and soil. Fade to black.

The boy is fishing from the top of a cliff when he notices something in the water. We have our first view of a basking-shark. There is a transition from this shark to one being harpooned by a crew in a boat, but the fish escapes.

In the next sequence, time has obviously passed, for the boat is now just a small spot in the ocean. We move closer as another shark is harpooned. A title card states that for two long days the men struggle with the creature. The boy and his mother are outdoors; they look at each other, smile, and run toward the water's edge. A brief shot of the boat far in the distance returning. A crowd of islanders run to the shore as the woman and her son prepare a cauldron in which to boil the shark's liver for oil. The shark is hauled ashore and cut up. Fade-out.

Crosscutting between a multitude of fins in the ocean and men launching boats. The Man of Aran refuses to allow his son to join the three-man crew, for he doesn't like the look of the sea. We see the boat at sea while the youngster and his mother with a basket on her shoulder are among the rocks. Fade to black.

The boy is sleeping in the house. Evidence of a storm awakens him, and quickly he dresses. The mother is outside working and watching the raging sea. She drops the basket and begins to run. The boy joins her. A montage follows of the foaming water, incredible waves climbing up the sides of the cliffs, and the two moving to the edges of those cliffs protruding farthest into the sea. The boat comes into view far in the distance. Finally the boat reaches shore. The men escape as it capsizes, then slams against the sandy beach and breaks apart. The five islanders save what they can.

Two of the men go their own way. Once again the Man of Aran and his family walk along the shore toward home.

### ANALYSIS

*Man of Aran* centers on only one vital aspect of the life of the Aran islanders: their struggle with and dependence on nature in its manifestations of sea, sky, and land. Flaherty strips his subject of the characteristics of civilization: technology, economics, politics, religion, art, and social mores. The result is a portrayal of human beings who through fortitude, courage, skill, and stubbornness survive in a hostile environment— the most elemental form of heroism. It is ironic that technology should supply the instrument whereby we are reminded that at one time human beings directly and individually challenged nature with their lives as the stakes, and even now in far corners of the earth man continues this type of struggle. We are led to wonder, a doubt intentionally planted in our minds by Flaherty in film after film, if in conquering so much of nature we have not gained a Pyrrhic victory. Have we lost the vitality and self-respect that comes when through the efforts of one's own body and spirit the right to exist is won from a worthy opponent? This is a romantic view of life, ignoring the costs of defeat and the advantages of advanced civilization, but one that keeps emerging in many forms from the deepest level of our psyche in dreams and art.

The first conceptual problem facing Flaherty was to individualize and dramatize life on the three Aran Islands. His solution was an approach he used in practically all his documentaries: follow for a period of time a few individuals who are occupied with activities that we are to assume are typical. In *Man of Aran,* our attention is focused on a family consisting of a man, wife, son, and baby living on one of the islands. We do see other people, but they appear so infrequently and tangentially that the independence and isolation of the family is emphasized. Although the boat crew must work as a unit, we come away from the film with an impression of the Man of Aran, with the help of his wife and son, struggling as an individual against nature.

Interrelations are muted not only between the family and the others but also within the family itself. Few emotions beyond those prompted by the need to survive are shown on the screen. The man is a distant, prototypal figure. We see him only at work, without once demonstrating tenderness toward his wife or, as does Nanook, instructing his son. The woman is anxious about the Man of Aran's safety, especially during the storm at the end of the film, but that is all we observe of her feelings for her husband. Once she places the baby in a sheltered area before turning to her tasks, conveying her maternal concern. Only toward her son is genuine warmth evident in the way she occasionally smiles at him or places a hand on his shoulder. The boy is the most expressive of the three: worried about his father at sea, protective of his mother during danger, awed by the sharks, and disappointed when he cannot join the boat crew. Perhaps Flaherty did not encourage his nonprofessional actors to convey more familial feelings because they were not in actuality related, or perhaps he was suggesting that the struggle for survival left no time for such intimacies.

The documentary consists of four sections: the sea, the land, the shark hunt, and the sea again (which begins as another shark hunt). These headings indicate that activities on the land are subordinated to those on the sea (at the most, the land section takes up 15 percent of the film). Yet while the sea sections convince us of the dangerous lives lived by the islanders, it is the farming sequence, if "farming" is an appropriate term for what they do, that reveals the stark bareness of their existence.

The sequence opens with a title card. Flaherty chose not to use a narrator or to allow dialogue to give us expository information. The titles serve this purpose. In a film made in 1934 containing a sound track, however, the cards seem outdated. John Goldman, the editor, tried to persuade Flaherty that they weakened the visual continuity of *Man of Aran,* but the director, as usual, was insistent on having his way.[20] He had a prejudice against the use of narrators and avoided them in his films. It may be that he associated this device with travelogues, a type of nonfiction film he was attempting to keep distinct from his documentaries.

After the title card, which indicates that potatoes are the only crop on the island, and two panoramic shots, we see the woman place her baby in a safe place. In the background, sheep are grazing at the edge of a cliff. The presence of these animals and later a horse and donkey carrying the seaweed indicate that there is grazing land on the island. Here is an example of how Flaherty eliminates whatever does not support his main intention in making a specific film. The Aran islanders must be shown struggling against a hostile environment. Any advantages, such as grazing land, are ignored. One wonders if there are other buffers between these people and a bare sustenance dependent only on fishing and potatoes that are not noted in the film.

The arduous process of gathering seaweed, collecting soil from crevices in the cliffs, breaking up boulders, and combining the three to make a bed for the potato plants is presented in detail. While the man crushes stones, his wife works to obtain soil and seaweed.

The Man of Aran breaking up the rocks with a sledgehammer is made by Flaherty into a symbol of an individual pitting his physical strength and determination against a hard environment. He is often shot from a low angle and is usually silhouetted against the sky.

The background music is dramatic, even sensational considering the occasion (one critic describes the music at this point as "silly"[21]). One series of four shots could be labeled as visually melodramatic. We see the man lifting a rock over his head (low angle, silhouetted) (Figure 7.13). This shot without change is repeated twice more, with the camera moving a bit to the right each time. The last image is of the rock thrown down and shattering against the ground. This device of repeated shots with slight or no variations of one action was used by Eisenstein, as in the pulling down of the statue of the czar at the beginning of *October.* Flaherty is never adverse to taking advantage of a nonrealistic series of shots to dramatize a scene.

**FIGURE 7.13**

*Man of Aran.* A dramatic view of the man of Aran breaking a rock, the pieces of which will be used in farming.

Although these people concentrate on their tasks on land, they and we never forget the sea. It is usually visible in the background. Periodically, no matter what they are doing, they (especially the Man of Aran) look toward the water and sky. The ocean, with all the threats and challenges it presents, is the main character in the documentary. A viewer comes away from the film with the impression that a third of its shots are of water rushing, rolling, spraying, and beating against the shore. There has never been, nor is likely to be, another motion picture that conveys with more conviction and immediacy the power, danger, and grace of the sea.

After a title card describing the Aran Isles, the opening sequence of the film is related to the sea, but a calm introduction: the boy at the water's edge catching a crab and placing it in his hat. The youngster is the most vivid human being in *Man of Aran,* for he reacts to his environment with an excitement and a spontaneity lacking in the others. We identify with him more than with either of his parents. This is intentional on the part of the director, and for good reason. We are unfamiliar with this world and need some sort of liaison between ourselves and what happens. A youngster is a person who is both a part of the foreign setting, thus needing no justification for being there, yet curious and adventurous enough to supply us with insights into his world. Flaherty discovered this type of third-person point of view in *Moana* (using a young man rather than a boy) and retained it in *Man of Aran,* in *Elephant Boy,* and, most successfully, in *Louisiana Story.*

After the introduction of the boy in the beginning of *Man of Aran,* we enter his family's house, where his mother is rocking a cradle. Cut to our first view of the sea and foaming waves. The camera shifts back and forth between the water and the interior of the hut. The transitions are cuts; however, the third of these cuts demonstrates that even with a conventional transition, Flaherty can be imaginative in his camera-editing dynamics. In the last of three shots that constitute our first view of the sea, the camera pans to the right, there is a cut, then the camera continues to pan within the house, thus fluently joining the two settings. A few minutes later the woman in profile looks out the window. The camera angle of the next image of the water suggests that it is a subjective shot from her point of view, again connecting the two settings.

The next sequence includes the landing of a boat. Certain cinematic approaches and devices that will be used throughout the film, especially in the lengthy final sequence, are introduced. A rhythm is built up from a series of three types of shots of varying numbers: the woman and boy on shore, the sea, the boat. Directional cutting is very important since the camera frequently shifts position and the two backgrounds of rocks and water do not have distinguishing features. Generally, the land is to the right and the sea to the left, so that when the mother and son are looking camera left, they are facing the sea, and the boat attempting to reach land moves toward the right.

We are impressed by the struggle necessary to land the boat in a rough sea. What we do not know at this point in the film is that the effort is Lilliputian compared to that required when there is a storm, and the director is preparing us for the final sequence. Yet the climax of this earlier scene is helped by the music, the sounds of the sea, and the snatches of the people's shouts on the sound track, as well as camera-editing dynamics. The closer the boat comes to shore, the briefer the shots become. A striking series of shots is repeated many times: The camera points into the base of a wave, pans as it moves to the right rising to a crest, and holds as the islanders are knocked about by the splashing water. We are as relieved as the crew, woman, and boy when the boat with a patched hole in its bottom is turned over on shore and they walk home.

After the section of the film devoted to the land, we are brought back to the boat and a man repairing the hole. There is crosscutting between the man and the boy fishing, then between the boy and men beginning a shark hunt. The shots of the boy hold our attention and are fused with a fluid continuity. We are thrilled when we realize that he is fishing, with nonchalant disregard of the danger to which he exposes himself, from the top of a high cliff. High-angle shots from above (some direct verticals) and low-angle ones from below make us fully aware of his precarious position. We hold our breath when later he edges his way down the side of the cliff to get a closer look at the shark.

The basking-sharks are awesome creatures in themselves, but in the film they also personify the sea. Unlike the sea, however, over which the islanders can only win the victory of survival, the sharks can be conquered. The two-day struggle of the boat crew against a single shark, thus, has a mythic connotation similar to Beowulf's day-long struggle with Grendel's mother. To this end, Flaherty gives them the aura of more than simply creatures of the deep; they are mys-

terious, almost supernatural monsters. We catch only glimpses of them—a fin, a tail, an eye, a gaping mouth —until one is dead. And our first view of a shark is through the eyes of the boy, the person most capable in his innocence and sense of wonder to be properly awed by the shadowy giants of the sea. The director suspensefully prepares us emotionally for the first sight of the shark before it is actually presented on the screen. The boy notices something below and starts to climb down the cliff without our having any idea what it is that has attracted his attention. The background music becomes ominous; we see and hear the agitated seagulls. Only after these clues are there shots of the monster.

The transition from the boy to the boat is cleverly edited. A series of five shots alternates between the fish and the youngster. The last one is of the shark with its tail out of the water. Before the shot ends, we hear adult male voices. Cut to a fin and a portion of a boat, then a pan along the side of the craft, ending with a tail splashing. We are now with the hunters. The struggle is intense but fairly brief. The excitement is intensified when one of the men starts to fall overboard, but he is pulled back. The shark frees itself, leaving behind evidence of its strength in the twisted harpoon.

Only then does Flaherty tell us about the sharks on a title card. What he does not mention is that the sharks were no longer hunted by the islanders at the time the film was being made and that these creatures were not man-eaters. If a portion of the truth does not serve the director's intention, it is omitted; critics of his approach rightly call this falsification by omission. Flaherty is also cavalier about indicating transitions of time. Only a fade to black distinguishes the first vain attempt to kill a shark and the second hunt. Both could occur on the same day or be separated by weeks. In any case, we first see the boat as a spot on the sea, then a shot of the crew surrounded by fins. Back to the shore, where the woman and the boy are staring out toward the left. The next shot we assume is subjective from their point of view, but it is one of a shark fin, impossible to be seen from shore. Either this is clumsy editing or Flaherty is contracting space in the same manner as has always been done with time in cinema.

The two-day battle with the harpooned shark, punctuated by crosscutting to the woman and her son, is an example of compressed physical time. When the shark is brought in, we see a large group of islanders for the first time as they all help to drag the creature on shore and to cut it up so that the liver can be boiled in the cauldron for its oil.

So the men of Aran have been victorious in one skirmish with the sea. Flaherty, however, wants his viewers to be fully conscious of the odds against which the islanders struggle, so the last third of the film is an unforgettable presentation of the sea when it is most dangerous—during a storm. It is fairly calm when two boats set out, with cutaways to fins in the water. At one point, a man looks out into the distance. Again space appears to be contracted, for the next shot is of the shark fins in the ocean. The boy is refused permission to join a crew. The reason the father gives, "I don't like the look of the sea," is the first of a series of foreshadowings (as with the initial appearance of the shark to the boy) of danger. The next one is solely visual. As the men prepare to leave, the woman is tending the cauldron. Twice there are cuts from the relatively calm sea to the inside of the pot of boiling, foaming water and shark flesh. The final foreshadowing occurs in the next scene, one of the most admirably constructed in the film, and leads to the storm.

There is a fade-in to a shot of the flame of a candle. We are inside the hut where the boy is sleeping, leaning against a wall. A shot of the animals also sleeping. Slowly the background music becomes agitated, the strings suggesting a whirling wind. The ashes in the hearth stir and shift; the candle flickers; the boy moves uneasily in his sleep. Shots of the sea at evening, the waves rising. Back at the hut, the boy awakens and looks down at his feet. A close-up of the ashes swirling, indicating that a draft is coming down the chimney, and it was this that disturbed the youngster. Cut to shots of agitated waves. The suggestion of wind in the music increases in volume; the candle is almost blown out; the lamb and dog, as well as the rooster in a basket, are awake; the boy rubs his eyes and looks up. There is a series of shots of turbulent waves, foaming and striking the rocks, the last one revealing the woman carrying a basket at the top of a cliff. Crosscutting between the woman, the water, and the boy in the house preparing to leave. The woman throws down the basket and begins to run; she is joined by her son. The two hurry along the edge of the cliffs.

Flaherty presents a multitude of shots of the sea during the storm from every conceivable distance and angle. Most remarkable are the long shots of spray rising hundreds of feet up the sides of cliffs [Figure 7.14(a)]. Repeatedly we return to the woman and boy as they move to the end of one protruding cliff, then inland and out to another cliff (a pattern followed three times), pausing only to stare out into the distance [Figure 7.14(b)]. After what some viewers might consider too long a time, we see the boat far away. It is like a toy bobbing in the boiling cauldron of the sea. Crosscutting between mother and son, ocean and rocks, and the boat inching its way to the right toward shore [Figure 7.14(c)].

Finally, after desperate efforts, the men reach the beach safely, but the boat is wrecked. The serious looks on the faces of the men and the cries of the woman indicate what a loss this is. Nothing can be done, so the three walk along the shore toward home as the ocean appears to calm somewhat. There are dramatic silhouette shots of them together or alone [Figure 7.14(d)]. The penultimate shot of the film is of the sea, which has triumphed in this instance. The last shot, however, is of the family walking away from the camera; they have won their own victory by surviving.

Flaherty's intention, implicit in the film, was to make vivid and real the hard life of these hardy Aran islanders. There can be no doubt that he succeeded. Even critics who object that the director isolated his subjects from the context of the life of their times, falsified by omission, and manipulated his material by staging events for dramatic effects—even these critics admit that *Man of Aran* is a moving, memorable film. For some of us, however, dogmatic genre criteria are less important than the experience of a film itself. Perhaps Flaherty's inner vision of the life of the Aran islanders projected on celluloid may be more true to the spirit of these people than would be possible through orthodox documentary adherence to facts.

(a)

(b)

(c)

(d)

**FIGURE 7.14**

*Man of Aran.* Images from the final sequence of the film. During a storm, the wife and son of the man of Aran watch as he and two other islanders attempt to reach shore (a, b, c). After the boat is wrecked, the family returns home (d).

## CINÉMA VERITÉ

### Titicut Follies

*My feeling is that if the films do anything, they may contribute information that people might not otherwise have, and may suggest things that some people may otherwise not think about. . . . I really have no particular propagandistic or social change solutions to offer, and I'm wary of them generally.*
Frederick Wiseman, 1970[22]

### CREDITS

*Producer, Director, Sound Technician, and Editor —Frederick Wiseman, Director of Photography— John Marshall, General Assistant—David Eames.*

1967/Bridgewater Film Production
Black & White/87 minutes

### BACKGROUND

Frederick Wiseman (1930–) did not enter professional filmmaking until his mid-thirties. Previously he was a lawyer engaged primarily in the teaching rather than the practice of law. His first participation in the creating of a motion picture was as producer of the feature film *The Cool World* (1964, directed by Shirley Clarke). In 1967 he directed, produced, and edited his first film; thereafter, he has continued to function in these three roles for approximately one documentary per year.

After *Titicut Follies* (1967), he completed *High School* (1968), which reveals the narrow-mindedness and conformity of the staff of an urban, middle-class high school in Philadelphia. The day-by-day activities of the Kansas City Police Department is the subject of *Law and Order* (1969). *Hospital* (1970) demonstrates the frustrations encountered by patients, doctors, and nurses at New York's Metropolitan Hospital in dealing with an incompetent, self-defensive city bureaucracy. The United States Army successfully transforms individual youths into automatous members of a fighting machine in *Basic Training* (1971). *Essene* (1972) was a departure for Wiseman in that it did not examine a public institution but life in a Catholic monastery. All our worst fears about the ineffectuality and callousness of city institutions are confirmed in *Juvenile Court* (1974) and *Welfare* (1975). Between these two

films Wiseman once again turned to a private organization by focusing on the experiments of scientists at the Yerkes Primate Research Center in Atlanta, Georgia, on the subject of animal sexuality in *Primate* (1974). *Meat* (1976) is a presentation of the practices of the meat-packing industry. *Canal Zone* (1977) concerns the way of life led by government employees at the American enclave at the Panama Canal. *Models* (1982) is one of Wiseman's more recent films.

What these documentaries have in common is that a central organization forces its members and people who come within its sphere of power to sacrifice humanity, individuality, and human dignity at the altar of a self-perpetuating and self-justifying system. Yet those committed to such organizations, each one without exception established originally for laudable or practical purposes, are not consciously villains. It is simply that bureaucracies can turn basically decent individuals into bullies and frightened defenders of the status quo, and human nature can be so weak and selfish that impulses of generosity, tolerance, and empathy can be stifled by rules and regulations.

The director makes no claims to being completely objective: "I think this objective-subjective stuff is a lot of bullshit. I don't see how a film can be anything but subjective."[23] In none of his films are we presented with a brief for a prosecution; we see both sides of a coin. The negative side, however, is more vivid and predominates. Wiseman is unquestionably subjective in this respect. He is a social critic, his intention is to uncover defects in an organization, and nothing that appears on the screen has not actually happened.

Wiseman creates his documentaries in two stages.[24] When the director chooses a subject, he has a notion but, he insists, no preconceived approach or theme. He obtains permission to shoot the film from the proper authorities, governmental or private. The two main filmmakers in the very small crew consist of the cameraman (directed by Wiseman), using 16mm film in a hand-held camera, and the sound man (a role the director usually assumes himself). There is no script, nor are any scenes staged. The crew remains at a locale for a period of 4 to 6 weeks, sometimes collecting as much as 400 hours of footage. Wiseman attempts to insert himself as unobtrusively as possible into the daily routine of an organization and point the camera at whatever attracts his attention. No effort is made to capture obviously dramatic or esthetically attractive shots.

The second stage is crucial. Wiseman is always his own editor, and the form and substance of his documentaries are molded in the editing room. Weeks or even months may be devoted to this task. His shooting ratio can be as high as 70 to 1; that is, 70 feet are shot for every foot used.[25] He does not include a voice-over narrator or background music.

Wiseman's approach to filmmaking has caused him to be associated with the *cinéma verité* or direct cinema, documentary style,* although the director vehemently denies that such a special style exists as more than a useless critical tag.[26] In the analysis of *Titicut Follies,* Wiseman's relationship to this style is considered.

Of all the many outstanding documentary filmmakers working today, Wiseman is probably the best known to the general public. The reason is not simply the quality of his films but that through his own distributing company, Zipporah Films, he has arranged to have his documentaries financed by and shown on educational television. WNET, while granting him complete artistic freedom, has supported his work since the early seventies. *Canal Zone,* in fact, was the first in a renewed 5-year, five-film contract.

The origin of *Titicut Follies* was the visits Wiseman made with his Boston University law students to the Bridgewater State Hospital for the Criminally Insane. He decided to make a documentary. After receiving permission from the Commonwealth of Massachusetts, with mostly his own money and a crew of two in addition to himself, he began shooting in 1966. He showed unedited footage to Bridgewater officials, who offered no objections. They did not view the final version.

When the film was presented to the public, state-level authorities reacted with outrage. They obtained a court order prohibiting the distribution of *Titicut Follies* in the state on the basis of a breach of

contract and invasion of the privacy of the Bridgewater State Hospital inmates. After five trials and over a decade later, the ban is still in effect. Since his experience in Massachusetts, Wiseman does not obtain written releases from participants. He simply asks a person if he or she has any objection to being included. If there is an objection, the material is eliminated. The edited version is *not* shown for approval to officials of an organization or those who appear on the screen. There have been many objections to his films but no additional legal action against them.

*Titicut Follies* has won a number of prizes in the United States and abroad, including First Prize for Best Documentary at the Mannheim Film Festival of 1967.

### SUMMARY OF EVENTS

A master of ceremonies introduces a group of male singers and tells a joke on a stage over which hangs a banner that reads "Titicut Follies." Cut to a large room in which men are taking off clothes that are searched by uniformed guards. From the glassy stare of some of the men and the incoherent monologue of a man who calls himself Borgia, we realize that the setting is a mental institution. There is crosscutting between the large room and an interview at which a psychiatrist questions a young man, the Child Molester (descriptive phrases are used to identify individuals who are not referred to by name in the film).

In an outdoor recreation yard, inmates are sitting, walking, and exercising. Cut back to the Follies. A man sings, and this same individual next appears with a towel over his shoulder on a staircase outside the cells. The Follies' master of ceremonies, who is a Chief Guard, talks to his colleagues. One of the patients, Jim, is brought into a room to be shaved. He is baited by a guard. A change of setting to guards discussing the lingering effects of gas after it has been used to subdue unruly prisoners. Once more we return to the Follies.

We are outdoors again. The psychiatrist attempts to respond to the accusations of the Talker, a forceful, discontented young man. After shots of other inmates, the camera settles on the Haranguer surrounded by a group as he discourses with more intensity than logic on Vietnam and world politics.

*pp. 343–344

The psychiatrist looks through the peephole of a cell and then telephones to arrange for the force-feeding of Joseph Cicoria. There is crosscutting between Joseph being force-fed and a corpse being prepared for burial; we assume that the latter are flashforwards.

The next sequence consists of a birthday party. Two of the women who organized the party speak of the satisfactions of their work.

The Director of the institution is on the telephone arranging an appointment for the next morning. A meeting of the Review Board chaired by the Director follows. They listen to the complaints of the Talker (seen earlier arguing with the psychiatrist). After he leaves, the board agrees that the young man must remain, and additional medication is prescribed.

A series of relatively brief scenes: an inmate being given a bath, a man screaming in his cell, a group in a large room, a priest giving extreme unction to a patient on a hospital bed, outside in the yard.

A corpse is placed in a coffin, carried to a cemetery, and buried. Return to the conclusion of the Follies.

━━━━━━━
ANALYSIS

*Titicut Follies* is an assault on our confidence that government institutions that take care of our sick and mentally ill are basically humane and attempt to treat those in their charge. If mankind has made any moral progress since primitive times, it has been in the belief that every human being has value and that it is a function of society to protect that value. Public institutions are a guarantee that our society accepts the responsibility of helping those who cannot help themselves.

Our illusions are shattered by *Titicut Follies*. In an institution for the criminally insane, inmates are not helped but degraded, dehumanized, and trapped in hopeless situations. It is not just that guards and officials are usually callous and at times sadistic; the bureaucratic system itself assists in blighting the lives of the people it is intended to protect. And we cannot escape the evidence of our eyes. We are not confronted by fiction or a report replete with cold statistics; we observe the actual experiences of human be-

ings in a real setting. There can be no doubt of the essential "truth" of the documentary. Questions do arise, however, as to whether that truth has been manipulated, the presence of the camera has influenced what appears on the screen, and the editing of footage has significantly distorted reality.

Wiseman makes every effort to convince us of his objectivity. There is no narrator telling us how to react, no prepared script, no background music to underscore a scene. The director avoids any appearance of artificiality. The hand-held camera is sometimes shaky and restless. Subjects are not neatly framed, and people move haphazardly between the camera and a person we are observing. The predominant angle is eye level. Occasionally a close-up is used for dramatic effect, as when the Talker is arguing with the psychiatrist and there is a close-up of his mouth. At one point the camera focuses on the observation slot of a cell door, then moves through it into the cell. At the end of the film there is a zoom shot. On the whole, however, camera techniques are as unobtrusive as possible.

The lighting is functional, just enough for clarity, without dramatic highlighting. It is obvious that portable sound equipment was used. Extraneous natural sounds at times blot out portions of a conversation. Volume levels can be erratic. There is not always parallel sychronization between a face and speech, so sometimes we are not sure who is speaking.

The camera is unobtrusive but not nonexistent. Wiseman does not attempt to disguise the fact that people, especially the inmates, are aware of the camera. Some look directly at it, and some—Jim, for example—cover their genitals. Awareness of the camera on the part of subjects is a major problem of direct cinema. Do people act as they appear on the screen because they are being filmed? Of course, to some degree reality is distorted by the presence of equipment and crew. We can only depend in determining this influence on our confidence in the director, the statements of subjects that after a while they *consciously* forget that the camera is operating, and internal evidence. In the case of the inmates in *Titicut Follies*, we sense that they are not acting, although probably extraverts like the Talker, Borgia, and the

Haranguer are reacting to an audience. The workers and officials at the institution also indulge, on occasion, in acting before the camera. At the birthday party, the woman who speaks of a letter of appreciation she received from a former inmate strikes a note of artificiality; one senses design rather than spontaneity in what she says. During the meeting of the Review Board, the Director and others self-consciously demonstrate their knowledge of psychiatry.

Reaction to the camera is understandable, even inevitable, but what surprises us is the willingness of the officials and guards at the institution to expose themselves. This is another question that often arises when a documentary in the direct-cinema style ends up being less than complimentary to participants. As indicated earlier, officials at Bridgewater State Hospital had the opportunity to insist on the deletion of any footage that they judged was detrimental to their reputations. Were the guards unaware that many of them appear as bullies with streaks of sadism or the psychiatrist as a voyeur and an incompetent? The only possible answer is that, encouraged by the indifference of a bureaucratic system, they felt what they were doing was proper.

When the state of Massachusetts, after more objective eyes than the participants' had seen what Wiseman had wrought, sought to prevent release of *Titicut Follies,* the chief legal argument was invasion of privacy. We are touching on still another controversial aspect of direct cinema. There is some validity to the view that the privacy of the inmates had been invaded, particularly someone like the Child Molester. No matter how laudable his intentions, the Director took advantage of the helplessness of those wards of the state. Arthur Knight is not the only person to pose the question: "Where does the truth stop and common decency begin?"[27] On the other hand, perhaps progress can be made only at the expense of victims of an indifferent system. And one is sympathetic to Wiseman's defense that if an institution receives tax support, citizens have a right to know what happens in it, and reportorial access is a constitutional right.[28]

The suit brought by Massachusetts implies that Wiseman manipulated his material to show Bridgewater State Hospital in the worst possible light. No one denied that what appears in *Titicut Follies* actually happened. Any documentary, however, especially one in the direct-cinema style which is not planned in advance, is subject to a selective process by the director and editor. Wiseman, who acts as his own editor, has not disclosed how much film he shot at Bridgewater, but he admits that he rarely uses more than 20 percent, and usually a good deal less, of the material he collects. A critic of the film could ask if the rejected footage might not have presented more positive aspects of the state hospital. A counterargument would be that this possibility exists, but the genre is inevitably a form of propaganda, and no documentary can contain the whole "truth," only an interpretation of reality grounded in actuality.

One of the reasons a viewer tends to trust Wiseman is that he does not indulge in simple stereotypes. The guards are not brutes; they do not physically torture the inmates. The Chief Guard even entertains them. The Follies itself is a commendable form of therapy and must have required a good deal of effort on everyone's part to prepare. The psychiatrist is not a monster; he simply does not have the skill, patience, or empathy to help his patients. The Director is officious and conceited, not a tyrant. At the birthday party—itself a diversion for a group of the inmates that is not a required activity for a public institution—the three women sincerely are trying their best, even if they do emit a bit of the self-congratulatory smugness of the do-gooder. The funeral could have been more perfunctory than it was.

Wiseman, therefore, does not strictly present a bill of indictment against Bridgewater. What we sense is his outrage—a feeling we very soon share—at the attitude toward and treatment of the inmates that appears intrinsic to the system itself. These charges of the state are dealt with as less than humans, almost as particularly bright animals. They are forced to walk around naked. Their cells are cages. If they do not perform properly, they are ridiculed. No shred of dignity or hope is left to them.

At the beginning of the film, when the inmates' clothes are taken from them and searched, the guards direct individuals with harsh, abrupt commands. When Jim, the former schoolteacher, is being shaved, one of the guards finds sadistic pleasure in harassing the man by pretending not to hear responses to his questions, so Jim is driven to scream in a hoarse, harsh voice. The most flagrant manifestation of this insensitive attitude toward the inmates is the force-feeding of Joseph, a sequence we will return to later.

The purpose of a hospital is to treat patients, but this is not the case at the Bridgewater State Hospital; it is a prison. Some of the patients are obviously hopeless. Others, such as Jim and Borgia, we do not see being treated, if they are at all. Two individuals, however, are presented as being "dealt with," and what we observe is, to say the least, discouraging. At the beginning of the film, we witness a session between the psychiatrist and the Child Molester. It is unfair to judge the doctor after listening to only a few minutes of an interview, but he hardly inspires confidence. It may be important to gather intimate information about a patient. The manner and type of questions asked by the psychiatrist, however, suggest on his part a puerile sexual curiosity and an ineffectual admonishing approach to his patient. When the Child Molester, so aware of his problems, says at the end of the session with poignant hopelessness that he knows he needs help but does not know where to get it, the doctor replies, "You get it here." We have profound doubts if the session we observed is any criterion.

Another patient of the psychiatrist, the Talker, is far more defensive. This young man's intense, aggressive volubility, on the borderline of the incoherent, indicates that he is disturbed. On the other hand, it is apparent that he is intelligent, and when his comments are shorn of their paranoia, there is a good deal of sense in what he is saying. In his confrontation with the psychiatrist in the yard, he appears more logical than the doctor, who himself has trouble speaking coherently.

Lest we assume that the psychiatrist is the only aberration in a sympathetic officialdom, we see the Talker before the Review Board. A few minutes earlier we heard the Director on the telephone. The conversation humanizes him somewhat as we learn that he has four children and doesn't feel well. This does not help very much to mitigate our dislike of this arrogant man. Even more distasteful is his narrow-mindedness during the proceedings of the board. The Talker is his own worst enemy by exaggerating what could be valid arguments until the diagnosis of schizophrenic paranoia does not seem farfetched. We cannot judge whether or not he is correct about his medication, but surely he is right to complain that there are no sports, recreation, or opportunities for study. One is reminded of the joke that sometimes paranoids are persecuted. If the Talker is wrong about being harmed by the institution (an objective observer might even agree with him), he is justified in feeling that he is definitely not being helped.

What is appalling is the conclusion the board reaches under the guidance of the Director. The Talker complains of adverse physical reactions to medication, so the Director prescribes an increase in the dosage of antidepressants. Then comes a "catch-22": the young man is making progress by releasing his aggression; however, the more aggressive he is, the more evident it is that he is "falling apart." At no time does anyone on the board consider a better environment and treatment in addition to medication. These people, especially the Director, are so unimaginative that they cannot see beyond the system as it is or any faults in that system.

Wiseman cannot be censured for presenting his vision of Bridgewater through the selection of his material, but open to question is his use of cinematic techniques, especially crosscutting, to manipulate the reactions of his audience. This is a violation of a cardinal rule of direct cinema.

The most obvious tampering with the events of the film is the use as a structuring device of the Titicut Follies (incidentally, Titicut is the Indian name for the Bridgewater area). The film opens and closes with shots of the show, and it is cut to twice during the main action (Figure 7.15). The participants appear so normal that we are all the more disturbed at their treatment when they are not onstage.

After the opening of the Follies, there is crosscutting between the inmates in a large room where they are stripped naked and their clothes collected and the psychiatrist with the Child Molester. The juxtaposition of these two events encourages us to recognize that the physical indignities and the search im-

**FIGURE 7.15**

*Titicut Follies.* The inmates of a state mental institution appear to be normal when they perform on a stage.

posed by the guards are similar to what on a mental level the psychiatrist is doing to his patient.

The force-feeding of Joseph is probably the most distressing sequence in the film [Figure 7.16(a–c)]. It is not the action itself, which might be justified, but the crude manner in which it is done that is disgusting. The helpless, naked old man is matter-of-factly held down and the greased tube shoved up his nostril while the psychiatrist makes stupid jokes. The gesture of covering the patient's genitals with a towel is surely for the benefit of the camera. During the procedure, the doctor has a cigarette dangling from his lips, and when he climbs on a chair and pours a syrupy brew into a funnel attached to the tube, we are sure the ashes from the cigarette will fall into the funnel and no one will care.

The sequence is powerful enough to make impressively clear that Joseph is not treated as a human being. Wiseman, however, underscores this point by crosscutting between Joseph on the table and a corpse being prepared for burial [Figure 7.16(d–f)]. The putting of the tube into Joseph's nose is associated with the placing of cotton under the eyelids of the corpse. Another of a number of correspondences is a placing of a towel over the face of the corpse and then a cut to the doctor wiping Joseph's face with a towel.

Later we see a priest in the most perfunctory

way giving extreme unction to a dying, indifferent man. Just before the concluding scene at the Follies, there is a burial, with the priest again in a bored voice going through the ritual. We assume that Joseph becomes the corpse, and Wiseman has manipulated time for dramatic effect. The two look similar, but we cannot be positive. We have learned Joseph's name (when the doctor speaks on the telephone to arrange for the force-feeding); on the other hand, when the guard bumps the coffin in placing it in the hearse, he remarks kindly, "Sorry, *Jim*" (italics added). It is not of great significance whether Joseph becomes the corpse, for even when he is alive, he is dealt with as though he were a living corpse.

In later films, Wiseman avoided such manipulation of his material, allowing an audience to draw its own conclusions without prompting. Perhaps, as advocates of direct cinema maintain, objectivity is the more effective, more honest way to move people. Yet the situation at Bridgewater was so offensive that any means seems justified to attract the attention of society. *Titicut Follies* reminds us that cinema has many purposes. One of them, the particular province of the documentary, whether by means of objectivity or manipulation, is to serve the cause of justice. Surely this cause is served by pointing an accusing finger at institutions and men who forget that the degree of our humanitarianism and respect for the individual in all circumstances is a touchstone of the type of civilization we have created.

**PROPAGANDA 1**

### Triumph of the Will
### (Triumph des Willens)

*I have never done anything I didn't want to do, and nothing I've ever been ashamed of.*
Leni Riefenstahl, 1965[29]

**CREDITS**

*Director, Producer, and Editor—Leni Riefenstahl, Directory of Photography—Sepp Allgeier, Head Cameraman—Arthur Kiekebusch, Composer—Herbert Windt, and others.*

1935/UFA
Black & White/120 minutes

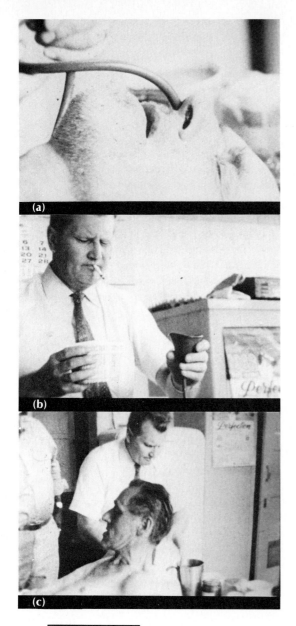

**FIGURE 7.16**

*Titicut Follies.* Crosscutting between Joseph being force-feed (a, b, c) and a corpse being prepared for burial (d, e, f). If the corpse is Joseph, then (d, e, f) would be examples of flashforward shots.

## BACKGROUND

Leni Riefenstahl (1902–) is a remarkable woman who demonstrated singularity even in her youth by studying dancing, painting, acting, and costume design, as well as being an enthusiastic sportswoman. Her career as a professional dancer was ended in her mid-twenties by a knee injury. Although offered an opportunity to star in Max Reinhardt's theater company, she decided to act in one of the "mountain films" that Arnold Fanck began directing in the early 1920s. This film genre presented melodramatic, sentimental stories of healthy, idealistic youths skiing and mountain climbing against the spectacular background of the Alps. Riefenstahl did so well in her first Fanck production that thereafter she starred in five other of his films. In 1931 she directed and wrote (with Béla Balázs) the script of *The Blue Light* (*Das Blaue Licht,* 1932), a superior mountain film that revealed her gift for conveying physical motion on the screen with visual elegance. A fervent admirer of the film was Adolf Hitler, soon to become chancellor of Germany.

Over the objections of Joseph Goebbels, Hitler selected Reifenstahl to direct a film of the fifth Nazi party rally at Nuremberg in 1933. Although relatively inexperienced, having only a few days for preparation, and continually harassed by Goebbels, she managed to put together *Victory of Faith* (*Sieg des Glaubens,* 1933) but was dissatisfied with the results. All prints of this work have disappeared.

Again through the influence of Hitler, she was commissioned to make a film on the sixth party rally, entitled *Triumph of the Will* (1935). At the insistence of the military, which felt it had not been given proper attention in this documentary, she put together a compilation film, *Day of Freedom—Our Armed Forces* (*Tag der Freiheit—Unsere Wehrmacht,* 1935).

Her next assignment came from the International Olympics Committee; it was to make the official record of the 1936 Olympic Games held in Berlin. The result was *Olympia* (1938), a two-part film that many consider the director's finest work. Although extravagant at points in her adoration of the athletic body in motion and projecting a pro-German bias, Riefenstahl created a magnificent tribute to the grace, beauty, and dedication of athletes that has had few equals.

During World War II Riefenstahl appears to have fallen out of favor with the Nazi party, and none of the film projects she planned was realized, except for shooting footage in the forties for *Tiefland.* After the war, she was imprisoned but released, and in 1948 and again in 1952 was absolved by denazification boards of collaboration activities that justified official action. In 1954 she completed *Tiefland,* based on a Eugène d'Albert opera set in eighteenth-century Spain. Since the sixties she has spent a good deal of time in Africa filming two documentaries—one of which ("Black Cargo") she abandoned and the other ("The Last of the Nuba") not yet completed—and doing still photography. She has published two volumes of photographs on Nuba and Sudanese tribes.

Riefenstahl's reputation is clouded by her association with Hitler and the Nazi party, but even her most unforgiving critics must admit that she infused each of her documentaries, primarily through brilliant editing, with a unity of tone and superb visual rhythms.

After accepting the commission to make *Triumph of the Will,* Riefenstahl worked through her own film production company (Leni Riefenstahl Studio-Film, established in 1931 to make *The Blue Light*). The financing and distribution was through UFA, a shadow of the great company of the twenties, ostensibly independent but susceptible to pressure from the Nazi party. The budget was 280,000 marks (approximately $110,600 at the time). The crew consisted of 172 people. This included 16 cameramen with 16 assistants using 30 cameras. Footage was also available from 29 newsreel cameramen.[30]

Riefenstahl insisted on independence in her shooting but had to contend with a preparation period of only 2 weeks and obstacles placed in her way by Goebbels, who resented her challenge of his authority, questioned her experience, and objected to a woman's having responsibility for recording such an important event. Nevertheless, she had a great deal of freedom in where she positioned her cameras and how she used them. She also found invaluable the advice of Walter Ruttmann, who had directed the renowned *Berlin: The Symphony of a Great City* (1927), and the assistance of her director of photography, Sepp Allgeier.

During 5 months of editing, Riefenstahl distilled

65 hours of film into 2 hours. The speeches were recorded directly; however, the score by Herbert Windt and most of the natural sounds were added in a studio. The premiere was held in Berlin on March 28, 1935.

The film was widely praised for its artistic merits even beyond the boundaries of Germany and was awarded prizes in Berlin and Paris. It was, however, considered by party officials as too sophisticated for extensive screening outside the big cities and did not have a very wide distribution.

*Triumph of the Will* is presently available for rental in the United States in both its original 120-minute version and in various excerpts that range in length from 40 to 60 minutes.

## SUMMARY OF EVENTS

After the credits and four titles giving the historical context of the Nuremberg rally, a plane floats through the sky, goes over the city, and lands. Hitler descends and is taken by motorcade to his hotel. There is a band concert and rally in the evening that Hitler and his entourage watch from the hotel balcony.

The camera takes us through Nuremberg and on the Pegnitz River as the city awakens. The scene shifts to the tent camps, where men and youths rise, wash, eat, and play games. A parade of supporters in regional costumes enters the city, and individuals are greeted by the Führer. He goes on to an informal review of young troops.

At the first party congress, Rudolf Hess opens the event, followed by 11 other speakers. The next sequence is the Labor Service rally. The laborers and farmers carry shovels instead of guns. From every region they pledge allegiance to one Reich. A dramatic flag ceremony salutes those who died in past battles. Hitler delivers a brief speech and the "work-soldiers" march before their leader.

The rally of storm troopers is held at night. After a few exhortative remarks by their chief, Viktor Lutze, there is a display of fireworks. In contrast to this open-air gathering by flickering lights is the youth rally, taking place in sunlight in a large stadium. Hitler speaks to the enthusiastic youngsters. The military parade of cavalry and artillery in another setting is briefly presented. In the evening there is an outdoor rally. Before an immense audience and a forest of flags and standards, Hitler delivers yet another speech, followed by a march of troops.

A memorable sequence at the war memorial is presented. Next is a very lengthy military parade. Hitler's longest and final speech takes place in a crowded hall at the closing party congress. A line of silhouetted marching men ends the film.

## ANALYSIS

*Triumph of the Will* is a controversial film because it succeeds so well in glorifying Hitler and the Third Reich, hardly a subject to be greeted with approval or even amiable tolerance by most viewers since World War II. Although certain moral dogmatists argue that the film should not be shown at all, this view has few supporters today. The question remains, however, of how to deal with a work with a repugnant theme. Most critics who examine the documentary separate form from content (an approach followed in this analysis) and focus their attention on the impressive cinematic techniques of the director. Many of us, however, feel uneasy in taking this stance, for we do not subscribe to a dichotomy of form and content as a critical principle and are wary of the implications that any artist in any medium can be relieved of responsibility for the ideological meaning and uses made of his work of art. This problem is too important to ignore, particularly in the case of *Triumph of the Will*, although it can only be defined rather than resolved in a couple of paragraphs.

Leni Riefenstahl is alive and active today and has defended her role in creating the documentary. She has repeatedly maintained, as suggested in the epigraph, that she acted solely as an artist meeting the challenge of recording a specific event as dramatically and esthetically as possible. Although she admits to being fully aware that the purpose of the documentary was the aggrandizement of the Führer and his party, she denies any specific *personal* political objective in directing the film. In other words, she fulfilled her commission to the best of her ability but cannot be blamed for the uses made by others of her creation.

Three conclusions seem reasonable: Riefenstahl is being devious, she was in the mid-thirties incredibly naive about politics, or artists, unlike the rest of us, cannot be held responsible for any of their actions that have political repercussions. The last position would find few advocates since World War II, even though the more fervent defenders of Ezra Pound, Louis-Ferdinand Céline, and Knut Hamsun often seemed to support this view. If either of the other two conclusions is accepted, Riefenstahl, no matter what her personal intention or how obliquely, is "guilty" of contributing to the success of the Nazi party in the thirties. Guilt suggests punishment, and here is the crux of the controversy surrounding the filmmaker. Some people insist that since she was absolved of officially punishable activities by two denazification hearings and was for years ostracized by the film industries of all countries, she has suffered sufficiently, and the past should be forgotten. Another opinion is that for the rest of her life she should be persona non grata as an artist and definitely not be allowed to lecture or, as has happened in recent years, be given awards. It is not likely that this controversy will be settled to everyone's satisfaction during Riefenstahl's lifetime. In any case, *Triumph of the Will* deserves to be analyzed for what it can tell us, as warning or prescription, about how an overt propaganda documentary can transform reality and direct the emotions of viewers.

The film is devoted entirely to events that occurred during the sixth Nazi party rally held in Nuremberg September 4 to 10, 1934. The footage consists primarily of marches, rallies, and congresses, but there are also three other sequences: Hitler arriving at Nuremberg by airplane, the city awakening in the morning, and the soldiers and workers in the tent camp. There are both night and day sequences. Objective photography of these events might have resulted in a lengthy newsreel. What Riefenstahl did instead was to manipulate her material through camera-editing dynamics and background music to the single purpose of glorifying Hitler and the Third Reich. It is the means of realizing this intention that is one of the fascinations of the film.

At the end of the closing party congress, Rudolf Hess proclaims, "The party is Hitler, but Hitler is Germany, just as Germany is Hitler!"[31] The Führer must be seen as not simply a human being but the personifi-cation of Germany—in fact, a demigod sent to lead the Chosen People to their manifest destiny. The opening sequence introduces this theme. After the title we see a plane floating through clouds, sky, and sunlight. We do not hear the sound of the engines, only an orchestrated version of "Horst Wessel," the anthem of the Nazi party. It is as if the music powers the plane, for though there are shots from within the machine looking out, we do not see the pilot or any other human being. We are meant to recall that the eagle is an emblem of the party and the personal symbol of Hitler. The plane is like a great eagle decending from the heights on Nuremberg. There is a superb shot of the shadow of the plane rippling along housetops and columns of the faithful marching into the city (Figure 7.17). The plane lands and, rather anticlimactically, Hitler appears.

FIGURE 7.17

*Triumph of the Will.* A view of Nuremberg as seen from the plane carrying Hitler.

Throughout the film the Führer is photographed primarily from low angles and whenever possible against the background of the sky or beneath one of the symbols of the party (see Figure 1.14). In the ride from the airport to the hotel, he lifts his hand, and sunlight reflects from it (Figure 7.18). Often the camera focuses on Hitler, leaving the people behind him slightly blurred. Rarely do we see him on the same visual plane with others; he is separate from his entourage, at a distance from others. He smiles infrequently. All these devices give Hitler a mythic aura: the lonely hero, more god than man, bearing with fortitude and courage the burden of leadership.

**FIGURE 7.18**

*Triumph of the Will.* Hitler as a demigod from whose hand flashes the energy of authority.

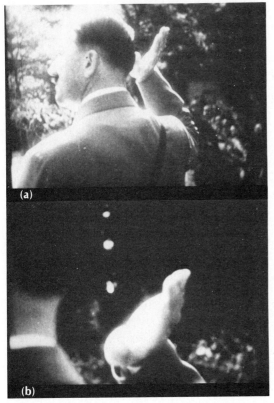

(a)

(b)

Yet this spirit of Germany is definitely incarnate. He can receive a bouquet of flowers from a child, chat with citizens dressed in regional costumes and soldiers in the ranks. The Führer of the film is simultaneously myth and a physical presence. As Richard Meran Barsam points out,[32] here lies Riefenstahl's chief problem in attempting an apotheosis of Hitler, one beyond her power to solve. The man is so physically unimpressive and his speeches are so mundane in substance and

delivered in such a shrill voice with exaggerated gestures that it is as if the myth and the man are out of synchronization. All the cinematic magic of the director could not completely transform the former house painter into a Wagnerian demigod.

Riefenstahl had an easier task in suggesting a fusion of the German people into a monolith of the Third Reich. Rallies by their very nature encourage a togetherness and a loss of individuality in a group. However, the director achieved this important objective by three interrelated means: indicating the character and range of the supporters of the Third Reich, taking advantage of staged events that blurred distinctions of time and space, and, most impressive, using camera-editing dynamics that dramatize the unity of the German people.

In contrast to the isolated Hitler, we usually see his followers as immense masses marching, standing, or shouting in unison, *"Sieg Heil!"* Panoramic shots, often from a high angle, and the moving camera at eye level sweeping past crowds are used throughout the film. The epitome of this approach, one that counterposes the isolation of leaders and the mass of followers, occurs at the war memorial. For many viewers this is the most memorable scene in the film. The setting is a stadium packed with uniformed figures at attention. From one end to the other of the memorial field is an empty, white road. Along this road walk in silence three men: Hitler in the center, on one side Himmler (head of the SS, the black-shirted *Schalzstaffel*), and on the other side Viktor Lutze (head of the SA, the brown-shirted *Sturmabeteiling*). The camera is behind them, very distant, and at a high angle [Figure 7.19(a)]. A cut to the camera facing the three, to the right of the center structure, again very distant, and then moving horizontally to the left, so the leaders are seen marching forward as the camera passes uprights of the memorial [Figure 7.19(b)]. After the wreath-laying ceremony, Hitler and the other two walk back between the two masses.

If Riefenstahl had confined herself to panoramic, sweeping shots of immense groups, the effect would have been of an abstraction, a blur of supporters. It must be established that human beings have committed themselves to the Third Reich and sac-

FIGURE 7.19

*Triumph of the Will.* Two shots from the scene of Hitler, Himmler, and Lutze laying a wreath at the war memorial in the Luitpold Arena.

(a)

(b)

rificed their individuality for a purpose that transcends the individual. So at every rally and march, the director cuts to shots of single persons or small groups. The civilians of all ages have healthy, Aryan faces, illuminated with the joy of being in the proximity of the Führer. The soldiers are earnest, their eyes stern with the fervor of dedication. Individual soldiers are often shot from a low angle.

The director goes further in humanizing Hitler's supporters. The morning after the arrival of the Führer, the camera seems to float over and through the waking city, even moving down the Pegritz River and photographing reflections of buildings and bridges. The strains of the hymn "Awake: The Dawn of Day

Draws Near" from Wagner's *Die Meistersinger von Nuremberg* are heard on the sound track. As the bell tower rings the hour of 7, the setting changes to that of the tent camp where troops and workers are housed for the period of the rally. The youths and men as they wash, eat, and play games are vigorous and vital. These scenes of city and individuals are intended to convey the impression that ordinary people in a typical city are joined together in the joy of their commitment to the Third Reich and the man-god who is their leader.

A number of events were staged at Nuremberg to emphasize not only the unity with the party of people of all ages, occupations, and areas but also of the past, present, and future. After the sequence in the tent camp, there is a parade of supporters dressed in regional costumes, many of them carrying agricultural tools. This indicates that the most traditional level of German society, the farmers and peasants, supports the party. Most of the paraders are middle-aged or older, and there are children and younger women. The young male farmers and other workers have their moment in the Labor Service rally, as they march carrying shovels as though they were rifles. At one point a leader of the workers repeatedly asks, "Comrade, where are you from?" The answers (with the camera cutting to each responder) represent every area of Germany. The ceremony that follows seems misplaced until we realize that the whole purpose of this gathering is to convince the members of the Labor Service that workers are an extension of the military, so they are called work-soldiers. No segment of society will be neglected—or their responsibilities lessened—in the new regime. The ceremony is very effective dramatically and consists of a flag being lowered to the ground as a famous battle of the past is named. At the cry "You are not dead, you are alive—in Germany!" all the flags are lifted to the sky (Figure 7.20). By this means, Germany of the past is presented in continuity with the present Reich.

Music also plays a role in evoking the grandeur of the past. The spirit of Richard Wagner, Hitler's favorite composer and creator of a mythos of Germanic heroism and demigods, haunts the sound track. Not only are there themes and passages from *Die*

**FIGURE 7.20**

*Triumph of the Will.* During a dramatic ceremony at the Labor service rally, flags representing battles of the past are raised in tribute to dead German soldiers.

*Meistersinger von Nuremberg,* appropriate to the setting of the rally, and other Wagnerian operas, but Herbert Windt's own score for the film is also neo-Wagnerian when not quoting German folk melodies and party anthems.

The future is stressed in the youth rally, yet another segment of society to be consecrated to the party. In his speech to this group, Hitler declares that what he and the party have accomplished will survive only if the youth of the present prepare themselves to carry the banner of the Third Reich into the future. The shots of individuals and small groups demonstrate that the Führer's message is accepted with enthusiasm.

As might be expected, most attention is paid to the military, both the traditional and the party's own "S" organizations. There are two military displays, the second of which is the longest sequence in the film. The first of the night events is for the storm troopers and includes a fireworks display.

We have already noted some of the techniques Riefenstahl uses to demonstrate that individual human beings have willingly submitted themselves to the goals of the state, such as intercutting between panoramic shots and shots of individuals. Another technique involves repeated cutaways to or lengthy shots of emblems and flags. Once again we have a means of fusing single units into a whole. Symbols of the whole are primarily the swastika, the iron cross, and the eagle. The flags and standards are predominantly representative of areas of Germany and units of the party. By having these flags swiftly pass by, the insignias on them are indistinct, and there is a sense of their flowing together. A similar approach is applied to marching men. More than once, the director places her camera at a great distance from the soldiers and at a high angle and adjusts her lens so that it is a bit out of focus. The result is a stream of light and shadows in which individual men become merely particles of that stream.

Flags and shadows are most effectively combined at the second evening rally and at the last party congress. Both begin with a flow of standards passing in a procession that fills the screen. The hall where the congresses take place, resembling a cathedral, is dimly lit, so the mass of people, in shots slightly out of focus, becomes a trembling field of shadows (Figure 7.21). There is a contrast in both cases to the clear shots of Hitler delivering his speeches.

**FIGURE 7.21**

*Triumph of the Will.* The final congress takes place in a hall that was as carefully designed as a movie set to inculcate in members of the Nazi party feelings of awe and solidarity.

The officials of the party stand halfway between the followers and their leader. They are generally in the background (we note how unimportant they appear when compared to Hitler in the last, lengthy military parade) until each makes a speech. These speeches possess a boring similarity; all exhort members of the party to subordinate themselves to the demands of the Führer and the country and present vague visions of a future of power and glory. Actually,

the most striking aspect of these speeches is the introductory titles at the first party congress. The name of each speaker appears in thick, hazy lettering that seems to catch fire and become clear for a few minutes (Figure 7.22), then indistinct again as the flames recede. Two speeches, however, do contain statements worth noting. Julius Streicher alludes to the need for racial purity in the nation. This ominous remark is the only one in the film that hints at a program of genocide. A little later, Goebbels refers to the power of propaganda as greater than that of guns. This attitude explains why so much money and effort would be expended to assist the making of *Triumph of the Will.*

Thus far we have not considered the element in the film that more than any other makes it cinematically impressive: the rhythms of scenes and sequences created through meticulous editing. It is impossible in words, without a shot-by-shot analysis and dozens of pages of stills, to convey Riefenstahl's creative power in this area. We recall that she was a professional dancer, for her footage is visual music that would not suffer by comparison with Eisenstein at his best. A small but typical example: The first shot of the fireworks is in reverse motion, so the gleams of light move toward the center of the frame, drawing our attention

**FIGURE 7.22**

*Triumph of the Will.* The graphic device of burning letters is used to indicate the name of the next speaker at the first party congress.

to that point. The next shot is normally photographed, and the lights move toward the edges of the frame. The effect is for us to feel kinetically as well as to see an explosion (emphasized by the boom on the sound track accompanying the second shot). On a broader scale, one marvels at how the director can hold our attention for almost 20 minutes while men simply march during the final parade.

Riefenstahl was to go even further in creating visual poetry in her film on the Olympics. *Triumph of the Will,* however, remains a prime example of how artistic genius can transcend, even transform, repellent subject matter.

### PROPAGANDA 2

#### Night and Fog
#### (Nuit et brouillard)

"Nacht und Nebel—niemand gleich!"
"Night and fog—hide me!"
Richard Wagner, Das Rheingold, 1869 [33]

### CREDITS

*Director and Editor—Alain Resnais, Commentary —Jean Cayrol (spoken by Michel Bouquet), Directors of Photography—Sacha Vierny and Ghislain Cloquet, Composer—Hanns Eisler, Assistant Directors—Chris Marker, André Heinrich, and Jean-Charles Lauthe, and others.*

1956/Argos Films/Como Films
Black & White and Color/30 minutes

### BACKGROUND

Alain Resnais (1922–) studied at France's leading film school, IDHEC (Institut des Hautes Études Cinématographiques), and was a professional editor before becoming a director of documentaries. He first attracted attention for his shorts on artists, one of the finest of which is his 11-minute *Guernica* (1950). Works on other subjects include *Les Statues meurent aussi* (1953, in collaboration with Chris Marker, on the disastrous influences of colonialism on African art), *Night and Fog* (1955), and *Toute la mémoire du monde* (1957, on the Bibliothèque Nationale).

In 1959 he completed his first feature, *Hiro-shima mon amour.* It is experimental in style and in its oblique means of revealing the psychological effects years later on a French actress and her Japanese lover of the German occupation of France and the dropping of the first atomic bomb. Resnais's next film, *Last Year at Marienbad (L'Année dernière à Marienbad,* 1961) had a success for such a complex film that surprised even its director. A woman and two men wander in a palace experiencing, recalling, or imagining (or all three) aspects of their relationships. Resnais continued to examine the ways in which illusion and reality intertwine in *Muriel, ou le temps d'un retour* (1963), *La Guerre est finie* (1966), and *Je t'aime, je t'aime* (1968). *Stavisky* (1974) takes place at the beginning of our century and is based on the life of a legendary swindler. The nightmares, fears, and hopes of a novelist in his last years is the subject of *Providence* (1976). *My Uncle in America (Mon Oncle d'Amérique,* 1980) is a delicate, carefully structured work, more accessible than most of the director's efforts. Through the lives of three fictional characters, he illustrates the theories of the French biologist Henri Laborit (who appears on screen and lectures to viewers) on aggression and defense mechanisms.

All of Resnais's feature films center on how human beings struggle to come to terms with memories that continually shift their meaning and validity as each new day changes these individuals' views of the past. Every moment a minute later becomes part of the past, and there is a continuity between what we were, are, and will be. The director, from the broadest perspective, is exploring, then, the ways in which we perceive our circumambient universe and react to our imperfect interpretations of the distinctions between illusion and reality.

This preoccupation with the subjectivity of experience influences both Resnais's method of characterization and his cinematic style. His characterizations are fragmented and tentative, presented in a nonsequential narrative. Often we are not sure which events in a character's life are real and which are dreams, hallucinations, or memories. One person's experiences may fuse with or echo another's. Motivations are obscure or even sometimes nonexistent. External occurrences are filtered through the sensibility of an individual, so that historical or political events are no more concrete or free of illusions than memories. Perhaps the most surprising aspect of Resnais's characters is that they are so fascinating. Part of their appeal may be that of emotional puzzles. Surely more entrancing, however, is the mythic dimension of the haunted landscapes of their minds, so that their conflicts, confusions, and doubts are ones we recognize, in different disguises and patterns, from encounters with our own subconscious worlds.

With such an unconventional approach to characterization and plot, it is appropriate that Resnais's cinematic style is experimental. He does not hesitate to use special effects, soft focus, unusual angles, abrupt transitions, and even close-ups that transform human beings into almost abstract patterns of light and dark (as in the opening of *Hiroshima mon amour*) or patches of color. One of his distinctive hallmarks is the extensive use of lengthy tracking shots. These devices, however, are means rather than ends, necessary to communicate the complex human experiences he chooses as subjects. Nothing is left to chance. Resnais structures his films with great care. He spends an unusually long period of time on preproduction and is equally meticulous in his editing. Any ambiguity or diffuseness in a final print is intentional on the part of the director. This preoccupation with structure carries over to filming. His shots and scenes demonstrate a concern with formal composition equaled among living major European directors only by Antonioni and Bresson. To describe his cinematic style as having a "cold beauty" is to define both the advantages and limitations of his approach.

Another distinctive quality of Resnais as a filmmaker is his ability to respect and integrate the contributions of his collaborators with his own. His screenwriters are invariably eminent writers of fiction and have included Marguerite Duras, Alain Robbe-Grillet, Jean Cayrol, and Jorge Semprun. The director rarely interferes with the author of a screenplay, always original, and follows a given plot closely. For every one of his features except *Je t'aime, je t'aime,* Sacha Vierny, who has also worked with Buñuel and Chris Marker, is his director of photography. Among

the famous composers who have contributed background music to his feature films are Hans Werner Henze, Penderecki, Hanns Eisler, Stephen Sondheim, and Giovanni Fusco. Resnais demonstrates that a director can surround himself with talented professionals and still retain his vision and integrity, or it is, in this case at least, in the visuals and editing that the hand of the *auteur* is discernible.

Resnais is often associated with the New Wave movement. He has shared with Godard, Truffaut, Rivette, and the others a willingness to experiment with new techniques, an uncompromising refusal to give mass audiences what they demand, a disdain of strictly sequential plots, a distrust of the time-honored modes of film characterization, and an existential belief that the revelation of subjective feelings is more significant than realistic delineations of causes and effects. On the other hand, Resnais's approach to filmmaking in many respects is different from that of members of the New Wave. He abjures spontaneity, the hallmark of his younger, nonconventional contemporaries. Instead, his style is grounded in formal, self-conscious composition. His insistence on a carefully constructed screenplay, dependence on the spoken word, and utilization of independent-minded collaborators also differentiates him from most of the *Nouvelle Vague* filmmakers.

*Night and Fog* foreshadows many of the themes and style of Resnais's feature films. Doubts that a horrendous experience of the past can be made real in the present are repeatedly voiced in the narration. The evil of Nazism becomes at the end a paradigm of the potential evil in all mankind. Resnais experiments with striking juxtapositions of images and the use of alternating color and black and white. In both the new footage (in color) and the compiled material, rhythm and tone are carefully controlled and developed through editing. A unifying device in the color sections, forcing the viewer to follow the filmmaker's lead, is the tracking shots insistently moving from left to right.

In *Night and Fog,* narration and music are almost as important as the visuals. The lyric script of Jean Cayrol is a most effective complement to the horrifying images. He also did the screenplay for

*Muriel* and directed films of his own, for example, *On vous parle* (1960) and *Le Coup de grâce* (1965). Hanns Eisler was a pupil of Arnold Schönberg. Because of his socialist politics and avant-garde style, the Nazi regime ordered the destruction of all his music. After leaving Germany in 1933, he devoted himself to film scores, working with such directors as Fritz Lang, Jean Renoir, Georg Pabst, and Joseph Losey. His chamber music score for *Night and Fog,* modernistic in style, has the same terse yet anguished musical rhythm and tone to be found in Schönberg's *Verklärte Nacht. Night and Fog,* therefore, is the result of a collaboration of true professionals, with Resnais as the guiding spirit.

## SUMMARY OF EVENTS

We see color shots of green fields and barbed wire, and the camera takes us into a preserved concentration camp as the narrator speaks of dried blood and silent tongues. Cut to black-and-white motion pictures of the Third Reich military in 1934, most of the footage from *Triumph of the Will.*

The building of the concentration camps is presented through still photographs. When the camps are ready, the deportees are rounded up and put on trains that pass through night and fog. Return to the present as the camera goes along a train track, broken and overgrown with grass, then moves toward the entrance to the camp.

Images of deportees naked in the cold, being shaved, tattooed, numbered, classified, and given uniforms. The hierarchy of the camp is described. In the present, the narrator refers to the cold and terrors of the night and the dead thrown out in the morning. This is a transition to the past: mustering for morning call, marching to work in the quarries and in the underground factories. Photographs follow of the inmates eating, and we learn from the narrator what food and utensils meant to them. In color, a view of the camp from inside an observation post. Photographs of bodies hanging from barbed wire, the humiliation imposed on naked men by a roll call that lasts for 2 hours, and a man being beaten. In color, the gallows and the execution yard.

Forms of resistance in the nightmare society,

such as men arguing with common criminals for control of camp life and the sickest prisoners being helped. Color shots of the outside of a hospital and black-and-white images of those who suffer within. Color footage of the surgical block and a description of the experiments that were carried out on human guinea pigs. Carefully kept passports and ledgers. On the life of those responsible for those records, from the Kapos to the Commandant. Color shots of the outside of a prison and telltale signs of what went on within.

The final stage began in 1942. Crematories are built. Color shots of a preserved one. Photographs illustrating that deportation has spread all over Europe. People who could not work are exterminated. In color, the inside of a gas chamber, accompanied by details on how it operated. Stacks of emaciated bodies and views of the incinerators. "Nothing is lost": a hill of women's hair and the rolls of cloth made from it; bones made into fertilizer; lines of headless bodies, the heads in buckets, to be turned into soap.

By 1945 there is no coal for the incinerators, and order has broken down. When the Allies arrive, camp streets are strewn with corpses. The cleaning-up operation: heads and corpses being carried to common graves and a bulldozer pushing stacks of naked bodies into a pit. Shots of deportees who survived staring uncomprehendingly at the camera. The camp officials are rounded up. At a trial, everyone denies responsibility.

The coda of the film is in color. Images of flowers, earth, and water are juxtaposed against ruins of the camp. The narrator questions whether we have forgotten this lesson from the past and thus are unprepared to resist the arrival of new executioners among us.

## ANALYSIS

*Night and Fog* is a companion piece to *Triumph of the Will,* an effort to document the dark underside of the Third Reich glorified in Riefenstahl's film. That Resnais had this objective in mind is evident from his use near the beginning of *Night and Fog* of footage from the earlier documentary. He is as intent on swaying the emotions of viewers as was the German director, so both works are overtly propagandistic. Our reactions to a director's intentions depends on our attitude toward the validity of the feelings and ideas about which the director is attempting to persuade us. Few viewers today do not feel revulsion toward the purpose of *Triumph of the Will* and applaud that of *Night and Fog*. On the other hand, the means by which a filmmaker dramatizes his material can be appreciated regardless of intention. Both works, separated by 21 years, are brilliant examples of the art of the propaganda documentary.

Although *Triumph of the Will* and *Night and Fog* are technically fascinating, the two have differences in approach that go beyond opposing themes. Riefenstahl photographed an actual event and edited the footage to her purposes. Resnais attempts to evoke an experience that occurred more than a decade earlier and to fathom the present and future significance of what happened in concentration camps. Time thus becomes a resistant medium with which he struggles.

Resnais's lack of confidence that anyone can fish in the sea of time past with the net of art and capture a lost reality is expressed at the very beginning of *Night and Fog*. As the camera moves into the camp, the narrator remarks, "The blood has dried, the tongues are silent." Later, following a train track, we hear: "Go slowly along it . . . Looking for what? Traces of the bodies that fell on the ground? Or the footprints of those first arrivals . . .?" Still later: "No description, no shot can restore their true dimension." Resnais realized that to convey the horrors of the camps while restricted to shadows and ruins of a reality required imaginative cinematic techniques. Fortunately, the director was equal to the challenge.

The film consists of two types of footage, alternately presented: in color, the present of 1955, a camera traveling through a deserted camp; in black and white, the past, stills and shots from motion pictures primarily taken by the Germans. The two types are unified by thematic associations (a situation in the past is related to an object or building in the present), but even more so by the narration. Narrations in a documentary are either an adjunct to images, background music, and natural sounds, a tangential commentary assisting in creating tone and clues to the intention of the director; or an indispensable explanation of the context of the visuals. The narration in *Night and Fog* falls into the latter category. Jean Cayrol's intense, expressive script supplies the matrix of the film, without which the images would not be unified nor the ultimate theme be apparent.

The present footage is in color to emphasize a living reality. The remnants of the camp (Auschwitz) exist today in red brick, rusted steel, and barbed wire. The concentration camps were not a nightmare dispersed by the light of day. Color also makes more vivid the contrast between the buildings and indifferent nature. The very first shot of the film begins with a verdant field with sky and clouds in the background ("a peaceful landscape"). The camera tilts down, and the shot ends with barbed wire in the immediate foreground. As we move into the camp, we note luxuriant grass, trees, and flowering bushes. The narrator makes a connection between nature's regenerating itself regardless of the horrors that occurred on the site with mankind's forgetfulness of the significance of the concentration camps.

From the beginning, the viewer identifies with the camera: "No footsteps are heard except *our* own" (italics added). No human being is seen in the present footage, yet the perspective of the camera can become that of those who are no longer there. After black-and-white shots of prisoners on trains, there is a color shot of tracks overgrown with grass. The camera moves along the tracks at a high angle, so we see as if we were the engineer on the train. Soon the camera tilts up, and the view of the entrance gates is as we imagine was the deportees' initial sight of the camp (Figure 7.23). Much later we are inside a guard house, and the moving camera at a high angle presents the camp as a guard would see it.

Resnais is imaginative in introducing a device that suggests that we are going on a journey into the past. During most of the color footage, the camera moves from left to right. Soon we feel that the camera is not haphazardly exploring the camp but is purposefully proceeding toward a destination. That destination is the heart of this darkness—the gas chambers and ovens (Figure 7.24).

The narrator more than once speaks of the camp as "haunted." His words, the camera, and the

FIGURE 7.23

*Night and Fog.* The entrance gates of Auschwitz as they appeared when the documentary was made (color), suggesting what might have been for deportees their first view of the concentration camp.

FIGURE 7.24

*Night and Fog.* An oven in an Auschwitz crematorium as preserved in the midfifties (color).

background music instill in us a conviction that the deserted camp is inhabited by unseen ghosts and the air is heavy with unheard screams and bursts of gunfire. It is as if at some subliminal level the black-and-white footage is superimposed on the color shots. Although the narrator, speaking for the filmmaker,

modestly denies the possibility, the film succeeds to a surprising degree in fusing past and present.

In *Night and Fog,* the black-and-white footage predominates, for, paradoxically, this material is the substance and the color section the shadow of the reality of the concentration camps. It consists of still photographs and films found in Third Reich archives. The first footage we see is primarily excerpts from *Triumph of the Will.* This is the face the Third Reich wished to present to the world. The narrator notes the underlying theme of this film: "The nation must sing in unison." Abruptly, without explanation, almost as if the concept is inherent in any system in which dissent is *verboten* and an outsider within is an enemy, we turn to the building of the concentration camps. The images of surveying, digging, and architectural styles introduces a major theme of the film. The camps were planned and operated with ruthless efficiency. Later we see the inmates shaved, tattooed, and recorded. Careful records were kept of work done and of deaths. Finally, hair was turned into blankets and bodies into soap and fertilizer. The technological, bureaucratic mind has triumphed; an idea is conceived and implemented. That idea is simple and logical if one accepts its premise: People who did not fit into the Third Reich by reason of race, religion, or independence of spirit were not human beings; like beasts of burden, they either worked for their masters or were destroyed. The fact that such subhuman creatures numbered in the millions was a problem, but one that could be solved by dedication, a will to succeed, organization, and attention to details. The less imaginative, the more narrow-minded an official, the greater the possibility for efficiency in carrying out the master plan. This is what Hannah Arendt meant by "the banality of evil."

Another advantage to this attitude could be summed up in an unacknowledged maxim of concentration camp officials: Dehumanize your victims before destroying them and you can do so with a clear conscience. Near the end of *Night and Fog* are shots from the Nuremberg trials, and from Kapos up the hierarchy of guards and officers to the Commandant comes the same statement: "I am not responsible." The narrator sarcastically asks, "Then who is responsible?'' One answer might be: ''The idea, the plan, the planners, the system.'' This is a reasonable defense only if one believes that men and women are not accountable for their choices, that any rationalization, no matter what its ramifications, absolves the participants from guilt. One of the purposes of *Night and Fog* is to restore humanity to the inmates of the camps that was denied them by their jailors and thus attach blame to those who saw and acquiesced to this barbarous crime against the human race.

The camps are finished, and rounding up of the deportees begins. The first image in this series is a famous still photograph of a boy with hands over his head next to an anguished woman and soldiers with rifles in the background. It is this photograph taken in the Warsaw Ghetto that haunts Elisabeth in Bergman's *Persona* (Figure 7.25). The narrator indicates that not only Jews but any resisters, actual or potential, to the Nazi regime were deported to the camps.

A scene at a railroad station prompts a question in the minds of many viewers. People are being herded like cattle into train cars, as many as 100 in each. In one shot, a door is being shut by a soldier and, to our amazement, the people within help him pull closed the sliding door. Although there was little the deportees could do and they were generally passive, it is surprising that Resnais never mentions (aside from statements that camp inmates organized themselves and contended with the Kapos for control) that there was some resistance, such as that by the Jews in the Warsaw Ghetto, and there were individuals in many countries—Denmark, for example—that helped the condemned. Perhaps the director and screen-

**FIGURE 7.25**

*Night and Fog.* A famous still photograph taken during a roundup of Jews in a Warsaw ghetto.

writer considered such material tangential and outside their subject matter, the concentration camp experience itself.

At the camps, deportees are shaved, numbered, and given blue-striped uniforms. Soon we see that the inmates are systematically terrorized and humiliated (for example, standing for hours naked in the cold— (Figure 7.26). This is part of a calculated plan of dehumanization. Not only must officials consider their prisoners less than human, but the inmates themselves should also come to share this view. To an extent, the Nazis succeeded. The narrator tells of food stolen from the weakest and of betrayals. As survivors have told us, for many of them the ultimate horror was not what was done to them but the capability for selfishness and brutality they found in themselves and those who shared their suffering (Figure 7.27). The Nazis, therefore, were truly diabolical, as the narrator implies. They not only inflicted pain and death on the bodies of their victims but also attempted to corrupt their spirits.

Hitler's regime was only partially successful in reducing camp prisoners to the condition of animals suitable only for work or death because "gradually a society developed, its form the image of terror." Ironically, it was the Nazis' own obsessions with organization and efficiency that encouraged a structuring of a

### FIGURE 7.26

*Night and Fog.* Humiliation of a group of concentration camp prisoners, a stage in the process of dehumanizing them.

### FIGURE 7.27

*Night and Fog.* Is the horror in these eyes caused by looking outward or inward?

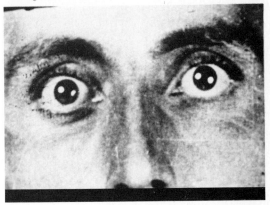

nightmare existence, which was preferable to the unpredictability of complete chaos. A good deal of *Night and Fog* is devoted to revealing how this society of terror operated.

The Nazis established a hierarchy that moved up the scale from the deportees wearing red triangles (Jews and other undesirables), those wearing green triangles (common criminals), Kapos (appointed leaders of the prisoners, usually criminals), SS soldiers and officers, and the Commandant. Work schedules were instituted, first in construction and underground factories and later in industry. Hypocritical signs, such as "Cleanliness Is Health" and "Work Is Freedom," were put up. "Each camp had its surprise": a symphony orchestra, zoo, greenhouse, orphanage. Hospitals, prisons, and brothels (for Kapos and soldiers) were built.

On their part, the deportees chose leaders and instituted a system of barter for food, utensils, and cigarettes. "They looked after those worse off than themselves." Secretly they constructed objects, wrote, and read. Most important of all, the emotionally and physically stronger learned to survive.

The odds were terribly against the concentration camp inmates. They had to struggle with not only the weaknesses within themselves and the insane system geared to destroy them but also the cruelty and sadism of the people in power. Bad as was the passivity of people like the Commandant, the architects, and others, even worse was the active evil of those in direct contact with the prisoners. The narrator points out the malevolence of the Kapos, torture in the prisons, and outlandish experiments in the hospitals. This was not simply a mad idea made concrete that demonstrates man's capacity to delude himself and commit any crime in the name of an ideology. It was an immediate, individual evil in which men beat and tore flesh, unmoved by screams of pain and anguish, capable of looking directly into the eyes of a terrified victim. That so many could allow themselves to be so possessed by the spirit of inhumanity is a challenge to any theory of human nature based on the innate goodness of man.

The black-and-white footage progresses from the building of the camps and the rounding up of the deportees to life in a grotesque society. As the color footage in having the camera moving from left to right appears to be purposefully advancing to a final statement, so the stills and shots from the past lead from one horror to another until the ultimate one. The last quarter of the film documents the extermination of millions of deportees. Once again we begin with the construction of the crematories, following the rules of order and efficiency. We see gas chambers and ovens. We stare with disbelief at piles of bodies and severed heads.

As the war draws to a close, official control breaks down, and an indiscriminate storm of death rages through the camps. We share the views of carnage that greeted the Allied soldiers. Finally, the climactic, unforgettable image: a bulldozer lifting hundreds of naked and emaciated bodies and dropping them into a pit (Figure 7.28).

The coda appropriately takes place in the present (1955) and contains the final message, the essential theme of the film. In color are presented images of blooming flowers, earth, and water as a setting for fallen-in roofs, broken piers of cement and wire, and a surrealistic metal object on a platform that looks like an instrument of torture (Figure 7.29). The narrator addresses those "who look at these ruins today as though the monster were dead and buried beneath them." Such complacency is unjustified and a danger,

**FIGURE 7.28**

*Night and Fog.* The final indignity imposed on victims of the "final solution."

**FIGURE 7.29**

*Night and Fog.* One of the last shots of the film is of this surrealistic object that somehow is almost as terrifying as the gas chambers.

for then who is "to warn us of our new executioners' arrival? Are their faces really different from ours?"

Resnais's ultimate intention is now clear. It is not simply to document a nightmare of twentieth-century civilization but to persuade us, to propagandize his belief that the dark beast within man that conceived and implemented the concentration camps is not dead but slumbering. It is the duty, Resnais implies, of men of goodwill not to allow it to awaken again in themselves or others.

# Western

## 8

More than most genres, a critical approach to the Western requires an understanding of its historical premises and the traditions it developed. In the following survey of characteristics and history, I have therefore emphasized three major topics: the relation of the film Western to the past it ostensibly depicts, the traits of the "classic Western," and departures from the conventional Western since the early forties.

John Ford's *Stagecoach* is a crucial film in the history of the Western. It contains both the major features, even clichés, of the classic Western and in incipient tendencies some of the new directions the genre was to take in the future. George Stevens's *Shane* superbly illustrates perhaps the major tension of the post–World War II Western, the contrast between romantic myth and uncompromising realism. The latter predominates in many contemporary examples of the genre and manifests itself particularly in presentations of physical violence and characterizations of the antihero. How these two characteristics can be combined with a flamboyant filmmaking style is demonstrated by Sam Peckinpah's *The Wild Bunch.*

## SURVEY OF CHARACTERISTICS AND HISTORY

The Western is the United States's only genuinely indigenous major motion picture genre. Musicals and gangster films may be associated with Hollywood, but they can take place, of course, in any age and in any country. The Western, however, is inexorably bound to American history and an American setting. To delineate the genre's characteristics, therefore, we must begin with its relationship to history and the significance of its setting.

Although some Westerns take place in modern times, they are a small percentage when compared to those that are basically historical films. This suggests that the genre possesses a certain factual authenticity. Only a naive viewer is not aware, however, that any Western is an artifice. It is historical in having as its time setting periods that actually existed, but a Western is a historical reconstruction of facts to degrees that range from the possible to the improbable. This is not entirely the fault of filmmakers, for each generation of historians revises views of the varied forces that influenced American frontier life, and they are continually uncovering additional material that results in new interpretations. The Western, then, is fundamentally based on myths in the sense of stories that are fiction or half-truths, although, as we will see later, the more profound meaning of the term *myth* also applies.

It is perhaps inevitable that this genre promulgate self-perpetuating illusions about the American frontier, for the earliest films were based, both literally and figuratively, on fictions. After the Civil War, a number of serious writers, inspired particularly by Bret Harte, wrote about the West. The myths about cowboys, outlaws, and gunfighters, however, were derived from more mundane sources. Dime novels devoted to Western heroes appeared as early as the 1840s. E. Z. C. Judson, for example, was not only a prolific writer of this type of popular fiction but also made famous a flesh-and-blood scout by writing about William F. Cody. Buffalo Bill's "Wild West Show," which toured the United States and abroad from 1883 to World War I, confirmed the stereotypes created by Judson and others. Newspapers were not far behind dime novels in proclaiming the West an area of adventure and profit, and they found it increased circulation to turn outlaws into folk heroes. These heroes and imaginary characters also strode through the pages of historical romances, especially popular at the turn of the century. Probably the most widely read work in this fictional genre was Owen Wister's *The Virginian* (1902).

The theater presented its share of Western melodramas. The plays were not created only by opportunists like Judson, who in 1872 wrote *The Scouts of the Plains.* Some of the most illustrious playwrights of the late nineteenth century turned to this new subject matter. Augustin Daley presented *Horizon* in 1871, and Clyde Fitch's *The Cowboy and the Lady* appeared in 1899. These plays, however, did not have the success of David Belasco's *The Girl of the Golden West* (1905), on which Puccini based his opera.

It was from these popular sources of fiction, journalism, and theater—essentially melodramatic, sentimental, and sensational—that the film Western took its cues in developing plots and traditions. Within the dimensions of this mythic world, however, some directors, screenwriters, and actors were more concerned with verisimilitude than others. The adjective *realistic,* amorphous enough when affixed to any type of motion picture, especially needs qualification when applied to the Western. First, complete historical accuracy is as unsuitable to the spirit of this genre as to the romances of King Arthur and his knights. Second, the areas that can be most authentically reproduced are the physical—costumes and settings. Finally, attitudes, situations, and relationships are most susceptible to any interpretation a filmmaker wishes to present. Yet we refer to a Western by John Ford as more "realistic" than one by Cecil B. DeMille. We are usually not simply alluding to matters of costume and setting or even of historical accuracy. We recognize, perhaps only intuitively, that Ford is closer than DeMille in portraying within the context of the Western the truths of human nature that do not change with time.

Setting is a more concrete common denominator of the Western film than shifting interpretations and approximate realizations of historical authenticity. Setting is restricted not only by time and place but also by situation. In this genre there must be a frontier, a sense that people are living in simultaneous contact with both civilization and the wilderness. That vague area of demarcation moved steadily from the western edge of the 13 colonies in the mid-eighteenth century

to the Pacific Ocean and south to the Rio Grande in the late nineteenth century. By World War I the American frontier had virtually disappeared. The temporal setting of most Westerns, however, is the four decades from 1850 to 1890, a period of individualism and optimism, yet also of conflicting attitudes, ideals, and life-styles. This diversity was encouraged by momentous historical events: the stream of wagon trains moving westward, the Civil War, the California gold rush, the building of transcontinental railroads, and Indian and range wars.

The most general opposition was between East and West. This was not simply a contrast of geographic areas; it included a multitude of values and associations. The East represented civilization, traditions, restrictions, industrialism, and class consciousness. The West symbolized nature, the future, freedom, individualism, agrarianism, and equality. Obviously, such distinctions are abstract and only suggest associations that repeatedly overlapped. Furthermore, as a frontier town grew, the values of the East became more prominent. The film Western takes place in its most dramatic form at that moment of greatest tension between individualism and community, nature and the town, freedom and restrictions. These dynamics and variations of them are seen in sharpest focus in the relationship of characters to the physical setting of a story.

The Western is usually permeated by what D. H. Lawrence termed "the spirit of place." And this perceptive British writer, in his *Studies in Classic American Literature,* recognized what was likely to have been the ambiguous feelings of frontiersmen toward the land and its natives. The prairies and plains, mountains and rivers could sustain and inspire human beings, yet also impersonally destroy the body and spirit of the weak. The negative forces were personified by the Indians, who appeared to be savages possessed by dark gods and seemed to survive because they were at one with everything in the landscape that threatened the white man. Yet contemporary memoirs and fiction (for example, *The Leatherstocking Tales* of James Fenimore Cooper) suggest that "redskins" not only frightened the white man but also awed and even, often secretly, aroused his admiration. What the frontiersmen saw as the spontaneity, freedom, and naturalness of the Indians, although appalling when manifested in violence, must have touched a sympathetic chord in the unconscious of travelers from the East, emotionally restrained by the civilization they carried with them like the clothes they wore and manufactured goods on which they depended. This ambiguity toward the American "savage" enters in disguised forms into the Western film from the beginning of its history.

Two extreme reactions to the physical ambiance of the West were possible: either conquer and exploit the land and its natives or give in to and become one with them. People who adhered to the former attitude established towns and had as their ambition to transform the West into a facsimile of the East. The chief instrument of transformation was the law, inflexible justice that protected the community from violence and Indians, encouraged business enterprise, and restricted antisocial individualism. The East was a nurturing mother whose umbilical cord was the railroads. The other radical alternative was the white man who lived like an Indian in harmony with nature. Often he was a half-breed or brought up by an Indian tribe. In films he appears as a scout, a trapper, or a "mountain man," sometimes living with a "squaw" and raising children of mixed race.

Between these two extremes was a range of combinations from which arose the themes and conventions of the Western founded on a tension between centripetal and centrifugal societal forces. Here lies the justification for applying to the genre the term *myth* in its most profound meaning: a story that reflects fundamental conflicts (and possible resolutions of them) in human nature and societies. The Western at its best is a paradigm of the opposition between the eternal dichotomies of nature and civilization, the individual and the group, Dionysian and Apollonian forces, the id and the superego. The Western, then, is set in a unique period of history in a special physical setting, yet can convey a significance that transcends that time and place.

Considering the importance of this genre in the history of American motion pictures, it is fitting that what is generally regarded as the first genuine narrative made in this country should be a Western. In 1903 Edwin S. Porter wrote and directed *The Great Train Robbery.* Today many of its effects are laughable, but for its time it was an astonishing breakthrough and can still hold the attention of an uncritical audience. Aside from its innovations (with individual precedents, especially in Great Britain) as a film per se (dependence on camera dynamics to tell a dramatic story, use of primitive crosscutting, tentative pans and tilts, and a striking medium shot of an outlaw firing his gun directly at the audience—see Figure 1.16), *The Great Train Robbery* established many of the fundamental elements of the Western. The outlaws are pitted against the law. At least half the film was photographed outdoors. During the last sequence of the 10-minute film, there is a chase ending in a shoot-out in which the outlaws are killed.

In retrospect, it is easy to perceive what was missing from Porter's Western and its numerous imitations if the genre were to develop. At the time, however, it took imagination to recognize that audiences needed a central character, a hero with whom to identify and for whom to cheer. G. M. Anderson had the insight to mold the first Western star. Although intending to serve only as director, he finally took over the acting of the role he had conceived, that of Broncho Billy. With *Broncho Billy and the Baby* (1910), he began the first Western series. During the next 8 years he produced 500 or more shorts featuring Billy, the "good bad man." The plots of these shorts were sentimental and contrived and the camera-editing dynamics rudimentary, but they contained a consistent main character, action, and, especially in setting and costumes, an aura of realism. Moreover, Anderson was one of the first to shoot his Westerns in California.

D. W. Griffith made the next significant contribution to the Western. As he developed in his one- and two-reelers new methods of filmmaking, he applied them to practically all genres, including the Western. The editing device of crosscutting for suspense was of particular importance for chase and rescue sequences. Griffith's Westerns (for example, *Fighting Blood,* 1911; *The Massacre,* 1912; and *The Battle of Elderbush Gulch,* 1913) were conventional for the day in plot and characterization, but they demonstrated that the genre could profit from creative directing. Unfortunately, aside from the uninspired

*Scarlet Days* (1919), Griffith never created a feature-length Western.

Thomas H. Ince, a contemporary of Griffith, directed such successful shorts as *War on the Plains* (1912) and *Custer's Last Fight* (1912), but after 1913 generally confined himself to producing. And it was as a producer that Ince influenced the Western in its formative stage. For this genre, as other types of motion pictures, he developed efficient means of organizing all stages of production. Probably of greatest significance was his emphasis on a detailed shooting script. He encouraged a solidity and consistency in characterization and a sharpening of focus on external and internal conflicts. The Western now had structure and unity.

At this propitious moment, William S. Hart (1870–1946) appeared on the scene. He had spent his early years on the frontier and had been a cowboy before becoming a stage actor. Through his friendship with Ince, he entered motion pictures. After two Westerns in which he played villains, he was allowed to star in a film whose script he helped to write. *The Bargain* (1914) was a resounding success, and Hart's career as a Western hero was launched. Most of his movies were done under the aegis of Thomas Ince, who was shrewd enough to relinquish a good deal of control to his star. From 1915 to 1925, when Hart retired, he, with a few exceptions, either solely or in collaboration wrote and directed his Westerns and supervised details of production.

It is always difficult to define the qualities that make a star, but in Hart's case his sincerity, his belief in what he was doing, evidently impressed his contemporaries and is discernible even to a modern viewer. He also was painstaking in attempting to convey what he had experienced or envisioned as the authentic West of the late nineteenth century. Hart's passion for verisimilitude in plots, costumes, setting, and acting is usually credited with bringing a new element of realism to the Western that went beyond the tentative efforts of Anderson and influenced the best films that were to follow his own. Furthermore, certain of the characteristics of the "good bad man" he portrayed were to appear in future heroes: commanding presence, intrinsic honesty, a restlessness

that made him essentially a lonely man, a suggestion of having endured hard times that left their marks on his long, lined face (he was 44 when he became a screen actor), and a romantic attitude bordering on treacly sentimentality toward women. Not all those who imitated Hart, however, had his acting ability, which included a surprising capacity for subtlety within the conventions of exaggerated silent-screen acting.

Among his successful films are *The Aryan* (1916), *The Narrow Trail* (1917), and *The Toll Gate* (1920). Superior to these, however, are two of the most fascinating silent-film Westerns. *Hell's Hinges* (1916) involves plenty of action and a confrontation between a "good bad man" and genuine villains.

**FIGURE 8.1**

William S. Hart. (a) As he appeared in a film of the early 1920s. (b) As a retired actor in his late sixties recalling how Westerns were made in his day.

What is exceptional about the film, however, is its religious and allegorical overtones. Although actually written by C. Gardner Sullivan, one could almost believe with a wild leap of imagination that the scenario was a collaboration of Zane Grey and Nathaniel Hawthorne. *Tumbleweeds* (1925) was Hart's last work and is considered by many admirers as his finest. It is an epic with a memorable land-rush sequence and a main character that is quintessential Hart. The film was rereleased in 1939 with added music, sound effects, and an 8-minute prologue delivered by Hart in which he recalls his experiences as a Western hero (Figure 8.1).

In the early twenties a dichotomy developed in the production of Westerns that was to last until the early fifties. A *program Western* was an expensively mounted production with a name director and stars not necessarily associated with the genre. The *"B" Western* was usually inexpensive, produced in a minimum of time, and featured a standard hero with individual traits who starred in a series. Although the two types will be dealt with separately in this survey, there was a good deal of cross-fertilization between them, and the lines of demarcation not always clear-cut. The conventions of the classic Western appeared in both, and often a star from "B" Westerns, such as John Wayne, was advanced to program Westerns.

The "B" Western very quickly developed its chief characteristics. The emphasis was on action, including a climactic chase sequence, and the films were obviously intended primarily for a juvenile audience. Most important was the star and the type of Western hero he had created as a persona. Moviegoers in the twenties did not refer to *Sky High* or *The Red Raiders* but a Tom Mix or Ken Maynard movie.

Anderson and Hart had established the basic traits of the Western hero, but those who followed added their own individual styles. Tom Mix was the best known of the next generation of heroes. Although he began his motion picture career before Hart, Mix did not become popular until the 1920s. Like Hart, he often acted in, wrote, and directed his own films; unlike Hart, he moved away from authenticity and character dramas toward sheer entertainment, escapism, and showmanship. In his Western hero persona,

he rejected the "good bad man" characterization of his two main predecessors and molded a sanitized, entirely virtuous hero immaculately costumed in white. Within this moralistic context, he emphasized comedy and action—fistfights, chases, and stunts—though minimizing realistic violence. Many of Mix's silent films were destroyed in a fire, but we still have such typical works as *Just Tony* (1922), *Sky High* (1922), and *Riders of the Purple Sage* (1925). Before his death in an automobile accident in the mid-thirties, Mix made a number of sound Westerns, less effective than his silent ones. Two of the best are *Destry Rides Again* (1932) and *Riders of Death Valley* (1932).

The silent era had other Western stars in addition to Hart, Mix, and Anderson. Chief among these were Ken Maynard, Buck Jones, Harry Carey, Fred Thomson, Tim McCoy, Jack Holt, and Hoot Gibson. Each major studio had its own stable of Western heroes, and Republic, RKO, and Universal in particular competed fiercely. The basic reason was commercial. B Westerns were in great demand and, in fact, released in surprising numbers. Fenin and Everson estimate that from 1923 to the early fifties the annual output of Westerns never fell below 150; most of them were "B" features.[1]

Although these "quickie" Westerns were popular and contributed to the traditions of the genre, they received little critical attention. This was reserved for the program Western, usually considered more complex and mature than the "B" type. One of the earliest was Cecil B. De Mille's *The Squaw Man* in 1913. The director followed this success the next year with *The Virginian,* the first version of Owen Wister's bestselling novel. The more notable of this type of silent feature also included Maurice Tourneur's *The Last of the Mohicans* (1920; Lake Champlain in 1757, the time setting of James Fenimore Cooper's novel, was then part of the American frontier), King Vidor's *The Sky Pilot* (1921), Irving Willat's *Wanderer of the Wasteland* (1924, the first feature-length film in the United States to be entirely in color—or at least two colors), and George B. Seitz's *The Vanishing American* (1927, based on a Zane Grey novel).

Two films released in the late 1920s shared with the earlier *Hell's Hinges* a fascination with symbolism and in tentative ways anticipated the psychological dramas that became a significant trend in Westerns after the mid-forties. William K. Howard's *White Gold* (1927) is a slow-moving melodrama of married life and murder on a sheep ranch that is almost expressionistic in its treatment of intense emotions. Victor Sjöström, the eminent Swedish director who worked in Hollywood during the twenties, turned to a Western setting for *The Wind* (1928). Georges Sadoul calls it "one of the masterpieces of the silent cinema and Sjöström's best American film, matching his Swedish achievements."[2]

A special category of the program Western came into being in the early twenties. The *epic Western* is sometimes defined simply as a film that has the frontier as its setting, with a large supporting cast and an emphasis on spectacle. This is a description of means and not ends. The epic Western depicts the scope and drive of frontier life, especially in its inexorable movement from East to West. Whether the plot centers on the building of a railroad or a telegraph line, a gold rush, a cattle drive, or a journey of covered wagons, the audience feels that it is participating in a proud moment in American history. Yet it still enjoys the excitement of the less elevated characteristics of the standard Western: a hero or heroes, villains, Indian attacks, and chases and rescues of various sorts.

The first epic Western that deserved the title was James Cruze's *The Covered Wagon* (1923). The plot of a wagon train's journey to California is less impressive, especially since it is so slow-paced, contrived, and cliché-ridden, than the film's attempts at authenticity, splendid settings, and fine photography (Figure 8.2). In addition, it was the first Western to attract a predominantly adult audience.

Of far more intrinsic worth was another epic released only a year later. John Ford's *The Iron Horse* is a classic and in the opinion of many aficionados of the Western, the greatest one made in the silent era (Figure 8.3). The film's very length is intimidating: 2 hours and 40 minutes at 18 frames per second (only 35 minutes less than *The Birth of a Nation*) and containing 1280 separate scenes and 275 title cards.[3] Length, however, is obviously no guarantee of a motion picture's merit. What earns our admiration even

FIGURE 8.2

*The Covered Wagon,* 1923, directed by James Cruze. An example of the panoramic shots that so impressed audiences when the epic was released.

a half century after its release is the masterful manner in which Ford controls and presents his sprawling story of the building of the Union Pacific Railroad. His effective use of the moving camera during action sequences was, at least in the United States, progressive for the early twenties. The crosscutting to heighten

FIGURE 8.3

*The Iron Horse,* 1924, directed by John Ford. Even in his early works, the director demonstrated a flair for dramatic visual effects. The hero (George O'Brien) is fighting his adversary (Fred Kohler), who is disguised as an Indian.

suspense illustrates how well the young director, 29 at the time, had learned from Griffith. The marvelous use of the striking Western landscape, however, is entirely the director's own and a trait that was to become characteristic of John Ford's style. On the other hand, *The Iron Horse* is not without faults: The comedy relief is too slapstick, the development of the romance too predictable, and the vindication and revenge of the hero too melodramatic.

Ford's and Cruze's epics were not followed by a deluge of imitations, perhaps because of the cost involved. James Cruze had little success with his next epic, *Pony Express* (1925), a showy but ponderous affair. In 1926 Ford directed *Three Bad Men* (the last of his Westerns until *Stagecoach*). Hart's *Tumbleweeds,* previously noted, had epic qualities unappreciated when it was released in 1925. Aside from these five films, the epic Western generally remained dormant until the advent of sound.

Another category of the program Western was the satirical comedy. Considering that comedy was a thriving genre during the silent period, it is surprising how few distinctive parodies of Westerns were made. Even more unexpected is the actor who starred in the most successful and subtle ones. In such films as *Manhattan Madness* (1916), *The Knickerbocker Buckeroo* (1920), and others, Douglas Fairbanks gave to his portrayal of the Western hero a wonderful vitality, especially in action scenes, and a refreshing sense of gently ridiculing the very conventions of the genre to which he was adhering. The only other silent Western comedies that did not have the buoyancy of lead balloons were "Fatty" Arbuckle in *The Round Up* (1920) and Buster Keaton proceeding at half steam in *Go West* (1925).

Sound did not require as radical a transformation for Westerns as other types of motion pictures. Dialogue was never that important in the genre, and it was relatively simple to include natural sounds and add background music. The first film to demonstrate convincingly what sound could do for a Western was Raoul Walsh's *In Old Arizona* (1929), a work that would have been popular without sound and probably is the best of the many films centering on the character of the Cisco Kid. Warner Baxter won an Academy Award—the first major one given to a Western—as Best Actor for his performance as the "good bad man."

By the time sound Westerns were released, the traditions of the "classic Western" had solidified. This is a major reason why the genre was less exciting than it might have been in the thirties except for the added dimension that resulted from sound: The formulas for making Westerns during the decade moved from solidification to stultification. To understand the classic Western and reactions to it in the forties and thereafter, it is necessary to be familiar with its characteristics.

Central to the classic Western was the hero. He was generally a loner, an individualist who survived in the dangerous world of the frontier by depending primarily on his physical strength and skills, especially in using a gun, and also his inner qualities of courage, resoluteness, integrity, and self-respect. In his relationships with each of the forces impinging on his world, he established a fixed stance and set of values.

Toward nature he was wary, adaptable, and respectful of its destructive potentials. He has learned to hunt, to scout, and to travel long distances across deserts and ranges during all seasons. Since he would have difficulty surviving in this environment without his horse, he took care of the animal and often had a strong attachment to it. A sure sign of a villain was a cowboy who mistreated his horse. In his adaptability, the Western hero was halfway between the townsman or Easterner who could not survive on the plains and the "renegade" who had deserted the white race to live completely in harmony with nature.

In the classic Western, the Indians were usually an extension of the destructive forces of nature. Like windstorms and a scorching sun, they were adjusted to by the hero. He would kill a "redskin" with as little compunction as he would a rattlesnake. In the films of Hart and Anderson, the Indian was often shown some respect at least as a worthy opponent, but in the late twenties and thirties, he was generally a villain to whom murder and treachery were instinctive.

Although the Western hero was primarily an individualist, he knew that situations arose in which he needed the help of friends. Friendship in this predominantly male society was a sacred bond. The appeal for help from a friend could not be denied, and it was axiomatic that one killed unfairly must be avenged. These duties were even more weighty responsibilities if they involved a member of the family, although most heroes appeared to have no living relatives. The hero's closest relationship was often with a "side-kick," a friend, usually comic, who aided him.

One of the reasons trustworthy friends were so essential was the violence indigenous to the frontier. As depicted on the screen, the law was usually in-effectual if existent at all. The gun was so essential in the lawless West that it became an extension of the cowboy and even a personification of the individual, so that a sheriff in forming a posse might announce, "I need a dozen guns" instead of men. The Western hero had to be an expert in handling a gun as well as in using his fists. This gave him great power, but he did not take advantage of it because being a hero, he follows "the code."

The code of honor was the unwritten law of the West. It suited the individualistic hero, for it was a set of restrictions he placed upon himself. Why and how the code came into existence has been argued for decades by historians. One theory suggests that there is an internal mechanism in any society that operates to preserve it. When there is no legal system that maintains order from without, there develops in the members of the society an unconscious need to re-strict dangerous, unbridled individualism. A set of rules or a code comes into being that is supported by the will of the community through its power to deter-mine what is good and what is evil. In medieval times the most powerful individual was the armed knight on horseback. He was accepted if he observed the chiv-alric code; otherwise, he was considered a villain. The parallel between the medieval knight and the Western hero has often been pointed out. The cowboy who was expert with his gun was admired by his peers only if he used his weapon in the service of the community, even if his commitment was, as we shall see, less than complete.

This theory, naturally, is a simplification of com-plex societal forces. And we are dealing in terms of ideals that may or may not have corresponded to

reality. That the Western code of honor was observed as faithfully as appears in films and fiction is question-able, just as the Knights of the Round Table were more likely the stuff of romance than of fact.

We have already noted one tenet of the code: Friendship is an inviolable bond. Equally important, the hero never backs down from a fight, no matter what the odds against him, and he must avenge any affront to his honor. In a confrontation, he faces his enemy and would never think of shooting him in the back; also, he allows his opponent to draw first. Con-sidering how important the horse was on the frontier, it is understandable that a rider is shot at, not his horse. Our hero is always a gentleman toward women, espe-cially one with whom he falls in love. Final in this selected list, he accepts pain and even death as stoi-cally as he does the changing fortunes of life.

The Western hero's attitude toward the law and the town and all they represent (civilization, the East, family, church, the feminine) is ambiguous. He sup-ports them when they are honest and necessary, but he avoids being hemmed in and tamed by them. Being an individual who knows instinctively the difference between right and wrong and who follows his own means to achieve the right earns him inner security and the respect of others. He may have a dubious past or even have been an outlaw—the "good bad man" —but he will still aid anyone threatened by danger. Although he may cooperate with a sheriff (and might be one himself) or the army, he prefers fighting evil alone. The cliché of the hero riding into the sunset at the end of a film underscores his restlessness and need for freedom.

What has just been summarized is a static image of the hero in a Western. Many "B" films were repetitive and dull, especially in the late thirties, be-cause they confined conflicts to those between the hero and the villains. The superficials of the Western were emphasized: gunfights, fistfights, chases, res-cues, and Indian attacks. Wrongdoers were unmiti-gated in their evil and often wore black costumes; heroes were unadulterated in their purity and often wore white. In the best "B" and program Westerns, however, there were internal conflicts, and the hero was a more equivocal figure. The essence of the frontier experience is found in moving beyond romances for adolescents to mature narratives. In such films, the hero has to make choices between diverse commitments.

For instance, the code requires that the hero be loyal to a friend as well as a defender of the right. Suppose, however, the friend is an outlaw. In *The Virginian* (1929), the hero (Figure 8.4) leads a posse in pursuit and capture of a gang of rustlers. One of them turns out to be a close friend who once saved his life, a very likable person who is morally weak. The hero must decide whether or not to hang his friend. Other examples: An Indian may be a person of noble character who cannot be dispatched casually. A cavalry officer is arrogant and stupid, refusing to listen to advice, so he leads his men toward an Indian ambush. Although the hero knows the danger ahead, can he desert those endangered troops? (Wild Bill Hickok faced this dilemma in *The Plainsman.*) Residual resentments from the Civil War and fights between ranchers and sheepherders or farmers also appeared in the classic Western and tested conflicting loyalties of the hero. Is the hero's honor more important than his responsibility to his beloved, who threatens to leave him if he rides into town to face the villains?

---

**FIGURE 8.4**

*The Virginian,* 1929, directed by Victor Fleming. When Gary Cooper as the Virginian first confronts the arrogant Trampas (Walter Huston), he drawls one of the most famous lines in the Western film genre: "When you call me that, smile."

These situations and many others like them could—and in many cases did—become stereotyped. Part of the interest for viewers of the classic Western is the variations conceived by filmmakers within the genre's traditions.

The same type of tension between the familiar and the unexpected existed in character stereotypes. Women in the classic Western play secondary roles and usually fit into two distinct categories. The "good women" consist mainly of those suitable for supplying romance to the Western but also include wives and mothers. The proper young woman represents family and town. She is attractive but not overtly sexual, frequently educated in the East, and courageous but pacifistic. In keeping with the cultural prejudice of Protestant countries, she is often blond. As a binding force, she tempts the hero to forsake his code of honor for the sake of love, family, and survival. On the other hand, there is also the woman who is basically a sex object. She is commonly associated with the saloon as a hostess or owner and is therefore knowledgeable about men and their physical needs. In many cases, she is brunette and may be Mexican or half Indian. As Robert Warshow has pointed out, she accepts the conditions and code of the frontier.[4] Unfortunately for her, she is inevitably rejected by the hero in favor of the "good woman."

Other character stereotypes include the vulnerable Easterner, the ruthless businessman, the villain who is instinctively cruel and sadistic, the comic sidekick, the corrupt or ineffectual sheriff, the arrogant cavalry officer, the bloodthirsty Indian, the virtuous or hypocritical preacher, the drunken doctor, the industrious but helpless farmer, and the shiftless cowboy. Directors of Westerns and their colleagues repeatedly wrought changes in these stereotypes to hold the interest of audiences, but not until after World War II were such changes radical.

The "B" Western, as noted earlier, was the most unsophisticated mode of the classic Western in that it played down the hero's conflict in favor of uncomplicated action. During the thirties it flourished under the Hollywood studio system. Most of the top stars, such as Tom Mix, Ken Maynard, Buck Jones, Harry Carey, and Hoot Gibson, took sound in their stride and continued to have devoted admirers, especially among young people. A few new stars made their appearances. George O'Brien, Johnny Mack Brown, and Warner Baxter are examples. There were, however, only two who, deservedly or not, rivaled the popularity of Tom Mix and William S. Hart.

William Boyd appeared in various Westerns before he found his proper persona in the Hopalong Cassidy series. His efforts were prodigious: Between 1935 and 1951 he starred as Cassidy in 66 features. Later, both films and hero were revived on television. These Westerns were geared to a young audience, so they included a great deal of action and little romance. To some degree the white-haired Boyd's popularity may have been due to the fatherly imagine he presented: He asserted quiet authority, was consistently gentlemanly, and was drawn into occasions to use his gun and fists, rather than seeking them out. He had none of the intensity of Hart or the barely suppressed arrogance of Mix.

Gene Autry introduced new elements into the "B" Westerns that sent shivers of revulsion down the spines of buffs. He was the first prominent singing cowboy. His lilting songs unrelated to plot halted the development of driving narrative action, one of the merits of the genre. Furthermore, it was incongruous for the typically lonely, taciturn hero to vocalize. As if this were not enough of a blow to the vitality of the Western, Autry was also responsible for the "Ten Commandments of the Cowboy." These edicts updated and improved on those of Moses: The hero does not drink or smoke, is a patriot, respects animals, elderly people, and children, helps those in distress, has clean thoughts and personal habits, and so on. If Tom Mix sanitized the Western hero, Autry sterilized him.

Somehow, though, Autry's films struck a responsive chord in contemporary audiences, for they were very popular. He was listed a number of times in surveys of Hollywood's 10 favorite stars. Autry made no pretense of being more than an ingratiating personality, and in the view of the more critical members of his audience, the best acting in his films was contributed by his horse Champion. As with others before him, Autry had found a formula that worked,

and he adhered to it from his first big success in *Tumbling Tumbleweeds* in 1935 until the early fifties. After World War II his films had fewer songs in them and even a soupçon of social consciousness, but by that time his crown had passed to Roy Rogers, and his financial profits were derived primarily from television and the Gene Autry Rodeo.

An offshoot of the "B" Western was the serial. Serials began in 1916 with a 20-episode series entitled *Liberty, A Daughter of the U.S.A.,* continued into the twenties, and reached their heyday in the thirties when a Saturday matinée with a double feature, cartoons, and serials was the climax of the week for school-oppressed youngsters. The most popular Western serial was first released in 1938, and the hero's name is one few Americans will not recognize —the Lone Ranger.

The thirties was not a vintage decade for the program Western. One of the reasons was that although many well-known directors had experience with silent Westerns, none, with the exception of James Cruze, was associated primarily with the genre or even, in the majority of cases, made his best Westerns during the decade. In addition, no major stars emerged who appeared in a series of outstanding Westerns, as later John Wayne, James Stewart, and Randolph Scott were to do in the forties and fifties, although Gary Cooper came closest by being in three fine Westerns. The conventions of the genre had become too rigid and predictable to allow filmmakers a range of creative possibilities.

Although the quality of the program Western in the thirties in sum was unimpressive, a number of distinguished individual films were released. William Wyler's first sound Western, *Hell's Heroes* (1929), is a superior variation of the "three godfathers" story, comparable to Ford's second version in 1948. In the same year appeared the more successful *The Virginian,* directed by Victor Fleming and starring Gary Cooper. It is a compilation of genre clichés, yet somehow is impressive in its total effect. In 1931 Cecil B. De Mille produced his third version of *The Squaw Man,* which attracted attention primarily because it had sound. The director, however, did better in 1937 with *The Plainsman,* an entertaining film that contains an exciting Indian attack. Also notable were Edward L. Cahn's *Law and Order* (1932, unusually realistic in approach for its time), Henry Hathaway's *Thundering Herd* (1934, a Zane Grey story, including one of the first sound versions of the famous gunfight at the OK Corral), and Howard Hawks's *Viva Villa!* (1934).

Perhaps because sound could add so much to visual spectacles, a number of films were made in the thirties that deserve to some degree the appellation of epics. Walsh's *In Old Arizona* has already been mentioned. In 1930 two films appeared with grandiose intentions; both, incidentally, were shot in 70mm gauge for wide screens. King Vidor's *Billy the Kid* is an admirable film, with outstanding performances by Johnny Mack Brown, who started and returned to being a "B"-Western star, and the always dependable Wallace Beery as Pat Garrett. It is generally recognized as the best of the film biographies of the Kid. Raoul Walsh's *The Big Trail* (starring John Wayne) followed basically the same trail as the silent *The Covered Wagon,* though with greater sophistication. In 1932 Wesley Ruggles directed *Cimarron,* with Richard Dix and Irene Dunne. Memorable for a striking land-rush sequence, it was a big commercial success. Disaster rather than success was the fate of *Sutter's Gold* (1936). Even a fine performance by Edward Arnold as Sutter could not compensate for the clumsy directing by James Cruze. In 1936 King Vidor's competent *The Texas Rangers* was released. Also no more than competent were *Wells Fargo* (1937), directed by Frank Lloyd, and James Hogan's *The Texans* (1938).

Nineteen thirty-nine was a watershed year for Hollywood studios. They presented their best face to the world before the transition years of the forties and early fifties, during which the studio system in effect lost its power and vitality. As with so many other genres, the classic Western had a spectacular moment of glory in 1939. In that one year was released *Stagecoach,* Henry King's *Jesse James* (starring Henry Fonda and Tyrone Power), Cecil B. De Mille's *Union Pacific* (Joel McCrea), Michael Curtiz's *Dodge City* (Errol Flynn), George Marshall's *Destry Rides Again* (James Stewart and Marlene Dietrich), John Ford's *Drums Along the Mohawk* (Henry Fonda and Claudette Colbert), Lloyd Bacon's *The Oklahoma Kid*

(Humphrey Bogart and James Cagney), Allan Dwan's *Frontier Marshall* (Randolph Scott and Cesar Romero), George Nichols, Jr.'s *Man of Conquest* (Richard Dix), and Hart's rereleased *Tumbleweeds.*

The most important on this impressive list is John Ford's *Stagecoach.* Like the others, the film was basically a conventional Western, but it also contained elements that anticipated and influenced a new approach to the genre that found its fullest expression in the post–World War II years. This Janus-faced quality is examined in the discussion of *Stagecoach* later in this chapter. Naturally, not every film after 1939 suddenly went beyond the conventions of the classic Western, but in the forties and the decades after, a new spirit pervades most of the finest works in the genre. The classic Western did not die; however, it did metamorphose into something that William S. Hart might have found "rich and strange."

These changes were so various that it is necessary to shift from the chronological approach by decades to a different one. After considering "B" Westerns, directors, actors, and forms of the program Westerns from 1940 to the present (sometimes designated as the post–World War II or modern Western), the remaining pages of this section will be devoted to themes.

The most conservative form of the genre has always been the "B" Western. After the thirties, it doggedly moved along familiar trails, featuring familiar faces, but it soon entered upon rocky terrain. Even in the early forties its popularity was beginning to wane. What kept these low-budget productions going were the singing cowboys, particularly Roy Rogers. During this decade, Rogers, helped by his horse Trigger and his wife Dale Evans, replaced Gene Autry as the "king of the cowboys." Boyish in appearance, dressed in elaborate, immaculate outfits, he was a better singer than cowboy and a better businessman than singer. There were many other singing cowboys in addition to Autry and Rogers, but only Dick Foran and Tex Ritter also achieved star status.

By the mid-fifties, the "B" Western had disappeared from the movie screens. The main reasons for its demise are not difficult to surmise. The rise in production costs and the aging of the most popular stars were factors; most decisive, however, was the rise of television as the chief source of entertainment in America. The Western TV series were not only able to fulfill the desire of audiences for the type of action and settings found in "B" Westerns and develop new heroes but also had the advantage of being free. The early years of television offered opportunities quickly grasped by stars of "B" Westerns. Gene Autry, Roy Rogers, and William Boyd (as Hopalong Cassidy) were especially successful on the small screen in shows for young people. More mature fare for adults as well as youngsters soon followed, and new reputations were made. Two TV series that attracted immense audiences were *Gunsmoke* and *Wyatt Earp,* with James Arness in the former and Hugh O'Brian in the latter. Other popular series included *Bonanza* (with Lorne Greene), *Wagon Train, Wild Bill Hickok* (starring Guy Madison and Andy Devine), *Laramie, Rawhide, Wells Fargo, The Cisco Kid,* and *The Virginian.*

TV Western series were so much in demand in the fifties and sixties that even unconventional forms of the genre were initiated. Action was combined with touches of satire and humor that on occasion approximated wit in *Maverick* (James Garner and later Jack Kelly), *Have Gun, Will Travel* (starring Richard Boone), and, to a lesser degree, *Alias Smith and Jones.* An Indian was one of the main heroes in *Broken Arrow.* Glenn Ford played a modern sheriff in *Cade's County.* During the seventies and early eighties, interest in the TV Western waned. It was not able to meet the challenge of situation comedy, police, and science fiction series. On the other hand, cycles in television are so erratic that the genre might regain its former popularity at any season in the future.

As the "B" Western declined, the program Western became more important and improved in quality; in fact, the decade and a half from the end of World War II to the beginning of the sixties was as close to a golden age as the genre is likely to have. Unlike the thirties, a number of directors associated with the Western did their finest work during this period. Chief among this group are John Ford, Howard Hawks, Anthony Mann, Budd Boetticher, Sam Peckinpah, Henry Hathaway, and John Sturges.

The contributions of John Ford, the director of

Westerns par excellence, are described in the "Background" section of the essay on *Stagecoach* that appears later in this chapter. Howard Hawks was outstanding in every genre he essayed. His fame as a director of Westerns rests primarily on two works, *Red River* (1948) and *Rio Bravo* (1959). The former is superb, and it demonstrates at their best Hawks's gifts for developing taut stories with striking visual effects centering on a group of men who through their camaraderie and courage survive repeated dangers (Figure 8.5). The director's other Westerns (*The Big Sky,* 1952; *El Dorado,* 1967; and *Rio Lobo,* 1970) are less distinguished than his two classics.

---

**FIGURE 8.5**

*Red River,* 1948, directed by Howard Hawks. In this great Western, representatives of two generations of cowboys come into conflict and then are reconciled. In the final sequence, Tom Dunson (John Wayne) and Matthew Garth (Montgomery Clift) end their fistfight when Tess Millay points a gun at them.

Anthony Mann (1906–1967) has become something of a cult figure among students of the Western. His films are filled with realistic action in which setting is of major importance and rendered on the screen with fine sensitivity. His consistent emphasis on violence, at times grisly, perpetrated by cynical, corrupt villains (some of the most fascinating in the modern Western), has caused controversy. In this aspect, as in others, he strongly influenced Sam Peckinpah. Of the 11 Westerns he directed between 1950 and 1960, the most distinctive are *Winchester '73* (1950), *The Naked Spur* (1952), *The Man From Laramie* (1955), *The Last Frontier* (1955), and *Man of the West* (1958).

For many Western buffs, the director with the most impressive oeuvre in the genre after Ford's is Budd Boetticher (1916–). Following his first Western, *The Cimarron Kid* (1951), he made five in 2 years, including *Horizons West* (1952) and *The Man From the Alamo* (1953). In 1956 he began a series of films that had scripts by Burt Kennedy, starred Randolph Scott, and, with the exception of the first one, were produced by Harry Joe Brown. They are sometimes called the "Ranown cycle" because of Brown's association with a company of that name. The cycle consists of seven works: *Seven Men From Now* (1956), *The Tall T* (1957), *Decision at Sundown* (1957), *Buchanan Rides Alone* (1958), *Ride Lonesome* (1959), *Westbound* (1959), and *Comanche Station* (1960). After working on other projects, especially the documentary *Arruza* (1968), on a Mexican bullfighter, Boetticher returned to the Western with *A Time for Dying* (1969).

All of Boetticher's films in the genre were made quickly and inexpensively, so spectacle and production values are at a minimum. He more than makes up for these limitations with unusually intelligent screenplays and a lean, unpretentious directing style. Although action is paramount, he also stresses the sensibilities of his heroes. Usually they are men of integrity who are eager to avoid violence but are forced by the code of revenge to confront evil. As is true of Mann's films, Boetticher's villains are among the most interesting of his characters, and extreme violence appears often. A quality of weariness and disillusionment suffuses most of these works, a sense of men driven into conflict by forces they cannot control and from which even the victor gains little satisfaction. Perhaps this is why Boetticher repeatedly cast Randolph Scott as his hero, an actor in his early fifties when they began their collaboration who even in his youth projected the persona of a strong, taciturn individual who never loses the dignity of a Southern gentleman.

The works of Sam Peckinpah are considered in the "Background" section of the essay on *The Wild Bunch* at the end of this chapter. Henry Hathaway began making Westerns as well as motion pictures in other genres in the early thirties. His most eminent films in the former category, however, appeared in the fifties and sixties, when he directed, among others, *Rawhide* (1951), *North to Alaska* (1960), *The Sons of Katie Elder* (1965), *Nevada Smith* (1966), and *True Grit* (1969). His Westerns are always exciting and competently done but rarely truly memorable. John Sturges is another craftsman who has directed many vigorous Westerns, including *Escape From Fort Bravo* (1953), *Gunfight at the OK Corral* (1957), *Last Train From Gun Hill* (1959), and *The Hallelujah Trail* (1965); his outstanding film in the genre is *The Magnificent Seven* (1960). Among dedicated but not especially distinguished directors of Westerns after 1939 are André de Toth, Burt Kennedy (a far better screenwriter than director), Andrew McLaglen, and George Sherman.

An indication of the popularity of the genre and its increased status after World War II was the number of directors prominent for their achievements in other forms who turned occasionally to the Western. Some of them had gained experience in the thirties and earlier and continued being active: King Vidor (*Duel in the Sun*, 1946, and *Man Without a Star*, 1954), William Wyler (*The Westerner*, 1940; *The Big Country*, 1958; and others), Michel Curtiz (for example, *Virginia City*, 1940, and *The Comancheros*, 1961), Raoul Walsh (*They Died With Their Boots On*, 1941, and more than a dozen others), George Marshall (*Destry Rides Again*, 1939; *The Sheepman*, 1958; and many others), Henry King (*Jesse James*, 1939; *The Gunfighter*, 1950; and *The Bravados*, 1958), and William Wellman (most notably, *The Ox-Bow Incident*, 1943, and *The Track of the Cat*, 1954).

Other well-known directors who made only a limited number of Westerns had little or no experience in the genre before the forties or fifties. Seniority must be granted to Fritz Lang, the great German director who settled in Hollywood in 1935. He made three Westerns in his career, each one to some degree outstanding: *The Return of Frank James* (1940), *Western Union* (1941), and *Rancho Notorious* (1951). John

Huston's efforts in the genre have been confined to *The Treasure of Sierra Madre* (1948), *The Misfits* (1961), and *The Life and Times of Judge Roy Bean* (1972). Nicholas Ray directed four Westerns, the most successful being *The Lusty Men* (1952) and *Johnny Guitar* (1954). Fred Zinnemann's sole effort was *High Noon* (1952) (Figure 8.6). George Stevens directed only two outstanding Westerns, *Shane* (1953), discussed later in this chapter, and *Giant* (1956). Delmer Daves was more prolific in the genre; his most popular works were *Broken Arrow* (1950), *3:10 to Yuma* (1957), and *The Badlanders* (1958). Arthur Penn turned to the Western for *The Left-Handed Gun* (1958), *Little Big Man* (1970), and *The Missouri Breaks* (1975). Of the five Westerns directed by Robert Aldrich, three should be mentioned: *Apache* (1954), *Vera Cruz* (1954), and *Ulzana's Raid* (1972). Samuel Fuller's other four excursions into the genre are not up to the level of *Run of the Arrow*

(1957). George Roy Hill did exceptionally well at the box office with his first Western, *Butch Cassidy and the Sundance Kid* (1969). Robert Altman rarely makes conventional films, and his two Westerns to date are not exceptions: *McCabe and Mrs. Miller* (1972) (Figure 8.6) and *Buffalo Bill and the Indians* (1976). Naturally, this list could be considerably expanded to include less prominent directors. Some of them are noted later.

Most male stars of the post–World War II decades appeared, if at all suitable, in at least one Western. Some of them, however, even if better

---

**FIGURE 8.6**

*High Noon,* 1952, directed by Fred Zinnemann. Marshal Will Kane (Gary Cooper) faces a group of outlaws without help from the frightened townspeople. In this masterful crane shot, the camera slowly moves upward until we see Kane as a small figure on a deserted street.

known for their work in other genres, were featured in a number of Westerns. John Wayne in John Ford's films immediately comes to mind. James Stewart starred in five of Anthony Mann's Westerns as well as those of other directors. Randolph Scott was Budd Boetticher's favorite actor. Among those who repeatedly turned to the genre were Gary Cooper, Henry Fonda, Joel McCrea, William Holden, Glenn Ford, Gregory Peck, Burt Lancaster, Robert Taylor, Richard Widmark, Kirk Douglas, Lee Marvin, and Charlton Heston. (This list could be doubled and tripled.) Mention must also be made of actors who regularly appeared in secondary roles, so important in the Western. A few among dozens of possible names: Walter Brennan, Andy Devine, Robert Ryan, Tim Holt, Arthur Kennedy, Harry Carey, Jr., Lee Van Cleef, George "Gabby" Hayes, John Ireland, Slim Pickens, and Warren Oates.

With outstanding directors and actors—as well as screenwriters, composers, and other filmmakers—working in the genre, it is not surprising that many exceptional program Westerns were released in the three decades following 1939. Also inevitable, considering the radical changes that occurred during this span of time in American history, culture, and methods of film production, were departures from the conventions of the classic Western in its forms and themes. The epic in particular was affected. As noted earlier, in the twenties and thirties, this form of the Western commemorated proud moments in the history of the frontier. This tradition continued in Cecil B. De Mille's *Union Pacific,* Michael Curtiz's *Santa Fe Trail* (1940), Fritz Lang's *Western Union,* Raoul Walsh's *The Tall Men* (1955), and William Wyler's *The Big Country.* Problems for the epic Western had developed, however, as exemplified by two films. *The Alamo* (1960, directed by and starring John Wayne) was a commercial success, but even the most indulgent critic found it old-fashioned and its blatant patriotism embarrassing. In *How the West Was Won* (1962, with individual sections directed by John Ford, George Marshall, and Henry Hathaway), a diffuseness and meretriciousness suggested that the three directors were themselves not convinced of the validity of what they were creating.

What undermined the effectiveness of these

two films was the development in the post–World War II era, especially in the sixties and seventies, of a skepticism about the virtures of the frontier heritage and the traditions of the classic Western. This meant that if the epic Western was to survive, it had either to be defensive about our past glories, as in *How the West Was Won,* or devise a new outlook. The latter approach has generally prevailed. Epic scope and spectacle have been preserved; however, major characters are far less heroic, and some are even antiheroes.

As early as the forties, a few epics were moving in this direction. King Vidor's *Duel in the Sun* has as its setting the immense cattle ranches that were being built in the early days of Texas; however, the code of honor is generally replaced by torrid sensuality (when the film was released, one wag referred to it as "Lust in the Dust"). In Howard Hawks's splendid *Red River,* the main character, played by John Wayne, is not only fallible and flawed, but his major conflict is with his foster son, representing a new generation of cattlemen, rather than outlaws or Indians. Only a matter of degree separates these two Western epics from Sergio Leone's *Once Upon a Time in the West* (1969), saturated with violent combat and sex, and Robert Altman's *Buffalo Bill and the Indians* (1976), in which one of the great heroes of the frontier is revealed as a poseur haunted by feelings of guilt about his past.

In the Altman film, the Indians are shown to have more fortitude and dignity than the white man. One of the fundamental traditions of the classic epic Western is thus reversed. This perspective is evident in two of the most spectacular Westerns of the sixties and seventies, classic epics in every sense except the identity of the heroes. In John Ford's *Cheyenne Autumn* (1964), the Indians rather than the cowboys and cavalry receive our admiration and respect. *Little Big Man* consists of the reminiscences of a 121-year-old frontiersman who was brought up by the Cheyenne. Through the eyes of a white man who is more survivor than hero, we see the massacres of Indians from the victims' point of view.

Another type of unconventional hero appears in Jan Troell's two-part *The Emigrants* (1969, 1972). It is by a Swedish director, and the opening sequences take place in Sweden. Yet there are few contemporary films that have captured with such realism and compassion the hardships and satisfactions of nineteenth-century pioneers in America. The Swedes settling in the wilderness of Michigan, contending with poverty, nature, loneliness, and Indians, are as much a part of the story of the opening and closing of the West as cowboys and Indians.

Different types of heroes, reversals of traditions, sex, violence—all have influenced the content of the modern epic Western. In our time this form of the genre will apparently be accepted by audiences only if it combines sophisticated realism, an infusion of irony, and heroes drawn to a human scale and presents this approach with the scope and spectacle that only the epic can supply.

The mode of the Western furthest removed from the serious, history-encrusted epic is, of course, the comedy. Most classic Westerns of any type contained some efforts at humor, especially as provided by the sidekick of the hero. As indicated earlier, however, Western comedy in the twenties and thirties was generally an impoverished form. Then in 1939 was released a spoof of the genre that was witty and projected a vitality not seen on the screen since the appearances of Douglas Fairbanks in Westerns. George Marshall's *Destry Rides Again* (Figure 8.7) took full advantage of the incongruity of a pacifist sheriff.

---
**FIGURE 8.7**

*Destry Rides Again,* 1939, directed by George Marshall. Tom Destry (James Stewart) has as much trouble calming Frenchy (Marlene Dietrich) as fighting the villains.

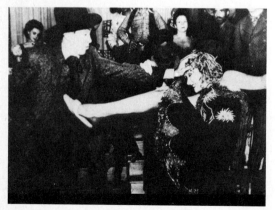

Since *Destry Rides Again,* the most popular Western comedies have been farces serving as vehicles for well-known comedians. The Marx Brothers, Bob Hope, Jack Benny, Martin and Lewis, and Abbott and Costello all created films in which they dressed as cowboys and acted as inept tenderfoots. The Marx Brothers in *Go West* (1940, not to be confused with Buster Keaton's 1925 film with the same title) and Bob Hope in *The Paleface* (1947) are two of the most enjoyable. More recent successful comedies are *Cat Ballou* (1964, directed by Elliott Silverstein) and Mel Brooks's *Blazing Saddles* (1973).*

Most Western comedies are farces, perhaps because there have been so many variations of conventional genre formulas that only gross exaggeration makes it clear that humor is intended. Some have been only mildly parodic, such as Stuart Heisler's *Along Came Jones* (1954, starring Gary Cooper) and Henry Hathaway's *North to Alaska* (starring John Wayne). More pointed satire is to be found in George Marshall's *The Sheepman,* with Glenn Ford as a crafty sheepherder who cons a cattle town into accepting him. Burt Kennedy has a talent for making Western comedies, as illustrated by *Support Your Local Sheriff* (1968) and *The Good Guys and the Bad Guys* (1969). The former, starring James Garner, is a particularly imaginative parody.

In the 1960s a category of the Western came into prominence that is not a separate form but contains certain emphases that set it apart from its contemporaries in the genre. The "spaghetti Western" is the best known of the "non-American Westerns" (actually a contradictory term), which includes not only those made in Italy and Germany ("sauerkraut Westerns") but also adaptations of the genre in countries throughout the world. It was in Italy, however, beginning with Sergio Leone's *A Fistful of Dollars* (1964), that a distinctive style developed. The spaghetti Western took specific traits that became prevalent in the genre in the United States during the late forties and fifties—focus on the antihero, sex, violence, other shock effects, and stark realism—and inflated them as much as censorship in Italy and the United States

---

*p. 316

allowed. As might be expected, this type of Western has been commercially successful.

At their worst, spaghetti Westerns have exploited the puerile desires of some contemporary moviegoers for indiscriminate sex and violence on the screen. At their best, they have created convincing nightmare worlds in which cruelty and brutality are rampant and "good bad men" are a cut above the villains only in their determination, passion for vengeance, and steely courage. Such super antiheroes were played repeatedly by Clint Eastwood and Lee Van Cleef. It is surprising, however, how many superior actors have also appeared in spaghetti Westerns, including Henry Fonda, Joseph Cotten, Jason Robards, Jr., Eli Wallach, and Arthur Kennedy.

Probably the finest of this type of Western has been Sergio Leone's *Once Upon a Time in the West* (starring Henry Fonda, Charles Bronson, Jason Robards, Jr., Claudia Cardinale, and Woody Strode). Although some critics have roundly condemned this work, it is a powerful, memorable film with a number of spectacular scenes. Some other examples of above-average spaghetti Westerns are Leone's Clint Eastwood trilogy (*A Fistful of Dollars, For a Few Dollars More,* 1965, and *The Good, the Bad, and the Ugly,* 1966); Duccio Tessari's *A Pistol for Ringo* (1965); Joaquin Romero Marchent's *Seven From Texas* (1964); Giuseppe Colizzi's *Revenge in El Paso* (1968); and Franco Giraldi's *Dead or Alive* (1968).

Since the beginning of the forties, whatever the form of a program Western, certain themes or emphases have appeared repeatedly. Central ones of the classic Western have been either discarded or, more often, retained but renovated. A prime force prompting these changes originated in the motion picture industry's competition from television. With the new medium presenting what amounted to a variety of weekly "B" Westerns, the genre had to offer qualities not to be found on the small screen. Spectacle in color on enlarged screens, sex, and violence were some of the devices filmmakers found effective, as well as more expensive productions and, whenever possible, the use of star actors and actresses not necessarily associated with the genre. Other pressures that encouraged new attitudes came from reactions of Americans to contemporary historical events and al-

tered social mores. Our resorting to atomic bombings, the Joseph McCarthy years, and the Korean and Vietnam wars, among other events, fostered revisionist views of the American heritage, which did not exempt myths about the frontier and its heroes. Ever-increasing freedom for the arts in dealing with once taboo subjects began in the early fifties. The civil rights movement and the militancy of other minority groups, including women, also had their effects on Westerns made after World War II.

For better or worse, the genre during the 3½ decades to 1980 underwent a bewildering number of changes. In fact, so many various new themes and emphases appeared in the modern Western (one of its characteristics is a search, at times desperate, for unusual approaches and novelties) that we can consider in this brief survey only seven significant ones: sex and women, violence, the new realism, changing images of the hero, Indians and social criticism, a focus on the disappearance of the frontier, and contemporary Westerns.

Sex was carefully differentiated from love in the classic Western and was rarely more than implied. Cracks had appeared in the taboo against sex before the 1940s, as in *Destry Rides Again* and *Stagecoach* (in which a prostitute is the heroine), but the first film to make a conspicuous point of sexuality in a Western (practically its only point) was Howard Hughes's *The Outlaw* (1943). Rio, played by Jane Russell, equipped with a superfluous special brassiere designed by her director, is a compliant sex machine for the gratification of Billy the Kid. Two years later, *Duel in the Sun* paired Gregory Peck and Jennifer Jones in scenes that burned to ashes most of the "Thou Shalt Nots" in Gene Autry's "Ten Commandments of the Cowboy." In the 1950s, viewers took in stride nude bathing in Lesley Selander's *Shotgun* (1955) and a nymphomaniac in Delmer Daves's *Jubal* (1956). By the 1960s and the advent of spaghetti Westerns, there hardly remained an explicit presentation of sex between man and woman that could not sneak past a lenient Production Code to shock audiences.

Many viewers, particularly males, approved of sexual explicitness. Others, however, especially females, strongly objected to at least one ramification of this new freedom: Although women became more central in the plots of Westerns, they were transformed from vapid virgins or wasted whores to exploited sex objects. This is not to assert that all female characters were complete stereotypes even in the classic Western. For example, in *The Plainsman,* Calamity Jane is a woman superior to most men in handling a gun or a whip. And there was Marlene Dietrich; somehow, whether in *Destry Rides Again, The Spoilers* (1942), or *Rancho Notorious,* she never gave the impression that she was an auxiliary personality used by men. Generally, however, even in the forties and fifties, women were secondary, undeveloped characters subordinated to the will of their fathers, brothers, husbands, and lovers.

In the mid-1960s, signs of a radical change began to appear. In *Cat Ballou,* Jane Fonda plays a young woman who holds her own with any male she meets. Cat would have been the most intriguing individual in the film if Lee Marvin had not upstaged Fonda with his bravura performance as the Shelleen brothers. More recently, a Western was released in which the main female character is as emancipated for the time setting of the film as any contemporary feminist. Less attention, unfortunately, was paid to this aspect of *The Missouri Breaks* than the self-indulgent overacting of Marlon Brando. It seems probable that these two films, and others, are not simply aberrations but harbingers of a type of Western of the future in which women will be presented as three-dimensional individuals instead of the stereotypes of the past.

Violence, like sex, was muted in the classic Western. Fights with guns and fists were taken for granted, yet the camera recorded them with discretion. Audiences did not see a bullet tear into flesh, only the victim's hand covering a blood-soaked spot and his body collapsing to the ground. Indian massacres were indicated by feet protruding from under blankets. Even these cautious visual statements were often considered too vivid by parents who sent their youngsters to matinées in the twenties and thirties. The response of Tom Mix and, to even a greater degree, Gene Autry was to minimize violence and substitute for it acrobatics, horsemanship, and fights with guns and fists that were unrealistically free of blood and pain. Program features followed "B" Westerns in

restricting violence as much as possible, using implicit means to suggest the ruggedness of frontier life.

All this changed after 1939. Increasingly, manifest violence became a component of Westerns, as it did in gangster and war films, other genres involving guns and struggles to the death. Some of the older directors, like Ford and Hawks, disdained using excessive violence in their films. On the other hand, the veteran King Vidor combined it and sexuality in *Duel in the Sun.* The two most prominent new directors of the fifties, Anthony Mann and Budd Boetticher, made graphic depictions of physical cruelty a characteristic of their styles. The best-known creator of Westerns during the sixties and seventies, Sam Peckinpah, does not hesitate to splatter blood and guts on the screen. Spaghetti Westerns sustain their popularity by exploiting violence and sex. A recent film, *The Return of a Man Called Horse* (1976, directed by Elliot Silverstein), repeats a sequence from its predecessor, *A Man Called Horse* (1970): an Indian initiation ritual in which the hero is hung up by his pectoral muscles. So long as explicit violence continues to appeal to audiences, as it obviously does, this type of intensified sensationalism will remain an integral part of most Westerns.

One of the justifications often offered by defenders of graphic violence in modern Westerns is the inevitability of this trend as the genre after World War II became more realistic. Individual efforts toward intensified realism (always keeping in mind the relativity of the term) within the rigid conventions of the classic Western have already been indicated. In the forties, some directors, such as John Ford and Howard Hawks, instilled in the classic Western at least a degree of psychological realism; that is, they went beyond stereotypes and presented characters, even legendary heroes, as flawed human beings with internal conflicts that went beyond those intrinsic in the code of honor.

What occurred in the fifties was that younger filmmakers (young in experience with the Western, not necessarily in chronological age), for example, Mann and Boetticher, built upon the innovations of the older generation that was active in the forties in exploring new areas of intensified physical and psychological realism. The problem faced by these directors was how far they could go in developing a new dimension of realism in the Western without completely undermining the myths of the genre. The tension that resulted supplied one of the major fascinations for discerning members of audiences of the modern Western. George Stevens's *Shane* epitomizes the conflict; later in this chapter, the film is examined particularly from this perspective.

Ambiguities proliferated: Heroes are subject to lust and doubts, Indians are not necessarily villains, villains are not always completely evil; the code of honor has not crumbled but is no longer inflexible; and representatives of the law are at times as corrupt as the outlaws they pursue. Though Shanes still wandered the land and patriots dedicated to Manifest Destiny continued to defend the Alamo, frontier life has generally been deromanticized since the fifties. It has become more barren, crude, and cruel, with fewer moments of genuine heroism, altruism, and patriotism to brighten the human landscape as impressively as the physical setting, the one element in the Western that has remained unchanged.

The contemporary generation, which sometimes finds pre–World War II works of the genre laughable and unrealistic, tends to forget that the violence in a Peckinpah Western or the cynicism in one by Altman is no less the result of a director's personal interpretation of the past, influenced by the attitudes of our time, than the artificial traditions of the classic Western. Perhaps Buffalo Bill was the fraud Altman depicts and the Wild Bunch a group of brutal, aging outlaws. We can never know without access to a model of H. G. Wells's time machine. What we have learned from historical scholarship, however, is that an age reconstructs the past in terms of its world-view of the present. Altman's Buffalo Bill is as much a product of the Vietnam debacle and the fall of Richard Nixon as he is of research that demonstrated the extent to which the most famous scout of the West was a creation of the imagination of the reporter E. Z. C. Judson.

So pervasive has been the new realism in the modern Western and so varied its manifestations that it is impossible here to do more than highlight a few

prominent examples. The first dark buds of iconoclasm began to appear in the forties. *The Ox-Bow Incident* is a Western without a hero, and its main character, played by Henry Fonda, vomits after excessive drinking, an action that would not have appeared on screen in a classic Western. *The Treasure of Sierra Madre* takes place in Mexico in 1920. It does belong to the genre, however, even though, in addition to its atypical time and place settings, nature is relentlessly oppressive and the major characters are consumed by avarice and selfishness. In the 1950s the films of Anthony Mann and Budd Boetticher were filled with shabby towns, sadistic villains, and reluctant heroes. The epitome of preoccupation with sex and violence was reached in the 1960s in the spaghetti Westerns, and Sam Peckinpah began his series of impressive Westerns, which feature graphic violence, betrayal, and cruelty.

Uncompromising details of Indian life and the crimes of the white man against this race are presented in *Little Big Man.* Perhaps no director has been more iconoclastic in his portrayal of frontier life than Robert Altman in *McCabe and Mrs. Miller* or deflated a national Western hero more completely than in his *Buffalo Bill and the Indians.* Other films of the early seventies that are notable for the extent to which they depart from whatever was romantic in the traditions of the classic Western include *Monte Walsh* (1970, directed by William A. Fraker), *Valdez Is Coming* (1971, Edwin Sherin), *The Great Northfield Minnesota Raid* (1972, Philip Kaufman), *The Culpepper Cattle Company* (1972, Dick Richards) (Figure 8.8), and *Jeremiah Johnson* (1972, Sidney Pollack).

Related to the new realism in the modern Western are changes in the standards whereby heroes and villains are judged. There were no questions in the classic Western about the characteristics of the hero or the people he fought against; if not literally, at least figuratively, the former wore white and the latter black. For purposes of plot complication, there might be doubts at some point about the virtues of the main character, but in the end he always demonstrated his courage, skill, adherence to the code, respect for women, and intrinsic goodness. During and after the fifties, however, the clay feet of a hero became almost

FIGURE 8.8

*The Culpepper Cattle Company,* 1972, directed by Dick Richards (color). This tale of a young man (Gary Grimes, standing to the right) growing up while working as a cook's helper on a cattle drive rises above the level of an average Western by virtue of its realistic presentation of the violent, grimy, impecunious life of ordinary cowboys.

as prominent as his accurate shooting hand. The term *antihero* in the Western usually does not refer to a character entirely devoid of admirable qualities or incapable of demonstrating courage but one who rejects the heroic ideal and acts from necessity rather than conviction and the need for self-respect.

There is a wide range of types of antiheroes and various degrees of antiheroic actions. Some filmmakers carry the concept of the Western antihero to extremes, so that he is either an unattractive person, as in *Johnny Concho* (1956, directed by Don McGuire), or a dangerous neurotic (for example, in *The Left-Handed Gun; One-Eyed Jack,* 1961, directed by Marlon Brando; and *The Hired Hand,* 1971, directed by Peter Fonda). Most directors and screenwriters, however, have confined their iconoclasm to creating characters who have at least one redeeming quality beyond a physical toughness—perhaps dignity, stubbornness, faithfulness, or courage—to compensate to some extent for cynicism, ruthlessness, greed, or self-doubt. It is sometimes necessary to scratch deep before being able to tell the difference between hero and villain. The film featuring a conventional hero has not disappeared—for every *The Naked Spur* and *The Deadly Companions* (1961, directed by Sam Peckin-

pah) there is an *Hombre* (1966, directed by Martin Ritt) and *The Magnificent Seven*—but the antihero has become increasingly prevalent.

Changing the characteristics of the hero has had a number of ramifications. An especially interesting one is a new perspective on the law and outlaws. Legendary lawbreakers, such as Jesse James, Billy the Kid, and Doc Holliday, appeared in innumerable classic Westerns, but in most cases their antisocial activities were justified or extenuated. The innovation of the sixties and seventies has been to present the law as morally dubious as the outlaws (another example of the influence of current events on the Western). In *The Wild Bunch, Butch Cassidy and the Sundance Kid,* and *The Missouri Breaks,* for example, we root for the criminals because they are at least no worse than the men who pursue them and possess a good deal more vitality.

Villains have not changed greatly in their negative qualities; they have simply become more brutal and sadistic since the fifties. In some films, however, they have been made three-dimensional characters rather than simply personifications of evil, as, say, Liberty Valance in the John Ford film. They may even be given a chance to explain, though rarely justify, their murderous acts; for instance, Ryker is given such an opportunity in *Shane.* *

The most radical revision of attitudes toward a category of villains in the classic Western involves a whole race. American Indians progressed in three decades from consistently being miscreants to either being heroes or at least belonging to a race with a heritage and way of life worthy of respect. One film more than any other initiated a trend toward more honest presentations of the white man–Indian conflict: Delmer Daves's *Broken Arrow.* Tradition was violated by a story of a white man (James Stewart) married—happily, no less—to an Indian princess. The film also contains an Indian warrior (Jeff Chandler) with the heroic qualities previously reserved for white men.

It took 4 years for the lesson to be absorbed; then, in 1954, two Westerns were released that were sympathetic to the plight of the "redskin": *Apache* starred Burt Lancaster as a noble Indian, and *Broken*

---

*p. 418

*Lance* (1954, directed by Edward Dmytryk) featured in its plot how the Indian wife of Spencer Tracy is subjected to the scorn of the prejudiced Richard Widmark. John Ford in *The Searchers* (1956) and then in *Cheyenne Autumn* did penance for his previous racial narrow-mindedness by creating two memorable films that described the dignity and integrity of the Indian people and the harassment with which they had to contend. *Run of the Arrow* is outstanding in its uncompromising honesty. A white man adapts himself to Indian life and marries an Indian; however, in the end he leaves when he cannot accept the savage treatment of an enemy. A decade later a similar conflict of cultures (that is, murder justified by Indian tradition but not by the white man's law) is the subject of Abraham Polonsky's *Tell Them Willie Boy Is Here* (1969).

Only one film sympathetic to the Indians, however, has the epic scope of Ford's *Cheyenne Autumn,* and that is *Little Big Man.* Other films of the seventies that made a major point of dealing fairly with Indians include *A Man Called Horse* and its sequel, *Soldier Blue* (1972, directed by Ralph Nelson), *Jeremiah Johnson,* and *Buffalo Bill and the Indians.*

Although less extensive than in the case of the Indians, portrayals of members of other minority groups have been more positive since the 1960s. Mexicans and Mexican-Americans have ceased to be exclusively comic characters or vulgar villains. They are presented as individuals and even heroes in, for example, *Valdez Is Coming* and many of the films of Sam Peckinpah. Blacks also have gone beyond prejudiced stereotypes and well-intentioned but condescending characterizations, as in *Sergeants Three* (1962, John Sturges). More than any other actor, Woody Strode, with his impressive physical presence and inveterate dignity, demonstrated the potentials of blacks in Westerns. In the early seventies appeared *Man and Boy* (1972, by E. W. Swackhamer) and *Buck and the Preacher* (1972, by Sidney Poitier). It is inevitable that other, more important Westerns featuring black actors and made by black filmmakers will be released in the future.

The growing awareness on the part of makers of Westerns during the post–World War II decades of a responsibility toward minority groups was part of an increasing consciousness of social issues. In the classic Western, moral choices and actions were based on the code and individual concepts of justice. The historical events of the forties dissuaded many filmmakers from blithely producing Westerns in which men with guns ignored the ramifications of taking the law into their own hands and the individual's deciding for himself the extent of his guilt in killing another human being.

The nature of this change in attitude becomes clearer if we compare the lynchings in two films separated by a decade and a half. In *The Virginian* (1929), the hero is torn between duty to the law and his friendship for one of a gang of rustlers. Not once does he, or even his friend, question that the cattlemen have the right to hang the thieves immediately after they are captured. The main theme of *The Ox-Bow Incident* (1943) is that group passions and prejudices are not a substitute for a duly appointed judge and jury and can result in irrevocable injustice. Such films as *High Noon* and *3:10 to Yuma* pose the problem of whether a community is worth saving if it refuses to face up to its responsbilities. On the other side of the coin, there are films (for example, *The Wild Bunch* and Ted Post's *Hang 'Em High,* 1968) in which we are led to wonder whether the most reprehensible "murderers" are not those who have the law on their side and order others to do the capturing and killing for them. These and similar social and moral dilemmas are to be found in the classic Western, but not with the same frequency or complexity and centrality as in the modern Western.

With the breakdown or transformation of many of the traditions of the classic Western, films appeared with heroes who felt that the old West was passing or had passed. Aging cowboys were not unknown before the forties. After all, William S. Hart was 44 when he made his first film in the genre, and he looked his age. What was relatively new in the post–World War II Western were heroes no longer young who looked with nostalgia to an earlier, simpler period. A list of outstanding films emphasizing the contrast of old and new might begin with Hawks's *Red River.* As discussed later in this chapter,* in many of the last West-

━━━━━━━━
*pp. 406–407

erns of John Ford, especially *The Man Who Shot Liberty Valance,* there is often an unstated question (to quote Wordsworth): "Where is it now, the glory and the dream?"

A longing for things past is not confined to directors in their advancing years, such as Hawks and Ford, both born before 1900, or Henry King in his mid-fifties when he made *The Gunfighter* (1950). Budd Boetticher, a post–World War II director, has as the hero of most of his best Westerns an aging, disillusioned gunfighter played by Randolph Scott. Sam Peckinpah also features cowboys and gunfighters who are past their prime.

One way in which a director and screenwriter could make this theme convincing was to have as a time setting the early twentieth century, when frontier life was near its end. Peckinpah's *The Wild Bunch* takes place in 1916 and describes the last exploits of a band of men who can no longer survive as outlaws in the American West. In the same director's *The Ballad of Cable Hogue* (1970), the hero, an old-time prospector, is killed, literally and symbolically, by a motorcar rolling over him. Lack of opportunities to practice their trade motivates the emigration of Butch Cassidy and the Sundance Kid to South America in George Roy Hill's film. And it is a white-haired Buffalo Bill and dying Geronimo we observe in Altman's *Buffalo Bill and the Indians.*

While a number of filmmakers concentrated their attention on the closing options for aging frontiersmen, others attempted to revitalize the Western by giving it a modern setting. This was not a new idea; as early as 1916 Douglas Fairbanks's *Manhattan Madness* had a contemporary setting. A trend toward this type of Western began in the fifties with Nicholas Ray's *The Lusty Men* (1952) and John Sturges's *Bad Day at Black Rock* (1954). It continued in the 1960s and 1970s: *The Misfits, Lonely Are the Brave* (1962, directed by David Miller), *Hud* (1963, Martin Ritt), *Monte Walsh* (1970, William A. Fraker), *Billy Jack* (1971, T. C. Frank) and its sequel, *The Trial of Billy Jack* (1975). Practically all these films, and others in this category, have one characteristic in common: a conflict between the qualities that won the West and still haunt those who live on ranches and participate

in rodeos and the aseptic, bureaucratic, materialistic values of our modern mechanistic age. Usually, representatives of the latter have the power, but those inspired by the former have the spirit that results in at least a moral victory.

So many radical changes have occurred in the Western since World War II that prophets of doom have declared it a dying genre, and they support this contention by pointing out that since the mid-seventies few Westerns of any distinction were released. The years 1970–1976 witnessed the last Westerns of Peckinpah, Altman's two distinctive contributions to the genre, Penn's *Little Big Man* and *The Missouri Breaks,* Troell's epic, Silverstein's *A Man Called Horse* and its sequel, Pollack's *Jeremiah Johnson,* Huston's *The Life and Times of Judge Roy Bean,* and other works mentioned earlier. Of somewhat less distinction were *The Hired Hand* (directed by Peter Fonda), *Ulzana's Raid* (Aldrich), *The Man Who Loved Cat Dancing* (1973, Richard C. Sarafian), *Bite the Bullet* (1975, Richard Brooks), *Posse* (1975, Kirk Douglas), *The Outlaw Josey Wales* (1976, Clint Eastwood), and *The Dutchess and the Dirtwater Fox* (1976, Melvin Frank), among others. In contrast, one is hard put to name a truly outstanding Western made since 1976. Respectable efforts include *Goin' South* (1978, Jack Nicholson), *Butch and Sundance: The Early Days* (1979, Richard Lester), *Comes a Horseman* (1978, Alan. J. Pakula), *Eagle's Wing* (1979, Anthony Harvey), *Tom Horn* (1980, William Wiard), and *The Long Riders* (1980, Walter Hill). Of dubious distinction is the fact that Michael Cimino's *Heaven's Gate* (1980), the most expensive Western ever made, had a disastrous premiere and had to be reedited before its official release. This is hardly an impressive list, so the pessimists on the fate of the genre may be right.

Perhaps we have grown so skeptical that we can only scoff at the idea that heroes, even ones with clay feet, once existed. Perhaps we have become jaded and blasé, so that we can no longer react to myths of unambiguous conflicts of good and evil, of ideals and reality unless wrapped in layers of cynicism, sex, and violence. If this is so, the Western is doomed. On the other hand, perhaps we can still respond to the idea that once upon a time in our history, men and women believed, no matter what the reality, in a vision of freedom and self-sufficiency. Perhaps we still retain enough innocence to enjoy last-minute rescues and gunfights between larger-than-life characters. If this is so, the Western will continue to thrill, entertain, and, at its best, move us.

## CLASSIC WESTERN IN TRANSITION

### *Stagecoach*

*To find the unusual in the commonplace, the heroic in the everyday, is a dramatic device that suits me.*
John Ford, 1956[5]

Q:          *Stagecoach is a landmark in the history of Westerns. Were you aware of that when you made the film?*
FORD:     *Of course not! I liked the story, it was a little bit different. A lot of action, a few good characters. The budget was low. We made the film in three weeks.*
Interview with John Ford, 1966[6]

**CAST**

*John Wayne (Ringo Kid), Claire Trevor (Dallas), Thomas Mitchell (Dr. Josiah Boone), John Carradine (Hatfield), Andy Devine (Buck), Louise Platt (Lucy Mallory), Donald Meek (Samuel Peacock), George Bancroft (Marshal Curly Wilcox), Berton Churchill (Henry Gatewood), and others.*

**CREDITS**

*Director—John Ford, Producer—Walter Wanger, Screenwriter—Dudley Nichols (from "Stage to Lordsburg," a short story by Ernest Haycox), Directors of Photography—Bert Glennon and Ray Binger, Composers—Richard Hageman, Frank Harling, and Louis Gruenberg, Second-Unit Director—Yakima Canutt, Editors—Dorothy Spencer and Walter Reynolds, and others.*

1939/United Artists
Black & White/96 minutes

### BACKGROUND

The list of films directed by John Ford (1895–1973), compiled during half a century, is one of the most impressive in the history of American cinema. As remarkable as the quality and quantity of his over 125 features is that much of his best work is in the genre

of the Western. In fact, he is the nonpareil director of Westerns, the standard by which all others are judged.

At the age of 18, Sean Aloysius O'Feeny (Ford's actual name) left Maine and went to Hollywood to join his brother Francis, who had adopted the name Ford for his work as an actor, director, and writer at Universal Pictures. Jack Ford, the name Sean assumed until 1923, started his motion picture career as a stunt man and bit actor. Soon, however, he was promoted to writer and assistant director. In 1917 he wrote and directed his first film, a short Western titled *Tornado*, for Universal. He became known for his work in this genre, particularly for a popular series (26 films) starring Harry Carey as Cheyenne Harry.

After moving to Fox Film Corp. in 1921, Ford continued to specialize in Westerns, his most important feature being *The Iron Horse* (1924).* *Three Bad Men* (1926) was the last Western he worked on until 1939. Included among the more than two dozen dramas he directed during the thirties were *Men Without Women* (1930), *Arrowsmith* (1931), *The Lost Patrol* (1934), *The Informer* (1935, for which he won his first Academy Award), *The Whole Town's Talking* (1935), *The Plough and the Stars* (1936), and *Wee Willie Winkie* (1937). The year 1939 was an annus mirabilis for Ford as well as the whole Hollywood film industry. He not only returned to the Western with the innovative *Stagecoach* but also directed *Drums Along the Mohawk* and *Young Mr. Lincoln*. The same year he began one of his most famous films, *The Grapes of Wrath* (1940, for which he received his second Academy Award).

In the early forties he completed, among others, *Tobacco Road* (1941) and *How Green Was My Valley* (1941, resulting in a third Academy Award for directing). During World War II he directed (with Robert Montgomery) the war drama *They Were Expendable* (1945), as well as documentaries for the U.S. Navy and Marines, most notably *The Battle of Midway* (1942). The first film Ford worked on after the war was a Western, the beginning of a series that constitutes a high-water mark in the history of the genre.

*pp. 388–389

*My Darling Clementine* (1946) (Figure 8.9) is the favorite of many devotees of Ford Westerns and definitely one of the most carefully structured and subtle in characterization of them. It is an account of the events in Tombstone that led to the gunfight at the OK Corral. Henry Fonda is excellent as Wyatt Earp, and Victor Mature gives one of his best performances as the consumptive Doc Holliday.

---
**FIGURE 8.9**

*My Darling Clementine,* 1946. In the last shot of this film, Wyatt Earp (Henry Fonda) rides away from Tombstone and Clementine Carter (Cathy Downs), though he hopes to return. It illustrates the impressive settings Ford found in Monument Valley, Arizona.

During the next 4 years, Ford directed five Westerns. Three of them are often bracketed together as a trilogy because they all deal with the U.S. cavalry. In *Fort Apache* (1948), Henry Fonda plays an arrogant, Indian-hating officer who leads his men into a massacre. *She Wore a Yellow Ribbon* (1949) is another of the director's Westerns that ranks among his very best. John Wayne is a captain close to retirement age who must face both a lonely future and a threatening Indian war. *Rio Grande* (1950) also stars Wayne, once again as an aging cavalry officer, who in the midst of an Apache uprising is reunited with his estranged wife (Maureen O'Hara). The two noncavalry Westerns are *Three Godfathers* (1948) and *Wagonmaster* (1950), the latter one of Ford's most lyric films. Although a simple story (conceived by the director

himself) of the trials of a wagon train journeying westward, it is magnificently photographed.

During the late forties and early fifties, the director also worked on dramas, the most prominent being *The Fugitive* (1947), *What Price Glory* (1952), *The Quiet Man* (1952, for which he won his fourth Academy Award), and *Mister Roberts* (1955, with Mervyn LeRoy). In 1956, he returned to his favorite genre with *The Searchers* (1956). The tone had changed from the optimism, communal unity, and unequivocal morality of the "cavalry trilogy." John Wayne is a Civil War veteran who, accompanied by a young man (Tab Hunter), spends years searching for a girl captured by Indians. The main character is a restless, lonely man who persists in his quest more out of stubbornness than dedication.

Ford continued to divide his time between dramas and Westerns in the late fifties and sixties. Although Ford was never less than professional and his motion pictures are always worth seeing, his imagination and vitality seemed to flag in such films as *The Last Hurrah* (1958), *Gideon's Day* (1959), *Donovan's Reef* (1963), and *Seven Women* (1965, his last feature). The same holds true for most of his Westerns: *The Horse Soldiers* (1959), *Sergeant Rutledge* (1960), *Two Rode Together* (1961), and an episode in *How the West Was Won* (1962). Two other Westerns of this period, however, are superior, not unworthy of being compared to his classics of the late forties.

*The Man Who Shot Liberty Valance* (1962) is a sad, nostalgic tale of the death of the old West, personified by Tom Doniphon (John Wayne). Doniphon kills a vicious outlaw (Lee Marvin) who is terrorizing the country. Credit for this heroic deed, however, goes to a young lawyer (James Stewart) and catapults him into political office. Ford makes clear his regret at the passing, inevitable though it may be, of Doniphon and all he represents and even adds a touch of bitterness that the courage, integrity, and modesty of these early heroes has not been appreciated. *Cheyenne Autumn* (1964) is Ford's final Western. It is an epic story of an Indian tribe's suicidal trek of a couple of thousand miles from a reservation in Oklahoma to their homelands in Wyoming, stubborn pride and fortitude their only defenses against hunger and a vengeful U.S. cavalry.

John Ford made so many Westerns that it is surprising, despite changes in his attitudes, how consistent he was in his themes and techniques. Permeating all his works in the genre is his acute sense of place. Monument Valley in Utah, the setting for *Stagecoach* and the principal location of his Westerns thereafter, was for him a microcosm of the land that could inspire, comfort, threaten, and even destroy his heroes. A measure of a frontiersman's character is how he meets the challenge of nature, a force, like fate, that is indifferent to man's personal needs and concerns.

Whether contending with the forces of nature or human enemies, a typical Ford hero is basically dependent on his own skills and inner resources to survive, yet he is not alone. Camaraderie, a group (for example, the army or a wagon train), the code of honor, family, community—all can be supportive to him. It is in dealing with the relationship of the individual and unifying forces that the director becomes ambiguous. Although the hero must defend to some degree societal pressures, they may also restrict or even attempt to stifle his independence and self-reliance. Conflicts can arise between strong-minded men *(She Wore a Yellow Ribbon);* the cavalry under a tyrannical, arrogant officer may be an instrument of oppression *(Fort Apache, Cheyenne Autumn);* adherence to the code can threaten the relationship between a man and a woman *(Stagecoach, Rio Grande);* a young man may have to leave his family to become an individual *(The Searchers);* in the wake of law and order may come political expediency and a shrinking of integrity *(The Man Who Shot Liberty Valance).*

What makes Ford's Westerns moving as well as exciting is his recognition that the encroachments of civilization are inevitable, perhaps even desirable, but that in the process the admirable qualities that won the West are sacrificed. This insight is the pulsating heart that nourishes the central myth of the director's Westerns: Regardless of historical accuracy, they dramatize a period in our past when the pros and cons of the constantly recurring conflict between the individual and society were revealed with unusual clarity.

People who meet the challenge of nature and men are heroes, but they are not the shimmering paragons that appeared in so many "B" Westerns. They are simply men with more courage, resourcefulness, and determination than those that surround them and are willing to risk death to preserve their integrity and beliefs. Once the nature of a hero or villain has been established at the beginning of a film, surprises of characterization rarely come forth. Because of this, some critics have maintained that Ford depends excessively on stereotyped characters. There is a good deal of validity in this accusation; on the other hand, as we shall see in examining *Stagecoach,* the director usually adds sufficient personal traits and variations to his stereotypes to individualize them.

Ford has also been criticized for other areas of his Westerns. The women are generally no more than two-dimensional, as so often are the villains in these films. With a few exceptions, such as Kathleen in *Rio Grande,* Laurie in *The Searchers,* and Hallie in *The Man Who Shot Liberty Valance,* most women fit into the three categories of the classic Western: the stalwart mother and wife, the gentle virgin or upright "widow woman," and the understanding, "heart-of-gold" prostitute. Sexual passion is always implied, never explicit, in a Ford film. His heroes are obviously most comfortable in the company of hard-drinking, hard-fighting, honor-bound men.

During most of his career, Ford presented "redskins" as no more than savages, personifications of the hostile face of nature. In his last Westerns, however, he paid tribute to the Indians as a proud people with their own worthy heritage and way of life, and he acknowledged the wrongs done to them by the white man. Ford more consistently adhered to racial stereotypes of Mexican-Americans that were typical of the classic Western. Blacks are also cliché figures. Prominent exceptions are Sergeant Rutledge and Pompey, the shrewd, independent servant in *The Man Who Shot Liberty Valance.*

Ford's camera-editing dynamics are basically classic. Decades of experience in making Hollywood motion pictures trained him to work efficiently and quickly. In his Westerns, he favored a stable camera, panoramic shots whenever possible, and a *mise-en-*

*scène* approach for everything but chases and gunfights. He rejected camera and editing pyrotechnics that call attention to themselves, so a striking shot (such as from under the wheels of a racing stagecoach or an unusual mirror reflection) appears somehow appropriate rather than self-conscious stylistic bravado.

However mythical the director's vision of his characters and situations, he was generally realistic in his elements of presentation. Costumes in his Westerns are accurate; the external sets are suitably worn and shabby; the interiors have a lived-in quality and even include the ceilings of rooms (an innovative practice for Westerns until the fifties). On the other hand, in interior lighting he was not adverse to using shadows to achieve dramatic effects. In dealing with actors, Ford was a tyrant. He preferred performers he knew would follow his commands and were natural and restrained in their acting, although he recognized when, as with Doc Boone (Thomas Mitchell) in *Stagecoach,* a more flamboyant interpretation was called for.

Only a few skeptics would deny that Ford was an artist, albeit not an ostentatious one. His style is so fluent and his choices appear so inevitable that audiences often miss the brilliance and subtlety of his scenes and sequences. Whether in photographing masses of people, as in *Wagonmaster* and *Cheyenne Autumn,* or a small group, as in the dinner in an early sequence of *The Searchers,* Ford reveals an artistry that viewers feel is impressive but can only appreciate intellectually by conscious attention to details and careful study.

*Stagecoach* was based on a short story by Ernest Haycox, "Stage to Lordsburg." From this straightforward tale, Dudley Nichols fashioned one of his typically tightly constructed, action-packed scripts. It also contains the weaknesses characteristic of the screenwriter's work: simplistic characterization, allowing for little ambiguity and shading of motivation or action, and a bent toward moralistic preaching. The screenplay for *Stagecoach* is the only Western that Nichols wrote for Ford, although they collaborated on 14 films, including *The Last Patrol, The Informer, The Plough and the Stars,* and *The Fugitive.*

Another member of Ford's filmmaking team for *Stagecoach* is notable. Yakima Canutt is generally considered to be the greatest stunt man that has worked in Hollywood; in 1967 he received a special Academy Award for his accomplishments in this field. For *Stagecoach,* Canutt was not only second-unit director in charge of the Indians, but he also personally performed the most dangerous stunt in the film: He was the Indian who leaps on the back of the racing team of horses, then falls under their hooves and between the wheels of the stage.

Over the years Ford repeatedly used certain actors in his films. Among those in his sound Westerns were John Wayne, Henry Fonda, James Stewart, Thomas Mitchell, Victor McLaglen, John Carradine, Harry Carey, Jr., Andy Devine, Tim Holt, Ben Johnson, and Francis Ford (his brother).

John Wayne was obviously the director's favorite actor. After playing bit parts, Wayne's first starring role was in Raoul Walsh's *The Big Trail* (1930). His career was quiescent in the thirties until *Stagecoach.* In addition to films by Ford, he starred in a number of Howard Hawks's Westerns, including *Red River* (1948) and *Rio Bravo* (1959). During World War II and after, he portrayed heroes in practically every branch of the armed forces. He won an Oscar for his performance as Rooster Cogburn in Henry Hathaway's *True Grit* (1969). *The Alamo* (1960) and *The Green Berets* (1968) both featured and were directed by Wayne. From 1929 to his death in 1979, he appeared in over 150 sound motion pictures. For many viewers, he was the personificaton of the slow-speaking, tough, self-sufficient frontier hero.

PLOT SUMMARY

The garrison in the town of Tonto learns that the Apache Geronimo is on the warpath and has cut the telegraph lines. The stagecoach to Lordsburg, driven by Buck (Devine), stops in Tonto. When departing, escorted by cavalry troops, it contains six passengers, Buck, and Marshal Curly Wilcox (Bancroft) "riding shotgun." The marshal has joined the group because he was informed that the Ringo Kid escaped from the penitentiary to avenge himself on the Plummer brothers, who are in Lordsburg. Lucy Mallory (Platt), a young, obviously pregnant Southern woman with an aristocratic bearing, is meeting her husband, a cavalry lieutenant, in Lordsburg. Dallas (Trevor), an attractive prostitute, is being run out of town by the ladies of the Law and Order League. She is accompanied by Doc Josiah Boone (Mitchell), a flamboyant, drunken medical doctor, who is forced by his landlady to leave for nonpayment of rent. Samuel Peacock (Meek) is a meek liquor salesman. At the last minute, Hatfield (Carradine), an elegantly dressed gambler, offers his protection to Mrs. Mallory and enters the coach. At the edge of town, they are stopped and joined by Henry Gatewood (Churchill), a florid, pompous banker. He has just received a deposit of $50,000 and leaves without informing anyone. Some distance outside of town, the Ringo Kid (Wayne), whose horse has been hurt, halts the stagecoach. He is arrested by Curly.

The coach arrives at Dry Forks, the first way station. The cavalry that was to meet them, led by Lucy's husband, has gone on to Apache Wells. The present escort must return; however, the passengers vote to continue the trip. At lunch, Dallas is snubbed by Lucy, Hatfield, and Gatewood but is befriended by Ringo, who is attracted by the young woman and unaware of her background. The stagecoach leaves.

On the trip along a high mountain trail, Curly tells Buck that although he is not indifferent to the reward, his real purpose in capturing Ringo is to protect the cowboy from the Plummers. Inside, Hatfield pours water for Lucy into a silver cup. It bears a crest that she recognizes as that of the Greenfields, an aristocratic Southern family, but the gambler maintains that he won it on a wager.

When the stage arrives at Apache Wells, the second way station, the travelers hear that the cavalry had a skirmish with the Indians, during which Lieutenant Mallory was hurt, and has left. The pregnant Lucy Mallory collapses. Doc sobers up. The men wait anxiously in the main room until Dallas brings out the newborn baby.

Ringo and Dallas talk together outside. We learn that Luke Plummer killed the cowboy's father and brother and that Dallas's parents were massacred by Indians, leaving her on her own. The young woman, however, does not reveal how she has lived since then. Ringo proposes marriage; she will not listen to him.

Chris, the stationmaster, announces the next

morning that his horse, rifle, and wife, an Apache (in that order of importance), are gone. Gatewood reveals anxiety when his valise is temporarily missing. In the hallway, Dallas tells Doc that Ringo wishes to marry her. The older man is skeptical but finally gives his approval. When Doc suggests that Ringo join Dallas in the kitchen, he learns that the cowboy was 17 when he was sent to the penitentiary. Dallas will marry Ringo if he attempts to escape. Reluctantly, he agrees. Ringo starts to ride away, pursued by Curly, but he stops. He points out war smoke signals in the distance. The coach hastily leaves Apache Wells.

When they arrive at Ferry Crossing, the third way station, they find the buildings burned down, the inhabitants killed, and the ferry destroyed. The stagecoach is floated across the river.

On the trail to Lordsburg, the moving stage is watched by Indians. A celebration inside the coach is interrupted by Peacock's suddenly being struck by an arrow. The Indians attack. The men on the stagecoach soon run out of ammunition. Just as Hatfield is about to shoot Lucy with his last bullet to save her from torture, he is wounded. At that moment, she hears the bugle call of the cavalry. The Indians are driven off. Inside the stage, Hatfield dies; his last words to Lucy are, "If you see Judge Greenfield, tell him his . . ." The stage coach is escorted to town by the cavalry.

In Lordsburg, Lucy is carried away to join her husband after expressing her appreciation to Dallas for the young woman's help. Gatewood is arrested for stealing bank funds (the telegraph lines have been repaired). Curly gives Ringo a rifle and releases him from his promise to remain in custody.

Luke Plummer, playing cards in a saloon, is informed of the arrival of the Kid. Crosscutting between the saloon, where Luke is joined by his two brothers, and Ringo with Dallas. Ringo insists on accompanying Dallas to her new residence. When he sees her "home," even the naive young man realizes his beloved is a prostitute, yet he still insists that they will be married. Ringo leaves her for a showdown with the Plummers. The conclusion of the gunfight takes place off-camera.

At the saloon, Luke enters but falls to the floor dead. Ringo joins Dallas and embraces her. Curly brings a buckboard, and Doc joins them. The marshal allows the two young people to escape to Ringo's ranch across the Mexican border. The closing shot is of the buckboard disappearing into the dawn.

### ANALYSIS

*Stagecoach* is an intrinsically exciting film with a workable screenplay, outstanding acting, and superb directing. It is, in addition, a milestone in the history of the Western because of its Janus-like quality of including many of the themes and techniques of the classic Western while also anticipating and influencing the new psychological and societal dimensions that appeared after the war.

The most obvious traditional element in the film is Ford's presentation of the Western landscape as awesome but also as a challenge that tests the mettle of individuals. We are made aware of how vulnerable the stagecoach is by panoramic shots from a high angle so that it appears like a bug creeping along a trail. After one such shot, Ford uses a device that was a visual cliché even in the late thirties, yet rarely fails to produce a shiver of excitement in a viewer: The camera pans from the high-angle long shot to a slightly low-angle view of Indians on a hilltop looking down at the stage (see Figure 1.21).

The Indians in the film are not individualized. They collectively represent external savagery (as opposed to that within the world of the settlers, exemplified by the Plummer brothers), capable of burning down the third way station, scalping, and attacking the stagecoach.

The hostile plain and hills and the Indians constitute one side of the tension inevitable in any Western between the wilderness and civilization. The latter is represented by the two towns, the cavalry, and the way stations. The stations are at the edge of the boundaries between the two forces. It is appropriate that the second station, halfway between the towns, should be operated by a Mexican with an Indian wife.

The characters in *Stagecoach* are generally types found in earlier Westerns. The use of these stereotypes prompts Richard Corliss to criticize this component of the film harshly:

. . . the character types whose every movement and motive we can predict as soon as they step

on-screen; the manipulation of emotions and conventions in the safest, most traditional ways; the absence of any genuine eccentricity, or anything dangerous, innovative, irresponsible, or disturbing.[7]

Corliss's strictures would be entirely justified if he had confined his criticism to the villains in the film—the Indians, the Plummer brothers, and the banker Gatewood. Luke Plummer, in fact, is so completely a villain that he is a caricature. From the moment we first see him in his large black hat playing cards and receiving a "dead man's hand," we anticipate his show of cowardice while waiting at the saloon, his attempt to use an illegal shotgun in a gunfight, and his lack of conscience about facing one man with two others at his side. Gatewood is also excessively transparent and one-dimensional. He is not only a thief and a pompous, blustering bully but a coward as well.

When we examine the other major characters in the film, Corliss's criticism is less valid. It is true that each person on the stagecoach is fundamentally a stereotype. Yet each has enough ambiguity of character or deviation from the traditional for anyone familiar with earlier Westerns to recognize that a new spirit, however cautiously expressed, is entering the genre. Buck, the stagecoach driver, is a standard comic character, but it is untypical in a classic Western for even a humorous Anglo-Saxon to be married to a Mexican. Curly, the marshal, is the personification of an admirable lawman—practical, courageous, and decisive. On the other hand, in the end he permits his prisoner to fight the Plummer brothers and then proves he is a sentimentalist at heart by allowing Ringo and Dallas to ride off into the dawn. Furthermore, his motives for capturing the outlaw, at least at the beginning, are not entirely unselfish, for he admits to Buck that he could use the reward of $500 in gold.

Peacock is described by the bartender in Tonto as an Easterner from Kansas City, Missouri, actually Kansas City, Kansas (in either case, a strange view of what constitutes "the East"). Wherever his home, the small man possesses the typical fears and caution of an Eastern tenderfoot, although finally he proves that he has a core of courage.

Doc Boone is another example of a prevalent cliché in the Western, the drunken doctor. We never learn why Boone turned to drink, but he does follow the standard pattern of redeeming himself by delivering Lucy's baby and helping Peacock when the salesman is wounded. He also functions as a means of presenting a repeated theme in the genre. The wounds of the Civil War did not heal completely during the period 1865–1890, which is the time setting of most classic Westerns. Boone, from the North, is in conflict with Hatfield, from the South. At the end of the film, however, shared danger and a growing respect for each other lead the two men to a subdued reconciliation, symbolic of what actually would happen on the frontier.

What brings Boone beyond the stereotype of the drunken doctor is his qualities as an older man of tolerance and understanding. In the Western, the archetype of the wise old man is usually one of two types: a primitive whose wisdom is gained through experience and natural shrewdness (a role often played by Walter Brennan, as in *Red River*) or an individual, originally from the East but completely adapted to the West, who has read and thought a good deal. Boone fits into the latter category. When forced out of town, he quotes Christopher Marlowe and alludes to the French Revolution. Both Ringo and Dallas ask his advice about getting married, and he warns them of the problems ahead. He has insight into the social conflicts among the passengers but usually remains an observer. The last significant speech in the film, one that sums up a major theme, is given to the doctor: "Well, that's saved them from the blessings of civilization."

Hatfield attracts our interest because of the incongruity between his impressive bearing and his occupation, as well as the mystery of his past. Of course, he is the Southern aristocrat turned gambler, a common figure in the Western. Cast over Hatfield as stereotype, however, is an intriguing sheen of ambiguity. He is a dangerous and unscrupulous man, perhaps even capable, as Doc Boone insinuates, of shooting a man in the back. He is a realist or a cynic, depending on one's point of view, who can describe the frontier world to some cowboys with whom he is playing cards as a jungle, a very wild jungle. Yet he sacrifices his life in the cause of chivalry by protecting Lucy Mallory, who represents for him the aristocracy of the South that he has lost. Even if the clues to Hatfield's past appear with contrived regularity and fit together with the mechanical clicks of the obvious, the gentleman-gambler does capture our imagination.

The two women in the coach hardly emerge as more than two-dimensional characters. Lucy Mallory is a strong-minded, brave person who is also a social snob. However, she has the grace in the end to admit to Dallas that she was wrong to snub the prostitute. The only mystery attached to her is her interest in Hatfield when she first sees him. Either his face stirs some vague recollection or the pregnant, straitlaced Southern lady is not immune to being attracted to a handsome stranger who admires her.

Dallas is basically the traditional gold-hearted prostitute. She is probably the most unbelievable of the major positive characters in the film. Her profession appears to have had no effects on her physically or on her manners. The refined features of Claire Trevor, who plays Dallas, have in other roles hardened with bitchiness, but one simply cannot imagine her as a frontier whore. The young woman is an exemplar of female modesty, humility, courage, and dedication.

Ford and Nichols were innovative in making a prostitute the heroine of a Western, no matter how romanticized. Before 1939, cowboy heroes simply did not ride into the sunrise with a whore beside them. Ford went further by adding what was for the day a shocking detail. Dallas and Ringo walk at night along a street of Lordsburg and then stop before a wooden walkway that leads down (naturally) to a brightly illuminated house that is obviously not a home. Even the incredibly naive Ringo understands. If a prostitute as heroine was unusual in a classic Western, to show a house of prostitution was even more uncommon.

The Ringo Kid is unquestionably the hero of the film. From the moment we first see him at the side of the road swinging his rifle and when in a wonderfully effective shot the camera swiftly tracks in from long to medium distance (see Figure 1.23), we know what role he is to play in the film. Generally he lives up to the appellation of hero. He is courageous, a fine shot, chivalrous, polite, gracious, always on the right side in arguments, and charmingly boyish. Ringo's appearance and good-naturedness, however, are deceptive. He possesses that quiet repose when not called upon to act that is often characteristic of Western heroes. Still, even in that state he can convey the potential danger in antagonizing him, as is evident when he silences an aroused Hatfield, no coward himself, with a determined look and a casual "Doc don't mean any harm." When decisive action is required, Ringo moves without fear and with steely determination, as when the stagecoach is attacked by Indians and in fighting the Plummers.

In every respect, Ringo would be a typical Western hero if it were not for his relationship with Dallas. The preliminaries of their courtship consist of exchanges of looks, especially in the stagecoach and later as Dallas shows the newborn baby to the men. It is when the relationship reaches a more advanced stage that two characteristics of Ringo are revealed that are unusual if not unique in a classic Western. Dallas is actually able to persuade him to give up his plan of vengeance against the Plummers; this is a major violation of the code. Fortunately for Ringo's credentials as a hero, he is stopped by evidence that Geronimo's Apaches are nearby.

Ringo's most surprising trait is his naiveté about women. He proposes to Dallas during their first private conversation. Even more incredible in face of all the hints that are given throughout the film, he does not realize that the woman he wishes to marry is a prostitute. That he unhesitantly holds to his proposal when the truth is forced upon him demonstrates that he is not only naive but a thorough romantic.

The plot is carefully arranged to assure the film a happy ending. In fact, aside from the excessive use of clichés in characterization, the chief criticism that can be leveled against *Stagecoach* is its contrived plot. Perhaps critics have made too much of the incredible circumstances that bring together a group of individuals so balanced in contrast of personality, background, and hopes for the future. On this basis, every story of a group journey, from Chaucer's *Canterbury Tales* to Steinbeck's *The Wayward Bus,* could be faulted. More crucial in this respect is the way in which each character, because he or she is more a piece in the screenwriter's plot mosaic than an indi-

vidual, restricts the development of the others. Group reactions and interrelationships within the group, rather than personalities, are in focus. The result is that our perceptions of each character are extremely limited beyond the fundamental stereotypes, as though the screenwriter parceled out one or two insights per person.

Contrivance is most conspicuous in single moments in the film. Credulity is strained to the breaking point when during the Indian attack, as the ammunition is exhausted, Hatfield points his revolver at Lucy's head but is himself shot just before he can pull the trigger. Moments later, in the nick of time, the sound of a bugle announces the arrival of the cavalry. Earlier, as the men drink to what they believe is a successfully completed journey, an arrow strikes Peacock. It is never explained how on an open plain an Indian could have gotten close enough to shoot an arrow through the window without being spotted by Curly and Buck. While dealing with the Indian attack from this critical perspective, William S. Hart's famous objection should be noted: The Indians were not imbeciles and could have stopped the coach by shooting one horse. Ford's reply was facetious: Then the film would have ended. He added more seriously that the Indians valued horses too much to kill one. One horse viewed as worth a dozen braves? It would have been more honest on Ford's part to admit that in the Western the plot presents whatever the plot requires for suspense and effects, no matter how unlikely. It has to be Lucy's husband who is wounded at Dry Fork. The baby had to be born at the next way station. The Indian smoke signals are noticed just as Ringo is escaping. Even the most timeworn clichés are allowed to remain: Luke Plummer receives a "dead man's hand" in cards before he dies; after the gunfight, he walks into the bar, suggesting that he has won, then falls to the ground dead. Any screenwriter has the right to use accidents and improbabilities in his script, but Dudley Nichols seems rather greedy in taking advantage of this prerogative.

The weaknesses in the plot, however, are more than counterbalanced by the distinctive acting, sound, and camera-editing dynamics. Each actor and actress is outstanding, although Berton Churchill as Henry

Gatewood does overdo the character's pomposity and bluster. It could also be argued that Ford was mistaken in choosing Claire Trevor for the role of Dallas. John Wayne as Ringo conveys the inexplicable presence that indicates he had the potential to be a star, a promise he fulfilled in the decades that followed. Thomas Mitchell as Doc Boone definitely deserved his Academy Award as Best Supporting Actor.

*Stagecoach* was Ford's first sound Western, and he included natural sounds and background music with an effectiveness that became characteristic of his future productions in the genre. The use of natural sounds are vigorous and straightforward—during the Indian attack, we hear the pounding of the horses' hoofs, the rattling of the stagecoach, and gunfire—or subtle and indirect, as when at the end of the film Dallas is waiting for Ringo and there is the sound of his slow, heavy footsteps before he appears on the screen. Sound anticipating visuals in this scene is an example of a device Ford used in other films and at least twice before in *Stagecoach:* The camera is on Doc Boone drinking when we hear the thud of an arrow striking, and only then is there a pan to the wounded Peacock, and later, during the Indian attack, Lucy's face is on-camera as she hears the sound of the cavalry bugle before we see the rescuers.

The idea of basing the musical score for the film on folk songs was suggested by Ford. In fact, the director utilized it again in two other Westerns *(Wagonmaster* and *Rio Grande).* The tunes are not simply background music but also leitmotifs. As J. A. Place points out,[8] in the opening sequence the stagecoach enters the town of Tonto to the strains of the ballad "Bury Me Not on the Lone Prairie," and it becomes the stagecoach theme. Later, when Doc and Dallas proceed to the coach, it is to a comic marching version of the song. Appropriately, the leitmotif for Lucy Mallory is "I Dream of Jeannie," whose composer is associated with the South.

Of all the innovations, large and small, in *Stagecoach,* the most impressive are those in Ford's brilliant camera-editing dynamics. Ford's ability to capture the majesty, starkness, and menace of the wilderness was noted earlier. This vision of nature is emphasized by the use of contrast. The freedom and loneliness of the prairie is juxtaposed with the confinement and bustle of the towns; during the trip, the open landscape is counterpointed to the closed area of the interior of the coach. Contrast is also involved in conveying the sense of a journey by changing perspectives. Ford repeatedly shifts the camera from inside the coach, with the passing landscape visible through the windows, to Curly and Buck on the driving seat outside, to the galloping horses, to panoramic shots of the stage rushing along the trail.

Viewers are so preoccupied with the journey that they often do not notice how much of *Stagecoach* takes place inside buildings in Tonto and Lordsburg and the first and second way stations. These interior scenes depend primarily on *mise-en-scène,* but montage is used when necessary. The luncheon at Dry Forks (Figure 8.10) during which Dallas is snubbed by Lucy and Hatfield is often referred to by admirers of Ford when they argue that the director could use expressive editing to make tangible the unspoken innuendoes of emotion and interrelations within a group.

**FIGURE 8.10**

*Stagecoach.* Ford uses the attitude of each passenger toward the prostitute Dallas during the luncheon at the Dry Forks way station to reveal characters and relationships.

The sequence at Apache Wells contains no scenes as taut and artful as the luncheon earlier in the day. An observant viewer, however, notices the care-

**FIGURE 8.11**

*Stagecoach.* The dramatic lighting and the striking perspective of this shot of the hallway in the Apache Wells way station suggest the intensity of the intimacy developing between Dallas and Ringo.

ful application of chiaroscuro, particularly in the hallway in front of Lucy's room, to heighten mystery and intensify dramatic events (Figure 8.11). The long shots, from floor to ceiling, convey the physical reality of the main room, and soon we share the beleaguered feelings of the travelers and their sense of relief, no matter what the dangers, when they are once more on the open road.

The scene of the Indian attack is justly considered classic footage that, in structure and rhythm, other Westerns have rarely equaled and never sur-

passed (Figure 8.12). For most directors, the attack and chase would have been the final climax of the film, but Ford goes on to the gunfight in Lordsburg. It is evidence of the director's genius that the encounter between Ringo and the Plummer brothers so soon after the Indian raid is not anticlimactic. Except for the first sequence, Ford uses little crosscutting until the end of the film. In the final sequence, this technique becomes the means of mounting suspense. Three scenes of the passengers, Ringo and Curly, and Ringo and Dallas alternate with three of Luke in the El Dorado Saloon. The setting of the last of the three saloon scenes shifts to outside, with Luke and his brothers walking the streets. We expect to return to Ringo, but an added measure of expectation is achieved by a scene in the office of the town newspaper, then shots of the emptying streets. Finally, the Plummers and Ringo appear in a single shot; then follow very brief

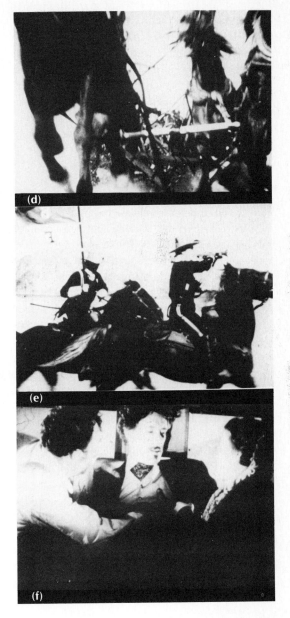

**FIGURE 8.12**

*Stagecoach.* Images from the sequence of the Indian attack on the stagecoach (beginning with the pan illustrated in Figure 1.21). In the last one (f), Hatfield murmurs to Lucy Mallory his incomplete dying message.

shots of Ringo, the brothers, and again Ringo, on the ground, firing.

The gunfight itself is realistic and admirably restrained. The confrontation is not at high noon, along a broad street, with frightened faces at windows but on a dark, lonely street with no observers visible. After lengthy scenes joined by parallel editing, this climax consists of four brief shots with heightened background music, and we do not see the Plummers killed. Perhaps it is just as well that we do not actually witness the improbable event of one man with a rifle finishing off three experienced killers with three bullets (all that Ringo carries with him).

The suspense continues: a shot of a despairing Dallas; Luke Plummer walking into the saloon, then collapsing; back to Dallas. The scene of the reunion is cleverly done, though requiring a bit of cinematic sleight of hand. Ford combines in a single shot two techniques used earlier in the film. Dallas, with her head in her hands, looks up as the sound of steps are heard on the sound track. This device, the auditory anticipating the visual, was noted above. Dallas's face lights up with relief and joy as she looks directly at the camera tracking in toward her and jiggling up and down to the rhythm of a man's gait. We assume that this is a subjective shot from the point of view of the man coming toward Dallas. Our assumption is correct; however, a rule of fluent change in point of view is now violated, for Ringo, whose eyes the camera represents, without transition walks into the frame from the right and embraces Dallas.

Ford is not above manipulating camera-editing dynamics for surprise and effect even if the content or technique of the shot had become a visual cliché of traditional Westerns. A number of examples have already been commented on. In the case of Ford, however—a trait he shares with Hitchcock—we tolerate these clichés because somehow they work in the context of the films, are acceptable, though hardly admirable, bridges between moments of true inspiration. There are many such moments in *Stagecoach*.

The film contains numerous other memorable individual shots or scenes. The reflection of the horses being hitched up to the stagecoach appear on the glass door of the bank, followed by a dissolve to a shot of Greenwood, thus subtly anticipating the banker's unannounced departure. Later, Dallas drinks from a canteen of water, she and Ringo exchange looks, and then, with the camera on him, the outlaw lowers his head, and the top of his round, wide-brimmed hat fills the screen. When Hatfield dies, the heads of Doc and Lucy are outlined in the stagecoach window on the other side of the gambler. In the final sequence, we first see Luke Plummer playing cards in an overhead shot, his face obscured until the next shot at eye level, when two hats separate to reveal Luke staring directly at the camera (Figure 8.13).

---

**FIGURE 8.13**

*Stagecoach.* A viewer's introduction to Luke Plummer. He stares belligerently directly at the camera, as though challenging the right of an outsider to be at his table.

John Ford is one of those remarkable directors who, given the proper opportunity, permeate a film with the vitality and perceptions of the artist and man. Perhaps this ability, more than any other, makes *Stagecoach* a classic. For all its romanticism, even sentimentality, contrived plot, stereotyped characterizations, and cliché images, the film has a driving force that not so much invalidates criticism as makes such objections less important than the overall pleasure and moments of emotional and esthetic satisfaction that the work offers.

## MYTH AND REALISM

### *Shane*

*The inquiry put to me was, if I could choose one Western as being typical of the entire tradition of the Hollywood West and was leaving on a long trip so I could only take one example, which would it be? My answer to that was* Shane.

Jon Tuska, 1976[9]

### CAST

*Alan Ladd (Shane), Jean Arthur (Marion Starrett), Van Heflin (Joe Starrett), Brandon De Wilde (Joey Starrett), Jack Palance (Wilson), Ben Johnson (Chris), Emile Meyer (Ryker), Elisha Cook, Jr. (Torrey), and others.*

### CREDITS

*Director and Producer—George Stevens, Screenwriter—A. B. Guthrie, Jr. (based on a novel by Jack Schaefer), Director of Photography—Loyal Griggs, Art Directors—Hal Pereira and Walter Tyler, Composer—Victor Young, Editors—William Hornbeck and Tom McAdoo, and others.*

1953/Paramount
Color/118 minutes

### BACKGROUND

George Stevens (1904–1975) is an example of a type of director particularly associated with Hollywood: a polished craftsman of unusual versatility whose work is usually underrated because it cannot easily be categorized with critical labels. Yet, as Georges Sadoul points out, "Some American critics include him among the greatest modern directors."[10]

A child actor at the age of 6, he was a professional cameraman at 17 and, somewhat later, a screenwriter for Hal Roach. Stevens directed his first film in 1933. During the thirties and forties he became known for such comedy-satires as *Woman of the Year* (1942), in which Katharine Hepburn and Spencer Tracy costarred for the first time. His versatility was demonstrated when he directed Fred Astaire in two musicals (*Swing Time,* 1936, and *A Damsel in Distress,* 1937), the adventure story *Gunga Din* (1939), the romance *A Penny Serenade* (1941, starring Irene Dunne and Cary Grant), and the light comedy *I Remember Mama* (1948).

In the fifties Stevens became more ambitious in subject matter and style, his social criticism more pointed, and his dramas more subtle and complex in characterization. He received an Academy Award for *A Place in the Sun* (1951), a version of Theodore Dreiser's *An American Tragedy. Something to Live For* (1952) dealt with alcoholism. *Shane* appeared in 1953. *Giant* (1956), based on Edna Ferber's novel, won Stevens another Academy Award. *The Diary of Anne Frank* (1959), although an honest effort, was generally disappointing.

Stevens directed two other films before he died. *The Greatest Story Ever Told* (1964) is pretentious and bloated. In *The Only Game in Town* (1969), he returned to comedy-satire, the genre in which he had had his first successes.

The common denominator in all of Stevens's films is his slow-paced, classic style. Even his comedies are restrained and controlled, to the extent that their lack of visual spontaneity and verve make them seem today somewhat staid and stagy. On the other hand, the director had a sharp, but gentle rather than savage, eye for the ridiculous in our society, which enlivens his satire, and he could draw sparkling performances from such actors as Katharine Hepburn, Spencer Tracy, and Jean Arthur.

The careful structuring and deliberate rhythms of Stevens's style are most effective when counterbalanced by plots that encourage action and vitality, as in *Gunga Din* and the Fred Astaire musicals. This method also works to the advantage of *A Place in the Sun* and *Giant,* where probing of psychological conflicts and a disclosing of the social and physical effects of a specific environment are important. *Shane* too gains from realistic action and setting in the mode of a mythic story.

Stevens was not an innovator or experimenter with new techniques. Once he discovered the value of a device, such as the slow dissolve, he employed it in many films. Viewers' reactions to this type of concentration on subtleties within self-imposed limitations are colored by their preferences for the classic or the romantic approach to filmmaking, similar to the factors determining a preference, to draw examples from a higher level of achievement than Stevens attained, for the works of Dreyer and Bresson or those of Cocteau and Godard.

Another critical problem relating to Stevens, and often a touchstone of a critic's own values, is whether the director was most significant in his genre films of the thirties and forties or his more challenging ones of the fifties. Andrew Sarris prefers the former, as is indicated in this witty but unkind statement: "George Stevens was a minor director with major virtues before *A Place in the Sun,* and a major director with minor virtues after."[11] Georges Sadoul disagrees: "Though his work in the Thirties and Forties is relatively minor, an undeniable talent is evident in *A Place in the Sun, Shane,* and *Giant.*"[12]

*Shane* was Stevens's second and last Western. The first was the easily forgettable *Annie Oakley* of 1935, starring Barbara Stanwyck. *Shane* was based on a novel by Jack Schaefer; however, it was molded into a superior screenplay by A. B. Guthrie, Jr., who had 6 years earlier written the best-selling Western novel *The Big Sky.* Ironically, the only other well-known member of the filmmaking team was Victor Young, whose musical score is the least distinguished aspect of the film.

All the major actors had already established their reputations before *Shane,* with the exception of Brandon De Wilde. This young man, 11 at the time, proved that his previous success in *The Member of the Wedding* (1953) was not a fluke.

The film was successful critically and has often been chosen by Western enthusiasts for their lists of 10 best.

## PLOT SUMMARY

Behind the credits we see a silhouetted rider entering a valley. A boy, Joey (De Wilde), observes the rider stop and talk to his father, Joe Starrett (Heflin). When Ryker (Meyer) and his men appear, Shane (Ladd) stands by Joe. At dinner, the rancher explains that he and other homesteaders have a legal right to the land; however, Ryker, who once owned the entire valley, is attempting to drive them out.

The next morning Shane agrees to work for the Starretts. Joe arranges for a meeting of the homesteaders that evening. In the town store, Shane purchases and changes into working clothes. When he goes into the adjacent saloon, he is bullied by Chris (Johnson),

one of Ryker's men; he does not respond. At the meeting that evening, Shane is branded a coward.

The homesteaders, traveling together for protection, go into town. Shane once again enters the saloon, only this time he accepts Chris's challenge and beats the bully in a fistfight. When the other men in the saloon attack Shane, Joe comes to his friend's aid.

Wilson (Palance), a ruthless killer hired by Ryker, arrives in town; it is the Fourth of July. At the homesteaders' party, there are fireworks and dancing. A ceremony celebrates the wedding anniversary of Joe and Marion (Arthur); the two kiss, watched by Shane and Joey. A little later, Shane dances with Marion. That night, Ryker, with his men, visits the Starrett ranch. He attempts to justify his position and proposes that Starrett join him. Joe refuses. Shane and Wilson size up each other.

Some time later, Torrey, a peppery Southerner, and another homesteader go into town. Wilson baits the Southerner into drawing his gun; Torrey is killed. At the burial, Joe makes an impassioned plea to the men to remain.

Ryker prepares a trap for Starrett by proposing that they talk together in town. Although aware of the danger, Joe agrees. Chris, however, warns Shane of the ambush. As Joe prepares to leave, Shane enters and declares that he is going in the place of Joe. The two men fight. Shane finally knocks out Joe with his gun. Joey condemns him for winning unfairly, but Shane rides away.

Joey runs after his hero. The gunman reaches town and enters the saloon. The youngster watches from under the swinging doors. Shane kills Wilson and Ryker, then, warned by Joey, shoots Ryker's foreman, who was hiding upstairs with a rifle. Shane says goodbye to the boy and, with Joey's voice pleading that he stay echoing in the hills, leaves the valley.

## ANALYSIS

The plot of *Shane* is a compilation of what had become, by the late forties, clichés of the classic Western. An aging cattle baron, who considers the valley his domain, attempts to drive out settlers who have legal claims to portions of the land. A stranger in white, a taciturn man with no known past or predictable future, enters the valley [see Figure 1.8(b)]. Eventually he saves the settlers by single-handedly killing the cattle baron, his foreman, and a hired gunman; the gunman, of course, wears a black hat and vest. The stranger then leaves to continue his wandering.

There are, on the other hand, elements of realism, especially in setting, and subtleties of characterization that were infrequently found in the pre–World War II Western. Ryker is not a one-dimensional scoundrel. In one scene (after the Fourth of July celebration), he attempts to justify his actions to Joe Starrett. From his point of view, he has demonstrated considerable patience by ordering his men not to use their guns. Whatever sympathy we may feel for him evaporates, however, when he allows the gunman Wilson to kill Torrey and attempts to trick Starrett into an unfair gunfight. Another unusual feature of the plot is the delicacy and restraint with which the love triangle of Joe, Marion, and Shane is presented. They are three decent people who could not easily betray love or trust. Joe is particularly admirable in the way he holds back his jealousy as Shane unintentionally threatens his roles of husband and father. Stevens only once reveals the settler's inner conflict overtly before his explicit statements as he prepares to fight Ryker: when he frowns as he watches Marion and Shane dancing together during the Fourth of July celebration. Finally, there is Chris's warning to Shane about Ryker's intentions. Although he bullied Shane in the saloon, anticipation of his change of heart appears in shots of the bewildered cowboy during Torrey's funeral. It is rare, however, in pre-forties Westerns for a villain to betray his boss on the basis of conscience.

We find in *Shane,* then, a combination of both the romantic and the realistic. What makes the film special is not only that these two approaches are inextricably joined but also that they implicate viewers by imposing upon them complementary points of view— one objective and the other subjective—that operate simultaneously.

As viewers, we observe objectively all that happens. Often Stevens uses high-angle, panoramic shots so that we look down on the ranch, wagons traveling to the town, or the town itself. We are not alone, though, in those scenes involving Shane. Joey first sees

Shane when he arrives and is the last person with him when he departs. With one exception (considered later), the youngster is physically present in every major incident involving the gunfighter. Lest we forget Joey's omnipresence when Shane is on the screen, Stevens cuts repeatedly from one to the other. Moreover, two of the three times when the stranger is in physical danger, Joey helps him: by calling for aid when Shane is attacked by Ryker's men in the saloon and by shouting a warning in the last sequence when his hero is about to be shot at from behind (Figure 8.14). Only when Shane and his father fight does Joey watch helplessly.

**FIGURE 8.14**

*Shane.* (a) Joey and his dog watch from under the swinging doors of Ryker's saloon as Shane has a showdown with Ryker and Wilson. (b) A subjective shot from Joey's point of view of the interior of the saloon just before the shooting starts.

We thus associate Shane with Joey. Although there are many subjective shots of Shane from the boy's point of view, a consistent subjectivism is not maintained. Rather *we* gradually come to see the gunfighter through Joey's eyes. Stevens encourages this perspective by usually shooting Shane from a low angle even when the shot is objective and the boy is in the frame or in another setting. A cynic might point out this was necessary because Alan Ladd was so short and slim that he hardly seemed capable of contending with the tall, burly Van Heflin (Joe Starrett) or robust Ben Johnson (Chris). A discerning viewer, in fact, notices that the director helped Ladd with more than camera angles. Near the end of the film, for example, when Shane stands in the doorway to prevent Joe from meeting Ryker, the lower part of his body is always hidden, and it is obvious that Ladd is standing on a platform. Practical reasons may necessitate this repeated use of low-angle shots of Shane, but there is also the psychological advantage of reminding us of Joey's idealization of the stranger.

There could be another reason why Stevens cast the unlikely Ladd in the role of Shane. Joey not only admires the gunfighter but also identifies with him. The youngster is at an age when he is impatient to be accepted as an adult and to challenge his father's authority. He would be encouraged by the example of his hero that he does not have to grow to the size of his father before attaining his dreams. Shane appears to have an insight into what is going on in Joey's mind. He is attentive to the boy, begins to teach him to shoot, and in his final speech in effect lays the responsibility for the future on the boy's shoulders.

If this film confined itself to presenting Shane as seen through the adoring eyes of Joey, it would not differ, except in quality, from the approach of the classic "B" Western. As was suggested earlier in this chapter, during the three decades prior to 1939, the Western had its defenders, but most adults considered the genre, especially when exposed to "B"-level works, as fare only for unsophisticated young people or as the secret vice of someone older, comparable to reading comic books. During and after World War II, many makers of Westerns attempted to capture a mature audience by instilling greater realism, violence,

sex, and spectacle into the genre. In the process, heroes became antiheroes, and innocence converted into the cynicism and corruption of, say, *The Wild Bunch*. Another possibility, developed by Ford, Hawks, and others, was to combine realism with the Western romance in such a way that an adult could safely respond to familiar formulae, yet be able to recognize real people in a real world. This is the approach taken by Stevens and Guthrie in *Shane*. Romance is represented by the subjective view of Joey; however, sufficient realism is also included—as well as the conflict between the two—so that a viewer can share the boy's perspective while at the same time maintaining an objectivity that makes possible an apprehension of a realistic dimension.

To some degree, everyone in the film is exposed to this type of stereoscopic presentation, particularly Shane. We recognize, as Joey does not, that he is a homeless wanderer who wants to give up gunfighting but must pay for his past. As soon as he exchanges his costume for a ranch worker's clothes— an unthinkable action for a traditional Western hero— he becomes vulnerable. Within a few minutes he is humiliated by Chris and branded a coward. Joey is not present at the scene in the saloon, for he only sees the hero in Shane, but we are. We realize that the man's open affection for the boy and suppressed feelings for Marion are expressions of his desire for a family and security. Joey cannot understand this, although, like his father, he obviously senses the undercurrent of attraction between his ideal and his mother. While we share with the boy the thrill of watching our hero destroy the villains in fair combat, we as adults also sympathize with someone who must wander like Cain, because as a man who kills, Shane is branded with shame.

Ryker's wrongheaded but roughly eloquent defense of his actions, the low-key love triangle, the conversion of Chris—elements that are departures from the traditional Western—are necessary if adult viewers are to preserve a dual vision. Also important to the realism of the story are the town, the killing of Torrey, and later his burial. The five ramshackle buildings fronting a dirt street on a flat plain fit our conception of how an actual frontier town might have looked.

The murder of Torrey on the muddy street, aside from melodramatic lighting and cloud shadows, has verisimilitude. It is appropriate that Joey is not present at the brutal killing. The burial of the Southerner also has touches that ring true, such as the women sitting on chairs and the plain white coffin with a large knot in it. This time the youngster is present, but his reactions reveal how much he would like to reject this stark consequence of the gunfighting that so fascinates him. At one point in the ceremony, he walks away, watched by Shane, to pet a suckling colt [see Figure 8.17(a,b)]. We sense that the boy unconsciously identifies with the colt and wishes for the security of a child that is threatened by the pine coffin.

The conflict in Joey between the comfort of childhood and the desire to be an adult, intensified by the arrival of Shane, has ramifications that become evident to a viewer who is willing to examine *Shane* from a psychoanalytical perspective. A Freudian interpretation in particular can help to illuminate a source of the youngster's tensions.

Joey is close to his mother and somewhat estranged from his busy father. Joe Starrett makes no secret of his sensual feelings for his wife. Under these circumstances, the youngster's natural Oedipal jealousy of his father would be intensified. Furthermore, he associates a gun with power and authority; he is allowed, however, to possess only a small, unloaded rifle. Throughout the film, he complains that his parents will not give him bullets for his gun. The sexual symbolism of the gun is obvious.

Shane appears on the scene. His pearl-handled six-shooter fascinates Joey. One can easily imagine the youngster thinking that if he had such a gun, his father would not be able to say deprecatingly of the boy's small rifle that it is no threat because "Heck, it's not even loaded." Joey has no conscious idea of how he might use Shane's gun. It is significant in a psychological context, however, that at dinner the boy reacts to only one statement by his father. He insists on knowing what Joe Starrett means by remarking that he will only leave the land—and his family—in a box. Marion, frightened, silences her son.

It is impossible for the boy to challenge his father in actuality, but he can through Shane, by identi-

fying with the mysterious outsider. Shane's small stature makes the identification easier. There is also the correspondence that as Joey is considered impotent by the adults, so too his alter ego is at first branded a coward and of little value in a showdown. The boy has no doubts that Shane is a hero and can handle Ryker's men, but the real challenge is his father, so Joey attempts to figure out who would win a conflict between the two men, that is, between himself and his father ("Pa, can you shoot as good as Shane? . . . Could you whip Shane?").

Joey watches and finds vicarious satisfaction in his mother's involuntary interest in Shane. Nothing overt happens in this suppressed affair, so the boy's psychic dream is not contaminated by distasteful reality, as in the case of Torrey's death. He can stand next to Shane and observe his father kiss his mother at the dance (Figure 8.15), yet know he is winning a victory of his own, one that does not involve a direct confrontation with his father. Meanwhile, Shane, unlike his father, is willing to teach him how to shoot. Marion watches the two and does not approve of her son's learning how to handle a gun.

The dreaded confrontation does occur, and the boy must face his guilt feelings. His Oedipal fantasies

---

**FIGURE 8.15**

*Shane.* At the Fourth of July celebrations, Joe and Marion acknowledge the congratulations of the homesteaders on their wedding anniversary. Joey and Shane look on. In a few moments, Joe will kiss his wife.

become reality as Joe Starrett and Shane fight, and Joey, a boy after all, has not the courage to make a choice until Shane uses his gun unfairly to hit Joe and win. The youngster verbally attacks the man he wants to be and helps his prostrate father. He cannot, however, completely give up his dream and runs after Shane.

At the end of the film, Shane in essence tells Joey to grow up (Figure 8.16). He should assume responsibility for his parents. Although the youngster calls after the man on whom he has projected his conscious and unconscious desires, we assume that Joey has completed his *rite de passage.* He will now enter a new stage in his development in which the most obvious manifestations of his Oedipus complex have been laid to rest. He will now meet his father as less a rival and more an ally and model. At least that is what we hope for Joey.

*Shane.* Shane bids farewell to Joey.

It is impossible to determine from the film, and there is no evidence in print, that Stevens and Guthrie intentionally planned to present this psychic drama. The overtones of the film, however, are consistent with such a Freudian interpretation. Shane, of course, exists as a concrete person on the screen; however, this perspective reveals how Joey, through projection, could make use of the stranger to deal with his—and, to the degree that each viewer identifies with the boy, our—innermost needs.

There are other aspects of *Shane* that contribute to making it a masterful Western: The acting is outstanding, the color vivid, and the background music serviceable (though at times overly lush and melodramatic). The camera-editing dynamics, however, are particularly impressive. George Stevens, as in all his best films, combines technical skill with scenes of imaginative photography.

Noteworthy are three devices used throughout *Shane.* The transition most often applied between scenes is the dissolve. This technique gives the film a dreamlike quality appropriate to Joey's romantic point of view. Second, a sense of spatial depth is achieved in individual shots by having an object close to the camera through which or beyond which distant action is presented. In the opening shot after the credits, a deer is in the foreground, and under its neck, far in the distance, a lone rider approaches the camera. Another example is the stamping horses' legs through which we see Joe Starrett and Shane fighting. Windows and doorways also serve as framing structures for deep-focus effects. Finally, a startling visual rhythm is attained by means of a succession of two or three swift tracking-in shots. The most dramatic instance (enhanced by the surging music and a low angle) is when Joe and Shane uproot an immense tree stump, but the device is used elsewhere, as in two shots of Ryker in the doorway of the saloon.

Every viewer will have a list of favorite scenes and sequences, such as Shane arriving at the Starrett ranch, the Fourth of July dance, Ryker talking to Starrett after the dance, the killing of Torrey, the Swede carrying Torrey's body home, the final gun battle, and Shane's departure. Our concern here, however, is not scenes and sequences whose effectiveness is based primarily on dramatic and contextual resonances, such as those just listed, but the ones that demonstrate particularly striking camera-editing dynamics. In this respect, probably the most impressive sequence in the film is the burial of Torrey.

After an establishing shot, the 26 shots that make up the burial sequence (excluding the epilogue of Joe and Shane exhorting the families to stay) begin and end with a dissolve to Ryker and his men in front of the saloon. The first and last shots of Cemetery Hill are long, lengthy ones. The remaining 22 shots,

FIGURE 8.17

*Shane.* The sequence of Torrey's funeral begins with the establishing shot illustrated in Figure 1.5a, continues with the parallel tracking shot illustrated in Figures 1.25a to 1.25c, and then includes these shots. (a) Joey escapes from the reality of the burial by petting a colt. (b) He is observed by Shane. (c) Shane stands with the mourners just before Joe attempts to persuade the homesteaders to remain.

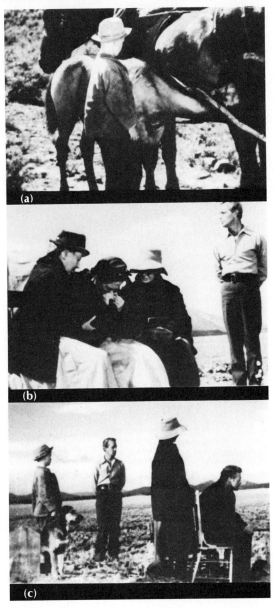

(a)

(b)

(c)

through a carefully paced visual rhythm, create a tone of touching sadness (Figure 8.17). Stevens combines pans and shots of individuals with close-ups and medium shots, as of the dog, the little girl, or Joe Starrett's foot on a shovel digging into the earth. In a number of group shots, a bit of the coffin is visible at the edge or base of the frame. Another visual motif is the harmonica player (playing dolorously the song associated with Torrey) in the foreground or background. Joey is not forgotten, for we see him with the others, as well as walking to the colt. High-angle shots provide a change of perspective, as in the second one in the series of the mourners singing, the coffin in the ground, and Joey with the colt. A fitting conclusion, before cutting to Ryker and his men, is a pan of the motionless mourners silhouetted against the sky, ending with a view of the plains and some of Ryker's men far in the distance (the significance of which—they will set fire to the house of one of the homesteaders—is anticipated by a dramatic rise in the background music).

The fight between Starrett and Shane is also extremely well done. The beginning is seen from within the house as Marion and Joey rush from one window to another. When the camera moves outside, there are cutaways from the two battling to horses and cattle agitated by the violence, as well as combinations of men and animals, with shots of stamping horses' legs in the foreground and Joe and Shane together in the background (Figure 8.18). The scene is photographed with much greater visual imagination than the more conventional but equally exciting earlier fight in the saloon.

The uprooting of the huge tree stump by Joe and Shane symbolizes a cooperation and comaraderie that can overcome the obstacles of nature, which Joe is attempting to instill in his friends in dealing with Ryker. These overtones of the scene are made dramatic and concrete not only by the dialogue and rousing background music but also by such cinematic techniques as low-angle shots of Shane and Joe separately and together and the climactic three rapid tracking-in shots noted earlier.

Some critics have suggested that *Shane* is entirely the dream of a boy. This interpretation is viable, related to the Freudian one advanced in this analysis, but only if a film can simultaneously be the dream of a character in it and a presentation of objective reality. The reality is convincing and enhances the value of the film. Most of us, however, find the romantic perspective more moving. We want to believe, against the evidence of history and common sense, that once upon a time and place, men like Shane existed. A dream, yes, but an innocent and exciting one realized with imagination and artistry. For this reason alone, *Shane* deserves its status as a Western classic.

**FIGURE 8.18**

*Shane.* The fight between Shane and Joe. By shooting through the legs of stamping horses, Stevens not only presents a striking visual image but also underscores how the violent struggle between two friends disrupts the security and unity of the Starrett farm.

## ANTIHERO WESTERN

### *The Wild Bunch*

*My idea was that* The Wild Bunch *would have a cathartic effect. No, I don't like violence. In fact, when I look at the film itself, I find it unbearable.*
Sam Peckinpah[13]

*The overriding effect is of a mania, the eccentric passion of a man who has found a medium that perfectly accommodates his passion. He likes killing, and he does it very well. His art makes it so generic, so tribal, that we can't even go through the usual self-flagellation, American style, about our American violence.*
Stanley Kauffmann, 1969[14]

### CAST

*William Holden (Pike Bishop), Ernest Borgnine (Dutch), Robert Ryan (Deke Thornton), Edmond O'Brien (Sykes), Warren Oates (Lyle Gorch), Ben Johnson (Tector Gorch), Jaime Sanchez (Angel), Emilio Fernandez (Mapache), Strother Martin (Coffer), L. Q. Jones (T.C.), Albert Dekker (Harrigan), and others.*

### CREDITS

*Director—Sam Peckinpah, Producer—Phil Feldman, Screenwriters—Walon Green and Sam Peckinpah (from a story by Walon Green and Ray N. Sickner), Director of Photography—Lucien Ballard, Editor—Louis Lombardo, Composer—Jerry Fielding, Art Director—Edward Garrere, and others.*

1969/Warner Bros.–Seven Arts
Technicolor/145 minutes

### BACKGROUND

Sam Peckinpah (1926–) is the preeminent American director of Westerns of the sixties and early seventies as Bud Boetticher and Anthony Mann were of the fifties. His most ardent admirers consider him to be the heir to the mantle of the grand master, John Ford. This may be a premature judgment, but he has established himself as an innovative and provocative filmmaker.

Born in California of pioneer stock, Peckinpah first worked in the theater as an actor and director. He entered filmmaking via the route of television Western series. In the fifties, he wrote and directed numerous episodes of "Gunsmoke," "The Rifleman," and especially "The Westerner."

The *Deadly Companions* (1961) was Peckinpah's first feature film. It is the story of a romance between a gunfighter (Brian Keith) and a widow (Maureen O'Hara) that develops as they travel through dangerous Indian territory. *Ride the High Country* (1962) has as its time setting the beginning of the twentieth century when there were men who still remembered the old frontier and willingly risked their lives to prove to themselves that their values and skills still had meaning in the modern world. Joel McCrea and Randolph Scott are outstanding as aged lawmen who embark on a dangerous adventure that leads to the death of one of them.

*Major Dundee* (1964) was intended to be a work of epic proportions and with major characters of a complexity and ambiguity rarely found in Westerns. Unfortunately, 1 hour of the original screenplay was never filmed, and 14 minutes were excised from the final print by the producers. Even the truncated version, however, is a remarkable motion picture. The essential plot, as in so many of Peckinpah's films, consists of a journey: the pursuit of a band of Apaches into Mexico by Union army troops and Confederate prisoners. Of central interest is the conflict between the inflexible, seemingly indomitable Dundee (Charlton Heston) and the proud, dashing Confederate leader, Tyreen (Richard Harris).

*The Wild Bunch* (1969) is usually considered to be Peckinpah's most impressive Western thus far in his career. It illustrates most of his major themes, approaches, and techniques. As will be discussed in the "Analysis" section, *The Wild Bunch* includes larger-than-life, individualistic, male-bonded antiheroes; a subordinate role for women; a controversial emphasis on and manner of photographing violence; and an attempt to extract contemporary significance from events that occurred when the frontier was fading.

The director's next film represents a change of pace. *The Ballad of Cable Hogue* (1970) tells of the redemption of a volatile, independent drunkard (played with gusto by Jason Robards, Jr.) through the discovery of a water hole in a desert along a stagecoach route and his romance with a prostitute (Stella Stevens). This cinematic idyll cloaked in realistic details is charming (the only film by Peckinpah to which this adjective can be applied) and humorous.

Peckinpah has directed to date only one other premodern Western. *Pat Garrett and Billy the Kid* (1973) contains the psychological insights and vivid camera techniques of the previous films, but its effectiveness is weakened by cuts unauthorized by the director and a diffuse narrative. His other motion pictures have contemporary settings at various locales and are in different genres: *Straw Dogs* (1971, a thriller in which an American professor on sabbatical in a primitive Cornish village must defend himself, his wife, and a mentally retarded murderer against an attack on his house by ruffians), *Junior Bonner* (1972, a modern Western dealing with rodeo riders), *The Getaway* (1973, a gangster film), *Bring Me the Head of Alfredo Garcia* (1974, another gangster film, much of it taking place in Mexico), *The Killer Elite* (1976, a spy story), *Cross of Iron* (1977, set at the front in Europe during World War II), and *Convoy* (1978, independent truckers battle a Southern police chief).

After *Straw Dogs,* the director's most perceptive and suspenseful non-Western film, Peckinpah's works show a deterioration of his powers as a filmmaker. He has increasingly opted for flashy surface effects rather than substantial, organic forms and feelings. His characters are frequently caricatures, two-dimensional creatures whose responses to adversity appear to be no more than hollow gestures rather than leading to revelations of inner needs and compulsions. Moreover, a stylistic problem emerges in his latest films.

The techniques are still striking, but they often possess an inert quality, a hollowness. They give the impression of being motivated by habit rather than artistic requirements; in short, they have become rhetorical in the negative sense of the term. For this reason, more than one critic has observed that in *The Killer Elite* and *Cross of Iron,* Peckinpah seems almost to be parodying himself. When a director's style loses the underpinnings of vitality and imaginativeness, distinctive techniques appear to be there for their own sake, calling attention to themselves, as a caricature points up the weakest physical characteristics of its subject.

One aspect of Peckinpah's style, however, has remained consistent. His emphasis on violence has consistently caused controversy. Extreme violence has become an accepted component of the work of most post–World War II directors of Westerns, but no one has presented unnatural death and mutilation more vividly than Peckinpah. In his films, bullets do not simply enter a body and lodge there; they explode, causing agony and spurts of red blood. For many viewers, Peckinpah compounds the horror of these scenes by counterpointing a rapid editing rhythm, sounds of gunfire, screams of pain, and bright splotches of blood with individual shots of men falling in slow motion. This technique both prolongs an image of dying and adds a grace note to the last moments of suffering.

As the epigraphs to this essay suggest, there are opposing opinions on why violence appears with such frequency and intensity in Peckinpah's films. The director defends himself by maintaining that a surfeit of brutal deaths will disgust audiences so that they will condemn violence. Others, led by Judith Crist, find in his work a perverted pleasure, an orgiastic reveling in mayhem. Even if the director is taken at his word, each viewer must judge the overall effect of this characteristic of Peckinpah's style, for there can be a vast difference between a director's intention and the effect of what appears on the screen.

*The Wild Bunch* was extensively cut in length by Warner Bros. before its release. This is typical of the problems Peckinpah has had with his producers. John Fell mentions that this film "is said to have sustained 3,500 studio cuts."[15] At its premiere in Great Britain, the film was 10 minutes longer than the 16mm prints available from American rental companies. Jim Kitses summarizes the contents of the two most important scenes, both flashbacks, omitted in the standard version.[16] Deke Thornton was deserted by Pike and Sykes and captured when lawmen sprung a trap while the three were in a bordello. The second scene explains why Pike has a weak leg. The woman he loved was killed by her husband, who also shot Pike.

The director of photography was Lucien Ballard, one of Hollywood's most distinguished cinematographers. He has worked with Peckinpah on *Ride the High Country, The Ballad of Cable Hogue, Junior Bonner,* and *The Getaway,* among other films. As usual, the director collaborated on the screenplay. The major actors—Holden, Borgnine, Ryan, and O'-Brien—were veterans in their profession when they appeared in *The Wild Bunch.* For secondary roles, Peckinpah tends to use the same actors repeatedly. A viewer who has seen a few of the director's Westerns will find familiar the faces of Warren Oates, Ben Johnson, Strother Martin, and L. Q. Jones.

With the exception of the Film Critics Award for Best Cinematography in 1969 to Lucien Ballard, *The Wild Bunch* did not win any major prizes. It was, however, fairly successful at the box office. Most critics praised the film, though some had qualifications about the violence in the opening and closing sequences, and its reputation has grown with the passing of time.

### PLOT SUMMARY

Behind and between the credits, we see a group of men in cavalry uniforms riding into the town of Starbuck. They pass a group of children. The men dismount before an office of the South Texas Railroad. When the credits end, there is crosscutting between the "soldiers" in the railroad office, who turn out to be outlaws, others positioned in the street, bounty hunters hired by the railroad on the roofs, and the members of a temperance union marching down the main street in front of the railroad office. When the men on the roofs are spotted, the outlaws gather up the loot and charge into the street. The result is a holocaust in which not only the gunmen on both sides but also townspeople are killed. Six members of the gang escape, passing the children again as they leave town.

Harrigan (Dekker), an official of the railroad, berates Deke Thornton (Ryan) for not killing Pike (Holden), the leader of the gang. We learn from their argument that Thornton was once a member of the Wild Bunch but was captured and sent to a penitentiary. He has been released to the custody of Harrigan in return for his promise to help to destroy Pike and his men. Meanwhile, one of the gang has been blinded and cannot ride; Pike shoots him. Thornton and his men are in pursuit.

The outlaws meet an old man, Sykes (O'Brien),

who has fresh horses ready for them. After an argument between the Gorch brothers—Lyle (Oates) and Tector (Johnson)—and Angel (Sanchez), a young Mexican, the stolen bags are opened. They contain only iron washers. The six ride off. At night, Pike and Dutch (Borgnine), second in command, talk. The next day, the gang rides across a desert; finally they cross the Rio Grande and enter Mexico. Thornton and his men also reach the river but turn back and return to Starbuck.

Angel brings the gang to his village to rest. They are welcomed warmly, but the young Mexican learns that his father was killed by the troops of General Mapache (Fernandez), the local bandit leader, and his girlfriend left with the murderers.

The Wild Bunch arrives at Agua Verde, Mapache's stronghold. When Angel sees his beloved kissing Mapache, he kills her and is taken prisoner. Pike makes a deal with the general and his German advisers to steal guns and ammunition from a U.S. Army train for $10,000 in gold. He insists that he requires the help of Angel, who agrees to join them if he receives one case of guns and another of ammunition for his people instead of his share of the gold.

In Starbuck, Thornton guesses where the gang will attack next. Cut to an Army train. Inside a coach are Thornton and his men and a group of very young Army recruits. Pike and his men cleverly separate the locomotive and equipment carrier from the two coaches. Farther down the line, they transfer the arms to a wagon and ride away. Thornton's group trails them.

In the hills on the road to Agua Verde, Pike and Dutch watch their pursuers through binoculars. That night, Angel's friends claim their two cases of arms. The next day a contingent of Mapache's troops attempts to appropriate the wagon without paying the gang. Pike, however, has rigged it with dynamite and threatens to blow it up if the troops do not withdraw. As the bandits ride away, there is a shot of Thornton watching what is happening. In the next scene, Pike enters Mapache's fortress alone. He will tell the general where a quarter of the crates are buried if he receives a quarter of the gold. This procedure will be followed until all the arms and payments have been exchanged. He presents to Mapache as a gift a machine gun found among the arms.

Dutch and Angel make the last exchange. Mapache has learned, however, what happened to the missing crates, and the young Mexican is once again captured; Dutch is forced to leave alone. At camp, the gang decides there is nothing they can do to help their friend.

Sykes is riding alone when he is attacked by Thornton's men and shot in the leg. He hides and is found by one of the hillmen to whom Angel gave the arms. Pike and Dutch watch Sykes being pursued through binoculars, and they agree that the safest place for them would be Agua Verde.

When the outlaws enter Mapache's fortress amid celebrations, they find a car dragging Angel along the ground. The general refuses to exchange the prisoner for Pike's share of the gold. The four are commanded to enjoy themselves. In the next scene, Pike is dressing after being with a Mexican woman. He reaches a decision and calls the others. Fully armed, they march to confront Mapache and his 200 men.

The general pretends that he will release Angel but instead slits the young man's throat. Pike shoots him, then the chief German adviser. Pandemonium breaks loose, with shooting on all sides. By gaining control of the machine gun, the four hold their own. One by one, however, they are killed; Pike is shot in the back by a youngster.

Thornton and his men enter the devastated fortress. The bounty hunters carry away the bodies of the outlaws, but their leader remains behind. A little later, there is the sound of shots. Sykes arrives with the Mexican hillmen; they have killed the bounty hunters. Sykes asks Thornton to join them; he agrees. They ride away.

The film concludes with a superimposition of the final credits over the Wild Bunch leaving Angel's village.

─────────────────
ANALYSIS

*The Wild Bunch* opens and closes with sequences of the slaughter of human beings. Although there are similarities between the massacres (for example, inno-

cent people are murdered in both), the context of the two sequences of violence differs. In Starbuck, the members of the Wild Bunch are motivated by greed and callousness; in Agua Verde, they kill to avenge the death of a comrade and to preserve their self-respect. Meanwhile, during a journey, we have gained insights into the characters of the five men, and this tempers an adverse judgment of the death and destruction that they perpetrate in the Mexican town.

Pike Bishop is the leader and brains of the gang. He plans their escapades and makes all their major decisions. More than any of the others, he recognizes, as he says after they discover that the bags stolen from the railroad contain washers, "We got to start thinking beyond our guns. Those days are closing fast." He holds authority over the others not only because he is the most intelligent but also because he takes on the responsibility of leadership and can be ruthless when the situation demands it.

On the other hand, Pike insists on the need for loyalty if the gang is to survive. When they are crossing a desert and an argument breaks out, he declares: "When you side with a man, you stay with him. And when you can't do that, you're like some animal. You're finished. We're finished. All of us." There is no contradiction between his dedication to the group and his willingness to desert Sykes and Angel. Pike is essentially a pragmatist. If the odds are too high against him, he will leave a man to his fate unless, as happens at the end of the film, more than loyalty is involved.

Like most of Peckinpah's Western "heroes," Pike has professional pride. On the way to Mexico after escaping from Starbuck, he tells Dutch that their next "score" might be a payroll. His friend remarks, "They'll be waiting for us." Pike's reply: "I wouldn't have it any other way." It is obvious that the challenge and danger as well as the money have made him an outlaw.

Pike has, however, a physical weakness and a psychological burden. For all his intelligence, bravery, pragmatic loyalty to his men, and lack of fastidiousness when it comes to killing—admirable qualities in outlaws and military leaders—he is getting too old for his trade. Peckinpah conceived with atypical understatement a superb visual moment to convey this problem facing Pike. The gang is on a desert during their flight from Starbuck. The outlaw chief has just lectured his men on the importance of loyalty and starts to mount his horse. The stirrup breaks, and Pike falls heavily on his game leg. While the Gorch brothers jeer at him, he slowly and painfully lifts himself into the saddle. His back is to the camera as he begins to ride away. While the background music consists of a wistful tune, the camera tracks in a little toward him, then holds in a lengthy shot as Pike, with shoulders hunched, rides slowly in the bright light away from the camera and over a mound of sand (Figure 8.19).

---

**FIGURE 8.19**

*The Wild Bunch.* A lovely shot of the aging, hurt Pike going (and being) over the hill.

Pike knows that he cannot endure the physical demands of an outlaw's strenuous life much longer. He plans to retire. What he wants, he tells Dutch, is to make "one good score and then back off." His friend's insightful reply is, "Back off to what?" Could Pike really tolerate the quiet life of a rancher or storekeeper, eking out his existence as a commonplace, aging ex-outlaw?

He is also psychologically burdened by an awareness of the emptiness of his past as well as his future. This apparently influences him in the most significant decision he makes in the film, one that results in his death: the attempt to rescue Angel. To escape the bounty hunters, he, Dutch, and the Gorch broth-

ers have sought refuge in Agua Verde, where they witness the torturing of their friend. In the next scene, Pike is with a Mexican woman. He is putting on his shirt, and she is gently patting water on his shoulders. A baby cries. The voice of Lyle is heard from the next room, arguing with a woman about payment for her services. Not a word passes between Pike and his woman. First there is a two-shot and then a series of separate shots, with cutting from one to the other. The outlaw looks at her with gentleness and warmth. Suddenly, he reaches a decision. He throws away the bottle from which he has been drinking, puts his gun belt over his shoulder, and calls to the brothers, "Let's go!"—the battle cry of the gang. Before he leaves, he places some money in front of the woman and looks at her sadly.

It is not too difficult to conjecture what was going through Pike's mind at some level of consciousness. His life has lacked fulfilling love with a woman and a family. All he has left is his ability as an outlaw leader, his self-respect, and his loyalty to his men. Mapache has put each of these supports in question by capturing and torturing Angel. Pike's command, "Let's go!" represents in effect his picking up the gauntlet thrown down by the disreputable bandit chief, and against overwhelming odds he sets forth with his men to regain his honor.

This allusion to a knight's entering the lists is not farfetched. Whatever his faults, Pike is a man of heroic dimensions. When T.C. says in an awed tone on seeing the body of the outlaw leader, "There's Pike!" and Thornton takes the pistol from the hand of his former friend and puts it into his own holster, we are witnessing homage being paid to an incipient legend. This aura is obviously the director's intention. As Francis Ford Coppola did with Vito Corleone in *The Godfather,* Peckinpah persuades us—no matter how reluctantly—to admire a murderer with some redeeming qualities, especially those of courage and dignity.

Dutch is completely devoted to Pike; he supports his leader on every occasion. There is even a faint suggestion of latent homosexuality on Dutch's part in his relationship with his friend. While Pike and the Gorch brothers are with women in Agua Verde, Dutch sits outside occupying himself with the sterile activity of whittling a piece of wood. He is as ruthless and pragmatic as Pike. On the other hand, Dutch is a moralist of sorts within the restrictions imposed by his trade. When the gang first enters Agua Verde and Pike remarks that both themselves and Mapache are bandits, Dutch insists, "We're nothing like him. We don't hang nobody." (After the massacre at Starbuck, this is a self-serving, sophistic logic.) When Pike defends Thornton by saying their former partner gave his word to pursue them, Dutch replies, "That ain't what counts. It's who you give it to."

Whereas the others, even Pike, have illusions about retiring from being outlaws, Dutch sees clearly that they have no place to which to "back off." Perhaps in addition to being clear-headed about their future, he is afraid of losing Pike, for their friendship is the keystone of his existence. With his last breath, he calls out his friend's name. If it is not extravagant to compare Pike to a knight, then Dutch is an Olivier to his leader's Roland.

Although Sykes, as Pike remarks, "did his share of killing," he is now an old man relegated to taking care of horses and serving coffee. He is resented by the Gorch brothers and is the butt of their cruel jokes. If Pike needed any reminder of the denigration that an aged outlaw must endure, Sykes is a living example. Since the old man is a straightforward character—a survivor who enjoys the challenge and camaraderie of the gang and is eager to get his hands on gold—it is surprising that at the end he joins the Mexican rebels. After all, there is no indication that he is wanted by the law and could not return to the United States. Perhaps, like Pike and Dutch if they had lived, he has nowhere to go, and the hill people are the only family available to him. As he says to Thornton in the last line of dialogue in the film, "Ain't like it use to be, but it'll do."

The Gorch brothers, Lyle and Tector, are vulgar, cruel, violent, and greedy. Yet even they are not completely worthless. They are loyal to each other, and when led by a strong leader like Pike, their unquestionable courage can be put to practical use in an outlaw raid. Their finest moment is when they willingly join the other two in challenging Mapache and his men.

It is in the final bloody battle that the two brothers assume a disturbing dimension. A viewer of that sequence may find them at this time both attractive and repulsive, but not everyone in an audience who so reacts would want to explore the reasons. The Gorch brothers live by their instincts, and two interrelated manifestations of those instincts are violence and sex. It is difficult to recall another Western in which violence is presented so graphically and explicitly as sexual expression. Lyle and Tector cry out ecstatically as they take turns in mowing down men and women with a machine gun [see Figure 8.21(e)]. Each is indulging in an orgy of murder that reaches a final climax in his own death. What is projected is a perverted cinematic *Liebestod*. Considering that during this sequence the brothers are represented by the director as heroes, it is no wonder that many viewers have been troubled by certain implied attitudes toward violence in *The Wild Bunch*.

Angel is different from the others in the gang. First of all, he is Mexican and has roots that the Americans do not. He has a home that he is willing to fight for and a village to which to return. Even more important, he is young and so is capable of being romantic and idealistic. He kills Teresa, now "Mapache's woman," when surrounded by the bandit leader's men. Earlier we had seen him playing a guitar and singing to another woman. The Mexican village elder sums up this aspect of the youth's character when he says, referring to Teresa, "Angel dreams of love while Mapache eats the mango."

He is allied with the hillmen in fighting against Mapache. In an impassioned speech to Pike, Dutch, and Sykes in the bathhouse, he declares that he cannot steal guns so that the bandits "can kill my people again." Although Pike calls Angel "a pain in the ass," we sense that the older men admire the commitment of the youth to an ideal, a quality they lack. It is not simply outrage at seeing a comrade being tortured that prompts Pike to offer Mapache his share of the gold for Angel; it is also a recognition that the young man is the best of them.

The Wild Bunch is a group of thieves and killers, yet they possess the virtues of loyalty to one another, courage, and resourcefulness. The same cannot be said of those who hunt and oppose them. Harrigan, the railroad manager and representative of the law, is a caricature of evil. He is arrogant, ruthless, and a bully. The band of bounty hunters hired by the railroad and led by Thornton is just what the former outlaw calls them: "gutter trash" and "scum." They are cowardly, bloodthirsty, and vulturine (appropriately, they enter Agua Verde during the final sequence at the same time as actual vultures attack the corpses).

Mapache and his officers are no better. He is crude, cruel, and a drunkard, yet in his own way also shrewd. He and his men are as much outlaws as the Wild Bunch, differing in the size of their bandit crew, disguise as a military force, and apparent lack of any moral principles. Behind Mapache is the gray eminence of the German military expert and his lieutenant, who are obviously manipulating the bandit chief for the purposes of their government (the time setting is World War I). In many ways these two Europeans are even more objectionable than the Mexican outlaws. Like Harrigan, they arrange for others to do their killing for them.

The victims of Harrigan and his bounty hunters and Mapache and his soldiers are the American and Mexican civilians. They are slaughtered, including women and children. The Mexicans are tyrannized by their leader, and their passivity is therefore understandable. Less comprehensible is the reaction of the Americans. A segment of the citizens of Starbuck march against the consumption of alcohol, a minor vice compared to murder. Yet when their main street is turned into a battleground and the citizens must protect the bodies of the slain from being stripped by the bounty hunters, the mayor and other officials ineffectually protest to Harrigan. Are they afraid of the man or of the power of the railroad he represents? Peckinpah appears to be saying that violence in the hands of evil men can oppress a people whether they live in a dictatorship or a democracy.

Outside of all groups—the true loner—is Deke Thornton. All we know of him in the version of *The Wild Bunch* available in the United States is that he was a member of an outlaw gang led by Pike, was captured and sent to prison, and in return for his freedom promised Harrigan that he would help to capture

the Wild Bunch. Although he relentlessly pursues the gang, he respects Pike. When Coffer asks Thornton what kind of man Pike is, the former outlaw replies, "The best. He never got caught." At the end of the film, he replaces his own pistol with Pike's as a tribute to his former friend.

Thornton's motivations are dealt with rather cursorily. Although he detests Harrigan and the bounty hunters in his charge, he has given his word to destroy the Wild Bunch. The reason he is determined to retain his freedom at any price is indicated by a fleeting flashback at the beginning of the film in which we see him being tortured in prison. (The original version of *The Wild Bunch* is more explicit about the relationship between Thornton and Pike, as noted earlier under "Background.") Thornton is a shrewd, brave, expert gunman, but like members of the gang, he is an anachronism in a fading frontier. Unlike the Wild Bunch, he is completely alone, torn by conflicting loyalties until the end of the film, when he joins Sykes and the Mexican hillmen.

Peckinpah concocted a rousing, bloody, realistic Western; however, he also invested his tale with implied comments on the propensity for violence in America's past and its influence on the present. It is crucial that the time setting of *The Wild Bunch* is 1916. An audience is not made aware of this fact until Pike and his men enter Agua Verde. Mapache has an automobile. When Sykes mentions a flying machine, Pike remarks, "Goin' to use them in the war, they say." There is a reference elsewhere to Pershing being present on the United States–Mexican border. The American general was there only in 1916, when he conducted punitive raids against Francesco Villa, and left in 1917 when the United States entered the European war. This is why the German advisers are directing the activities of Mapache.

By the second decade of the century, the challenge of the frontier has disappeared. The character traits of independence, bravery, integrity, and camaraderie are no longer necessary and respected. The law does not attract the allegiance of the outsider (the position of the typical classic Western hero, who lives by a code of honor supported by those who believe as he does) because the forces of civilization have become selfish, commercial, and bureaucratic, as represented by Harrigan and the railroad. Violence without integrity or honor is perpetrated by killers hired by companies that exist solely to preserve their privileges and bow only before Mammon. Individuals who retain lingering allegiances to past traditions (even if they are outlaws tainted by the corruption of their age) are the last outsiders who will risk death in defense of their self-respect.

There can be a relevance of this concept to our times. Violence is the heritage of our frontier decades, encouraged by individualism, democracy, and capitalistic free enterprise. When there are no ideals and respected codes of honor, as existed during frontier days, violence becomes indiscriminate or manipulated for its own ends by a government controlled by business interests. The results are Vietnam, assassinations, and crime in the streets. This perspective is arguable, but it is advanced by many critics who admire Peckinpah's Westerns.

The idea of a heritage of violence in America is supported in *The Wild Bunch* by the persistent presence in the film of children. In practically every sequence in which they can logically appear, either the director focuses attention on children or they are in the background observing the action. The film opens with crosscutting between the gang entering Starbuck and a group of youngsters who have placed two scorpions in a nest of ants. There is more intended than the possible symbolism that the scorpions represent the Wild Bunch destroyed by the ants of Harrigan's bounty hunters (also symbolized by vultures at the end of the film) and Mapache's men, for Peckinpah in this scene repeatedly cuts to the faces of the children. These faces are lovely and innocent [see Figure 8.21(a)]. Is the message that children, and by extension mankind, are inherently prone to sadistic violence, or are they corrupted by the lessons of cruelty taught by adults? The latter interpretation is encouraged by what follows.

When the gunfight in Starbuck is over and the Wild Bunch gallop out of town, they once again pass the children who were torturing the scorpions and now are burning the ants. A connection is thus made between the violence of the adults and the cruelty of

the youngsters. At the farm where the outlaws meet Sykes and discover that they have been tricked by Harrigan, the men are observed by Mexican-American children. That night, while the outlaws rest on their trip to the border, Angel plays a guitar and sings to a woman with two children. Angel's village, a place of innocent and simple people, is filled with romping, happy children. Even the Gorch brothers are tranquilized by this idyllic atmosphere and learn the game of cat's cradle from a young girl. The village elder remarks, "We all dream of being children again. Even the worst of us." This is the way life should or could be, but it is not the way of the world. The next sequence, which takes place in Agua Verde, opens with an expressive shot. A baby is sucking at a woman's breast. The camera tracks back to reveal that crisscrossed on the mother's chest are two bandoleers filled with bullets. Symbolically, the child is being weaned on violence.

In the holocaust at the end of the film, it is demonstrated that the outlaws have lived by the sword and die by it, but even more important in the long run, they have unknowingly sharpened the sword and passed it on to another generation. Pike is shot in the back by a boy. The look of satisfaction on the youngster's face reminds us of the children destroying the scorpions and ants in the opening sequence of the film.

It is appropriate that the elder of the Mexican village should remark on the dream of being a child again, for the sequence in Angel's home assumes the proportions of a visit by the gang to a type of Eden. In many of Peckinpah's films, Mexico is symbolic on the one hand of a place of primitive innocence where there is still commitment to integrity, communal unity, and dedication to family and land (Angel's village) and on the other hand of a country susceptible to the corrupting influence of American materialism and violence (Agua Verde).

The problem with the Mexican village sequence in *The Wild Bunch* is that it is so idyllic as to cause a disconcerting shift in the tone of the film. Although recently raided by Mapache's men, the villagers are incredibly happy and friendly, and the elder is as remarkably wise as the head lama in *Lost Horizon*. The departure of the gang is accompanied by heartwarming, inflated music that could have been borrowed from a thirties musical with painted backdrops that are supposed to represent Mexico. At the very end of the film, images of the procession and the background music are repeated, as though a spectral director were creating a triumphal march for the semiheroes into the land of the dead (Figure 8.20). One recognizes what Peckinpah is attempting to do: contrasting the sterile, desperate lives of Pike and his colleagues with a paradise lost, ending on the uplifting note of a sort of redemption for them by a suicidal act of heroism. This

concept, however, is implemented with such extravagance and sentimental flourishes as to constitute a major weakness in the film.

Unlike John Ford, Peckinpah is not adept in convincingly presenting the advantages of a family and a home. He is capable of portraying strong, self-possessed women. They are usually of secondary interest, however, to male characters preoccupied with preserving their integrity and meeting life-and-death challenges that test their manhood and the skills necessary for survival. The American version of *The Wild Bunch* is one extreme in Peckinpah's Westerns of denying woman a significant role in men's lives. Aside from the ersatz Mexican village and Pike in a momentary physical relationship in Agua Verde, women are simply members of crowds, betrayers, and whores. Like Howard Hawks in his Westerns, the director is at his best in projecting the vital interflow of camaraderie among men.

**FIGURE 8.20**

*The Wild Bunch.* This shot appears twice in the film: first when the members of the Wild Bunch are leaving the Mexican village and again at the conclusion of the Western, when all (with the exception of Sykes) are dead.

The germ of most of Peckinpah's themes, from an emphasis on violence to an aging antihero, can be traced to earlier directors of Westerns. Uniquely his own, however, is a baroque use of cinematic techniques, although he had a competitor in this respect during the sixties in Sergio Leone. There is no doubt that he is immensely skillful in manipulating his medium and taking full advantage of its resources.

Peckinpah's forte is orchestrating large groups in action sequences. In this ability, he probably has no equal among living directors, with the exception of Federico Fellini. The gun battles that open and close the film, whatever one may think of the explicitness with which bullets tear into human flesh, are superbly shot and edited (Figure 8.21). With expert pacing and shifting centers of attention, the director admirably fulfills the cardinal rule for presenting cinematically a large group in action: a balance between repeated overviews of what is happening and a focus on a few prominent individuals or minor moments within the major action. Another example of remarkable camera-editing dynamics is the robbery of the Army munitions train.

In any fast-paced sequence or scene of intense drama, the director usually brings into play his entire arsenal of cinematic techniques. The two most noticeable of his camera-editing dynamics, because so distinctive, are his repeated use of slow motion and zoom shots. Peckinpah is addicted to presenting wounded men falling to the ground in slow motion. More than a dozen times in the opening and closing gunfights, the death of men is extended in time by this special effect. The technique is not confined to group gunfights. When Pike and his men return to Mexico with the stolen guns and are met by a contingent of Mapache's men, one of the bandits prematurely fires on the Wild Bunch. The hapless youth is ordered shot by his own leader, and his body floats down from a cliff where he was stationed. Earlier, the gang is crossing a desert, and they and their horses tumble down a sand dune; this is presented in slow motion. Generally, however, it is violent deaths that are photographed in this manner. Critics of Peckinpah maintain that slow motion extends and adds gracefulness to an ugly event. Defenders insist with equal fervor that the

director is forcing audiences to confront the horror of a bloody death, as Arthur Penn did at the conclusion of *Bonnie and Clyde* (1967).

As noted in Chapter 1, the zoom shot is a form of visual exclamation mark. Repeated use of this device tends to lessen its ability to startle us. This is what happens in *The Wild Bunch.* Peckinpah utilizes the zoom shot not only during gun battles but also when something important is occurring or could happen. At one point, for instance, when Thornton is trying to instill caution in his undisciplined men, he remarks that their quarry might be hidden anywhere waiting to kill them. The camera zooms in on some rocks, pans quickly to the right, swish-pans to the left, then zooms out. Peckinpah's indiscriminate dependence on the zoom shot adds a histrionic stylistic element to a film in which the plot is already melodramatic.

Although the director periodically attempts to overwhelm us with pyrotechnic cinematic techniques, he is capable of straightforward photography that is completely effective. The shots of Pike in the desert with a broken stirrup in a scene that was described earlier is an instance of uncomplicated yet memorable camera-editing dynamics. Another is the scene of the outlaw with the Mexican woman in Aqua Verde. Also presented with restraint, allowing the images to speak for themselves, are panoramic shots of the imposing landscapes in the United States and Mexico.

Peckinpah may be a master, if often a self-indulgent one, of camera-editing dynamics; however, he is apparently not particularly sensitive to music. The background music he approved for *The Wild Bunch* —as in all his films—is conventional, without subtlety or distinction. Color is another matter. There is a striking counterpoint in this film between browns, grays, and blacks (earth, towns, and dress) and yellows and reds (the brightness of the desert, the red car of Mapache, and seeping or spurting blood).

The acting in the film is uniformly praiseworthy, though more so in some cases than others. Ernest Borgnine (Dutch), Warren Oates (Lyle Gorch), and Ben Johnson (Tector Gorch) are excellent. Edmond O'Brien's performance as Sykes is mannered but convincing. Robert Ryan's Thornton is perhaps too low-key, not conveying sufficiently the ambiguity and

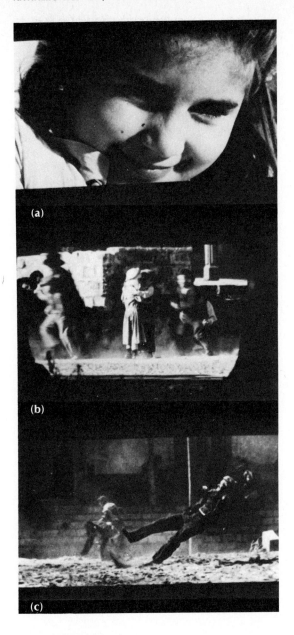

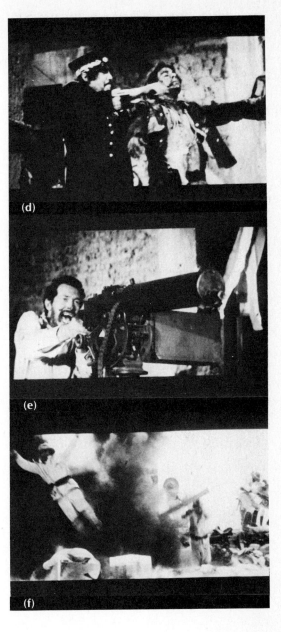

**FIGURE 8.21**

*The Wild Bunch.* From the opening and closing sequences. In the opening sequence, the Wild Bunch has a gunfight with Deke Thornton and his men. (a) The face of a child as she watches two scorpions being destroyed by red ants. (b) Two frightened children cling to each other in the middle of the street as may-hem erupts around them. (c) A man is killed. The final sequence begins with the shot illustrated in Figure 1.24 and continues as (d) Mapache cuts the throat of Angel, (e) Lyle Gorch fires a machine gun, and (f) one of Mapache's soldiers is killed (see also Figure 1.22).

inner conflicts of the most complex character in the film. Most criticism of the acting in *The Wild Bunch* has centered on William Holden. Few would deny the actor's talent; however, the question is whether or not he is too suave and graceful as the worn and ruthless Pike. Holden does not carry himself like a man who has spent most of his life in a saddle or suggest at least a streak of vulgarity one might expect in a realistic portrayal of an outlaw leader. On the other hand, he conveys well the sensitive side of Pike's nature.

*The Wild Bunch* is an exciting film in both its narrative dimension and its cinematic techniques. No one who has seen it is likely to forget the experience. Peckinpah demonstrates in this film that the Western is still capable of vitality and even with antiheroes as its main characters can draw an audience into a mythic world in which why and how a man challenges death is a measure of his integrity and his ultimate value as a human being.

# Musical

## 9

Although many moviegoers have some misconceptions about the functions and forms of the musical, the essential characteristics of this genre are not difficult to define. Its history, however, is more complex to survey. Individual works tend to be less important from a historical perspective than the general approach during a period and the vital contributions of more key people than in any other genre. For these reasons, my survey in this chapter includes, especially for the American musical, commentaries that cover the style of a period, types of musicals, and not only directors but also singers, dancers, composers, lyricists, and choreographers.

Each of the three films analyzed is representative of an era in the history of the American musical. *Top Hat* is typical of the thirties musical. *Singin' in the Rain,* a satirical musical, is an outstanding example of the integrated, energetic productions of "the golden age" that extended generally from 1940 to 1953. *West Side Story* demonstrates an expansion of the genre's subject matter to include serious social and psychological problems and offers an opportunity to compare a film musical with a stage drama from which it is derived.

## SURVEY OF CHARACTERISTICS AND HISTORY

The two essential components of a film musical are plot and music, yet not all film narratives with music are musicals. The most important distinction in relation to plot is that the narrative dimension of a musical be fictive. A motion picture recording actual musical events, such as *Woodstock,* is a documentary. Performers may play themselves, as in the all-star revues popular in the thirties. There was always, however, a framework plot, flimsy though it might be, to justify the appearance of the stars.

Background music is added to most sound films. In a musical, however, the characters on the screen respond to that music (whether the source is on or off the screen) by singing and/or dancing. Once again, there are motion pictures that include these responses and are not musicals. The criterion is the essentiality of the singing and dancing to the purpose of the film. In other words, would the removal of the songs and dances still leave a viable motion picture? Sternberg's *The Blue Angel* is an instance of a film in which songs are important but not indispensable. On the other hand, eliminate the production numbers (any routine involving singing and/or dancing) from *Top Hat* and what would remain is a silly plot with stereotyped characters and a few jokes that no one would pay money to see.

The criterion of essentiality is, however, open to subjective judgment. Are the early thirties films of René Clair musicals or comedies? And what of the typical Shirley Temple film? Take away the songs and dancing and in the opinion of many viewers there is nothing worthwhile left, while others will find sufficient satisfaction in the maudlin story. There are, then, borderline cases, and the fact of their existence should remind us of the limitations of neat genre definitions and categories.

The music in a musical is not only indispensable but also of a certain type. It must be popular and the songs and dances accessible to the majority of an audience. Most critics distinguish between musicals, opera films, and ballet films. This does not mean that there is no cross-fertilization among the three genres, that one is more "entertaining" than another, or that the musical cannot be as sophisticated and complex in style as an opera (though it rarely is). Film biographies ("biopics") of composers and performers also offer difficulties. Sometimes they are considered a separate genre, but usually they are classified according to the type of music, so that a film on the life of Giuseppe Verdi is labeled an opera film and one on Lorenz Hart a musical.

By an indirect route we have reached a definition of the film musical: a fictive narrative containing popular music to which the characters in the story respond by singing and/or dancing, responses that constitute the primary justification for the existence of the film. Within the boundaries of this definition, the musical has developed a variety of characteristics, conventions, and techniques through its principal elements: comedy, plot, characterization, conflict, spoken dialogue, song, dance, and music.

In searching for information on the musical in film books, dictionaries, and encyclopedias, one often finds only the heading "musical comedy." It is understandable why certain writers should couple the musical with comedy, for 90 percent or more of these films are comic in mode, ranging from the farcical to the ironic, and very few do not contain some humorous scenes. To restrict a definition of the genre to comedy, however, is to ignore some of the most exciting films that few would deny are musicals. For instance, *The Umbrellas of Cherbourg* contains little humor, and it would make a travesty of our terminology to designate *West Side Story* or *Oh! What a Lovely War* as comedies. The musical, therefore, is usually comic in approach, but not invariably so.

Plot and characterization (as well as other elements of the narrative dimension) have been of secondary importance in a certain type of musical, exemplified by those made in Hollywood during the thirties. Stories simply provided justification for production numbers, and the personae of stars replaced characterization. Although this form of musical continues to be released (for example, *The Boy Friend,* 1971), a change occurred, as we shall see, during and after the forties. Attempts were made to integrate production numbers with the narrative and to present,

within the artificiality inherent in the genre, believable people in believable situations and even to deal with complex characters, deeper emotional problems, and significant social issues.

The presence of spoken dialogue in musicals is a convention; that is, it is not essential to the genre. A few of the earliest experiments in sound and *The Umbrellas of Cherbourg* illustrate that a valid musical can contain only lyrics. There are a number of reasons, however, for the prevalence of this convention. Alternating songs and dialogue adds variety; unlike opera, the musical usually does not contain sustained intense emotions that justify uninterrupted singing; popular music is rarely complex and substantial enough to hold our attention for as long as $1\frac{1}{2}$ or 2 hours; and comedy, exposition of plot, and subtleties of ideas and situation (rather than expressions of deep feelings) are easier to achieve through dialogue than lyrics. Spoken dialogue, therefore, is an important component of the typical musical. Unfortunately, too often it has not received the attention it requires and has been consigned to hacks with little imagination and less wit. Only when superior writers like Bertolt Brecht, Comden and Green, Arthur Laurents, and Ernst Lehman create screenplays for musicals do we admire rather than simply tolerate the spoken dialogue.

Song, dance, and music constitute the heart of any musical. They also make the musical the most artificial of film genres. All others are at least consistent from beginning to end, no matter how radical an adjustment we must make to their conventions. Musicals, on the other hand, with a few exceptions, alternate between realistic representations of situations and the unnatural acts of people bursting into song or dancing on a street. Filmmakers of musicals have two choices. Either they ignore the problem of improbability and depend on audiences' accepting the convention that in a musical a person can at any time be moved to sing or dance, or they can attempt to justify these means, unusual in our culture, of publicly expressing emotions.

One obvious way of justifying singing and dancing is for the main characters to be professional entertainers. In what has come to be described as the *backstage musical,* there is an opportunity for presenting production numbers that are supposedly appearing on a stage in a theater (as in *Top Hat*) or a movie lot (for example, in *Singin' in the Rain*). Moreover, we are willing to accept the legend that entertainers are uninhibited exhibitionists and likely at any moment to perform offstage, as Al Jolson is known to have done. This does not mean that all artificiality is banished, for the camera does not represent the eyes of a person in a theater audience or an observer. It may assume positions and move in a manner no human being could achieve. Among other forms of justification are dreams, hallucinations, memories, and a person singing to a child or leading a group (perhaps marching men or celebrants). Once again, simulation creeps in when we consider the skill of the participants, so that the members of a typical Midwestern family in *Meet Me in St. Louis* are atypical in their singing and dancing abilities.

The source of musical accompaniment is another problem. Often there is a visible orchestra or band, radio or phonograph. In most musicals, however, we accept music to which the characters respond as originating from a source unrepresented on the screen, just as we do background music in other genres.

Songs and dances are primarily intended to entertain us, as in the title song of *Top Hat*. At their best, however, they also reveal the feelings of a character with a vividness and intensity rarely possible through spoken words. Since most musicals are romances, a song or dance often expresses the joys and pains of love. An example is Gene Kelly in the production number "Singin' in the Rain" in the film of the same title. Different emotions, of resentment against society and a dream of revenge, prompt Jenny in her "song" in *The Threepenny Opera*. In theory, there is no strong feeling that cannot be communicated in songs and dances; in practice, however, few musicals have gone beyond the conventional and predictable.

Song and dance function in another area in addition to entertainment and the expression of deep emotion. Hollywood musicals of the forties and early fifties were particularly effective in presenting satires and parodies in musical forms. *Singin' in the Rain* satirizes silent and early sound films. *The Band Wagon* has as one of its highlights a travesty of Mickey Spillane thrillers.

The film musical is closely related to its stage counterpart, especially since it depends on the theater so extensively for source material. In fact, they share many characteristics. Both must contend with difficulties of artificiality and the limitations of what has been considered suitable subject matter. Film by its very nature, however, accentuates the need for viewers to adjust to the unrealistic action of actors shifting from speaking to singing and dancing. By coming close to an actor, a camera enlarges every facial expression and body movement, so that in the movie theater we are more conscious of singing, for example, than in a stage presentation. There is another aspect of the problem, as Stephen Sondheim once pointed out:[1] The theater has the tradition of the soliloquy, but film does not; therefore, a person singing a solo on the stage is more easily accepted than a person singing in a motion picture. Sondheim went on to note that the most unnatural experience in a stage musical—and even more so in a film—is two people singing to each other instead of speaking.

There is no point in belaboring the artificiality of stage and film musicals. Every genre in any medium has its conventions to which audiences learn to adapt. It is noteworthy, however, that whereas many stage musicals, especially since World War II, have taken advantage of this artificiality inherent in the genre, film musicals have less frequently resisted the ties of the medium to realism and not explored fully the potentials of stylized, innovative, nonrealistic approaches and devices.

Another advantage the stage musical has over its counterpart in film is that the original version is usually created in the theater. At least four out of five film musicals are adaptations of stage musicals, and the average has risen since the mid-fifties. Moreover, stage musicals have smaller, generally more sophisticated audiences. In adapting a stage production for the screen, there is a tendency on the part of filmmakers to expand a work's appeal by lessening the unconventional and the possibly offensive elements in a stage musical and to substitute spectacle for substance. An example is the film version of *Pal Joey,* which contains little of the bite and irony of the original. On the other hand, *The Sound of Music* was more effective as film than play because it is so fundamentally sentimental and reassuring in its moral certitudes that the screenwriter and director could preserve its plot and tone, as well as add cinematic dimensions. While it is true that many of the finest film musicals are adaptations of Broadway successes, such as *West Side Story* and *Cabaret,* the genre is most provocative when working with original material, as in *Singin' in the Rain, An American in Paris, New York, New York,* and *All That Jazz,* or material derived from another medium, as with *Summer Holiday* and *Gigi.*

A film musical does, of course, have certain advantages over a stage production. Spectacle is an important element in the genre, and film is incomparable in this regard. However critical one may be of Busby Berkeley's style, he offered a visual excitement few stage numbers could rival. A film also can "open up" a story, that is, increase the number of settings and the size of choruses. Being able in a motion picture to re-create a medieval joust in *Camelot* or a mob of beggars at a coronation during the ending of *The Threepenny Opera* increases the texture of a story's atmosphere. The "magic" of the camera is another plus factor in a film musical. We can easily enter into a dream or a flight of imagination. The opening of *The Sound of Music,* featuring aerial shots of the Alps and ending with a zoom in to the figure of Julie Andrews below, is another instance of a dramatic effect possible only in film. Finally, a compensation for the loss of the immediacy of living people performing is always having a "front and center" seat in a movie theater with no worries about poor acoustics, sight lines, or an actor's having an off night.

Knowledge about the characteristics of film musicals and the problems filmmakers must overcome to create an outstanding one can increase a person's enjoyment of the genre and sharpen critical awareness. What is often forgotten, however, even by professional critics, is that a film musical is a film as well as a musical. This statement does not simply restate the obvious. To examine a film musical with any acumen requires a focus of attention on cinematic techniques, to go beyond the personalities of stars, voices, dancing, and scores to how these vital components are communicated to viewers through the narrative dimension, camera-editing dynamics, and elements of presentation. Viewing a musical on the screen is a different experience from encountering the same one in a theater. By exploring the similarities and differences between the two, especially in the context of evolving cinematic techniques and conventions, it is possible to establish criteria for evaluating both individual works and the film musical as a genre.

Although songs and background music were heard in motion pictures released in the United States during 1926–1928, most notably in *The Jazz Singer* (1927), *The Broadway Melody* (1929) is usually credited with being the first genuine musical, "all-talking, all-singing, all-dancing" film. Made at MGM, it was directed by Harry Beaumont and promoted in Bessie Love the first in a series of film musical stars. Original songs were written by Arthur Freed and Nacio Herb Brown. Its story of two sisters who rise to stardom on Broadway initiated the backstage musical plot. It received Hollywood's highest accolade by being the first sound film as well as first musical to win an Academy Award for Best Picture (1928–1929).

During the first period of the history of the American screen musical, the years 1929 and 1930, *The Broadway Melody* was atypical in being an original film. Most studios, desperate for material, turned to the stage. Among the most popular of these adaptations were *Rio Rita, Sally, Gold Diggers of Broadway* (all 1929), *Whoopee,* and *Viennese Nights* (both 1930). Stage stars—Ruth Chatterton, Marilyn Miller, Jack Buchanan, Maurice Chevalier, Jeanette MacDonald, George Jessel, Eddie Cantor, Al Jolson, Fanny Brice, John Boles, and a flock of others—journeyed to the West Coast to appear on the screen. Few stayed longer than for a couple of films. Even fewer musical stars discovered by Hollywood, with such exceptions as Bebe Daniels and Nancy Carroll, sustained their popularity into the mid-thirties. Composers of the caliber of George Gershwin, Sigmund Romberg, Oscar Strauss, Richard Rodgers, and Lorenz Hart fared little better at this time.

Another type of musical devised during these early years was the all-star review. A tenuous plot was simply a net with which to hold together a series of appearances of actors, musicians, singers, and comedians. Some examples: *Hollywood Review, The Show of Shows, On With the Show* (all 1929), *King of Jazz, Paramount on Parade,* and *Happy Days* (all 1930). The casts were truly impressive. *Hollywood Review* included Buster Keaton, Jack Benny, Marion Davies, Bessie Love, Marie Dressler, Norma Shearer, and John Gilbert (the last two doing a scene from *Romeo and Juliet*), among others.

Operettas were primarily showcases for certain stars, including Jeanette MacDonald, Maurice Chevalier, and Jack Buchanan (Nelson Eddy did not become known until the mid-thirties). They did, however, offer Ernst Lubitsch an opportunity to demonstrate that musicals could be done with style and wit. *The Love Parade* (1929, starring Jeanette MacDonald and Maurice Chevalier) was his first sound film. It has a mythical European setting and involves the taming of a queenly shrew by her prince consort (Figure 9.1). This film is properly regarded as the first screen musical to be truly cinematic rather than basically a photographed stage play. Three others followed in quick succession: *Monte Carlo* (1930, teaming MacDonald with Jack Buchanan), *The Smiling Lieutenant* (1931), and *One Hour With You* (1932). They were superior to most contemporary American musicals not only in technique and style but also in Lubitsch's mature, risqué attitude toward sex and love. He directed one other musical. *The Merry Widow* (1934, with MacDonald and Chevalier together for the last time) was not as popular as Stroheim's silent version of Franz Lehár's operetta, and Lubitsch had already turned to nonmusical comedy.*

Original Hollywood musicals of the period generally did not come up to the standards of those adapted from the stage and Lubitsch's operettas. There were, however, exceptions. *The Broadway Melody* was one of them. King Vidor contributed another with *Hallelujah!* (1929). This film, the first all-black musical, is remarkably honest for its time. But

**FIGURE 9.1**

*The Love Parade,* 1929, directed by Ernst Lubitsch. Queen Louise of Sylvania (Jeanette MacDonald) glowers at her prince consort, Count Alfred (Maurice Chevalier), as he uses binoculars to look at a lovely dancer on the stage.

the plot is hackneyed, and film stereotypes of blacks are not entirely discarded. The songs consist of Negro spirituals and additional tunes written by Irving Berlin (added over Vidor's objections).

Rouben Mamoulian (1898–), like Lubitsch, recognized from the beginning the potentials for drama in the musical. In contrast to most directors who traveled from Broadway to Hollywood, he quickly learned the techniques of motion pictures, then struck out in bold, new directions. His first film, *Applause* (1929), was a drama with songs and a theater setting rather than a musical, and it is one of the most significant of its time in combining the visual imaginativeness of silent films with innovations in sound to tell a believable human drama. After a gangster film, *City Streets* (1931), he made his first genuine musical, *Love Me Tonight* (1932), with a Rodgers and Hart score and starring MacDonald and Chevalier. A striking quality in this work, unusual for the early thirties, is the fluency with which songs are integrated with the narrative. The opening sequence of a city awakening is remarkable. Mamoulian's other musicals appeared later in the decade.

By the end of 1930, American audiences had become satiated with musicals, especially since so many of them had been shabby, insipid productions. There was still enough tolerance to welcome a Lubitsch work or *Love Me Tonight,* but audience resistance was so strong that distributors advertised a film with the notice "This is *not* a musical." Thus ended the first period of the American musical, and the second was not to begin until 1933.

European filmmakers of the late twenties and early thirties also recognized that the advent of sound made musical films possible. Most of these musicals were similar to those made in the United States, but a director in one country and a film in another devised a variation that, unfortunately, was not developed by others. René Clair,* after resisting the use of sound, made his first three sound films in the form of musical comedies (although they are often classified more as comedies than as musicals). In *Under the Roofs of Paris (Sous les toits de Paris,* 1930), a street singer loses his mistress to his best friend but gallantly accepts the new situation. *Le Million* (1931) deals with a mad search for a lost winning lottery ticket. *A nous la liberté* (1931) is the best known of the three and is generally regarded as a classic. Two friends plan to break out of prison. One sacrifices himself so that the other can succeed. The escaped convict becomes a millionaire manufacturer of phonograph records. When the two meet years later, the millionaire helps his friend, but after a series of adventures involving lost love and blackmail, the two travel the open road as vagabonds. One of the characters is a Chaplinesque figure who cannot adjust to a dehumanizing assembly line and who loses a woman he adores to another man (in fact, there is no doubt that Chaplin was influenced by the film in making *Modern Times*). A sequence in which paper money floating in a wind is chased by staid officials in formal suits and top hats is a cinematic gem.

All three Clair films contain songs that are more important in expressing the feelings of the characters than the spoken dialogue. The director's approach differs from that of his American musical-making contemporaries in many respects. The songs are not justified by a person's being a professional singer (except in *Le Million*) or performing before an audience.

*p. 269

There are no production numbers aggrandized by dancing, impressive sets, and lighting. The singing voices of the actors are no more than pleasant, and the songs themselves are charming, without the sheen that a self-conscious writer for the stage gives to lyrics and melodies. Finally, the characters involved are primarily lower-class, ordinary people caught in extraordinary situations. Clair was not to return to this style of musical after 1931.

In Germany, G. W. Pabst made an unusual musical based on a very successful stage play. The film, *The Threepenny Opera (Die Dreigroschenoper,* 1931), retains, with some changes, the plot and lyrics of Bertolt Brecht and the music of Kurt Weill. The adaptation does not have the bitter satirical bite of the original (and Brecht repudiated Pabst's version), but it is still a distinctive film. As with the René Clair works, the story of Mack the Knife's courting of Polly and betrayal by Jenny (Lotte Lenya) is presented with spoken dialogue and songs and deals with lower-class characters. Unique in the German film, however, is the street singer, who looks directly at the camera while commenting on the action. He could be described as a one-man, cynical Greek chorus. The deft directing of Pabst, superb cinematography of Fritz Arno Wagner, and striking sets by Andrei Andreiev fuse basic realism with Expressionistic devices, especially chiaroscuro effects. As a musical, it was exceptional in its time for the acerbity of its wit, antiromanticism, and social criticism.

In Germany, one director of talent specialized in musicals for a few years. Wilhelm Thiele anticipated Clair's use of ordinary people as the chief characters in *Three From the Gas Pump (Die Drei von der Tankstelle,* 1929) and *Private Secretary (Privatsekretärin,* 1930). He also directed the more conventional operetta *Liebeswalzer* (1930) before coming to Hollywood and a much less distinguished career. Most German and Austrian musicals were operettas, such as *Kongress tanzt* (1931, directed by Erik Charell and starring the leading German musical team of the decade, Lilian Harvey and Willy Fritsch) and *Amphitryon* (1935). Just before and during World War II, German musicals were confined to mediocre operettas, reviews, and star vehicles for such singers as the deep-voiced Zarah Leander.

The only other country to create musicals that won a measure of international attention during the thirties was Great Britain. The sole director of note was Victor Saville. His light, ingenuous touch is evident in his first work in the genre, *Sunshine Susie* (1931). He is remembered, however, primarily as the director of the finest motion pictures in which England's leading musical star was featured. Jessie Matthews enhanced numerous films with her dancing, singing, and comic talents, including *The Good Companions* (1933), *Friday the Thirteenth* (1933), *Evergreen* (1934, probably her most memorable performance), *First a Girl* (1935), *It's Love Again* (1936), and *Climbing High* (1939). Other English stars, most of whom eventually appeared in American films, included Anna Neagle, Gracie Fields, Gertrude Lawrence, Jack Buchanan, Noël Coward, and George Formby.

In the United States, audiences, after 3 years of aversion toward the musical, were ready in 1933 for a revival of the genre. It began with *42nd Street* (1933, directed by Lloyd Bacon for Warner Bros.). Many of the characteristics of this trend-setting musical were imitated in various forms in other films of the decade. *42nd Street* had a "clothesline plot": The story was less important to it for its inherent drama than as a means of attaching songs and musical numbers (Figure 9.2). Not many viewers were inclined to challenge the credibility of a chorus girl's replacing an ailing Broadway star at the last minute and not only becoming an instant success but also winning the leading man. As this one-sentence synopsis indicates, the film was a backstage musical.

*42nd Street* initiated a whole set of stereotyped characters that with or without variations appeared repeatedly in musicals of the thirties. There had to be two young lovers separated by misunderstanding but joined together by the final number. The chorus girl did not make her debut in this film; however, she became a mainstay thereafter, especially in backstage musicals. There was also usually a hard-driving yet fair director or producer. And not to be forgotten is the aged moneybags happily in the clutches of a chorus girl.

Ruby Keeler and Dick Powell made their reputations in *42nd Street* and appeared together or sepa-

**FIGURE 9.2**

*42nd Street*, 1933, directed by Lloyd Bacon, choreographed by Busby Berkeley. This still has been printed so often in film histories that it has become a visual signature for the musical. Director Julian Marsh (Warner Baxter) is instructing Peggy Sawyer (Ruby Keeler), one of the girls in the chorus (though not for long). To the left of Marsh is "Anytime Annie" Lowell (Ginger Rogers).

rately in many musicals of the decade. The pattern was established of featuring stars and familiar faces in these films. The king and queen of this royal company from 1933 (*Flying Down to Rio*) to 1939 (*The Story of Vernon and Irene Castle*) were Fred Astaire and Ginger Rogers,* but many other stars, in addition to Keeler and Powell, became popular with screen audiences, including Joan Blondell, Ann Sothern, Irene Dunne, Ruth Etting, Ethel Merman, Ray Bolger, Dennis Morgan, Eddie Cantor, Buddy Rogers, and John Boles. A few stars of the earlier musicals, most prominently Maurice Chevalier, Bebe Daniels (who was featured in *42nd Street*), and Nancy Carroll, continued to perform. Eleanor Powell confined herself to dancing, but she was truly outstanding in this art. She usually did solo numbers, and one understands why: Aside from Fred Astaire and Ray Bolger, few male dancers at the time could be her partner without looking clumsy by comparison. Vera Zorina at the end of the thirties made a more classic style acceptable in musicals.

*pp. 461–462

One star of the 1930s American musical did not appear before the cameras. More than anyone else (with the possible exception of Astaire), the style of this period of the genre is associated with the name of Busby Berkeley (1895–1976). When not actually directing a film, he was listed in the credits as choreographer. Since staged numbers were the spine of a musical, however, his contribution was often more important than that of the director. He began as a Broadway stage director, then was hired by MGM for the early Eddie Cantor musicals. His particular style blossomed when he went to Warner Bros. and choreographed the production numbers for *42nd Street.*

In 1933 Berkeley also contributed to *Footlight Parade,* then *Dames* (1934), *Fashions of 1934,* and *In Caliente* (1935). Some of his best work appeared in the *Gold Diggers* series (1933, 1935, 1937, 1938); he himself directed *Gold Diggers of 1935.* After an excursion into drama, he returned to musicals and directed *Broadway Serenade* (1939). He continued to be active during the forties.

Berkeley created production numbers that were, from one point of view, spectacular and dynamic and, from another perspective, as gaudy and tasteless as wedding-cake decorations. No one could deny, however, that he had flair and that he more than any other person vitalized the second period of the American musical. He had immense sets constructed, on which he placed a bizarre architectural structure and peopled it with 100 or more chorus girls and boys. One of his trademarks was to transform pulchritudinous young women into objects, such as blossoming flowers, harps, and caryatids. Costumes ranged from the barely visible to the enormously elaborate. Always there were pageantry and surprises.

His camera-editing dynamics were restless. Tracking and panning shots, abrupt angle changes, and extensive use of a crane were joined in every possible combination. Berkeley's favorite shot, especially associated with his style, was a very high one, often a direct vertical, with the camera focused on a chorus that, like a kaleidoscope, repeatedly changed design before a viewer's eyes.

There is no doubt that Berkeley was a master craftsman, and his choreography often captivated

through its very audacity. Yet there is a disturbing element in his transformation of lovely human beings into precise machines for the purposes of spectacle. More than one critic has pointed out that Berkeley's techniques have a kinship in this respect with those of a contemporary in another country, Leni Riefenstahl.*

The extent of Berkeley's success can be gauged by the numerous imitators of his approach. It became almost de rigueur for a musical of the period to contain at least one number in his style. An example of a pseudo-Berkeley production number is "The Piccolino" in *Top Hat.* † This number, as with other imitations, lacked the brio and daring of such genuine Berkeley stagings as "42nd Street" in the film of the same title, "Remember My Forgotten Man" in *Gold Diggers of 1933,* "By the Waterfall" in *Footlight Parade,* "No More Love" in *Roman Scandals* (1933), and many viewers' favorite, "Lullaby of Broadway" in *Gold Diggers of 1935* (Figure 9.3).

Directors were generally less prominent than production-number choreographers. Only a movie

---

**FIGURE 9.3**

*Gold Diggers of 1935,* 1935, directed by Busby Berkeley. "Lullaby of Broadway" (in which this shot appears) is considered by many critics to be the most imaginative production number of thirties American musicals.

---

*pp. 368–369
†pp. 466–467

buff would know that *42nd Street* was directed by Lloyd Bacon or recognize the names of Ray Enright, Mark Sandrich, and William Keighley. Aside from Lubitsch, one exception to the ranks of Directors Anonymous was Rouben Mamoulian. *The Gay Desperado* (1936, starring Nino Martini) is less witty and vivacious than *Love Me Tonight,* but it is still a pleasant musical satire on films that had their setting south of the border. *High, Wide and Handsome* (1937, with music by Jerome Kern and Oscar Hammerstein II and starring Irene Dunne, Randolph Scott, and Dorothy Lamour) is one of the few musicals of the thirties that dealt with American history—oil prospectors in the West during the mid-nineteenth century—intelligently and without sentimentality.

*42nd Street* contained original songs by Al Dubin and Harry Warren. Like Herb Nacio Brown and Arthur Freed, this team was unusual in having developed its talents in Hollywood. Most of the popular musicals of the decade depended on the efforts of composers and lyricists who had made their reputations on Broadway. In fact, the majority of film musicals of the thirties were adaptations of stage successes. Among the most famous of those who brought musical style to the songs of these films were George and Ira Gershwin, Irving Berlin, Cole Porter, Jerome Kern, Richard Rodgers, and Lorenz Hart.

Nineteen thirty-three was a vintage year for film musicals. Not only was *42nd Street* released, but also *Gold Diggers of 1933* and *Flying Down to Rio.* The second of the *Gold Diggers* series illustrates two aspects of the thirties musical not mentioned earlier. Berkeley's production number "Remember My Forgotten Man" is the most striking statement about the problems of the Depression in this genre. The Hollywood studios had decided that people went to musicals to escape their troubles, so any more than the most casual reference to the economic problems of the day was prohibited. "Remember My Forgotten Man" and a later film, *Hallelujah, I'm a Bum* (1934, with Al Jolson), were rare in reminding audiences that the United States and most of the rest of the world were suffering from a lengthy economic crisis.

The "Pettin' in the Park" number in *Gold Diggers of 1933* demonstrates how near Berkeley and other choreographers of the time came to being sala-

cious. Attitudes toward sex in films in the thirties were two-faced. On the one hand, the "Hays Office" (Studio Relations Committee) could be outraged by the honest sensuality of Mae West and insist on adherence to its ridiculously rigid Production Code (instituted in 1930). On the other hand, hints and titillation were acceptable. A heroine of a musical, even if a chorus girl, was faithful to her beloved, and it was taken for granted that the relationship between the two would end in marriage. Yet her friends in the chorus evidently but not overtly might live by other standards. For example, Ann Lowell (Ginger Rogers) in *42nd Street* never did anything on the screen that the Hays Office or the League of Decency could condemn; however, only a cloistered virgin from a small Midwestern town, say Gopher Prairie, would not understand what "Anytime Annie" was ready for anytime. Lubitsch alone among directors of the decade was able to suggest by clever, subtle innuendo that sex and marriage did not always go together like a horse and carriage. Busby Berkeley could be more openly provocative in production numbers because he dealt with groups, and sensuality was confined to the physical appeal of the female body. While there is a superficial pleasure in watching those lovely creatures posing or moving provocatively, there is also a sense that being titillated by these mannequins and clockwork dolls is puerile.

Among the outstanding musicals of the thirties not previously mentioned or associated with stars and directors of the forties were *Dancing Lady* (1933, with Joan Crawford, Fred Astaire, Nelson Eddy, Clark Gable, and Franchot Tone), *Folies Bergère* (1934, starring Maurice Chevalier and Ann Sothern), *Bolero* (1934, starring Carole Lombard and George Raft), *George White's Scandals* (1934, with Alice Faye and John Boles), *Wonder Bar* (1934, with Dolores Del Rio and Ricardo Cortez, choreography by Busby Berkeley), *The Singing Kid* (1936, starring Al Jolson), *Born to Dance* (1936, starring Eleanor Powell and James Stewart, songs by Cole Porter), *Showboat* (1936, starring Irene Dunne, Helen Morgan, and Paul Robeson, from the Jerome Kern musical), *Rosalie* (1937, starring Eleanor Powell and Ray Bolger), *On the Avenue* (1937, starring Dick Powell and Madeleine Carroll, songs by Irving Berlin), *Goldwyn's Follies* (1938, with

Vera Zorina and the Ritz Brothers), and *On Your Toes* (1939, starring Vera Zorina).

Other American musicals of the thirties fitted into special categories or were subgenres. The all-star reviews that first appeared in the late twenties were revived. Two examples are *The Big Broadcast of . . .* (1936, 1937, and 1938) and *Broadway Melody of . . .* (1936, 1938, and 1940). Another revival from the first period of the film musical was the creation of vehicles for opera stars. This idea was no more successful the second time around than the first. With the possible exception of Grace Moore in such films as *One Night of Love* (1934), Lawrence Tibbett (as in the *New Moon,* 1930, with Moore), John McCormack (*Song O' My Heart,* 1930), Lily Pons (*I Dream Too Much,* 1935), Gladys Swarthout (*Romance in the Dark,* 1938), and others never captured the loyalty of American moviegoers.

One series of films that included singing and dancing was unique only because of its star. Shirley Temple (1928–) was a national institution; in poll after poll during the decade, she was chosen as America's favorite movie star (even above Astaire and Rogers). Her films were not truly musicals, but the highlight of each was her singing and tap dancing. It is difficult today to understand her immense success. She was undeniably talented and unquestionably pretty, but her dimpled cuteness quickly became cloying, and the plots of her films were sickeningly sentimental. After seeing a Temple film, one can appreciate as never before W. C. Fields's caustic comments on children. She was most tolerable when, as in *The Little Colonel* (1935), she danced with Bill Robinson.

Biographies of popular composers and performers have not constituted a particularly distinguished subgenre of the musical. In the thirties, only *The Great Waltz* (1937) is worth noting. Based on the life of Johann Strauss, it starred Fernand Gravet, Miliza Korjus, and Luise Rainer.

Many of the animated films of Walt Disney, both shorts and features, also qualify as musicals. After all, the songs "Who's Afraid of the Big Bad Wolf," from a short, *Three Little Pigs* (1933), and "Heigh-ho," from *Snow White and the Seven Dwarfs* (1937), were as popular in the United States as any by Jerome Kern or Cole Porter. Disney's other major features were not released until the early forties.

The one type of screen musical that during the thirties challenged the conventional form in terms of popularity was the operetta. Ernst Lubitsch, as we have seen, was appreciated for his efforts in this subgenre. Rouben Mamoulian's *Love Me Tonight, The Gay Desperado,* and *High, Wide and Handsome* are sometimes described as domestic operettas (with songs by Rodgers and Hart and Kern and Hammerstein, they were departures from the European tradition of Strauss, Youmans, and Romberg). The only musical directed by Josef von Sternberg was an operetta entitled *The King Steps Out* (1936).

This is a respectable but not particularly impressive record. The fortunes of the film operetta suddenly soared, however, with the discovery of a team that soon rivaled the appeal of Astaire and Rogers. Jeanette MacDonald and Nelson Eddy appeared in *Naughty Marietta* (1935, their debut together), *Rose Marie* (1936), *Maytime* (1937), *Sweethearts* (1938), *New Moon* (1940), and *I Married an Angel* (1942), among other films. By the end of World War II, they were considered passé. After the two went their separate ways, the operetta generally disappeared from the American screen.

There is no question that Jeanette MacDonald (1901–1965) was the more talented partner of the team. She made her first screen appearance in *The Love Parade* opposite Maurice Chevalier and again joined with the inimitable Frenchman in *One Hour With You* (1932), *Love Me Tonight,* and *The Merry Widow.* MacDonald was to star without Eddy or Chevalier in a number of films in the thirties and forties, most prominently in *San Francisco* (1936). She had not only an impressive voice but also a gift for comedy.

Nelson Eddy (1901–1967) possessed a fine baritone voice and was an attractive man, but he was woefully inadequate as an actor (his expressions were limited to being seriously resolute and happily smiling). He had some success without MacDonald in such films as *Rosalie* (1938, costarring Eleanor Powell), but his appeal declined after 1942.

The thirties ended with a war in Europe that was

to spread to the United States in 1941. Hollywood anticipated problems with the diminishing of foreign markets and wartime restrictions, but motion picture production flourished during the war years. This was especially true of musicals, which turned out to be the favorite type of screen entertainment for people seeking distraction. In 1943, 40 percent of the motion pictures made in Hollywood were musicals.[2] Most of them, in the spirit of escapism, did not directly deal with the war. There were, however, exceptions, for instance, *The Fleet's In* (1942, starring Dorothy Lamour and introducing Betty Hutton), *Stage Door Canteen* (1943), and the blockbuster musical of the war years, *This Is the Army* (1943, with songs by Irving Berlin).

After World War II, euphoria and optimism spread throughout the nation. Once again the musical was the preferred form of motion picture entertainment, and the genre reached full maturity. The years 1940–1953 are referred to as "the golden age" of the American musical. There has never been (and probably never again will be) a comparable period with such a profusion of memorable musicals that even today impress us with their vitality and distinctive styles. Filmmakers of musicals had learned during the thirties the value of distinguished stars, big production numbers, and humor. What they added was a closer integration of plot and musical numbers, a surer sense of sophistication and taste, the need for the controlling vision of a masterful director, and the advantages of having original screenplays, lyrics, and music. Furthermore, a new element of presentation had been perfected; most of the forties musicals had the benefit of color. Still lacking was the realization that the genre was capable of dealing with serious social and psychological problems. On the other hand, genuine style on the part of directors, composers, actors, and others compensated for any weaknesses that were evident to a critical eye.

No factor was more responsible for the superiority of the forties musicals than the rise in the importance of directors. So due credit must be given to a man who never directed a musical but who in the role of producer encouraged originality in the members of the filmmaking teams he assembled, especially care-

fully chosen directors. Arthur Freed (1894–1973) entered the Hollywood scene as a lyricist.* In 1938 he was made executive producer in charge of musicals at MGM. He recognized and cultivated the talents of such directors as Vincent Minnelli and Stanley Donen and such performers as Judy Garland, Gene Kelly, and Cyd Charisse. The musicals he personally produced from 1939 *(The Wizard of Oz)* to 1960 *(Bells Are Ringing)* include many of the finest created in Hollywood.

The only producer in the area of the musical who rivaled the success of Freed was Joseph Pasternak. He discovered Deanna Durbin while at Universal Studios and produced 10 of her films before moving to MGM, where his romantic, conventional approach to musicals complemented the more sophisticated, experimental efforts of Freed. Pasternak played an important role in the careers of Kathryn Grayson, Esther Williams, Jane Powell, Mario Lanza, and others. Among his best-known musicals are *Anchors Aweigh* (1945), *The Great Caruso* (1951), and *Jumbo* (1962). He continued to work as a producer into the late sixties.

It was no accident that both Freed and Pasternak were under contract to Metro-Goldwyn-Mayer. Other studios did musicals, but the most popular, imaginative, and star-studded ones were released by MGM.

The most important director sponsored by Freed at MGM in the forties was Vincente Minnelli (1913–). His early experiences as a Broadway art director are evident in all his films. He brought an unusual sensitivity to design and color to his directing. Another benefit of his theatrical background was a mastery of *mise-en-scène* that was missing from musicals since those of Lubitsch and Mamoulian. Moreover, he rejected clothesline plots in favor of a fusion of story, songs, and dances. Of all the characteristics of his style, the most easily identifiable are a bouncing exuberance, unpretentiousness, and optimism that one associates with grass-roots America. These qualities, which Minnelli shared with the best of his directing peers, more than any others distinguished the mu-

*p. 440

sical of the forties from the artificial, contrived approach promulgated by Berkeley and his imitators.

    *Cabin in the Sky* (1943, with songs by John Latouché and Vernon Duke) was an auspicious film debut for Minnelli. This all-black musical, starring Ethel Waters, Lena Horne, and Louis Armstrong, was less naive than King Vidor's *Hallelujah!,* although still burdened with racial sterotypes. More typical of the director's work is *Meet Me in St. Louis* (1944), with an original screenplay. It starred Judy Garland (whose second of five husbands was Minnelli) and featured Margaret O'Brien, for a time considered the heir to the mantle of Shirley Temple. This Technicolor production is a charming, nostalgic view of the turn of the century that only occasionally descends into sentimentality.

    Between 1945 and 1951, Minnelli directed four major musicals. *Yolanda and the Thief* (1945) is notable, in addition to its successful fantasy and high spirits, as the first musical in which he directed Fred Astaire (partnered by Lucille Bremer). *Ziegfield Follies* (1946) is an extravaganza done with taste and imagination. In *The Pirate* (1947), he turned from Astaire to the other major male dancer of the decade, Gene Kelly, who had to be on his toes to match the verve of his costar, Judy Garland. When the director and Kelly again joined forces, it was to create the extraordinary *An American in Paris* (1951), considered by many connoisseurs of musicals as Minnelli's finest. In the film, an American painter in Paris gives up a wealthy patroness (Nina Foch) for a charming French girl (Leslie Caron, in her film debut). This conventional plot is offset by superb color and sets that echo great French painters (Figure 9.4), the vibrant choreography of Kelly, the songs of George and Ira Gershwin, and, most of all, the guiding hand of Minnelli. The film richly deserved the five Academy Awards it won.

    Minnelli is primarily associated with musicals, which he continued to direct into the sixties and seventies (for example, *Bells Are Ringing,* 1960, and *On a Clear Day You Can See Forever,* 1970). His many nonmusicals have been far less impressive, often static and uninspired.

    Although no one challenged Minnelli's preeminence in directing musicals in the forties and early

**FIGURE 9.4**

*An American in Paris,* 1951, directed by Vincente Minnelli (color). In one of his daydreams, Jerry (Gene Kelly), an American painter in Paris, imagines that he is dancing with Lise (Leslie Caron), the woman he loves, in a Montmarte setting inspired by the paintings of Toulouse-Lautrec.

fifties, he did receive some competition from Gene Kelly, Stanley Donen, and Charles Walters. Gene Kelly's achievements in directing are considered elsewhere in this chapter.* Stanley Donen was a choreographer and assistant director in the forties. He made his directing debut with *Royal Wedding* (1950, starring Fred Astaire and Jane Powell). He was codirector with Gene Kelly before for *On the Town* (1949) and after for *Singin' in the Rain.* His reputation, however, rests to a large degree on his films after 1953.†

    Charles Walters generally has been disparaged by film critics and historians. One reason may be that after making a series of prominent musicals, the quality of his work declined precipitously in the fifties. His first outstanding musical was *Easter Parade* (1948, starring Fred Astaire and Judy Garland). Walter's acute feeling for visual rhythms and the ability to preserve a driving pace also enhanced *The Barkleys of Broadway* (1949, the reunion after 10 years of Astaire and Rogers) and *Summer Stock* (1950, Judy Garland's last film for MGM).

*pp. 468–470
†p. 454

Not many directors who had established their reputations in the thirties continued to be active in the forties. Busby Berkeley directed *Strike Up the Band* (1940) and *Babes on Broadway* (1941)—both of which teamed Judy Garland and Mickey Rooney— *For Me and My Gal* (1942, in which Gene Kelly made his film debut), and *Take Me Out to the Ball Game* (1949), among other films. Lesser-known directors did not fare so well. Some, such as William Keighley, moved to other genres. A few continued with only occasional major assignments. Mark Sandrich lost his monopoly on films starring Fred Astaire and Ginger Rogers but did make *Holiday Inn* (1942, starring Astaire and famous for introducing the song "White Christmas") and *Here Come the Waves* (1944, with Betty Hutton).

Rouben Mamoulian's accomplishments in this genre are unique in at least one respect. No director has created so few musicals (less than half a dozen) over such an extended range of time (1932–1957) and still been acknowledged as a master of the form. His only contribution in the forties was *Summer Holiday* (1948, an adaptation of Eugene O'Neill's *Ah, Wilderness!*). This story of an adolescent's initiation into manhood is hardly the typical stuff of which successful musicals are made. Through sheer brilliance of style, however, Mamoulian, aided by the talents of Mickey Rooney, Gloria DeHaven, and Marilyn Maxwell, transformed an unlikely prospect into a moving experience. Unfortunately, the work was ahead of its time and was roundly condemned by both critics and audiences.

Directors and producers, of course, were not solely responsible for the success of the forties musicals. With perhaps the exception of the music, all other elements that made up those musicals were done with greater skill and sophistication than during the thirties. Music is an exception because from the beginning songs had been of a high caliber, and composers of the previous decade—Irving Berlin, Cole Porter, Richard Rodgers, Jerome Kern (until 1945)— continued to work in the forties or, as in the case of George Gershwin, who died in 1937, had scores made up of earlier songs. In addition, Hollywood encouraged the talents of songwriters who wrote exten-

sively for the screen, for instance, Harold Arlen, Jimmy Van Heusen, Howard Dietz, Arthur Schwartz, Roger Edens, and Hoagy Carmichael.

The screenplays of musicals of any period have infrequently been marvels of dramatic construction and scintillating dialogue. Filmmakers of the forties preserved this tradition but were easily able to improve on the inane plots of the majority of thirties musicals. Most of the screenwriters were little known outside of the industry. Even enthusiasts of the genre would be hard put to name the authors of the scenarios for, say, *The Wizard of Oz* or *Meet Me in St. Louis* (the former was written by Noel Langley, Florence Ryerson, and Edgar Allan Woold and the latter by Irving Brecher and Fred F. Finklehoffe). However, in the late forties emerged one writing team who demonstrated that a screenplay for a musical could be as intelligent and witty as one for another genre. Betty Comden and Adolph Green, who wrote the screenplays and lyrics for *On the Town* and *Singin' in the Rain,* among other works, are discussed elsewhere in this chapter.*

The stranglehold of Busby Berkeley and his imitators on production numbers in the thirties was broken by a group of young, vigorous choreographers who had more taste and respect for the humanity of their dancers but not always the flair for spectacle of Berkeley. In the lead were Gene Kelly and Stanley Donen. Hermes Pan had moved out from under the shadow of Berkeley in the late thirties and developed his own dependable, if not always imaginative, choreographic style. His best work appeared in the fifties and sixties. Michael Kidd and Eugene Loring began as film choreographers in the early fifties but were also most prominent later in the decade.

Although audiences in this period were becoming increasingly aware of individuals who contributed from behind the camera to the making of musicals, their devotion and enthusiasm still centered on the actors and actresses. Especially among the women there were numerous glamorous stars, most of whom had begun their careers in the thirties. Foremost in the

---

*p. 470

forties was the incomparable Judy Garland (1922–1969).

Frances Gumm began as a child actress in vaudeville and earned a contract with MGM when she was only 13. As Judy Garland she attracted attention in the Hardy family series as the girlfriend of Mickey Rooney. But it was *The Wizard of Oz* (1939) that made her a star. It is surely the most popular musical, rereleased repeatedly in theaters and on television. Based on Frank L. Baum's children's classic, it tells of the dream adventures of Dorothy (Garland) after she had been made unconscious by a tornado sweeping through Kansas. She is accompanied on her way to the Emerald City to consult the Wizard of Oz by a scarecrow (Ray Bolger), a lion (Bert Lahr), and a tin man (Jack Haley). The film was directed by Victor Fleming (that jack-of-all-genres, who was the final director of *Gone With the Wind,* also released in 1939), produced by Mervyn LeRoy for MGM, with music by Harold Arlen and lyrics by E. Y. Harburg. One of the most memorable moments in American cinema as well as the musical is Garland singing "Over the Rainbow."

Garland's main partner while she was still an adolescent was Mickey Rooney in the musicals *Babes in Arms* (1939), *Strike Up the Band* (1940), *Babes on Broadway* (1941), and *Girl Crazy* (1943). She was a young woman in *Meet Me in St. Louis.* During the forties, Garland was MGM's most popular star as she appeared in numerous musicals, including *The Harvey Girls* (1946), *Ziegfeld Follies, The Pirate, Easter Parade,* and *Summer Stock.* In the early fifties, the strain of her hectic, driven life became too much. She left motion pictures for a series of personal appearances in New York and London, returning to the screen in *A Star Is Born* (1954). This film demonstrated her abilities as a dramatic actress as well as a phenomenal singer. Garland's reputation for undependability kept her out of films until the sixties, when she played dramatic roles in *Judgment at Nuremberg* (1960) and *A Child Is Waiting* (1962). At the relatively young age of 47, she died of an accidental overdose of sleeping pills.

Garland had many rivals in the forties for her place as the brightest star of film musicals. One of the earliest—and quickest to leave the scene—was Deanna Durbin. She was Universal Pictures' major musical star until she retired in 1949. Her semi-operatic voice and "nice girl" persona graced, among other films, *Spring Parade* (1940) and *Can't Help Singing* (1944). Another singer with an exceptional voice was Kathryn Grayson. A dark-haired beauty, she was guided in her career, as was Durbin at Universal, by Joe Pasternak when he moved to MGM. Among the films in which she starred were *That Midnight Kiss* (1949, with Mario Lanza), *Show Boat* (1951, the third version of Jerome Kern's classic), and *Kiss Me, Kate* (1953, with Howard Keel).

If MGM had a host of stars and the finest musical filmmakers and Universal had Deanna Durbin, 20th Century-Fox had "the blondes." These included not only June Haver, Vivian Blaine, Vera-Ellen, and Carole Landis but also Betty Grable and Alice Faye. Grable had passable abilities as a dancer, singer, and actress as well as a striking figure. Her pinups, circulated during World War II, encouraged GIs to end the war quickly and return home. Among the more than four dozen films in which she appeared are *Million Dollar Legs* (1939), *Down Argentine Way* (1940), *Pin-Up Girl* (1943), *Mother Wore Tights* (1947), and *How to Marry a Millionaire* (1953). Alice Faye had a better voice and a more likable personality than Grable, but also a tendency toward chubbiness that became more obvious in the late forties. She was very popular in *Alexander's Ragtime Band* (costarring Tyrone Power and Ethel Merman), *In Old Chicago* (1938), *Tin Pan Alley* (1940, with Betty Grable), and *Hello, Frisco, Hello* (1943).

Certain actresses in musicals had special characteristics that earned them a reputation. Betty Hutton's specialty was being frenzied, as in *The Fleet's In, Incendiary Blonde* (1945), and *Annie Get Your Gun* (1950). Sonya Henie had little else to offer beyond her ice-skating expertise, in which skill she had competition from Vera Ralston and Belita. Esther Williams was a champion swimmer and attractive woman who could sing on key when forced to and substituted a winsome smile for acting abilities. Two of her most popular films were *Neptune's Daughter* (1949) and *Easy to Love* (1953, with production numbers by

Busby Berkeley). Dorothy Lamour was always ready to swim in her sarong but rarely did. She was most effective as a comedienne in the Hope-Crosby "Road" series. Carmen Miranda was the "Brazilian Bombshell." Wearing headdresses almost larger than her diminutive body, she belted out songs with a Latin-American accent and had an explosive personality in such films as *Down Argentine Way, That Night in Rio* (1941), and *Copacabana* (1947).

Female dancers constitute another special category. Practically every actress or singer in a musical had to be able to dance to some degree, but there were stars who were primarily dancers. Eleanor Powell, tap-dancing dervish of the thirties, continued to appear in musicals in the forties. Only two dancers who became known during and after World War II could compare to her. Cyd Charisse was one.* Ann Miller was closer to the zestful tap-dancing tradition of Powell. Three examples of the many films in which she has danced are *Easter Parade, On the Town,* and *Kiss Me, Kate.* Lucille Bremer, Vera-Ellen, and Marge Champion were principally dancers who never attained the fame they deserved. Rita Hayworth was unusual in that she began her film career as a dancer and was outstanding in a number of musicals (including *You Were Never Lovelier,* 1942, and *Pal Joey,* 1957) but is chiefly remembered as a dramatic actress and sex symbol. Although some actresses were not professional dancers, they demonstrated special skill, for example, Betty Garrett, Betty Hutton, Debbie Reynolds, Judy Garland, Nanette Fabray, and Jane Powell.

In the forties and early fifties, the two major male musical stars were Fred Astaire† and Gene Kelly.‡ Among the better-known stars of the thirties who continued into the forties were Jack Buchanan, Ray Bolger (best remembered as the scarecrow in *The Wizard of Oz* and in *Where's Charley?,* 1952), and George Murphy. Mickey Rooney (1922–) belongs in this group, for the short, dynamic, cocky dancer-singer-actor has appeared in dozens of films since 1932. During and after playing a perennial adolescent in the

seemingly endless Andy Hardy series (1937–1946, plus another in 1948), he starred in musicals. The most successful were those that also featured Judy Garland. He was impressive also in Mamoulian's *Summer Holiday.* In the sixties and seventies, Rooney turned increasingly to television. Two other multitalented actors who made their reputation in musicals during the forties were Donald O'Connor* and Dan Dailey.

Among the stars of the golden age of the American musical were singers who were also adequate actors (sometimes even superior ones) and could dance enough not to appear completely awkward. At the top of the list would be Bing Crosby (1904–1977). Although he made his film debut in 1932, he became well known on the screen in the forties. His "Road" series films (1941–1952) with Bob Hope were not really musicals, but they always contained many songs and dances. In *Birth of the Blues* (1941), *Holiday Inn* (1942), and *White Christmas* (1954), he demonstrated how relaxed and casual a singer can be and still project a distinct personality. In the same style, he played a dramatic role in *Going My Way* (1944, for which he won an Academy Award for Best Actor) and was surprisingly moving as an alcoholic actor in *The Country Girl* (1955).

Bing Crosby's place as the number one big-band singer was challenged in the forties by Frank Sinatra (1917–), an emaciated young man with a phenomenal gift for phrasing that made even the most mundane song lyrics seem emotionally significant. He costarred in *Anchors Aweigh* (1945) and *On the Town* (1949). The latter is an example of the type of lively, creative musical MGM could make with its storehouse of talent. Sinatra is one of three sailors (the others are Gene Kelly and Jules Munshin) on a 24-hour leave who spend their time courting or being courted by three attractive young women (Betty Garrett, Vera-Ellen, and Ann Miller). After a swift decline in popularity in the early fifties, Sinatra made a sensational comeback in a straight acting role as Maggio in *From Here to Eternity* (1953) and returned to musicals. He starred in *Guys and Dolls* (1955), *High Society* (1956), and *Pal Joey* (1957), among others. Sina-

---

tra has played in numerous dramas and comedies, directed a film, and produced a few.

Reliable singers who did not achieve the fame of Crosby and Sinatra included Dick Haymes, Dennis Morgan, Gordon MacRae, and Howard Keel. The most powerful and compelling voice of the forties, however, belonged to Mario Lanza, who died in 1959 at the age of 38. During the decade in which he appeared on the screen, from his debut in *That Midnight Kiss* (1949) to his death, he attracted a multitude of devoted fans. His most memorable performance was in *The Great Caruso* (1951).

Actors who neither sang nor danced (or at least not enough to be noticeable) were also mainstays of forties musicals. The most prominent were Tyrone Power, Don Ameche, William Powell, John Payne, George Montgomery, Larry Parks, and Peter Lawford. Some dated from the thirties; practically all of them became known for their work in other genres. Outstanding comedians in musicals included Phil Silvers, Jack Carson, and Jack Oakie.

Of the three major musical subgenres, the operetta was no longer a viable form, and the biography musical was generally ignored until the mid-fifties. However, the period 1940–1953 was the heyday of animated features created by Walt Disney Studio. Although it is arguable whether or not *Dumbo* (1941), *Bambi* (1942), *Alice in Wonderland* (1951), and *Peter Pan* (1953) should be labeled musicals, the songs sung by cartoon figures were, to many viewers, young and old, the highlights of the films. In other features (for example, *Saludos Amigos,* 1942; *Make Mine Music,* 1946; and *Melody Time,* 1948), music played an even more central role. (*Fantasia,* 1940, does not fit our definition of the musical because the music included is entirely classical.) After 1953 Disney produced as many live-action films, especially comedies, as animated ones.

While Hollywood was creating dozens of musicals, European studios after World War II continued, in the main, to disregard the genre. Some related forms, however, did flourish. Russia released ballet films and spectacles based on the music and lives of its national composers. In Italy, opera films were more popular with audiences than Neorealistic works.

Many postwar French films contained songs, but they were not integrated into the plots, and the films rarely qualify as musicals. Only Jacques Demy (1931–) made a valid excursion into the genre, and his efforts were confined to two motion pictures. *The Umbrellas of Cherbourg* (*Les Parapluies de Cherbourg,* 1964) tells of two young lovers (Catherine Deneuve and Nino Castelnuovo) who are separated when he is forced to leave for military service. Through a misunderstanding, each one marries another person, and they meet briefly years later. The sentimentality of Demy's screenplay is reinforced by Michel Legrand's lush, lilting score. Everything else about the film, however, is extraordinary. Not only are there individual songs, but even the dialogue is sung. There are no production numbers as such. The use of color is bold and captivating. The sets by Bernard Evein are impressive, as is the directing. The film was deservedly an international success.

Demy appeared to have hit upon a new approach to the musical that with a plot of more substance and less shallow charm could develop the unique combination of realism, calculated artificiality, and vigorous artistry initiated by René Clair in his early sound films and Pabst in *The Threepenny Opera*. However, Demy's next film, *The Young Girls of Rochefort* (*Les Demoiselles de Rochefort,* 1966), was a disappointment. Despite an all-star cast (including Catherine Deneuve, Françoise Dorléac, Danielle Darrieux, Gene Kelly, and George Chakiris) and once again a score by Michel Legrand, the film has a rambling, inconsequential plot about two dancing sisters that is not redeemed by any of the virtues of its predecessor. Demy then turned to other genres, and no one to date, in France or elsewhere, has followed the lead suggested by *The Umbrellas of Cherbourg*.

Great Britain's film industry attempted but never succeeded in discovering a musical star of the caliber of Jessie Matthews and Gracie Fields. The closest possibility was Anna Neagle. This remarkable woman not only appeared in stage and screen musicals but has also been an outstanding actress specializing in historical film roles (for example, Nell Gwyn, Queen Victoria, and Florence Nightingale) and a motion picture producer. She was notable in a series of musicals made in the late forties, beginning with *Piccadilly Incident* (1946), in which she costarred with Michael Wilding. More successful than musicals of the forties were two motion pictures from a related genre, the ballet film: Michael Powell and Emeric Pressburger's *The Red Shoes* (1948) and its successor, *The Tales of Hoffmann* (1951).

British musicals were in the doldrums during the fifties, enlivened somewhat by Peter Brook's version of John Gay's *The Beggar's Opera* (1953, starring Laurence Olivier) and the films of pop singer Tommy Steele. In the mid-sixties a gust of spontaneity and irreverence rattled this staid world. Richard Lester's *A Hard Day's Night* (1964) presented a day and a half in the life of the Beatles, the most electrifying rock group of the postwar era. There was a calculated madness appropriate to the antics of the group on- and offstage in the director's frantic, sweeping camera, use of the zoom lens, and disorienting transitions and angles. More careful planning and editing than is evident to the casual eye went into the film, but the overall effect was of freedom and a snubbing of social and cinematic conventions. *Help!* (1965) was a more sedate sequel, or perhaps the director's shock techniques were beginning to wear thin. Lester then stopped making musicals and turned to comedies.* The Beatles were represented in and supplied the songs for a unique musical, *Yellow Submarine* (1968). It is an animated film in which the four singers experience a series of unbelievable adventures, each one related to a specific song.

Another startling musical was released a year later. Richard Attenborough's *Oh! What a Lovely War* (1969) was adapted from a stage presentation. This survey of World War I from a British perspective is unified by songs of the period and a narration. The film highlights with bitter humor the futility, waste, and stubborn stupidity that prevailed among military leaders and officers during the Great War. More than two dozen stars, including Laurence Olivier, John Gielgud, John Mills, Vanessa Redgrave, and Susannah York, played cameo roles. *Oh! What a Lovely War* is a

musical that can be compared in its savage irony only to *The Threepenny Opera*.

These late-sixties films had little competition in quality from other contemporary British musicals. Although Carol Reed has been one of England's leading directors, his *Oliver!* (1968) was conventional and uninspired as a film. Ken Russell's *The Boy Friend* (1971) possesses the director's typical heavy-handed extravagance. It has some merit as a visual parody of Busby Berkeley's style, but the ponderous spectacle suffocated a modest plot and a very fragile star, Twiggy.

In the United States, the momentum of the forties musical carried into the mid-fifties, when a massive roadblock stood in its way: Television came into its own and challenged motion pictures as the number one popular form of entertainment in the nation. Hollywood studios panicked and instituted drastic retrenchments. Musicals bore the heaviest brunt because they were the most expensive type of motion picture to make. Contracts with stars, directors, choreographers, and other filmmakers were terminated or allowed to lapse. The effect of these new conditions on the musical was not only that fewer were made, and more cautiously, but also that experienced talent was no longer consolidated and new talent lost opportunities to train.

It is impossible, naturally, to pick one year in which "the golden age" ended and a less adventurous, less vibrant form of musical began to appear. The convenient decade designation simply does not apply, especially when two of the finest musicals in the forties style, *An American in Paris* and *Singin' in the Rain,* were released, respectively, in 1951 and 1952. The year 1953 is the best candidate. In this year appeared *The Band Wagon,* the last Minnelli–Astaire combination, and *Gentlemen Prefer Blondes,* which featured Marilyn Monroe, one of the top stars of the fifties, in her first major role.

The best forties musical filmmakers and stars did not go gently into retirement at the end of 1953, but, with a few notable exceptions, the number of musicals they made, as well as the quality of their work, declined. Vincente Minnelli directed *Brigadoon* (1954, with music by Lerner and Loewe, starring Gene

Kelly, Van Johnson, and Cyd Charisse), *Kismet* (1955, based on music by Borodin, starring Howard Keel and Dolores Gray), *Bells Are Ringing* (1960, with Judy Holliday and Dean Martin), and *On a Clear Day You Can See Forever* (1969, with music by Lerner and Burton Lane and starring Barbra Streisand). All four musicals lacked the director's usual sparkle and taste and were more effective in their original stage productions. In *The Band Wagon* and *Gigi* (1958), however, Minnelli met the high standards he set in *Meet Me in St. Louis* and *An American in Paris*. *The Band Wagon* has a screenplay by Comden and Green and stars Fred Astaire, Cyd Charisse, Oscar Levant, Nanette Fabray, and Jack Buchanan (Figure 9.5). The story of an aging dancer, no longer a bright star in films, who attempts a Broadway comeback is a backstage musical with some wonderful production numbers, such as "That's Entertainment," "Dancing in the Dark," "Triplets," and a burlesque of Mickey Spillane mysteries. The songs are derived from a Schwartz-Dietz thirties musical, with lyrics updated by Comden and Green. *Gigi* has an original screenplay by Alan Jay Lerner based on a novel by Colette; Lerner also provided the lyrics to Frederick Loewe's music. Leslie Caron, Maurice Chevalier, Louis Jourdan, and Hermione Gingold are the stars. Although a bit sentimental, *Gigi* is one of the

most delightful musicals of the fifties, and it won nine Academy Awards.

For *It's Always Fair Weather* (1955), Stanley Donen (1924–) was for the third time codirector and cochoreographer with Gene Kelly (the previous musicals were *On the Town* and *Singin' in the Rain*). The plot has Kelly, Dan Dailey, and Michael Kidd as World War II veterans having a wild reunion, with Cyd Charisse as chief romantic interest. Comden and Green, as usual, supplied a sprightly script. Donen also collaborated with George Abbott on *Pajama Game* (1957, starring Doris Day) and *Damn Yankees* (1959, with Gwen Verdon).

After his solo directing debut in 1950 *(Royal Wedding)*, Donen did a few films on his own. His two finest efforts in the musical genre are *Seven Brides for Seven Brothers* (1954) and *Funny Face* (1957). The former (Figure 9.6) features music by Gene de Paul, lyrics by Johnny Mercer, superb choreography by Michael Kidd, and Cinemascope, a novelty at the time. Based on a short story by Stephen Vincent Benét ("Sobbin' Women"), it transfers the classic story of the rape of the Sabine women to Oregon. The film is one of the few musicals to capture the ambiance of the nineteenth-century American West with authenticity and honesty, a distinction it shares with Mamoulian's *High, Wide and Handsome*. *Funny Face* is less zestful and imaginative than *Seven Brides for Seven Brothers* but more sophisticated and witty. In addition to striking French settings, it took advantage of the talents of Fred Astaire and Audrey Hepburn, especially in the choreography by Eugene Loring and Fred Astaire.

Like Minnelli and Kelly, Donen integrated plot with songs and dances. What is uniquely his own, however, is his cinematic style: inventive, dynamic, and vigorous, in which the camera seems to become a participant in the action rather than a passive observer. After 1958 Donen left for England and devoted himself to social comedies and mysteries. He did return to Hollywood to direct *The Little Prince* (1974).*

As a director, Gene Kelly created an adventurous work in *Invitation to the Dance* (1956)† but later proved how unadventurous he could be in *Hello,*

**FIGURE 9.5**

*The Band Wagon,* 1953, directed by Vincente Minnelli (color). Even in the fifties, stars such as these were the backbone of a musical (left to right, Oscar Levant, Cyd Charisse, Jack Buchanan, Fred Astaire, and Nanette Fabray).

*p. 459
†p. 469

*Seven Brides for Seven Brothers,* 1954, directed by Stanley Donen (color). Milly (Jane Powell) gives an etiquette lesson to her six brothers-in-law in the exuberant production number "Goin' Courtin'."

*Dolly* (1969, starring Barbra Streisand). Charles Walters was not at his best in *High Society* (1956), a musical version of George Cukor's film comedy *The Philadelphia Story,* which even Bing Crosby and Frank Sinatra could not salvage. He was somewhat more effective in *The Glass Slipper* (1955, with Leslie Caron); however, he was again pedestrian in *The Unsinkable Molly Brown* (1964, starring Debbie Reynolds). The always dependable Rouben Mamoulian directed *Silk Stockings* in 1957. This is a film version of the Cole Porter Broadway success, in turn based on Lubitsch's *Ninotchka* (1939). While not as piquant as *Love Me Tonight* or as dramatic as *Summer Holiday,* it is a superior musical that supplied a visual showcase for the dancing of Fred Astaire and Cyd Charisse. Walter Lang is a conventional professional whether directing comedies or musicals. His phlegmatic touch dulled *Call Me Madame* (1953), *There's No Business Like Show Business* (1955)—both with Irving Berlin scores and starring Ethel Merman—*The King and I* (1956, with Yul Brynner and Deborah Kerr), and *Can-Can* (1960, starring Frank Sinatra and Shirley MacLaine).

Many directors of film musicals in the fifties and sixties were inexperienced in the genre, and their efforts were confined to one or two such films. No matter what their abilities in other types of motion pictures, their directing of musicals was rarely more than competent. Some examples: Howard Hawks (*Gentlemen Prefer Blondes,* 1953), Otto Preminger (*Carmen Jones,* 1954, and *Porgy and Bess,* 1959), Fred Zinnemann (*Oklahoma!,* 1955), Richard Quine (*My Sister Eileen,* 1955), Joseph L. Mankiewicz (*Guys and Dolls,* 1955), Jean Negulesco (*Daddy Longlegs,*

1955), Robert Lewis (*Anything Goes,* 1956), Henry King (*Carousel,* 1956), Henry Koster (*Flower Drum Song,* 1961), Mervin LeRoy (*Gypsy,* 1962), Richard Fleischer (*Doctor Dolittle,* 1967), and William Wyler (*Funny Girl,* 1968).

A few directors showed a flair for musicals but did not go beyond a single one in Hollywood. *Mary Poppins* (1964), an original film musical, is sheer entertainment and no more, imaginatively directed by Robert Stevenson. Richard Lester found an appropriate vehicle for his free-wheeling, exuberant style in *A Funny Thing Happened on the Way to the Forum* (1966). *Thoroughly Modern Millie* (1967), another original film musical, stylishly directed by George Roy Hill, should have been more popular than it was. Francis Ford Coppola's *Finian's Rainbow* (1968) was made with a fluency and sureness astonishing in a director only in his mid-thirties.

Two directors devoted themselves particularly to adapting stage musicals for the screen. One of them, Joshua Logan, was responsible for *South Pacific* (1958), *Camelot* (1967), and *Paint Your Wagon* (1969). He is an eminent director and producer of stage plays but has a limited cinematic imagination. His work has the static, stilted quality of filmed stage musicals. Although George Sidney has more verve and finesse, his approach was basically routine in *Kiss Me, Kate* (1953), *Pal Joey* (1957), and *Bye Bye Birdie* (1963).

George Cukor was from the early 1930s one of Hollywood's most versatile, dependable, and intelligent filmmakers. With a sure hand, he directed Judy Garland and James Mason in *A Star Is Born,* a drama with songs. *Les Girls* (1957, starring Gene Kelly) and *Let's Make Love* (1960) are genuine musicals created with taste and vitality. It was, however, in *My Fair Lady* (1964) that Cukor proved he was one of the finest directors of musicals in Hollywood in the sixties. It is difficult to imagine that the Lerner and Loewe Broadway hit based on George Bernard Shaw's *Pygmalion* could fail as a film. Cukor, however, not only drew superior performances from Rex Harrison, Audrey Hepburn, and Stanley Holloway but also neatly balanced the pleasure of a lavish, expensive spectacle with a preservation of the ambiguous relationship of the two main characters and the intellectual wit of the stage production. It is regrettable that Cukor directed only three musicals in his career.

In the 1960s two directors came to prominence who gave hope to those who feared that the film musical was becoming a moribund genre. The background and contributions of Robert Wise to *West Side Story* (1961) and *The Sound of Music* (1965) are discussed later in this chapter.* Bob Fosse (1925–) was initially a stage dancer and actor. He continued these activities in films in the early fifties (for example, in *Kiss Me, Kate*). In the mid-fifties he turned to choreography, then directed his first musical, *Sweet Charity,* in 1968. It is an adaption of a stage comedy by Neil Simon and others, in turn derived from Federico Fellini's *The Nights of Cabiria.* The film appeared to have all the components that would make it a success. The songs by Cy Coleman and Dorothy Fields, including "Rhythm of Life" and "Hey, Big Spender," are captivating. Shirley MacLaine as Charity Hope Valentine is splendid and is surrounded by such talent as Chita Rivera, Paula Kelly, Sammy Davis, Jr., and Ricardo Montalban. Bob Fosse's directing (he also did the choreography) is superb, with a facility in manipulating camera-editing dynamics that recalls Stanley Donen and a sensitivity to color values comparable to that of Vincente Minnelli. Yet the film was a financial failure and, though one of the finest musicals since *West Side Story,* has been underrated except by a few enthusiasts.

Fosse was more fortunate with his next film, *Cabaret* (1972). The original stage musical, with songs by John Kandor and Fred Ebb, was derived from both Christopher Isherwood's *Goodbye to Berlin* and John Van Druten's play *I Am a Camera,* adapted from Isherwood's novel. The setting is Berlin in the early thirties, when the Nazi party was rising to power. A sexually ambiguous Englishman finds himself part of a triangle including Sally Bowles, an emotionally vulnerable but generous American cabaret singer, and a young baron. The stage version was more incisive and dramatic in dealing with this tangled relationship and others, but Fosse is splendid in capturing the decadent

---

*pp. 477–478

ambiance of the Kit Kat Klub where Sally sings. Liza Minnelli as Sally and Joel Grey as the master of ceremonies at the club are remarkable (Figure 9.7). They both won Academy Awards for their performances, as did Fosse for his directing.

**FIGURE 9.7**

*Cabaret,* 1972, directed by Bob Fosse (color). Sally Bowles (Liza Minnelli) and the Master of Ceremonies (Joel Grey) sing the cynical song "Money, Money, Money" at the Kit Kat Klub.

The situation in regard to composers and lyricists of film musicals released from 1953 to 1969 can be illuminated by a statistic. In the foregoing discussion of American directors, 47 works are noted. Of these, 35 are adaptations from stage musicals, and only 12 original Hollywood musicals. *Funny Face* uses earlier George and Ira Gershwin songs. *Gigi* (Lerner and Loewe) and *Sweet Charity* (Cy Coleman and Dorothy Fields) are engaging throughout, and there are memorable songs in *Les Girls* (Porter), *Daddy Longlegs* (Johnny Mercer), and *There's No Business Like Show Business* (Berlin). *Mary Poppins* (Richard and Robert B. Sherman) has some charming moments, and *Thoroughly Modern Millie* (Elmer Bernstein and others) has some witty ones. The music for the remaining four are on the mediocre level of Leslie Bricusse's for *Dr. Doolittle.*

Adaptations, on the other hand, provided a good deal of exciting music, if only sporatically provocative cinematic experiences. Dominating the scene during these years were Richard Rodgers (1902–1979) and Oscar Hammerstein II (1895–1960): *Oklahoma!, The King and I, Carousel, South Pacific, Flower Drum Song,* and *The Sound of Music.* Almost as prolific and no less distinguished in quality are the musicals of the team of Alan Jay Lerner (1918–) and Frederick Loewe (1904–). In addition to their original *Gigi,* they supplied the scores for *Brigadoon, Paint Your Wagon, My Fair Lady,* and *Camelot.* Cole Porter (1891–1964), who wrote musicals from 1916 to the late fifties, contributed songs to *Kiss Me, Kate, Anything Goes, Silk Stockings,* and *Can-Can,* as well as the original films *High Society* and *Les Girls.* Porter's only rival in productivity was Irving Berlin (1888–). He slowed down in his late sixties, and his only film musicals after 1953 were *Call Me Madame* and the original *There's No Business Like Show Business.*

Other prominent composers and lyricists whose stage musicals were adapted to films include Richard Adler and Jerry Ross *(Pajama Game, Damn Yankees),* Leonard Bernstein and Stephen Sondheim *(West Side Story),* Jule Styne and Stephen Sondheim *(Gypsy),* Frank Loesser *(Guys and Dolls),* Burton Lane and E. Y. Harburg *(Finian's Rainbow),* and Meredith Wilson *(The Unsinkable Molly Brown).*

Most outstanding choreographers of this period had begun in films in the forties or earlier. Gene Kelly and Stanley Donen were still active either separately (for instance, Kelly in *Invitation to the Dance*) or in collaboration (as in *It's Always Fair Weather*). Hermes Pan, who dated back to the thirties, choreographed the dances for *Pal Joey, Porgy and Bess, My Fair Lady, Finian's Rainbow,* and others. Jerome Robbins and Michael Kidd were known as innovators in ballet and stage musicals before working in Hollywood. Robbins was responsible for the dances in *The King and I* and *West Side Story* (he was also codirector of the latter). Michael Kidd contributed to *The Band Wagon, Seven Brides for Seven Brothers,* and *Guys and Dolls.* Among Bob Fosse's credits are *My Sister Eileen, Pajama Game,* and *Damn Yankees,* as well as the major films he has directed.

Many new female stars came to the fore after 1953, though no one actress dominated the American musical as did Judy Garland in the forties. The most popular often were as well known for their comedies as their musicals. In her 13 years as a film actress, Marilyn Monroe appeared in only three musicals (Gentlemen Prefer Blondes, There's No Business Like Show Business, and Let's Make Love), but she sang numbers in many of her comedies. Although she had a no more than adequate voice, she had a unique way of interpreting a song, projecting a personality of overwhelming sexuality protecting a core of vulnerability and naiveté. Doris Day was the direct opposite of Monroe, the personification of the healthy, attractive girl next door. She was at her best in Pajama Game. She has confined herself to comedies since the late sixties. Julie Andrews, with her relentless cheerfulness, handsome face, and polished voice, has always been popular in musicals, including Mary Poppins, The Sound of Music, and Thoroughly Modern Millie. She also starred in Star! (1968) and such comedies as The Americanization of Emily (1964) and "10" (1979). Barbra Streisand overcame the disadvantages of plain features and a strident personality with determination and a big, expertly controlled voice to become one of the half dozen highest-paid stars in Hollywood today. After winning an Academy Award for her first musical, Funny Girl, she went on to Hello, Dolly and On a Clear Day You Can See Forever. During the seventies, she proved to be a very gifted comedienne.

Other female stars of these two decades were usually better dancers than singers. Audrey Hepburn is a fine actress, particularly delightful in comedies, a tolerable dancer, and sings on occasion. She brought freshness and style to Funny Face and My Fair Lady (for which her singing voice was dubbed by Marni Nixon). Leslie Caron, a professional ballet dancer before appearing in films, was outstanding in An American in Paris and Gigi. She successfully made the transition to comedies and straight dramatic roles. Shirley MacLaine was remarkable in Sweet Charity but also communicated her vivid personality in the earlier Can-Can as well as in nonmusical roles. Debbie Reynolds and Natalie Wood* made their reputations in drama and comedies but appeared in hit musicals.

Other outstanding female performers in musicals of the period include Mitzi Gaynor, Juliet Prowse, Zizi Jeanmaire, Ann-Margret, Gwen Verdon, Dolores Gray, Rita Moreno, Janet Leigh, Paula Kelly, Chita Rivera, Mary Tyler Moore, and Vanessa Redgrave.

There was a paucity of new male stars in musicals after 1953. Fred Astaire, Gene Kelly, Frank Sinatra, Bing Crosby, Howard Keel, and others continued to be active until the early sixties. Gordon MacRae achieved a measure of acclaim in Oklahoma! and Carousel, as did John Raitt in Pajama Game. The versatile and energetic Sammy Davis, Jr. appeared in Porgy and Bess and Sweet Charity. Other professional singers in musicals include Dean Martin (Bells Are Ringing), Harry Belafonte (Carmen Jones), and Dick Van Dyke (Bye Bye Birdie and Mary Poppins). Among male professional dancers, only Russ Tamblyn was notable in Seven Brides for Seven Brothers and West Side Story. Both he and Bobby Van (Kiss Me, Kate) never had the opportunities to develop commensurate with their talents.

During this period, the basically nonsinging, nondancing male star began to appear in musicals. Rex Harrison (My Fair Lady and Dr. Dolittle) and Yul Brynner (The King and I) compensated for limited vocal abilities with personality and stylish acting. In this category also belong Christopher Plummer, Richard Harris, Tab Hunter, Rossano Brazzi, and Louis Jourdan.

A number of films that belong in subdivisions of the musicals were released in the fifties and sixties. Biography films focused on popular composers, band leaders, and performers. The best of the composer "biopics" were Stars and Stripes Forever (1953), with Clifton Webb as John Philip Sousa, and Deep in My Heart (1954), with Jose Ferrer as Sigmund Romberg. James Stewart played the title role in The Glenn Miller Story (1954). Most of the biography films were devoted to performers: I'll Cry Tomorrow (1955, with Susan Hayward as Lillian Roth), The Seven Little Foys (1955, with Bob Hope as Eddie Foy), The Eddie Duchin Story (1956, starring Tyrone Power), The Joker Is Wild (1957, with Frank Sinatra as Joe E. Lewis), The Five Pennies (1959, with Danny Kaye playing Red Nichols, the jazz trumpeter), Funny Girl (1968, star-

---

*p. 478

ring Barbra Streisand as Fanny Brice), and *Star!* (1968, with Julie Andrews as Gertrude Lawrence). To this list could be added two films loosely based on living performers: *Gypsy* (1962, which deals more with Mama Rose, played by Rosalind Russell, than the young Gypsy Rose Lee, a singer of sorts) and *The Sound of Music* (1965, on the Trapp family).

The films of Elvis Presley are in a special category. Between 1956 and 1977, when Presley died, he made over two dozen movies that were very successful financially. A cut below even the Presley films were the "beach party" movies popular with adolescents in the sixties.

The seventies was not a propitious decade for the film musical. Aside from *Cabaret* (1972), noted earlier, the remarkable *All That Jazz*, three works of more than passing interest, two compilation films, and the phenomenon of the rock musical, the record is an undistinguished one for a period of 10 years. Hollywood has remained the capital of productions in this genre. Other countries of the world have yet to learn how to make exportable musicals.

England, however, has been unusually active in recent years in releasing respectable, though not resourceful, musicals. Ken Russell's *The Boy Friend* (1971) was mentioned. *Bugsy Malone* (1976, written and directed by Alan Parker), a spoof of gangster films acted by youngsters, made no pretense of offering more than charming entertainment and succeeded admirably in being just that. *Aces High* (1975, directed by Jack Gold) was a muted echo of *Oh! What a Lovely War*. The German "street film" was resurrected and updated, and music was added in *Moon Over the Alley* (1975, directed by Joseph Despins). British popular songs of the thirties constitute the foundation of Dennis Potter's *Pennies From Heaven* (1977, originally made for BBC TV).

In the United States, mediocrity prevailed in *Song of Norway* (1970), *Man of La Mancha* (1972), *1776* (1972), *Tom Sawyer* (1973), and Peter Bogdanovich's *At Long Last Love* (1975). *Fiddler on the Roof* (1971, directed by Norman Jewison) though admirable, was disappointing when compared to the Broadway success. In Sidney Lumet's *The Wiz* (1978, starring Diana Ross), spectacle overwhelmed the

imaginativeness and ingenuousness that characterized the stage production of this black version of *The Wizard of Oz*.

The talent involved in *The Little Prince* (1974, based on Antoine de Saint Exupéry's fable) recalled the golden age of the musical: directed by Stanley Donen, with screenplay by Alan Jay Lerner and songs by Lerner and Loewe, starring Richard Kiley and the young Steven Warner, featuring Gene Wilder and Bob Fosse. Many critics found it pretentious and discomforting in its straining for whimsy, but there were those, admittedly a minority, who felt it deserved a better reception than it received.

One of the most controversial musicals in the last decade was Martin Scorsese's *New York, New York* (1977), starring Liza Minnelli and Robert De Niro. Through visual echoes and its production numbers, the film evokes the musicals of the thirties. The plot, humor, and style, however, seem to be haunted by a sadness, an aura of nostalgia turned sour. Perhaps this is why some critics felt Scorsese was conducting a public wake for the musical as a genre. *New York, New York* lingers in the memory like an ambiguous dream that was both pleasurable and depressing.

*A Little Night Music* (1978, directed by Harold Prince) is an adaptation of Stephen Sondheim's enchanting stage musical, in turn based on Ingmar Bergman's *Smiles of a Summer Night*. Diana Rigg and Hermione Gingold are outstanding. Unfortunately, the directing is only adequate, and Elizabeth Taylor is miscast as Desirée. Sondheim, the most provocative creator of stage musicals today, deserved to be served with greater distinction.

If *New York, New York* caused controversy, Bob Fosse's *All That Jazz* (1979) provoked violent debate. While few viewers have denied its visual power or dramatic intensity, many have doubted the appropriateness of its subject matter for a musical—the last days of a director-choreographer (played by Roy Scheider)—and the alternately honest and self-justifying plot that is obviously autobiographical (a sort of musical *8½*). To enthusiastic viewers, however, it is in the tradition of *West Side Story, Sweet Charity,* and *Cabaret* (the latter two also directed and choreographed by Fosse) in expanding the potentials of the conventional musical to include exploration of serious social and psychological themes. Whatever the weaknesses of *All That Jazz,* it is a stirring cinematic experience (Figure 9.8), and for some critics the film demonstrates, if there was any question before, that Bob Fosse ranks with Minnelli, Donen, and Kelly as a grand master of the musical genre.

**FIGURE 9.8**

*All That Jazz,* 1979, directed by Bob Fosse (color). Just before he dies, director-choreographer Joe Gideon (Roy Scheider) stages in his mind a spectacular farewell to the theater, which features the song "Bye Bye Love."

It is a sign of the times that two of the most enjoyable musicals in the seventies were compilations: *That's Entertainment* (1974) and *That's Entertainment, Part 2* (1976), which consist of excerpts from the best of the MGM musicals.

Optimists on the future of the conventional musical in the United States were not encouraged by the major releases of the early eighties. *Pennies From Heaven* (1981) contains superb production numbers in the style of Hollywood thirties musicals, but its creators were not able to fuse the dimensions of stark realism and romantic fantasy. *Annie* (1982) is dull and unimaginatively directed by John Huston.

A vital innovative development in the genre was the rock musical. Both *Godspell* (directed by David Greene) and *Jesus Christ, Superstar* (directed by Norman Jewison) were released in 1973. Charac-

teristics of the two films are vitality, driving (and loud) music, and inventiveness, as well as a certain awkwardness, self-righteousness, and faulty structure (each has a striking opening, sags in the middle, and is monotonous by the end). Ken Russell's *Tommy* (1975), a British-American production, is never monotonous. This expanded version of a "rock opera" composed by Peter Townshend of The Who is, however, brash, crude, extravagant, and shocking. As with most of Russell's recent efforts, beneath the flash and glitter is—flash and glitter. The main actors—Ann-Margret, Roger Daltrey, Oliver Reed, and Jack Nicholson—struggle courageously with bizarre ·material. Elton John is bizarre enough to begin with to be comfortable in his role. Only the music stands on its pounding feet and demands respect.

Perhaps the most intelligently and sensitively made rock musical to date has been Milos Forman's adaptation of *Hair* (1978). Unfortunately, for reasons that only a sociologist is qualified to explain, this classic play of the sixties (1968) was not a commercially successful film of the seventies. *The Rocky Horror Picture Show* (1975) should at least be mentioned because of its popularity among those addicted to bizarre cult films. By a strange coincidence, 1978 was the premier year of rock film musicals in quantity if not in quality. Not only was *Hair* released, but also *Grease,* a splashy but dull adaptation of the stage play; *Sgt. Pepper's Lonely Hearts Club Band,* a fantasy that failed, based loosely on songs from the great Beatles album; *American Hot Wax,* an effective evocation of the fifties when Alan Freed was the king of rock disk jockeys; *The Buddy Holly Story,* a biopic of the singer with an outstanding performance in the lead role by Gary Busey. The previous year a film appeared that was fabulously profitable. *Saturday Night Fever* qualifies as a contribution to the genre unless one insists that there be a separate category for rock dance films. Though overwrought and contrived, its dance sequences are exciting, and John Travolta conveys intimations of authenticity in portraying an immature young man with a gift for rhythm.

The rock musical is one answer to the stultification—always allowing for such exceptions as *All That Jazz*—that has apparently gripped the genre since the early seventies. Adaptability would seem to be the means to overcome the problems of high production costs, the competition of television, and changing audience tastes in popular music. Of course, the value of the end product rather than the means is the criterion of whether the genre deserves to survive. One anticipates with apprehension the first major science fiction film musical.

## HOLLYWOOD THIRTIES MUSICAL

### Top Hat

*Passion . . . is usually confused with emoting or going primitive. With Astaire and Rogers, it's a matter of total professional dedication; they do not give us emotions, they give us dances, and the more beautifully they dance, the more powerful the spell.*
*Arlene Croce, 1977[3]*

### CAST

*Fred Astaire (Jerry Travis), Ginger Rogers (Dale Tremont), Edward Everett Horton (Horace Hardwick), Helen Broderick (Madge Hardwick), Eric Blore (Bates), Erik Rhodes (Beddini), and others.*

### CREDITS

*Director—Mark Sandrich, Producer—Pandro S. Berman, Screenwriters—Dwight Taylor and Allan Scott, Director of Photography—David Abel, Composer (music and lyrics)—Irving Berlin, Director of Dance—Hermes Pan, and others.*

1935/RKO Radio
Black & White/101 minutes

### BACKGROUND

For most moviegoers in the thirties, the personification of the American musical was the team of Fred Astaire (1899–) and Ginger Rogers. The two separated in the last year of the decade (although they were to be reunited for one film in the forties). Rogers went on to other genres. Astaire, however, continued to perform in musicals during the forties and fifties.

It is not difficult to explain why Astaire remained a top musical star for three decades. There had never appeared on the screen—and probably never will again—a dancer with a style to equal his grace, agility, and suavity. He seems to have been constructed differently from other human beings. Where the rest of us have bones articulated together by fibrous tissue, Astaire has some fluid material that allows his long, thin limbs to swivel in any direction (an ability shared by Ray Bolger). Moreover, he has a special dispensation from the full effect of gravity. Gene Kelly, for example, overcomes the pull of gravity by muscular strength and exuberance; Astaire's problem, it appears, is to remain in contact with the ground.

No matter what Astaire's physical advantages, he would be less impressive if he did not possess the additional qualities of intelligence, charm, and inventiveness. An observant viewer notices that the dancer never indulges in wasted or tentative movements. Everything has been carefully thought out, from the best means of highlighting a variation in a step pattern to the overall rhythm of an entire number. Yet Astaire dances so effortlessly that we could be fooled into believing that he is almost improvising. This is a demonstration of the art of concealing art. People who attended his rehearsals report that they were grueling sessions at which Astaire spent hours experimenting with a seemingly simple routine until it met his exacting standards.

If charm can be defined as the quality or power of pleasing, Astaire has it in abundance. His screen persona, no matter what role he plays, is consistently that of a likable person who is casual, witty, and confident. And he has a gift for conveying this pleasing personality in his dancing. He appears to enjoy dancing so much that a viewer cannot help but share his pleasure.

Astaire deserves most of the credit for the inventiveness of his dances. Although his name is not always listed as choreographer, he created most of the numbers in which he appeared, especially the solos. No one can object to this prerogative because he has the imagination to surprise us in film after film. He is especially ingenious in taking advantage of props during his solo dances.

As with most superior artists, Astaire had his roots in a tradition that he went on to transcend. Actually, his style is founded on two traditions: European ballroom dancing and American tap dancing. It is appropriate that he appeared with Ginger Rogers in a film biography of Vernon and Irene Castle, for this team in the second decade of the century introduced Americans to the artistic potentials of ballroom dancing. Astaire and his sister Adele were consciously imitating the Castles (as he tells us in his autobiography, *Steps in Time*) when they danced as a stage team in the twenties. After he began making films, Astaire not only grafted the rhythmic tap dancing of vaudeville to the more sinuous forms of ballroom dancing but also adapted his style to the new medium. He took advantage of both the intimacy possible by bringing a camera close to a dancer and the spectacle that no legitimate stage could contain. Moreover, he introduced into his solo dances some of the basic vocabulary of modern dance and ballet, such as the pirouette, that were foreign to popular dance. The result is a style that is flexible and eclectic and bears the stamp of a distinct personality.

Astaire's genius as a dancer compensates for the fact that he is not handsome, his acting abilities are limited, and his voice is no more than pleasant (though he has a sure sense of rhythm and pitch and a gift for projecting personality into the lyrics of a song).

When Fred and Adele Astaire ended their successful vaudeville and stage dancing team, Fred made his film debut in *Dancing Lady* (1933). It was, however, in another film that same year, *Flying Down to Rio,* that he and his partner for the first time, Ginger Rogers, were a sensation dancing "The Carioca." Astaire and Rogers went on to make eight more musicals between 1934 and 1939: *The Gay Divorcee* (1934), *Roberta* (1935), *Top Hat* (1935), *Follow the Fleet* (1936), *Shall We Dance* (1937), *Swing Time* (1937), *Carefree* (1938), and *The Story of Vernon and Irene Castle* (1939). They were reunited once more in *The Barkleys of Broadway* (1949).

Although he never found a partner quite as stylish and compatible as Ginger Rogers, he came closest with Cyd Charisse in *The Band Wagon* (1953) and *Silk Stockings* (1957) and, to a lesser degree, with Lucille Bremer in *Ziegfeld Follies* (1945) and *Yolanda and the Thief* (1946). Judy Garland danced and sang

with Astaire in the memorable "Just a Couple of Swells" in *Easter Parade* (1948). In one film or another he appeared with Rita Hayworth, Joan Crawford, Leslie Caron, Ann Miller, Vera-Ellen, Eleanor Powell, and Betty Hutton, among others. Astaire also starred in two other noteworthy films, *Holiday Inn* (1942) and *Funny Face* (1957). After *Funny Face,* he retired from musicals to play dramatic roles, as in *On the Beach* (1959). At the age of 69, as lithe and graceful as ever, he returned to dancing in *Finian's Rainbow* (1968).

Ginger Rogers (1911–) first attracted attention playing hardened, wisecracking, heart-of-gold chorus girls in such musicals as *42nd Street* (1933) and *Gold Diggers of 1933*. Then came *Flying Down to Rio* and Fred Astaire. In addition to her obvious talents as a dancer, attractive face and figure, and fair singing voice, she had special qualities as an actress. These went into the making of a persona which, as with Astaire, changed only in name from film to film. There was no doubt that she was an intelligent woman and a match for her partner in making witty comments (supplied by the script) seem natural. She had a gift as a comedienne that she also demonstrated in nonmusical comedies. What made her particularly appealing in any role in which she acted was the conflict between the independence and honesty that shone from her clear, wide eyes and her vulnerability as a woman susceptible to love for a man who might delude and hurt her. Fortunately for the characters she played and the sense of well-being of audiences, Fred Astaire in the musicals might confuse her but in the end never disappointed her. She had the opportunity to project heartache from the screen when she turned to dramatic roles.

In the forties and fifties, Rogers divided her acting career between serious roles and comedies. The climax of the former was reached in *Kitty Foyle* (1940), for which she received an Academy Award for Best Actress. Many of her admirers, however, preferred her as a delightful comedienne in, for example, *Bachelor Mother* (1939) and Billy Wilder's *The Major and the Minor* (1942).

Irving Berlin (1888–) is not only one of the most prolific and admired composers of Broadway musicals (21 since 1914, including *Annie Get Your Gun* and *Call Me Madame*) but is also equally esteemed as a creator of original songs for film musicals. A list of his scores, even excluding stage productions adapted for motion pictures, reads like a roll call of some of the best Hollywood musicals of three decades. A half dozen titles of his most successful are *Top Hat, Follow the Fleet, Alexander's Ragtime Band* (1938), *Holiday Inn, Easter Parade,* and *There's No Business Like Show Business* (1954).

### PLOT SUMMARY

Jerry Travis (Astaire), American musical comedy star, is to appear in London in a show produced by Horace Hardwick (Horton). After meeting in the producer's staid club, they go to Horace's hotel suite, where the entertainer is to stay. Bates (Blore), Horace's valet, is carrying on a feud with his employer over a question of proper dress.

Horace announces that his wife Madge (Broderick) is in Venice and that he and Jerry are to join her for a weekend after the opening of the show. When Horace suggests that his friend should marry, Jerry declares his commitment to independence in the song "Fancy Free." His dancing awakens Dale Tremont (Rogers) in the apartment below. Although she complains directly to Jerry, he is quite taken by the lovely young woman.

The next morning, Jerry buys all the flowers in a shop and sends them to Dale. From the florist's gossip, we learn that Dale's clothes and hotel bills are paid by a Mr. Beddini. Through various manipulations, Jerry joins Dale in a band pavilion in a park. He sings "Isn't It a Lovely Day," and they dance together.

Dale tells Beddini (Rhodes), a dress designer who has hired her to advertise his clothes, that she will not go to Italy to join her friend Madge Hardwick because she has met a fascinating man. A telegram from Madge informs Dale that her husband Horace is in London and will look her up. While at the hotel desk, Dale mistakenly assumes that a clerk has identified Jerry as Horace Hardwick. When Jerry joins her, she slaps his face without explanation.

The slap has ramifications. To protect his friend from what he considers a designing woman, Horace assigns Bates, with whom he is now reconciled, to follow Dale. Meanwhile, she leaves for Italy with Beddini.

During an intermission on the opening night of the show, Jerry learns from his producer that Dale is with Madge. He insists that he and Horace fly to Venice. Cut to onstage, where Jerry sings and dances "Top Hat" with a male chorus.

At a hotel on the Lido, Dale informs Madge that her husband is a philanderer. This information does not disturb the blasé Madge. A shot of Bates in the canal spying on them. On the plane, Horace tells an uninterested Jerry about Beddini. The two groups come together, and confusion is compounded as Dale runs to her room, Beddini threatens Horace, Horace maintains he never met Dale, and he and Jerry end up in the bridal suite.

A vengeful Dale attempts to embarrass Jerry by pretending that they had an affair in Paris years earlier, but the tables are turned, and it is Dale who is flustered and bolts from the room. At dinner that night, Madge encourages a romance between her friend and Jerry, to the latter's delight and Dale's bewilderment, since she still believes Jerry is Horace. On the dance floor, Jerry sings "Cheek to Cheek" to Dale, and then, in the privacy of a terrace, the two dance. When Jerry proposes marriage, Dale once again slaps his face but inadvertently admits she loves him.

Madge hears about the proposal while Dale is packing. When she sees her husband, she punches him in the eye. Beddini also proposes marriage to the unhappy Dale and is accepted. The two leave, followed by Bates.

At the request of the manager, Jerry and Horace give up their bridal suite. The two are with Madge when Dale telephones that she is married. The three finally realize what has disturbed the young woman. Jerry resolves to set things right. While the dress designer is occupied with challenging Horace to a duel, Jerry persuades Dale to leave with him.

All has been explained when we see the young lovers in a gondola rowed by Bates. The inexperienced rower falls off, and the boat floats out to sea. Meanwhile, back at the hotel, Madge has calmed Beddini when Bates enters to inform them of the lost gondola. Beddini and the Hardwicks depart in a motorboat, but it runs out of gas. Cut to Jerry and Dale returning and being told by Bates that he has removed the gas from the tank of the motorboat.

At the wedding reception, Jerry takes the place of the bridegroom. ''The Piccolina'' production number follows. The motorboat returns with its three chilled and tired passengers. The confrontation scene is in the bridal suite. The dress designer is adamant in refusing to give up Dale until Bates joins them. The valet explains that, disguised as a clergyman, he married Dale and Beddini, so there has been no legal wedding. The final shots of the film are of Jerry in top hat and tails and Dale in formal gown dancing together.

## ANALYSIS

*Top Hat* is superior entertainment in itself, but it is also of particular value in surveying the history of the American musical as a typical example of the genre in the thirties. Plot is of minor importance; characterization is superficial and dependent on stereotypes; the chief actor and actress are Hollywood stars; the production numbers constitute the spine of the film; two of these numbers are justified in the plot as appearing on a stage of some sort, and one is in the style of Busby Berkeley; humor sustains our interest between production numbers; the milieu is upper-class in foreign settings, without the slightest indication that the United States is in the middle of an economic depression.

A clothesline plot, as noted earlier, is one whose sole purpose is to move the action along from one production number to the other. The typical pattern is for young people to meet, to separate through a misunderstanding, and finally to come together at the end of the film. In *Top Hat,* the misunderstanding is based on a mistaken identity so ridiculous that irony must have been intended. One does not expect verisimilitude in a thirties musical. But the fact that Dale and Jerry encounter each other frequently, yet from the time she mistakes him for Horace to her discovery of the truth, not one person mentions Jerry's name in the young woman's presence strains our credulity to a point usually reserved only for farce. The

denouement, in which we learn that Bates pretended to be a parson, is equally absurd. The plot line of *Top Hat,* therefore, is somewhat sillier than that of most musicals of the time.

Jerry Travis is a famous stage dancer (a conventional ploy in thirties musicals to justify a character's dancing at the drop of a top hat). We learn nothing else about his background. He is bold, enterprising, and determined and has a sense of humor. From the moment he meets Dale Tremont, he falls in love with her and allows nothing to stand in the way of his winning her. Even when he hears that she is married, he continues to pursue her. More startling is his complete indifference to rumors that she is being supported by another man (which is true, but, of course, an innocent arrangement). That Jerry is not even curious, much less concerned, about how the woman he loves earns her living indicates that he is either very sophisticated or unusually tolerant for a male of his day. Another possibility is that nothing fazes this cardboard character. In fact, although many surprising things happen in the film, Jerry never reacts with more than a smile, a joke, or the raising of an eyebrow.

Dale Tremont at least has a genuine dilemma: What is she to do if she has fallen in love with the husband of a close friend? She never confronts Jerry directly, and her solution to her problem, to marry Beddini, suggests either that she is very confused or that she is a masochist. It is difficult to understand Dale because, as with Jerry, we know little about her background. Why is she working for Beddini? Where did she learn to wear clothes with such style, carry herself with such confidence, and dance with such grace? How did she meet Madge?

To probe the portrayals of Jerry and Dale is an exercise in futility and is unfair to the film, which was not intended to present believable people. It does, however, demonstrate how vacuous characterization was in most thirties musicals, for *Top Hat* in this regard is typical. The other characters in the film are stereotypes that appeared over and over again in musical after musical. Edward Everett Horton (Horace) made a long career (from silent films to the mid-sixties) of playing a bungling husband who reacts four beats too late with a double take to any ambiguous statement addressed to him. Helen Broderick (Madge) repeated in a number of musicals her version of a wise-cracking, self-possessed, domineering wife of a rich man or older friend of the heroine. Beddini is played by Erik Rhodes, an American comic actor who commuted between stage and screen and, eventually, television. The Italian dress designer is another stock character: the foreigner whose fractured English is filled with malapropisms and unintentional puns (a couple of examples: "Adam, this gardener of Eden" and "The little birdies come flying back to the rooster"). The last of the major stereotypes in *Top Hat* is the eccentric gentleman's gentleman. As portrayed by Eric Blore, Bates is a delightful caricature of a servant who insists that he should have at least as many privileges as his inept master. Blore presented this type of English butler or valet in many musicals and comedies.

These stock characters revolve like satellites around the twin stars, Astaire and Rogers, who generate light and heat through their star personae. In the thirties musical, the substitute for characterization was the personalities of the lead actor and actress. For this reason, *Top Hat* could have basically the same plot and actors as *The Gay Divorcee,* released a year earlier. All that was changed were the songs, dances, and jokes, but that "all" is the essence of a musical of that decade. To be able to persuade audiences to accept the transfer of stars, stock characters, and even plots from one film to another is the ideal of a motion picture studio. There is much to be said for the view that the thirties musical was the fullest realization of the potentials of the Hollywood studio system.

*Top Hat* contains five production numbers. Their contexts and the ways they are filmed encompass most of the cinematic approaches of the pre–World War II musical. "Fancy Free" takes place in Horace's apartment. From the moment the two enter, there is music in the background (either a radio or a phonograph). After the introduction of Bates and some conversation, Horace suggests that his friend should marry. Jerry first responds with spoken words, then a rhythmic patter, and finally song. Meanwhile, the background music rises in volume. He sits on the edge of a couch, looking at Horace as he sings. Standing up, he makes a drink and hands it to his host, still

singing. The camera shifts from medium shots to a long shot as he stops singing and begins dancing. The visual continuity of the dance is broken, although the sound continues, as the camera moves to Dale in the room below. There is crosscutting between Dale's and Horace's suites. Jerry uses a mirror and a statue as props while he dances until Dale knocks on the door. There is a hiatus as they converse. After she leaves, he spreads sand on the floor and does a soft-shoe dance that puts Dale, Horace, and himself to sleep.

The characteristics of this pattern are a movement, with a continuation of the same verbal idea, from speech to song; music from a natural source; singing first, then dancing; lengthy long shots, but cuts to different angles and camera positions; and breaks in the visual continuity.

"Isn't It a Lovely Day" follows a similar pattern: Speech becomes a song: a song leads to a dance (Figure 9.9). The major differences involve the source of musical background and the type of filming. There is no possible source for the orchestra; we accept as a convention of the genre that music can magically be heard on the sound track. In filming, there are no cutaways, and the number of shots is kept to a minimum. The song is delivered in one shot. From the moment Dale rises and begins dancing with Jerry until

**FIGURE 9.9**

*Top Hat.* From the production number "Isn't It a Lovely Day." The setting is a band pavilion in a park during a rain shower.

the end of the scene there are only two shots, including a good deal of tracking in and out and panning. In the choreography of the dancing, no props are used, and the form is primarily repeats of imitation and combination steps: One of the partners does a step, which is imitated by the other; then they dance together.

A second approach characteristic of the thirties musical is illustrated by "Top Hat." The title song is sung and danced by Jerry at the premiere of the musical that Horace has produced and so supposedly is appearing on a stage. The number, with Jerry and a male chorus dressed in top hats, white ties, and tails, contains some spectacular effects, particularly Jerry's using his cane as if it were a machine gun (Figure 9.10).

**FIGURE 9.10**

*Top Hat.* The title song of the film is sung by Jerry in a musical on a London stage.

"Cheek to Cheek" begins on the dance floor of a restaurant in a Venetian hotel, so the music comes from the hotel orchestra. Jerry sings the song, then guides Dale to an open terrace. Here they dance (Figure 9.11). The shots are lengthy, either full-figure or very long, showing a good deal of the setting; the only camera movement is panning to keep the two in the center of the frame.

**FIGURE 9.11**

*Top Hat.* After Jerry sings "Cheek to Cheek," he and Dale dance on the terrace of a hotel in Venice.

The most elaborate production number in the film is "The Piccolino." Like "Top Hat," it is supposedly a public entertainment, but it takes place on a stage, with elaborate choreography that no hotel in the world could offer. And there are cinematic shots; that is, the effects could not be seen by an audience seated at tables. The number begins with a dancing chorus dressed in ersatz gondolier and peasant-girl costumes. After a high-angle shot of the group, there is a cut to Dale singing "The Piccolino" (the only song Rogers sings in the film). There is a clever transition back to the dancers: A skirt rises, revealing shapely legs; in the background, on the other side of a canal, is the chorus [Figure 9.12(a)]. After closer shots of the singing dancers, another interesting effect appears: a reflection of them in the water. The influence of Busby Berkeley is then evident as the camera looks down in a direct vertical on the chorus and a pattern on the floor of a circle and the points of the compass. The men come together in the center, and the white sash of each is drawn out by a female dancer, so that the sashes form the spokes of a wheel and the women the rim of a spinning circle [Figure 9.12(b)]. Two additional designs are created using the sashes as props [Figure 9.12(c)]. Finally, the women return to the men, and they dance together.

### FIGURE 9.12

*Top Hat.* From ''The Piccolina'' production number. (a) Opening shot. (b, c) Two dance patterns influenced by the style of Busby Berkeley. (d) Jerry and Dale dance together in the concluding sequence.

Cut to a shot of the feet of a man and woman dancing. Naturally, when the camera tracks back, we see that those flashing feet belong to Jerry and Dale. The chorus watches as the two dance [Figure 9.12(d)]. One eye-level shot, with the camera panning left and right to keep them in the center of the frame, is sufficient until they collapse into chairs at their table.

Aside from the production numbers, the cinematic techniques in the film are efficient without being imaginative. The only exceptions are two transitions. After Jerry discovers that Dale has vacated her London hotel room, he leaves for the theater. A maid taps a vase against a metal wastebasket. The sound contin-

ues as there is a cut to the orchestra conductor at the theater tapping his baton against a music stand. At the end of the song ''Top Hat,'' there is a final shot of the orchestra leader conducting the finale. Dissolve to black, but the background music continues. The fade-in leads to shots of a small orchestra in a new setting, the hotel on the Lido, playing the same song.

While the five production numbers are the heart of *Top Hat,* the time in between them is made tolerable by the humor of the dialogue. Sight gags are few, and most of them are supplied by Bates. The chief sources of verbal comedy are the silly case of mistaken identity and Horace's relationships with Bates and with Marge. The range of humor includes the awful malapropisms of Beddini, the slow-witted responses of Horace, the incongruous speech pattern of Bates, the wisecracks of Marge, and the sophisticated wit of Jerry. There is something for everyone, and not too much for anyone. If the production numbers and personalities of Astaire and Rogers are the thick icing on the cake and the plot and humor the cake itself, the latter is unsubstantial and half-baked.

The subjects of humor and conversation center chiefly on the relationship between the sexes, the stuffiness of Horace, the conceit of Beddini, and the pretentiousness of Bates. The one topic never mentioned is the Depression. The film takes place in the thirties; however, the setting is not only hundreds of miles physically from the United States but equally distant from the concerns of our nation during that period. Everyone is either rich or living in this sphere of affluence. Although some musicals of the decade referred to the economic and social problems of the day—such as Lewis Milestone's *Hallelujah, I'm a Bum* (1933), King Vidor's *Hallelujah!* (1929), and the "Remember My Forgotten Man" number in Mervyn LeRoy's *Gold Diggers of 1933*—most were sheer escapist fare.

It is tempting to be condescending about the musicals of the thirties, especially when they are compared to the more realistic and sophisticated post–World War II examples of the genre. On the other hand, only a very hypercritical viewer would not admit that they are entertaining even today. In *Top Hat,* one of the best, there is a tolerable naiveté and unpretentiousness in the narrative dimension, a delightful vigor in the music, and an impressive craftsmanship in the production numbers. The reason most of us remember the film with pleasure, however, is the dancing of Astaire and Rogers: the epitome of grace, elegance, and, by any definition of the term, style.

![black bar]

## SATIRICAL MUSICAL

### Singin' in the Rain

*But, in [Kelly's] pas de deux with O'Connor ("Fit as a Fiddle"), in his own solo ("Singin' in the Rain"), and in O'Connor's knockabout knockout ("Make 'Em Laugh"), the combination of comic invention, technical expertise and an exhausting manic energy produced elegant, surrealistic balletics worthy of a Ballanchine [sic], a Nijinsky, a Keaton.*
*Richard Corliss, 1974[4]*

**CAST**

*Gene Kelly (Don Lockwood), Donald O'Connor (Cosmo Brown), Debbie Reynolds (Kathy Selden), Jean Hagen (Lina Lamont), Millard Mitchell (R. F. Simpson), Cyd Charisse (Dancer), Rita Moreno (Zelda Zanders), and others.*

**CREDITS**

*Directors—Stanley Donen and Gene Kelly, Producer—Arthur Freed, Screenwriters—Betty Comden and Adolph Green, Choreographers—Stanley Donen and Gene Kelly, Director of Photography—Harold Rosson, Composers—Nacio Herb Brown, Arthur Freed, Roger Edens, and others, Musical Director—Lennie Hayton, Art Directors—Cedric Gibbons and Randall Duell, Editor—Adrienne Fazan, and others.*

1952/MGM
Color/103 minutes

### BACKGROUND

One method of gaining a perspective on the achievements of Gene Kelly is to compare him to Fred Astaire. Both men have no more than adequate singing voices and limited acting abilities. As popular dancers, however, they are the finest that have appeared on the screen. They share amazing technical facilities, boundless energy, fluidity of movement, and an uncompromising concern for perfecting the details of a step or a whole dance. Otherwise, their styles are as different as their physiques. Kelly is short, stocky, and muscular. Whereas the energy of the tall, thin Astaire appears to be dispersed throughout his body, animating all his limbs, Kelly's drive seems to pulse chiefly from his torso, commanding the muscles of his legs, arms, and head. As noted in the discussion of *Top Hat,* Astaire apparently defies gravity and moves effortlessly through nonresistant space; Kelly conquers gravity with an effort of will and strength. Astaire's dancing is the personification of grace and wit, Kelly's of exuberance and power.

Although Astaire's style has roots in popular American dance forms, an aura of the sophistication and self-consciousness of European ballroom dancing clings to it. Kelly has to a greater degree tapped indigenous American rhythms and movements as transformed by a group of choreographers and dancers in the early forties to serve as the basis of ballets. Agnes De Mille, Eugene Loring, Jerome Robbins, Michael

Kidd, among others, molded an athletic, robust, "fancy free" type of dancing that not only resulted in distinctive ballets but also influenced the choreography for stage and screen musicals. All four of these innovators worked in Hollywood. Among their disciples were Stanley Donen, Bob Fosse, Marge and Gower Champion—and Gene Kelly.

Kelly's choreographic style is intelligent and carefully thought out, often to the extent that his dances appear too rigidly planned, lacking the air of spontaneity of those created by Astaire. Kelly is very much at home in elaborate production numbers, yet never allows the setting and chorus to overwhelm him and his partner. Perhaps this is so because he is usually inventive in relating himself to what surrounds him, even to dancing with the cartoon figures Tom and Jerry in *Anchors Aweigh.*

Athletic energy is the most obvious characteristic of Kelly's choreographic style. Even among ardent admirers, however, are those who feel that at times this dynamism becomes frantic. Such vigorous motion is most appropriate to comedy. And it is in projecting healthy physical humor that Kelly is practically without peer among film choreographers and dancers. Astaire's elegant movements cause us to smile in appreciation; Kelly's, when he is working in the comic mode, instill in us a desire to laugh and shout encouragement. This confident, almost show-off exuberance is all the more impressive when one realizes that a perceptive mind and strong will are in control.

Gene Kelly (1912–) was a dancer in and choreographer of Broadway musicals, as well as director of his own dancing school, before he made his film debut in *For Me and My Gal* (1942). After being featured in three other musicals, including *Cover Girl* (1944), he became a star in *Anchors Aweigh* (1945). Among his outstanding films during the next 5 years were *The Pirate* (1947), *Take Me Out to the Ball Game* (1949), and *On the Town* (1949). Many consider the climax of his acting career his performance in Vincente Minnelli's *An American in Paris* (1951), which contains a 17-minute semiballet danced by Kelly and Leslie Caron and choreographed by the actor.

Kelly, however, was too versatile and ambitious to remain solely a performer. From the time he entered films, he had assisted in choreographing his own dances and soon received screen credit as choreographer (for example, for *On the Town* and *An American in Paris*). He went further: He codirected, with Stanley Donen, *On the Town, Singin' in the Rain,* and *It's Always Fair Weather* (1955, in which he also starred). After appearing in a number of other films, including Minnelli's *Brigadoon* (1954, for which he was choreographer), he finally obtained backing from MGM for *Invitation to the Dance* (1956), a film he conceived, starred in, choreographed, and directed. It is undoubtedly the most uncompromising musical made in Hollywood. There is no dialogue, and the film consists of three separate stories in three different dance styles. Unfortunately, the film was called, with some justification, pretentious by some critics and boring by others. It was a financial failure. *Invitation to the Dance* was the culmination of Kelly's repeated efforts to expand the boundaries of dancing in film musicals. Obviously, he overestimated the tolerance of motion picture audiences, who would support his innovations only so far as he went in *Singin' in the Rain* and *An American in Paris.*

Kelly was apparently discouraged by the negative reception given to what he considered the most important work of his career. After *Invitation to the Dance,* he appeared in only two major musicals: *Les Girls* (1957) and Jacques Demy's *The Young Girls of Rochefort* (1960). He turned to straight acting roles, for instance, in *Inherit the Wind* (1960). In the late sixties, he returned to directing, doing both comedies (for example, *A Guide for the Married Man,* 1967, and *Gigot,* 1963) and one musical (*Hello, Dolly,* 1969). In the seventies, he appeared in television specials and was, with Fred Astaire, cohost for *That's Entertainment* (1974) and *That's Entertainment, Part 2* (1976). Gene Kelly, then, has been a dancer, choreographer, director, and actor. Few Hollywood stars have equaled him in accomplishments, versatility, and intelligence.

*Singin' in the Rain* was a success as soon as it was released, immediately recognized as one of the finest musicals made in Hollywood. That the film was outstanding was no surprise, considering the talent involved. The first step in the right direction was to have Stanley Donen and Gene Kelly as codirectors and cochoreographers.

The significance of Arthur Freed as head producer of musicals at MGM was indicated earlier in this chapter.* In addition to being producer, however, he also contributed the lyrics to most of the songs in *Singin' in the Rain.* With the exception of "Moses" (with music by Roger Edens and lyrics by Comden and Green), "Beautiful Girl," and additional music by Lennie Hayton for "Broadway Rhythm," all the songs are by the songwriting team of Nacio Herb Brown and Freed. They included six songs from their earlier collaborations: *The Broadway Melody* (1929—"You Were Meant for Me" and "Wedding of the Painted Doll"), *The Hollywood Revue of 1929* ("Singin' in the Rain"), and *Broadway Melody of 1936* ("Broadway Rhythm," "You Are My Lucky Star," and "I Gotta Feelin' You're Foolin' ").

The ingenious plot and the intelligence and irony of the script of the film are to the credit of Betty Comden and Adolph Green. This team first attracted attention in the mid-forties with their Broadway musical *On the Town* (which they adapted for the screen in 1949). Moving to Hollywood in 1946, they wrote the lyrics for the songs in *Take Me Out to the Ball Game* (1949) and the screenplays for *The Barkleys of Broadway* (1949), *The Band Wagon* (1953), and *It's Always Fair Weather* (1955). They adapted their stage musical *Bells Are Ringing* for the screen in 1959 and wrote the scenario for *What a Way to Go!* (1964). Their screenplays have been uniquely imaginative, leavened by a gift for satire and parody, and among lyricists of songs for original musicals, only Cole Porter is their peer for literate wit and Alan Jay Lerner for grace and charm.

The performances in *Singin' in the Rain* are on a par with the other outstanding components of the film. Gene Kelly is at his best. Donald O'Connor as Cosmo Brown adds vigor and humor to the action. He has been always an exceptional dancer (as he demonstrates especially in "Make 'Em Laugh") and a natural comedian. Of the 47 films in which he appeared, a

*p. 447

number were musicals, including *On Your Toes* (1939), *Call Me Madame* (1953), *There's No Business Like Show Business* (1954), and *Anything Goes* (1956).

Debbie Reynolds is an attractive woman with a high-spirited personality. She has a flair for comedy and is an effective, though rarely remarkable, singer and dancer. Cyd Charisse, one of the finest female dancers in screen musicals, and surely one of the most beautiful, starred or was featured in, among others, *The Band Wagon* (1953), *Brigadoon* (1954), *It's Always Fair Weather* (1955), *Invitation to the Dance* (1956), and—probably her best performance—*Silk Stockings* (1957). Jean Hagen, so delightful as Lina Lamont in *Singin' in the Rain,* never had another major role in a Hollywood motion picture.

### PLOT SUMMARY

The time is 1927; the setting is the Hollywood premiere of the silent film *The Royal Rascal.* We are introduced to Cosmo Brown (O'Connor). He is the best friend of Don Lockwood (Kelly) and plays mood music on the sets during shooting. Finally, the stars of the film, Don Lockwood and Lina Lamont (Hagen), make a royal entrance.

Don is prevailed upon by a radio announcer to describe his rise to stardom. There is an ironic contrast between what he is describing (going to the finest schools, concert tours, friendship with Lina) and realistic flashbacks (poolrooms; appearances in a speakeasy and on a vaudeville stage, with Cosmo, singing "Fit as a Fiddle and Ready for Love"; a stint as a stunt man; conflicts with Lina).

We see the ending of *The Royal Rascal,* a ridiculous pastiche of romance and adventure. Don and Lina appear on the theater stage, but only he addresses the audience. Backstage it becomes clear why Don prevented his costar from speaking in public: She has a shrill, grating voice, with a mind and personality to match.

On the way to the producer's party, Cosmo's car breaks down, and Don is assaulted by overenthusiastic fans. He escapes to the top of a passing streetcar and jumps into a car driven by Kathy Selden (Reynolds). She squelches his advances by pretending to sneer at movies from the lofty pinnacle of her commitment to the legitimate theater.

At his party, the producer, R. F. Simpson (Mitchell), screens a demonstration of a "talking picture." Everyone, except Cosmo, dismisses it as an impractical novelty. Kathy and a group of chorus girls sing and dance "All I Do Is Dream of You." Although Don attempts to date her, they have an argument, and Kathy runs away.

Three weeks later Don is at Monument Studios to begin filming *The Dueling Cavalier.* We learn from Cosmo that Kathy has lost her job and that Don has attempted in vain to locate her. Cosmo makes an effort to cheer up his friend with the spirited "Make 'Em Laugh." R. F. stops production. *The Jazz Singer* has been such a great success that all the studios are converting to sound, so *The Dueling Cavalier* is to be transformed into a talking picture.

After a montage of shots of actors and actresses dancing and singing amid Busby Berkeley effects, there is a full production number, "Beautiful Girls," with Kathy as a member of the chorus. Don arrives as R. F. decides to advance Kathy to an acting role. The two young people walk together; their conversation, once some misunderstandings have been cleared up, indicates that they are romantically involved. On an empty studio set, they express their feelings in "You Were Meant for Me."

A headline in *Variety* indicates that there is a "big bonanza" for diction coaches. Cosmo joins Don at his lessons, and the two mock the pretentiousness and exercises of the diction coach, ending with a robust rendering of "Moses."

The shooting with sound does not go smoothly, and the preview of *The Dueling Cavalier* is a fiasco. Later, in the kitchen of Don's house, Kathy and Cosmo attempt to cheer up the dispirited actor. They come up with the idea of turning the film into a musical. With buoyant spirits the three sing "Good Morning" as they dance through the house. Dejection returns as they remember Lina's limitations, but Cosmo suggests dubbing Kathy's voice for Lina's. Don brings Kathy home. After he leaves her, he sings the title song, "Singin' in the Rain."

R. F. is enthusiastic about *The Dancing Cava-*

*lier,* the new title of the film. He insists, however, that Lina not be told that her voice is being scrapped. After scenes of the dubbing process, Don describes the final sequence, yet to be shot. The camera moves toward the screen, and we see the production number "Broadway Rhythm" as Don envisions it.

The tenuous story line of the number describes how a young dancer comes to the big city. He is attracted to a beautiful woman (Charisse) in a speakeasy but is spurned by her in favor of a gangster. The young man becomes a success and once again encounters the mysterious woman. And again he loses her to the gangster. At the end appears another ambitious young dancer.

Lina learns about the dubbing. Using her contract as a weapon, she forces R. F. to eliminate Kathy's credit from the titles of the film and to restrict the singer's future career to being her voice.

At the successful premiere of *The Dancing Cavalier,* the deception of the dubbing is revealed, and Don informs the audience that Kathy is the true star of the picture. The two again sing "You Were Meant for Me." The last shot is of Don and Kathy kissing before a billboard in the countryside advertising *The Dancing Cavalier,* starring Don Lockwood and Kathy Selden.

### ANALYSIS

Among the multitudes who have seen *Singin' in the Rain,* there must have been viewers with hearts so cold and minds so dry that they did not enjoy the film, but such a reaction is difficult to imagine. With memorable songs, superb choreography and dancing, an intelligent screenplay, delightful comedy, and masterful directing, it is no wonder that the film is usually listed as among the half dozen best musicals produced by Hollywood. Its faults, such as a flatness in characterization, are more than compensated for by its virtues.

The most evident of these virtues is its vitality. There is not one moment when the energy of the film flags or one feels that the actors are marking time until the next big scene. The visual effects during certain scenes, as when Don is a stunt man and the first attempt to record sound while filming, are hilarious precisely because they are intentionally exaggerated. But the driving vitality is most palpable in the singing and dancing numbers. Donald O'Connor's Cosmo Brown contributes his own frenetic quality, especially in "Make 'Em Laugh"; however, it is principally Gene Kelly who sets the pace and tone of the production numbers.

Kelly's short, compact body appears a human dynamo of such power that no confined space can contain it. Only in the semiballet sequence in "Broadway Rhythm," with its seemingly endless vistas, does he have an adequate area for his movements. More typical are the numbers "Singin' in the Rain" and "Moses." Both reach climaxes of explosive energy that are almost demonic, as though controlled choreography is too restrictive to express physically the dancers' intensity of feelings. In "Singin' in the Rain," Kelly ends by pounding his feet in a large puddle of water. Only the appearance of a policeman, representative of society's disapproval of Dionysian frenzy, restrains him (Figure 9.13). At the conclusion of "Moses," Kelly and O'Connor take apart a room, piling up everything detachable on a desk and over the diction coach (like the policeman, a symbol of social decorum).

FIGURE 9.13

*Singin' in the Rain.* Near the end of the famous "Singin' in the Rain" production number, Don's frenzied expression of love for Kathy is curtailed by the appearance of a policeman.

FIGURE 9.14

*Singin' in the Rain.* One of the stars who appears at the premiere of *The Royal Rascal* obviously represents Theda Bara, who in her day gave currency to the term *vamp.*

Another impressive quality of *Singin' in the Rain* is the self-mocking, parodic approach that pervades both plot and camera techniques. Although the film is fun even if its allusions are not recognized, a full appreciation of its humor requires an acquaintance with the pretensions, conventions, and production methods of Hollywood studios in the late twenties and early thirties.

The opening sequence sets the tone of parody and satire. The radio announcer at the premiere of *The Royal Rascal* sounds and looks like gossip columnist Louella Parsons. The two female stars who enter before Don and Lena bring to mind Clara Bow and Theda Bara (Figure 9.14). The silent film itself caricatures those that starred Douglas Fairbanks. Specific allusions of this sort continue throughout the film. For instance, in the montage of shots preceding "Beautiful Girl," the singer with a megaphone obviously represents Rudy Vallee. In "Broadway Rhythm," the gangster who flips the silver dollar is impersonating George Raft, who made this gesture famous in *Scarface* (1932).

Most of the parody in *Singin' in the Rain* is more generally of situations and types typical of the transition period in Hollywood from silent to sound films. The end of the career of Lina Lamont reminds

**FIGURE 9.15**

*Singin' in the Rain.* In the megaphone of a Rudy Vallee–type crooner appear chorus girls in a flower-blossom pattern. This is a parody of one of Busby Berkeley's favorite devices.

us that such stars as Pola Negri and Norma Talmadge were unable to meet the demands of sound. The success of Don Lockwood suggests perhaps the ability of Ramon Novarro, originally trained in singing and dancing, to move from stardom as a romantic hero in the silent era to moderate success in singing roles. One historical footnote that supports this supposition is the fact that for "The Pagan Love Song," sung by Novarro in *The Pagan* (1929), the music was composed by Nacio Herb Brown (is it simply a coincidence that the name is so similar to Cosmo Brown?) and the lyrics by Arthur Freed, who once again collaborated for *Singin' in the Rain.*

Spectacular premieres, parties with chorus girls popping out of cakes, skepticism about sound films, technical difficulties in synchronizing sound and visuals, diction lessons for actors, headlines in *Variety,* transforming silent films to sound, the discovery of dubbing—these are part of the legend of Hollywood

in the late twenties that are incorporated into the plot of *Singin' in the Rain.* More cinematic is the parody of the style of early musicals. The presiding spirit evoked, naturally, is Busby Berkeley, particularly when a mobile camera shoots down at a direct vertical on a chorus that creates an intricate pattern. There are many examples in the montage sequence preceding "Beautiful Girl"; one shot is of a flower blossom made up of girls superimposed on the inside of a megaphone (Figure 9.15). "Beautiful Girl" itself is a clever rendering of a Berkeley production number with just enough exaggeration in the lyrics, elaborate sets, scantily clad women, and restless camera to qualify as parody rather than simply imitation.

All the stops are pulled out in "Broadway Rhythm" (designated in the screenplay as a "ballet"), and the result is the type of spectacle associated with Berkeley musicals (Figure 9.16). More than one critic has suggested that this number is a flaw in *Singin' in the Rain* because "except for its score [the ballet] has no real relationship with the rest of the film and even has a different leading lady."[5] These critics have

___

**FIGURE 9.16**

*Singin' in the Rain.* From the number "Broadway Rhythm." (a) Establishing shot. (b) A young dancer-singer (Gene Kelly) arrives on Broadway to make his fortune. (c) While working in a nightclub, he dances with a gangster's moll (Cyd Charisse). (d) Later he dances with her again in a fantasy setting. The concluding shot of this series of production numbers is illustrated in Figure 1.29.

missed the point that the big production numbers in musicals of the thirties usually had only the flimsiest justification for being included.

"Broadway Rhythm," as with "Beautiful Girl," is a gentle, affectionate, even nostalgic form of parody. It conceivably could have appeared in an early thirties MGM musical, though it is doubtful if so many clichés, conventions, and humorous touches (such as the coin-flipping gangster) would have been combined in one production number without some degree of self-mockery intended. In this respect, the tone of *Singin' in the Rain* is unique. The filmmakers manage to convey to viewers an attitude akin to what a person in his fifties might feel on recalling an adolescent romance: laughing indulgently at one's own gaucheries and illusions, yet also a little sad that the romance, vitality, confidence, and innocence of youth are past.

Parody is a type of satire, an imitation in spirit and details of a specific subject for the purposes of

ridicule. The broader mode can be the means of criticizing a general attitude, ideology, or situation. The satire in *Singin' in the Rain* focuses on an aspect of cinema that could be summed up in the phrase "Hollywood, the dream factory." Hollywood—particularly in the twenties and thirties, with its star system, studio production-line approach, and commercial orientation—devoted most of its efforts to producing dreams of glamour, adventure, and ideal love. Musical comedy was the perfect vehicle for presenting an unrealistic world in which love always triumphed, goodness was rewarded, selfishness was punished, and talent was recognized. The very artificiality of people expressing their emotions through song and dance was a not very subtle signal to viewers that any similarity between the screen world and the real world was purely coincidental.

This dichotomy between illusion and reality in *Singin' in the Rain* is established in the initial sequence. Don Lockwood first appears in a shimmering white coat and hat (a delightful touch is when, as he walks toward the microphone, he pushes someone out of his way with the most brilliant, amiable smile). For his fans, he describes his rise to fame and proclaims his motto, "Dignity, always dignity." We as viewers, however, through flashbacks, are privy to the truth. The contrast is a comic use by Comden and Green of dramatic irony.

It is clearly demonstrated that the genuine emotions of actors are divorced from those they project to a camera, as when Don and Lina say nasty things to each other during a passionate silent love scene. The process of dubbing is the epitome of this type of pretense: An actor's voice can be taken away, and viewers are unaware of the substitution. The difference between Lina on the screen and off is additional satire on the unsubstantiality of the public image of Hollywood stars.

Comden and Green underscore that the make-believe of the dream factory is accepted not only by moviegoers but also by many of the participants. Lina is convinced that Don loves her because that is what studio publicity has announced. Characters are constantly pretending to be what they are not. Lina is an obvious example, but Kathy also lies to Don on their first meeting that she is a dramatic actress who sneers at motion picture actors, and R. F. insists on his authority but is afraid of Lina.

More subtle is the way in which the screenwriters poke fun at the unreality of Hollywood films, particularly the musical genre, through the plot itself of *Singin' in the Rain*. The escape of Don from his overenthusiastic fans by jumping to the top of a streetcar and then into a car is as ridiculous as his athletic dueling scenes in *The Royal Rascal*. And, of course, he leaps into the car of Kathy, who just happens to be going to R. F.'s party. The denouement at the premiere of *The Dancing Cavalier* is equally farfetched. The last shot of the film underlines the artificiality of life on the screen even when presented as a behind-the-scenes musical. Don and Kathy embrace in a pastoral setting before a billboard advertising *Singin' in the Rain*. This one shot embodies the whole spirit of the film (Figure 9.17).

**FIGURE 9.17**

*Singin' in the Rain.* The final shot of the film.

Even the one sequence in the film that comes closest to being serious is permeated with illusion. Don has finally found Kathy, and the two are reconciled during a walk from the set of "Beautiful Girl." As he stumbles verbally to convey his feelings, he makes a statement that, like the final shot, epitomizes the characters in the film: "I'm such a ham, I need a proper setting." The two enter a deserted stage, and Don supplies with lights and a wind machine the proper Hollywood romantic atmosphere in which to express his love in song and dance (see Figure 1.39).

Since the main objective of *Singin' in the Rain,* aside from entertaining, is good-natured parody and satire, it is perhaps inevitable that the characterization be two-dimensional and the plot contrived. Don is the amiable, faithful hero. Cosmo is the comic sidekick who seems to have no personal life. R. F. is the heart-of-gold boss with a rough exterior. Kathy is the lovely, innocent ingénue with just enough spirit to prevent her from being cloyingly sweet. The most interesting character is Lina: At least she has a streak of nastiness. She is not a villainess, however, because her monumental stupidity and selfishness can be no real threat to the hero and heroine. We assume that the hackneyed nature of the main characters is intentional, a derisive commentary on the flatness of characterization in thirties musicals, but this approach does limit our interest to *what* is happening—the spectacle and humor—rather than *why*.

The reason we are not concerned with why the characters act as they do, accepting obvious motivations, is that there is no genuine conflict in the film. Don and Kathy have a misunderstanding that is straightened out during a single conversation. The problem of what to do about the failure of *The Dueling Cavalier* is solved early one morning. Lina represents an obstacle rather than a danger since she is not intelligent enough to use her power effectively. So the viewer settles back, confident that all difficulties, since they are so superficial, will be resolved, in no matter how contrived a manner, and content with a clothesline plot on which periodically are hung imaginative production numbers.

These numbers are done with a professionalism and expertise that sums up what Hollywood filmmakers had learned during two decades about the camera-editing dynamics and elements of presentation that would be most effective in a musical. Sound, choreography, color, mobile camera, and creative editing combine to make *Singin' in the Rain,* on a sheer technical level, a masterpiece of the genre.

Although a critic would be hard put to find faults in the technical aspects of the production numbers, he might be uneasy about their unrelenting exuberance. Vitality, as we have seen, is one of the virtues

of the film, but there can be too much of a good thing. Aside from "You Were Meant for Me," every number either is an overwhelming spectacle, as "Beautiful Girl" and "Broadway Rhythm," or possesses a physical drive that is exhausting just to watch and can, in "Make 'Em Laugh," for example, border on the hysterical. The same criticism could be leveled against the machine-gun verbal humor, especially when Cosmo is present.

There are admirers of the film who refuse to admit it has any faults and argue that those who criticize the characterization or rhythm are imposing criteria of evaluation inapplicable to musicals. Whether *Singin' in the Rain* is perfect or simply a joy within its limitations, the film looks to the past and sums up in the early fifties the best and worst characteristics of earlier Hollywood musicals. It was left for the sixties, with such films as *West Side Story,* to explore new directions and dimensions of the genre.

## SOCIAL CRITICISM MUSICAL

### *West Side Story*

> *Two such opposed kings encamp there still*
> *In man as well as herbs, grace and rude will;*
> *And where the worser is predominant,*
> *Full soon the canker death eats up that plant.*
> Shakespeare, Romeo and Juliet *(2.3. 26–30)*

**CAST**

*Natalie Wood (Maria), Richard Beymer (Tony), Russ Tamblyn (Riff), Rita Moreno (Anita), George Chakiris (Bernardo), Tucker Smith (Ice), Tony Mordente (Action), Eliot Feld (Baby John), Sue Oakes (Anybodys), David Winters (A-Rab), Joe De Vega (Chino), Ned Glass (Doc), Simon Oakland (Lieutenant Schrank), and others.*

**CREDITS**

*Directors—Robert Wise and Jerome Robbins, Producer—Robert Wise, Screenwriter—Ernest Lehman (based on the stage play by Arthur Laurents, from an idea by Jerome Robbins), Choreographer—Jerome Robbins, Composer— Leonard Bernstein, Lyrics—Stephen Sondheim, Director of Photography—Daniel L. Fapp, Art Director—Boris Leven, Editors—Thomas Stanford and Marshall M. Borden, Titles—Saul Bass, and others.*

1961/Mirisch/Seven Arts for United Artists
Color/155 minutes

## BACKGROUND

A good deal of the credit for the film *West Side Story* must be given to the contributors to the original theater musical. Although in the film adaptation, dialogue was added, the dances restaged, and the placement of some songs changed, the basic plot remained intact, and all the music and songs were included. Arthur Laurents did the book for the stage musical. He is a successful Broadway playwright (for example, *The Home of the Brave* and *A Clearing in the Woods*) who also has written screenplays, including *The Snake Pit* and *Anastasia.* He did not, however, do the screenplay for *West Side Story.* This assignment was given to Ernest Lehman, one of Hollywood's leading screenwriters. Among his best known works are *Sabrina, North by Northwest,* and *Who's Afraid of Virginia Woolf.* He is recognized as a specialist in adapting theater musicals for the screen; *The King and I, The Sound of Music,* and *Hello, Dolly* are among his credits.

Leonard Bernstein is a famous American conductor and composer. He has the unusual gift of being successful in creating both classic music (symphonies, ballets, operas, and other forms) and musicals. The latter category includes *On the Town* (made into the fine Kelly-Donen film musical), *Wonderful Town,* and *Candide.* He has also done original film scores, such as for Elia Kazan's *On the Waterfront.* Bernstein adapted his own theater score for the screen version of *West Side Story.* Stephen Sondheim made his Broadway debut at the age of 25 as a lyricist for this musical. Since 1957 he has emerged as today's most sophisticated and talented composer of musicals. He did the music and lyrics for *A Funny Thing Happened on the Way to the Forum* (made into a hilarious film in 1966), *Company, Follies, A Little Night Music* (also transferred to the screen), *Pacific Overtures,* and *Sweeney Todd,* among other works.

Considering the praise received by the cast of the original production in New York of *West Side Story,* it is surprising that so few of the actors and actresses were retained for the film. In the theater musical, the main roles of Maria and Tony were played by Carol Lawrence and Larry Kert. Chita Rivera was Anita; Mickey Calin, Riff; Ken Le Roy, Bernardo; and Art Smith, Doc. Only Tony Mordente (Action)

and David Winters (A-Rab) appeared in both versions, although a few others, notably George Chakiris, were in the London production.

In addition to Bernstein, the other major figure involved in both play and film was Jerome Robbins. He not only conceived the idea for *West Side Story* but also directed and choreographed (with Peter Gennaro) the theater production. He was intended to repeat these assignments for the film. After shooting had begun, however, a series of disagreements with Robert Wise, the producer, led to Wise's taking over as director. In the credits, Robbins is listed as codirector and choreographer. Newspaper interviews at the time indicate that he was entirely responsible for the restaged dance production numbers.

Jerome Robbins has been one of the most prominent artists in the history of both American ballet and the musical. As a choreographer he contributed to the development of a robust, athletic American ballet style and has created a series of works that rank in significance just below those of the great choreographers George Balanchine and Anthony Tudor. His most famous ballets include *Fancy Free, The Age of Anxiety, Fanfare,* and *The Cage.*

Robbins has been equally productive in choreographing musicals. He has contributed to *The King and I* and *On the Town* (Broadway and screen versions of both), *Call Me Madame,* and *High Button Shoes,*, among others. His versatility extends to directing in the theater (for example, *Pajama Game, Bells Are Ringing,* and the *Peter Pan* production starring Mary Martin); *West Side Story,* however, was his first film directing assignment.

Robert Wise began his career in motion pictures as a sound editor and then a chief editor at RKO. Among his credits in this area are Welles's *Citizen Kane* and *The Magnificent Ambersons* (both with Mark Robson). He first directed thrillers, such as *Curse of the Cat People* (1944), but went on to many other genres. Wise's finest early film was *The Set-Up* (1949), on boxing, which won the Critics' Prize at Cannes.

With *Odds Against Tomorrow* (1959), Wise began producing as well as directing films. *West Side Story* was his first musical. Four years later (with *Two for the Seesaw,* 1962, and *The Haunting,* 1963, in between), he returned to the genre. *The Sound of Music* (1965) is a screen version of the Rodgers and Hammerstein stage musical on the early years of the Trapp family. Critics praised many of the cinematic techniques, especially for the opening, but were far less enthusiastic about the sentimental story and bland production numbers. Moviegoers thought otherwise. Within 10 years its earnings had surpassed those of *Gone With the Wind*. It also won five Academy Awards, including Best Picture and Best Director. Wise's next musical, *Star!* (1968), a "biopic" of Gertrude Lawrence, was a financial and critical failure. He continued to direct and produce films in the seventies, including *The Andromeda Strain* (1971) and *The Hindenburg* (1976).

Wise is a complete professional, in the best sense of the term. One doubts if there is any type of film he could not direct with competence. In addition to his consistent craftsmanship, he demonstrates a special ability to reveal in details of action and expression how a stress situation affects an individual. Although he never developed a unique cinematic style as a director, his work since *The Sound of Music* has been particularly undistinguished in this respect.

Of the actors in *West Side Story,* Natalie Wood is the best known. She made her debut on the screen at the age of 5. After she appeared in *Rebel Without a Cause* (1955), she specialized in performing as a confident but vulnerable adolescent and young woman. Although she starred in the musicals *West Side Story* (for which her voice was dubbed) and *Gypsy* (1962), she was primarily a dramatic actress and comedienne rather than a singer or dancer. After 1962, Wood advanced to playing mature women in, for example, *Love With the Proper Stranger* (1963), *Inside Daisy Clover* (1966), and *Bob and Carol and Ted and Alice* (1969). She was an active and popular star at the time of her death in 1983.

Rita Moreno has not attained the star status of Natalie Wood, although she has an exciting personality and is a fine dancer. She has divided her time between the stage and film. Most of her appearances on the screen have been in adventure films and Westerns or in secondary roles in major productions.

As noted in the survey section of this chapter, Russ Tamblyn is an extraordinary dancer who has had few opportunities to demonstrate his talents. George Chakiris began as a singer and has made records. He also played Riff in the London stage production of *West Side Story.* Since 1961, however, he has appeared in only second-rate films. The same fate awaited the less talented Richard Beymer.

After *West Side Story's* lengthy run of 3 years on Broadway and an almost equal success of a second cast in London, United Artists had high hopes for the film version, so they invested $6 million in the project, a substantial sum for the early sixties. Five weeks were spent on location in New York with Robbins as director; the time was devoted to shooting street scenes. An additional 6 months was spent on studio-constructed sets. It was at this time that producer Wise took over as director. After production, the voice of Marnie Nixon was dubbed for that of Natalie Wood and Jimmy Bryant contributed the songs of Richard Beymer. The film was finally edited to a little over 2½ hours.

*West Side Story* fulfilled its promise in being a financial and critical success not only in the United States but also abroad. The New York Film Critics chose it as Best Motion Picture of 1961, and the National Board of Review named it one of the 10 best of the year. At the Academy Award ceremonies, *West Side Story* won eight Oscars, including Best Picture, Best Supporting Actor (Chakiris), Best Supporting Actress (Moreno), Best Director, and Best Film Editing.

---

PLOT SUMMARY

After a striking opening, including the main title, we are introduced through a combination of realistic scenes and ones of dance and song to two Manhattan West Side street gangs—the "American" Jets and the Puerto Rican Sharks. A fight between them is stopped by Lieutenant Schrank (Oakland), a crude, bullying plainclothes policeman, and Officer Krupke. When they are alone, the Jets sing the "Jet Song," and their leader, Riff (Tamblyn), decides to challenge the Sharks to a decisive rumble.

Tony (Beymer) is working for Doc (Glass), the kindly owner of the local drugstore. Although Tony is a cofounder with Riff of the Jets and a successful streetfighter, he feels that he has outgrown the gang and does not want to be involved in their fights. At the back of Doc's store, Riff finally persuades Tony to join him that night at the high school gym dance, at which he is going to challenge the Sharks. Tony tells his friend that he feels a strange sense of anticipation. After Riff leaves, he sings, "Something's Coming."

Dissolve to Maria (Wood) having a new dress fitted on her by Anita (Moreno). Maria has been in the United States only a few weeks, and the dance that evening will be her first in this country. It is expected that she will marry Chino (De Vega), lieutenant of the Sharks. Bernardo (Charkiris) enters the room. He is the leader of the Sharks, Maria's brother, and Anita's boyfriend.

At the gym, the groups remain separated and dance in different styles ("Dance at the Gym"). Maria meets Tony; the two are overwhelmingly attracted to each other. An angry Bernardo comes between them. He willingly accepts Riff's challenge and agrees to meet at Doc's store at midnight to make arrangements for the rumble. As Tony leaves the high school and wanders down streets, he sings "Maria."

After lecturing Maria in her room, Bernardo joins his gang and their girlfriends on the roof of a tenement, where they sing "In America." It is time for the meeting at Doc's store. Meanwhile, Maria is in her room. Tony, in the alley below, calls out her name. On the fire escape, they declare their love ("Tonight") and arrange to meet the following afternoon at the bridal shop where Maria works.

Outside Doc's store, the Jets satirize the efforts of adults to understand and control them in "Officer Krupke." They enter the store, and a few minutes later Bernardo arrives with his fellow Sharks. Tony joins the negotiations and persuades them to settle for a fistfight between a champion from each side. Lieutenant Schrank interrupts and is nasty to everyone in his efforts to find out the time and location of the rumble (which is to take place the next night under the West Side Highway).

It is the following afternoon, and Maria sings "I Feel Pretty" to her coworkers in the bridal shop. After the others have gone, Anita tells Maria about the rumble. Tony enters, and although Anita disapproves of

their affair, she promises to remain silent. When the two lovers are alone, Maria makes Tony promise to stop the fight. They conduct an unofficial wedding ceremony ("One Hand, One Heart").

Crosscutting between brief shots of the Jets, Sharks, Anita, Maria, Tony, and Schrank preparing for the rumble or thinking about what the evening will bring. Under the highway, Bernardo and Ice (Smith) prepare to fight. Tony interferes and attempts to calm Bernardo, who responds by ridiculing the peacemaker and finally slapping him. Riff can stand it no longer, and he hits Bernardo. The two young men draw knives. Tony again comes between them, inadvertently causing Riff to be stabbed. Before he dies, Riff hands his knife to his friend, and Tony kills Bernardo. A general fight ensures ("The Rumble") until a police siren is heard, and everyone escapes.

Maria is on the tenement roof dreaming of seeing Tony when Chino bursts in upon her reverie and tells her that Bernardo is dead. When she asks about Tony, Chino realizes their relationship, and jealousy is added to his hatred of the youth who stabbed his leader. He runs down the stairs. Maria is in her room praying when Tony enters. He explains what happened and asks her to go off with him ["Somewhere (There's a Place for Us)"]. They find solace and hope in each other's arms.

The Jets have hidden in a garage. Ice, their new leader, calms down his gang ("Cool"). When they are on the street again, Anybodys (Oakes) tells them that Chino is looking for Tony with a gun. They separate to search for their friend.

Back in Maria's room, the two lovers agree to meet later that night at Doc's. Tony leaves. Anita enters and spies him running down the alley. The young woman warns Maria ("A Boy Like That"), and Maria defends herself ("I Have a Love"). Lieutenant Schrank arrives to question Maria. The young woman conveys to Anita that she is to go to Doc's store and tell Tony that Maria will be delayed.

At the store, the Jets have learned that Tony is hiding in the cellar. When Anita enters, they refuse to allow her to talk to Tony. They manhandle her and are about to rape her when Doc stops them. In her rage, Anita cries that Chino shot Maria and she is dead. Doc goes downstairs with money and tells Tony what Anita has said.

The distraught Tony rushes out into the street, shouting that Chino should kill him too. In the playground he sees Maria. As the two lovers rush toward each other, Chino appears and shoots Tony. After Maria and Tony sing a few lines of "Somewhere (There's a Place for Us)," he dies. The Jets and Sharks surround Maria. She accuses them of being responsible for the deaths of her brother and Tony. The police arrive. After Maria gives Tony a farewell kiss, his body is carried away by members of the two gangs. Everyone leaves the playground. Cast and credit titles follow.

---

ANALYSIS

When *West Side Story* opened on Broadway in 1957, some critics and members of the audience had difficulty in categorizing a play with songs and dance on New York street gangs that ends tragically. There had been previous musicals with serious themes and tragic endings (such as *The Cradle Will Rock, Street Scene, The Consul,* and *Lost in the Stars*), but generally the Broadway musical was musical comedy. So *West Side Story* was something of an anomaly, not "Broadway opera" and surely not typical of the genre.

Four years later the musical was brought to the screen, and this problem was made more acute, for the concept of the musical as musical comedy was even more entrenched in Hollywood than on Broadway. In fact, the motion picture *West Side Story* was almost unique for the United States in being a tragic musical with its setting in a slum, although there had been precedents in Europe. Many people felt that the essence of the cinematic genre had been violated and criticized the film on this basis. Stanley Kauffmann summarizes these objections before denying their validity:

Occasionally specific arguments were adduced, but most of them seemed to spring from an a priori conviction that such a film must be an abortion. . . . The commentators prefer musicals in which credibility of plot and quality of acting are irrelevant and beyond criticism (as they are not in *West Side Story*), which exist for their music and dance.[6]

Although *West Side Story* was popular with audiences and was critically acclaimed, it did arouse controversy as to the function of the genre and its capability to present social problems.

Another burden *West Side Story* as play and film had to support was that the book is based on Shakespeare's *Romeo and Juliet.* Too many people ignored the point Arthur Laurents made in interview after interview at the time of the theater opening. He insisted that he was not "translating" the drama into a musical but only using Shakespeare's plot as a framework for his own development of a modern story. It is easy enough to identify, in addition to the obvious principals, Riff with Mercutio, Bernardo with Tybalt, Chino with Paris, Anita with the Nurse, and Doc with Friar Lawrence. Equally recognizable are parallel situations: the gym dance with the Capulet festivity, the lovers singing "Tonight" on the fire escape with the balcony scene, the sequence in the bridal shop ("One Hand, One Heart") with the prelude to the wedding ceremony in Friar Lawrence's cell, the knife fight with the sword fight, and the playground at night with the tomb. Echoes of the Renaissance play are in the musical; however, they should not be used in comparing the two works as a weapon for indiscriminately attacking the musical as an unworthy version of Shakespeare.

One perspective based on comparing the drama and musical, however, can give us insights into the approach taken by the creators of *West Side Story. Romeo and Juliet* is a romantic tragedy, containing many improbabilities and plot contrivances. We willingly suspend disbelief in the instantaneous passion of the lovers because of the extreme youth of Juliet (not quite 14) and the nature of Romeo, a young man in love with love. We first meet him as he bewails the loss of the favor of Rosaline, but he quickly recovers at the sight of Juliet, and she responds, having a potential equal to his own for transforming their surroundings through love into places of beauty and joy. This power of transformation is the true subject of the drama, with the enmity between the Capulets and the Montagues symbolic of the adult world that has lost innocence and replaced love with hate. Shakespeare convinces us of the reality of the lovers' vision and holds our attention while others are on stage through the magnificence of his poetry. His art is the means whereby the amorphous feelings of love and its transfiguring power are made concrete and believable. Reduce *Romeo and Juliet* to prose, and you have a hackneyed melodrama.

The same problem is inherent in any modern story based on Shakespeare's play. If its setting is a slum area in New York, difficulties are compounded, especially with regard to the question of how to have entirely consuming passion convincingly conveyed in words by two verbally unsophisticated youngsters. The modern version, therefore, could not depend solely on the spoken word and staging, just as the original *Romeo and Juliet* required more than prose and staging. What the creators of *West Side Story* did was to substitute dance, songs, and music for Shakespeare's poetry. It is to the credit of Laurents and his associates that they were able, no matter what the weaknesses of individual elements and scenes, to fuse seamlessly the two components of a realistic tale of contemporary tragedy and nonrealistic expressions of fervent emotions, primarily love and hate. To appreciate how they accomplished this, however, it is necessary to examine the narrative structure into which they infused the requisite nonverbal poetry and song lyrics.

The plot consists of two narrative patterns: the conflict of the gangs and the love story. There is a balance between presentations of the Jets and the Sharks, but different emphases. We come to know best the individual members of the "American" gang (children or grandchildren of European immigrants). Most prominent are Riff, a natural leader dedicated to preserving the integrity of the group, loyal and affectionate (demonstrated by his friendship with Tony); Ice, "cool," shrewd, laconic, the inevitable replacement for Riff; Action, vicious, nearly psychopathic, jealous of Riff's friendship with Tony; Baby John, weak, naive, the innocent of the gang; and A-Rab, who takes upon himself the protection of Baby John. Their girlfriends play minor roles. The tomboy, Anybodys, belongs to no one and wants only to be "one of the boys."

The opposite is true of the Sharks, the Puerto Rican gang. Aside from Bernardo and Chino, the rest of the group are barely distinguishable. Bernardo is an assured, domineering, rather elegant young man whose intense pride makes him sensitive to prejudice against Puerto Ricans. Chino is quiet and unassuming, devoted to Bernardo, and has a perpetual look of bewilderment on his face that suggests he is a born loser. The Sharks' girlfriends, particularly Anita, are more individualized than the other members of the gang. Anita is a striking, vivacious, intelligent, generous young woman. Although she is Bernardo's girlfriend, she has no hesitation in standing up to him.

Whereas the Jets seem to have no home life, and their sexuality, aside from Tony's, appears muted and casual, the Sharks conform to the stereotype of Puerto Rican family orientation and sensuality. They apparently all live in the same tenement and meet on its roof. Bernardo acts as a father to his sister, and his relationship with Anita is clearly passionate. The contrast between the attitude of the women toward their situation in New York and that of the men is set forth in the production number "In America" on the roof before the war council. Anita and the other young women want to be integrated into the United States, while the males hope to return to Puerto Rico. Anita also represents the view of the females that the conflict between the gangs is futile, yet they cannot restrain their boyfriends.

The Jets and Sharks are basically engaged in a power struggle for "turf," but the reasons why control of a few blocks is so important reflects social problems endemic in an urban "melting pot." For the Jets, their gang is a substitute for their families. Lieutenant Shrank's brutal comments to Action about a prostitute mother and A-Rab about an alcoholic father, as well as, in exaggerated form, the home problems listed in the song "Officer Krupke," indicate that the youngsters come from broken and disturbed family backgrounds. A family of any sort can give purpose to life and security. Yet a family must have a home, a base, a territory that is physical evidence of its right to respect from other peer groups and the ability to defend itself from outsiders. For the Jets, in their world of the adolescent slum dweller, their territory is a few blocks, with Doc's store as its capital. As Riff says to his gang,

"It ain't much, but all we got." The Sharks are outsiders, foreigners, endangering the Jets' self-respect and their power to protect the individual, without which the group cannot sustain itself.

For the Sharks, the "turf" is symbolic of their problems as immigrants to the United States, even though they are officially citizens of this country. The young men may dream of returning to Puerto Rico, but while in New York, they want to have equal opportunities and to be accepted. This has not happened, so they are determined to fight for their rights. Control of the streets represents power and the concomitant respect from the "Americans" that they regard as their due.

The scenes involving the Jets and Sharks are completely believable and ring true in tone and rhythm. What strains an audience's credibility, however, is the suggestion in the last scene of a reconciliation between the two gangs. There are no clues earlier in the play that forgiveness could come from within the combatants themselves. Shakespeare understood human nature better. His plays may end in peace, but it is imposed by an authority from without that has the power to control the opposing groups. For example, in *Romeo and Juliet,* it is Escalus, prince of Verona; in *Hamlet,* it is Fortinbras; in *Macbeth,* it is Malcolm. In his book for the musical, Laurents has excluded this possibility by his characterizations of the two representatives of the adult world that could control the gangs. Lieutenant Schrank, unlike Escalus, is a vicious, prejudiced, crude arm of the state who has not earned the respect of the juveniles. Doc is an ineffectual, timid voice for reason and humanity. The dubiousness of the "upbeat" ending is the price the creators of *West Side Story* paid for weakening the authority of adults.

In counterpoint to the power struggle of the gangs is the love affair between Tony and Maria. Both the lovers and their relationship on a realistic level are unconvincing. Tony is idealized, having no discernible faults. Maria is pert, desperate to break out of the cocoon of family restrictions, delightful in her obvious pleasure in being admired and loved. She almost persuades us to accept without skepticism the most implausible scene in the play and film: Maria's giving herself to Tony the same night that he killed her brother. Shakespeare made it easier for Juliet by having Romeo kill Tybalt, only a cousin to the young woman. Yet, as pointed out earlier, this scene and the instantaneous love that grips the two after a glance across a crowded floor cannot be judged by the criteria of logic. With the characters and actions of Tony and Maria we enter the province of romance, where feelings and imagination transcend reason.

In adapting the musical drama for the screen, Ernest Lehman and his colleagues made a number of changes in the placement and settings of songs. Some of these seem arbitrary, but most are obviously arranged to take advantage of the possibilities in the film of "opening up" a scene. In the motion picture "In America" is sung in a production number by the Sharks and their girlfriends, not solely by Anita and a few young women; "Cool" occurs after the rumble, not before the council of war; "I Feel Pretty" is sung in the bridal shop before the rumble, not in Maria's room after the fight; and "Officer Krupke" appears before the council of war, not after the rumble (thus the intensity of the last third of the film, without the comic interlude, is greater than on the stage). Moreover, the roles of Ice and Anybodys are expanded; for example, the former is the lead singer in "Cool" rather than Riff.

These changes do not constitute the chief difference between the play and film. A theater production is, naturally, more real and immediate because of the presence of living actors. The advantage of the film is the ability of the cinematic techniques to supplement the poetry of songs and dance, so that another dimension of transfiguring imagination is added.

In the very beginning, the superb opening graphics by Saul Bass establishes the theme of a repeated shifting from illusion to reality as well as the importance of color and sound. With a black screen, whistling and the snapping of fingers (two important auditory rhythmic devices used throughout the film) issue from the sound track. An abstract design suggesting the lower end of Manhattan appears as the "Jet Song" is heard. The colors of orange, white, and blue melt into one another. As we will see, a blurring of colors is a means in the film of indicating a romantic dream world. "Maria" replaces the previous song before it returns again, contrasting the two realities of the gangs and the lovers. After the title, "West Side Story," is superimposed (the credits and cast are listed at the end of the film), the design changes into a helicopter view of lower Manhattan. The camera moves from right to left (east to west), passing over landmarks of the city. A zoom shot in almost a direct vertical brings us to a school playground where some fellows are playing basketball. A couple of more shots and we are introduced to the Jets, snapping their fingers.

The first sequence of the motion picture continues on the same high level of excellence; in fact, probably no other American musical begins with greater vitality and creativity. The line of action is a series of chases and confrontations between the Jets and the Sharks. There is an intertwining of realistic movements and dancing. This dual approach is exemplified by two fights: The first is basically a ballet; the second (just before the police arrive) is an actual group fistfight. The transitions between certain scenes are distinctive. In one, the Jets are dancing along the street, and a close-up of their hands fills the screen. Cut to those same hands, only now they are under a basketball net in the playground. Another effective transition device is the use of swish pans to move in time and space from one situation to another as the two gangs chase each other.

Opening the film proper with dancing indicates its importance. Since *West Side Story* is a musical, we accept the artificiality of these unsophisticated youths moving with the grace of professionals and unselfconsciously dancing along slum streets (Figure 9.18), on rooftops, and in a garage. Only at the high school gym is the dancing realistically justified, and even this scene is a production number. Robbins developed a

**FIGURE 9.18**

*West Side Story.* The Jets, led by Riff, dance down a New York West Side street.

choreographic style that is athletic and vigorous, reflecting the vitality and restlessness of the youths.

Each large production number, with the exception of the high school dance and the comic "Officer Krupke," involves a group singing at some time as well as dancing. What these numbers ("Jet Song," "In America," and "Cool") share in content is that they express group cohesion. Dance and group singing in the film, then, symbolize unity, a repressing of the individual in favor of the security and power possible in a social unit.

In contrast, the two lovers do not dance, except for a few moments at the high school and Maria in a small way when singing "I Feel Pretty." Instead, the two communicate their intense inner emotions in the more personal and individual form of the song as duet or solo: "Something's Coming," "Maria," "Tonight," "One Hand, One Heart," and "Somewhere." The two songs that do not directly express the lovers' feelings for each other but are related to their love, "A Boy Like That" and "I Have a Love," are solos sung, respectively, by Anita and Maria.

Color is used expressionistically throughout the film. It especially indicates the romantic milieu that Maria and Tony create through their love. When they first meet at the high school dance, the other dancers become blurred figures, and the two come toward each other surrounded by a swirl of bright reds and cool greens (symbolizing the two main components of their relationship, passion and peace).

In the bridal shop, where the unofficial marriage of Tony and Maria takes place, not color but bright light (more ethereal than color) conveys the transcendental sphere they have entered. As they exchange vows and sing "One Hand, One Heart," the circular window above them begins to glow, forming a sort of halo (Figure 9.19). This touch is sentimental, but then so is the whole scene, a tone not unsuitable to two star-crossed lovers. When they finally consummate their "marriage" in Maria's room, in the background is a wall of decorative squares of red and blue (instead of green as at the dance). The two embrace and sink below the bottom of the frame, while the camera holds on the squares of color.

Whereas vivid colors are especially associated

**FIGURE 9.19**

*West Side Story.* The sentimentality of the glowing circular window over the heads of Tony and Maria (like a celestial benediction) as they exchange vows of love is mitigated by the scene's context of romantic love.

with the lovers, natural sounds usually indicate external reality. The scene in the high school gym where Maria and Tony meet for the first time ends, just as their lips are about to touch, with a whistle, and Bernardo comes between them. The dissonant sound of whistles (the device the Jets use to signal each other), the snapping of fingers, and sirens (announcing the arrival of the police) represent the world of conflict and authority as opposed to the lyric songs of the lovers' private world. The sound of Chino's gun is the final intrusion into that world.

The camera-editing dynamics in *West Side Story* are also often striking. The directors take full advantage of the wide screen. They tend to confine action to the central area of the frame, occupying the two ends (often in soft focus) with props or portions of a static setting. A number of high-angle shots are memorable. Examples include those in the opening sequence, the crane shot of Tony after the dance, and the direct vertical of the stairwell when Maria calls to Chino after she has been informed of her brother's death. Tilted shots during and immediately after the rumble and near the end of the film suggest that the lives of the young people have gone askew with the deaths of Riff and Bernardo.

**FIGURE 9.20**

*West Side Story.* The crosscutting between people in six different settings is unified by each individual's preoccupation with the rumble that will soon take place.

Crosscutting is necessary in a story with a number of plot lines and is effectively utilized throughout the film. There is one use of the technique, however, that is remarkable in interlocking visuals, sound, and directional cutting in an exciting rhythm. After the sequence in the bridal shop, there is a cut to a rooftop and a bright moon. It is hours later, just before the rumble is to take place. First there is parallel editing between shots of the Jets and the Sharks striding toward and looking directly at the camera as they gather weapons and sing the "Jet Song." Cut to Anita dressing and anticipating her date with Bernardo after the fight [Figure 9.20(a)]. Cut to Tony in front of Doc's store [Figure 9.20(b)], beginning "Tonight." Cut to Maria in her apartment continuing the song [Figure 9.20(c)]. As she sings, there is a cutaway to Lieutenant Schrank in a police car [Figure 9.20(d)], then a long shot of the Jets coming down an alley. We hear a counterpoint on the sound track between the "Jet Song" and "Tonight" (suggesting, as during the title footage, a contrast between violence and love), and there is a return to Maria. Following is a succession of brief shots and a vocal blending: Sharks, Anita, Tony, Jets, Sharks. The Jets are moving from left to right and the Sharks from right to left, giving us a feeling of the two gangs heading toward each other [Figure 9.20(e, f)]. The scene ends with a square of red filling the screen, symbolizing violence instead of passion. This is superb organic montage, exceptional in a musical.

Two instances of ingenious transitions in moving across space and time were noted earlier. Some others: After Tony has sung "Something's Coming," the camera tilts up; there is a dissolve and the camera tilts down to Maria, thus visually joining the two who have not yet met. At the end of the scene, Maria twirls in her new dress of white and red. Her figure blurs until all we see are masses of white and red that slowly coalesce again into vague, swirling figures and, finally, dancers. We are at the high school gym hours later. When Tony leaves the dance, he is singing "Maria," facing the camera, with the dancers behind him. They disappear and are replaced by the background of the street as the camera continues to lead Tony.

These are only a few illustrations of what cinematic techniques have added to the stage musical. The weaknesses in the original version, discussed earlier, are present in the film, and a few others are made more prominent. The chief of these is a sliding at times from sentiment into sentimentality, such as the glowing circular window above the lovers in the bridal shop. On the other hand, it is a driving, exciting motion picture that skillfully blends adolescent conflict and love, comedy and tragedy. *West Side Story* has met the test of time. Two decades after its release, it still ranks as one of the half dozen most impressive American film musicals.

# Afterword

The future of film in, say, the remaining two decades of this century depends on so many variables that only a very audacious or foolhardy person would presume to play the role of Nostradamus on cinema. Startling new explorations of the art of the medium usually depend on the achievements of especially creative individuals, and no one has yet been able to determine the conditions that favor the appearance of a Griffith, Gance, Renoir, Welles, or Bergman. Current tendencies are, of course, likely to continue and perhaps be augmented in the years to come. One need not gaze into a crystal ball or probe the viscera of sacrificed animals to prophesy that, for example, film production will remain expensive, women will play an increasing role as filmmakers, and motion picture production in the countries of the Third World will become more significant than at present.

There is, however, a component of film production in which the media subdivision of futurology is more than a sophisticated guessing game. Developments in technology have initiated a revolution that will inevitably transform the creation and distribution of motion pictures. In the former area, such inventions as Steadicam (trade name for a mechanism that holds a camera steady under all circumstances) and film stock so light-sensitive that a minimum of artificial illumination is necessary have already improved the quality of what appears on the screen. More than anything else, however, computers and video will profoundly influence production and editing practices.

Without computer systems, the spectacular special effects that have enlivened recent science fiction films such as the *Star War* series and *The Black Hole* would have been difficult if not impossible. Other systems are being devised that will make feasible the retrieval of individual frames of developed stock and thus facilitate and decrease the expense of editing a motion picture. This ability of computers also plays a vital role in editing procedures that use videotape.

Video has the advantages of equipment and tape that are relatively inexpensive when compared to film production, reusable tape, and immediate screening of what has been shot. Its disadvantages include weak resolving power (that is, quality of the details of an image), poor representation of depth, and difficulty of editing without sophisticated equipment. Whatever its present inadequacies, video has become the standard medium for television newscasts (with notable exceptions, such as the program "60 Minutes"), is used in creating documentaries by amateurs and increasingly by professionals, and for some years has been accepted as an avant-garde art form. Although video has yet to prove itself as a viable form for feature fiction motion pictures, it is being used today as a supplement in various stages of the production of conventional films.

Many directors shoot simultaneously with film and video cameras. It is thus possible by looking at a video monitor to determine if there are any major faults in a shot without waiting to view rushes the next day. At an experimental stage is the computerized coding of video images with corresponding film frames. After the tape is edited, the selected images are retrieved from the complete film footage, forming the rough cut of a feature.

An exciting application of video was developed at the now defunct American Zoetrope Studios and is used elsewhere. Francis Ford Coppola called his system *previsualization* and worked with it to a degree on the preproduction stage of *One From the Heart.*

A videotape for a feature is made, consisting of sketches from the storyboard, rehearsals of actors, and other material. The director and his associates study this preproduction tape and make decisions on what will be shot and how. The system is still in its formative stage, but it obviously has high potentials as a money saver when it is perfected.

Efforts to incorporate video images into standard films are still tentative and only sporadically successful. Michelangelo Antonioni's attempt in this direction for *The Mystery of Oberwald* (1980) is an instance of an imaginative experiment that was more admirable as an idea than in realization. What truly intrigues those who believe that the future of film is inseparable from that of video, however, is research, especially in the United States and Japan, toward developing the means whereby a feature film can be shot on videotape and then transferred to film without any discernible difference in quality. Should this ever be achieved, the ramifications on motion picture production could be as far-reaching as the advent of sound.

Most amazing of all are attempts to take extant video images and to mold them solely by means of computers into a new sequence of events. It is doubtful, though, that even within a few decades, an individual will, without shooting on film or videotape, be able to sit in front of a computer and create a new fiction narrative.

More immediate—in fact, right now—are radical changes in motion picture financing, screening, and distribution. Since the fifties, television has become the major source of information and entertainment. This medium has affected the motion picture industry not only as a competitor but also as a source of financing and production. In countries where TV is subsidized by the state, such as Germany and Italy, this industry has generously supported commercial and noncommercial filmmaking. In the United States, made-for-television motion pictures and miniseries have increased in number each year since the mid-seventies. The influence of television on the documentary has already been indicated.

Decisive for the future of the movie industry are the ramifications of new dimensions of television on film distribution. Cable TV is now an important outlet for fiction films after distribution in theaters. If this mode of broadcasting continues to increase the number of subscribers, it is conceivable that cable systems, especially subscription pay-television, will subsidize film production. It has been estimated that if 2 million homes paid $5 each for a new film, most of the cost of a $10 million motion picture could be recouped even before it was screened in a theater. This means that a relatively small audience could support a film with limited appeal. The same situation applies to videocassettes and videodisks. Perhaps the present pattern of preoccupation on the part of producers with potential blockbusters to the exclusion of any other type of film will be broken. A recent article in the *New York Times Magazine* summed up the attitude of producers in Hollywood: "Troubled by roller-coaster economics, studio insiders are betting on a golden future based on the new technology behind pay-per-view cable television and videocassettes."[1]

Both filmmakers and audiences hope for a "golden future." Probably the most dependable characteristic of all "golden futures" is that they are never quite as glittering as we had anticipated. However, if this medium continues, as it has in the past, to entertain, inform, thrill, and deepen our understanding of ourselves and our world, we can't complain.

*Notes*

## CHAPTER 1

**1/** Aristotle, *On the Art of Poetry,* tr. S. H. Butcher (New York: The Liberal Arts Press, 1950), pp. 12–13.
**2/** Vladimir Nilsen, *The Cinema as a Graphic Art,* tr. Stephen Garry (New York: Hill and Wang, n.d.), chap. 1.
**3/** Aeneas MacKenzie, *"The Secret Sharer: A Screenplay,"* in *Media for Our Time: An Anthology,* ed. Dennis DeNitto (New York: Holt, Rinehart and Winston, 1971), p. 99.
**4/** Jean-Luc Godard, "Montage my Fine Care," in *Godard on Godard,* ed. Jean Narboni and Tom Milne (New York: Viking Press, 1972), p. 39.
**5/** Siegfied Kracauer, *Theory of Film: The Redemption of Physical Reality* (New York: Oxford University Press, 1965), p. 103.
**6/** Rudolf Arnheim, *Film* (London: Faber and Faber, 1933), p. 213.
**7/** Kracauer, pp. 111–124.
**8/** Anthony Heightman, "Special Effects," in *Focal Encyclopedia of Film and Television Techniques,* ed. Raymond Fielding (New York: Hastings House, 1969), p. 723.

## CHAPTER 2

**1/** William Froug, *The Screenwriter Looks at the Screenwriter* (New York: Dell, 1974), p. vii.
**2/** Roger Graef, "Decisions, Decisions," *Sight and Sound,* Winter 1975–1976, p. 3.
**3/** This topic is discussed in Donald Chase, *Filmmaking: The Collaborative Art* (Boston: Little, Brown, 1975), pp. 268–270.

## CHAPTER 3

**1/** André Bazin, *"Le Journal d'un curé de campagne* and the Stylistics of Robert Bresson," tr. Hugh Gray in *What Is Cinema?* (Berkeley, Calif.: University of California Press, 1971).
**2/** Pauline Kael, "Raising Kane," in *The Citizen Kane Book* (Boston: Little, Brown, 1971).
**3/** Will Wright, *Six Guns and Society* (Berkeley, Calif.: University of California Press, 1975).
**4/** Harry M. Geduld and Ronald Gottesman, *An Illustrated Glossary of Film Terms* (New York: Holt, Rinehart and Winston, 1973), p. 73.
**5/** John Mercer, *Glossary of Film Terms,* The University Film Association Monograph No. 2 (Philadelphia: Journal of the University Film Association, 1978), p. 40.
**6/** Beograd Film Institute, *Film Genre: An Essay in Terminology and Determination of Film Genres* (Belgrade, Yugoslavia: Beograd Film Institute, 1964).
**7/** *The American Film Institute Catalogs: Feature Films: 1921–1930* and *Feature Films: 1961–1970* (New York: Bowker, 1971).
**8/** J. Dudley Andrew, *The Major Film Theories: An Introduction* (New York: Oxford University Press, 1976), p. 4.
**9/** André Bazin, *"Bicycle Thief,"* tr. Hugh Gray, in *What Is Cinema,* vol. 2 (Berkeley, Calif.: University of California Press, 1971), p. 60.
**10/** Andrew Sarris, "Notes on the *Auteur* Theory in 1962," *Film Culture,* Winter 1962–1963, pp. 6–7.
**11/** Andrew, p. 229.
**12/** Christian Metz, *Film Language: A Semiotics of the Cinema,* tr. Michael Taylor (New York: Oxford University Press, 1974), p. 137.
**13/** Christian Metz, "Entretien sur la sémiologie du cinéma," *Semiotica* (1971): 4, 1. Quoted in John G. Hanhardt and Charles H. Harpole, "Linguistics, Structuralism, and Semiology," *Film Comment,* May 1973, p. 52.
**14/** Siegfried Kracauer, *From Caligari to Hitler: A Psychological History of the German Film* (Princeton, N.J.: Princeton University Press, 1971), chaps. 4–10.

## CHAPTER 4

**1/** Siegfried Kracauer, *From Caligari to Hitler: A Psychological History of the German Film* (Princeton, N.J.: Princeton University Press, 1971), chap. 5.
**2/** The print presently available from rental companies in the United States is the shortened version—77 minutes at silent speed.
**3/** Andrew Sarris, *The American Cinema* (New York: Dutton, 1968), chap. 1.
**4/** Cesare Zavattini, "Some Ideas on the Cinema," in *Film: A Montage of Theories,* ed. Richard Dyer MacCann (New York: Dutton, 1966), pp. 216–228.

**5/** Statistics from Cobbett Steinberg, *Reel Facts: The Movie Book of Records* (New York: Vintage Books, 1978).

**6/** Quoted in Georges Sadoul, *Dictionary of Film Makers,* tr. and ed. Peter Morris (Berkeley, Calif.: University of California Press, 1972), p. 33. Original source not indicated.

**7/** Michael Pye and Lynda Myles, *The Movie Brats* (New York: Holt, Rinehart and Winston, 1979).

**CHAPTER 5**

**1/** Georges Sadoul, *Dictionary of Film Makers,* tr. and ed. Peter Morris (Berkeley, Calif.: University of California Press, 1972).

**2/** Sergei Eisenstein, "Dickens, Griffith and the Film Today," in *Film Form: Essays in Film Theory,* tr. and ed. Jay Leyda (New York: Harcourt Brace Jovanovich, 1949), p. 204.

**3/** John Gassner, *Masters of the Drama,* 3d ed. (New York: Random House, 1954), p. 637.

**4/** Thomas Burke, "The Chink and the Child," in *Limehouse Nights* (New York: Robert M. McBride, 1919), pp. 26–27.

**5/** George C. Pratt, *Spellbound in Darkness: A History of the Silent Film* (Greenwich, Conn.: New York Graphic Society, 1973), p. 251.

**6/** Quoted in Pratt, p. 252.

**7/** Robert M. Henderson, *D. W. Griffith: His Life and Work* (New York: Oxford University Press, 1972), p. 201.

**8/** Gerald Mast, *A Short History of the Movies,* 2d ed. (Indianapolis: Bobbs-Merrill, 1976), p. 87.

**9/** Quoted in Pratt, p. 251.

**10/** Henderson, p. 205.

**11/** Lewis Jacobs, *The Rise of the American Film: A Critical History* (New York: Columbia University Teachers College Press, 1968), p. 307.

**12/** Ivan Butler, *Cinema in Britain: An Illustrated Survey* (New York: Barnes, 1973), pp. 86–87.

**13/** Lotte H. Eisner, *The Haunted Screen* (Berkeley, Calif.: University of California Press, 1969), p. 284.

**14/** Pratt, p. 377.

**15/** Siegfried Kracauer, *From Caligari to Hitler: A Psychological History of the German Film* (Princeton, N.J.: Princeton University Press, 1971), pp. 123, 125–127.

**16/** Eisner, p. 281.

**17/** Eisner, p. 282.

**18/** Kracauer, p. 127. The Dawes Plan was proposed by an American Committee under the chairmanship of Charles G. Dawes and accepted by Germany in 1924. One of its conditions was that Germany pay reparations of 1 billion gold marks annually for 5 years, after which payments would more than double.

**19/** Quoted in *The Complete Films of Eisenstein,* Dutton Paperback Original (New York: Dutton, 1974), p. 51. Original source not indicated.

**20/** Harry M. Geduld and Ronald Gottesman, eds., *Sergei Eisenstein and Upton Sinclair: The Making and Unmaking of "Que Viva Mexico!"* (Bloomington, Ind.: Indiana University Press, 1970).

**21/** S. M. Eisenstein, V. I. Pudovkin, G. V. Alexandrov, "A Statement on the Sound-Film," in *Film Form,* pp. 257–260.

**22/** Eisenstein, "The Cinematographic Principle and the Ideogram," p. 37.

**23/** Lincoln F. Johnson, *Film: Space, Time, Light and Sound* (New York: Holt, Rinehart and Winston, 1974), p. 115.

**24/** Eisenstein, "Methods of Montage," p. 73.

**25/** Ibid., p. 80.

**26/** *The Complete Films of Eisenstein,* p. 51.

**27/** Eisenstein, "A Dialectic Approach to Film Form," p. 55.

**28/** Eisenstein, "Methods of Montage," p. 75.

**29/** "October," in *Eisenstein: Three Films,* ed. Jay Leyda (New York: Harper & Row, 1974), pp. 59, 63.

**30/** Eisenstein, "A Dialectic Approach to Film Form," p. 58.

**31/** Ibid., p. 61.

**32/** André Bazin, *"Bicycle Thief,"* tr. Hugh Gray, in *What Is Cinema?,* vol. 2 (Berkeley, Calif.: University of California Press, 1971), p. 60.

**33/** Bazin, "De Sica: Metteur en Scène," tr. Hugh Gray, in *What Is Cinema?,* vol. 2, p. 69.

**34/** Cesare Zavattini, "Some Ideas on the Cinema," in *Film: A Montage of Theories,* ed. Richard Dyer MacCann (New York: Dutton, 1966), p. 225.

**35/** Quoted in *The Bicycle Thief: A Film by Vittorio De Sica,* tr. Simon Hartog, Modern Film Scripts (New York: Simon & Schuster, 1968), p. 6.

**36/** Bazin, *"Bicycle Thief,"* p. 52.

**37/** Quoted in *The 400 Blows: A Film by François Truffaut,* ed. David Benby, Film Book Series (New York: Grove Press, 1969), p. 245.

**38/** Both quotations appear on the back cover of *The 400 Blows: A Film by François Truffaut.* Original sources not indicated.

**39/** Ibid., pp. 172–174.

**40/** Ibid., p. 171.

**41/** C. G. Crisp, *François Truffaut,* Praeger Film Library (New York: Praeger, 1972), p. 40.

**CHAPTER 6**

**1/** Ingmar Bergman, *"Smiles of a Summer Night,"* in *Four Screenplays of Ingmar Bergman* (New York: Simon & Schuster, 1960), p. 47.

**2/** Henri Bergson, "Laughter," in *Comedy: Meaning and Form,* ed. Robert W. Corrigan (San Francisco: Intext, 1965), p. 477.

**3/** James K. Feibleman, *Aesthetics* (New York: Duell, Sloan and Pearce, 1949), p. 82.

**4/** James Agee, "Comedy's Greatest Era," in *Film Theory and Criticism,* ed. Gerald Mast and Marshall Cohen (New York: Oxford University Press, 1974), p. 449.

**5/** Gerald Mast, *The Comic Mind: Comedy and the Movies* (London: New English Library, 1974), p. 199.

**6/** Ibid.

**7/** Agee, p. 445.

**8/** Charles Chaplin, *My Autobiography* (New York: Simon & Schuster, 1964), p. 303.

**9/** Ibid.

**10/** Ibid., p. 304.

**11/** Reported by Jean Cocteau in *Cocteau on the Film* (New York: Roy Publishers, 1954), p. 94.

**12/** Stig Björkman, Torsten Manns, and Johnas Sima, *Bergman on Bergman: Interviews with Ingmar Bergman* (New York: Simon & Schuster, 1973), pp. 104–105.

**13/** Ibid., p. 195.

**14/** William Wordsworth, "Ode. Intimations of Immortality," (Stanza 10).

**15/1** Vernon Young, *Cinema Borealis: Ingmar Bergman and the Swedish Ethos* (New York: David Lewis, 1971), p. 142.

**16/1** Robin Wood, *Ingmar Bergman* (New York: Praeger, 1969), pp. 68–72.

**17/** Quoted in Gene Lees, "The Mel Brooks Memos," *American Film,* October 1977, p. 16.

**CHAPTER 7**

**1/** Quoted in Richard Meran Barsam, *Nonfiction Film: A Critical History* (New York: Dutton, 1973), p. 1.

**2/** Ibid., p. 6.

**3/** John Grierson, *Grierson on Documentary,* ed. Forsyth Hardy (New York: Harcourt Brace Jovanovich, 1947), p. 13.

**4/** Quoted in Barsam, p. 2.

**5/** John Grierson, "Flaherty's Poetic *Moana,*" in *The Documentary Tradition,* 2d ed., ed. Lewis Jacobs (New York: Norton, 1979), pp. 25–26.

**6/** John Grierson, "First Principles of Documentary," in *Film: A Montage of Theories,* pp. 209–210.

**7/** Quoted in Georgés Sadoul, *Dictionary of Film Makers,* tr. and ed. Peter Morris (Berkeley, Calif.: University of California Press, 1972), p. 104, s.v. "Grierson, John." Original source not indicated.

**8/** Grierson, *Grierson on Documentary,* p. 179.

**9/** Ibid.

**10/** Grierson, "First Principles of Documentary," p. 214.

**11/** Georges Sadoul, *Dictionary of Films,* tr. and ed. Peter Morris (Berkeley: University of California Press,

1972), p. 115, s.v. *"Fires Were Started."*

**12/** Quoted in Jay Leyda, *Kino: A History of the Russian and Soviet Film* (New York: Collier Books, 1973), p. 176. Original source "a speech in 1929."

**13/** Quoted in Sadoul, *Film Makers,* p. 264, s.v. "Vertov, Dziga." Original source not indicated.

**14/** Sadoul, *Films,* p. 292, s.v. *"Primary."*

**15/** Stephen Mamber, *Cinema Verité in America* (Cambridge, Mass.: MIT Press, 1974), pp. 209–210.

**16/** Jay Chapman, "Two Aspects of the City: Cavalcanti and Ruttmann," in *The Documentary Tradition,* p. 41.

**17/** Arthur Calder-Marshall, *The Innocent Eye: The Life of Robert J. Flaherty* (New York: Harcourt Brace Jovanovich, 1966), p. 229.

**18/** Quoted in Ben Achtenberg, "Helen van Dongen: An Interview," *Film Quarterly,* Winter 1976–1977, p. 51.

**19/** Calder-Marshall, p. 151.

**20/** Barsam, p. 145.

**21/** Ibid.

**22/** Quoted in G. Roy Levin, "Frederick Wiseman," in *Documentary Explorations* (New York: Doubleday, 1971), p. 326.

**23/** Ibid., p. 321.

**24/** Description of two stages based on material in David Eames, "Watching Wiseman Watch," *New York Times Magazine,* October 2, 1977, pp. 96–106.

**25/** Roger Graef, "Decisions, Decisions," *Sight and Sound,* Winter 1975–1976, p. 3.

**26/** Levin, p. 318.

**27/** Arthur Knight, "Cinéma Verité and Film Truth," *Saturday Review,* September 9, 1967, p. 44.

**28/** Erik Barnouw, *Documentary* (New York: Oxford University Press, 1974), p. 246.

**29/** Quoted in Gordon Hitchens, "An Interview with a Legend," *Film Comment,* Winter 1965, p. 7.

**30/** Richard Meran Barsam, *Filmguide to "Triumph of the Will"* (Bloomington, Ind.: Indiana University Press, 1975), p. 23.

**31/** Ibid., p. 65.

**32/** Ibid., p. 32.

**33/** These lines are spoken by Alberich at the beginning of scene 3 of the opera. The greedy dwarf has stolen the Rhinegold. He refers to "night and fog" as he puts on the tarnhelm, which makes its wearer invisible. Later Wotan and Loge capture him, his hoard of treasure, and the ring made from the Rhinegold.

It is possible that the Wagner-worshiping Nazis had these lines in mind when classifying many concentration camp prisoners under the strange heading *"Nacht und Nebel."* They could have associated Alberich with the Jews and Wotan with Hitler, but I can find no evidence to support this supposition.

The *Nacht und Nebel Erlass* ("Night and Fog"

Decree) was issued by Hitler himself on December 7, 1941. See William L. Shirer, *The Rise and Fall of the Third Reich* (New York: Simon & Schuster, 1960), p. 957.

**CHAPTER 8**

1/ George N. Fenin and William K. Everson, *The Western,* rev. ed. (New York: Penguin Books, 1977), p. 131.
2/ Georges Sadoul, *Dictionary of Films,* tr. and ed. Peter Morris (Berkeley, Calif.: University of California Press, 1972), p. 420, s.v. *"The Wind."*
3/ Fenin and Everson, p. 136.
4/ Robert Warshow, "Movie Chronicle: The Westerner," in *Film Theory and Criticism,* ed. Gerald Mast and Marshall Cohen (New York: Oxford University Press, 1974), p. 403.
5/ Quoted in Georges Sadoul, *Dictionary of Film Makers,* tr. and ed. Peter Morris (Berkeley, Calif.: University of California Press, 1972), p. 89, s.v. "Ford, John," ". . . told Jean Mitry in 1956."
6/ Axel Madsen, "John Ford: American (1895–1973): An Interview," *1,000 Eyes,* July-August 1976, p. 11.
7/ Richard Corliss, *Talking Pictures: Screenwriters in the American Cinema* (Woodstock, N.Y.: Overlook Press, 1974), p. 228.
8/ J. A. Place, *The Western Films of John Ford* (Secaucus, N.J.: Citadel Press, 1973), p. 36.
9/ Jon Tuska, *The Filming of the West* (New York: Doubleday, 1976), p. 529.
10/ Sadoul, *Film Makers,* p. 240, s.v. "Stevens, George."
11/ Andrew Sarris, *The American Cinema* (New York: Dutton, 1968), p. 110.

12/ Sadoul, *Film Makers,* p. 240, s.v. "Stevens, George."
13/ Quoted in Michael Parkinson and Clyde Jeavons, *A Pictorial History of Westerns* (New York: Hamlyn, 1973), p. 184. Original source not indicated.
14/ Stanley Kauffmann, *"The Wild Bunch,"* in *Figures of Light* (New York: Harper & Row, 1971), pp. 182–183.
15/ John L. Fell, *A History of Films* (New York: Holt, Rinehart and Winston, 1979), p. 423.
16/ Jim Kitses, *Horizons West* (Bloomington, Ind.: Indiana University Press, 1970), p. 166.

**CHAPTER 9**

1/ Stated in a lecture given by Stephen Sondheim at the Andiron Club, New York, on December 17, 1976.
2/ Richard Griffith and Arthur Mayer, *The Movies* (New York: Simon & Schuster, 1957), p. 379.
3/ Arlene Croce, *Afterimages* (New York: Knopf, 1977), p. 436.
4/ Richard Corliss, *Talking Pictures: Screenwriters in the American Cinema* (Woodstock, N.Y.: Overlook Press, 1974), p. 198.
5/ *The Oxford Companion to Film*, Liz-Anne Bawden, ed., (New York: Oxford University Press, 1976), p. 635, s.v. *"Singin' in the Rain."*
6/ Stanley Kauffmann, *"West Side Story,"* in *A World on Film* (New York: Dell, 1966), p. 136.

**AFTERWORD**

1/ Aljean Harmetz, "Hollywood's Video Gamble," *The New York Times Magazine,* March 28, 1982, p 40.

# Selected bibliography

The literature of film studies has expanded so rapidly since the 1960s that only a book-length bibliography deserves to be designated as comprehensive. My listing is selective, but it encompasses what I consider the fundamental volumes in English for a student of cinema who is not a specialist.

The first main section, titled "Specific Subjects," is divided into nine categories that correspond to the nine chapters of *Film: Form & Feeling*. Material on directors is confined to those whose films are analyzed in Chapters 5 through 9. Items referred to in my notes also are recorded; however, a title noted in a chapter in some cases (for example, an encyclopedia) may be listed in the second part of this bibliography.

The second main section, titled "General Sources," is divided into the following categories:

*Introductions to Film*
*Analyses of and Commentaries on Individual Films*
*General Anthologies*
*Reference and Research, (Encyclopedias, Dictionaries, and Guides; Glossaries; Bibliographies and Catalogues; Periodicals; Guides to Periodical Literature; and Miscellanea)*

I do not, unfortunately, have the space to annotate my listing. Information on individual books can be found in George Rehrauer's *The Macmillan Film Bibliography,* 2 vols. (New York: Macmillan, 1982), which annotates practically every volume I cite.

## SPECIFIC SUBJECTS

### 1/ THE COMPONENTS OF FILM

*General*

Arnheim, Rudolf. *Film as Art.* Berkeley, Calif.: University of California Press, 1966.

Balázs, Béla. *Theory of the Film: Character and Growth of a New Art.* Trans. Edith Bone. New York: Dover, 1970.

Braudy, Leo. *The World in a Frame: What We See in Films.* New York: Doubleday, 1977.

Durgnat, Raymond. *Films and Feelings.* Cambridge, Mass.: M.I.T. Press, 1971.

Eidsvik, Charles. *Cineliteracy: Film Among the Arts.* New York: Random House, 1978.

Huss, Roy, and Norman Silverstein. *The Film Experience.* New York: Delta, 1968.

Kracauer, Siegfried. *Theory of Film: The Redemption of Physical Reality.* New York: Oxford University Press, 1965.

Lawson, John Howard. *Film: The Creative Process: The Search for an Audio-Visual Language and Structure.* 2d ed. New York: Hill & Wang, 1967.

Mast, Gerald. *Film/Cinema/Movie: A Theory of Experience.* New York: Harper & Row, 1977.

McLuhan, Marshall. *Understanding Media: The Extensions of Man.* New York: McGraw-Hill, 1964.

Spottiswoode, Raymond. *A Grammar of the Film: An Analysis of Film Technique.* Berkeley, Calif.: University of California Press, 1969.

Stephenson, Ralph, and J. R. Debrix. *The Cinema as Art.* Rev. ed. Baltimore, Md.: Penguin, 1969.

*The narrative dimension*

Aristotle. *On the Art of Poetry.* Trans. S. H. Butcher. New York: Liberal Arts Press, 1950.

Armes, Roy. *The Ambiguous Image: Narrative Style in Modern European Cinema.* Bloomington, Ind.: Indiana University Press, 1976.

Beja, Morris. *Film & Literature: An Introduction.* New York: Longman, 1979.

Booth, Wayne C. *The Rhetoric of Fiction.* Chicago: University of Chicago Press, 1961.

Gassner, John. *Masters of the Drama.* 3d ed. New York: Random House, 1954.

Gessner, Robert. *The Moving Image: A Guide to Cinematic Literacy.* New York: Dutton, 1968.

Luhr, William, and Peter Lehman. *Authorship and Narrative in the Cinema: Issues in Contemporary Aesthetics.* New York: Putnam, 1977.

MacKenzie, Aeneas. "The Secret Sharer: A Screenplay." In *Media for Our Time: An Anthology.* Ed. Dennis DeNitto. New York: Holt, Rinehart and Winston, 1971, pp. 93–130.

Murray, Edward. *The Cinematic Imagination: Writers and the Motion Pictures.* New York: Ungar, 1972.

Winston, Douglas Garrett. *The Screenplay in Literature.* Cranbury, N.J.: Fairleigh Dickinson University Press, 1973.

*Camera-editing dynamics
and elements of presentation*

Alton, John. *Painting with Light.* New York: Macmillan, 1962.

Cameron, Evan William, ed. *Sound and the Cinema.* Pleasantville, N.Y.: Redgrave, 1979.

Chierichetti, David. *Hollywood Costume Design.* New York: Harmony, 1977.

Coe, Brian. "The Development of Colour Cinematography." In *The International Encyclopedia of Film.* Ed. Roger Manvell. New York: Bonanza Books, 1975, pp. 29–48.

Culhane, John. *Special Effects in the Movies: How Do They Do It?* New York: Ballantine, 1981.

Johnson, Lincoln F. *Film: Space, Time, Light and Sound.* New York: Holt, Rinehart and Winston, 1974.

Leese, Elizabeth. *Costume Design in the Movies.* New York: Ungar, 1977.

Limbacher, James L. *Four Aspects of the Film.* New York: Brussel & Brussel, 1969.

Mascelli, Joseph. *The Five C's of Cinematography.* Hollywood, Calif.: Cine/Graphics, 1965.

McConathy, Dale, and Diana Vreeland. *Hollywood Costume.* New York: Abrams, 1976.

Myerscough-Walker, Raymond. *Stage and Film Decor.* London: Pitman, 1940.

Nilsen, Vladimir. *The Cinema as a Graphic Art.* Trans. Stephen Garry. New York: Hill & Wang, n.d.

Reisz, Karel, and Gavin Millar. *The Technique of Film Editing.* New York: Hastings House, 1968.

Rovin, Jeff. *Movie Special Effects.* Cranbury, N.J.: Barnes, 1977.

Schechter, Harold, and David Everitt. *Film Tricks.* New York: Harlin Quist, 1980.

See also Section 2; Pudovkin in Section 4, under *Movements;* and Eisenstein in Section 5.

━━━━━━━━

## 2/ THE FILMMAKING TEAM

*General*

Butler, Ivan. *The Making of Feature Films: A Guide.* Baltimore, Md.: Penguin, 1971.

Chase, Donald. *Filmmaking: The Collaborative Art.* Boston: Little, Brown, 1975.

Watts, Stephen, ed. *Behind the Screen: How Films Are Made.* New York: Dodge, 1938.

*Specific aspects of filmmaking*

Albertson, Lillian. *Motion Picture Acting.* New York: Funk & Wagnalls, 1947.

Ash, Rene L. *The Motion Picture Film Editor.* Metuchen, N.J.: Scarecrow, 1974.

Bare, Richard L. *The Film Director: A Practical Guide to Motion Picture and Television Techniques.* New York: Macmillan, 1971.

Barsacq, Léon. *Caligari's Cabinet and Other Grand Illusions: A History of Film Design.* Rev. & ed. Elliott Stein. Boston: New York Graphic Society, 1976.

Baumgarten, Paul A., and Donald Farber. *Producing, Financing, and Distributing Film.* New York: Drama Book Specialists, 1973.

Bluem, A. William, and Jason E. Squire, eds. *The Movie Business: American Film Industry Practice.* New York: Hastings House, 1972.

Brady, John. *The Craft of the Screenwriter.* New York: Simon & Schuster, 1981.

Braudy, Leo, and Morris Dickstein, eds. *Great Film Directors: A Critical Anthology.* New York: Oxford University Press, 1978.

"Cameramen." *Film Comment,* March–April 1984, pp. 31–41.

Carrick, Edward. *Designing for Films.* London: Studio Publishers, 1949.

Corliss, Richard. *Talking Pictures: Screenwriters in the American Cinema.* Woodstock, N.Y.: Overlook Press, 1974.

————, ed. *The Hollywood Screen-Writers.* New York: Avon, 1972.

Field, Syd. *Screenplay: The Foundations of Screenwriting.* New York: Dell, 1979.

Froug, William. *The Screenwriter Looks at the Screenwriter.* New York: Dell, 1974.

Geduld, Harry M., ed. *Film Makers on Film Making: Statements on Their Art by Thirty Directors.* Bloomington, Ind.: Indiana University Press, 1971.

Hagen, Eric. *Scoring for Films.* New York: Criterion Music Corp., 1971.

Higham, Charles. *Hollywood Cameramen.* Bloomington, Ind.: Indiana University Press, 1970.

Lees, David, and Stan Berkowitz. *The Movie Business.* New York: Random House, 1981.

Limbacher, James, ed. *Film Music: From Violins to Video.* Metuchen, N.J.: Scarecrow, 1974.

Maltin, Leonard. *The Art of the Cinematographer.* New York: Dover, 1978.

Marner, Terence John, ed. *Film Design.* Cranbury, N.J.: Barnes, 1974.

"The Motion Picture Art Director." *Film Comment,* May–June 1978, pp. 25–60.

Noose, Theodore. *Hollywood Film Acting.* Cranbury, N.J.: Barnes, 1979.

Pate, Michael. *The Film Actor.* Cranbury, N.J.: Barnes, 1970.

Prendergast, Roy M. *A Neglected Art: A Critical Study of Music in Films.* New York: New York University Press, 1977.

"The Producers." *Film Comment,* July–August 1982, pp. 33–48.

Pudovkin, Vladimir. *Film Acting* [1935]. Reprint in *Film Technique and Film Acting.* New York: Grove Press, 1960.

Reynertson, A. J. *The Work of the Film Director.* New York: Hastings House, 1970.

Rosenblum, Ralph, and Robert Karen. *When the Shooting Stops . . . the Cutting Begins: A Film Editor's Story.* New York: Viking Press, 1979.

Smith, Frederick Y. *The American Cinema Editor's Decade Anniversary Book.* 2 vols. Hollywood, Calif.: American Cinema Editors, 1961, 1971.

Thomas, Tony. *Music for the Movies.* Cranbury, N.J.: Barnes, 1973.

Young, Freddie. *The Work of the Motion Picture Cameraman.* New York: Hastings House, 1972.

## 3/ CRITICAL APPROACHES TO FILM

### The review and principles of criticism

Critics whose reviews have been collected in individual volumes include James Agee, Renata Adler, Peter Bogdanovich, Judith Crist, Manny Farber, Penelope Gilliatt, Graham Greene, Pauline Kael, Stanley Kauffmann, Arthur Knight, Dwight Macdonald, Andrew Sarris, Richard Schickel, John Simon, Susan Sontag, Parker Tyler, Robert Warshow, and Vernon Young.

Bowles, Stephen E., ed. *Index to Critical Film Reviews.* 2 vols. New York: Franklin, 1975.

Boyum, Joy Gould, and Adrienne Scott. *Film as Film: Critical Responses to Film Art.* Boston: Allyn & Bacon, 1971.

English, John W. *Criticizing the Critics.* New York: Hastings House, 1979.

Heinzkill, Richard. *Film Criticism: An Index to Critics' Anthologies.* Metuchen, N.J.: Scarecrow, 1975.

Kauffmann, Stanley. *Figures of Light.* New York: Harper & Row, 1971.

―――. *A World on Film.* New York: Dell, 1966.

―――, ed. *American Film Criticism.* New York: Liveright, 1972.

Monaco, James. *A Standard Glossary for Film Criticism.* New York: Zoetrope, 1975.

Murray, Edward. *Nine American Film Critics: A Study of Theory and Practice.* New York: Ungar, 1975.

*The New York* Times *Film Reviews, 1913–1974.* 8 vols. New York: Arno.

Salem, James M. *A Guide to Critical Reviews—Part IV: The Screenplay from "The Jazz Singer" to "Dr. Strangelove."* 2 vols. Metuchen, N.J.: Scarecrow, 1971.

Samples, Gordon. *How to Locate Reviews of Plays and Films.* Metuchen, N.J.: Scarecrow, 1976.

Variety *Film Reviews: 1913–1970.* 9 vols. New York: Arno, 1972.

### Cinematic and noncinematic perspectives

Andrew, J. Dudley. *Concepts in Film Theory.* New York: Oxford University Press, 1984.

―――. *The Major Film Theories: An Introduction.* New York: Oxford University Press, 1976.

Bazin, André. *What Is Cinema?* 2 vols. Trans. Hugh Gray. Berkeley, Calif.: University of California Press, 1971.

Beograd Film Institute. *Film Genre: An Essay in Terminology and Determination of Film Genres.* Belgrade, Yugoslavia: Beograd Film Institute, 1964.

Burch, Noel. *The Theory of Film Practice.* New York: Praeger, 1973. [Semiotic perspective]

Cavell, Stanley. *The World Viewed: Reflections on the Ontology of Film.* New York: Viking Press, 1971.

Dreyer, Carl. *Dreyer in Double Reflection: Translation of Carl Th. Dreyer's Writings "About the Film" ("Om Filmen").* Trans. & ed. Donald Skoller. New York: Dutton, 1973.

Eberwein, Robert T. *A Viewer's Guide to Film Theory and Criticism.* Metuchen, N.J.: Scarecrow, 1979.

Godard, Jean-Luc. *Godard on Godard.* Ed. Jean Narboni and Tom Milne. Trans. Tom Milne. New York: Viking Press, 1972.

Grant, Barry K., ed. *Film Genre: Theory & Criticism.* Metuchen, N.J.: Scarecrow, 1977.

Greenberg, Harvey R. *The Movies on Your Mind: Film Classics on the Couch, from Fellini to Frankenstein.* New York: Dutton, 1975. [Freudian perspective]

Hanhardt, John G., and Charles H. Harpole. "Linguistics, Structuralism, and Semiology." *Film Comment,* May 1973, pp. 52–57.

Henderson, Brian. *A Critique of Film Theory.* New York: Dutton, 1980.

Houston, Beverle, and Marsha Kinder. *Self and Cinema: A Transformalist Perspective.* Pleasantville, N.Y.: Redgrave, 1980.

Kael, Pauline. "Raising Kane." In *The Citizen Kane Book.* Boston: Little, Brown, 1971.

Kaminsky, Stuart. *American Film Genres.* Dayton, O.: Pflaum, 1974.

Kawin, Bruce F. *Mindscreen: Bergman, Godard, and First-Person Film.* Princeton, N.J.: Princeton University Press, 1978.

MacBean, James Roy. *Film and Revolution.* Bloomington, Ind.: Indiana University Press, 1975. [Marxian perspective]

Metz, Christian. *Film Language: A Semiotics of the Cinema.* Trans. Michael Taylor. New York: Oxford University Press, 1974.

Sarris, Andrew. "Notes on the *Auteur* Theory in 1962." *Film Culture,* Winter 1962–1963, pp. 1–8.

―――. "Notes on the *Auteur* Theory in 1970." *Film Comment,* Fall 1970, pp. 6–9.

Solomon, Stanley. *Beyond Formula: American Film Genres*. New York: Harcourt Brace Jovanovich, 1976.

Tudor, Andrew. *Theories of Film*. Cinema One. New York: Viking Press, 1973.

Wollen, Peter. *Signs and Meaning in the Cinema*. 3d ed. Cinema One. Bloomington, Ind.: Indiana University Press, 1972.

*Audience responses and popular culture*

Austin, Bruce A. *The Film Audience: An International Bibliography of Research*. Metuchen, N.J.: Scarecrow, 1983.

Deer, Irving, and Harriet Deer, eds. *The Popular Arts: A Critical Reader*. New York: Scribner, 1967.

Hall, Stuart, and Paddy Whannel. *The Popular Arts*. New York: Pantheon Books, 1965.

Jarvie, I. C. *Movies and Society*. New York: Basic Books, 1970.

Jowett, Garth. *Film: The Democratic Art*. Boston: Little, Brown, 1976.

Mayer, J. P. *Sociology of Film*. London: Faber & Faber, 1946.

Powdermaker, Hortense. *Hollywood: The Dream Factory*. Boston: Little, Brown, 1951.

Seldes, Gilbert. *The Great Audience*. New York: Viking Press, 1951.

Sklar, Robert. *Movie-Made America: A Cultural History of American Movies*. New York: Random House (Vintage Books), 1975.

Thomson, David. *America in the Dark: The Impact of Hollywood Films on American Culture*. New York: Morrow, 1977.

Tudor, Andrew. *Image and Influence: Studies in the Sociology of Film*. New York: St. Martin's Press, 1975.

Warshow, Robert. *The Immediate Experience: Movies, Comics, Theater, and Other Aspects of Popular Culture*. New York: Doubleday, 1962.

**4/ FILM HISTORY AND MOVEMENTS**

*General*

Armes, Roy. *Film and Reality: An Historical Survey*. Baltimore, Md.: Penguin, 1974.

Bardèche, Maurice, and Robert Brasillach. *The History of Motion Pictures*. Trans. & ed. Iris Barry. New York: Norton, 1938. Reprint: New York: Arno, 1970.

Beaver, Frank E. *On Film: A History of the Motion Picture*. New York: McGraw-Hill, 1983.

Casty, Alan. *Development of the Film: An Interpretive History*. New York: Harcourt Brace Jovanovich, 1973.

Ceram, C. W. *Archeology of the Cinema*. New York: Harcourt Brace Jovanovich, 1965.

Clair, René. *Cinema Yesterday and Today*. Trans. Stanley Appelbaum. Ed. R. C. Dale. New York: Dover, 1972.

Cook, David A. *A History of Narrative Film*. New York: Norton, 1981.

Cowie, Peter. *Seventy Years of Cinema*. Cranbury, N.J.: Barnes, 1969.

———, ed. *The Concise History of the Cinema*. 2 vols. Cranbury, N.J.: Barnes, 1971.

Griffith, Richard, and Arthur Mayer. *The Movies*. New York: Simon & Schuster, 1957.

Fell, John L. *Film and the Narrative Tradition*. Norman, Okla.: University of Oklahoma Press, 1974. [Early history]

———. *A History of Films*. New York: Holt, Rinehart and Winston, 1979.

Jacobs, Lewis, ed. *The Emergence of Film Art*. New York: Hopkinson & Blake, 1969.

Knight, Arthur. *The Liveliest Art: A Panoramic History of the Movies*. New York: Macmillan, 1957.

Macgowan, Kenneth. *Behind the Screen: The History and Techniques of the Motion Picture*. New York: Dell, 1965.

Mast, Gerald. *A Short History of the Movies*. 2d ed. Indianapolis: Bobbs-Merrill, 1976.

Pratt, George C. *Spellbound in Darkness: A History of the Silent Film*. Greenwich, Conn.: New York Graphic Society, 1973.

Rhode, Eric. *A History of the Cinema from Its Origins to 1970*. New York: Hill & Wang, 1976.

Robinson, David. *The History of World Cinema*. New York: Stein & Day, 1973.

Rotha, Paul. *The Film till Now: A Survey of World Cinema*. Rev. & enlarged by Richard Griffith. Norwich, England: Fletcher & Son, 1967.

Schickel, Richard. *Movies: The History of an Art and an Institution*. New York: Basic Books, 1964.

Taylor, John Russell. *Directors and Directions: Cinema for the Seventies*. New York: Hill & Wang, 1975.

Wenden, D. J. *The Birth of the Movies*. New York: Dutton, 1975.

Wright, Basil. *The Long View*. New York: Knopf, 1974.

*National*

Anderson, Joseph I., and Donald Richie. *The Japanese Film: Art and Industry*. Rutland, Vt.: Charles E. Tuttle, 1959.

Armes, Roy. *A Critical History of British Cinema*. New York: Oxford University Press, 1978.

———. *French Cinema Since 1946*. 2 vols. Cranbury, N.J.: Barnes, 1970.

————. *French Film.* New York: Dutton, 1970.

Babitsky, Paul, and John Rimberg. *The Soviet Film Industry.* New York: Praeger, 1955.

Balio, Tino, ed. *The American Film Industry.* Madison, Wis.: University of Wisconsin Press, 1976.

Barnouw, Erik, and Subramanyam Krishnaswamy. *Indian Film.* New York: Columbia University Press, 1963.

Battcock, Gregory, ed. *The New American Cinema.* New York: Dutton, 1967.

Betts, Ernest. *The Film Business: A History of British Cinema, 1896–1972.* New York: Pitman, 1973.

Birkos, Alexander. *Soviet Cinema: Directions and Films.* Hamden, Conn.: Archon Books, 1976.

Bjorkman, Stig. *Film in Sweden: The New Directors.* Cranbury, N.J.: Barnes, 1977.

Bock, Audie. *Japanese Film Directors.* New York: Kodansha International, 1978.

Bordwell, David. *French Impressionist Cinema: Film Culture, Film Theory, and Film Style.* New York: Arno, 1980.

Brownlow, Kelvin. *The Parade's Gone By . . .* New York: Bonanza Books, 1968.

Bucher, Felix. *Germany.* Cranbury, N.J.: Barnes, 1970. [Guide to German filmmakers and films]

Butler, Ivan. *Cinema in Britain: An Illustrated Survey.* Cranbury, N.J.: Barnes, 1973.

Cameron, Ian, ed. *Second Wave.* New York: Praeger, 1970.

Cowie, Peter. *Sweden I.* Cranbury, N.J.: Barnes, 1970.

————. *Sweden II.* Cranbury, N.J.: Barnes, 1970.

Dickinson, Thorold, and Catherine De La Roche. *Soviet Cinema.* London: Falcon Press, 1948.

Durgnat, Raymond. *A Mirror for England: British Movies from Austerity to Affluence.* New York: Praeger, 1971.

Earley, Steven. *An Introduction to American Movies.* New York: New American Library, 1978.

Gelmis, Joseph, ed. *The Film Director as Superstar.* New York: Doubleday, 1970.

Gifford, Denis. *British Cinema.* Cranbury, N.J.: Barnes, 1968.

Hardy, Forsyth. *Scandinavian Films.* London: Falcon Press, 1952.

Harmetz, Aljean. "Hollywood's Video Gamble." *New York Times Magazine,* March 28, 1982, pp. 40–54.

Hibbin, Nina. *Eastern Europe.* Cranbury, N.J.: Barnes, 1969. [Guide to filmmakers and films]

Higham, Charles. *The Art of the American Film.* New York: Doubleday, 1974.

Hillier, Jim. *Cinema in Finland.* New York: Zoetrope, 1975.

Hochman, Stanley, ed. *American Film Directors: A Library of Film Criticism.* New York: Ungar, 1974.

Hull, David Stewart. *Film in the Third Reich: A Study of the German Cinema, 1933–1945.* Berkeley, Calif.: University of California Press, 1969.

*Italian Cinema: Literary and Socio-Political Trends.* 4th ed. Los Angeles: Center for Italian Studies of the Department of Italian, UCLA, 1975.

Jacobs, Lewis. *The Rise of the American Film: A Critical History.* New York: Columbia University Teachers College Press, 1968.

Jarratt, Vernon. *The Italian Cinema.* New York: Falcon Press, 1951.

Kindem, Gorham, ed. *The American Movie Industry: The Business of Motion Pictures.* Carbondale, Ill.: Southern University Press, 1982.

Kolker, Robert Phillip. *A Cinema of Loneliness.* New York: Oxford University Press, 1980. [Penn, Kubrick, Coppola, Scorsese, Altman]

Kracauer, Siegfried. *From Caligari to Hitler: A Psychological History of the German Film.* Princeton, N.J.: Princeton University Press, 1971.

Kurzewski, Stanislaw. *Contemporary Polish Cinema.* London: Stephen Wischhusen, 1980.

Leprohon, Pierre. *The Italian Cinema.* Trans. Roger Greaves and Oliver Stallybrass. New York: Praeger, 1972.

Leyda, Jay. *Kino: A History of the Russian and Soviet Film.* New York: Collier Books, 1973.

Liehm, Antonin J. *Closely Watched Films: The Czechoslovak Experience.* White Plains, N.Y.: International Arts and Sciences Press, 1974.

Liehm, Mira, and Antonin Liehm. *The Most Important Art: East European Film After 1945.* Berkeley, Calif.: University of California Press, 1977.

Manvell, Roger. *New Cinema in Britain.* New York: Dutton, 1969.

———— and Heinrich Fraenkel. *The German Cinema.* New York: Praeger, 1971.

Mellen, Joan. *Voices from the Japanese Cinema.* New York: Liveright, 1975.

Molin-Foix, Vicente. *New Cinema in Spain.* New York: Zoetrope, 1977.

Monaco, James. *American Film Now: The People, the Power, the Money, the Movies.* New York: Oxford University Press, 1979.

Oakley, Charles. *Where We Came In: Seventy Years of the British Film Industry.* London: Allen & Unwin, 1964.

Peetz-Schou, Morten. *The Cinema in Denmark.* Copenhagen: Danish Government Film Foundation, 1970.

Pye, Michael, and Lynda Myles. *The Movie Brats.* New York: Holt, Rinehart and Winston, 1979.

Reade, Eric. *History and Heartburn: The Saga of Australian Film, 1896–1978.* Rutherford, N.J.: Fairleigh Dickinson University Press, 1979.

Richie, Donald. *Japanese Cinema.* New York: Doubleday, 1971.

Rondi, Gian Luigi. *Italian Cinema Today.* New York: Hill & Wang, 1966.

Sadoul, Georges. *French Film.* London: Falcon Press, 1953.

Sandford, John. *The New German Cinema.* New York: Barnes & Noble Books, 1980.

Sarris, Andrew. *The American Cinema.* New York: Dutton, 1968.

———, ed. *Hollywood Voices.* New York: Bobbs-Merrill, 1971.

Schnitzer, Luda, Jean Schnitzer, and Marcel Martin, eds. *Cinema in Revolution: The Heroic Era of the Soviet Film.* Trans. David Robinson. New York: Hill & Wang, 1973.

Spears, Jack. *Hollywood: The Golden Era.* Cranbury, N.J.: Barnes, 1971.

Stoil, Michael. *Cinema Beyond the Danube: The Camera and Politics.* Metuchen, N.J.: Scarecrow, 1974.

Svensson, Arne. *Japan.* Cranbury, N.J.: Barnes, 1971. [Dictionary of Japanese filmmakers and films]

Tucker, Richard. *Japan: Film Image.* London: Studio Vista, 1973.

Whyte, Alistair. *New Cinema in Eastern Europe.* New York: Dutton, 1971.

Wollenberg, Hans. *Fifty Years of German Film.* London: Falcon Press, 1948. Reprint: New York: Arno, 1972.

Youngblood, Gene. *Expanded Cinema.* New York: Dutton, 1970.


*Movements*

Armes, Roy. *Patterns of Realism.* Cranbury, N.J.: Barnes, 1972.

Barlow, John D. *German Expressionist Film.* Boston: Twayne, 1982.

Byrne, Richard. *Films of Tyranny.* Madison, Wis.: College Printing and Typing Co., 1966. [Expressionism]

Durgnat, Raymond. *Nouvelle Vague: The First Decade.* Loughton, England: Motion Publishers, 1966.

Eisner, Lotte H. *The Haunted Screen: Expressionism in the German Cinema and the Influence of Max Reinhardt.* Berkeley, Calif.: University of California Press, 1969.

Gould, Michael. *Surrealism and the Cinema.* Cranbury, N.J.: Barnes, 1976.

Graham, Peter, ed. *The New Wave: Critical Landmarks.* New York: Doubleday, 1968.

Huaco, George A. *The Sociology of Film Art.* New York: Basic Books, 1965. [German Expressionism, Soviet "expressive realism," Italian Neorealism]

Kuleshov, Lev. *Kuleshov on Film.* Trans. & ed. Ronald Levaco. Berkeley, Calif.: University of California Press, 1974.

Matthews, J. H. *Surrealism and Film.* Ann Arbor, Mich.: University of Michigan Press, 1971.

Monaco, James. *The New Wave: Truffaut, Godard, Chabrol, Rohmer, Rivette.* New York: Oxford University Press, 1976.

Overby, David, ed. *Springtime in Italy: A Reader on Neo-realism.* Hamden, Conn.: Archon, 1979.

Pudovkin, Vladimir. *Film Technique and Film Acting.* Rev. ed. New York: Grove, 1960.

Silver, Alain, and Elizabeth Ward, eds. *Film Noir.* New York: Overlook Press, 1979.

Willett, John. *Expressionism.* New York: McGraw-Hill, 1970. [Film and other arts]

Williams, Christopher. *Realism and the Cinema.* Boston: Routledge & Kegan Paul, 1980.

Zavattini, Cesare. "Some Ideas on the Cinema." In *Film: A Montage of Theories.* Ed. Richard Dyer MacCann. New York: Dutton, 1966. [Neorealism]

See also Section 5.


## 5/ INDIVIDUAL FILMS AND MOVEMENTS

Allen, Don. *Truffaut.* New York: Viking Press, 1974.

Barna, Yon. *Eisenstein.* Bloomington, Ind.: Indiana University Press, 1973.

Barry, Iris. *D. W. Griffith: American Film Master.* Rev. ed. New York: Museum of Modern Art, 1965.

Benby, David, ed. *The 400 Blows: A Film by François Truffaut.* Film Book Series. New York: Grove Press, 1969.

*The Bicycle Thief: A Film by Vittorio De Sica.* Trans. Simon Hartog. Modern Film Scripts. New York: Simon & Schuster, 1968.

Burke, Thomas. "The Chink and the Child." In *Limehouse Nights.* New York: Robert M. McBride, 1919.

*The Complete Films of Eisenstein.* Dutton Paperback Original. New York: Dutton, 1974.

Crisp, C. G. *François Truffaut.* Praeger Film Library. New York: Praeger, 1972.

Eisenstein, Sergei. *Film Form: Essays in Film Theory.* Trans. & ed. Jay Leyda. New York: Harcourt Brace Jovanovich, 1949.

———. *The Film Sense.* Trans. & ed. Jay Leyda. New York: Harcourt Brace Jovanovich, 1975.

———. *Notes of a Film Director.* New York: Dover, 1970.

Geduld, Harry M., ed. *Focus on D. W. Griffith.* Englewood Cliffs, N.J.: Prentice-Hall, 1971.

——— and Ronald Gottesman, eds. *Sergei Eisenstein and Upton Sinclair: The Making and Unmaking of*

*"Que Viva Mexico!"* Bloomington, Ind.: Indiana University Press, 1970.

Henderson, Robert M. *D. W. Griffith: His Life and Work.* New York: Oxford University Press, 1972.

Indorf, Annette. *François Truffaut,* Boston: Twayne, 1978.

Leyda, Jay, ed. *Eisenstein: Three Films.* New York: Harper & Row, 1974.

Moussinac, Leon. *Sergei Eisenstein: An Investigation into His Films and His Philosophy.* Trans. D. Sandy Petrey. New York: Crown, 1970.

O'Dell, Paul. *Griffith and the Rise of Hollywood.* New York: Castle Books, 1970.

Petrie, Graham. *The Cinema of François Truffaut.* Cranbury, N.J.: Barnes, 1970.

Samuels, Charles Thomas. "Vittorio De Sica." In *Encountering Directors.* New York: Putnam, 1972.

Truffaut, François. *The Films in My Life.* Trans. Leonard Mayhew. New York: Simon & Schuster, 1975.

———. *Hitchcock.* New York: Simon & Schuster, 1967.

Wagenknecht, Edward, and Anthony Slide. *The Films of D. W. Griffith.* New York: Crown, 1975.

Zavattini, Cesare. *Sequences from a Cinematic Life.* Trans. William Weaver. Englewood Cliffs, N.J.: Prentice-Hall, 1970.

## 6/ COMEDY

### General

Byron, Stuart. *Movie Comedy.* New York: Grossman, 1977.

——— and Elisabeth Weis, eds. *The National Society of Film Critics on Movie Comedy.* New York: Viking Press, 1977.

Corrigan, Robert W., ed. *Comedy: Meaning and Form.* San Francisco: Intext, 1965.

Durgnat, Raymond. *The Crazy Mirror: Hollywood Comedy and the American Image.* New York: Horizon Press, 1970.

Feibleman, James K. *Aesthetics.* New York: Duell, Sloan & Pearce, 1949.

Jordan, Thomas H. *The Anatomy of Cinematic Humor.* New York: Revisionist Press, 1975.

Kerr, Walter. *The Silent Clowns.* New York: Knopf, 1975.

Montgomery, John. *Comedy Films.* London: Allen & Unwin, 1954.

Robinson, David. *The Great Funnies: A History of Film Comedy.* New York: Dutton, 1969.

Treadwell, Bill. *Fifty Years of American Comedy.* New York: Exposition, 1951.

### Individual films and directors

Adler, Bill, and Jeffrey Feinman. *Mel Brooks: The Irreverent Funny Man.* Chicago: Playboy Press, 1976.

Bergman, Ingmar. *Four Screenplays of Ingmar Bergman: Smiles of a Summer Night, The Seventh Seal, Wild Strawberries, The Magician.* New York: Simon & Schuster, 1960.

Bergom-Larsson, Maria. *Film in Sweden: Ingmar Bergman and Society.* Cranbury, N.J.: Barnes, 1979.

Björkman, Stig, Torsten Manns, and Jonas Sima. *Bergman on Bergman: Interviews with Ingmar Bergman.* New York: Simon & Schuster, 1973.

Callenbach, Ernest. "Classics Revisited: *The Gold Rush.*" *Film Quarterly,* Fall 1959, pp. 31–37.

Chaplin, Charles. *My Autobiography.* New York: Simon & Schuster, 1964.

Cowie, Peter. *Ingmar Bergman: A Critical Biography.* New York: Scribner, 1982.

Donner, Jörn. *The Films of Ingmar Bergman: From "Torment" to "All These Women."* Trans. Holger Lundbergh. New York: Dover, 1972.

Gibson, Arthur. *The Silence of God: Creative Response to the Films of Ingmar Bergman.* New York: Harper & Row, 1969.

Holtzman, William. *Seesaw: A Dual Biography of Anne Bancroft and Mel Brooks.* New York: Doubleday, 1979.

Huff, Theodore. *Charlie Chaplin.* New York: Henry Schuman, 1951.

Kaminsky, Stuart M., and Joseph F. Hill, eds. *Ingmar Bergman: Essays in Criticism.* New York: Oxford University Press, 1975.

Lees, Gene. "The Mel Brooks Memos." *American Film,* October 1977, pp. 10–18.

Livingston, Paisley. *Ingmar Bergman and the Rituals of Art.* Ithaca, N.Y.: Cornell University Press, 1982.

Lyons, Timothy. *"The Gold Rush." Cinema,* Summer 1968, pp. 17–44. [Screenplay compiled from the film]

Manvell, Roger. *Chaplin.* The Library of World Biography. Boston: Little, Brown, 1974.

McCaffrey, Donald W., ed. *Focus on Chaplin.* Englewood Cliffs, N.J.: Prentice-Hall, 1971.

Payne, Robert. *The Great God Pan: A Biography of the Tramp Played by Charles Chaplin.* New York: Heritage House, 1952.

Petrić, Vlada, ed. *Film & Dreams: An Approach to Bergman.* South Salem, N.Y.: Redgrave, 1981.

Simon, John. *Ingmar Bergman Directs.* New York: Harcourt Brace Jovanovich, 1972.

Steene, Brigitta. *Ingmar Bergman.* Boston: Twayne, 1968.

Tyler, Parker. *Chaplin: Last of the Clowns.* New York: Vanguard Press, 1947.

Tynan, Kenneth. *Show People.* New York: Simon & Schuster, 1980. [Includes interviews with Mel Brooks]

Wood, Robin. *Ingmar Bergman.* New York: Praeger, 1969.

Young, Vernon. *Cinema Borealis: Ingmar Bergman and the Swedish Ethos.* New York: David Lewis, 1971.

## 7/ DOCUMENTARY

### General

Assari, M. Ali, and Doris Paul. *What Is Cinema Verité?* Metuchen: N.J.: Scarecrow, 1979.

Barnouw, Erik. *Documentary.* New York: Oxford University Press, 1974.

Barsam, Richard Meran. *Nonfiction Film: A Critical History.* New York: Dutton, 1973.

——, ed. *Nonfiction Film: Theory and Criticism.* New York: Dutton, 1976.

Graef, Roger. "Decisions, Decisions." *Sight and Sound,* Winter 1975–1976, pp. 2–7.

Grierson, John. *Grierson on Documentary.* Ed. Forsyth Hardy. New York: Harcourt Brace Jovanovich, 1947.

Ivens, Joris. *The Camera and I.* New York: International Publishers, 1969.

Jacobs, Lewis, ed. *The Documentary Tradition.* 2d ed. New York: Norton, 1979.

Knight, Arthur. "Cinéma Verité and Film Truth." *Saturday Review,* September 9, 1967, p. 44.

Levin, G. Roy. *Documentary Explorations: 15 Interviews with Film-Makers.* New York: Doubleday, 1971.

Mamber, Stephen. *Cinema Verité in America.* Cambridge, Mass.: M.I.T. Press, 1974.

Rosenthal, Alan. *The New Documentary in Action: A Casebook in Film-Making.* Berkeley, Calif.: University of California Press, 1971. [Interviews]

Rotha, Paul. *Documentary Film.* 3rd ed. London: Faber & Faber, 1952.

### Individual films and directors

Achtenberg, Ben. "Helen van Dongen: An Interview." *Film Quarterly,* Winter 1976–1977, pp. 46–57.

Armes, Roy. *The Cinema of Alain Resnais.* Cranbury, N.J.: Barnes, 1968.

Atkins, Thomas R. *Frederick Wiseman.* New York: Simon & Schuster, 1976.

Barsam, Richard Meran. *Filmguide to "Triumph of the Will."* Indiana University Press Filmguide Series. Bloomington, Ind.: Indiana University Press, 1975.

Berg-Pan, Renata. *Leni Riefenstahl.* Boston: Twayne, 1980.

Calder-Marshall, Arthur. *The Innocent Eye: The Life of Robert J. Flaherty.* New York: Harcourt Brace Jovanovich, 1966.

Eames, David. "Watching Wiseman Watch." *New York Times Magazine,* October 2, 1977, pp. 96–106.

Ellsworth, Liz. *Frederick Wiseman: A Guide to References and Resources.* Boston: G. K. Hall, 1979.

Flaherty, Frances Hubbard. *The Odyssey of a Film-Maker: Robert Flaherty's Story.* Urbana, Ill.: Phi Beta Mu, 1960.

Griffith, Richard. *The World of Robert Flaherty.* Boston: Little, Brown, 1953.

Hinton, David. *The Films of Leni Riefenstahl.* Metuchen, N.J.: Scarecrow, 1978.

Hitchens, Gordon. "An Interview with a Legend." *Film Comment,* Winter 1965, pp. 4–11.

Infield, Glenn B. *Leni Riefenstahl: The Fallen Film Goddess.* New York: Crowell, 1976.

Kreidl, John. *Alain Resnais.* Boston: Twayne, 1978.

Monaco, James. *Alain Resnais.* New York: Oxford University Press, 1979.

Mullen, Pat. *Man of Aran.* Cambridge, Mass.: M.I.T. Press, 1970.

Murphy, William T. *Robert Flaherty: A Guide to References and Resources.* Boston: G. K. Hall, 1978.

Schreivogel, Paul. *Night and Fog.* Dayton, O.: Pflaum, 1970. [Study guide]

Shirer, William L. *The Rise and Fall of the Third Reich.* New York: Simon & Schuster, 1960.

Ward, John. *Alain Resnais: The Theme of Time.* New York: Doubleday, 1968.

## 8/ WESTERN

### General

Brownlow, Kevin. *The War, the West, and the Wilderness.* New York: Knopf, 1979.

Eyles, Allen. *The Western.* Rev. ed. Cranbury, N.J.: Barnes, 1975. [Dictionary format]

Fenin, George N., and William K. Everson. *The Western.* Rev. ed. New York: Penguin Books, 1977.

Kitses, Jim. *Horizons West.* Cinema One. Bloomington, Ind.: Indiana University Press, 1970.

Maynard, Richard A., ed. *The American West on Film: Myth and Reality.* Rochelle Park, N.J.: Hayden, 1974.

Meyer, William. *The Making of the Great Westerns.* New Rochelle, N.Y.: Arlington House, 1979.

Nachbar, Jack, ed. *Focus on the Western.* Englewood Cliffs, N.J.: Prentice-Hall, 1974.

Parkinson, Michael, and Clyde Jeavons. *A Pictorial History of Westerns.* New York: Hamlyn, 1973.

Pilkington, William T., and Don Graham, eds. *West-*

*ern Movies.* Albuquerque, N.M.: University of New Mexico Press, 1979.

Tuska, Jon. *The Filming of the West.* New York: Doubleday, 1976.

Wright, Will. *Six Guns and Society.* Berkeley, Calif.: University of California Press, 1975.

*Individual films and directors*

Anderson, Lindsay. *About John Ford.* London: Plexus, 1980.

Anobile, Richard, ed. *John Ford's "Stagecoach."* New York: Avon Books, 1975. [Complete dialogue and 1200 frame enlargements]

Bogdanovich, Peter. *John Ford.* Berkeley, Calif.: University of California Press, 1968.

Evans, Max. *Sam Peckinpah: Master of Violence.* Vermillion, S. D.: Dakota Press, 1972.

Madsen, Axel. "John Ford: American (1895–1973): An Interview." *1,000 Eyes,* July–August 1976, pp. 9–11.

McBride, Joseph, and Michael Wilmington. *John Ford.* New York: Da Capo, 1975.

Place, J. A. *The Non-Western Films of John Ford.* Secaucus, N.J.: Citadel Press, 1979.

———. *The Western Films of John Ford.* Secaucus, N.J.: Citadel Press, 1973.

Richie, Donald. *George Stevens: An American Romantic.* New York: Museum of Modern Art, 1970.

Sarris, Andrew. *The John Ford Movie Mystery.* Bloomington, Ind.: Indiana University Press, 1976.

Seydor, Paul. *Peckinpah: The Western Films.* Urbana, Ill.: University of Illinois Press, 1980.

## 9/ MUSICAL

Croce, Arlene. *Afterimages.* New York: Knopf, 1977.

Green, Stanley. *Encyclopedia of the Musical Film.* New York: Oxford University Press, 1981.

Hirschhorn, Clive. *The Hollywood Musical.* New York: Crown, 1981.

Kobal, John. *Gotta Sing, Gotta Dance: A Pictorial History of Film Musicals.* New York: Hamlyn, 1970.

Kreuger, Miles, ed. *The Movie Musical from Vitaphone to "42nd Street."* New York: Dover, 1975.

Pike, Bob, and Dave Martin. *The Genius of Busby Berkeley.* Reseda, Calif.: Creative Film Society, 1973.

Springer, John. *All Talking, All Singing, All Dancing.* Secaucus, N.J.: Citadel Press, 1966.

Stern, Lee Edward. *The Movie Musical.* New York: Pyramid Books, 1974.

Taylor, John Russell, and Arthur Jackson. *The Hollywood Musical.* New York: McGraw-Hill, 1971.

*West Side Story.* New York: Program Publishing Co., 1961. [Program notes]

## GENERAL SOURCES

### INTRODUCTIONS TO FILM

Blumenberg, Richard M. *Critical Focus: An Introduction to Film.* Belmont, Calif.: Wadsworth, 1975.

Bobker, Lee R. *Elements of Film.* 2d ed. New York: Harcourt Brace Jovanovich, 1974.

Bordwell, David, and Kristin Thompson. *Film Art: An Introduction.* Reading, Mass.: Addison-Wesley, 1979.

Dick, Bernard F. *Anatomy of Film.* New York: St. Martin's Press, 1978.

Giannetti, Lewis. *Understanding Movies.* 3d ed. Englewood Cliffs, N.J.: Prentice-Hall, 1982.

Harrington, John. *The Rhetoric of Film.* New York: Holt, Rinehart and Winston, 1973.

Lindgren, Ernest. *The Art of the Film.* Rev. ed. New York: Collier, 1970.

Monaco, James. *How to Read a Film: The Art, Technology, Language, History and Theory of Film and Media.* New York: Oxford University Press, 1977.

Montagu, Ivor. *Film World: A Guide to Cinema.* Baltimore, Md.: Penguin Books, 1967.

Perkins, V. F. *Film as Film: Understanding and Judging Movies.* Baltimore, Md.: Penguin Books, 1974.

Scott, James F. *Film: The Medium and the Maker.* New York: Holt, Rinehart and Winston, 1975.

Sobchack, Thomas, and Vivian C. Sobchack. *An Introduction to Film.* Boston: Little, Brown, 1980.

Solomon, Stanley. *The Film Idea.* New York: Harcourt Brace Jovanovich, 1972.

### ANALYSES OF AND COMMENTARIES ON INDIVIDUAL FILMS

Bayer, William. *The Great Movies.* New York: Grosset & Dunlap, 1973.

Bellone, Julius, ed. *Renaissance of the Film.* New York: Macmillan, 1970.

Bowser, Eileen, ed. *Film Notes.* New York: Museum of Modern Art, 1969.

Crowther, Bosley. *The Great Films: Fifty Golden Years of Motion Pictures.* New York: Putnam, 1967.

———. *Vintage Films.* New York: Putnam, 1977.

DeNitto, Dennis, and William Herman. *Film and the Critical Eye.* New York: Macmillan, 1975.

Kinder, Marsha, and Beverle Houston. *Close-up: A Critical Perspective on Film.* New York: Harcourt Brace Jovanovich, 1972.

Klein, Michael, and Gillian Parker, eds. *The English Novel and the Movies.* New York: Ungar, 1981.

Lennig, Arthur, ed. *Classics of the Film.* Madison, Wis.: Wisconsin Film Society Press, 1965.

Magill, Frank, ed. *Magill's Survey of Cinema.* 4 vols. Englewood Cliffs, N.J.: Salem, 1980.

Murray, Edward. *Ten Film Classics: A Re-viewing.* New York: Ungar, 1978.

O'Connor, John E., and Martin Jackson, eds. *American History/American Film.* New York: Ungar, 1979.

Pickard, R. A. E. *Dictionary of 1000 Best Films.* New York: Association Press, 1971.

Peary, Gerald, and Roger Shatzkin, eds. *The Classic American Novel and the Movies.* New York: Ungar, 1977.

———. *The Modern American Novel and the Movies.* New York: Ungar, 1978.

Solomon, Stanley. *The Classic Cinema.* New York: Harcourt Brace Jovanovich, 1973.

Tyler, Parker. *Classics of the Foreign Film: A Pictorial Treasury.* New York: Cadillac, 1962.

Wagner, Geoffrey. *The Novel and the Cinema.* Rutherford, N.J.: Fairleigh Dickinson University Press, 1975.

Walz, Eugene P., John Harrington, and Vincent Di Marco, eds. *Frames of Reference: Essays on the Rhetoric of Film.* Dubuque, Ia.: Kendall/Hunt Publishing, 1972.

Wolf, William, and Lillian Kramer Wolf. *Landmark Films: The Cinema and Our Century.* New York: Paddington Press, 1979.

Zinman, David. *50 Classic Motion Pictures: The Stuff that Dreams Are Made Of.* New York: Crown, 1970.

## GENERAL ANTHOLOGIES

Denby, David, ed. *Awake in the Dark.* New York: Vintage, 1977.

Harrington, John, ed. *Film and/as Literature.* Englewood Cliffs, N.J.: Prentice-Hall, 1977.

Jacobs, Lewis, ed. *Introduction to the Art of the Movies.* New York: Farrar, Straus & Giroux, 1960.

———. *The Movies as Medium.* New York: Farrar, Straus & Giroux, 1970.

MacCann, Richard Dyer, ed. *Film: A Montage of Theories* New York: Dutton, 1966.

———. *Film and Society.* New York: Scribner's, 1964.

Mast, Gerald, and Marshall Cohen, eds. *Film Theory and Criticism.* New York: Oxford University Press, 1974.

Nichols, Bill, ed. *Movies and Methods.* Berkeley, Calif.: University of California Press, 1977.

Robinson, W. R., ed. *Man and the Movies.* Baltimore, Md.: Penguin Books, 1974.

Ross, T. J., ed. *Film and the Liberal Arts.* New York: Holt, Rinehart and Winston, 1970.

Samuels, Charles Thomas, ed. *A Casebook on Film.* New York: Van Nostrand Reinhold, 1970.

Talbot, Daniel, ed. *Film: An Anthology.* Berkeley, Calif.: University of California Press, 1959.

## REFERENCE AND RESEARCH

*Encyclopedias, dictionaries, and guides*

Bawden, Liz-Anne, ed. *The Oxford Companion to Film.* New York: Oxford University Press, 1976.

Cawkwell, Tim, and John M. Smith, eds. *The World Encyclopedia of the Film.* New York: Collins, 1972.

Cowie, Peter, ed. *International Film Guide.* London: Tantivy Press, 1964 to present. [Yearly]

Fielding, Raymond, ed. *Focal Encyclopedia of Film and Television.* New York: Hastings House, 1969.

Gottesman, Ronald, and Harry Geduld, eds. *Guidebook to Film: An Eleven-in-One Reference.* New York: Holt, Rinehart and Winston, 1972.

Graham, Peter. *A Dictionary of the Cinema.* Cranbury, N.J.: Barnes, 1964.

Halliwell, Leslie. *The Filmgoer's Companion.* 6th ed. New York: Avon Books, 1978.

Katz, Ephraim. *The Film Encyclopedia.* New York: Crowell, 1979.

Maltin, Leonard, ed. *The Whole Film Sourcebook.* New York: New American Library, 1983.

Manchel, Frank. *Film Study: A Resource Guide.* Rutherford, N.J.: Fairleigh Dickinson University Press, 1973.

Manvell, Roger, ed. *The International Encyclopedia of Film.* New York: Bonanza Books, 1975.

Paul, Michael. *The American Movies Reference Book: The Sound Era.* Englewood Cliffs, N.J.: Prentice-Hall, 1969.

Roud, Richard, ed. *Cinema: A Critical Dictionary.* 2 vols. New York: Viking Press, 1980.

Sadoul, Georges. *Dictionary of Film Makers.* Trans. & ed. Peter Morris. Berkeley, Calif.: University of California Press, 1972.

———. *Dictionary of Films.* Trans. & ed. Peter Morris. Berkeley, Calif.: University of California Press, 1972.

Thompson, David. *A Biographical Dictionary of Film.* New York: Morrow, 1976.

*Glossaries*

Beaver, Frank E. *Dictionary of Film Terms.* New York: McGraw-Hill, 1983.

Geduld, Harry M., and Ronald Gottesman. *An Illustrated Glossary of Film Terms.* New York: Holt, Rinehart and Winston, 1973.

Jordan, Thurston C., Jr., ed. *Glossary of Motion Picture Terminology.* Menlo Park, Calif.: Pacific Coast Publishers, 1968.

Mercer, John. *Glossary of Film Terms.* University Film Association Monograph No. 2. Philadelphia: Journal of the University Film Association, 1937.

Miller, Tony, and Patricia George Miller. *"Cut!*

*Print!": The Language and Structure of Filmmaking.* Los Angeles, Ohara Publishers, 1972.

Quick, John, Tom LaBau, and Herbert Wolff, comps. *Dictionary of Motion Picture and Video Terms.* Boston: Herman, 1978.

### Bibliographies and catalogues

*The American Film Institute Catalogs: Feature Films.* 4 vols. New York: Bowker, 1971–1976

Armour, Robert A. *Film: A Reference Guide.* Westport, Conn.: Greenwood, 1980. [Bibliographies]

British Film Institute Staff, comps. *Catalog of the Book Library of the British Film Institute.* 3 vols. Boston: G. K. Hall, 1975.

Bukalski, Peter J., comp. *Film Research.* Boston: G. K. Hall, 1972.

*Cinemabilia: Catalogue of Film Literature.* New York: Cinemabilia, 1972.

Dyment, Alan R. *The Literature of the Film: A Bibliographical Guide to the Film as Art and Entertainment, 1936–1970.* London: Whitelion, Publishers, 1975.

Leonard, Harold, ed. *The Film Index: A Bibliography.* Vol. 1: *The Film Art* [1941]. Reprint: New York: Arno, 1966.

Lubovski, Git. *Cinema Catalog.* Hollywood, Calif.: Larry Edmunds Bookshop, 1970. [Cinemabilia as well as books and magazines]

MacCann, Richard Dyer, and Edward Perry. *The New Film Index.* New York: Dutton, 1975. [Supplement to Leonard, 1941]

McCarty, Clifford. *Published Screenplays: A Checklist.* Kent, O.: Kent State University Press, 1971.

Monaco, James, and Susan Schenker. *Books About Film.* New York: Zoetrope, 1976.

*Motion Pictures: A Catalog of Books, Periodicals, Screen Plays and Production Stills.* Boston: G. K. Hall, 1973.

Poteet, G. Howard. *Published Radio, Television and Film Scripts: A Bibliography.* Troy, N.Y.: Whitston, 1975.

Rehrauer, George. *Cinema Booklist.* Metuchen, N.J.: Scarecrow, 1972. Supplement 1, 1974; Supplement 2, 1977.

———. *The Macmillan Film Bibliography: A Critical Guide to the Literature of the Motion Picture.* 2 vols. New York: Macmillan, 1982.

Welch, Jeffrey. *Literature and Film: An Annotated Bibliography, 1900–1977.* New York: Garland, 1979.

### Periodicals

**U.S.A./** *Film Comment, Film Quarterly, American Film, Quarterly Review of Film Studies.* Also: *Action, American Cinematographer, Cineaste, Cinema Journal, Film Culture, Film Facts, Film Heritage, The Film Journal, Film Library Quarterly, Journal of Popular Film, Journal of the University Film Association, Jump Cut, Literature and Film Quarterly, Millimeter, Wide Angle.*

**GREAT BRITAIN/** *Sight and Sound.* Also: *Cinema Studies, Films and Filming, Focus on Film, Movie, Screen.*

### Guides to periodical literature

Batty, Linda. *Retrospective Index to Film Periodicals.* New York: Bowker, 1975.

Gerlach, John C., and Lana Gerlach. *The Critical Index; A Bibliography of Articles on Film in English, 1946–1973.* New York: Columbia University Teachers College Press, 1974.

*International Index to Film Periodicals.* 3 vols. New York: Bowker, 1973, 1974; New York: St. Martin's Press, 1975.

Schuster, Mel. *Motion Picture Directors.* Metuchen, N.J.: Scarecrow, 1973. [Articles on directors, 1900–1972]

———, ed. *Motion Picture Performers: A Bibliography of Magazine and Periodical Articles, 1900–1969.* Metuchen, N.J.: Scarecrow, 1971. Supplement, 1976.

### Miscellanea

*American Film Institute Guide to College Courses in Film and Television.* 7th ed., Washington, D.C.: American Film Institute, 1980.

Cowie, Peter, ed. *World Filmography 1967, 1968.* 2 vols. Cranbury, N.J.: Barnes, 1967, 1968.

Dimmitt, Richard. *A Title Guide to the Talkies.* Metuchen, N.J.: Scarecrow, 1965.

Emmens, Carol A. *Short Stories on Film.* Littleton, Colo.: Libraries Unlimited, 1978.

Limbacher, James, comp. *Feature Films on 8mm, 16mm and Videotape.* 6th ed. New York: Bowker, 1979.

Parish, James Robert. *Film Directors Guide: Western Europe.* Metuchen, N.J.: Scarecrow, 1976. [Filmographies]

——— and Michael Pitts. *Film Directors: A Guide to Their American Films.* Metuchen, N.J.: Scarecrow, 1974. [Filmographies]

Steinberg, Cobbett. *Reel Facts: The Movie Book of Records.* New York: Vintage, 1978.

# Index of film terms

This index includes the film terms introduced in Part One and the pages on which these terms are defined. Some of these terms are also listed as either main entries or subentries in the Index of Subjects. **Boldface** indicates an illustration or a series of illustrations.

# Index of subjects

This index is organized into general topics and subtopics. Specific film terms, and the page numbers on which these terms are defined, are listed in the Index of Film Terms. Names of personalities are listed in the Index of Names. Titles of films are listed in the Index of Film Titles. **Boldface** indicates an illustration or a series of illustrations.

## ℐ𝓃𝒹ℯ𝓍 𝑜𝒻 𝓃𝒶𝓂ℯ𝓈

When there are numerous entries for a major filmmaker, the main entry is indicated by a page number or numbers in *italic*.

# Index of film titles

The original title of a foreign film is indicated in the text (with some exceptions for motion pictures of the seventies and eighties) on the first page listed in an entry for references to and beyond page 99 (the beginning of Chapter 4). There are, however, cross-references in this index for foreign films known by their original titles and their alternate English-language titles. **Boldface** indicates an illustration or a series of illustrations.